SWEET LAND OF LIBERTY

SWEET LAND OF LIBERTY

THE FORGOTTEN STRUGGLE FOR

CIVIL RIGHTS IN THE NORTH

Thomas J. Sugrue

RANDOM HOUSE

NEW YORK

Published in the United States by Random House, an imprint
of The Random House Publishing Group, a division
of Random House, Inc., New York.

RANDOM HOUSE and colophon are registered trademarks
of Random House, Inc.

The author and Random House, Inc., wish to thank the Crisis Publishing
Co., Inc., the publisher of the magazine of the National Association for the
Advancement of Colored People, for the use of "Mr. Roosevelt Regrets"
(from the August 1943 issue of *The Crisis*) and "I Believe in Democracy
So Much" (from the September 1942 issue of *The Crisis*).

LIBRARY OF CONGRESS CATALOGING-IN-PUBLICATION DATA
Sugrue, Thomas J.
Sweet land of liberty: the forgotten struggle for civil rights in the
North/Thomas J. Sugrue.
p.   cm.
Includes bibliographical references.
ISBN 978-0-679-64303-6
1. African Americans—Civil rights—Northeastern States—History—20th
century.   2. African Americans—Civil rights—History—20th century.
3. Civil rights movements—Northeastern States—History—20th century.
4. Civil rights movements—United States—History—20th century.
5. African American civil rights workers—Northeastern States—Biography.
6. Civil rights workers—Northeastern States—Biography.   7. Northeastern
States—Race relations—History—20th century.   8. United States—Race
relations—History—20th century.   I. Title.
E185.9.S95 2008
323.1196'073074—dc22   2008002081

Printed in the United States of America
on acid-free paper

www.atrandom.com

2 4 6 8 9 7 5 3 1

FIRST EDITION

Book design by Simon M. Sullivan

To Anna and Jack

History, as nearly no one seems to know, is not merely something to be read. And it does not refer merely, or even principally, to the past. On the contrary, the great force of history comes from the fact that we carry it within us, are unconsciously controlled by it in many ways, and history is literally *present* in all that we do. It could scarcely be otherwise, since it is to history that we owe our frames of reference, our identities, and our aspirations.

—JAMES BALDWIN, "White Man's Guilt," *Ebony*, 1965

CONTENTS

INTRODUCTION

"THE RACIAL ISSUE WE CONFRONT IN AMERICA IS NOT A SECTIONAL BUT A national problem. Injustice anywhere is a threat to justice everywhere." So proclaimed the Reverend Martin Luther King, Jr., in 1960. Nearly a half century later, our histories—and our collective memories—of the civil rights era do not reflect the national scope of racial inequality and the breadth of challenges to it. The near library of books on the black freedom struggle is full of empty shelves. Most histories focus on the South and the epic battles between nonviolent protestors and the defenders of Jim Crow during the 1950s and 1960s. *Sweet Land of Liberty* turns our attention northward.

Conventional histories of the civil rights movement begin with 1954 and the landmark Supreme Court decision *Brown v. Board of Education,* and they culminate in the passage of the Civil Rights Act of 1964 and the Voting Rights Act of 1965, which together unraveled southern-style racial segregation. They tell a story of tragedy but ultimate triumph. As a result of litigation, legislation, and grassroots activism, the Jim Crow buses, lunch counters, and drinking fountains are artifacts of a vanquished racial order. Southern blacks enjoy the right to vote. Lynchings are rare.

The story of the southern freedom struggle is fundamentally a morality play, one that pits the forces of good (nonviolent protestors) against evil (segregationist politicians, brutal sheriffs, and rednecks). It is a story of suffering and redemption, with larger-than-life martyrs and prophets. Southern civil rights activists literally put their bodies on the line, willing to make the ultimate sacrifice to advance the cause of racial equality. Through protest and moral suasion—a call to conscience—activists reinvigorated the "American Creed," a belief in the fundamental equality and humanity of all people that is supposedly enshrined in our nation's founding documents. Through these activists' heroism and uncompromising faith, the civil rights movement cleansed America of its sins.

The commonplace accounts turn northward only in the mid- and late 1960s, when cities exploded in riots and black power advocates burst onto the national scene. Our accounts of this period are bleaker and briefer, focusing on King's frustrated attempt to "bring the movement North" to Chicago; the contentious New York City school strikes of 1968; the rise and fall of the Black Panthers; and the infamous battle in the 1970s against court-mandated busing in Boston. The North is the tragic denouement of the otherwise triumphant civil rights struggle.

These histories are as much the product of forgetting as of remembering. To understand the history of civil rights—indeed, to understand modern America—it is essential to bring the North back in. As a battleground in the struggle for racial equality, the North mattered enormously. The Great Migration of blacks from the South, which began with a trickle in the 1890s and accelerated rapidly with the outbreak of World War I, meant that the North was home to millions of African Americans by 1920. Fifty years later, almost half of American blacks lived north of the Mason-Dixon Line. Yet northern blacks loom in the shadows, absent from the historical stage until the mid-1960s, when they serve as spoilers: rioting, embracing a divisive identity politics, and sparking a white backlash against an alleged consensus in support of racial equality. Northern whites—especially those who joined the interracial struggle for equality—are also largely missing from these accounts.

The exclusion of the North—or its selective inclusion as a foil to the southern freedom struggle—comes at a cost. It ignores the long and intense history of racial violence and conflict in northern towns and cities. Though the differences between North and South were real, our emphasis on southern exceptionalism has led historians, journalists, and political commentators to overlook the commonalities across regions. The long and well-publicized history of racial atrocities in the South gave northerners a badge of honor, a sense that they were not part of America's troubled racial history. In his 1944 bestseller, *An American Dilemma*, Gunnar Myrdal remarked on a pervasive sense of "innocence" among northern whites. "It is convenient for Northerners' good conscience," wrote Myrdal, "to forget about the Negro." Myrdal did not spend much time investigating the North, but he could not miss the yawning gap between white northerners' self-understanding and their practices. "The social paradox in the North is exactly this, that almost everybody is against discrimination in general but, at the same time, almost everybody practices discrimination in his own personal affairs."

As the national news media turned their attention to civil rights and black power, white denial turned into defensiveness. With charges of racism hurling past them in the 1960s and early 1970s, northern whites fiercely proclaimed their racial innocence. "If I hear the four hundred years of slavery bit one more time," complained a white man to journalist Pete Hamill in 1970, "I'll go outta my mind." Michael Novak, who passionately defended "white ethnics" against "sanctimonious" civil rights activists, likewise saw the question of race and injustice as a distinctly southern problem. "Racists?" he asked with incredulity. "Our ancestors owned no slaves. Most of us ceased being serfs only in the last two hundred years." Racial inequality was someone else's problem—it was not the North's responsibility.

Racial inequality took different forms on each side of the Mason-Dixon Line in the twentieth century. Most northern communities did not erect signs to mark separate black and white facilities; only some northern schools were segregated by law; and black voters were not systematically disenfranchised in the North. But in both regions, private behavior, market practices, and public policies created and reinforced racial separation and inequality. Northern blacks lived as second-class citizens, unencumbered by the most blatant of southern-style Jim Crow laws but still trapped in an economic, political, and legal regime that seldom recognized them as equals. In nearly every arena, blacks and whites lived separate, unequal lives. Public policy and the market confined blacks to declining neighborhoods; informal Jim Crow excluded them from restaurants, hotels, amusement parks, and swimming pools and relegated them to separate sections of theaters. All but a small number of northern blacks attended racially segregated and inferior schools. As adults, blacks faced formidable obstacles to economic security. They were excluded from whole sectors of the labor market. And, as a result of the combined effects of segregation, discrimination, and substandard education, they remained overrepresented in the ranks of the unemployed and poor.

Impoverishment and exclusion engendered despair. But they also fueled righteous indignation. Throughout the twentieth century, black and white activists (and occasionally Latino and Asian allies, who were a minuscule segment of the region's population until recently) rose to challenge racial inequality in the North. Their struggles defied easy categorization at the time—and still do. Activists used the term "civil rights movement" more broadly than do many historians, social scientists, and legal commentators. The "movement"—narrowly defined—consisted of challenges to officially sanctioned, legally enforceable racial segregation. But few activists at the time saw the battle to strike down legally mandated segregation as an end in itself. Rather, it was one part of a larger, multifaceted battle that at its broadest included fights for prohibition against discrimination in the workplace, the opening of housing markets, the provision of quality education, the economic development of impoverished communities, and untrammeled access to the consumer marketplace. The keyword linking these battles was "rights."

For most of the period, activists (and ordinary Americans) embraced a capacious definition of rights. Rights talk—the evocation of "inalienable" rights attached to citizens and groups—is as old as the American republic itself. The very notion of rights was, from the beginning, fiercely contested. Were rights to be granted only to citizens? Only to those who were independent or those who held property or those who were virtuous? To women or African Americans? These were fundamental questions throughout most of American history. Notions of rights—and who was entitled to them—expanded in two crucial periods. In the aftermath of the emancipation of slaves, the Reconstruction amendments guaranteed African Americans the fundamental rights of citizenship, including the right to vote, serve on a jury, and be tried by a jury of one's peers. But those rights were more often than not honored in the breach—and remained a target of civil rights activists for most of the century following the Civil War.

During the New Deal and World War II, a new, broader conception of rights pervaded American politics. Blacks and whites alike came to view an empowered federal government as the guarantor of positive as well as negative rights. At the heart of the later New Deal was a sweeping redefinition of the relationship of government, entitlement, and citizenship, perhaps best summarized in Franklin Delano Roosevelt's "Second Bill of Rights," in 1944. Roosevelt offered a sweeping revision of the freedoms guaranteed in the first ten constitutional amendments. Under the Bill of Rights, government power was to be checked; the government could not interfere in a citizen's lawful exercise of the enumerated rights such as free speech, religion, and assembly. Under the Second Bill of Rights, an activist government guaranteed the positive rights to "a useful and remunerative job," "to earn enough to provide adequate food and clothing and recreation," "to a decent home," and "to adequate protection from the economic fears of old age, sickness, accident, and unemployment." The twin pillars of these newly enumerated rights as President Roosevelt defined them were "equality" and "security."

The "rights revolution"—that is, the extension of citizenship to include positive rights—fundamentally shifted the terms of debate in the civil rights movement, particularly in the period from the 1930s to the 1970s. Often such expansive notions of rights came into conflict with more traditional understandings: Did a black's right to a decent home trump the property rights of whites to rent or sell to whom they chose? Did the right to a decent, remunerative job override the employer's prerogative, long recognized in American law, to hire and fire at will? Was there a right to welfare? Was there a right to equal education? Were rights restricted to the lifting of negative restraints on an individual's freedoms—the equality of opportunity—or were they to be expanded to include equality of results, such as truly integrated schools, workplaces, and neighborhoods? All these questions moved to the center of national political debate—and black activists and their white allies kept them there.

This book focuses on the moment in modern American history when activists, especially in the North, fought for their rights broadly conceived. This book uses the term "civil rights" in that sense; and it uses "civil rights" interchangeably with "freedom struggle" and "struggle for racial equality," as did many activists throughout the twentieth century. To separate these terms artificially, or to favor one over the others, would obscure more than clarify.

The stories of the black freedom struggle are both ordinary and extraordinary. Northern activists successfully challenged Jim Crow in public accommodations. To an extent unimaginable in 1940, it is now commonplace to see blacks and whites in the same restaurants, hotels, and theaters. Through protest and legislation, civil rights organizations chipped away at the problem of employment discrimination, opening up whole sectors of the workforce to people of color. And through pickets, litigation, and moral suasion, integrationists transformed white attitudes about segregation in housing and in schools—even if the practice of racial separation proved much more difficult to uproot. Black radicals also launched an extraordinary grassroots movement to gain hold of the mechanisms of economic and political power—through the ballot box and through community economic development. By threatening disruption, they gained control, sometimes fleetingly, sometimes enduringly, over the levers of power.

At their most effective, northern civil rights activists forged unlikely coalitions that fused critiques of racial, political, and economic inequality, motivated by a common vision of a just society. During the Depression and World War II, activists overcame political, cultural, and social differences, forging a remarkably united front to demand full political and economic citizenship. Devout churchwomen, lawyers, laborers, Democrats, Republicans, Socialists, and Communists marched together on picket lines, lobbied public officials, and joined in lawsuits against segregated housing and schools. Civil rights organizations developed increasingly sophisticated strategies to influence local, state, and federal policy making. They championed litigation and legislation that advanced their goals. Black activists made alliances—often awkward and contentious, but nonetheless productive—with white unionists, religious activists, and elected officials. Interracial organizing was never easy: It was plagued by misunderstanding and miscommunication and riddled with compromises. But it was also fruitful. Laws that prohibited workplace and housing discrimination—even if they were often watery—were the result of interracial organizing. The shift in racial attitudes and practices in modern America cannot be understood without telling the stories of myriad northern civil rights activists and their organizations, most of them unknown and forgotten.

In ways that I can only suggest here, northern and southern activists influenced one another. The topic—still mostly unexplored—is worth its own book. Northern activists shared their experiences with their southern counterparts, and by turn, they were moved to action by the example of the southern civil rights movement. Many veterans of the battles against segregated facilities in the North participated in the well-known southern sit-ins of the 1950s and 1960s. They disseminated pamphlets, wrote articles, and advised southern activists, offering lessons from their own hard-won victories. The black press served as an indispensable resource for civil rights activists around the country. Widely circulating (many papers had readerships across several states) black newspapers informed their readers of racial injustices around the country and reported extensively on those who challenged racial inequality. As a result, activists in Detroit could learn lessons from their counterparts in suburban New Jersey, who in turn followed the progress of protests in places as far away as Cincinnati, Atlanta, or Birmingham. Also linking black activists around the country were national organizations, from fraternities and women's clubs to civil rights organizations to churches. Their local chapters—at times more militant than their parent organizations—often set the agenda for protests and experimented with new strategies for social change.

While the situation of blacks—north and south—was unmistakably better at the turn of the twenty-first century than it had been at the turn of the twentieth, the history of the black freedom struggle, especially in the North, is not just one of victories. It is full of paradoxes and ambiguities, of unfinished battles and devastating defeats. At the opening of the twenty-first century, the fifteen most segregated metropolitan areas in the United States were in the Northeast and Midwest. A half century after the Supreme Court struck down separate, unequal schools as unconstitutional, racial segregation is still the norm in northern public schools. The five states with the highest rates of school segregation—New York, New Jersey, Illinois, Michigan, and California—are all outside the South. Rates of unemployment, underemployment, and poverty reach Third World levels among African Americans in nearly every major northern city, where the faces in welfare offices, unemployment lines, homeless shelters, and jails are disproportionately black.

TO UNDERSTAND THE black freedom struggle requires going back further in time than most histories have—to the 1920s and 1930s—and also forward into the 1990s. I am inspired by the work of a new generation of civil rights historians, most of them focusing on the South, who have challenged the tired chronologies of that region's battle over Jim Crow. Jacquelyn Dowd Hall calls for the history of a "long civil rights movement" that took root in the liberal and radical milieu of the late 1930s, was intimately tied to the "rise and fall of the New Deal order," accelerated during World War II, stretched far beyond the South, was continuously and ferociously contested, and in the 1960s and 1970s inspired a "movement of movements" that "def[ies] any narrative of collapse." The history of the northern freedom struggle told here also pushes at conventional boundaries and in the process greatly complicates our understanding of the underlying causes of racial equality, the creative strategies black and white activists deployed to challenge it, and the obstacles they faced.

It is, of course, futile to search for one single moment of origin. The North was never a place of primeval racial innocence. It had a long—if mostly forgotten—history of chattel slavery. Many northern fortunes in banking, textiles, and shipping were built on the backs of unfree laborers. Cities such as New York, Philadelphia, and Providence rose to economic power because of the trade in slaves and the products of plantations in the South and Caribbean. As slavery waned in the nineteenth-century North, racial inequality persisted and, in many places, hardened. In 1835, Alexis de Tocqueville trenchantly observed that "in the North the white no longer clearly perceives the barrier that is supposed to separate him from this debased race, and he shuns the Negro all the more assiduously for fear that he might one day become indistinguishable from him." Even in those northern states that had abolished or prohibited slavery, Tocqueville observed that "the Negro is free, but he cannot share the rights, pleasures, labors, or sorrows—not even the tomb of him whose equal he has been declared to be. There is no place where the two can come together, whether in life or death." Northern abolitionists worked to destroy slavery both in their own region and in the South. Black and white activists, sometimes working separately, at other times collaboratively, participated in the Underground Railroad, valiantly fought the South to liberate the slaves, and struggled to abolish racially separate schools and racially restricted voting throughout the nineteenth century.

Deeply rooted, the scope and scale and form of racial protest changed dramatically as millions of African Americans moved northward in the 1920s, in search of the "promised land," the "New Canaan," or the "sweet land of liberty." The Great Migration was—for many—in itself a political act. It was an assertion of independence from the economic and legal chains of semifreedom in the South. In the wake of the influx, northern cities became hothouses of organizing. Newcomers discovered that the North was a far more troubled and unequal place than they had been led to believe. Many disillusioned northern blacks compared their region unfavorably with the South. Cleveland became "Alabama North." Detroit was "the northernmost Southern city." Philadelphia was "Up South." During World War II, a Brooklyn minister bluntly argued that "when it comes to the way the Negro is treated, the only difference between the North and the South is the weather."

The period from the Depression through World War II, in particular, cannot be seen solely or primarily as a "prelude" or "foreshadowing" of what was to come later. Black militancy, especially on economic issues, reshaped local and national politics. The emergence of interracial coalitions, an emphasis on the intersection of race and class, and the explosion of organized and unorganized protests give this era importance in its own right. The vast majority of northern whites cared little about African Americans and racial justice; many were overtly hostile to blacks. Yet a small but growing number, most of them religious activists or secular leftists, joined the struggle during the Depression and World War II. Sometimes working together, sometimes apart, black activists and their allies accomplished change.

Likewise, the postwar years were not, as conventional wisdom has it, a sleepy period of consensus. Rather, it was in the 1940s and 1950s that the frames that would shape the struggle for civil rights in the United States emerged: the belief in racial inequality as a moral and psychological problem and the emphasis on racism as an individual pathology. The postwar years spawned notions about racial inequality, its causes, and its solutions that have remained influential for the last half century, namely the belief that changing images and representations of race, by fostering tolerance and promoting diversity, would purge whites of their prejudices and uplift blacks from the "inferiority complex" that was believed to be the root of their subordinate status in American society.

By beginning in the pre–World War II years and carrying the story through to the present, *Sweet Land of Liberty* challenges the tired clichés of recent books that fixate on the 1960s as the fundamental turning point in the history of race in modern America. Many prominent analysts of race relations argue that the ideal of a color-blind society met its demise in the destructive 1960s. The nonviolent vision of Martin Luther King, Jr., gave way to the angry rhetoric of Malcolm X. Blacks wanted too much, too fast. Whites recoiled at the angry militancy of black power. When cities exploded in riots, the "silent majority" gave up all hopes of racial reconciliation. In the aftermath of the bloody summers of the late 1960s, minorities and their well-intentioned liberal supporters embraced a pernicious identity politics that deepened America's racial divide and destroyed the integrationist dream of a land where character, not skin color, mattered most. This story is powerful for its simplicity. It has been influential in shaping national politics. It is also terribly incomplete.

The 1960s matter, but the period was profoundly shaped by what came before. Black radicalism did not burst onto the scene in 1966 when Stokely Carmichael famously uttered the words "black power." It had a deeper history. Contrary to the conventional story of the decline of civil rights, postwar integrationism reached its crescendo, not its doom, in the 1960s. Activists who had cut their teeth in Depression and World War II–era protests (as well as the strategies they devised) did not simply disappear. In the 1960s, they pushed once again for policies that would solve racial and economic inequality simultaneously. The history of social movements in the 1960s also confounds the sharp dichotomy between black power and civil rights. The travails of black power had less to do with its challenge to the supposedly color-blind consensus and more to do with its acceptance of the very structures of local government and grassroots self-help that were embraced by the resurgent conservative movement.

Most histories of the civil rights movement peter out in the late 1960s. Commentators write of a "post–civil rights era" when "the marching stopped," but in the post-sixties years, civil rights activism did not cease. However, it did take new forms and faced an increasingly hostile political climate. Beginning in the 1970s, thousands of blacks were elected to office in northern cities, an unprecedented shift in the color of local and national politics. By 1996, sixty-seven cities with populations over 50,000 had elected black mayors. Unprecedented numbers of blacks served on city councils, school boards, in local and federal courts, and in statewide offices. The surge in black political power may have been the most enduring consequence of the civil rights revolution, but the gains came with ever-growing burdens. Just as blacks took the helm, federal expenditures on cities and social welfare programs began to plummet; suburbanization continued apace; and the flight of jobs and capital accelerated. Scrutinized closely by the news media, held to high expectations by their black constituents, and viewed with deep skepticism by white suburbanites, black elected officials found themselves in paradoxical situations. Out-numbered and politically marginal, black mayors and local elected officials largely sought to preserve their fragile gains, while watching angrily as civil rights and social welfare programs atrophied.

"COLOR IS NOT a human or a personal reality," wrote novelist James Baldwin in 1962, "it is a political reality." It is now axiomatic in biology that race is a meaningless concept. It is a term that describes skin tone variation but little else. The genetic and physiological variations among members of supposedly homogeneous racial groups are as great as the differences among the so-called races. What race means varies widely from society to society and in different periods of history. Yet its pretense to being anthropological or scientific allows race to persist as a means of classification, as a system for allocating power and resources, and as a tool for depriving one segment of the population of the full perquisites of citizenship. Race is a political construction, one whose pernicious consequences can be unmade only through political action.

This book is a political history. The battle for racial equality in modern America has had high political stakes and real material consequences. I define politics broadly, to encompass organized and unorganized protests, riots, grassroots organizing, intellectual advocacy and engaged journalism, electoral politics, policy making, and litigation. *Sweet Land of Liberty* explores efforts by ordinary citizens and civil rights activists to push at the boundaries of citizenship, to incorporate African Americans into an economy that had marginalized them, into a consumer culture that held out false promises of inclusion, into schools that deemed them uneducable, into neighborhoods where they were viewed as pariahs. It is a history of efforts to change the law, to gain a voice in electoral politics, to influence public debate. It explores the social movements that civil rights activists created, joined, and transformed—from churches to civil rights advocacy groups to political parties.

Social movements have an impact on public policy. Public policies and national politics shape and constrain the options available to activists. Many histories of civil rights artificially separate the local and the national, the micro and the macro. Policy makers at the local, state, and federal levels were influenced by grassroots activists. Most protestors did not draft civil rights laws, propose legislation, or enact regulations. But they raised the issues of racial exclusion in public forums, through demonstrations, pamphlets, and newspaper articles. They also organized politically—both inside and outside normal electoral channels. They marched through the courts, using the law as a weapon to overturn racial segregation. Their victories were seldom complete or wholly satisfying. Grassroots activists faced their opponents on an uneven playing field. Their movements were shaped and constrained by political and economic institutions over which they often had little control. Advocates of racial equality—and their opponents—were both very much products of their times, of a history not always of their own making.

The history of civil rights activism is inseparable from that of national-level political and economic history. Northern blacks—and their allies—made their own history, but on a contested terrain. Events in such far-flung places as Delhi and Addis Ababa affected activists in Chicago and Harlem. Shifting politics in Washington, D.C.—from the New Deal to the New Right—created moments of political possibility and, just as often, limited or foreclosed them. And the decisions of policy makers about where to allocate tax dollars, where to build housing, how to distribute welfare, how to fund schools, and what procedures should be in place to determine who is hired and who is fired—all of these seemingly distant, impersonal, bureaucratic decisions affected people's everyday lives. They could be seen in overcrowded urban schools. They could be seen in the slow opening of the American workplace to nonwhite people. They could be seen in the rutted streets of the inner cities that were home to a majority of the region's blacks. And they could be seen in the ring of suburban white prosperity, what Philadelphia reformer Richardson Dilworth called the "white noose" around the neck of the city. Even the ostensibly private realms of shopping, dining, leisure, and recreation were the product of public contests over white power and black autonomy. No issue was the subject of greater political contestation in the twentieth-century North than race.

Several currents made their way through northern politics—overlapping and reinforcing one another at some points, conflicting at others. Just as it cannot be confined to a brief historical period, the northern black freedom struggle cannot be reduced to a single impulse or political current. Except for in the pages of social science, where we try to find universal, generalizable rules of behavior, political actors and ordinary citizens seldom hold consistent views. Their motivations vary; their ideologies shift; their sense of what is possible and impossible, pragmatic and impracticable changes with the times.

One of the most deeply rooted themes in black politics was that of racial uplift and respectability. It manifested itself in the view that black elites—churchwomen, members of fraternities and sororities, ministers, educators, and organizational leaders—had the duty to use their privilege to better the black masses. Other activists embraced interracialism, arguing that collaboration across the divides of black and white was a moral imperative and a political necessity. Still others tapped a long current in black political thought, one that emphasized self-determination and self-help through the creation of all-black institutions. Weaving through these diverse positions, sometimes undermining them, at other times reinforcing them, were arguments about the root causes of racial inequality. By the 1930s, a wide range of activists—interracialists and separatists, advocates of uplift and those who promoted black unionism—were bound together by a common belief in the inseparability of questions of race and class.

Social movements for equality struggled with important questions: Should blacks organize separately or in collaboration with other groups? Should protests deploy the strategies of nonviolence and persuasion or self-defense and coercion? Should they combine them into something altogether different? Again and again, the history of northern activism confounds the simple dichotomies between integrationism and black power that shape conventional narratives of the movement. As we shall see, ordinary blacks, as well as activists and political leaders, moved fluidly between the strategies of race consciousness and interracialism. The northern civil rights movement was characterized by improvisation and reformulation. Activists and ordinary citizens could—and did—hold seemingly contradictory ideas simultaneously: working for the creation of an interracial society in the long run but supporting separatism in the short run, or deploying the tactics of peaceful persuasion but turning to more coercive forms of protest in the face of changing political circumstances. Many blacks fashioned a politics not easily defined as nonviolent or violent, integrationist or separationist.

The tensions between integration and separation also shaped white politics. Many northern whites supported integrationism in rhetoric but rejected it in practice. One of the most important stories of race in modern America is the widespread acceptance of racial separation as natural, as the result of ostensibly race-neutral market decisions, of individual choices, rather than of public policy. Among whites, racial separatism was widely practiced but, especially in the aftermath of the campaigns to discredit overt racism, dared not speak its name.

Northern civil rights activists also struggled over profound questions of morality and political theory that still have implications for the ways we think about race and inequality. From the 1930s to the present, an important cadre of northern activists argued that racial inequality was embedded in American economic, legal, and political institutions: Racial differences were not solely or primarily a matter of personal beliefs or prejudiced attitudes. In this view, achieving racial equality required contesting power—reforming or fundamentally transforming key American institutions, including the real estate industry, city governments, the welfare system, and, in the view of the most radical, the very system of American capitalism itself. Another strand of activists—those who have been most influential in modern American history—emphasized racism as an individual moral and psychological problem: one in the hearts and minds of misguided whites. Racial inequality would be solved by eliminating prejudice, by persuading whites to tolerate or accept blacks as their equals. These efforts focused on changing the boundaries of discourse and of modifying representations of race, through therapy, advertising, education, and the media. In this view, eliminating racial inequality was a matter of changing attitudes and beliefs; institutional change would follow.

Activists also grappled with another major issue: the matter of race itself. Should we accept the timeless and enduring reality of racial separation? In the North, the commitment to racial equality was often symbolic and rhetorical—and it grew as the result of civil rights activism. But at the same time, a growing number of blacks and whites accepted—even embraced—the idea that there were permanent, ultimately irreconcilable racial differences. Should blacks trouble themselves with whites, or should they imagine themselves as an oppressed colony, a nation within a nation? Should whites continue to make sacrifices for black folks, who should pull themselves up by their bootstraps and help themselves? Even as science and social science discredited notions of race as real and essential, many Americans clung to notions of race and identity as permanent, fixed, unchanging.

The pages of this book are peopled with figures—some forgotten, some famous—whose careers embody many of the major currents of racial politics in the twentieth century. Some of the stories that follow will be familiar to specialists but unfamiliar to nearly everyone else. Some give voice to activists, movements, and organizations that do not fit into conventional narratives about civil rights and black power. Many recast the histories of well-known organizations and political figures, offering new vantage points on well-researched topics. More so than most scholars, civil rights historians have emphasized individual acts of resistance, single acts of defiance, moments of sheer courage and heroism. But most of the actors in the black freedom struggle north and south did not act alone. They were part of collective efforts to accomplish change, and, however heroic, they were part of something much larger than themselves.

Political change did not happen as the sum of individual actions. Advocates of racial equality (and, for that matter, their opponents) worked collectively, through an extraordinary web of organizations. Perhaps more than any other group in American society, African Americans were joiners. Over the course of the twentieth century, black activists founded and supported a remarkable array of institutions, pressure groups, political organizations, religious congregations, fraternities, sororities, and social clubs. Most of them advocated the cause of racial equality. And when they were most successful, they forged alliances, built unlikely coalitions, often across the lines of race, religion, and class, and linked local, national, and international issues.

The North is, of course, vast. By some definitions, it encompasses everything outside of the former Confederate States of America; by others, it simply includes the Midwest and Northeast. By necessity, this book focuses on the states with the largest black populations outside the South: New York (which had the largest black population of any state in 1960), Pennsylvania, New Jersey, Ohio, Michigan, and Illinois; but, occasionally, California, Indiana, Minnesota, Washington, Massachusetts, and Connecticut appear. The battle for racial equality in the North played out with special intensity in the major cities that were home to nearly four-fifths of the black population outside Dixie. But struggles for civil rights also reshaped small towns and suburbs—a part of the northern story that has been almost completely overlooked.

The northern battles over civil rights raised fundamental questions that we still grapple with today—in the North as well as the South. Who is responsible for racial inequality, for interracial hostility, for poverty, for crime and violence, for persistent racial divisions? To understand *our* America, we must give as much attention to the unheralded struggles for civil rights in the factories, churches, and neighborhoods of Philadelphia, New York, and Detroit, the schools of Harlem and New Rochelle and Gary and Chicago, and the movie theaters of Cincinnati as we have to the now-epic events of Greensboro, Birmingham, Montgomery, and Selma. The history of the struggle for racial equality in the North—its triumphs and failures, its ironies and unexpected outcomes—opens up new ways of exploring the most important, and still unfinished, history of race, rights, and politics in modern America.

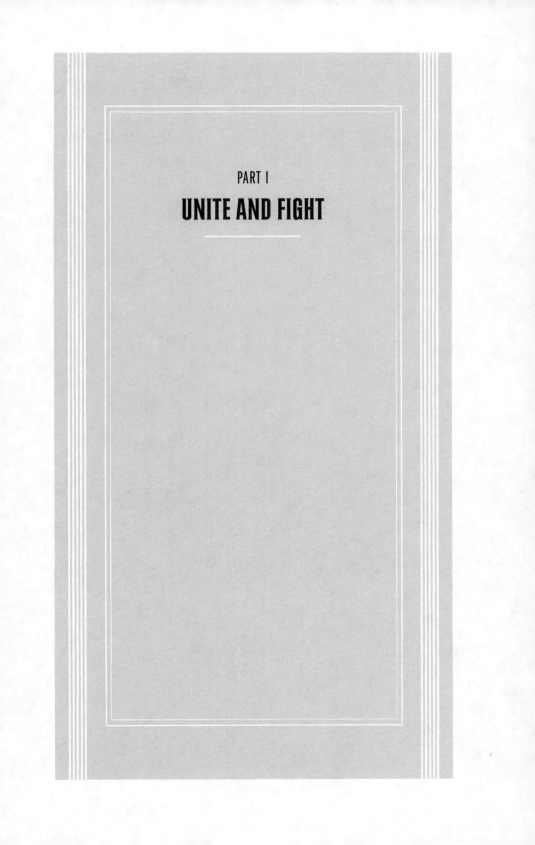

PART I

UNITE AND FIGHT

CHAPTER 1

"SWEET LAND OF LIBERTY"

And this will be the day—this will be the day when all of God's children
will be able to sing with new meaning:

> *My country 'tis of thee, sweet land of liberty, of thee I sing.*
> *Land where my fathers died, land of the Pilgrim's pride,*
> *From every mountainside, let freedom ring!*

And if America is to be a great nation, this must become true.
And so let freedom ring from the prodigious hilltops of New Hampshire.
Let freedom ring from the mighty mountains of New York.
Let freedom ring from the heightening Alleghenies of Pennsylvania.
Let freedom ring from the snow-capped Rockies of Colorado.
Let freedom ring from the curvaceous slopes of California.
But not only that:
Let freedom ring from Stone Mountain of Georgia.
Let freedom ring from Lookout Mountain of Tennessee.
Let freedom ring from every hill and molehill of Mississippi.
From every mountainside, let freedom ring.

AS THE REVEREND MARTIN LUTHER KING, JR., BROUGHT HIS SPEECH AT THE
1963 March on Washington for Jobs and Freedom to a thundering close,
Anna Arnold Hedgeman sat a few feet away. It was a long-overdue moment of recognition for the sixty-four-year-old civil rights activist, though
it was bittersweet. The only woman on the steering committee for the
march, Hedgeman had a place of honor on the dais at the base of the Lincoln Memorial. It was only at the last minute, at her insistence, that
march organizers gave a few minutes on the program to Little Rock
leader Daisy Bates and "casually" introduced Rosa Parks to the crowd.
Hedgeman remained unacknowledged, her presence mute testimony to
the importance of decades of grassroots organizing, much of it in the

North, that had brought a quarter of a million people to the greatest demonstration in the nation's history. It is safe to say that most of the marchers gathered that hot August afternoon had no idea who she was. At a moment when the black freedom struggle was growing younger and more militant, Hedgeman was part of a largely forgotten generation of activists, women and men, black and white, religious and secular, whose lives embodied the long history of civil rights in the North.

Anna Arnold Hedgeman's journey began in the small-town Midwest at the dawn of the twentieth century, took her through the North, and brought her into the heart of a remarkable and diverse political and social movement to challenge racial inequality in America. She came of age as millions of blacks headed north in search of opportunity but faced a regime of racial proscription there that was every bit as deeply entrenched as the southern system of Jim Crow. During her lifetime of activism, she encountered grassroots school desegregation activists and angry Klansmen; black and white churchwomen committed to dialogue on race relations; poor black migrants and struggling women workers; hypocritical white liberals who mouthed their commitment to racial equality but continued to profit from it; musicians, activists, and intellectuals who created the Harlem Renaissance; black separatists dreaming of a proud black nation; and blue-collar activists committed to building an interracial labor movement. A tireless woman of political savvy and considerable charm, she worked with nearly every important civil rights activist in the first half of the twentieth century.

Hedgeman started life born into the "talented tenth," a term coined by W.E.B. Du Bois for the highly educated, deeply religious, and well-connected black men and women who saw their mission as uplifting the race. Pious and proper, she was the embodiment of the black churchwoman, sometimes prone to self-righteousness but deeply committed to leading a life of faith in service of social change. For Hedgeman, as it was for many early-twentieth-century black activists, there was no boundary between politics and piety, between prayer and protest. Her calling was both spiritual and practical but also open to the dramatically changing circumstances of America as it was remade by the massive black diaspora. Hedgeman's encounter with the troubled and unresolved history of race and inequality in the North profoundly altered her vocation. She found herself drawn to the plight of poor and working-class Americans, especially the black women born in circumstances far less fortunate than her own. Even if she never jettisoned her intense religiosity or her sense of propriety, she came to see that the project of uplifting the poor into bourgeois respectability by prayer, admonition, or moral education would never be sufficient. Because of her encounter with racial and economic injustice, she came to argue that the plight of the black poor would be overcome only through a wholescale political and economic transformation.

ANNA ARNOLD'S CHILDHOOD was anything but ordinary. She grew up in a nearly all-white world. Born in Marshalltown, Iowa, in 1899 and raised in Anoka, Minnesota, in a devout household, she was the daughter of a college-educated southern migrant so light-skinned that he could pass for white. William Arnold was a preacher and educator committed to the prohibition of alcohol. A stern, devout man, he had high ambitions for his children. When Anna was still an infant, the Arnolds found their way to Anoka, a relatively prosperous lumber and mill town on the northernmost reaches of the Mississippi River, twenty miles northwest of Minneapolis. Only 8,809 blacks lived in the entire state in 1920. Anoka's tiny black population had risen from only 15 to 41 in the first two decades of the twentieth century. The only blacks Arnold knew for most of her childhood were immediate family members. Minnesota was relatively liberal, its white population more indifferent than hostile to the small number of blacks who peppered the state. Anna Arnold did not recall facing any racial hostility as a child, but it did affect others. In 1931, less than ten years after she left her hometown, a black Anokan barely escaped a lynch mob.

Comfortable as the only black person in a room full of whites, she became the first black student at Hamline University, a small Methodist school in St. Paul. It was there, in Minnesota's capital, where racial tensions were soaring, that she had her first serious encounters with other African Americans. Several thousand blacks had moved into the Twin Cities in the early 1920s, leading to a tightening of racial restrictions in schools, housing, and employment. One member of Arnold's social circle in St. Paul was Roy Wilkins, two years her junior and later president of the National Association for the Advancement of Colored People (NAACP).

Fresh from college, Wilkins wrote a scathing account of their home state, decrying the "complacency" and "indifference" of its black leadership. "The most regrettable and almost tragic feature of life in Minnesota," wrote Wilkins, "is that Negroes are so satisfied with their condition that they are blind to the signs of a new time."

In the 1920s, blacks faced growing hostility in the North. Throughout the region, restrictive covenants—clauses in home deeds that forbade blacks and other minorities from purchasing or renting homes—proliferated. Nearly every new housing development built during the booming 1920s was closed to blacks. Those who attempted to breach the invisible color lines that separated neighborhoods faced violent reprisals. The result was a steep rise in housing segregation. The Ku Klux Klan gained strongholds in nearly every northern city in the 1920s. Chicago's Klan, for example, had nearly forty thousand members, and nearly one in three white men in Indiana belonged to the group at its peak in the mid-1920s. In Detroit, a Klansman lost election to the Detroit mayoralty on a technicality in 1924. Blacks faced growing restrictions. Shopkeepers, restaurant owners, and theater managers proclaimed their premises for whites only. And racially separate schools proliferated, particularly in northern towns that attracted large numbers of black migrants. Nearly all of these proscriptions—as Wilkins called them—were defended by law enforcement authorities.

Anna Arnold had her first serious encounter with discrimination as a twenty-two-year-old. An ambitious student, she pursued one of the few professions open to educated black women—teaching. But St. Paul had a very small black population, and its school district had no interest in placing a "colored" teacher in one of its white schools. (With few exceptions, hardly any black teachers taught white students in the North until the mid-1950s.) Frustrated by her experience and eager to see the larger world, she took a teaching job at Rust College in Holly Springs, Mississippi, a small, all-black "citadel of moralistic Methodism." The students at Rust were, for the most part, poorly educated; the school had a small budget; and Holly Springs could not have been more different from Anoka or St. Paul. Arnold found the indignities of southern-style Jim Crow difficult to negotiate, though she learned a great deal about the history of race relations from her mentor, Rust College dean J. Leonard Farmer, whose son James would later move north and spearhead the

Congress of Racial Equality (CORE). Embittered by the "overwhelming difficulties" of life in the segregated South, she headed back north after two years, feeling a "deep hate" toward southern whites.

In 1924, Anna Arnold was hired by the YWCA, starting out in Springfield, Ohio. The town was hardly a refuge from the indignities that she had experienced in the South, but the Y provided a springboard for her ambition. A bastion of liberal Protestantism amid the fundamentalist revival of the 1920s, the Y attracted young, idealistic, churchgoing women who used their talents to reform and uplift poor and working-class women through continuing education, moral training, cultural events, and physical fitness programs. By the 1920s, the YWCA movement was also tentatively interracial, drawing together churchwomen who began to experiment with "interracial dialogues." One of the few white-dominated institutions that hired black women to positions of leadership, the Y became the base for a whole generation of ambitious black social workers, educators, and administrators. Building on a Christian understanding of the "brotherhood of all mankind," the Y's moral integrationists worked within churches and religious organizations toward the goal of interracial cooperation. It was a daunting challenge when, as the old adage went, Sunday services were the most segregated hour in America. Most whites listened to white ministers, imagined Jesus as white, and could scarcely envision a heaven without segregation. Religious interracialists had modest goals: to foster "tolerance" of racial difference, to encourage whites to grapple with the presence of "the Negro problem" in their midst, and to create spaces for interracial dialogue through what one skeptical observer called "tea, touch, and talk." To white interracialists, the very prospect of attending conferences with blacks was heady. And to black interracialists, especially those who aspired to respectability, interracial meetings were a rare opening to a white world mostly forbidden to them.

When Arnold started with the Y, it was part of a still-tentative religious interracialist movement. Beginning in the 1920s, the Federal Council of Churches, an umbrella organization of mainline Protestant denominations, created a Department of Racial and Cultural Relations. Through the mid-1960s, it published a bimonthly newsletter, the *Interracial News Service*, and sponsored "Race Relations Sunday," an annual event in which pastors were encouraged to bring up questions of racial inequality in sermons or, for the less adventuresome, in church newsletters or afternoon seminars. However symbolic such efforts were, they attracted a dedicated cadre of activists, committed to the ideal of persuasion, who envisioned the problem of racial inequality as a moral problem. Their vision of "brotherhood," that all were equal in the eyes of Christ, would lead a small but growing number of whites to embrace the goals of the fledgling struggle for black equality.

Protestant interracialism, especially in the Y, drew much of its vision from the missionary movement. Missionaries were often agents of American imperialism, men and women who dedicated their lives to bringing civilization and Christianity to the unchurched, uneducated, and undemocratic peoples of the world. As the United States extended its political, military, and economic reach abroad in the early twentieth century, missionaries were often on the front lines. However, overseas mission work had unintended consequences. By the 1920s, many returning missionaries, particularly white women, had been transformed by their encounter with foreign people of color. Though most were incapable of wholly jettisoning their sense of moral and political superiority, many returned from these stints humbled by their experiences and outraged at the suffering, deprivation, and political oppression they had witnessed. A small, vocal, and growing segment of churchwomen began to compare the situation of American blacks to that of the oppressed peoples overseas. Haltingly, they began to demand that their own churches extend their mission work to Negroes—and, even more important, they began to argue for the full recognition of blacks within their own churches. By the late 1920s, they began to push even further, forging alliances with like-minded black churchwomen.

The Y movement was influenced by similar interracial currents, but like most institutions in the early twentieth century—even the most progressive—YMCAs and YWCAs were still strictly segregated by race. Any self-respecting northern city had its "White-WCA" and, if its black population was large enough, its Negro Y, a place that provided social services, housing and food, and education for urban blacks. The Negro Y was one of the most visible manifestations of a politics of respectability and race uplift that had infused black politics since the late nineteenth century. In this vision of social reform, the black elite had a special duty to promote a new vision of "the race," one that challenged prevailing white assumptions about innate black inferiority. Well-to-do blacks emphasized the importance of propriety, embracing a set of Victorian values of decorum, restraint, and caution that distanced them from the black masses, whose dress was garish; music profane; religion overly emotional; accents backward and folkish; and habits feckless and irresponsible. Respectability required abstinence from the pleasures of the flesh, a proper and restrained religion, and conservative dress. The politics of uplift was deeply condescending, but also hopeful that the poor and working classes could be redeemed through the charitable efforts and good example of their betters.

Black women such as Arnold played a special role in the politics of uplift and respectability. Since the late nineteenth century, black women had created an extraordinary base of sororities and clubs. At lunches and teas, they gathered to socialize and to build lasting networks of friendship. As much as clubwomen liked to don their fine dresses, hats, and gloves, they were motivated by a higher purpose, a deep sense of responsibility toward their disadvantaged sisters. As "race women," they had a twofold duty: first, to embody the very virtues that whites believed were inherently lacking in black culture, and, second, to instill those virtues in the downtrodden. Through their moral example, but also through reform institutions, churches, and schools, black women hoped to modify the behavior and values of the poor and thus undermine the racial stereotypes that prevented the full recognition of Negroes as citizens. To be sure, early-twentieth-century black elites had no monopoly on the ideology of uplift. Progressive-era reformers—black and white alike—condescended toward the poor and created a bevy of institutions to control and discipline the ill-behaved, the "uncultured," and the unruly. But because of the deep currents of racial oppression, blacks viewed uplift as a distinct task to be performed by blacks themselves. At the very core of the politics of uplift was a belief in racial solidarity and self-help. It was up to Negroes to pull their disadvantaged people out of spiritual and economic impoverishment.

One of the most established women's groups, the National Association of Colored Women (NACW), had more than one hundred thousand members, including Anna Arnold, in 1924. Its motto, "Lifting as we climb," expressed its members' aspirations. Working through their churches, they provided food, clothing, and other supplies to impoverished families, paying special heed to the needs of new migrants to northern cities. Under the leadership of Mary Church Terrell, the NACW did more than provide charity. It also joined women's voices in a collective demand for political reform. NACW members pushed for antilynching and antidiscrimination laws, demanded an end to racially inferior education, and collaborated with a wide range of black and white groups to push for social welfare policies that would benefit poor and working women, regardless of race.

The Great Migration gave a real sense of urgency to advocates of racial uplift. Established northern blacks—the "old settlers"—recoiled at the influx of southerners, many of whom arrived with few skills, little education, and little familiarity with urban life. But many blacks pooled their resources to create charities and reform organizations—usually with the support of white philanthropists—to facilitate the "adjustment" of newcomers to the North. The Travelers Aid Society and other local charitable organizations fanned out through train stations to rescue women arrivals from the lures of illicit life in the city. Settlement houses provided migrants with social services and education. And one of the most important black reform organizations, the Urban League, was founded in 1910 to provide job training and economic opportunity to penniless southern migrants. Urban League chapters—often in collaboration with Y's and church groups—conducted studies of the newcomers and, armed with data, set forth to rescue them, particularly the young women, from the disreputable boardinghouses, dance halls, and bars that they believed would lure migrants into a life of crime and vice. One of the league's most innovative programs was to instill black migrants with the values of thrift and discipline and, through connections with white employers, find them steady employment. The Y also put an emphasis on the transformative power of uplift. Through Christian education, edifying lectures, courses on hygiene, and camping and recreation programs, the Y would transform simple country women into upstanding, respectable urban citizens.

A natural leader, Anna Arnold rapidly moved up the ranks of the YWCA. Her Springfield posting was eye-opening. An industrial city of 60,000, Springfield was part of a belt of Ohio towns that had been bastions of abolitionism and Republicanism and, because of that, magnets for black southerners—first slaves, then impoverished southern blacks—in search of freedom. Its long-established black population of nearly 8,000 supported a Negro Y, a thriving NAACP chapter, and a black newspaper. But despite its storied past, Springfield was racked with black-white conflict in the early twentieth century. By the time Arnold arrived, race relations were raw. Three years earlier, whites had rampaged through the city's black section after rumors spread that a black man had attacked a white girl. It was the third riot that had devastated the town in two decades. In the aftermath of the 1921 riot, Springfield's newly organized Ku Klux Klan chapter attracted many of the town's most respectable, middle-class Protestant citizens, just as Klaverns did throughout the North. Its membership, numbering about three thousand, even included the school board president, who led the school district—against Ohio law—to create an all-black elementary school in 1922.

Springfield's blacks did not sit back passively. As the 1922–23 school year began, a large group of black parents boycotted the colored school. While parents held their children from classes, the local NAACP branch filed a lawsuit against the district for violating Ohio law. Not all Springfield blacks supported the boycott and litigation. A minority—led by black educators—supported separate education because the new school provided teaching jobs for women who did not stand a chance of employment in the town's white-dominated schools. The Springfield school controversy was a foreshadowing of how divisive the issue of race and education would become in the North. The parents won their suit—a judge ruled that the separate school was illegal—but were powerless to enforce the ruling. The district retaliated by firing its black schoolteachers. Arnold was surely outraged, given her experience in St. Paul. Springfield's elementary schools remained almost completely segregated by race because of the growing concentration of the town's black population in its new "Negro ghetto."

Separate and unequal was not just the rule in Springfield's schools. Jim Crow northern-style also pervaded the town's everyday life. The town's hotel, white-owned restaurants, and theaters excluded blacks. Although she was a YWCA official, Arnold could not even take a meal in the cafeteria of Springfield's central Y. The segregation of public accommodations was the norm in the North in the early twentieth century. It outraged Arnold, and shortly after she arrived in Springfield, she made common cause with Springfield's civil rights activists. With a small group of black women, she demanded the desegregation of the well-equipped central YWCA. As a fallback—if Springfield's Y's remained separate—she demanded funding to bring the facilities at the Negro Y up to the white standard. Arnold and her fellow activists pursued a strategy common among northern advocates of racial equality in the early twentieth century. They wanted access to first-class facilities, but if integration failed, they would settle for a separate but equal solution. The all-white board of the Community Chest (the white-led group that funded the Y) rebuffed their demands. Springfield's Y, like most of the town's institutions, would remain separate and unequal. "There were no signs 'colored' and 'white,' " she recalled, "but the wall of separation was as vivid in the minds of Negroes and whites as though the signs were present."

Arnold did not stay in Springfield for long. She was a young woman of great talent, destined for a more prominent post. With the encouragement of her colleagues, she won a position at the Jersey City, New Jersey, YWCA. There she gained more bitter experience with northern poverty and discrimination and sharpened her critique of racial inequality. A gritty riverfront town full of small factories, warehouses, and wharves, Jersey City had a rapidly growing black population. Many YWCA members were washerwomen and recent migrants who toiled in the city's industrial laundries. It was grueling work, "hot and disagreeable and . . . poorly paid." In the drying rooms, temperatures regularly rose over one hundred degrees. You could tell a laundress by her hands, chapped by exposure to water or raw with contact with lye and bleach. Striving to overcome her privileged background, Arnold worked a weeklong stint in a laundry, where she jettisoned her "dearly cherished Midwestern ideas about the ability of the individual to accomplish on his own." Slaving shoulder to shoulder with black workers entrapped by discrimination, she grew increasingly distrustful of northern whites. "Good Christian white people who thought of themselves as 'liberal' if they invited a Negro speaker to their meetings" turned blind eyes to workers pushed into the "lowest paid and the most menial" jobs. She also came to realize that Jersey City's poor and working-class women needed uplift much less than they did good pay and workplace safety. Economic injustice and pervasive discrimination knew no regional boundaries. "The North and the South" shared a "basic philosophy," she concluded. "In the South the weapon was a meat axe; in the North, a stiletto. Both are lethal weapons."

Between 1927 and 1933, as the Harlem Renaissance gave way to the ravages of the Great Depression, Arnold joined the staff at the segregated YWCA on New York's West 137th Street, in the capital of black America. No place was more exciting for a single, black woman in her late twenties and early thirties than Harlem, and no place more challenging to a young social reformer. The 1920s had witnessed a black political and cultural awakening in the North. As millions of blacks migrated to New York, Chicago, Philadelphia, and Detroit, a remarkable cadre of "New Negroes"—black artists, writers, activists, and intellectuals—celebrated the distinctive contributions of black culture. Like Chicago's Bronzeville or Detroit's Paradise Valley but on a larger scale, Harlem was institutionally rich, home to the churches, political clubs, jazz clubs, and speakers' corners that created a public space for the "New Negro," assertive, race-conscious, and politically engaged.

Anna Arnold was too prim, too much of a small-town midwesterner to be drawn into Harlem's bars and dance halls, as alluring as they were. But she was never isolated from the city's vital cultural life. The Harlem YWCA was a social, political, and intellectual hub. Nearly every major and minor poet, politician, civil rights leader, and minister made an appearance there. Poets Langston Hughes and Countee Cullen gave readings; NAACP founder and towering black intellectual W.E.B. Du Bois addressed its assembled members; Paul Robeson filled its auditorium with song and black classical musicians held packed recitals; A. Philip Randolph, founder of the Brotherhood of Sleeping Car Porters, rallied for support of the trade union movement. Black clubwomen Mary Church Terrell and Mary McLeod Bethune, both staunch advocates of women's welfare, offered inspiring lectures. Black travelers from all over the country—even celebrities—took rooms at the Y because they were excluded from nearly all white-owned hotels. In its meeting rooms, religious groups prayed, labor activists organized, and civil rights organizations planned demonstrations.

Arnold also reveled in the rich cultural life of Harlem outside the walls of the Y. Brilliant, socially graceful, and well positioned, she quickly found herself a part of New York's black elite. She frequented soirées in the elegant ballroom of Harlem's Hotel Theresa, where, like many "society ladies," she took an apartment. There, she socialized with writers, musicians, and artists. And in 1933, she married former Fisk Jubilee singer Merritt Hedgeman, a well-regarded member of Harlem's artistic circles.

Even as she led the charmed life of a socialite, Anna Arnold Hedgeman walked through the grim streets and alleys of New York misery. Wrenching poverty was inescapable in Depression-era Harlem. Unemployment skyrocketed to 60 percent and employers slashed wages for those lucky enough to keep their jobs. As an administrator at the Y, she heard countless stories of families forced to beg and steal, living on the brink of starvation amid the country's worst economic downturn. She walked past the corners where hungry men and women gathered, desperate for jobs as day laborers. She felt the anguish of the emaciated women and children who "searched in garbage cans for food, foraging with dogs and cats." And she grew increasingly frustrated that the Y, like most private charities during the Depression, simply did not have the resources to provide for the legion of poor people it valiantly struggled to serve.

Harlem provided Hedgeman with a crash course in politics. In Springfield, she had been introduced to grassroots organizing around equal education. In Jersey City, she had had her first experience with the labor movement. But it was in Harlem where she experienced northern black politics in all its complexity and diversity. Hedgeman arrived in New York when black political life was in a state of flux. The 1920s had marked the zenith of post–Civil War black separatism. Harlem was the movement's center. From at least the nineteenth century, an influential current of black activists had advocated the creation of separate, all-black communities within the boundaries of the United States; others held a vision of black people liberated by their return to Africa. In the 1870s and 1880s, freed blacks had created separate towns scattered throughout the South. Others had migrated westward to Kansas, and later, Oklahoma, where they hoped to free themselves from the chains of southern peonage and Jim Crow. Some former slaves headed to Liberia, where black American colonists created their own republic. Many southern migrants had carried northward a deep sympathy for the vernacular separatism of the emigrationist societies; others had a sense of nationhood that had been nurtured in the fraternal lodges and churches of the post-Emancipation South. All these currents came together in Harlem, where emigrationists and advocates of Pan-Africanism, religious nationalism, and black economic self-determination debated on Harlem's street corners, published tracts, and held mass meetings.

The largest of the separatist movements was led by Marcus Garvey, a Jamaican immigrant and entrepreneur whose Harlem-based Universal Negro Improvement Association (UNIA) called for black economic independence. Garvey encouraged American blacks to reclaim their African identity and laid the groundwork for what he hoped would be a mass migration back to Africa. Founded in 1916, Garvey's movement reached its pinnacle of influence just after World War I, fueled by black discontent at the limitations of black progress both in the rural South and in northern cities. The postwar experience proved an especially bitter pill for blacks. Leaders such as W.E.B. Du Bois had supported the war effort, hoping that blacks would be rewarded with the full rights of citizenship in exchange for their service. And hundreds of thousands of former sharecroppers, manual laborers, and household servants had migrated north, hoping that wartime employment would lead to real economic advancement. Blacks found themselves among the proverbial "last hired and first fired at war's end" and faced a torrent of racial violence in the aftermath of the war (including bloody race riots in East St. Louis and Chicago) and routine police abuse on the streets of nearly every major city. In this climate of intense racial hostility, Garvey's call for black dignity and self-determination resonated deeply. "No more fear," he proclaimed, "no more cringing, no more sycophantic begging and pleading."

Garvey offered a powerful alternative vision—one that combined a popular critique of imperialism with a call for black self-determination and independence. Few Garveyites actually seriously considered leaving the United States, but the UNIA offered a compelling vision of self-help and a celebration of the pride of African ancestry. More than any black leader in the early twentieth century, Garvey galvanized audiences with his powerful rhetoric and built an enormous, if short-lived, mass movement. "Being satisfied to drink of the dregs from the cup of human progress," proclaimed Garvey, "will not demonstrate our fitness as a people to exist alongside of others, but when of our own initiative we strike out to build industries, governments, and ultimately empires, then and only then will we as a race prove to our Creator and to man in general that we are fit to survive and capable of shaping our own destiny." At the core of Garveyism was a vision of the empowered, militant black man defending the black homeland of Africa against European imperialists. Garvey organized paramilitary units, including the Universal African Legion, to be served by Black Cross nurses and the Black Star shipping line. On a smaller scale, local Garveyites founded black cooperative stores and self-help community institutions, all vehicles for economic independence, short of emigration.

The separatist impulse ran like a black thread through northern politics in the 1930s, even if it was sometimes only barely visible. By the onset of the Great Depression, when Hedgeman arrived in Harlem, the Garvey movement was greatly diminished. Garvey himself was jailed in 1925 and deported in 1927 on fraud charges. In his absence, the UNIA shattered. But many of Garvey's supporters, who gained political experience and revolutionary zeal in the UNIA, remained vocal grassroots activists. Harlem's remaining Garveyites staked out the famous "Speakers' Corner" at 125th Street and Seventh Avenue, where they harangued passersby. But the marginality of the UNIA did not mean that such sentiments had disappeared among African Americans. Many former Garvey supporters, such as Audley "Queen Mother" Moore, recast their race-conscious politics in the Communist Party, in black-led trade unions, and in other radical groups. Ex-Garveyites played a leading role in the "Don't Buy Where You Can't Work" boycotts that proliferated in the 1930s and influenced the budding cooperative movement, an effort to create independent, member-owned black stores in Harlem during the Depression. Even if most Garveyite businesses and cooperatives disappeared, the idea of black self-help enterprises remained powerful throughout the 1930s and beyond.

Separatist politics also remained alive among small cadres of black nationalists, religious separatists, and advocates of race pride. A lesser-known contemporary of Garvey, Noble Drew Ali, had launched the Moorish Science Temple of America in Newark during World War I. Ali's followers rejected their slavish Negro past for a newly assertive "Asiatic" identity. In Detroit, a peripatetic prophet named W. D. Fard, probably influenced by Ali, launched the Lost-Found Nation of Islam in 1930. By the mid-1930s, the Nation of Islam movement, led by Fard's successor, Elijah Muhammad, had outposts in a number of northern cities, including Harlem. Other separatists, most of them not as godly, embraced the "Forty-ninth State" movement, demanding that the United States set aside land for a separate Negro-controlled government.

Even if these movements remained small, separationism continued to appeal in a commonsensical way to ordinary blacks. Whatever their views on Garvey or religious nationalism, most northern blacks, especially in large cities, lived in a deeply segregated world. Between 1920 and 1940, blacks found themselves confined to neighborhoods left behind by fleeing whites, usually the most decrepit and overcrowded. Working-class whites often violently defended their neighborhoods against the "Negro invasion." In rapidly growing urban black neighborhoods, racial separation was an everyday reality, even for those who did not adopt it as an ideal. "There come times when the most persistent integrationist becomes an isolationist, when he curses the white world and consigns it to hell," wrote James Weldon Johnson during the depths of the Depression. "This tendency toward isolation . . . springs from a deep-seated, natural desire—a desire for respite from the unremitting, grueling struggle; for a place in which refuge might be taken."

All-black churches, social clubs, fraternities and sororities, and civic groups provided solidarity in the face of racial oppression. A later generation of activists (and scholars following them) drew a bright line between separationism and integrationism, between those who called for black self-determination and those who hoped to work with whites to demand civil rights and racial equality. But few could be so easily pigeonholed. Even Hedgeman found herself in a wholly black world, with only the most perfunctory contact with whites. She found solace in Harlem's blackness. "I developed no white friends," she recalled, "and wanted none." Hedgeman would never repudiate her commitment to racial integration, but throughout her career she argued that racial solidarity was a necessary precursor to racial equality. Later in life, she recalled hearing Malcolm X at Speakers' Corner. "I stood and I listened and I had to admit to myself that I was deeply moved." In 1966—nearly forty years after she arrived in Harlem—she joined a group of black religious activists who offered a critical endorsement of what they called the "anguished cry for 'black power.'"

Immersed in Harlem, Hedgeman grew ever more impatient with whites for their lack of comprehension of "the Negro." How could even the most well-meaning whites who lived in racially homogenous neighborhoods have the slightest idea about blacks' everyday tribulations? She could barely conceal her annoyance with white benefactors who visited the Harlem Y asking condescending questions like "What do Negroes want?" and "Don't you agree that intermarriage is bad for Negroes and for whites?" Their inevitable counsel of "patience" infuriated her. "It actually suggests that the Negro accept rejection on the basis of color as his lot until such time as white people decide that he can have rights which every other American expects on birth and on sight. How dare any man ask a Negro to wait for his rights when he has only one life to live?"

Hedgeman's Harlem was full of race-conscious activists, but it was also the nation's center of interracialism. Just a short walk from the YWCA was the headquarters of the National Association for the Advancement of Colored People. Many of the nation's most prominent black politicians and intellectuals—and a cadre of liberal whites—belonged to the venerable organization, and even more read the provocative, well-written articles, poems, and short stories published in *The Crisis*. Founded in 1909 for the purpose of achieving racial equality, the NAACP had increasingly turned its energies toward fighting segregation through litigation. Beginning in the 1920s, the NAACP leaders fashioned a legal strategy intended to undermine racial inequality through systematic litigation in voting, transportation, and education. The plan was to pick away at Jim Crow on a case-by-case basis, undermining the legal underpinnings of segregation or setting precedents in the local courts that would eventually work their way through the federal courts. A reform organization birthed in the Progressive era, the NAACP also served as a clearinghouse of information on the status of blacks. The old guard of the NAACP believed that the assiduous gathering of facts and data would provide formidable weapons in the struggle for equality.

Despite its visibility, the "N double A" failed to gain a mass following. Its top-down, reformist agenda generated little passion except among black professionals. Its membership stagnated throughout the early years of the Depression. As militant protests swept through nearly every segment of American society—from marches of the unemployed to sit-downs and strikes in heavy industry to mass movements for pensions and public works—the NAACP seemed out of step with the working-class black majority. Would cautious, incremental change within the system really transform everyday lives? A growing cadre of young leaders began to argue to the contrary. By the mid-1930s, the NAACP was increasingly divided over the issue of activism. The "Young Turks," an insurgent group, challenged the NAACP leadership for its failure to create a mass organization. However, not all of the NAACP's critics were youthful. W.E.B. Du Bois, by then in his sixties, was moving sharply leftward in the Depression years. He lamented his organization's stasis and called for "a frontal attack on race prejudice" before resigning from its leadership in 1934.

Hedgeman befriended many NAACP leaders through her community work and socializing, but she gravitated toward the insurgents. In August 1933, she joined thirty-one activists and intellectuals—among them Du Bois, sociologist E. Franklin Frazier, economist Abram Harris, and political scientist Ralph Bunche—at the Amenia, New York, estate of NAACP board president Joel Spingarn. Most of the Amenia participants, like Hedgeman, were young and impatient. The goal of the meeting was nothing less than rethinking the tired "methods and philosophy" of organizations dedicated to the advancement of African Americans. The four days of deliberation took on a leftist cast. In a statement released after the conference, the Amenia delegates called for a "new labor movement with Race workers as active participants." Organizing across class divisions among blacks, this "new labor movement" depended on interracial alliances with white workers. "Its activities," stated the delegates in a published report, "must be political as well as economic for the purpose of effecting such social legislation as old age pensions, unemployment insurance, the regulation of child and female labor, etc." It was, in the view of the Amenia delegates, impossible to separate race and class. The subordination of workers in an industrial society was the core of America's intertwined problems of racial and economic inequality.

Amenia had highlighted the failure of "race" institutions to deal with the structural causes of black poverty. Philanthropic and voluntary associations of all varieties struggled to meet the needs of their clients during the bleak Depression years. Black organizations faced even greater hurdles. Hedgeman's experience at the Y was disheartening. As the economy collapsed, she saw firsthand the limits of the charitable approach to social problems. Appalled by the crushing poverty in Harlem, she found herself overwhelmed by the lack of relief funds to deal with the "elemental need" of the poor. "I found myself making decisions on the basis of the number of children immediately in need of milk."

As the Depression worsened, the federal government began to fill the gap left by charitable organizations. Federal officials worked closely with nonprofits such as the YWCA. Both the Emergency Work Bureau and the Works Progress Administration placed unemployed workers in Harlem's Y and used its facilities to distribute relief checks. Fired up by a desire to accomplish larger-scale social change, Hedgeman left the Y in 1934 to join the New Deal. Her first post was in the Brownsville, Brooklyn, office of the Federal Emergency Relief Administration (FERA), where she could more effectively provide assistance to the poor. Blacks were disproportionately represented on New York's welfare rolls—the proportion on relief was nearly three times that of whites. By 1935, in the mid-Atlantic region, which included New York, a remarkable 55.6 percent of black families received relief because they were so destitute. After her stint with FERA, Hedgeman joined New York's welfare department, which was under intense pressure to provide better service to the city's impoverished black population. After four years in government service, she returned to the Y with a new vision of leadership and activism, and served as executive director of the Negro branch in Brooklyn.

Hedgeman joined the New Deal just as millions of blacks were beginning to shift their allegiance away from the Republican Party. However, jumping from the GOP onto the Roosevelt bandwagon was a leap of faith. Neither the Democrats nor the Republicans had established their bona fides on questions of concern to blacks. With few exceptions, those who advocated racial equality came from the fringes of American politics. Some atavistic members of the Grand Old Party still looked longingly at the days when the party of Lincoln was the party of emancipation and citizenship. The Democrats, so beholden to their powerful southern wing, had made mostly symbolic gestures toward African Americans, but President Roosevelt, appealing to the growing population of northern blacks who were still tentative converts to the New Deal, had gone so far as to appoint a "Negro Cabinet" of advisers. To the closest observers of electoral politics, there were signs of hope in some northern cities with large black populations, where urban machines had begun incorporating blacks, or where politicians with statewide ambitions calculated the advantages of winning the black vote. But the problems of black Americans were at best a minor issue, even among the most enlightened northern Democrats.

Civil rights did not have much traction as an issue for white elected officials. But the New Deal unleashed great expectations about government and a rhetoric of rights that became increasingly empowering. By pushing national politics leftward, the New Deal made room for dissenters on moral, religious, and economic issues to organize. Depression-era left liberals, of both the religious and the secular variety, moved closer to the political mainstream than they had been in decades. A small but growing cadre of activists, among them Hedgeman, began to argue that racial inequality was fundamentally intertwined with larger problems of systemic, economic injustice that they believed were the root cause of the Depression. While activists on the spectrum from liberal to leftist diverged on many points—splitting and fracturing over politics and dogma—they shared a common orientation toward American society. They believed that economic justice, morality, and racial equality could be achieved only through the mobilization of the oppressed—workers, African Americans, and immigrants alike.

Like so many young people in the Great Depression, Hedgeman found her verities under nearly constant siege. A deeply religious woman, Hedgeman was attracted to the YWCA precisely because of her sense of responsibility to the black working class and poor. Hedgeman never lost her deep sense of piety, nor her maternalist belief in the power of uplift. Her views of the black masses were often sanctimonious. (As late as 1954, she rallied New York's blacks to "catch the full impact of the simple, direct, and holy life of Jesus," rather than the debauchery of a black world "drenched with jump and jive music" and an obsession with "material goods" and "the city's so-called glamour.") But to view Hedgeman as a Christian moralist is to overlook her complex transformation as she—and a whole generation of northern black activists—struggled to come to grips with the Depression. Increasingly she came to see the race problem as one of jobs and economic power. She fused religion and radicalism.

Hedgeman's growing interest in the problems of workplace discrimination and black unemployment brought her into the widening circle of the political left. Between the early 1930s and the mid-1940s, it was nearly impossible to find a civil rights cause that did not include a sizeable number of partisan leftists. While established black organizations struggled to redefine themselves during the Depression, radical activists were rushing in to fill the void of leadership. Hedgeman recalled Communist organizers who held corner meetings near her office "protesting the lack of jobs in a nation with such great resources." During the Depression, the lines between civil rights activism, religious uplift, and political radicalism blurred. Left-wing organizations, the Communist and Socialist parties in particular, attracted a growing number of black activists and intellectuals. Dorothy Height, a contemporary of Hedgeman and an equally devout churchwoman who would have a distinguished career in the YWCA and other black women's groups, rejected Communists' atheism but was attracted by their politics. "I went to all kinds of Young Communists groups' meetings, I was in everything," she recalled, "but I knew I was not and never would be a Communist."

Hedgeman and Height found themselves in meetings with a wide range of black and white activists—including radical trade unionists and pacifists who formed the left flank of the New Deal. Those who had believed that poor and working-class blacks should emulate their betters found common ground with militants who called for the "self-liberation" of the black working class. Black churchwomen shared the platform at civil rights rallies with Communists and Socialists. Members of the Federal Council of Churches signed petitions circulated by sleeping car porters and autoworkers and leftist partisans. The period from 1935 to 1943 was one of fusion and convergence, a moment when, in service of the common cause of racial equality, civil rights activists forged unlikely coalitions and alliances—some enduring, others ephemeral. Those alliances gave participants in the struggle for black equality a collective voice that was far more powerful than that of individual leaders and organizations.

It was not self-evident that churchwomen and leftists, advocates of racial uplift, and radicals calling for the overthrow of American capitalism would find common ground. But they did. The secular left in the United States in the 1930s had more in common with liberal Protestantism than most at the time would have admitted. Just as Protestant churches witnessed a simultaneous rebirth and fragmentation during the Great Awakenings of the eighteenth and nineteenth centuries, so too was the left revivified by the Great Depression but still divided into many small, competing sects. Itinerant Communist and Socialist activists roused audiences throughout the country. Their intellectual rigor and moral fervor won them a small, dedicated band of followers wherever they spoke. Even when they did not win over converts, their fiery calls for activism and their fervent denunciations of businessmen spoke to the concerns of millions of ordinary people reeling at the collapse of the economy. Critics of capitalism, hounded to the margins during the prosperous and conservative 1920s, found that their ideas had new currency during the nation's deepest economic crisis. Left-wing authors and critics gained a respectful hearing in the nation's press. When the private sector seemed incapable of reconstituting itself, when impoverishment and unemployment were ubiquitous, and when political leaders around the world were expanding welfare programs, socialism made more sense to more Americans than ever before.

Of the many lefts of the 1930s and 1940s, the most important was the Communist Party. "The Party," as it was known by its supporters, had established itself as a forceful advocate for black equality. It was, by the mid-1930s, one of the only truly interracial organizations in the United States, a fact that did not go unnoticed by its right-wing critics and by civil rights activists alike. Communists, wrote Harlem congressman and minister Adam Clayton Powell, Jr., "fought vigorously, courageously and persistently for the rights of the Negro people through the years of the Depression." Although few blacks became "card-carrying" party members, many were "fellow travelers" who made common cause with Communists in the struggle for civil rights. When *The Crisis* surveyed black newspaper editors in 1932, most striking was their openness to the Party. A veritable Who's Who of black intellectuals and activists, among them W.E.B. Du Bois, Langston Hughes, Mary McLeod Bethune, Ralph Bunche, Bayard Rustin, Richard Wright, Paul Robeson, and Dorothy Height, found themselves in the Communist orbit in the 1930s. For some, such as Hughes, Rustin, Wright, and Bunche, party affiliation was a short-lived phase. Too independent-minded to tolerate the doctrinal shifts and strategic evasions of the Party, they left quickly. Others, such as Bethune, Height, and Powell, supported the Party in its antiracism efforts but declined membership. Du Bois and Robeson, in contrast, made communism a lifelong commitment. Even the CP's black critics—and there were many—could not help but admire the Party's outspoken pro-civil-rights stands when racial equality was otherwise almost entirely off the table in national politics.

A mix of ever-changing dogma propagated by Moscow and delivered to its American adherents in the form of newspapers, tracts, speeches, and clandestine directives, American communism was less a coherent ideology than a way of life. It attracted members committed to social change who worked with missionary zeal. Beginning in 1928, when the Sixth World Congress of the Communist International declared the South's plantation Black Belt an oppressed nation and championed the right of southern blacks to self-determination, the CP directed its energies toward the South. The Party targeted sharecroppers and peons, the nearly enslaved laborers whose toil was essential to the southern economy, in such places as the Mississippi delta and the Alabama black belt. Party members also attempted to organize laborers in the coalfields of Alabama, the tobacco plants of North Carolina, and the laundries of Birmingham. Communist writers built a powerful case against Jim Crow, documenting the everyday brutality that southern white power rested upon. Of particular interest to propagandists was the southern penal system, the chain gangs whose very appearance was a grim reminder of the shackles of slavery.

Nothing brought the Party to prominence among blacks more than its vocal defense of the Scottsboro Boys, nine young men charged with rape aboard a train they had hopped. In 1931, nearly every black newspaper sent correspondents to cover the case in Alabama, where the defendants were jailed. Rallies in support of the young men brought thousands of blacks in Chicago, Detroit, Philadelphia, and New York into contact with CP organizers for the first time. At the same time, the Communists formed Unemployed Councils in industrial centers throughout the country, providing food to impoverished families, demonstrating for increased poor relief, and organizing on behalf of evicted tenants.

Beginning in 1935, the Party entered its "Popular Front" period, building close alliances with non-Communist organizations such as churches, trade unions, and civil rights groups—and particularly with New Deal Democrats. To widen its appeal, the Party embraced the rhetoric of Americanism, arguing that it was the true heir to the spirit of liberty, equality, and democracy embodied in the American Revolution and the Civil War. Key to the strategy was coalition building with groups the Party had long denounced as bourgeois. "We Communists," argued party strategist James W. Ford, "desire to do everything possible in building and broadening the movement of the Negro people in conjunction with the NAACP, the National Negro Congress, the Urban League and other organizations." The result was the creation of all sorts of unlikely coalitions. Party member Audley Moore, for one, joined the National Association of Colored Women and used her position there to build an alliance between middle-class clubwomen and the fledgling industrial union movement. By rejecting overtly sectarian organizing strategies (but not sectarian principles), party officials believed that they could reach a wider segment of the population.

Never a particularly large organization, in good part because of its doctrinaire politics and intolerance of dissent, the CP saw its membership peak at a little over one hundred thousand in the late 1930s. But despite the Party's small numbers, its members were a ubiquitous presence at civil rights rallies. Carefully trained in parliamentary skills, well schooled in the art of organizing, and often so committed to their cause that they simply put in more hours than most activists, CP members infiltrated many trade unions and civil rights groups and assumed leadership positions. Party members were tireless in their advocacy of racial equality, protesting workplace discrimination, advocating tenants' rights, demanding black inclusion on WPA projects, and pushing for interracial unionization. Behind the scenes, the Party provided the grunt workers of the movement: those who spent hours duplicating and distributing leaflets, plastering storefronts and telephone poles with posters, and joining picket lines. CP activists gained credibility for their very omnipresence and their careful work building alliances with mainstream civil rights leaders. A red taint could, in certain circles, be a political liability, but in the era before McCarthyism took hold, Communist civil rights advocates appeared on the same stages, in the same newspaper advertisements, and at the same rallies as non-Communists, to an extent unimaginable in the chilly days of the Cold War.

The Communist Party was the most influential of the left-wing organizations of the 1930s, but by no means was it alone. Often at ideological war with the Communists was a welter of small Socialist factions, many of them only a few hundred or a few thousand strong. Riven by intensely held but often minute ideological differences, the American left broke into fragments, whose politics and ideology were indistinguishable to most outsiders, even as they reflected enduring partisan enmities. Many American Socialists grew increasingly disaffected with revelations of the brutality of Stalin's regime; others would be pushed over the brink by the Hitler-Stalin pact. They felt justified in arguing that communism and fascism were nothing but mirror totalitarian images. Several sects owed their existence to factional divisions within the Communist Party, most notably the followers of the exile Leon Trotsky and the apostate Jay Lovestone. The various leftist sects—too various and fractious to catalogue—still had an impact that extended beyond their meager ranks. Even if they diverged from communism, quibbled over whether or not to support the concept of black self-determination, and debated the relationship of racial and class solidarity, they shared many of the CP's Popular Front sensibilities, including its deep antifascism, its commitment to racial equality, and its sense of solidarity with people of color battling European colonialism. Most important, the fractious left attracted intellectuals whose ideas about race would circulate in newspaper, pamphlet, and book form. Leftist groups served as a training ground for activists who would bring their skills to the civil rights struggle.

Leftist intellectuals shared a broad, international perspective, one that linked the struggle of African Americans to the battles of oppressed peoples worldwide. They forged links with the anticolonial struggles of Mohandas K. Gandhi in India, Kwame Nkrumah in Ghana, and Haile Selassie in Ethiopia. This cosmopolitan leftism made its way out of the partisan sects in countless ways. The black press regularly covered the anti-imperialist movements of Asia and Africa (and several papers had correspondents in places as diverse as Addis Ababa, Moscow, Paris, and London); black leaders regularly visited and corresponded with their counterparts abroad; and black activists were convinced that there was something about their largely local struggles that transcended the narrow politics of Harlem or Detroit or Chicago and put them in the same league as the freedom fighters of South Africa or the satyagrahis of India.

It was a measure of how little most white Americans cared about civil rights that the cause of racial equality remained largely the province of the political left. Of the tiny number of white Americans who cared in the least about racial injustice, most were members of various left-of-center, usually far-left-of-center, political and religious organizations. Yet, over the course of the 1930s and 1940s, through sheer persistence, through publications (particularly through their journalistic contributions to the mainstream media), and through tireless efforts to shape the agendas of influential organizations (whether religious sects or trade unions), the various lefts gained a measure of influence during the Depression and World War II that was nearly without precedent in American history. To a great extent, the story of northern civil rights in the mid–twentieth century is the story of how a fractious interracial left came together—tentatively—and brought the question of racial injustice to the political mainstream.

The milieu of left-labor militancy shaped Anna Arnold Hedgeman's politics. Hedgeman came to supplement her vision of race uplift with an increasingly radical, labor-oriented analysis of black women's plight. She came to see that their problems were economic—and only adequate welfare and good jobs would provide a step up. In the mid-1930s, both at the Y and as a welfare official, Hedgeman grew increasingly concerned with the woes of black women in New York's labor market. "The majority of the miserably poor and low-skilled people we met wanted work," she recalled, "but there was none." The situation was grim even for those lucky enough to find paid labor. The vast majority of black workers in the 1930s were concentrated in a handful of jobs. Seventy percent of black women worked in the service sector, the majority as domestics. Many of the remainder worked in equally degrading jobs as laundry workers, kitchen helpers, and cleaners. "Slavery is the only word that could describe the conditions under which we worked," recalled Evelyn Macon, a laundry worker in Depression-era New York City. What was most galling about women's work was that it harked back to the days of the South's "peculiar institution." Black women were largely trapped in the sorts of jobs that their enslaved mothers and grandmothers had performed. Federal employment programs provided some black women with work but did little to change the status quo. Still beholden to the stereotypical view of black women as "mammies," these agencies trained black women in the skills of ironing, cooking, and washing clothes.

No issue galvanized black women reformers in Harlem more than the abysmal working conditions of black working women. The YWCA was the home base for a loose network of activists who found common cause in their opposition to the exploitation of black domestics. Ella Baker, an idealistic recent graduate of North Carolina's Shaw University, focused on the abusive Bronx "slave market." At the corner of Prospect Avenue and 167th Street, wealthy housewives picked up black women for temporary employment cleaning houses and doing laundry. (There were similar informal, outdoor labor markets in most major cities.) Baker had moved to New York in 1927 and moved into the YWCA just as Hedgeman was starting there. While living at the Y, Baker gained "post graduate experience" working as a domestic and factory worker, building bridges with working-class women and using her experience as a tool for political organizing. She also joined the lively discussions over meals in the Y's cafeteria. Baker became a well-known figure in radical and civil rights circles in Harlem, befriending a wide range of activists, from Social Gospel advocates to Socialists to Garveyites. In 1935, Baker paired up with black

Communist Marvel Cooke to write a searing exposé of the Bronx slave market.

Hedgeman joined in the challenge to the slave market. In a reprise of her stint as a laundry worker in Jersey City, she went undercover as a prospective domestic, hanging out at the notorious Bronx corner. There she learned firsthand about the exploitation black women faced. She was advised to bring a clock to the job, because employers regularly "stole time" from household servants by turning back their own clocks. She also discovered that employers—in a ritual reminiscent of nineteenth-century slave auctions—checked out women's knees and hands (those that were rough and calloused provided evidence of their work experience). Outraged at the slave market, she redoubled her efforts to open up better-paying work for black women. Other YWCA activists lobbied the New York City Council to regulate informal labor markets. Dorothy Height testified before a "stunned" council, which created a Committee on Street Corner Markets to investigate and regulate the industry.

Hedgeman used her post as the executive director of the Brooklyn Y to push for economic opportunity for black women, joining the Brooklyn chapter of the National Negro Congress (NNC), a broad-based coalition of labor unionists, churchwomen, liberals, and Communists. Many clubwomen like Hedgeman (who served as one of the Brooklyn chapter's vice presidents) played roles in the NNC, among them her friends Dorothy Height in Manhattan and YWCA executive Crystal Bird Fauset, who was a leader of the Philadelphia chapter. One of the key members of the Brooklyn chapter—and a Communist—was Jessie Scott Campbell, who worked under Hedgeman at the Y. (In her memoir, published in 1964, Hedgeman did not mention the Congress, probably because of the political liability of association with leftism during the Cold War.) Hedgeman coordinated a campaign bombarding the New York welfare commissioner with postcards urging the city to appoint black welfare workers, which resulted in the city eventually hiring 150 black women.

While in Brooklyn, Hedgeman joined militant protests. The Brooklyn NNC chapter directed most of its energies toward challenging workplace discrimination. It picketed and boycotted employers who refused to hire black workers. In more than thirty-five cities, mostly in the North, grassroots organizers staged "Don't Buy Where You Can't Work" campaigns throughout the 1930s. The strategy was easy to execute: Activists identified stores in black neighborhoods with no black employees. They set up pickets, handed out pamphlets, and coordinated boycotts of the offending businesses. Most campaigns were short-lived, but some—including those led by black nationalists and Communists in New York—extended for several years. Outraged at persistent discrimination and inspired by similar protests, Hedgeman led a group of young women from the Y on a picket line in front of a Brooklyn dime store. Hedgeman then forged a coalition with the NAACP, the NNC, the Urban League, and local white churchwomen to demand the hiring of black women department store clerks, through a combination of picketing and persuasion. She also joined protests against inferior education for black students in Bedford-Stuyvesant.

However, picketing and protest were not common tactics in the YWCA, which continued to emphasize education, training, and uplift. Hedgeman's embrace of militant strategies was a sign of how much she had changed over the course of the 1930s. Like most "Don't Buy" campaigns, Hedgeman's was a synthesis of black pride and a commitment to hard work and racial uplift. Her efforts also reflected the growing influence of the labor movement—with its picket lines and sit-downs—on grassroots black organizations. Hedgeman's newfound militancy rubbed the Brooklyn Y's "old guard" the wrong way. Both the "old Brooklyn" black board members and their white associates were "disturbed" by Hedgeman's appearance on picket lines. It was "not their idea of suitable leadership for the young people of the community." Hedgeman had become a "symbol of revolt." At odds with her board, she resigned her post.

Hedgeman's antidiscrimination activism brought her into new circles, just as the United States was on the brink of war. In particular, she gravitated toward the Socialist cadre around A. Philip Randolph, ten years her senior and an already legendary labor activist. She soon joined his wartime efforts to challenge workplace discrimination and would head the National Council for a Permanent Fair Employment Practices Committee. Hedgeman maintained her affiliation with black women's clubs and religious groups, but she also collaborated closely with groups such as the Workers' Defense League (WDL). Randolph and the WDL had focused their energies primarily on male workers, but Hedgeman continued to emphasize that blacks' economic woes knew no sex. "Although all women have serious employment problems," Hedgeman told an audience in 1941, "Negro women carry the additional handicap of color with its attendant discrimination with regard to training, apprenticeship opportunities, and job opportunities." During the war, Hedgeman joined pickets at a Brooklyn defense plant, and she used her new post as race relations director for New York's civil defense agency as a platform to demand the full inclusion of blacks in the war effort. At a "Victory Through Unity" meeting in New York in 1942, Hedgeman called for a "mixed combat division of men of all faiths, creeds, and colors." She also rallied black women to contribute to civil defense as a step toward full citizenship.

Looking out onto black America at the outbreak of World War II, journalist Roi Ottley found a "united front" among black Americans. "Negroes may differ among themselves on minor issues concerned with day-to-day living, but on the question of their rights—political, economic, and moral—and the right to integration in American life, they present an almost solid bloc." Even if Ottley papered over political and ideological divisions among advocates of racial equality, he captured the sense of hope and excitement that pervaded civil rights politics in the North. To an extent unimaginable five years earlier or even a decade later, black activists found common ground, particularly in their emphasis on black economic opportunity. Anna Arnold Hedgeman's journey from uplift to militancy was but one of thousands of similar journeys over the 1930s and 1940s that would collectively bring the struggle for racial equality to a national audience during World War II. Calls for "jobs and freedom" and for the end of Jim Crow, north and south, would get a hearing at the very highest levels of government, in the mass media, in mainstream religious and political organizations, and even in popular culture. The various lefts did not accomplish their goals of creating God's kingdom on earth or ushering in the Revolution. They were no more powerful in 1945 than they had been at the nadir of the Depression. But they did succeed beyond their greatest hopes in raising popular consciousness about race and unleashing a mass movement. That they reached their success in the midst of the Second World War is no coincidence. Advocates of racial equality got a hearing—and had an impact, however limited—precisely because their rise coincided with the American battle against fascism abroad.

The unexpected shift in the politics of race during World War II was not, as any good Depression-era leftist might have acknowledged in a reflective moment, wholly of the radicals' own making. The secular and religious lefts forced Americans to confront the pressing and still unresolved question of racial inequality, but they had unwitting allies. The civil rights impulse had been deeply rooted in the American past, yet it came to the surface in America at one particular moment, the 1940s. And it did so because of a shift in national politics and a simultaneous grassroots struggle from below. The left aided and abetted both, but ultimately the interracial left came in from the margins and made its mark on American history because of good timing. Its leaders and activists alike vocally decried injustice when the world was convulsed in a battle against one of history's most violent and racist regimes. And their message found a reception among a newly empowered black working class that had, in unprecedented numbers, migrated northward. The vanguard had—it seemed—found the moment of world-historical change it had long been waiting for. And after years of theorizing about rights and revolution, left activists found the foot soldiers who, both hopeful at their newfound freedom and prosperity and frustrated at their ongoing deprivation, took the struggle for civil rights into their own hands. America would never be the same.

CHAPTER 2

"PRESSURE, MORE PRESSURE
AND STILL MORE PRESSURE"

"DEAR FELLOW NEGRO AMERICANS," BEGAN A. PHILIP RANDOLPH, IN AN open letter published on May 1, 1941, "be not dismayed in these terrible times. You possess power, great power. Our problem is to harness and hitch it up for action on the broadest, daring and most gigantic scale. In this period of power politics, nothing counts but pressure, more pressure and still more pressure." With those words, Randolph, the most visible black activist in the United States, issued a call to join the March on Washington Movement, an effort to open the ranks of defense employment to the Negro. Randolph threatened to bring ten thousand blacks to Washington, D.C., to protest discrimination in federal contracts. At the heart of Randolph's audacious gambit was an astute sense of the root causes of racial inequality. Without jobs, there would be no freedom. Without full economic participation, blacks would continue to be denied fundamental rights. More than two decades of agitation and organizing had taught Randolph that old strategies of moral suasion or racial uplift would not open America's military and its burgeoning defense industries to blacks. Whites would not yield the advantage of their race without a fight. Only the threat—or the actuality—of political disruption would.

To propose a mass march of blacks on Washington would have seemed madness just a few years earlier. Black activists during the Depression had been too fragmented, too fractious, and too intensely localistic in their orientation to be able to mount a credible threat to disrupt the nation's capital. But the growing militancy of black organizations and the proliferation of grassroots protests had transformed the political climate. A grassroots challenge to a popular president in a nation on the brink of war was only possible because of a remarkable reconfiguration of civil rights politics in the mid- and late 1930s—one that Randolph himself helped engineer.

In February 1936, not quite five years before Randolph issued his challenge to Roosevelt, one of the most remarkable assemblages of civil rights activists in American history took place in Chicago. During the day, 817 delegates, black and white—the vast majority from northern cities— gathered to form the National Negro Congress (NNC). Thousands more attended its evening sessions. Urban League official Lester Granger colorfully described the heterogeneity of the congress. "There were representatives of New Deal departments and agencies," he recalled. "Old line Republican wheel horses and ambitious young Democrats exchanged arguments; Communists held heated altercations with proponents of the Forty-ninth State Movement; and Garveyites signed the registration book immediately after the Baha'ists." Several prominent bishops worked the corridors. Members of the fledgling National Housewives' League, which called for self-help cooperatives to battle high prices in inner-city stores, found kindred spirits among both leftists and nationalists, who, for their own reasons, sought alternatives to white-dominated capitalism. Black clubwomen mingled with their peers in black fraternities, but also with Pullman porters, meatpackers, and steelworkers. The lively congress stood in sharp contrast to the serious and stodgy atmosphere that prevailed at the annual meetings of the Urban League and NAACP. Roy Wilkins, Anna Arnold Hedgeman's old friend, now an NAACP official, marveled that the congress "enlisted great sections of young colored and white people" largely "from the so-called working class and mass organizations." For all their differences, what the participants had in common, noted Granger, was a "deep-rooted and nationwide dissatisfaction" and "flaming resentment" at the racial status quo.

In its first three years, the congress drew support from a wide range of black and white intellectuals and activists. Randolph served as its first president, and Ralph Bunche helped organize it. Ella Baker, fresh from her victory exposing the Bronx slave market—who would later be famous as an advisor to Martin Luther King, Jr., and a mentor to the Student Nonviolent Coordinating Committee (SNCC)—served as its director of publicity. The congress was the brainchild of John P. Davis, a young black Harvard graduate who had close ties to both New Deal reformers and the Communist Party. Davis's goal, echoing the CP's Popular Front ideology, was to assemble the broadest possible coalition of advocates for racial equality. That strategy paid off.

At its first two conventions, the congress passed a wide-ranging set of resolutions: It denounced segregation in New Deal programs, supported antilynching legislation, demanded a minimum wage for farmworkers, and lashed out at Social Security as "inadequate and discriminatory." But at the core of its program—endorsed by Randolph in his inaugural address and reinforced in a series of resolutions from the floor—was the recognition that the problem of racial inequality was fundamentally economic and that the solution required addressing the impoverishment and exploitation of black and white workers alike. "No black workers can be free so long as the white worker is a slave and by the same token, no white worker is certain of security while his black brother is bound." To evoke slavery two-thirds of a century after the Emancipation Proclamation was a pointed reminder of blacks' continued subordination. But Randolph's comment that white workers too were enslaved was even more radical. Freedom for both blacks and whites would come only in a "movement in aid of industrial unionism."

The rise of the NNC was the consummation of the proletarian turn in 1930s-era black politics. What had been a marginal position among civil rights activists—that class and race were intertwined, that jobs were necessary for freedom, that unionism was a prerequisite to civil rights—moved to the center of the black freedom struggle. It would remain there for another dozen or so years, before it was eclipsed by an even more influential paradigm, one that emphasized the moral and psychological roots of racial inequality.

It was unthinkable, even five years before the first meeting of the NNC, that such a wide range of black activists would find common ground in support of the labor movement. In the early twentieth century, northern blacks and leading civil rights organizations had been deeply skeptical about trade unionism as a strategy for black advancement. They had good reason. The American Federation of Labor had an abysmal record of excluding blacks from membership and, as a result, of keeping crucial sectors of the economy all-white. The pervasiveness of discriminatory practices in unions (from attacks on black "scabs" to the separation of blacks into inferior locals to the countenancing of racially separate job and seniority lines) made unionization a hard sell. Further hindering unionization efforts, many black elites cast their lot with white employers. The Urban League, which had as its primary task expanding economic opportunities, did so by accepting close, often paternalistic relationships with corporate leaders in exchange for a small number of jobs. The key part of this bargain was opposition to unionization. Upwardly mobile black ministers often curried favor with white philanthropists and business leaders, hoping to open a few well-paying jobs to members of their congregations. In Gary, Indiana, "the churches," lamented one clergy leader, "have become subsidiaries of the steel corporation and the ministers dare not get up and say anything against the company." In Detroit, where Henry Ford made generous donations to black congregations, pastors provided his plants with reliable black workers. To break down the deep-rooted antiunion sentiment among blacks would require simultaneous efforts to overcome union-sanctioned racism and to wean black leaders from their dependence on white business.

By the early 1930s, as the nation plunged into depression, a growing number of blacks joined the chorus of skeptics of big business and began, gradually, to embrace working-class organizations. No organization was more important than the fledgling Congress of Industrial Organizations (CIO) in shaping the direction of black politics in the late 1930s. Many of the industries targeted by the CIO—steel, automobile manufacturing, and meatpacking, to name three—had sizeable black workforces. From the CIO's creation in 1935, many of its member unions reached out to black and white workers alike, even if their efforts to break down the barriers of race were often halting and fraught with difficulty. In left-led CIO unions, Communists saw the organization of workers across racial lines as an essential prerequisite to forging class consciousness. But for many CIO unionists—Communist or not—interracialism was also a practical matter. There were enough black workers in key northern industries that it would be difficult to organize plantwide or industrywide unions without their support. And given the high rates of unemployment during the Great Depression, companies could easily resort to the time-honored practice of hiring black strikebreakers to replace white workers, using the wedge of race to undermine workplace solidarity.

By the mid-1930s, support for unionism had taken hold, even among relatively conservative black organizations. A bellwether of change was the Urban League. In 1934, Urban League leaders Lester Granger and

T. Arnold Hill announced the creation of Workers' Councils, to bring blue-collar blacks together to give rise to a "new deal for labor" by mobilizing black workers to challenge segregated unions. By 1935, forty-two Workers' Councils together had nearly thirty thousand members. The league did not give up on its strategy of negotiating with employers, but in the midst of the Depression, its leaders saw for the first time the utility of labor organizing. At the same time, industrial unions, most notably the Steel Workers Organizing Committee, were making headway in Chicago, Gary, Youngstown, and Pittsburgh, in an industry with a sizeable black workforce. When the Steel Workers and other industrial unions forged the Congress of Industrial Organizations in 1935, many of the Young Turks embraced it—including economists Robert C. Weaver and Abram Harris, sociologists E. Franklin Frazier, Horace Cayton, and St. Clair Drake, and political scientist Ralph Bunche.

The National Negro Congress represented the culmination of the proletarian turn in black politics. For all their differences, the diverse constituents of the congress embraced the goal of unionism as central to black emancipation. For Randolph and his compatriots, race and class were fundamentally intertwined. The black freedom struggle was not separate from the quest for workplace security and dignity, decent wages, and the right to organize and strike. The argument that racial inequality was fundamentally an economic problem resonated throughout the NNC. It shaped demands for higher Social Security payments to blacks and whites equally; it prompted NNC delegates to endorse the National Housewives' League and its efforts to battle "the high cost of living"; and it led to demands for union wages on WPA relief projects. Among the most prominent NNC delegates were religious activists who argued for the need to "preach an economic and social gospel as well as a spiritual gospel."

"Let us build a united front of all Negro organizations, of varying strata, purpose and outlook," charged Randolph in a stirring address at the second meeting of the congress. "Let us build a united front in cooperation with the progressive and liberal agencies of the nation whose interests are in common with Black America. Let us build a national coalition of diverse black organizations and forge links with sympathetic white-dominated groups that together would forge a grassroots social movement for racial equality." Whether the congress could ever have

held together groups as diverse as black bishops, Urban League supporters, steel and packinghouse workers, and the remnants of Marcus Garvey's Back to Africa movement—much less racial liberals and leftists of
various stripes—was a doubtful proposition. On the national level, the
NNC was little more than a paper organization; Randolph was a powerful
orator but directed most of his energies toward organizing the Brotherhood of Sleeping Car Porters rather than turning the NNC into a national
voice in civil rights politics. And some mainstream civil rights leaders, notably NAACP executive secretary Walter White, distanced themselves
from the congress, in part because of its encroachment onto what had
been the NAACP's turf, and in part because of their suspicions of the links
between the congress and the Communist Party. Still, Randolph, Bunche,
and many black leaders remained committed to the congress precisely
because of its "big tent" approach.

As long as the NNC remained, in Randolph's formulation, officially
nonpartisan, it was the most promising vehicle for black liberation in the
Depression era. At a moment when the NAACP was still struggling to become a mass-membership organization, the NNC had the potential to
create an unlikely coalition of activists, all dedicated to the common
cause of advancing racial equality through economic advancement.
When the congress held a massive rally in Philadelphia in 1938 to commemorate the seventy-fifth anniversary of the Emancipation Proclamation, an audience of nearly ten thousand listened to Crystal Bird Fauset, a
close associate of Anna Arnold Hedgeman at the YWCA, John Edelman,
a CIO leader, and none other than the First Lady, Eleanor Roosevelt, who
gave a rousing speech denouncing the persistence of "slaves of many
kinds" in America. Nearly every important left and liberal group was represented on the program.

Weak at the top, the NNC had its strength in its nearly seventy local
chapters. In the late 1930s, the NNC had robust chapters in a number of
cities, such as Chicago, whose members played a crucial role in building
bridges between black workers and the left-led packinghouse, steel, and
garment workers' unions while also battling slumlords, supporting public
housing, and pushing for welfare reform. The NNC did more than support union organizing efforts. On the local level, it was as diverse as its
constituent groups, and its activities ranged from radical to meliorist. In
Detroit, it pushed for the integration of the ranks of public employees. In

Boston, the NNC chapter challenged the depiction of blacks in school textbooks and pushed for the inclusion of blacks in the local orchestra and in a local hospital staff. In Oakland—not coincidentally one of the major bases of the Brotherhood of Sleeping Car Porters—the local chapter battled discrimination at the nearby Berkeley campus of the University of California. Many NNC chapters were more aggressive and militant in the late 1930s than their NAACP counterparts. At the grassroots level, the NNC drew much of its energy and leadership from Communist Party organizers, but many local chapters were too heterogeneous to be described as "front" organizations. Brooklyn's chapter, where Anna Arnold Hedgeman served, was broad enough to include open Communists, but also liberals and churchwomen. The NNC's local rallies and protests continued to attract ordinary blacks, many of whom had little or no interest in Marxism. Even if the NNC's chapters were eclectic in their membership and tactics, the organization gave coherence to a congeries of local struggles—a sense of unity of purpose that loosely tied together activists across the North.

Perhaps the NNC's most important contribution to the fledgling civil rights movement was its staunch antifascism. At a time when antifascist rhetoric had not moved to the center of mainstream American politics—as it would during the war—black organizations found that it gave meaning to their local battles by linking their aspirations to an international political struggle. Hovering as a shadow over the first NNC meeting was Mussolini's 1935 invasion of Ethiopia. The fascist domination of Ethiopia became a metaphor for the racial oppression of black Americans. A. Philip Randolph advocated a boycott of Italy, and the NNC issued a forceful denunciation of Il Duce. Hitler's invigoration of theories of racial supremacy gave further credibility to the NNC's charges that America's white supremacists were homegrown fascists. Through its antifascist rhetoric, the NNC offered a holistic vision of political and economic change that appealed to a wide cross section of the black population. By the late 1930s, antifascist language had become ubiquitous in the black press and authors reported sympathetically about Republican fighters in the Spanish Civil War and critically about Mussolini and Hitler. The black freedom struggle in America was part and parcel of the struggle against fascism abroad.

All of that changed in late 1939, when the NNC abruptly repudiated its antifascism—toeing the Communist Party line in support of the Hitler-Stalin nonaggression pact. At the April 1940 meeting of the NNC, Randolph angrily resigned his presidency, taking with him many NNC delegates. Torn asunder by its rigid adherence to Communist foreign policy, the NNC lost most of its non-Communist members and much of its credibility as a civil rights organization, although it gained strength again when the Soviets allied with the United States in 1941. During the war some NNC chapters, especially in New York, joined broad antidiscrimination protests, but the NNC would never be the "big tent" organization that it had aspired to be. Finally, in 1947, greatly weakened, it dissolved as the Communist Party turned its attention to other strategies.

If the NNC lost its organizational clout, it had nonetheless played an important role in changing the tone of civil rights politics in the late 1930s. Its founders had envisioned the congress as an alternative to the stodgy, mainstream civil rights organizations. The very existence of the NNC forced established groups to become more militant as a matter of survival. By the late 1930s and early 1940s, following the example set by the NNC, Urban League members joined picket lines and held mass rallies. In Chicago, in the late 1930s, the city's "accepted leadership" organized the Council of Negro Organizations as an alternative to the NNC. "The organization, led by upper and upper-middle-class, middle-aged men and women," wrote St. Clair Drake and Horace Cayton in a tone of surprise, "was itself organizing demonstrations in the proletarian style."

The shift to the "proletarian style" was most pronounced in the NAACP. Shortly after the NNC was founded, Ralph Bunche argued that "the NAACP does not have a mass basis. It never has assumed the proportions of a crusade, nor has it attracted the masses of people to its banner." But many of the same activists attracted to the NNC joined an insurgency within the NAACP. Abram Harris offered a pointed critique of the "18th century liberalism" that undergirded the NAACP's civil rights strategy. Individual political rights meant little in an economy dominated by the "persistent growth of corporate wealth, consolidations, and monopoly in industry." Harris argued for a broad-based understanding of racial inequality as one of the "extreme manifestations of the exploitation of labor." At its 1936 annual meeting, the NAACP embraced Harris's recommendations for reorganizing the NAACP, including supporting worker education and interracial union-organizing efforts.

While the Young Turks were challenging the NAACP's leadership, a "new crowd" of younger, more militant activists led insurgencies throughout the North, pushing local branches to organize blue-collar workers, stage visible protests, and support industrial unionism. In Detroit, for example, a group of prounion militants, working first through the NAACP's half-dozen youth councils, supported the United Automobile Workers in its battle to unionize Ford. Young NAACP activists drove sound trucks and went door-to-door in the city's black neighborhoods to promote unionism.

The NAACP's grassroots insurgency paid off. NAACP membership doubled between 1935 and 1940. Between 1940 and 1946, the NAACP gained more than seven hundred branches nationwide and saw its membership rise from just over 50,000 to nearly 450,000. Local branches complained of the lack of envelopes to collect membership dues. The NAACP made its biggest inroads in cities where it was most closely associated with organized labor. Detroit's membership spiked to 25,000 in 1944. More than at any time in its history, the NAACP became a mass membership organization with a populist orientation.

The NNC—largely by dint of its visibility and militancy—had opened a space in black politics that pulled the entire movement leftward. Four important themes emerged from the NNC's short history, all of which would shape the next ten years of civil rights organization in the North. First, the NNC played a crucial role in orienting the struggle for civil rights as a question of power—economic and political. Second, the NNC ushered in a period of creative coalition building among black and white antiracists. During World War II, even small, local civil rights organizations built bridges across racial and organizational divisions around nearly every important civil rights issue, although the issue of communism would remain divisive. Third—as a corollary to the first two—industrial unionism was the core of the movement for racial equality. Wartime activists in the North targeted Jim Crow in public accommodations, unequal education, and segregated housing, but the fight for remunerative work galvanized civil rights activists nearly everywhere. Fourth, in the aftermath of the 1930s, the struggle for civil rights, for better and for worse, would be inextricably bound up with events far from American soil. By linking the black freedom struggle with socialism, antifascism, and colonial liberation, civil rights activists would find their movement rising and falling with events overseas. Activists in the late 1930s and 1940s thought globally and acted locally. But their fate was often decided—and their credibility supported or undermined—by the fate of political struggles continents away.

NO ONE HAD played a more important role in the rise of the NNC than A. Philip Randolph, and no one would play a more decisive role in carrying forward its agenda, even as the organization imploded because of Soviet political machinations. Randolph had deep ties to the non-Communist left of the postwar era, but also to nearly every other strain of black activism, from Social Gospel Protestantism to Garveyism. As a student at the City College of New York in the 1910s, Randolph supported Eugene V. Debs, and in 1916, joined the Socialist Party. In the pages of *The Messenger*, a journal that he started in 1917, Randolph promoted socialism, provided a forum for many leading black intellectuals and artists, and offered searing analyses of racial inequality and capitalism. Despite his inexperience as a laborer, Randolph took the helm of the fledgling Brotherhood of Sleeping Car Porters in 1925. Over the course of the 1920s and 1930s, Randolph, like many in the American left, grew disillusioned with the Soviet Union and its American followers—but he never veered from his commitment to working-class empowerment and racial equality.

The Socialist Party was a natural home for Randolph, who found himself attracted to its antiwar and anti-imperialist politics. But until the 1930s, racial equality remained on the margins of socialism. In 1926, Socialist leader Norman Thomas had memorably argued that "what the Negro worker wants and needs, the white worker wants and needs, neither more nor less. This is what we Socialists stand for." It was a position that reflected the widespread belief in the necessity of interracial collaboration in the class struggle, but it was a position that alienated many black activists. Thomas bitterly complained in 1931 that "Socialists have earned a degree of Negro support that they have not received." But over the course of the 1930s, they paid more attention to black concerns in response to the inroads that their Communist Party foes had made among blacks, and in part because of the growing interest leftist intellectuals took in the "Negro problem." Thomas came to view the oppression of blacks as part of an insidious process of "human exploitation." Under Thomas's leadership, the Socialists forged close links with civil rights organizations and, like the Communists, began to link American racial discrimination with "Hitlerism." "The war against fascism," he thundered in 1938, should begin "at home in our own country."

Never a large party, the Socialists—often in fierce competition with the Communists—established beachheads in the labor and civil rights movements during the Depression. In 1936, the Socialist Party launched the Workers' Defense League (as a counterpoint to the Communists' International Labor Defense, which had made its reputation in the defense of the Scottsboro Boys). Like its Communist rival, the WDL turned its attention to civil liberties and, increasingly, civil rights. The WDL attracted an interracial coterie of young activists, among them Morris Milgram (a leading open-housing advocate in the 1950s), Pauli Murray (a feminist who would become a prominent civil rights lawyer and the first black woman Episcopal priest), James Farmer (a founder of the Congress of Racial Equality), and James Peck (whose bloodied face during the 1961 Freedom Rides would make him an international icon of the nonviolent civil rights movement). Together they formed a political counterculture. WDL activists worked closely with Randolph, helped to coordinate the wartime March on Washington Movement, and supported organizing efforts among sharecroppers, textile workers, and anti-death-penalty activists north and south.

Randolph forged important and enduring ties—with great consequence for the direction of the civil rights movement—with members of the religious left, particularly advocates of the "Social Gospel," who applied Christianity to the pressing social problems of the age. At the core of Social Gospellers' vision were religious egalitarianism and a profound hopefulness about the possibility of large-scale societal change. Social Gospellers believed in the fundamental goodness of humanity and deployed the tactics of "moral suasion" rather than coercion to win the hearts and minds of their opponents. For many Social Gospellers, socialism provided a compelling political home, in part because Norman Thomas himself had come to socialism from the religious left and never jettisoned its moral rhetoric.

Religious activists in another day would draw a harsh contrast between "atheistic socialism" and "godliness," but in the depths of the Great Depression and the turmoil of World War II, religious and secular leftists found much common ground. They joined together in a common denunciation of industrial capitalism and often found themselves working side by side in support of industrial unions. Many found common ground in the burgeoning antiwar movement and met in student antiwar groups that proliferated in the 1930s. When the United States entered World War II, Socialists and members of peace churches found themselves together in conscientious objector camps or in prison because of their draft resistance. Their common bonds—over exploitation and injustice—led many to join the burgeoning movement for racial equality.

A small movement, the Social Gospel was influential far beyond its numbers. By the 1930s, many of its most ardent supporters had established themselves on the faculties of liberal theological seminaries throughout the country and in the religion departments of many denominational colleges. Social Gospel theologians also had a strong presence at many traditionally black colleges and universities, including Morehouse College and Howard and Atlanta universities. The Federal Council of Churches, founded in 1908 as the leading ecumenical organization of mainstream Protestant churches, propagated the Social Gospel. And individual denominations, from the Presbyterians to the Congregationalists, ran their own social action departments, which became havens for activists who believed in the religious imperative to transform the world. As the Great Depression worsened, and as theologians confronted growing political and social unrest, the ideals of the Social Gospel seemed more relevant than ever. Social Gospel activists finally found themselves at the forefront of systematic social change and seized the opportunity to play a role in the construction of a new, just social order. Haltingly, they found themselves drawn toward civil rights.

Many Social Gospel advocates were attracted to socialism because of their shared belief in the fundamental evil of acquisitive capitalism and unchecked industrialization. Socialists and Social Gospellers believed in the perfectibility of human nature. Both groups struggled to revolutionize American society along the principles of social equality, and both realized that liberation would not come about without struggle, even if they sometimes diverged on the forms that struggle would take. The left-religious faith in the "beloved community" or the "imminent Kingdom of God" and the secular Socialist vision of a society free from capitalist domination reflected a shared "here and now" commitment to social change.

Black Social Gospel preachers, in particular, brought together themes of biblical liberation in their critique of economic and racial injustices.

Randolph's alliance with religious activists did not temper his view that the root causes of racial inequality were economic and the solutions were political. The son of an African Methodist Episcopal minister, Randolph learned the art of oration, which he put to good use in union halls and churches and on street corners. He spoke with a preacherly cadence and used religious metaphors un-self-consciously. As a young man, Randolph rebelled against the black church, using the pages of *The Messenger* to publish scathing denunciations of the black ministry, but by the 1930s he had softened his criticism of organized religion. He remained an atheist, but he saw that religious commitment to racial equality could be a powerful impetus for activism. Randolph differed from religious activists who saw their goal as "changing the hearts and minds" of white Americans: Blacks would not attain first-class citizenship through strategies of "uplift" or conversion. They could not wait for an outpouring of white goodwill. They would rise from their subordinate status only if they seized power and fundamentally altered the political system.

SOCIALISTS AND RELIGIOUS leftists found common cause in the plight of industrial workers. World War II provided Randolph the opportunity to connect the demand for the "right to work" to the larger goal of racial equality. War requires the mass mobilization of labor—to serve as soldiers and to provision troops with weapons, clothing, and food. When Randolph threatened to march on Washington in 1941, the war buildup was lifting the United States out of the depths of the Depression, ensuring for many Americans—at least whites—freedom from want in service of freedom from fear. In the year leading up to Pearl Harbor, massive federal expenditures flowed toward defense production, soon to make it the largest de facto government job creation program in American history. More than one million draftees were inducted in 1941, further tightening the labor market. Unemployment rates plummeted and pent-up consumer demand fueled an economic boom. But for blacks, the Depression was not over. In 1940, more than one in three black workers in the Northeast and Midwest were unemployed or working in New Deal work relief programs. Even those blacks lucky enough to make inroads into meatpacking, steel, and auto manufacturing—the major northern industries open to them—remained confined in race-specific jobs, almost always the most dangerous and unpleasant.

Randolph argued, "Well-nigh 99 and %₀ percent of the Negro people are workers of hand and brain who earn their living in the sweat of their brow by selling their labor in the market for wages. Hence, the biggest business of the Negro consists in his selling at the highest price that which he has the most of, namely his ability to work." But work was the source of so much more than money or food. It was a symbol of status: What you do is what you are. Work could provide a sense of community. "To have a 'sense of belonging,'" wrote Ida Coker Clark, a black clubwoman, "is as important to the Negro woman worker as getting and holding a job." For black migrants north, the battle for equal opportunity in the workplace was a matter of dignity as much as it was of economic power. Northern blacks reviled servile employment—preferring industrial to domestic work. But servile employment remained the norm, especially for the 70 percent of black women who worked in the service sector in 1940. Those women and men lucky enough to get factory work were disproportionately clustered in what one observer called "the meanest and dirtiest" occupations.

As the defense industry rolled into high gear, northern blacks looked at the boom from the outside. If the federal government could open defense jobs to blacks—without discrimination in hiring or promotion—the benefits would be legion. For one, many defense industry jobs were unionized. Under union-negotiated contracts, work rules protected the health and safety of workers, protected them from arbitrary firing, and offered them an array of benefits. Industrial employment also brought black workers under the umbrella of the welfare state. Agricultural workers, domestics, and railroad workers were unprotected by unemployment insurance and were ineligible for Social Security payments in the case of disability and old age. Industrial workers, by contrast, contributed to social insurance and could collect its benefits. Defense work also had great symbolic importance: It was in service of the broader struggle against fascism. And, more than most employment, it was an expression of a longing to be recognized as full, empowered citizens. Finally, if the government enforced antidiscrimination in war-related industries, other industries that excluded blacks would surely follow. Opening up the military had equal promise—particularly if blacks were no longer "Jim Crowed" into inferior positions. Military service provided many men, particularly from blue-collar backgrounds, with the opportunity to pick up all sorts of new skills, from electronics to machine repair to engineering. But those were white jobs, closed to black inductees—who were stuck doing "colored work" in the kitchens, latrines, and stockrooms of military bases.

Randolph's decision to propose a march on Washington was a response to months of mobilization around the issue of discrimination in defense industries. In spring 1940, *The Pittsburgh Courier*, the largest black newspaper at the time, launched the Committee on National Defense to demand the inclusion of blacks in military-related employment. The NAACP demanded that Roosevelt issue an executive order barring discrimination in defense plants. Over the summer, the Urban League signed on. Notably missing from the effort was the National Negro Congress, which, under the Hitler-Stalin pact, opposed America's military buildup. The NNC belatedly joined the chorus in late June 1941, when Hitler suddenly turned against his erstwhile Soviet allies.

"There was every temptation for Negroes to jump aboard the bandwagon of empty patriotism," wrote Lester Granger, recalling the hard-won lessons of World War I, when many blacks had uncritically supported the war effort in a vain hope that loyalty to country would open up the long-closed doors of citizenship. From the outset, Granger and other civil rights activists worked to ensure that blacks would be part of "a democratic crusade." In an organizational division of labor, Urban League officials began gathering information about defense contracts and attempted to negotiate with employers to open positions to blacks. Beginning in the fall of 1940, NAACP and Urban League officials lobbied for a more coercive mechanism to open defense jobs to blacks—namely a nondiscrimination clause in federal defense contracts. Only "strong measures" would "break down traditionally hostile attitudes" that kept blacks unemployed.

Civil rights groups with Washington connections began to lobby the Roosevelt administration, working their way through FDR's "Negro Cabinet." NAACP president Walter White, Urban League executive T. Arnold Hill, and Randolph pressed for a meeting with the president. When Congress debated the introduction of the military draft in September, Randolph and his colleagues saw a propitious moment to propose the desegregation of the army and won a meeting with FDR. Always cordial—if a bit patronizing—toward his black visitors, Roosevelt professed his sympathy to the goal of breaking down the color line in the armed services. But just two weeks later, the War Department announced that its policy was "not to intermingle colored and white enlisted personnel in the same regimental organizations." Black papers around the country were outraged. Randolph fumed. "Calling on the president and holding those conferences are not going to get us anywhere." The meeting with FDR reinforced Randolph's belief that "only power can effect the enforcement and adoption of a given policy, however meritorious it may be. The virtue and rightness of a cause are not alone the condition and cause of its acceptance."

While employers and the federal government stonewalled, activists pursued a twofold strategy of protest and publicity. Building on the momentum generated by local protests during the Depression, grassroots activists staged demonstrations and rallies throughout the country, demanding an end to discrimination in the military and in the defense industry. Six thousand blacks in Kansas City, Missouri, gathered at a "monster protest demonstration" sponsored by the Urban League. In January 1941, NAACP branches in twenty-three states held "National Defense Day" protests. *The Pittsburgh Courier* "threw its whole influence" behind the cause; New York's left-liberal daily *PM* ran a special section on blacks and the defense program; *The Nation, The New Republic,* and *Survey Graphic* all supported antidiscrimination efforts; and Walter White pulled strings to publish an article critical of defense industry and military discrimination in *The Saturday Evening Post.* The combination of protest and publicity gave traction to Randolph's threatened march.

The burgeoning black protest movement had no stauncher ally than the black press. By World War II, the United States had 155 black newspapers, which together formed what one observer called a "crusading press which serves the special needs of a militantly struggling people." The two giants—*The Pittsburgh Courier* and *The Afro-American* in Baltimore, with their multi-city editions—were closely followed by *The Chicago Defender* and the *Amsterdam News.* What was most important about the black press as a tool for publicity and organization was its wide circulation. Sixty percent of black newspapers circulated across state lines. By one historian's estimate, black papers had nearly four million readers during the early 1940s—nearly one-third of the entire nation's adult black population.

"The Negro press," wrote one observer, "goes out to cooks, servants, elevator boys, and truck drivers." The result was a virtual web of information about black life, politics, and grassroots protests that linked ordinary readers, activists, and leaders.

While the politics of black editors and columnists ranged widely, from Republican to Socialist, they shared an emphasis on stories of the everyday slights blacks faced and the grassroots efforts against them. E. Franklin Frazier described the papers as "an organ of protest" that "reflects the growing race consciousness of the Negro." Editors saw their role in crusading terms. The goal of *The Afro-American*, recounted its longtime editor, John Murphy, Sr., was to "really unify the black people." Conservative white columnist Westbrook Pegler saw the political orientation of the black press as a scourge and charged it with "obvious inflammatory bias in the treatment of the news." But Pegler overlooked bias by neglect in the white press. The front-page stories in black papers rarely made it into the white-owned dailies. Whites, unless they were devoted readers of leftist newspapers such as the *Daily Worker* or *PM*, were left to the occasional article on blacks that appeared in liberal periodicals. As Gunnar Myrdal noted, northern newspapers minimized "all Negro news, except crime news. The Northerners want to hear as little as possible about the Negroes, both in the South and in the North."

Randolph and his army of supporters used the press as one weapon in the struggle. In the age before superhighways, railroads were the lifeblood of the country. As head of the Brotherhood of Sleeping Car Porters, Randolph could call on his members, Pullman porters, to spread word of the march nationwide. In the 1930s and 1940s, the ideals of civil rights rode the rails. The Sleeping Car Porters formed a veritable national network. On southbound trains, they carried copies of *The Chicago Defender* and the *Amsterdam News* to eager readers in small delta towns and to workers in the shotgun-shack villages that surrounded the mills and mines of northern Alabama. Near almost every important train station there was at least a bar or a diner—or in Jim Crow towns both north and south, a back table or restaurant kitchen—where porters gathered to socialize, listen to music, and talk union. In their hometowns, now that they held well-paying union jobs under Randolph's leadership, the porters were a blue-collar elite. Their wives organized into what was likely the largest organization of working-class black women in the country, the

Ladies' Auxiliary of the Brotherhood of Sleeping Car Porters. Often the same shop stewards and union officials who worked for Randolph and the regulars of the Ladies' Auxiliary meetings were also the pillars of their local churches, the leaders of neighborhood political clubs, and members of black fraternities and sororities.

The best-connected and best-known man in black America, Randolph made no idle threat when he proposed the March on Washington. Roosevelt and his advisors had no idea whether Randolph could mobilize thousands of black protestors, but the White House had reason to fear the worst. "Both were strategists of high order," wrote Pauli Murray, who worked closely with Randolph throughout the 1940s. Perhaps Randolph was bluffing, but he had a strong hand to play. A popular speaker in black churches, fraternal organizations, and political clubs, Randolph was a household name. His stirring speeches had been heard by tens of thousands. Only popular singers Paul Robeson and Marian Anderson and boxer Joe Louis were better known among black Americans than the ubiquitous Randolph.

Roosevelt and his advisors probably did not fully appreciate the extent of Randolph's connections, particularly at the grass roots, but they knew he spoke for a sizeable and vocal segment of blacks. And unlike his predecessors, who had largely ignored the "Negro vote," FDR knew that the Democratic Party had regained power, at least in part, because of the defection of blacks from the Republicans. The most popular president among blacks since Abraham Lincoln, Roosevelt had danced a delicate two-step around the issue of civil rights since 1932. By the election of 1936, photos of Roosevelt appeared in Negro Elks halls in Chicago and in shops and homes "in the black belts in every Midwest city of any size." The Great Migration of blacks northward made them an important swing vote in several states above the Mason-Dixon Line, and Roosevelt could not ignore them. (In 1940, Roosevelt's opponent, Wendell Willkie, hoping to make inroads among wavering black voters in key northern states, had taken a pro-civil-rights position more forceful than any that had come from the party of Lincoln since the last days of Reconstruction.)

In ways that he could not have anticipated, Roosevelt's policies helped give momentum to Randolph and to the rising black insurgency and set the groundwork for the confrontation in 1941. Roosevelt courted black voters, but did so behind the scenes. FDR's meetings with black leaders usually occurred without comment or notice, at least in the white-dominated newspapers, which paid little attention to blacks except when they committed crimes or won prizefights. By contrast, FDR's overtures to blacks were covered extensively in the black weeklies. Had FDR chosen to make civil rights a national issue, he could have, but overt support for racial equality would have exacted a high political price. The fate of the New Deal was held in the balance by the powerful southern wing of the party. Southern Democrats, beneficiaries of their party's long monopoly of power in the region, had amassed the seniority that allowed them to control key congressional committees. They used that control to thwart any legislation that even indirectly threatened Jim Crow. Throughout the 1930s, civil rights groups pressed FDR to support antilynching laws, but the president maintained a studied silence, fearful that if he alienated the South, his increasingly fragile New Deal would come unglued.

Because of the southern veto, the New Deal cut both ways for blacks. Like most Americans at the bottom of the economic ladder, ordinary blacks saw real promise in Franklin Roosevelt and his party. A black minister in Chicago exhorted his congregants: "Let Jesus lead you and Roosevelt feed you!" An interventionist federal government that put blue-collar and social welfare issues front and center was bound to benefit blacks—even if unequally. For the first time since Reconstruction, blacks came to see the federal government as an ally. FDR was, after all, no Woodrow Wilson, who had segregated government offices and who had endorsed the racist film *The Birth of a Nation*. And FDR offered blacks more than his Republican predecessors Theodore Roosevelt, William Howard Taft, Warren Harding, Calvin Coolidge, and Herbert Hoover. Despite their membership in Lincoln's party, they had been content to appoint a few Negroes to patronage positions while southern Jim Crow grew increasingly violent and exclusive. Although Hoover had won a majority of black votes in 1932, it was the GOP's last hurrah. More than two-thirds of black voters turned out for Roosevelt in 1936 and 1940, their loyalty cemented by the New Deal.

"For the first time in their lives," intoned the NAACP's *Crisis* in the midst of Roosevelt's third campaign, "government has taken on meaning and substance for the Negro masses." During a period when the executive branch expanded enormously—and when the federal government expanded employment in offices nationwide—the most important breakthrough for blacks was the opening of government jobs to them. Quietly, the Roosevelt administration forbade discrimination in many federally administered jobs programs. Harold Ickes, former president of Chicago's NAACP branch, used his authority overseeing the Public Works Administration to set aside jobs for blacks in proportion to their percentage in the local population, something very similar to what would later be called affirmative action. More important than antidiscrimination orders was the opening of federal employment to blacks—in part a reward for their support of the Democrats. The number of black federal workers tripled during Roosevelt's first two terms to nearly 150,000, turning government employment into a major economic foothold for blacks, even if most of them were confined to lower-level jobs. Employment aside, most of the New Deal's other gestures to blacks were symbolic. Desperate for recognition in government, African Americans celebrated the administration's efforts to reach out to black leaders; FDR's appointment of the "Negro Cabinet," including Mary McLeod Bethune and Robert C. Weaver; and, perhaps above all, the omnipresence of Eleanor Roosevelt, the administration's most vocal proponent of racial equality, who addressed the National Negro Congress, the NAACP, and the Urban League. When she resigned from the Daughters of the American Revolution in 1939 over their refusal to allow Marian Anderson to sing in Constitution Hall, Eleanor Roosevelt entered the small pantheon of whites, including Abraham Lincoln, whom nearly every black admired.

Northern blacks had a mixed experience with the New Deal's alphabet soup programs. The most important social welfare programs, those created by the Social Security Act of 1935, disproportionately excluded blacks. Old age insurance (the program that earned the moniker Social Security) did not extend benefits to agricultural workers and domestics, two of the largest categories of black workers in the North. Other programs created by the Social Security Act, including Unemployment Insurance (UI), Old Age Assistance (OAA), and, most important, Aid to Dependent Children (ADC), were funded by federal matching grants and administered locally. Overall, sociologist Charles S. Johnson found that blacks "receive less attention the farther the control of relief is removed from Washington."

The act also left General Relief or General Assistance, cash payments to the nonworking poor (predominantly men), wholly funded and administered at the state level. All these programs were potentially open to African Americans, but black applicants for relief had to negotiate a welter of regulations that varied by state. And their fate was left to local officials' discretionary authority. Blacks were overrepresented on the rolls of Old Age Assistance (a stingier program) in the largest northern states and, on average, received larger payments than whites in New York, New Jersey, Ohio, Illinois, and California. More uneven was the experience of black recipients of ADC, whose benefit levels were determined at the state level and whose eligibility requirements were administered by local welfare authorities. Black women applicants for ADC suffered the brunt of locally administered restrictions, among them "suitable homes" and morality clauses. But northern states offered more generous benefits than their southern counterparts and, overall, fewer restrictions on aid. Between 10 and 24 percent of ADC recipients in northern states were black, at a time when the population of black children in those states ranged from 2.8 to 5.1 percent of all children. Altogether, northern blacks were disproportionately dependent on local and federal relief programs.

Job relief programs also provided greater opportunities for northern blacks than for their southern counterparts. Southern members of Congress worked to guarantee that New Deal jobs programs did not overtly challenge the racial division of labor. Works programs tended to be better administered and fairer in the North—even if blacks often found themselves in race-typed jobs. Most notably, a provision that works programs pay the local prevailing wage rather than a national standard meant that Works Progress Administration projects paid better in northern cities than they did in the South. In 1935, the proportion of blacks on relief ranged from 33.5 percent in New England to 55.6 percent in the mid-Atlantic, compared to 13.3 percent of whites in New England and 14.5 percent of whites in the mid-Atlantic.

Of the social programs created during the Great Depression, housing policies discriminated most overtly against African Americans. Ambitious in their scope, federal housing programs utterly transformed metropolitan America beginning in the 1930s. Federal programs to underwrite home mortgages made possible a dramatic increase in rates of home ownership. But the two leading federal agencies—the Home Owners' Loan Corporation and Federal Housing Administration (and their World War II counterpart, the Veterans Administration)—deemed black neighborhoods uncreditworthy and, with few exceptions, denied blacks access to federally backed loans and mortgages. Compounding the discriminatory effects of housing policy were federal experiments in public housing during the New Deal and Truman's Fair Deal. The 1937 Wagner-Steagall Housing Act created the U.S. Housing Authority (USHA), fulfilling Roosevelt's pledge to assist the "one third of a nation ill housed." The USHA made real inroads in providing affordable housing for blacks—but, with few exceptions, it was done by segregating public housing projects. Public housing programs, while federally funded, were locally administered. Public officials in northern cities chose the sites for housing projects and enforced eligibility requirements. In every major northern city, public housing projects were sited in deference to local housing patterns. The few "colored" projects usually adjoined segregated neighborhoods or were built on marginal land near waterfronts, industrial sites, railroad tracks, or highways. Blacks' pent-up demand for housing remained unfulfilled.

Of the many federal agencies created or restructured by the Roosevelt administration, only one, the newly created Civil Liberties Unit of the Department of Justice, handled racial matters explicitly. Created by attorney general and later Supreme Court justice Frank Murphy, the Civil Liberties Unit took on important cases, defending blacks entrapped in the southern peonage system and those denied the right to vote. But the Civil Liberties Unit struggled for funding and legitimacy, faced congressional harassment, and eventually lost some of its most committed members to anti-Communist purges in the late 1940s.

New Deal programs did not have to be race-specific to benefit blacks. New Deal labor legislation brought real economic gains to both black and white workers, especially in the occupations that were aggressively organized by the AFL and CIO in the 1930s. A. Philip Randolph's own Brotherhood of Sleeping Car Porters provides a good example. The passage of the Amended Railway Labor Act of 1934, which gave unionists the right to strike without reprisal and required that firms negotiate with duly elected unions, greatly boosted the Brotherhood. The National Labor Relations Act of 1935, also known as the Wagner Act, brought federal government power behind trade union organizing for the first time and, by legalizing the "closed shop," provided a real opening for the unions that organized black and white workers in auto manufacturing, steelmaking, and meatpacking. But labor legislation was not a silver bullet for the problem of racial equality in the workplace, for it did not regulate union membership rules. Randolph's Brotherhood of Sleeping Car Porters, the NAACP, and the Urban League had pushed for the inclusion of an anti-discrimination clause in the Wagner Act, but the bill's sponsors quashed the effort and FDR refused to intervene. Still, black union membership increased fivefold between 1935 and 1940.

Whatever the benefits of federal welfare and labor policies, New Deal rhetoric provided blacks with a robust language of rights and democracy that they made their own. Beginning with the New Deal, advocates of racial equality came to view the empowered federal government as the guarantor of positive as well as negative rights. At the heart of the later New Deal was a sweeping redefinition of the relationship of government, entitlement, and citizenship, and the language of rights would be a powerful tool in the hands of black activists. Much of the story of the black freedom struggle in the 1940s was that of black activists pushing the federal government to give meaning to those rights, to make the commitment more than rhetorical.

No formulation of rights was more influential—or timely—than Franklin Delano Roosevelt's "four freedoms." On January 6, 1941, Roosevelt launched war preparations with a call for the defense of the "four freedoms"—the freedom of religion and speech, the freedom from fear and want. Few presidential speeches have ever had such currency. Roosevelt reaffirmed long-standing negative rights, namely the checks on government power enumerated in the Bill of Rights that resonated strongly amid reports of fascists' clampdown on civil liberties. But Roosevelt also pushed rights talk in a new direction, one that foreshadowed his expansive 1944 Second Bill of Rights. He envisioned an activist government that offered citizens protections from insecurity and poverty.

For blacks, those freedoms had been parceled out parsimoniously for most of American history. However, even if these were rights honored in the breach rather than in practice—at least for blacks—they symbolized a whole new world of possibility. The New Deal introduced a new, thicker conception of the rights of citizenship—of social and economic citizenship. Civil rights activists pushed to broaden the very understanding of who was a citizen entitled to these new rights. The rights revolution would be sadly truncated if its benefits flowed simply to whites. For black

Americans they were freedoms that would have to be won. *The Chicago Defender* editorialized of the four freedoms: "We have had none, we will fight if we have some, nor will mere promises suffice." Rights would come only with struggle.

The question of citizenship and rights intensified with the coming of war. In war, the boundaries of national identity—of who is in and who is out—are clearer than ever. Above all, wartime sacrifice raised the question of just rewards. How could a nation demand that its citizens serve on the battlefront and on the home front without rewarding them for their service? Did not fulfillment of duty to the state entitle a citizen to all the perquisites of citizenship? These were questions that blacks had raised during and after World War I, only to be frustrated by their ongoing status as second-class citizens. But in the context of World War II, a war that targeted foes who were explicitly racist in their national ideologies, the question of black citizenship took on new resonance. Well into the 1950s, civil rights activists would use wartime rhetoric and draw from wartime experience to demand full citizenship. Black Americans could not help but make an analogy between their struggle for equality and the war against fascism. The United States battled regimes in Germany and Japan whose rise to power was premised on notions of racial superiority. Black soldiers returned home from the "good war" emboldened to demand democracy and an end to racism at home.

The rights revolution expanded black activists' sense of the possible. And no one played a more crucial role in pushing at the boundaries of that unfinished revolution than black advocates of equal opportunity in the workplace. Throughout early 1941, Randolph and his "efficient couriers"—the Pullman porters—built momentum for the March on Washington. Black newspapers carried nearly weekly accounts of the progress toward the march. Sleeping car porters also provided both money and legwork to build support for the campaign. Randolph himself spread the word in bars, barbershops, and beauty parlors. Other unionists sold buttons, took up collections in churches, and circulated leaflets in nearly every public place where blacks congregated, from pool halls to neighborhood groceries.

Randolph insisted that the March on Washington be exclusively black, and he vigorously defended the decision against charges of reverse racism. For him, it was both a matter of realpolitik and ideology. Randolph was fearful that the Communists would hijack the march for partisan gain. Excluding whites would keep party members away—at least the whites who made up the vast majority of the CP's membership. But Randolph was also shaping a new vision of black political power, one that would put him at odds with many interracial groups. The march was a necessary step in what he called black "self-liberation." Randolph argued that "white liberals and labor may sympathize with the Negro's fight against Jim Crow, but they are not going to lead the fight. They never have and they never will. The fight to annihilate Jim Crow in America must be led by Negroes with the cooperation and collaboration of white liberals and labor." To that end, Randolph garnered the support of leading civil rights groups, but also black churches, the black YWCA, and black-only fraternities—most notably the Elks.

Randolph's insistence that the March on Washington be all black had some unintended consequences. The movement ended up attracting black nationalists and alienating some otherwise sympathetic white liberals. Randolph distanced himself from what he called the "Back to Africa" tendency, but he steadfastly refused to exclude black nationalists from the movement. In the end, Randolph recognized that the issues of race and class were inseparable and that an economic policy that benefited blacks and whites alike would be necessary but not sufficient to overcome the enduring effects of racial discrimination in the workplace. And he recognized that blacks could use their sense of racial identity—one that had been imposed upon them but also chosen—as the basis of political mobilization.

Fearful of the specter of mass protest on the eve of war, Roosevelt sought to squelch the protest through symbolic gestures. Hanging like a cloud over Randolph's threat were memories of the last large-scale march on Washington—the descent of the twenty-thousand-strong Bonus Army of unemployed World War I veterans on the capital in 1932. The Bonus March had gone very badly. Police shot two demonstrators, dozens were injured, and thousands were teargassed before federal troops dispersed the protestors and destroyed their encampment. The march also hobbled the already weakened Herbert Hoover. Now Roosevelt's associates tried various gambits to deter Randolph and his allies. Sidney Hillman, unionist and director of the federal Office of Production Management, and Roosevelt himself sent notices to defense contractors, encouraging them to open their doors to "all loyal and qualified workers, regardless of race, creed, or color." Civil rights leaders refused to be mollified by high-minded rhetoric. Eleanor Roosevelt tried to talk Randolph out of the march for fear it would backfire. Randolph did not budge. The march was on unless FDR issued an antidiscrimination order "with teeth in it." Meeting with Roosevelt and key aides, along with the NAACP's Walter White, on June 18, Randolph upped the ante, pledging that a hundred thousand blacks were poised to march on the capital. Roosevelt caved to the pressure. The risk of a massive display of internal dissent on the eve of war was too great.

On June 25, less than a week before the proposed march, Roosevelt issued Executive Order 8802, which forbade discrimination on the basis of "race, creed, color, or national origin" by defense contractors and created a Committee on Fair Employment Practices to monitor compliance. For the first time since Reconstruction, a president intervened decisively on behalf of black civil rights. Randolph declared Roosevelt's order the "Second Emancipation Proclamation" and called off the proposed march. Some leftists chastised Randolph for selling out. The Socialist Workers' newspaper, *The Militant*, denounced the "obvious shortcomings" of the order and called for "greater militancy" to force "real concessions" from the federal government. The black press, however, generally hailed the success of Randolph's strategy. With some hyperbole—and a historical chronology that omitted Emancipation and Reconstruction—*The Chicago Defender* lauded Executive Order 8802 as "one of the most significant pronouncements that has been made in the interests of the Negro for more than a century." Randolph had succeeded in changing the course of the federal government through "mass pressure." An editorial in the *Amsterdam News* concurred that "we get more when we yell than we do when we plead." Grassroots activists heeded the lesson.

If FDR believed that his order would buy off black discontent, subsequent events proved him terribly wrong. During the summer of 1941, clashes between blacks and whites broke out in dozens of cities. Major papers in New York and Washington published sensationalistic stories about a Negro crime wave. Whether or not crime rates were rising, interracial tensions were. In South Philadelphia, blacks clashed with whites leaving a church picnic; in Santa Monica, California, black and white youths brawled in city parks. "Throughout the urban areas of the country," wrote black journalist Roi Ottley just a month before Pearl Harbor, "the Negro communities are seething with resentment." The *Amsterdam News* concurred that "now the Negro is showing a 'democratic surge of rebellion,' bordering on open hostility." The face-off between Randolph and Roosevelt was the first battle of a war at home over the full inclusion of blacks into the ranks of American citizenry. Ironically, by hoping to defuse black protest, Roosevelt ended up providing an arsenal to the combatants in the black freedom struggle. Armed with Roosevelt's own rights rhetoric and with the powerful language of antifascism, civil rights activists would push hard for change. Ordinary blacks, increasingly frustrated at the gap between the wartime rhetoric of freedom and Jim Crow, would also take to the streets in a wave of mass protest that would eventually dwarf the March on Washington Movement.

CHAPTER 3

"1776 FOR THE NEGRO"

TOTALING 1,483 PAGES IN TWO HEFTY VOLUMES (AND PRINTED ON CHEAP paper because of wartime rationing), Gunnar Myrdal's *An American Dilemma: The Negro Problem and American Democracy* hit the bookstores in January 1944. It met with immediate acclaim in the black and liberal white press alike. In 1937, Myrdal had been commissioned by the Carnegie Corporation to conduct a comprehensive study of the condition of the American Negro. A Swedish social democrat and economist, Myrdal had penned virtually nothing about the problem of race and inequality, but he was an internationally respected social scientist. Carnegie sought someone who could write from a detached perspective, unconnected to the scholarly debates that swirled in American universities. That Myrdal was an outsider who had spent some time in the United States and written little on race would allow him to be a sort of Alexis de Tocqueville of American race relations. Armed with more than three hundred thousand dollars, Myrdal hired a veritable Who's Who of black academics to conduct research. Ralph Bunche, Allison Davis, Kenneth Clark, St. Clair Drake, E. Franklin Frazier, Doxey Wilkerson, and many others produced an extraordinary array of books, articles, and memos that Myrdal synthesized for his massive study.

Few people have the time or inclination to read table-laden, citation-heavy, social scientific tomes. Myrdal wrote compellingly, often lyrically about race in America, but *An American Dilemma* was still heavy going, more likely to be mined for its innumerable insights than to be voraciously consumed. For those unwilling to pay the hefty $7.50 list price or too busy to read it, Myrdal offered a brief prepublication summary in the *Negro Digest*. Just a few months later, the liberal Public Affairs Committee published a handy pamphlet summarizing its arguments. Opinion writers and editorialists offered even briefer snippets. To their good fortune, Myrdal provided readers cues about what he wanted them to take away from his book, such as italicized passages and pithy chapter summaries. They invariably turned to the introduction—and probably more than a few closed the book at that point. Few introductions have ever made a more powerful argument for their case.

"The Negro problem," wrote Myrdal, all in italics, *"is a problem in the heart of the American. It is there that the interracial tension has its focus. It is there that the decisive struggle goes on."* American values, which he called "boundless, idealistic aspirations" of the "American Creed," stood in sharp contrast to "personal and local interests; economic, social, and sexual jealousies; considerations of community prestige and conformity; group prejudice against particular persons or types of people; and all sorts of miscellaneous wants, impulses, and habits." Americans were fundamentally "moralistic" and deeply "rationalistic." These traits, in Myrdal's words, were the "glory of the nation, its youthful strength, perhaps the salvation of mankind." The challenge to solving America's "Negro problem" would be to appeal to the moral sentiments and the reason of ordinary white Americans. Faced with evidence of the appalling gap between the national rhetoric of equality and opportunity and the bleak reality of race relations, white Americans would jettison their prejudices.

Myrdal was aware of the depth of racial inequality in the United States and of black resentment at the status quo, but he remained profoundly optimistic. In his view, racism was a pathology, a deformed version of the American national character. But Myrdal believed that because Americans were a deeply moral people, whose self-understanding fused a sense of national mission with a Judeo-Christian understanding of the unity of humanity under God, there was great hope for solving America's race problem. Above all, Myrdal tapped a deep root in the American social reform tradition: a faith in human perfectibility. If people were fundamentally good, then moral suasion—appeals to their deepest, most humane sentiments—could transform society.

Myrdal had relatively little to say about race relations in the North, despite the fact that many members of his research team had offered astute observations. Statistician Richard Sterner found that black unemployment rates in cities above the Mason-Dixon Line exceeded those in the South. Doxey Wilkerson, who became a Communist in 1942, documented the persistent problem of racially separate education in the northern states, even those with long-standing laws forbidding segregated schools. St. Clair Drake, in the midst of preparing his own landmark study of black life in Chicago, provided an unparalleled account of the richness of black institutional and cultural life in America's Second City. And Ralph Bunche, Myrdal's closest black associate, examined black leadership and institutions—but also drew from his Depression-era leftism to offer a chastening critique of Myrdal's optimistic notion that concepts like "the Land of the Free" had an impact on white behavior.

Despite the extensive information at hand, Myrdal's primary concern was the South. It was there, of course, that the gap between the "American Creed" and everyday race relations was so blatant. But for many reasons, Myrdal was hopeful about the state of race relations in the North. For one, the absence of Jim Crow laws meant that segregation and discrimination "have not acquired the strength, persuasiveness, or institutional fixity found in the South." The lack of state-sponsored racial discrimination, however, had the ironic effect of blinding northern whites to the Negro problem. Northern whites lived blissfully unaware of racial inequality or of their role in perpetuating it. "White Northerners," observed Myrdal, "are surprised and shocked when they hear about such things" and "are moved to feel that something ought to be done to stop it. They often do not understand correctly even the implications of their own behavior and often tell the interviewer that they 'have never thought of it in that light.' " Northerners' sense of innocence may have been naïve in Myrdal's view, but it also provided social reformers with an opening— for their ignorance could be "fought with education." Had he known more about the depth of racial animosity in the North, Myrdal would not have been so optimistic.

Myrdal looked at the situation in the North from the perspective of a Swedish social democrat, deeply sympathetic toward America's version of the welfare state. The migration of blacks northward—in effect from America's South Africa to America's Sweden—boded well for the future of the Negro. "We foresee that the trend of unionization, social legislation, and national planning will tend to break down economic discrimination, the only type of discrimination which is both important and strong in the North." What Myrdal could not, of course, foresee was that the very premises of the New Deal state that he so admired would come under siege in the mid- and late 1940s. As unionization efforts weakened, as social legislation came to a virtual halt, and as national planning was denounced as un-American and Socialist, the very underpinning of at least one part of Myrdal's optimistic vision would collapse.

An American Dilemma provided a data-laden overview of the state of race relations in America. But Myrdal was not content to pile detail upon detail. Believing in the fundamental responsibility of social scientists to change the world, he offered a blueprint for reform. He unabashedly called for "social engineering," using language that would, only a few decades later, become taboo in American politics. From the Progressive period on forward, American social scientists and policy makers shared a deep faith in the power of expertise to solve social and economic problems. Deeply technocratic in its vision—only those who truly understood social problems could devise their solution—social engineering captured the minds of planners, economists, sociologists, and the health professions. Anticipating his critics, Myrdal justified social engineering in terms of American optimism and pragmatism. "Social engineering . . . will be nothing but the drawing of practical conclusions from the teaching of social science that 'human nature' is changeable and that human deficiencies and unhappiness are, in large degree, preventable." What made Myrdal's analysis so novel was that he combined high social science with commonsensical folk wisdom. "People are all much alike on a fundamental level," argued Myrdal. "And they are all good people. They want to be rational and just." Social engineering was merely a strategy that appealed to the best in people—their innate moral sensibility, their desire to be fair and just.

In Myrdal's view, the struggle for black freedom would be waged by moderate, reasonable activists—ones informed by social science—who would remake America into the truly just society that it was meant to be. Despite the findings of his politically connected research associates, especially Bunche and Wilkerson, Myrdal downplayed the strength and vitality of black political activism in the North and eschewed the left's critiques of labor and public policy. *An American Dilemma* advocated social change, not structural change; Myrdal and his popularizers did not want to remake American politics or economic institutions. They were not revolutionaries or even radicals. Their goal was individual change. One by one, racist but essentially well-meaning white Americans would have to be persuaded, cajoled—educated—to accept a race-blind society.

AS MYRDAL FINISHED his writing in late 1942, events in the North called his optimism into question. Racial tensions hardened in the northern cities that had attracted so many war workers. Northern blacks were rising in the streets, civil rights groups were exploding in membership, black activists of all stripes were challenging the political status quo and above all challenging the very premise of Myrdal's argument: that education and persuasion would resolve America's "dilemma." Ideologically, civil rights activists—particularly those on the left—complicated Myrdal's understanding of the "American Creed" by highlighting the commonalities between fascist regimes and race relations in the United States. Indeed, the ubiquity of anti-imperialist and anticolonialist rhetoric in the wartime black press undermined the sense of American exceptionalism that pervaded Myrdal's book. The freedom struggles in India and Ethiopia inspired civil rights activists as much as the still-unachieved promises of equality and liberty dating from the early American republic. Civil rights activists offered a powerful grassroots critique of American democracy, one that was far more challenging to the status quo than anything Myrdal could have imagined.

"Negroes," reported the *Chicago Sun* in January 1943, just as Myrdal's book was going to press, are "in a very explosive frame of mind." To its allies and enemies, America presented a united front, but behind the scenes—on military bases, at overseas encampments, and on ships—blacks were bristling with discontent. Civil rights activists held the government responsible. "You must be aware, Mr. President," wrote A. Philip Randolph and a diverse group of black activists, which included Anna Arnold Hedgeman and Pauli Murray, to Franklin Roosevelt in July 1942, "of the complete disillusionment and embittered resentment of the Negro masses in this country, a discontent which is taking organized form. . . . Don't you see, Mr. President, this is not a repetition of anything that has happened before in the history of Negro-white relations?"

At every turn, blacks confronted persistent racial inequality. The wartime draft brought a huge number of black men into the military, where Jim Crow became a flash point of conflict. The vast majority of enlisted blacks found themselves in race-typed jobs in service units, as one observer reported, "cooking, shoveling coal, waiting on white officers." Blacks served in segregated units, lived in segregated quarters, used separate latrines and showers, and exercised in separate gyms. The racial hierarchy was strict: Black officers could never outrank or command a white officer in the same unit. Charles H. King, Jr., who grew up in Pottstown, Pennsylvania, sardonically described his experience in the Jim Crow military: "I became a highly trained member of the U.S. Navy: trained to serve white officers their dinners in the officers' mess." Bitter that he was "a servant, a non-person, invisible," King and his fellow mess hands engaged in on-the-job subterfuge, what he described as a "kind of black warfare, waged with a vengeance," like drinking milk out of the officers' glasses and dropping steaks on the dirty floor and covering the grit with gravy. In a fit of rage, King struck a noncommissioned officer who called him a "black nigger."

The military took segregation to its absurd, logical extreme. Black and white blood was segregated, lest whites be contaminated by inferior hemoglobin and plasma. The most literal symbol of the "one-drop rule," which determined racial identity in the United States, Jim Crow blood banks outraged blacks and fueled a campaign of resistance. Rumors spread that Negroes who "passed" for white defiantly donated their blood to "white only" blood banks. In New York, where the local chapter of the Red Cross segregated its blood donations by race, many blacks simply refused to donate. "I will give no blood to the war effort and will not appeal to my workers to give until the practice of the segregation of Negro blood is stopped," proclaimed Laundry Workers Union official Charlotte Adelmond at a New York Civil Defense conference. When black students at a New York school whose parents refused to donate blood were harassed by their white classmates for being "unpatriotic," their teacher turned the dispute into a class science experiment. Students looked at black and white blood under a microscope, noted that it was identical, and presented their findings to the Red Cross. "All blood is the same," they wrote on a poster that they mounted on the school bulletin board. "Our dying soldier needs it that he may live."

Jim Crow extended off base as well, usually with the approval of white commanders. Black soldiers chafed at petty racial restrictions. Brawls broke out near southern encampments, where uniformed blacks proudly defied such southern "customs" as moving off the sidewalk for passing whites, avoiding eye contact with whites, sitting at the back of the bus, and using inferior, black-only facilities. But racial indignities were not restricted to the land of Dixie. In Walla Walla, Washington, where few blacks had lived before the war, a base commander ordered black soldiers to stay out of the town's restaurants. At Fort Dix, New Jersey, which had constructed new separate housing and recreation facilities for the many black soldiers stationed there, white soldiers defended Jim Crow in the row of restaurants and bars that sprang up just across the street from the base. Small encounters could turn deadly. In April 1942, seven black soldiers stationed at Fort Dix were shot, two fatally, after an altercation about their use of a pay phone at an off-base bar. Put in the position of enforcing "law and order" on bases, the military police defended strict segregation, north and south. Many blacks who challenged segregation were rewarded with less than honorable discharges.

On the home front, wartime America was boiling with racial conflict, much of it spontaneous and unorganized. As hundreds of thousands of blacks migrated northward and westward, city streets, defense plants, and even shops and restaurants became racial battlegrounds. Northern whites found the very presence of thousands of black newcomers unsettling. One observer noted the "almost guerilla-like warfare that occurs on busses, trains, streetcars, in restaurants and any place where 'prejudice as usual' meets head on with [blacks'] new belligerency." Even more bothersome was a shift in black attitudes. Weren't blacks supposed to be docile and deferential? Northern whites complained about "bump and push" squads of young, "uppity" blacks, who they believed deliberately jostled whites in crowded buses and ration lines. Even if the charges were exaggerated, black and white youths clashed in public spaces, often violently. In June 1944, fifteen black youths were arrested in Brooklyn after pushing their way through a crowded subway, insulting white passengers, and shooting a white man who chastised them. Young black men wore zoot suits and flaunted a new assertive style, deliberately unsettling whites. The zoot suit was not only a sartorial statement of difference; in the midst of wartime rationing, wearing clothes tailored from yards of fabric directly flouted the notion of sacrifice. In Los Angeles in 1943, white mobs attacked black and

Mexican American men wearing the suits; and in Evansville, Indiana, in 1944, zoot-suit-wearing black men attacked white soldiers.

The black rebellion even made its way into the confines of white, suburban homes. White housewives complained about the growing insolence of black domestics, and some believed that they had formed into "Eleanor Clubs" (named for Eleanor Roosevelt) or "Disappointment Clubs," whose members supposedly organized to disrupt white households and steal from their employers. Blaming Eleanor Roosevelt's allegedly pernicious influence on black women put a conspiratorial, human face on what was an enormous economic and political shift. Wartime work liberated black women from domestic labor—from the "slave markets" of northern cities—by providing them new opportunities. What whites perceived as impudence was the product of a newfound political assertiveness. Wartime democracy meant not having to trade dignity for meager wages. Many observers attributed the hardening of racial segregation in stores and restaurants to the growing presence of blacks asserting their rights in public places. Not surprisingly, public accommodations, as we shall see, became one of the major battlegrounds for racial equality in the wartime North.

No place was as tense as Detroit. Labeled the nation's "arsenal of democracy" for its concentration of defense factories, Detroit attracted more than sixty thousand black migrants in the first few years of the war. Housing was so scarce that black war workers slept in "hot sheet" boardinghouses, where beds turned over every eight hours as one shift set out for work and the last returned home. Because of pervasive housing segregation, shelter was seldom available outside the small, densely packed neighborhoods that had been home to Detroit's blacks since the 1920s. Most blacks were crammed into the decrepit wood-frame buildings of the city's Black Bottom or its ironically named Paradise Valley, where basements, firetrap attics, and even closets were hastily converted into apartments.

In Detroit, as elsewhere in the urban North, the housing crunch became the source of intense racial conflict. The Detroit branch of the NAACP and the United Automobile Workers lobbied hard for the construction of affordable housing for the new migrants but met with fierce resistance. When the city announced that the new Sojourner Truth Homes, a public housing project, would be open to blacks, a firestorm of protest ensued. White neighbors—with support from prominent elected officials—demanded that the project be white-only. Six weeks before the Sojourner Truth Homes were to open, federal housing officials capitulated to their demands. But black activists fought back. The fate of Sojourner Truth was, in the words of a black observer, "a symbol of the whole question of Negro rights" and "a test for democracy itself." Sojourner Truth was not just a matter of providing a little additional housing for blacks who faced overcrowding; it was a test of the meaning of the New Deal's enumerated right to "a decent home." The question at stake on the streets of northeast Detroit was to what extent blacks would be included in the state. Local black activists put pressure on federal housing officials, who were flooded with letters and telegrams opposing the last-minute decision to exclude blacks from the project. Black picketers, their ranks full of trade unionists and leftists, established a "permanent picket line" at the city housing commission offices. They couched their demands in the patriotic rhetoric of the war. "Together We Fight! Together We Live!" The protests were successful: Federal officials backtracked and announced that Sojourner Truth would be open for "Negro occupancy."

White Detroiters, bearing American flags and demanding their "Rights to Protect, Restrict, and Improve Our Neighborhood," picketed the project throughout the month prior to its opening. A large billboard graced a vacant lot overlooking the project, proclaiming, "WE WANT WHITE TENANTS IN OUR WHITE COMMUNITY." When the first black families moved into the project on February 28, 1942, a crowd of a few hundred blacks and whites gathered near the project, and by the end of the day, more than a thousand demonstrators had gathered. Enraged whites barricaded the street to defend their turf. Black counterprotestors fought back, until they were dispersed by the police. At least 40 people were injured, 220 arrested, and 109 held for trial—all but three black—before police restored order in the area. The NAACP's *Crisis* lambasted the riot as an "open revolt against the Federal government" by "Nazi-minded mobsters who would sacrifice their country for a Hitlerite principle."

"Detroit is dynamite," wrote a reporter for *Life* magazine after the Sojourner Truth battle. "It can either blow up Hitler or blow up the U.S." In the summer of 1943, the arsenal exploded. On a hot summer day in late June, the worst race riot since the Tulsa, Oklahoma, massacre of 1921 (where as many as three hundred blacks had been killed) erupted in Detroit. The conflagration began on Saturday, June 20, at the city's Belle Isle Park, an oasis of meadows, woods, and beaches on the Detroit River. Nearly one hundred thousand picnickers and swimmers, many of them black, gathered there to escape the sweltering heat. Over the course of the day, fights broke out between blacks and whites in the park and tensions rose. As the day wound down, thousands jostled across the bridge that connected the park to the city, to catch buses home. Cars crept even more slowly away from the park, dodging pedestrians who poured off the sidewalks onto the roadway. Tempers flared and fights of all sorts broke out in the park and on the bridge. In the already racially tense atmosphere, black-white confrontations took on new, ominous meaning. Rumors of an impending race war spread throughout black and white neighborhoods. Over the next day, thousands of whites descended on Hastings Street, many armed and ready to fend off the black "invasion." On major thoroughfares, white mobs stopped buses and trolleys, pulled off black passengers, and beat them. The city's overwhelmingly white police force sided with white rioters, infuriating blacks. "Those police are *murderers*," charged one black eyewitness to the riot. "They were just waiting for the chance to get us. We didn't stand a chance. I hate 'em, oh God, how I hate 'em." Altogether, thirty-four people were killed, all but nine of them black. The police were responsible for half the riot-related deaths.

Attorney Thurgood Marshall, who headed the NAACP Legal Defense and Educational Fund, bitterly wrote of Detroit's "Gestapo." Many other observers blamed homegrown Nazis for the violence, and still others saw the riot as the result of the migration of southern whites to the Motor City. Even if the riots gave succor to the Axis, as one observer argued, most of the rioters were neither Nazi sympathizers nor southerners. It may have reassured native Detroiters to believe that white rioters were southern migrants, outside agitators who had imported their racism to the North, but the whites who took to Detroit's streets were mostly homegrown racists who needed little tutelage from their southern counterparts. The Detroit riot made it clear that the North had its own, very serious race problem.

Just a month later, a quite different riot shook Harlem. Detroit had witnessed a pitched battle between blacks and whites, one of hundreds of bloody battles between blacks and whites that had rocked American cities since the bloody anti-Negro riots of Boston, Philadelphia, and New York a century earlier. In the early twentieth century, as blacks migrated to cities in ever-increasing numbers, whites attacked black newcomers and torched black neighborhoods in places as diverse as Atlanta, Tulsa, Chicago, and Springfield, Illinois. By contrast, Harlem in 1943 exploded in a black insurrection that foreshadowed the long hot summers of the 1960s. Thousands of blacks took to the streets, enraged by an all-too-plausible rumor that the police had killed a black soldier (he had been injured by an arresting officer, not killed). Suspicion of the police was at an all-time high; Harlem residents had protested police brutality throughout the 1930s and early 1940s. Adding fuel to the fire was the widespread outrage against police involvement in the Detroit riot. The precipitating event—a clash between a black soldier and the police—was yet another reminder of blacks' second-class citizenship. A military uniform offered a black soldier no protection from vindictive white police officers. Harlemites took out their anger on the most visible white institutions in their community—shopkeepers. "The angry mob," wrote novelist Ralph Ellison, "wreaked its revenge on pawnshops, grocery stores, second-hand furniture stores, shoe stores, fish stores, liquor stores, jewelry stores, hardware stores, and corner bars," breaking windows and looting. Six blacks died and hundreds more were wounded.

The black and white press alike denounced Harlem's "hoodlums," but most civil rights activists and black writers put the event into the context of simmering wartime discontent. In a series of acerbic letters to white shopkeepers, published in *The Chicago Defender* in the wake of the Harlem riot, Langston Hughes explained the mounting black anger: "We know you live in nice neighborhoods with trees and lawns, where we cannot live. And we see you at the bank with those big bags of our hard-earned money—so that makes us mad." The *Amsterdam News* argued that the Harlem riot was a harbinger of worse to come. The only antidote to further violence was equal citizenship. "Negroes must be made to feel that they are part of this country." Pointing to the fact that Harlem's riot had started with the attack on a soldier, Walter White pointedly blamed the riot on "the fury born of repeated, unchecked, unpunished, and often unrebuked shooting, insulting, and maiming of Negro troops." Pauli Murray walked the streets in the wake of the looting and found that "people who participated in it do not think they did wrong. . . . I know there were people who participated in the looting who never before had the desire to steal, and probably never will again. In the few hours of that wild night, they purged themselves of bitterness which had piled up in them for years."

President Roosevelt took increasing heat for what many perceived as his inaction on civil rights as wartime racial tensions mounted. "Why, in these months when the peril of open race war hung upon the air, hasn't Mr. Roosevelt come to us with one of his greatest speeches?" asked Thomas Sancton in *The New Republic,* just days after the Detroit race riot. "The race situation is not okay, Mr. Roosevelt." Roosevelt's response to urban unrest gave little comfort to civil rights advocates: "The recent outbreaks of violence in widely spread parts of the country endanger our national unity and comfort our enemies. I am sure that every true American regrets this."

Pauli Murray rejoined with a scathing poem, "Mr. Roosevelt Regrets," published in *The Crisis* in August 1943.

> *What'd you get, black boy,*
> *When they knocked you down in the gutter,*
> *And they kicked your teeth out,*
> *And they broke your skull with clubs,*
> *And they bashed your stomach in?*
> *What'd you get when the police shot you in the back,*
> *And they chained you to the beds*
> *While they wiped the blood off?*
> *What'd you get when you cried out to the Top Man?*
> *When you called on the man next to God, so you thought,*
> *And you asked him to speak out to save you?*
> *What'd the Top Man say, black boy?*
> *"Mr. Roosevelt regrets . . ."*

Of all the problems facing blacks during the war, "discrimination in employment," wrote black historian L. D. Reddick in 1944, "is the number one problem among Negroes, North and South." There had been so much publicity around Roosevelt's signing of Executive Order 8802 that many held out hope that the barriers to black equality in the workplace would quickly fall. But the Committee on Fair Employment Practices faced serious hurdles. The order itself, for all its rhetorical power against workplace discrimination in the defense industry, was quite toothless. In its first year, the FEPC (as it came to be called) had a part-time staff of six and a budget of only eighty thousand dollars. In addition, it had no enforcement powers. The committee's limitations were clearest when it ventured forth to hold much-publicized hearings in Chicago, New York, and Los Angeles in the winter of 1941–42. In each of those hearings, the FEPC uncovered egregious examples of workplace discrimination against black workers. Sometimes the FEPC's pressure did open up formerly closed jobs to blacks. For example, in the weeks leading up to the Los Angeles hearings in October 1941, Lockheed-Vega Aircraft hired its first black workers, 54 of them, in a workforce of 48,000. In the aftermath, the company hired nearly 500 more. Similarly, after the Chicago FEPC hearings, several defense contractors hired black workers for the first time and the state hastily passed a law (which was not enforced) prohibiting discrimination in defense employment. Still, there was little that the FEPC could do other than publicize discrimination and hope that defense contractors, under the glare of public scrutiny, would modify their hiring practices. In New York, which topped the country in receipt of defense appropriations, Fairchild Aviation, located in a section of Queens with a large black population, tripled its workforce after the FEPC hearings but hired hardly any blacks: They were 1 percent of the firm's workforce.

Despite the FEPC's weaknesses—or perhaps because of them—its very existence had a galvanic effect on civil rights activists. The FEPC hearings raised the public consciousness of the pervasiveness of workplace discrimination and gave writers and editorialists ammunition to keep the struggle for jobs and freedom in the public eye. Accounts of workplace discrimination were rife in the black press; liberal periodicals carried detailed accounts of the FEPC's findings. More than that, the committee gave black activists, particularly in the trade union movement, a focal point. The lesson from the hearings only reaffirmed Randolph's vision of change: It would take more than hearings or publicity to change the workplace status quo. It would take pressure, pressure, and more pressure.

The battle for a stronger, permanent federal fair employment practices law led to the creation of an interracial alliance that spanned the left flank of the Democratic Party, various religious groups, many CIO unions, and various Socialist and Communist organizations. When the Soviet Union entered World War II as an American ally, many civil rights organizations overcame their earlier divisions over communism, particularly on the local level. Most noteworthy was the political breadth of coalitions around civil rights issues during the war. More often than not, Communist-front organizations joined forces with suspected Communists, with other leftists, with religious activists, and with liberals—papering over their different interpretations of international issues and class struggle in service of the common goal of racial democracy on the home front.

Some of the most vocal advocates of fair employment came from left-labor circles, particularly from unions with many black members. In New York, a group of left-labor activists, mostly members of the National Maritime Union and the State, County, and Municipal Workers, founded the Negro Labor Victory Committee (NLVC) in February 1941. The NLVC began modestly as a sort of left-wing Urban League, helping black workers find defense-related employment, but it soon broadened its goals and deployed more militant tactics. Building on the momentum of black discontent at the war effort, the NLVC held mass rallies, publicized FEPC hearings, and lobbied for stricter enforcement of antidiscrimination regulations. Its Popular Front strategy brought it support from politicians as diverse as New York mayor Fiorello La Guardia and Roosevelt advisor Mary McLeod Bethune, the Reverend Adam Clayton Powell, Jr., and singer, actor, and Communist Paul Robeson.

While the Negro Labor Victory Committee worked in a high-profile way to challenge workplace discrimination, many left-wing organizations worked behind the scenes. Socialists and Communists alike moved into blue-collar jobs, attended union meetings, and organized their fellow workers. Perhaps the most vocal and interesting of the many leftist factions active during the war was the Forest-Johnson tendency, a Trotskyist group headed by Trinidad-born black intellectual C.L.R. James (known by his party pseudonym, James Johnson) and by Trotsky's former secretary Raya Dunayevskaya (also known as Freddy Forest). A small cell based in New York and Detroit, it had perhaps fifteen hundred members at its peak, but nonetheless drew some of the most brilliant leftist minds of the era, including memoirist Charles Denby, who penned a scathing account of racial inequality and alienation in Detroit's factories; philosopher and activist Grace Lee Boggs, who organized factory workers while providing the first English translations of the early works of Marx; and James Boggs, a shop-floor activist who spearheaded a campaign to open up restaurants to blacks, who led union insurgents, and whose political writings would inspire a whole generation of black power advocates in the 1960s and 1970s.

At the center was C.L.R. James, who wrote hundreds of articles for sectarian periodicals after he arrived in the United States in 1938. The pages of *The Militant*, the Socialist Workers' Party newspaper, to which James regularly contributed, extensively covered grim working conditions, anti-black hate strikes, and wartime hypocrisy. James traveled incognito throughout the United States speaking to labor and civil rights groups, and even if he won few converts to his esoteric brand of socialism, he inspired many grassroots activists to join black workers' struggles for dignity and security on the job. James had two qualities that brought his work to an audience far beyond his tiny sectarian circle: He was a brilliant writer and a charismatic speaker. Over the course of the 1940s, James developed a trenchant critique of the subordination of American blacks in the industrial economy. To James, racism was not an aberrant strain of Americanism, it was the natural outgrowth of an economic system that depended on the exploitation of people of color. But James also offered a hopeful reinterpretation of black resistance. He found in the self-organization of blacks, such as wildcat strikes against workplace discrimination, a more powerful model of social change than Stalinist bureaucracy or liberal models of social engineering and education. More so than any other observer in wartime America, James recognized the power of what he called "self activity," the everyday resistance and small-scale organization of black workers against oppression. In the 1960s and 1970s, James would be hailed as a prophet of black radicalism, largely for his emphasis on black self-determination.

The most visible—even if short-lived—wartime grassroots organization was the March on Washington Movement (MOWM). A. Philip Randolph was always better at starting organizations than keeping them alive and vital, but the Movement bounced back to life in the spring of 1942, when Randolph pledged to fight for the "democratic rights of Negroes now, during the war" with a series of massive rallies around the country. In June, the MOWM organized a mass rally in New York's Madison Square Garden that coincided with a two-hour blackout in Harlem.

"While the Garden blazes with light and rocks with oratory and song," wrote the *Black Worker*, "every home and place of business and entertainment in Harlem will be darkened" to "dramatize the economic and political blackout through which our people still stumble and fall in their too-slow progress toward the light in half-free America." In the aftermath of the rally—twenty-five thousand people participated—a group of young organizers took to the city's streets, building momentum for a parade on behalf of Odell Waller, a young sharecropper who had been sentenced to death on dubious charges in Virginia. From July 9 to July 25, organizer Pauli Murray reported, "we kept a running fire of street meetings every night." Local activists joined with dignitaries Hedgeman and Bethune to address street corner rallies. Some of the protests were creative and spontaneous. Murray joined a "truckful of young radicals" who "skittered down 125th St, shouting in jitterbug rhythm, 'HEY JOE—WHADDYE KNOW—OLE JIM CROW—HAS GOT TO GO!'" New York was a hotbed of MOWM protest, but it was not alone. "Vast throngs"—sixteen thousand in Chicago in late June and nine thousand in St. Louis in early August—gathered at MOWM rallies. Randolph proudly reported that they "were drawn from all walks and levels of Negro life," including "businessmen, teachers, laundry workers, Pullman Porters, waiters and red caps; preachers, crapshooters and social workers; jitterbugs and Ph.Ds."

Building on the momentum from the summer rallies, MOWM activists gathered in Detroit in a small "policy conference" to set the direction for future protests. Randolph gave a stirring speech that set a high tone for the proceedings. "Never have the principles of freedom," proclaimed Randolph, "had so vital a meaning to so many millions of human beings." The war—and the freedom struggle at home and abroad—demanded unity and sacrifice. "Rather than continue to exist in the gutter of second-rate citizenship, we Negroes are ready to . . . offer the gift of human life in the cause of freedom here." In its "8 Point Program," the MOWM drew explicitly from Roosevelt's rhetoric of rights but framed it in the larger context of anticolonialism. "For the masses of people," its preamble declared, "abstract principles have meaning only in concrete expression: 'Freedom from want' is only real when it means a chance to work for sufficient food, clothing, and shelter. Likewise for the Negro and for all oppressed people everywhere, the fight for democracy has meaning only when it grants them the full measure of every right as well as of every obligation for which democracy stands."

The wartime battle for the FEPC came to a head in the winter and spring of 1943. Less than two years after Roosevelt had signed his antidiscrimination order, many observers believed that the FEPC was doomed to extinction. Southern Democrats reviled the committee as a haven for advocates of racial mixing and intermarriage. Probusiness Republicans cared little for any government agency that meddled with "private enterprise," even in symbolic ways. It seemed unlikely that Congress would authorize the release of funds to keep the FEPC alive. But civil rights activists also joined the fight, flooding the White House with letters and petitions, and Randolph mobilized the March on Washington Movement to stage nationwide protests demanding that the government "Save FEPC." Roosevelt was caught in a vise: The most influential members of his own party, those southerners who controlled the lion's share of congressional committees, hoped to eviscerate the FEPC. But at the same time, the specter of black-led protests threatened his goal of wartime unity at whatever cost. In the midst of war, could the nation afford mass disruption in the streets?

In Detroit, on April 11, 1943, ten thousand marchers, led by the Detroit NAACP and the United Automobile Workers' Interracial Committee, marched from the Sojourner Truth monument near the Detroit Institute of Arts to Cadillac Square, the traditional parade destination in the heart of downtown. They challenged the "slow upgrading of trained Negro men, the reluctance of war industries to utilize available Negro women power." Banners read "Down with discrimination," "Jim Crow must go," and "Bullets and Bombs are Colorblind." To show their involvement in the war effort, many blacks marched in civil defense uniforms and were joined by black soldiers on weekend leave. The parade ended with the endorsement of the "Cadillac Charter," which demanded "abolition of discrimination in government, housing, the armed forces; abolition of the poll tax; security from mob violence, lynching, police brutality, and physical violence; equal treatment in hiring upgrading and training." The preamble was that "as people of all races," we "declare ourselves wholeheartedly behind the effort of the government to prosecute the war to an ultimate victory." But that support came with a caveat: "Discriminatory practices cannot be maintained if America is to hold out to the world hope of freedom."

Amid growing black unrest and relentless political pressure, the FEPC won a new lease on life. On May 27, 1943, Roosevelt issued Executive Order 9346, reiterating the government's commitment to nondiscrimination in defense industries and reorganizing and strengthening the FEPC. As always, Roosevelt walked a fine line, unwilling to alienate his party's ever-powerful southern wing but also fearful that inaction would generate further black unrest and jeopardize national unity in the midst of total war. The southern Democrats won a key concession: The FEPC would not have any enforcement powers against discriminatory employers. The flip side was that the newly reorganized FEPC had a larger budget, which it used to create field offices in fifteen cities. For the next two years, the FEPC conducted a record number of public hearings, further publicizing workplace discrimination. Some employers, unwilling to undergo public scrutiny by FEPC investigations, opened their doors to blacks. And most notably, the FEPC intervened to help squelch twenty-five hate strikes in the Midwest in 1943 and 1944, restoring defense production after whites walked off the job to protest the hiring or upgrading of black workers. But the major gains in black employment were the result of economic forces well beyond the control of the still-small federal agency.

World War II wrought enormous transformations for African Americans. It kick-started the second great migration, as black refugees from the still-depressed rural South sought opportunities and, most of all, the comparative freedom of the North. The catalyst of change was economic: America's military-industrial complex had a nearly insatiable demand for workers. Fueled by workers' rapidly rising incomes, aggregate consumer demand spiked during the war, putting pressure on industries as diverse as food production, garment making, and electronics. Government employment at all levels also expanded exponentially during the war. The tremendous shortage of labor, the result of military mobilization, led employers to tap workers once viewed as unreliable or undesirable. Among the greatest beneficiaries were African Americans. By late 1942, over a year after Roosevelt signed Executive Order 8802 but before it was extensively enforced, blacks began to enter defense industries in great numbers. FEPC intervention mattered, but not nearly as much as economic necessity.

The results of the wartime economic boom were dramatic. In the large cities of Pennsylvania, New Jersey, and Delaware in January 1942, only 4 percent of the defense workforce was black; by November 1943, 7.2 percent of war workers in Trenton, 8.8 percent in Newark, 13 percent in Philadelphia, and 7.2 percent in Pittsburgh were black. Other cities also witnessed startling gains in black employment. In Chicago in March 1940, slightly over 80,000 blacks were employed; by January 1945, 222,500 blacks were at work; in New York, blacks in war work rose from 1.6 percent in May 1942 to 6.6 percent of workers in March 1945. Detroit's auto industry workforce—which had retooled to build tanks, jeeps, and aircraft during the war—was 3 percent black in 1940 and 15 percent black in 1945. Economist Robert C. Weaver noted that "these changes . . . represented more industrial and occupational diversification for Negroes than had occurred" since the end of the Civil War. The mass migration of blacks to industrial centers and their growing economic clout would, over the long term, change the balance of power between blacks and whites in many northern cities and unleash ongoing conflicts over turf, politics, and, ultimately, economic power.

WARS IN THE American past had often unleashed domestic conflict, from the bloody draft riots of the Civil War to the angry racial clashes in East St. Louis and Chicago around World War I. But racial conflict was even more pronounced during World War II as a growing number of blacks saw the struggle against fascism as one front in a global war against racist empires—building on the Depression-era rhetoric of groups such as the National Negro Congress. In addition to its extensive antifascist coverage, the black press carried articles on South Africa, India, and the British Empire. "It may seem odd to hear India discussed in poolrooms on South State Street in Chicago," wrote Horace Cayton, but blacks took growing pride in the rising tide of revolution worldwide. L. D. Reddick encapsulated the increasingly global view of democracy and rights that reshaped wartime black politics. "The northern Negro," he wrote, "seems to have developed a definitely international outlook." America did not have a monopoly on democracy: It resided in "the struggle of India for independence and of China for national equality." This international vision, Reddick hoped, would "lead the American nation to a broader and deeper approach to human relations." The challenge to the United States was not primarily one of calling the nation's leaders to abide by the timeless verities of the "American Creed." Rather, it was expanding the meaning of a creed that reflected the two-ness of American nationalism, at once egalitarian and inclusionary toward some and inegalitarian and exclusionary toward others, particularly people of color.

A quirky term emerged in the hot political debates of the Cold War, still far off on the national horizon at the outbreak of World War II. In investigations of suspected "Reds," McCarthyites hurled charges of "premature antifascism." Those who had gone on the record as critics of Hitler, Mussolini, and Franco in the mid-1930s—"premature antifascists"—were presumed to be "Reds." But whether "Red" or not, a disproportionate number of black intellectuals and activists were staunchly antifascist during the 1930s. If premature antifascism would become a handicap in the acidic climate of the McCarthy era, it was still a powerful rhetorical weapon during World War II. Advocates of black civil rights in the 1930s had powerfully linked second-class black citizenship to the Nazis' vision of Aryan supremacy. As America turned its wartime propaganda toward demonizing Hitler and his minions, the black and leftist comparison of racism and fascism moved in from the political margins to the political mainstream.

Black activists throughout the war developed a particularly broad and inclusive notion of democracy. To some extent, they highlighted the discrepancy between America's democratic "creed" and its undemocratic practices. Most black intellectuals and journalists and their comrades harbored no illusions about a supposedly egalitarian national creed. In nearly every form of political utterance, from letters sent to elected officials to poems in the black press to civil rights tracts to speeches, activists linked American racism with Nazism. This was at once a rhetorical move—one to shock white Americans and political leaders into action—and a heartfelt repudiation of the myth of American democracy. Blacks believed that they were struggling to make America democratic for the first time. More than that, in the aggregate, they embraced a vision of democracy that was far broader than the narrow notion of individual civil rights: They demanded the full economic and political rights of citizenship. This meant inclusion in American institutions that had long excluded blacks or relegated them to second-class status, as well as the embrace of a rhetoric of rights that encompassed the right to a decent job, to a decent home, and to economic security. They were the vanguard of an unachieved American democracy.

World War II, wrote Louis Martin, a black journalist who would soon move to a career as a prominent Democratic Party strategist, must become "truly a war of universal liberation." "In a sense," wrote Thomas Sancton in *The New Republic*, "it is 1776 for the Negro. Perhaps a more accurate analogy is 1789." Wartime rhetoric is often high-minded, but so much of the language of "sacrifice" in World War II was parochial in its interests. White American boys fought the good war for their families at home, for the "girl next door." But black Americans had a much broader understanding of the battle against fascism: They were fighting for a "double victory" against fascism, homegrown and international. Although some black critics of World War II denounced the "white man's war," many more black activists held a broad, universalistic understanding of what the war meant. Adam Clayton Powell, Jr., in his little book *Marching Blacks*, published at the end of the war, anecdotally described blacks' sense that they were on the cutting edge of democracy. "Two Negroes would pass each other on the street now and one would cry to the other, 'How are things going?' The other would reply, 'Colored folks in the lead.'"

During the war, Americans clung to a triumphalist notion of American liberty and democracy. But black activists were far more likely to look at their nation's history and find there a grim, illiberal history of racial oppression. "Most Americans were more solicitous about the woes of the oppressed of Europe than about the tribulations of the oppressed of America," lamented *The Call*, a Socialist periodical that promoted the March on Washington Movement. "There are thirteen million Czechs ... and Americans were deeply moved. There are about thirteen million Negroes in America. And among them there has been a slaughter of the innocents—a tragedy extending over two centuries. Democratic America has not done much about it." Activists regularly compared the United States to Nazi Germany. "History and tradition combine to form a bulwark for native fascism that is no less dangerous than that of Hitler," argued NAACP official Gloster Current in 1943. When a group of white clergymen organized to prevent blacks from moving into their North Philadelphia neighborhood, *The Philadelphia Tribune* denounced the efforts as "precisely the technique which Goebbels . . . has employed so effectively in crushing Germany under the heel of brutal Nazism." Detroit's branch of the NAACP rallied its members around the goal of defeating the city's "fascist forces." "Jim Crow Uber Alles," screamed the headline of a *Crisis* article in 1943. And NAACP officials labeled Inkster, a blue-collar suburb of Detroit with a rapidly growing population of black migrants and defense workers, "Michigan Sudetenland" when the town's whites proposed to secede and form their own government, taking with them all the public buildings but leaving blacks with the $750,000 village debt. Black newspaper editorials railed against America's "homegrown fascists," and ordinary blacks, writing to elected officials or to local newspapers, echoed the anti-Nazi theme. Those who did not stand up to Jim Crow were "appeasers," just as pusillanimous as the European leaders who had stood cravenly by as Hitler vanquished Czechoslovakia.

Many black wartime workers viewed their labor as part of the struggle for liberation, and part of that battle was winning white recognition that blacks were indispensable citizens. "We brown women of America need victory so much, so desperately," wrote Leotha Hackshaw in the Urban League's *Opportunity* magazine. "We must prove it to white Americans as well—that our country can't get along without the labor and sacrifice of her brown daughters." Hortense Johnson, who worked as an inspector in a munitions factory in New Jersey, found purpose in the skills that her job required—and above all in its contribution to the struggle against both Hitler and American racists, "who will run the country if Hitler wins." Hackshaw, who inspected binocular lenses, wrote that "work today is more than just livelihood. It is a sharp weapon useful in bringing the day of victory nearer."

The flip side of blacks' criticism of fascism was their positive vision of "democracy"—one that was more robust than Myrdal's notion of a timeless "American Creed." In the official war rhetoric of the United States, *democracy* was one of those taken-for-granted words, one that was synonymous with America and its allies. But for African Americans, democracy was not a reality, it was an aspiration. Rhoza Walker, who regularly contributed poetry to *The Crisis*, powerfully captured the reality that for blacks American democracy existed only in the future tense:

I believe in democracy, so much,
That I want everybody in America,
To have some of it.
Negroes,
Denounced and deprived of Democracy,
Insulted and inveigled in Industry,
Shunned and shamed in Society,
Murdered and mangled,
On the very land for which they must fight!
They shall have some of it.

The gap between the wartime rhetoric of freedom and the day-to-day reality of Jim Crow became a persistent theme in black politics. One year after America entered the war, the Bureau of Public Sentiment, the polling operation of *The Pittsburgh Courier*, found that 82.2 percent of black respondents replied "no" to the question "Have you been convinced that the statements which our national leaders have made about freedom and equality for all peoples include the American Negro?" A survey of black residents of Chicago and Detroit in the spring of 1943 found that 78 percent were dissatisfied that they did not "get as much chance as they should to help win the war." Federal government officials also fretted about the problem of "Negro morale." Office of War Information surveys revealed that blacks supported the war effort but were deeply disaffected by the persistence of racial inequality on the war and home fronts. Louis Martin catalogued the "resentment and despair" that blacks felt about wartime race relations. Blacks "want to feel that this is their war and that their contribution to the war will also be a contribution to their own liberation. The mounting bigotry of white America reflected in farm, field, and factory as well as in the armed forces of the nation clouds this hope and obscures their vision."

Wartime antifacism cut two ways. Antifascist rhetoric, combined with denunciations of white political and economic power, gave a radical edge to wartime black protests. In this view, World War II was the beginning of a global revolution against racism and empire. But a growing number of civil rights activists drew from an alternative vision of the war, one that emphasized the fundamental democracy of the United States and eschewed comparisons between Americans and Nazis as unpatriotic. The war against fascism was a moral war, pitting an egalitarian, democratic, forward-looking America against its undemocratic, sinful foes. The key to racial equality was capturing that moral fervor and using it as a call to judgment against the sinful remnant in America, a pathological, immoral minority of whites whose racial views violated American ideals. In this view, America was an imperfect—but perfectible—nation whose core principles embodied universal ideals of individual liberty and freedom. Racial inequality and segregation were anomalous features of the republic that needed to be eradicated—and were not, as radicals had contended, a constitutive part of the nation's economic and political institutions.

UNTIL THE 1960s, very few black intellectuals and activists offered a fundamental critique of Myrdal's *An American Dilemma*. The few dissenting voices after the book's publication, however, offered telling criticism. Oliver Cromwell Cox, a leading Marxist sociologist, took Myrdal to task for downplaying the connection between race and economic exploitation. Cox singled out Myrdal's "mystical" belief that changing individual attitudes would end the "exploitation" at the heart of racial inequality. "In the end," wrote Cox, "the social system is exculpated." Historian Herbert Aptheker pointed out that Myrdal overestimated the hold of the "American Creed," especially in the South, and underestimated the power of black resistance. But these were increasingly marginal opinions. There was so much useful in the book—its detailed anatomy of racially divided labor markets, its fine-grained analysis of white racial prejudices, its searing portrayal of police brutality, its graphic descriptions of separate, unequal education, its unparalleled synthetic overview of black political, social, and religious institutions—that it became an indispensable companion for activists, editorialists, and social scientists.

But the outsider critics of Myrdal probably had their finger more closely on the political pulse of black America than he did. Myrdal's framework for social change—his emphasis on education, persuasion, and conversion—was, at best, a secondary emphasis of militant advocates of black equality during World War II. To most wartime activists, Myrdal's "American Creed" was a myth belied by the long history of African American enslavement and second-class citizenship. Their America was not one of the soaring rhetoric of equality and liberty; it was one of dashed hopes. Myrdal's optimism that white Americans would concede power when confronted with moral arguments ran against everything that Randolph believed. Whites, in Randolph's view, would not give up their privileges until they were forced to do so, by concerted political pressure, in the form of protest and the threat of disruption. Equality required mass action, not polite discourse.

The war had unleashed black demands for inclusion in America's economy, and it had given civil rights activists a powerful new language to express their grievances and their aspirations. But Myrdalian arguments would wholly reshape the postwar struggle for racial equality in the North, especially as America entered the Cold War. The wartime critique of American democracy was no less relevant at war's end. In fact, as the New Deal came under sustained siege by both Dixiecrats and northern Republicans, it grew even more timely. Black activists would continue to express their discontent in the wartime language of antifascism (indeed, it would appear in letters to elected officials from ordinary blacks well into the 1950s). And, to an extent unthinkable among whites, black activists continued to frame their freedom struggle in international terms. As countries as diverse as India, Nigeria, and the Congo struggled for independence after World War II, black activists would continue to think globally. But the Cold War and the growing suspicion of mass protest and politics would give increased credence to the Myrdalian framework. The welling anticommunism of mainstream black organizations, grassroots activists, and public opinion leaders would squeeze black radicalism to the margins. And it would wholly reshape the direction of the northern freedom struggle through the 1950s in ways that would have profound implications for the direction that the black movement would take in the 1960s and beyond.

Myrdal's emphasis on morality touched a nerve in America, on the cusp between World War II and the Cold War. In the mid- and late 1940s, "intergroup relations" agencies proliferated, nearly all of them dedicated to fostering "toleration" among different racial and ethnic groups through education, exhortation, and negotiation. By 1949, there were more than 1,100 such agencies nationwide, nearly two-thirds local. "Most of them," wrote one analyst, "showed a strong concentration on what may be called inspirational talks and pamphlets . . . to arouse opinion against prejudice and discrimination . . . by appeals to decency, morality, and a sense of justice." Above all, intergroup agencies devised programs to "awaken the conscience and stimulate consideration" of racial inequality. From the White House to local pulpits to op-ed pages, opinion leaders described the battle against communism in crusading terms. In the eyes of the establishment, to contain Soviet communism may have been part of a struggle for power. But in the vernacular, fighting communism transcended politics. It was a moral battle for the heart and soul of mankind.

The Cold War world was one of moral absolutes, where good and evil faced off in potentially mortal combat. Thus, in the perfervid atmosphere of the late 1940s, with America triumphant but gravely threatened by the Red Menace, the battle for racial equality took on even greater urgency, and civil rights activists took up Myrdal's emphasis on the American Creed with a crusading zeal. America could embark on two crusades simultaneously: to persuade Americans to be truthful to the promise of life, liberty, and the pursuit of happiness, and to remake the world in the image of the redeemed American nation. While Randolph and many grassroots activists saw World War II as a new 1776, a struggle over power that required mass action to wrest control of America's political institutions from those who profited through the exploitation of a divided, multiracial working class, a growing number of civil rights advocates saw the struggle in profoundly different terms: The battle for civil rights was a battle for the soul of America. They eschewed the idea of revolution. The key was not a contest over the social structure, it was not an effort to redistribute economic power from blacks to whites; rather, it was an effort to perfect the United States, to hold the nation to its truest ideals and to deploy them against the Communist foe. These activists touched on deep, perfectionist religious ideals in American politics. They were fundamentally optimistic about the possibilities of change but believed that racial equality would come about ultimately on the individual level—not through protest or disruption but rather by moral suasion, education, and conversion.

PART II

HEARTS AND MINDS

CHAPTER 4

"BALANCE OF POWER"

NO ONE LEARNED THE LESSONS OF PROTEST POLITICS MORE ACUTELY THAN Henry Lee Moon, a journalist, labor organizer, government official, and longtime NAACP activist who became one of the most influential black political strategists of his time. The child of southern migrants to Cleveland, Ohio, Moon came of age in an intensely political household. His father, Roddy Moon, a government employee, was the first head of the Cleveland branch of the NAACP. His mother, Leah, despite her humble roots, moved into the ranks of the black bourgeoisie and, through her affiliation with black women's clubs, worked to lift as she climbed. An avid gardener who spent hours tending her prizewinning perennials, she did not draw a bright line between her flourishing social life and her commitment to helping the black poor.

Strivers both, the Moons encouraged their son Henry to achieve academically. As a student and well-known campus journalist at Howard University, he discovered his gift for writing. From there, he went to Ohio State, earning a master's in journalism. Moon's career mirrored the leftward trajectory of black activism between the 1920s and the 1940s. He started his career as a publicist for the Tuskegee Institute in Alabama, a bastion of Negro self-help, accommodationism, and conservative politics. But Moon did not remain long in Booker T. Washington's shadow. Never at home in Dixie, he returned north in 1930, joining the migration of young black intellectuals and activists to Harlem. There he became a reporter for the *Amsterdam News*, covering city politics. He also contributed occasional stories about Harlem and Africa to *The New York Times*. In 1932, a year when many black intellectuals were flirting with communism, Moon traveled to the Soviet Union with an entourage of prominent black actors and writers, including Langston Hughes, to make a film about the "American Negro at work and play." When the Soviets canceled the film—allegedly to appease American business interests hoping to expand into the USSR—Moon reacted bitterly. The experience left him suspicious of the Soviets. But in the Popular Front period, his shift to anticommunism was gradual. In 1935, Moon joined a group of liberals and leftists as an officer of the greater New York "sponsoring committee" for the National Negro Congress.

The New Deal provided Moon with a real political education. Like many young blacks, especially on the left, Moon saw the liberatory possibilities of the rights revolution. Joining other struggling writers, Moon found temporary employment with the Federal Writers' Project. He became a strong advocate of the New Deal's efforts to provide housing for America's neediest population and eventually joined the Federal Public Housing Authority as a race relations specialist. The alignment of the New Deal and organized labor was for Moon the most encouraging development. But he also saw firsthand the political limitations of New Deal liberalism, particularly agencies' willingness to "accept local patterns" of discrimination "in violation of basic democratic principles." Through bitter experience he learned that the "claims of the Negro, however sound, just, and legal, are seldom granted when they happen to be in conflict with the claims of a white group."

By the mid-1930s, Moon identified the issue that would drive much of his later career: black political empowerment. In a 1936 article for the *Times*—published just a few weeks before the hotly contested presidential election pitting the incumbent Roosevelt against Kansas governor Alf Landon—Moon became one of the first writers to highlight the defection of blacks from the party of Lincoln to the New Deal. Would they remain loyal to FDR? Or would they drift back to the Republican Party? In 1936, the question was still open, and as a good journalist, Moon left it that way. But he hinted at an answer: The Democrats could not afford to take the Negro vote for granted, as they had in the 1936 party platform, which "remains silent on the problems of the race." Over the next twenty years, the black vote—and black political power—became Moon's crusade.

After his stint in the New Deal, Moon joined the CIO Political Action Committee (CIO-PAC) as a southern field organizer in 1944. It was a natural move for an activist committed to economic and racial justice. The alliance of civil rights groups and industrial unions had paid off mightily for black workers. By war's end, the industries that had attracted them—steel, auto and aircraft, shipbuilding, and meatpacking—were heavily unionized. Even if many CIO unions were white-dominated, no institution in wartime America was as racially diverse as the CIO. The leadership of the United Steelworkers of America, the United Automobile Workers, and the United Packinghouse Workers of America had all taken strong antidiscrimination positions and supported the creation of a permanent FEPC. Leftist locals, in particular, were often bastions of racial progressivism. In meatpacking, where blacks made up more than a third of all workers after the war (and more than a half of the meatpackers in Chicago), blacks assumed union offices and benefited from upgrading. In steel and auto, black workers found themselves frozen out of most skilled jobs, but nonetheless garnered generous wage and benefit packages.

Committed to the left-liberal side of the New Deal, the CIO-PAC pushed a "People's Platform," which emphasized labor and economic rights, to counter the Democrats' increasingly conservative southern wing. It also staunchly supported racial equality and publicized its civil rights efforts in an expensively produced and widely distributed booklet, *The Negro in 1944*. Enthusiastic about the CIO-PAC, Moon traveled through the South, organizing black voters in the aftermath of the Supreme Court ruling, in *Smith v. Allwright*, that the all-white primary was unconstitutional. Embracing the stirring rhetoric of FDR's Second Bill of Rights, CIO-PAC pushed for the renomination of Vice President Henry Wallace, whose pro-labor and civil rights positions were anathema to many southern whites. Newly enfranchised blacks, Moon hoped, would pull the Democrats leftward and break Dixie's stranglehold on the New Deal. Working to register black voters and campaign in South Carolina and Alabama, Moon was struck by the energy and power of the budding southern black electorate. When he returned north in 1946 to take a job as the NAACP's publicist, Moon turned to electoral politics on the northern front.

Moon was a rare activist who had the writing skills to publicize his vision of political change while putting it into practice. While working for the CIO and the NAACP, Moon penned what would be the period's most influential book on black politics, *Balance of Power*. Published in 1948, on the brink of one of the most hotly contested presidential elections of the twentieth century, Moon's book laid out a series of questions that would shape black politics for at least the next half century. How could a minority—only one-tenth of the population—influence mainstream politics? Should blacks, by necessity, remain on the outside, using protest and the threat of disruption to accomplish political change? Moon placed his bet on electoral politics. He calculated that blacks were a swing vote, and as a result, neither party could ignore civil rights issues lest it alienate a key constituency. As a left-liberal Democrat, Moon hoped black support for the Democrats would pull the party leftward, but he knew that civil rights laws would not pass without Republican support and argued that competition for black voters would compel Republicans to heed black concerns. In highly competitive states, blacks could use the vote to move the civil rights agenda to center stage.

The power of Moon's book was its commonsensical position. Moon was no social scientist, but he was a superb polemicist. His key lessons were straightforward. He highlighted the remarkable shift of black voters to the Democratic Party. He also reminded readers that "the vote of Negro citizens in 1948 will certainly not be a bloc vote." The Negro vote, he argued, held the balance of power in seventy-five congressional districts outside the South. A shift of only three hundred thousand black votes in fifteen states would have resulted in Roosevelt's defeat in 1944. The key to the Democrats' success would be getting out the black vote. Widely reviewed and praised, *Balance of Power* brought a key point home to a national audience: Blacks were not marginal to American politics. They were major players whose ballots would have national implications. Ignore them at your peril.

MOON LAUNCHED HIS book amid the "fluid and confused political milieu" of the mid-1940s. The real economic gains that blacks had won during World War II were tenuous. As the nation demobilized, the economy entered a period of great uncertainty. Many feared that the United States would plunge into another Great Depression. Without massive military spending, labor markets would collapse, consumption would fall, and the economy would tailspin downward. Without the external pressures of war, would fragile programs such as FEPC survive? How would blacks continue the momentum generated by wartime protests? Would black economic gains survive the postwar "reconversion" from military to civilian production?

As the war drew to a close, black activists focused on the fundamental question of employment security. In 1944, an intense debate broke out over a small, seemingly technical issue—workplace seniority. It had grave implications for blacks' still-uncertain economic status. Given that they had been last hired, would they be the first fired when defense production slowed down and stopped? Would black war workers be replaced by white veterans who would return to claim the positions that they had left behind? Historically, employers could hire and fire at will, leaving employees vulnerable to managerial whim. The result had been a stunning degree of workforce turnover up through the 1930s. However, unionization changed that. During the Depression and war, as unions gained strength in nearly every major northern industry, nearly every collectively bargained contract contained protections for workers based on how long they had been on the job. Some firms offered seniority on a plantwide basis; others in particular departments of plants; others by occupation. Many offered a combination of the two. The longer a worker held his or her job, the more secure it would be. Those who were newcomers to the workforce would be the first to be laid off during economic slumps or if a company restructured or relocated. Seniority was no trivial matter for black workers.

Leading the call for a rethinking of seniority rules were leftist and black unionists who demanded "super-seniority," that is, a modification of seniority rules to account for the fact that blacks were often at the bottom of the seniority queue because of longtime, systemic racial discrimination in hiring. "Unmodified and unadjusted seniority rules," argued the National Negro Congress, could "become an instrument whereby pre-war discrimination may be frozen into post-war industry." Leftist unionists contended that "the right to a job is one thing, but it is no good if we do not give jobs to those who have a right to them." In lieu of strict seniority, they argued for a system of "proportional" cutbacks: That is, "lay-offs in any plant or department of a plant must be in proportion to the number of minorities in plants or departments."

By contrast, most unionists, including black and white liberals and Socialists, defended strict, inviolable seniority rules. As one advocate of seniority argued, "it is the cornerstone of the labor movement." If it were violated, "workers with seniority will be made responsible for the faults of management in not hiring Negroes in the first place." NAACP activists took a middle ground—accepting the principle of seniority but calling for the creation of a plantwide system. The Workers' Defense League, directly challenging its Communist rivals, argued that full employment would obviate the need for changes to the seniority system. In an argument that foreshadowed later debates about affirmative action, the WDL rejected both super-seniority and veterans' preferences. The seniority debate was settled on the side of a strict reading of union contracts (with the exception of special provisions to hire returning soldiers), although Communist-affiliated groups continued to demand super-seniority through the late 1940s.

The postwar economic boom rendered these questions moot for the time being. By late 1946, it became clear that postwar reconversion would not adversely affect the economy. Most African American men hired during the war retained their toehold in northern labor markets. However, African American women faced more serious obstacles. Many employers used a two-tiered seniority system, with women at the bottom. In the rush to provide employment for returning veterans, even the most progressive unions displaced women workers. Defense work had provided unprecedented wage gains and benefits to black women, allowing many to attain a degree of financial independence unimaginable when they were primarily employed as domestics, washerwomen, and cooks. But when they lost their factory jobs, many black women returned to the service sector, most of them employed in jobs without benefits and uncovered by Social Security, unemployment insurance, or disability payments. The insecurity of black women's work was particularly acute for those who were the primary breadwinners for their families. Because many lived economically precarious lives, northern black women were disproportionately represented in the ranks of recipients of Aid to Dependent Children. But the question of workplace discrimination remained unresolved and even more pressing than ever.

The central question at the end of the war, for male as well as female black workers, was "Whither the FEPC?" Even if the wartime FEPC had not lived up to its potential, it represented a fundamental departure. If it remained in place—and were strengthened to include nondefense industries—the FEPC could be a powerful tool in ensuring that blacks' wartime gains would not be ephemeral. Many CIO unions, especially those with large black memberships, were, however, unwilling to stake their futures on the FEPC alone. Facing pressure from leftist and black insurgents, many CIO unions created their own fair employment practices departments to hear the grievances of workers, to investigate discrimination, and to fight for workplace equality. The UAW's fair practices department, for one, tackled hate strikes and shop-floor discrimination, while championing an expanded FEPC. The Steelworkers, by contrast, created a fair practices department that did little else than run educational workshops for white workers.

While unions fought internal battles, FEPC activists also organized nationally. Building on the energy of the March on Washington Movement, A. Philip Randolph appointed Anna Arnold Hedgeman head of the National Council for a Permanent FEPC in September 1943. Hedgeman directed the National Council from the top down, putting tight reins on local organizing and preferring behind-the-scenes negotiations to pickets and protests. The National Council lobbied Congress, staged letter-writing campaigns, worked with sympathetic journalists, and provided information to national and local civil rights groups. Unlike the NNC, however, the National Council was a single-issue interest group. Hedgeman put her energies into coordinating the activities of established organizations in service of a single issue. Hedgeman's model of political change became increasingly common over the remainder of the twentieth century: Advocacy groups without a mass base claimed to speak for a large segment of the population. It also put her at odds with younger, more protest-minded activists, who preferred grassroots organization and agitation to quiet lobbying.

For all her connections and clout, Hedgeman and the National Council faced an uphill battle in Congress, compounded by internal funding problems. Increasingly, they made their appeals on moral terms, arguing that the passage of antidiscrimination laws was essential to America living up to its democratic ideals. They won the support of some prominent members of Congress, but the National Council failed to prick the conscience of the powerful southern congressional committee chairs and senators who set the legislative agenda. In early 1946, Mississippi senator Theodore Bilbo, in one of his politer moments, lashed out at the FEPC as a "damnable" law, one that "forced" black and white "affiliation and association" based on "the craziest, wildest, most unreasonable illogical theory." Bilbo and other southern members of Congress fiercely resisted even the weakest antidiscrimination laws on the grounds that they would foster social equality—that is, the sexual intermingling of blacks and whites.

While Hedgeman and her associates lobbied, more militant pro-FEPC activists rallied. In late February 1946, nineteen thousand people gathered at New York's Madison Square Garden to support the creation of a permanent FEPC. NAACP members flooded the Senate with telegrams. Both tactics were insufficient. The filibuster prevailed. In a scathing editorial, *The Chicago Defender* labeled the first day of the filibuster "Fascist Wednesday." FEPC supporters mustered only forty-eight votes, well short of the two-thirds needed to bring the bill to a vote. In the House, a similar FEPC bill languished in committee. Moon and his colleagues at the NAACP lamented the "sham battle" over the nondiscrimination law and reserved special criticism for "the 'friends' of the FEPC, [who] with a few exceptions, put up no fight for the measure." For Moon, the long-term lesson was clear: It would take more than lobbying efforts or protest marches. Success required mass political mobilization, to build a coalition that would thwart Bilbo and his ilk. But again, that was a long-term strategy. In the short run, the FEPC movement faltered, demoralized by its defeat. In August, Hedgeman resigned from the National Council, frustrated at its financial condition. The organization struggled for the next few years before it went defunct.

"FEPC was a frail war-baby," wrote one prominent activist. It had suffered "blitzkrieg attacks." It would not survive. Between 1944 and 1963, 114 fair employment bills were introduced in Congress. None were enacted. The debate over the creation of a permanent FEPC became drearily repetitive as it played out year after year in the nation's capital. Northern Democrats spoke forcefully against racial discrimination, arguing that equality of opportunity was necessary to democracy, while southern Democrats in turn railed against what they saw as "Gestapo" measures to foist racial "amalgamation" on their region. But the southern Democrats could not have thwarted FEPC laws alone: They needed northern allies—most of whom were in the erstwhile party of Lincoln. In the 1946 debate over the reauthorization of the FEPC, eight northern Republicans joined the southern Democrats in voting against cloture. The Dixie-GOP alliance would only grow stronger after the 1946 midterm elections. For the first time since 1930, Republicans gained control of both the Senate and the House. As national politics veered rightward, the struggle for a permanent FEPC faltered.

By the 1940s, the Republican Party found itself in a complicated position on civil rights. Historically, the party had supported—at least symbolically—black advancement. Since the 1870s, however, the GOP had gone into full retreat from the civil rights laws that Radical Republicans had crafted during the Civil War and Reconstruction. A Republican minority continued to push for racial equality, but the issue became increasingly marginal in party politics by the early twentieth century. Other than patronage appointments to loyal black partisans and the occasional symbolic meeting with a black leader (such as Theodore Roosevelt's much-vaunted summit with Booker T. Washington), the Republican Party maintained the loyalty of black voters out of inertia. The Democrats made their job easier; their party had never shaken off its association with slavery, and popular Democratic leaders such as William Jennings Bryan and Woodrow Wilson supported segregation. During the 1930s and 1940s, when the Republicans scrambled to defeat the New Deal, they sought to win back Negro voters who had defected to FDR. In 1940, Republican Wendell Willkie—whose hometown of Elwood, Indiana, had notoriously mounted a sign that read "Nigger Don't Let the Sun Go Down on You Here"—worked strenuously to overcome his background, campaigned extensively among African American voters, and uncompromisingly supported civil rights laws. His 1943 book, *One World*, sold more than a million copies and was nearly as important as Gunnar Myrdal's *American Dilemma* in bringing the question of race and civil rights out of the political shadows. For Willkie, civil rights for blacks in the United States were part and parcel of the larger project of global democratization. America, he argued, could not battle "the forces of imperialism abroad and maintain any form of imperialism at home." In 1944, the Republican convention adopted a platform that included strong support for the creation of a permanent Fair Employment Practices Committee. And in 1946, some Republicans still hoped that they would capture black voters alienated by the Dixiecrats, despite the GOP equivocation on fair employment practices.

The Republican Party had its share of Wendell Willkies, but they were a distinct minority. A vocal cadre of GOP moderates pushed the party to support fair employment—some out of principle, others hoping to outflank the Democrats on an issue that might give them traction in key districts. By the 1940s, though, the GOP was more the party of business than the party of emancipation. At best, Republicans argued for moderation, gradualism, and educational efforts to mitigate workplace discrimination, in lieu of using federal power. But when civil rights conflicted with business interests, the latter won. Northern corporations, particularly those opening new factories in the South, where they benefited from a low-wage black labor force, had little to gain from the passage of a permanent FEPC. As black columnist J. A. Rogers reported at the end of World War II, for "the past fifteen years or so, northern manufacturers have been moving to the South to be nearer to . . . the ill-paid labor common to most agricultural regions." A national FEPC would disrupt the southern labor market, raise wages, and undermine the "alliance" of northern manufacturers and the "jim-crow interests of the South."

A growing number of black activists saw the intense partisan competition of the late war years as an opportunity instead of a disaster. Appeals to the electoral self-interest of northern politicians—especially those seeking statewide office in states with large black populations—might help break the congressional deadlock on civil rights. "The large Negro vote," opined the *Defender*, echoing Moon, "is an unattached reservoir that could be tapped by either party that had the foresight to merit it. As matters now stand, Negroes, theoretically, are partyless." In the fall of 1946, the NAACP, following Moon's strategy, encouraged its members to vote against those who refused to support the FEPC bill. The NAACP was too small to have much of an impact in the 1946 midterm elections, particularly in a year when liberals came under siege at the ballot box, but the strategy that it advocated—the deployment of the black vote to accomplish racial change—had a growing number of advocates. If black voters, particularly those in northern swing states, used their franchise instrumentally, they could shift the outcome of national elections and force the passage of long-overdue civil rights laws.

CIVIL RIGHTS ACTIVISTS challenged congressional conservatives but also went after the biggest political target of all, President Harry S Truman. By 1946, Truman was at the nadir of his popularity. In that year's midterm elections, both the House and the Senate had fallen to the Republicans. The national economy was ravaged by inflation. The Cold War was intensifying, and Truman's critics denounced him for failing to prevent Soviet expansion in Eastern Europe. At home, the New Deal coalition was fracturing. Southern Democrats were in outright revolt. Labor unions were bitter at Truman's use of federal power to thwart the steel strike of 1946 and his failure to defeat the Taft-Hartley Act, which in 1947 rolled back New Deal gains for unions. Many observers wrote Truman off as unelectable. He faced a seemingly insurmountable challenge from Republican Thomas Dewey, New York's popular governor. And renegade Democrats challenged Truman from the left and the right. Former vice president Henry Wallace marshaled support from disaffected civil rights and labor activists who hoped to reinvigorate the Popular Front. Running under the Progressive Party banner, Wallace campaigned aggressively among black voters, with Paul Robeson often at his side. Black Democrats in New York worried that voters would defect to Wallace, and the head of the Indiana NAACP and key black leaders in San Francisco and Philadelphia endorsed him. Truman, recalled the NAACP's Roy Wilkins, "did need help to keep Negroes from wandering off toward Henry Wallace." To Truman's right, embittered southern whites rallied around Dixiecrat Strom Thurmond, who mounted an independent campaign for the White House.

When Moon's *Balance of Power* came off the presses, the NAACP's Walter White sent a copy to President Truman with a brief note: "You will enjoy and profit from it." Truman, not much of a reader, probably never cracked the book's spine, although his aides, particularly campaign mastermind Clark Clifford, found its argument compelling. In a late 1947 memorandum outlining Truman's campaign strategy, Clifford reminded the president of the importance of the black vote. In early 1948, Clifford warned that the "northern Negro . . . under the tutelage of Walter White" was a "cynical, hardboiled trader" who could easily "swing back to his traditional moorings—the Republican party." Moon put an exclamation point on Clifford's argument.

That black voters entered into Truman's calculations was a sign of how much had changed during the 1940s. Most accounts of Truman overemphasize his personal "conversion" on the matter of race and civil rights. In the Senate, Truman's civil rights record was mixed. He had supported antilynching legislation and advocated the repeal of the poll tax, but had done so as a matter of political calculation, not principle. Senator Truman hoped to capture the black vote in Kansas City and St. Louis, and he knew that not many white Missourians would hold antilynching or electoral reform against him. Still, the thinness of his record on civil rights led many blacks to worry. Would they suffer rollbacks with an "untested haberdasher from Klan country" in the Oval Office? But from his first days in the White House, Truman defied expectations that he would be a reliable ally of the Democrats' southern wing. Like many nonsouthern Democrats, Truman was swept along by the wartime shift in the perception of race and injustice. As the Cold War chilled, Truman grew increasingly concerned about the impact of the "Negro problem" on America's reputation abroad. The Soviets had long reported on riots, lynchings, and racism in the United States. The contrast between blacks' second-class status and the American celebration of democracy and prosperity became a central element of Russian propaganda. To combat communism meant to deprive the Reds of one of their weapons in the battle for the hearts and minds of the world: America's abysmal record on civil rights.

Truman's "conversion" would have been unlikely in the absence of systematic political pressure. From nearly his first week in office, civil rights activists tested Truman's commitment to racial equality, pouncing on nearly every one of his pronouncements on race. Truman faced a wave of demonstrations—most orchestrated by northern activists—unprecedented in the history of the White House. When A. Philip Randolph suggested a march on Washington in 1941, official Washington reeled at the prospect of angry Negroes descending on the capital. But by Truman's time, organized protests at the White House and in Washington—none on the scale of the proposed March on Washington, to be sure—had become commonplace. In the summer of 1946, antilynching protestors descended on Washington, a thousand members of the National Negro Congress marched on the White House and met with one of Truman's aides, the NAACP held large civil rights rallies in New York, and four hundred members of the National Association of Colored Women picketed outside the White House for a week.

Civil rights activists engaged in an elaborate dance with Truman. He hesitated, they pushed, he gave, they praised, he paused, they pushed for more. Truman raised expectations at a political moment when far-reaching change seemed possible. Thus, after every step Truman took toward civil rights, activists pushed him to take a bigger one. Truman came under relentless criticism in the black press, and civil rights activists, above all, capitalized on Truman's political vulnerability. He was an accidental, increasingly unpopular president who needed every vote he could get at home; at the same time, as the United States entered a leadership position in the postwar world, he needed international political legitimacy. Mainstream civil rights organizations began to embrace the rhetoric of anticommunism to push their cause. Both efforts were part of a large-scale postwar mobilization for racial equality, one that built on the successes of the wartime movement.

By 1946, Truman had dissipated any remaining doubt that he was committed to civil rights. He had some political cover. Governor Dewey, his likely Republican challenger, advocated racial equality and had signed the first state fair employment practices law. And Wallace, still a Democrat, had outflanked Truman on civil rights to the left. With room to maneuver, Truman supported, at least in principle—how hard he would push was another matter—legislation to create a permanent Fair Employment Practices Committee. And he used the occasion of the NAACP's 1946 convention to support efforts to extend the black franchise in the South. In December 1946, Truman took an even bolder step, announcing the creation of the President's Committee on Civil Rights (PCCR), a blue-ribbon, interracial commission to "safeguard the civil rights of the people." A diverse body, it included blacks and whites, representatives of major religious denominations (Protestant, Catholic, and Jewish), and both corporate and trade union leaders. The PCCR met throughout 1947, gathering evidence about segregation and discrimination in the United States.

The PCCR's final report, *To Secure These Rights*, issued in October 1947, deployed the language made familiar by Gunnar Myrdal. It emphasized racial inequality as a moral problem and argued that civil rights was a Cold War imperative. "The central theme in our American heritage," contended the report, echoing Myrdal, "is the importance of the individual person. From the earliest moment of our history we have believed that every human being has an essential dignity and integrity which must be respected and safeguarded." The report briefly acknowledged slavery, religious persecution, and mob rule in the American past, not as systematic parts of American history, but rather as aberrations, as evidence of a "gulf between ideals and practice," the consequence of "individual outrages" and "moral erosion." The report unflinchingly depicted the second-class status of blacks, particularly in the South and in Washington, D.C. The PCCR offered a wide-ranging set of suggestions for reform, affirming the agenda of racial liberals. It called for the extension of fair employment practices laws, for "equality of opportunity" in the housing market, and for a strengthening of the weak federal agencies, especially the Department of Justice, that handled civil rights matters. In stirring, italicized words, the commission summed up: *The United States can no longer countenance these burdens on its common conscience, these inroads on its moral fiber.*

As Myrdal's *American Dilemma* had done, the president's commission addressed whites. The moral fiber of America was a white one; the burdens were the white man's; the vision of America's glorious history of egalitarianism had been, for most of the nation's 170 years, for whites only. But Truman also intended *To Secure These Rights* to reach a black audience as a symbol of his administration's unflagging commitment to civil rights, part of a preelection strategy to appeal to black voters. He had good reason. Many of the black elite still had ties to the Republican Party, and many new migrants from the South were reluctant to pull the lever for the party of notorious segregationists such as Theodore Bilbo, John Rankin, and Strom Thurmond. Even in such Democratic strongholds as Chicago, it took some effort to attract southern newcomers into the party of FDR. Compounding Truman's concerns, black newspapers in New York, Philadelphia, Cleveland, Milwaukee, and Newark all endorsed Dewey, despite their enthusiastic reception of *To Secure These Rights. The Pittsburgh Courier,* with seventeen local editions, also joined the Republican bandwagon. Only *The Chicago Defender* and a host of small black papers endorsed Truman.

Adding to the pressure was Henry Wallace's maverick campaign. Barnstorming through the South, Wallace denounced Jim Crow to angry white crowds, who regularly pelted him with eggs and rotten fruit. His fearless attacks on segregation increased his popularity among black voters. To deflect Wallace's appeal, Truman deployed key surrogates to drum up black support throughout the North. Among them were Anna Arnold Hedgeman and Judge William Hastie, the only black federal jurist at the time. Social Security official Oscar Ewing keynoted the Urban League's annual conference, arguing that blacks who did not support the incumbent would be "betraying their own race." To solidify his standing, Truman himself appealed to black voters with celebrated executive orders to desegregate the military and enforce nondiscrimination on government contracts. And in October, Truman's campaign swung through large northern black neighborhoods. During a campaign stop in North Philadelphia, Truman addressed a "huge throng" in front of the all-black Richard Allen Homes. In a symbolic gesture with national resonance, he became the first Democratic president to campaign in Harlem.

Truman's efforts in the North paid off. When the votes were tallied, 69 percent of black voters in twenty-seven cities supported the incumbent. Wallace proved to be a "general without an army," in the words of *The Chicago Defender*. And Dewey's track record on civil rights as governor of New York could not compete with Truman's dramatic civil rights program. But the jury was still out on whether black voters were responsible for Truman's upset victory over Dewey. Truman lost four key northern states with large black populations—New York, Michigan, New Jersey, and Pennsylvania—despite winning a comfortable majority of black voters in each of those states. Truman barely edged out Dewey in California, Ohio, and Illinois, states that were home to large black populations, providing support for Moon's balance of power argument. But throughout the North, blacks were not the only swing voters whose ballots may have provided Truman with his narrow margin of victory. In Chicago, Truman won black wards with over 84,000 out of nearly 110,000 votes cast, but he also swept heavily white neighborhoods where the Democratic machine worked overtime. Moon attributed Truman's razor-thin victory in California to black voters in Los Angeles, three-quarters of whom voted to re-elect the president. But who is to say that it was black votes that pushed Truman over the top? After all, Truman's advisors cast their net widely in the last months of the campaign to target "independent" liberal-minded voters, as well as "large groups . . . which can swing the election . . . workers, veterans, and Negroes." In the tight race, labor union get-out-the-vote drives, last-minute appeals to rural Democrats, and party machine chicanery may well have provided Truman's edge.

After the election, Truman did not live up to Moon's expectations, especially regarding fair employment practices. Hamstrung by the increasingly powerful Dixie-GOP congressional coalition, Truman supported antidiscrimination laws for naught. Civil rights activists continued to lobby relentlessly for a permanent federal FEPC. In January 1950, four thousand activists from fifty organizations descended on Washington in the National Emergency Civil Rights Mobilization. The vast majority were black, most were northern, and more than half were NAACP members. They fanned out over Capitol Hill, meeting with members of Congress to push the bill and pledging, à la Henry Lee Moon, to mobilize "pressure from the voters in the blocks, precincts and the wards" of their home-towns. That pressure began to yield results, but not in Washington, where southern Democrats and their northern Republican allies threw up obstacle after obstacle. Still, Truman's outreach to black voters—and Moon's swing vote arguments—indelibly shaped Democratic Party poli-tics. Pundits offered variations of Moon's argument well into the 1960s, and no Democratic presidential candidate would again ignore black vot-ers. Moon himself used his NAACP post and his writing to promote voter registration campaigns throughout the North, for he knew that black clout depended on black turnout. "If we vote," he argued, "we have a voice in determining the policies of government. If we don't vote we give up that right to participate."

MOON'S BALANCE OF power argument—and his belief that the future of racial equality rested with the mainstream political parties—was not ac-cepted by all black activists. Moon raised profound questions that would rise again and again in black politics over the next half century. Would blacks be more effective as party insiders, pushing for incremental change? Or would they be better off continuing the politics of pressure and protest, working from the outside, forcing the hand of government in moments of crisis? While activists such as Moon and Hedgeman worked within the two-party system, leftist activists, including the Socialists around A. Philip Randolph, and the Communists, continued to advocate mass protest politics and often supported third- or fourth-party candi-dates. But the differences between liberals and leftists were often over matters of rhetoric and strategy, not over matters of substance—with the notable exception of foreign policy.

In the fluid political climate of the mid-1940s, the hardest leftists (par-ticularly Communists) were often indistinguishable from liberals and even moderate Republicans when it came to their support for particular civil rights policies. Perhaps the biggest difference between liberals and leftists in the mid- and late 1940s was in emphasis. Communists and other leftists put a much greater priority on racial inequality than did Democrats and moderate Republicans, for whom civil rights was still decidedly a political issue of secondary or even tertiary importance. Even Moon, who lambasted Communists for "their subservience to policies formulated in Moscow," could not help but admire their energy and commitment. "It is a matter of record," he wrote, that the "Communists have generally fought for full recognition of Negro rights. . . . They have dramatized his problem. They have risked social ostracism and physical violence on his behalf. They have challenged American hypocrisy with the zeal, if not the high principle, of the Abolitionists. In all of this they have performed a vital function as an irritant to the American conscience."

To be sure, Communists were inconsistent. During World War II, the Party faced accusations that it had backpedaled on civil rights, for fear of embarrassing the Roosevelt administration and thus jeopardizing the victory of America's Soviet ally. By the late 1940s, the Communists refused to join in calls for the desegregation of the military because of their opposition to aiding American armed forces in the Cold War. Still, despite some deviations, racial equality remained a central issue for postwar leftists. Communists saw protests and publicity as a tool to delegitimize the United States worldwide by laying bare the contradictions between American democratic rhetoric and undemocratic practices. Finally, as decolonization efforts, many of them Communist-led, were under way throughout Asia and Africa, many leftists interpreted the black freedom struggle in the United States as part and parcel of the struggles of nonwhite peoples worldwide.

Communists and various Socialists were ubiquitous in civil rights battles in the 1940s, despite their small numbers. A glance at the letterheads of umbrella organizations advocating fair employment practices made clear the centrality of political leftists. Joining the roster of groups that lobbied for fair employment were such organizations as the Communist-dominated Civil Rights Congress (the successor to the National Negro Congress) and leftist National Lawyers Guild, the Workers' Defense League (Socialist), and various left-led unions. NAACP branches in cities as large as Detroit and Philadelphia and as small as Great Neck, New

York, and Grand Rapids, Michigan, were led by charismatic Communists. Left-led unions made major contributions to civil rights groups, and leftists regularly joined picket lines and rallies.

By the mid-1940s, however, as the Cold War intensified, leftists of all varieties came under siege. In 1947, Truman issued Executive Order 9835, requiring government employees to take oaths that they were not members of the Communist Party. The U.S. attorney general's office prepared a list of "subversive" organizations, including the National Negro Congress, the Civil Rights Congress, and the Negro Labor Victory Committee. Any affiliation to these groups, past or present, could trigger an investigation. The Taft-Hartley Act, which the Dixie- and GOP-dominated Congress enacted over Truman's veto, required unions to certify that their officers were not Communists. The CIO began purging Communists and suspected Communists and in 1949 expelled eleven member unions that remained unrepentantly left-led. Union factionalism often dampened civil rights efforts. Many black unionists and their white allies—who rose with the support of the Communist Party or who were themselves Communists—found themselves on the political margins. The unions' purge of suspected leftists drove out many rank-and-file activists deeply committed to workplace racial equality.

Mainstream civil rights organizations also struggled with charges— often accurate—that they were infiltrated by Reds and their sympathizers. In many NAACP branches, suspected Communists and their critics battled for organizational control. With few exceptions, the leftists lost. The NAACP's Walter White, deeply suspicious of the political left since the early days of the National Negro Congress, grew even more resolutely anti-Communist in the late 1940s. White had good reason to be fearful of communism. The NAACP, like other civil rights groups, battled against charges that they were in the orbit of the left. To many anti-civil-rights activists, support for racial equality was prima facie evidence of leftism. In postwar Detroit, for example, white neighborhood associations and conservative papers regularly denounced "Communist-inspired Negroes" who attempted "to penetrate white residential sections" and lashed out at liberal civil rights proponents as "fringe disruptionists, political crackpots," and "socialist double-domes." More ominously, although the NAACP was not on the federal government's list of subversive organizations, some federal loyalty investigations flagged NAACP members for closer scrutiny.

The NAACP's shift to anticommunism was not just reactive. As U.S.-Soviet relations chilled, many civil rights leaders strategically deployed Cold War rhetoric to win support for the goals of racial equality. The Truman administration, facing the dual challenge of Soviet expansionism and the rising tide of decolonization in Africa and Asia, worried that civil rights violations would taint America's image abroad. American racism was a liability that undermined U.S. credibility and gave the Soviets ammunition. The Cold War rationale, however, turned attention southward, where lynchings, the denial of the right to vote, and legally mandated Jim Crow were obvious embarrassments. Northern civil rights issues were a little harder than their southern counterparts to wrap in the mantle of Cold War moralism—and throughout the 1940s and early 1950s, northern activists were just as apt to use antifascist as anti-Communist language to discredit white racism. Still, a growing number of northern advocates of fair employment, open housing, and equal education argued that the failure to eradicate discrimination, like Dixie's atrocities, played into the hands of the Reds.

The dangers of the red taint and the opportunity provided by Cold War rhetoric pulled the NAACP toward a position of liberal anticommunism. In 1947, the NAACP condemned "the attempts of various groups, particularly Communists, either to secure control of our branches outright, or to use the branches as sounding boards for political or other ideas." It also turned on two of its most visible Communist members. Founder W.E.B. Du Bois lost his position as director of special research projects in 1948 over his differences with Walter White on Cold War foreign policy, and after Paul Robeson's passport was revoked for his leftist sympathies in 1949, the NAACP rescinded his Spingarn Medal (the group's highest award) and rebuked him in the pages of *The Crisis*. The attacks on Du Bois and Robeson sent a chilling message about the risks of leftist taint. In Boston in 1950, the NAACP's annual convention passed a resolution—after two hours of "acrimonious debate"—to take "necessary steps to eradicate Communist infiltration and, if necessary, to suspend, reorganize, lift the charter of, or expel any branches that came under Communist control." Worried that the mandate would lead to bruising factional disputes in local branches, White issued a memorandum clearly defining the process by which those steps should be taken. "The resolution adopted in Boston," he wrote, "does not give branches the right to call anybody and everybody a Communist. . . . We do not want a witch-hunt in the NAACP, but we want to be sure that we and not the communists are running it."

The NAACP's directive to expel Communists did not lead to wholesale purges; only about a dozen branches came in for close scrutiny. But the specter of anticommunism irrevocably altered the grassroots culture of the organization. Leftists and liberals who shared common views on workplace discrimination or segregated housing and schools found themselves squabbling over Soviet expansionism and the Chinese Revolution. In some cases, Communist activists did not help their cause, because of their penchant for secrecy and their ideological rigidity.

Bruising factional disputes tore apart many of the NAACP's largest and most effective branches. In Detroit, where the NAACP had a strong proletarian cast during World War II because of its close ties to the left-led locals of the United Automobile Workers, suspected Communists were hounded out. The Reverend Charles Hill, a practitioner of the Social Gospel who believed in the power of coalitions between secular leftists and the church, led the Detroit branch through a period of phenomenal growth. Hill worked closely with the March on Washington Movement, even though he never embraced Randolph-style socialism. He opened his church to union organizers and forged close links with the CIO. And he led thousands of blacks in protesting the segregation at the Sojourner Truth Homes, in backing the United Automobile Workers, and in protesting hate strikes. But despite his record, when Hill refused to sever ties with Communist-affiliated groups such as the Civil Rights Congress, he was expelled from office. Hill continued to fight for civil rights and was hauled before the House Un-American Activities Committee (HUAC) in 1952. But once he lost his institutional base in the NAACP, Detroit's period of coalition building came to an end. The Detroit branch adopted less militant tactics and appeared less relevant to the rank and file, who left in droves. Membership in Detroit's branch plummeted from a peak of nearly 25,000 in 1944 to only 5,162 in 1951.

By the early 1950s, the NAACP had lost much of its activist edge in the North. Many northern branches became what one observer called "tax bases" for the NAACP's southern litigation campaign. The purge of leftists and the shift to litigation support meant that in many cities, once-militant NAACP chapters became havens of middle-class respectability whose members put most of their energy into fund-raising. Tea parties, dances, and fashion shows became the public face of many branches. The loss of a mass base led some observers—such as the editors of *The Pittsburgh Courier*—to argue that the NAACP's survival depended on its adopting "new means and methods to interest a much larger number of members." But, with a few exceptions, that would not happen until the early 1960s, when insurgents challenged the "old guard" throughout the North and resuscitated an emphasis on working-class concerns.

The NAACP was not alone in its internal struggles over communism. The Urban League also issued denunciations of "Reds." The league had long been a more conservative organization than the NAACP, but during the Great Depression, both the national headquarters and local affiliates had occasionally collaborated with left-leaning organizations, including the National Negro Congress, though it never attracted many overt leftists. Still, the Urban League burnished its anti-Communist credentials. At its 1949 annual meeting, delegates repudiated "those totalitarian groups, of whatever persuasion which are exploiting the issue of race for their own selfish ends." Throughout the 1950s, the Urban League kept close tabs on its employees and board members, tracking their affiliations and their positions on Communist-related issues. "Fortunately," wrote an Urban League official, "the frequent and sudden changes in the Communist Party line, particularly with respect to the race question, provide handy reference points for checking attitudes and sympathies of individuals."

By the early 1950s, there were still two prominent left-led organizations pushing for racial equality, even as they grew increasingly isolated. One was the Civil Rights Congress (CRC), founded in 1946 out of the ashes of the National Negro Congress and the International Labor Defense, the Communist group famous for publicizing the Scottsboro case. The CRC combined protest and litigation, especially involving issues such as police brutality, that more mainstream groups were reluctant to handle. In New York and Oakland, the CRC spearheaded a campaign against what it called "legal lynchings" perpetrated against blacks by law enforcement officials. In Los Angeles and Detroit, where it also had strong bases, the CRC continued efforts begun by the National Negro Congress to publicize workplace discrimination and enact fair employment laws. But the CRC increasingly acted alone, as the NAACP branches, Urban

League affiliates, and religious groups that had collaborated with its predecessor organizations in the 1930s and early 1940s stayed away.

The fate of the Civil Rights Congress's efforts to petition the United Nations was an indication of how much the political climate had changed in the early years of the Cold War. In 1951, the CRC presented the United Nations with a lengthy petition titled "We Charge Genocide." The document forcefully linked the black freedom struggle—north and south—with human rights battles abroad. The term "genocide," coined by human rights advocate Raphael Lemkin in 1944, attracted the attention of black commentators, who quickly applied it to lynching, police brutality, and, more broadly, the systematic oppression of blacks in American society. When the United Nations proposed an international genocide treaty in 1947, many black activists embraced the idea. Willard Townsend, a longtime labor and civil rights activist—and a staunch anti-Communist—offered an expanded definition of the term: "If it becomes a crime to destroy the cultural and spiritual life of a nation, racial, or religious group, by the very same means social and economic genocide cannot be less immoral or less barbaric. The deliberate practice of social and economic genocide against Negroes in America gets its result in disease-ridden communities, high mortality rates, and a collective group frustration that slowly destroys the spiritual and moral fibre of the victim." In December 1948, when the United Nations adopted the antigenocide convention, many civil rights activists saw it as another weapon in the black freedom struggle.

In "We Charge Genocide," the CRC offered a pointed argument. "Out of the inhuman black ghettos of American cities, out of the cotton plantations of the South, comes this record of mass slayings on the basis of race, of lives deliberately warped and distorted by the willful creation of conditions making for premature death, poverty, and disease." Cataloguing police brutality, the petitioners noted that "the wanton killing of Negroes . . . is no longer a sectional phenomenon." The CRC also highlighted the "super-exploitation" of black workers and denounced the "profit from Negro ghettos" that benefited "insurance companies, mortgage concerns, and realty corporations" while entrapping blacks in overpriced, inferior housing. The petition denounced the "theory of 'gradualism,'" namely "the concept of gradual evolutionary improvement of the plight of the Negro." The petition pointedly concluded that "three hundred years is a long time to wait."

Whether the list of atrocities and everyday segregation compiled by the CRC constituted genocide, even by the fairly broad definition adopted by the United Nations, was an open question. But it would not be answered. The petition was one of the CRC's last grand gestures, as it reeled under anti-Communist scrutiny. American diplomats, unwilling to have the charges aired, squashed the petition. Other civil rights activists—even those who would have supported the concept of accusing the United States of human rights violations just a few years earlier—did not endorse the petition. The Civil Rights Congress grew only more marginal in the early 1950s. Many of its members were hauled before HUAC investigators and jailed. Several CRC members were tried on charges that they violated the Smith Act, which made it illegal to "advocate, abet, advise or teach" the "overthrowing [of] the government of the United States . . . by force or violence" or to support any group that did so. The battered organization put most of its energies into mounting costly and time-consuming legal defenses.

The other leading leftist civil rights organization, the National Negro Labor Council (NNLC), pledged to engage in "militant struggle" on behalf of blacks' economic rights. The NNLC grew out of Detroit's still-vibrant labor–civil rights alliance and spread to other cities, such as Cleveland and Baltimore. Most of its members hailed from left-led unions—many fighting for survival in the early 1950s. Blacklisted unionist Coleman Young (later Detroit's mayor) described the NNLC as a reincarnation of the "leftist labor movement . . . smaller, peskier, and more focused than ever." However pesky, the NNLC made demands similar to those of the Urban League and NAACP. It agitated for fair employment practices legislation and sought the inclusion of blacks in high-visibility jobs, including as airline stewardesses and pilots. But the NNLC also offered a political economic analysis missing from most postwar anti-discrimination efforts. Most notably, it warned of the devastating consequences of the flight of jobs from union-dense northern cities to the low-wage Sunbelt. In its pamphlet "Give Us This Day Our Daily Bread," the organization used religious language to make a radical argument, namely that the fate of northern and southern workers was bound together. So long as Dixie remained a bastion of poorly paid, nonunion labor, northern industry would relocate there—profiting from Jim Crow and victimizing northern urban blacks, too.

Tainted red, the NNLC's protests were shunned by other civil rights groups and nonleftist unions. The NAACP ordered its members to avoid the NNLC. Many NNLC members were called before HUAC, faced jail time, and lost their jobs. But the group also served as a springboard for future black activism, most notably in Detroit, where HUAC hearings in 1952 inadvertently launched Coleman Young's political career. Willful and defiant, Young chided Georgia Dixiecrat John Wood for using the southernism "Nigra." "I said to myself," Young later recalled, "Why should I take any shit off a son of a bitch from Georgia? How can he question my Americanism?" Young was just as unsparing with California Republican Donald Jackson. "You can't tell me that Jim Crow doesn't exist in California. There is a whole lot wrong with California that has got to be straightened out." Young's defiance made him a folk hero among Detroit blacks. But the NNLC fought an uphill battle with few allies. In 1956, facing further accusations that it was a Communist organization, the NNLC disbanded.

The collapse of the left–civil rights alliance had serious implications for the northern movements for racial equality, particularly around issues of housing and employment. The shift away from an economic understanding of racial inequality channeled activists down the narrower path that had been blazed by Myrdal. Anticommunism marginalized those who emphasized racial inequality as a matter of power and empowered those who emphasized individualism and morality. The Red Scare drove activists away from strategies of protest and confrontation to those of conciliation and persuasion. Beginning in the late 1940s, the unlikely coalitions of leftists and religious activists that had shaped the politics of the Depression and war fractured.

Dorothy Height best captured the corrosive impact of anticommunism on the movement. She lamented the disappearance of the big tent of activists in the late 1940s, in contrast to "a few years before, when we were more of an open society, and a Republican, a Communist, a Socialist, a Democrat, whoever else, could all sit down together." She described a climate of fear that pervaded civil rights groups. The McCarthy era, she recalled, "was a terrible period, because it meant that if you protested against the lack of jobs or against discrimination, immediately you were considered a Communist. You were considered unpatriotic." Even fundraising efforts suffered. "Outstanding women, particularly those who were in teaching jobs . . . just got absolutely frightened, and they would say 'Well, I like Mrs. Bethune, and I'm sending this contribution, but I'm sending a money order.' They wouldn't send a check." In her view, the freedom struggle "lost ground" as the chill of anticommunism "contributed to a kind of withdrawal from social action." The narrowing of the civil rights movement in the North in the late 1940s would leave many unresolved issues for the activists of the 1960s—including an enduring suspicion of arguments that racial and economic inequality were fundamentally intertwined.

"IMPORTANT NATIONAL POLICIES and issues," wrote Henry Lee Moon, "may be debated, developed and formulated on the national level, but in America, they are settled only in the community—back home in the neighborhoods, precincts, and wards where the people live." In no respect was this truer than in racial politics. While civil rights activists continued their uphill battle for a federal FEPC, they increasingly turned their energies to northern state legislatures and city halls, where their chances of victory were greater. In America's federal system, states and localities are often incubators of innovative public policy—and that was particularly true in the case of civil rights. Between 1945 and 1964, twenty-nine states outside the South enacted fair employment practices laws. The age-old doctrine of "states' rights" in America cut two ways. In the South, it became the mantra of supporters of Jim Crow, a way to oppose federal civil rights initiatives in the guise of defending America's federal system of government. But in the North, state and local autonomy gave civil rights activists new arenas for struggle. Unwilling to wait for a reluctant Congress to act, activists set out for such places as Albany, Trenton, Lansing, Harrisburg, and Springfield, to lobby, write letters, testify, and negotiate for the passage of state fair practices laws. And when the states failed to pass laws, they turned to the localities to plant the seeds of civil rights.

Moon argued that blacks could reorient American politics by playing the "balance of power" card. For the moment, at the national level, he was wrong. But his arguments made much more sense on the state and local levels, particularly in the large northern states that had attracted a disproportionate number of black migrants. If Truman and his advisors paid heed to Moon's argument about the power of the black electorate, northern state and local elected officials had even more reason to take it seriously. The black majority had shifted to Democrats by 1936, but no one knew whether that allegiance would endure. Many key northern black civil rights leaders, ministers, and businesspeople remained Republicans despite the New Deal. White elected officials assumed that black voters were fickle and could be lured back to the GOP. Hoping to capture the swing vote, both parties began to court blacks.

Moderate northern Republicans, particularly those seeking statewide office, endorsed civil rights to win black votes or at least maintain the loyalty of those who had not defected to the Democrats. But most Republicans represented rural and suburban areas with few blacks and had little to gain in local races by supporting racial equality. By contrast, Democratic elected officials had good reason to court blacks. Across the North, the Democratic Party was largely urban. As their black constituencies grew, mayors and other local elected officials began to pay heed to their black constituents. In many cities, municipal governments became the employer of first resort for blacks. During the Great Depression and the war, for example, Chicago mayor Ed Kelly forged extensive links with the city's South Side blacks through patronage, the construction of new schools in predominantly black neighborhoods, and efforts to integrate the city's public housing. A consummate party builder—every bit as astute electorally as he was corrupt—Kelly knew from his "cold, pragmatic look at the numbers" that the black votes were essential to consolidating his power. His efforts paid off: He outpaced Franklin Delano Roosevelt among Chicago's black voters in 1936 and 1940. Pittsburgh's incumbent mayor David Lawrence and Detroit's incumbent Edward Jeffries both won the fealty of black voters by opening municipal jobs to blacks. By 1946, over one-third of Detroit's city workers were black.

Urban mayors walked a fine line between winning black support and alienating their white base. From the New Deal until the early 1960s, blacks were a small enough minority in most northern cities that their interests mattered most during election season and least afterward. Northern politicians who identified too closely with "the colored" often paid a steep political price or backed down in the face of white opposition. When Chicago's Kelly intervened on behalf of black families who tried to move into the all-white Airport Homes in 1946, he faced ferocious white opposition. In 1947, Kelly lost his berth as the head of Chicago's machine to conservative, anti-civil-rights politico Martin Kennelly. And Detroit's Jeffries stood by his white constituents over matters of "Negro housing." During his 1945 reelection campaign, after three years of white battles against "mixed housing," Jeffries ran a race-baiting campaign in which he denounced his opponent as a "red" who would support "racial invasions" of white neighborhoods. Still, by the mid-1940s, even conservative white mayors kept blacks on city payrolls with hopes of cementing their loyalty at the ballot box. It is impossible to underestimate the importance of municipal employment as a niche for urban blacks, particularly in an economy where workplace discrimination was still widespread. Blacks may have been concentrated in the lowest-level municipal jobs, particularly maintenance work, but their inroads into public employment testified to their newfound electoral clout.

The tug-of-war for black voters was most intense in politically competitive states, where Republicans and Democrats vied for state legislatures, senate seats, and governorships. By the mid-1940s, New York, New Jersey, Michigan, Pennsylvania, and Illinois—the northern states with the largest black populations—were all up for grabs. These five states became testing grounds for civil rights legislation. The flood of black migrants northward during and after World War II had fundamentally shifted the political demography. The passage of a strongly pro-civil-rights plank at the 1948 Democratic National Convention, which prompted a walkout by most southern delegates and gave fire to Strom Thurmond's insurgent campaign, was largely the result of growing black political power in the North. Big-city bosses, reported the NAACP's Roy Wilkins, "were looking to score what consolation points they could with their minority home folks."

Northern civil rights activists, attentive to the political calculus of state and local elected officials, saw localities and states as key battlegrounds for the passage of fair employment practices laws (FEP). The model law was New York's, passed in 1945. New York's prominent Communists and Socialists exerted significant influence over city politics and pulled many Democratic party activists leftward. New York's Republicans—from Fiorello La Guardia to Thomas Dewey—were among the nation's most liberal. All of them responded to pressure from the state's well-organized civil rights organizations.

The wartime rhetoric of antiracism also touched a deep nerve among nonblack New Yorkers, especially Jews, who made up about a quarter of the city's population. During the war, Jewish groups were at the forefront of the battle for civil rights throughout the North. The American Jewish Congress, the Anti-Defamation League of B'nai B'rith, and the Jewish Labor Committee spearheaded national efforts to pass antidiscrimination laws; they joined with Hedgeman and the National Council for a Permanent FEPC to lobby Congress; and they were involved in nearly every state and local battle to pass laws prohibiting workplace discrimination. Like other religious groups, Jewish organizations embraced the rhetoric of brotherhood, but they also mobilized out of self-interest. Discrimination by "creed" and "national origin" affected large numbers of Jews, secular and religious alike, particularly in the professions and the upper echelons of corporate America. The alliance between Jews and blacks in New York provided a template for FEPC advocates elsewhere. Rather than pitching the FEPC as a "Negro" law, they emphasized its broad constituency. The prohibition against workplace discrimination would also benefit Catholics and Jews, not to mention Latinos and Asians (whose populations were still minuscule in the North) and the descendants of southern and eastern European immigrants. Calls for the prohibition of discrimination on grounds of "race, creed, color, or national origin" became a civil rights mantra.

That New York's state law was introduced during the war proved to be a boon. Wartime antifascist rhetoric was the glue that held together a coalition of diverse groups including the National Negro Congress, the American Labor Party, the Workers' Defense League and other Socialist groups, the New York Council of Churches, the American Jewish Congress, and a wide range of leftist and more moderate trade unions. By contrast, FEPC efforts in Michigan and Pennsylvania during the McCarthy era squandered energy dealing with factional squabbles among Communist-dominated groups and other left and liberal organizations—despite the fact that they shared virtually identical goals. Antifascism united, whereas anticommunism divided.

The battle over New York's FEP law foreshadowed later conflicts over civil rights legislation in the North. The proposed law's staunchest critics were Republicans. The New York Chamber of Commerce, various business and manufacturing groups, and small-town Republicans led the charge against the FEPC. Conservative journalist Westbrook Pegler gave prominent billing to their concerns in his nationally syndicated column. What was most striking about New York's critics of FEP was their denunciation of "quotas"—language that would be echoed decades later in conservative critiques of affirmative action. Master builder Robert Moses (who later designed parkways to connect New York City to suburban beaches that could not accommodate buses—in part to keep blacks and Puerto Ricans out) made the point bluntly. "The most vicious feature" of the proposed FEPC, he argued, "is that it will inevitably lead to the establishment of what in European universities and institutions, from the Middle Ages to World War II, was known as the 'numerous clauses,' that is, the quota system under which Jews and other minorities were permitted only up to a fixed number proportionate to their percentage of the total population.... It means the end of honest competition, and the death knell of selection and advancement on the basis of talent." Not all Republicans shared Moses's skepticism. New York was an intensely competitive state, where statewide elected officials could not ignore the votes of blacks and Jews. Republicans did not form a united front against the FEP law: Its co-author, Irving Ives, was a Republican, and Governor Thomas Dewey was one of its staunchest supporters. Rural and suburban Republicans largely opposed FEP legislation, but with the support of Jewish groups and Democrats it passed with a strong majority.

The politics of New Jersey's 1947 constitutional convention, where a proposal to prohibit discrimination generated intense debate, makes clear the shifting politics of the 1940s. New Jersey's largest cities—Newark, Trenton, and Camden—had rapidly growing black populations. The Garden State also had sizeable black enclaves in older suburbs such as Montclair, East Orange, and Plainfield, and long-standing rural black communities were dotted throughout the rich agricultural land, especially in its southern section. Henry Lee Moon himself highlighted the growing political clout of New Jersey's black population. In particular, New Jersey's Democrats and Republicans, eager to gain statewide offices, were receptive to blacks. When Republican Alfred Driscoll assumed the governorship of New Jersey in 1947, he pledged to rewrite New Jersey's century-old state constitution, whose antiquated language had given "good government" reformers grief for decades. Driscoll did not have civil rights in mind; rather, he wanted to uproot political corruption, modernize the state's court system, reform taxation policies, and strengthen the power of the executive branch. New Jersey's civil rights leaders, however, seized the opportunity of a constitutional convention to push for broad civil rights provisions. Leading the charge was the state NAACP. Lobbying delegates to the convention, with special attention to moderate Republicans and Democrats, the NAACP used the state's competitive party politics to its advantage.

When the NAACP demanded that the New Jersey constitution include antidiscrimination language that July, Republican-dominated business groups rallied against it. The New Jersey Chamber of Commerce argued that "the interest of special groups should not be written into the basic law but should remain subjects of legislative determination." The Small Business Association of New Jersey worried that the antidiscrimination laws would force employers to hire what the association spokesman called "personally objectionable help." Myra Hacker, a leading Republican delegate, denounced antidiscrimination as "a totalitarian concept" that "would create racial animosities." Civil rights, she argued, would come about "through a process of slow adjustment to be solved by education rather than imposed from above." Oliver Randolph, a prominent attorney, a lifelong Republican, and the convention's only black delegate, tailored a compromise that included only public education and militia service. To defuse fears that the constitution would favor one "special group" over others, he drafted language that forbade discrimination by religion, race, color, ancestry, or national origin. Randolph's amendment succeeded by a 50–18 vote. In the opposition were largely small-town Republicans, mostly from the southern half of the state. With bipartisan endorsement, the state constitution passed in the November 1947 general election by a comfortable three-to-one majority. The NAACP hailed New Jersey's voters as "torchbearers for justice."

In Philadelphia, rapid growth in the black electorate and intense local political competition also made possible the passage of civil rights laws. Philadelphia's black voters, like their counterparts throughout the North, had begun to shift to the Democrats during the New Deal, but many were still closely bound through patronage to the local GOP. Civil rights groups took advantage of the city's unusually competitive political climate. Hundreds of blacks showed up at rallies and flooded public officials with petitions demanding the right to jobs. The Committee on Equal Job

Opportunity, the city's umbrella organization of fair employment practices advocates, lobbied city council members. Reform Democrats embraced the cause of fair employment, and local Republicans knew that it would be necessary to "corral the votes of minority groups" to fend off the reformers' challenge. The result was bipartisan consensus. Philadelphia's city council unanimously passed a local FEP ordinance in 1948. In Philadelphia, Moon's balance of power argument accurately described the political reality.

By the late 1940s, Republicans tended to support—at least in principle—symbolic, gradualist civil rights legislation. Every state FEP law passed with some Republican backing, sometimes even with Republican majorities. But the Republicans had a double consciousness when it came to civil rights that was exacerbated when civil rights laws came into conflict with "free enterprise." Key GOP interest groups, particularly state affiliates of the National Association of Manufacturers and local chambers of commerce, came out against the proposed laws. With big business lining up in opposition and with few black constituents to keep happy, many northern Republicans felt little urgency to pass the laws, even when they supported civil rights in principle. Often, proposed FEP laws pitted Republican against Republican. In Pennsylvania, for example, a 1951 effort to pass the antidiscrimination law was supported by moderate Republican governor John Fine but opposed by fellow GOP members such as Representative William McMillen, who charged that a state fair employment practices commission would become "the Commissar or the Gestapo of both labor and capital in America."

The Republicans' resort to a probusiness, antigovernment campaign reflected the changing place of corporations in postwar American politics and popular culture. From the earliest days of industrialization through the Depression, most Americans had been deeply suspicious of "robber barons." The bloated plutocrat, bursting out of his tuxedo, had become a stock caricature. But during the 1940s, especially as the Cold War intensified, business leaders began to link their fortunes with the struggle against communism. Through well-placed advertisements, school curricula, and opinion pieces, groups such as the National Association of Manufacturers recast the image of American business. Free enterprise, in their view, was the antithesis of socialism; regulation, by implication, was the beginning of a slippery slope toward totalitarianism.

In the case of fair employment practices laws, the conflict between African American and business interests was crystal clear. Proposed FEP laws threatened the sacrosanct "freedom of contract." National Time & Signal Corporation president George Fulton argued, "If I apply for a job and any prospective employer does not want to hire me . . . that is his business. And thank God for this." Business groups such as the Pennsylvania Manufacturers Association and the Philadelphia Hotel Association led the charge against that state's FEP law. Laws that forbade discrimination in hiring and promotion directly threatened "managerial prerogative" to hire and fire at will. One Michigan legislator argued that the proposed FEP bill would bring Michigan "into the realm of a Socialistic state." Government should not meddle with the free market—particularly in service of a far-fetched scheme of social engineering.

That some of the earliest and most vocal supporters of the FEPC had been Communists—and that the first state and local FEP organizations were almost always Popular Front coalitions that included Communist-dominated groups such as the Civil Rights Congress—was a double-edged sword. Leftists provided the most consistent support for state and local FEPCs and tirelessly coordinated letter-writing, protest, and lobbying campaigns, but the very presence of suspected Communists in the antidiscrimination movement led opponents to taint anti-Communist FEP supporters as red. The fact that FEP had been, in the words of a Michigan legislator, "conceived in the halls of the Communist Party" gave the law's Republican foes more ammunition.

Even Republicans who continued to support civil rights increasingly embraced the rhetoric of gradualism. *The Saturday Evening Post,* which appealed to suburban, moderate Republicans, set the tone in a 1950 editorial opposing FEP laws. "Force is always a tempting device, but in the long run, the results of persuasion are sounder." Such arguments resonated widely. As civil rights politics heated up during the early and mid-1950s, President Dwight D. Eisenhower recoiled at what he saw as the movement's excesses. Eisenhower expressed his regret that he had appointed Earl Warren to the Supreme Court, counseled patience in the aftermath of the *Brown v. Board of Education* decision, and intervened only reluctantly in such controversies as the mob violence that accompanied the desegregation of the Little Rock public schools. Above all, Ike believed that coercion would not accomplish racial change. Republican congressman William Broomfield, of suburban Detroit (and later a staunch opponent of school busing), offered a typical Republican critique of FEP laws on the grounds that "educational and religious advancement," not legislation, would solve the problem of racial discrimination. Ford Motor Company vice president Benson Ford, an opponent of Michigan's proposed FEP law, proclaimed in words that could have come from Eisenhower's mouth that "you cannot legislate good human relations." Fearful of the coercive power of the government, Republicans argued that the strong arm of the law would not change hearts and minds; there would need to be a long, gradual process of appeals to morality and education.

Republicans were not alone in their go-slow politics. By the early 1950s, many staunch advocates of antidiscrimination laws began to embrace the rhetoric of education and gradualism—in large part out of a sense of pragmatism. In 1952, Herbert Northrup, a prominent labor economist who had once supported the creation of a permanent FEPC, argued in the pages of then-liberal *Commentary* magazine that antidiscrimination advocates should moderate their position to win Republican support. Because of their "intransigent stand," their "all or nothing attitude," civil rights groups had "killed all chances" for a fair employment practices law on the federal level. In the place of agitation and lobbying, Northrup advocated "an educational or voluntary program" of fair employment practices, and not compulsory nondiscrimination regulations. His calls for voluntarism and education echoed a shift that was occurring in civil rights law in the states and localities.

State by state in the North, FEP bills ground their way through legislatures. The process and timing of enactment varied, reflecting the peculiarities of state-level partisanship, the effectiveness or division of pro-FEPC lobbying groups, and the larger political climate. It is noteworthy that nearly every state FEPC law was passed in a nonelection year—a signal that state legislators feared that the laws would alienate constituents or campaign donors. One by one, however, FEPC advocates prevailed, largely by framing their arguments in moralistic terms, by appealing to the electoral self-interest of politicians in swing districts, and, most important, by drafting compromise legislation that minimized controversy.

State FEP laws had two key characteristics. First, most were noncoercive. Every state fair employment practices law that passed in the postwar years put an emphasis on gradual change. Nearly every state FEPC had a mandate to mount educational programs to persuade employers and unions and white workers to accept the principle of nondiscrimination. In the same vein, they relied on conciliation rather than punishment. Most state FEPCs did not have enforcement powers: They could not fine employers for noncompliance. (Only three states, Idaho, Vermont, and Iowa, all with tiny black populations, included civil or penal enforcement powers in their laws.) Second, the laws were individualistic. They relied on aggrieved workers to file specific complaints against employers suspected of discrimination. Frustrated job seekers could claim that they were improperly turned away at the hiring office or that they were denied a placement or promotion on the ground of race, creed, or ethnicity. But the individualistic model put the costs and burden of proof squarely on the shoulders of aggrieved workers, who often did not have the time, the money, or the education to file discrimination claims. All too often, cases devolved into "he said/she said" arguments. Complicating matters, state FEPCs were always understaffed and underfunded. State legislatures simply did not put a priority on funding agencies to combat discrimination.

A typical state FEP law was Pennsylvania's. Enacted in 1955 after more than ten years of lobbying and grassroots activism, it was the product of legislative compromise. Fearful of a law that would interfere with managerial prerogative, Republicans thwarted efforts to pass a state FEP law five times between 1945 and 1955, before a tepid version of the bill (emphasizing the then largely uncontroversial issue of "age discrimination") passed in October. Liberals, already inclined toward gradualism, watered down the legislation to win over moderate Republicans. The law was passed in a nonelection year in a session marked by unusually high absenteeism.

Underfunded and understaffed, most state FEPCs made a small dent in the problem of workplace discrimination. Adjudication was time-consuming and difficult. Under Pennsylvania's law, the state Commission on Human Relations heard 1,416 employment discrimination cases in its first seven years and ruled on behalf of the complainants in 564 cases. Under such constraints, it was virtually impossible to attack the systematic exclusion of blacks from certain jobs. At best, state FEPCs accomplished the token placements of blacks. But however ineffective state FEP laws

were, they had unintended consequences. Above all, they raised expectations that job discrimination would soon be a thing of the past. By
enlisting the power of government in the battle against workplace discrimination, FEP laws made states into allies—however weak—of civil
rights groups in the struggle for equal employment opportunity.

BY THE MID-1950S, the radical demand for "jobs and freedom" had given
way to a restrained integrationism. Whereas wartime activists had targeted discriminatory employers with protests and walkouts and had
pressured the FEPC to enforce antidiscrimination regulations, postwar
activists turned to the quieter tactics of moral suasion and education. Motivated by a desire to challenge white assumptions about the inherent inferiority of blacks, activists set out to persuade employers to hire blacks in
"breakthrough" jobs, primarily white-collar and skilled positions formerly reserved for whites. Civil rights organizations also prepared extensive media campaigns to promote the most visible success stories—such
as the hiring of the first black airline stewardess, or the most celebrated
breakthrough of all, in Major League Baseball.

In 1947, when the Brooklyn Dodgers fielded Jackie Robinson, the
event became a barometer of changing race relations and a reminder of
how deeply entrenched racial hostility remained in the North. Most
players—four out of five by the best estimate—supported integration, but
white fans regularly heckled the rookie, and in an infamous incident,
members of the Philadelphia Phillies catcalled the rookie as "nigger."
But baseball officials and most of the press rallied around Robinson, por-
traying him as the exemplar of a postracial America. By the time of his re-
tirement in 1957, Robinson had become a celebrity whose personal life
was fodder for the black press and whose compelling story of triumph
over racial injustice turned him into the white media's feel-good example
of America's changing racial order. But Robinson's breakthrough, however celebrated, was largely symbolic. It would take much more than a
handful of black sports heroes to transform race relations in postwar
America.

While Robinson vaulted to fame, the Urban League led the effort to
place less-heralded black pioneers in prominent places throughout the
American economy. "We no longer think," stated the Urban League's

Lester Granger in 1950, "of finding many thousands of Negro workers to place in a dozen plants." Instead, the Urban League placed "a man here and there, and over there, at strategic points." It was a striking shift in emphasis from the Depression and World War II, when the Urban League had joined the effort to open up whole industries on a nondiscriminatory basis. Granger was optimistic that "a dozen strategic placements in industry can mean within a five-year period the employment of 5,000 workers—this through the change of thinking on the part of those who are responsible for policymaking and administration." In St. Paul and Minneapolis, social worker Whitney Young (later head of the National Urban League) engaged in behind-the-scenes negotiations with employers to place blacks in "pioneer" positions, mostly in retail and white-collar employment. In Cincinnati and Detroit, local Urban League branches held conferences with employers throughout the 1940s and 1950s to persuade them to hire blacks for retail and clerical jobs. Throughout the North, the Urban League circulated the résumés of well-educated blacks to prospective employers, hoping that the presence of respectable blacks in skilled and professional positions would erode whites' irrational prejudices.

The Urban League was not alone in its strategy. A coalition of religious groups and local race relations agencies—spearheaded by the American Friends Service Committee (AFSC), the activist branch of the Society of Friends—launched a "merit employment" program that spread nationwide in the late 1940s and 1950s. Starting with the premise that racial progress would come only when whites were able to see blacks as their equals, "merit employment" advocates put a lot of energy into symbolic hires of usually overqualified black workers. However, the placement of token blacks in high-visibility positions did little to change the stark reality of postwar black employment, and it left open the question of what constituted "merit"—a term that masked employers' often capricious decisions as seemingly objective. Most Americans got their jobs on the basis of personal networks. A few highly skilled jobs excepted, there were no tests to measure objectively a prospective worker's merit or qualifications. By the late 1950s, grassroots activists throughout the North grew increasingly frustrated at what they saw as the limitations of both the fair employment practices paradigm and civil rights groups' uphill struggle to persuade employers to jettison discriminatory practices.

Philadelphia's grassroots campaign to open up jobs provides a good example. Between the mid-1940s and the early 1960s, Philadelphia's major civil rights groups—led by the AFSC, the Armstrong Association (the local Urban League affiliate), and the Committee on Equal Job Opportunity (CEJO)—all struggled for the hearts and minds of the city's employers. Civil rights activists regularly met with individual employers, encouraging them to hire blacks. To deal with employers who were skeptical of blacks' native intelligence and ability or who were hostile to equal employment demanded tremendous patience. In 1954, a typical year, Armstrong Association officials met with eighty-nine employers, gaining about 150 jobs, primarily for "those with above average skills." Most of the jobs were sales and clerical, often involving contact with a white clientele.

The CEJO, the NAACP, and a number of liberal religious groups also mediated between employers and individual workers who suffered racial discrimination. As with the Armstrong Association, these groups handled complaints and negotiations on a case-by-case basis and used the tactics of moral suasion to open jobs to blacks. In 1950 and 1951, the CEJO and the AFSC planned an "educational program" to persuade Philadelphia area banks to hire carefully screened black applicants for clerical and teller positions. Bank officials were usually skeptical, although a few hired a handful of blacks as messengers, office machine operators, and clerks. CEJO activists spoke to business groups and churches, screened *Fair Play*, a film that depicted the travails of a frustrated black job seeker, and distributed pro-civil-rights publications to employers.

Occasionally, postwar civil rights activists practiced a cautious militancy with regard to hiring policies. Between 1945 and 1948, a coalition led by AFSC and CEJO targeted Philadelphia's six major department stores, to urge the employment of black salespeople. Their efforts yielded little. In 1953, thirteen civil rights organizations engaged in a ten-month campaign to persuade city department store managers to hire black saleswomen and clerks. Fearful that protest would alienate prospective employers (perhaps reflecting back on the limited successes of the Depression-era "Don't Buy Where You Can't Work" campaigns), they kept a low profile, "avoiding all publicity and keeping clear of any coercive action such as picketing and boycotts." Certain that managers had refused to hire blacks because of fears of "unfavorable reaction on the part of white employees or customers," they argued that "their customers actually *wanted* the change." White integrationists returned their monthly bills emblazoned with stickers that read "I should like to see qualified Negroes included in your sales force." Activists met behind the scenes with store officials, wrote letters to store heads, and enlisted the aid of a prominent white judge, Curtis Bok, who held a dinner party for department store officials to persuade them to hire black staff. After great effort, Gimbels placed one black woman in its sales training program. Civil rights leaders also pushed "specialty store" managers to hire carefully selected black workers for the 1953 and 1954 holiday seasons. Only a handful were hired, most to fill a staff shortage during the Christmas rush. Nearly all were laid off shortly thereafter.

BY THE LATE 1950s, astute observers noted a growing impatience among black workers about the seemingly glacial progress of racial equality on the job. The postwar years witnessed some gains, particularly in industrial employment, but in the increasingly affluent, suburbanizing North, blacks remained mostly confined to the least-secure, least-remunerative jobs. Relative to their share in the population, blacks were overrepresented in unskilled industrial and service jobs and underrepresented in sales, management, and the professions. The number of blacks in the skilled trades rose significantly, but most of the gain came in traditionally black crafts such as bricklaying and roofing, and in nonunionized construction. Stuck overwhelmingly in the lowest-level jobs, they were vulnerable to layoffs, particularly when firms moved to white-dominated suburban and rural areas. Black unemployment in Philadelphia mirrored a nationwide trend: it hovered at one and a half to two times that of whites in the boom years from 1946 to 1953, and double that of whites from the 1954 recession through the late 1960s.

The stagnation in black employment prospects and the persistence of workplace discrimination generated growing discontent. Black workers led a rebellion against racial gradualism, unwilling to wait for the Urban League or merit employment campaigners to change the hearts and minds of their employers. Already by the mid-1950s there were rumblings of shop-floor insurgencies. Warner Bloomberg, Jr., a labor journalist who spent time with black factory workers in Chicago in 1956, found that "a shift of power is beginning to take place among the Negroes. . . .

The younger, more militant leaders increasingly challenge the older group whenever it resorts to techniques now considered a form of 'Uncle Tommin'.'" Black workers, frustrated at the pace of change, had "increased solidarity and a more intense sense of identity." A. Philip Randolph reported "an upsurge among Negroes in all walks and callings of life against tokenism—and it is spontaneous, self-generating, leaderless."

The simmering shop-floor rebellion did not remain leaderless for long. Never content to be on the margins—particularly at a moment of incipient rebellion—Randolph jumped into the debate about workplace discrimination. Having long advocated fair employment practices laws, he increasingly came to see the problem of discrimination as a problem in the house of labor. "Negro trade unionists, and workers generally," he argued, "are in no mood to look with toleration upon 'tokenism' in the elimination of racial discrimination by the unions today." In 1959, Randolph founded the Negro American Labor Council, an all-black caucus, to push for union reform and to spearhead a campaign to organize among working-class blacks. Randolph's position brought him to loggerheads with George Meany, president of the newly merged AFL-CIO. Randolph challenged the lack of black leadership in the union movement, blamed Meany and his staff for indifference to black workers, and demanded that organized labor take a more aggressive role in combating discrimination within its own ranks.

By the early 1960s, Randolph did not have much of a movement under his aegis. The labor council was largely a paper organization. But Randolph's call for full employment and fair employment won the support of grassroots labor activists throughout the North. Black union caucuses sprung up in Chicago, Pittsburgh, Youngstown, Gary, Jersey City, and Detroit, in unions as diverse as the United Steelworkers, the Building Services Employees, and the United Automobile Workers. The most important was the Trade Union Leadership Council (TULC). Begun as an insurgency within the United Automobile Workers to challenge the lack of black union leaders and the exclusion of black workers from skilled employment in the auto plants, the TULC expanded to other industrial cities in the early 1960s. The TULC presented itself as the loyal opposition within both the mainstream union movement and the Democratic Party. In 1960, the TULC endorsed John F. Kennedy's bid for the White House (Randolph, by contrast, refused to join the Democrats). But from the first days of Kennedy's term, TULC activists challenged him. Robert J. "Buddy" Battle III, the TULC head, put pressure on administration officials so that "the solemn campaign pledges and promises" would not "become a mockery."

The TULC also targeted white union leaders such as the UAW's Walter P. Reuther. Widely hailed as a progressive on civil rights (the UAW was one of the first unions to provide support for Martin Luther King, Jr., and the southern freedom struggle), Reuther faced criticism for his unwillingness to negotiate antidiscrimination clauses in auto industry contracts. The TULC also demanded the proportional representation of blacks in union offices and pushed for the inclusion of black workers in the white-dominated skilled trades. Over the course of the early 1960s, the TULC grew increasingly militant in its denunciation of racism in the trade unions. "The old clichés, the syrupy sentiments are no longer saleable," wrote the TULC in an open letter to George Meany in 1962. "The pious platitudes about patience and fortitude we leave to the Uncle Toms.... A man either has full equality or he doesn't—there is no satisfactory twilight zone in between." By 1963, the TULC had shifted its emphasis toward unemployment. TULC activists challenged what they saw as the hypocrisy of northern liberals on the matter of discrimination and unemployment. "Talk alone, good intentions, sterile resolutions, and blustering timidity bring only stagnation." Calling for "a storm of coordinated day-to-day agitation" throughout the country, the TULC demanded "equality of opportunity for employment in all places and at all levels. And we will win because we will settle for nothing less."

While Randolph's NALC and the TULC turned their attention to organized labor, another insurgency, based in Philadelphia, issued a direct challenge to employers. No one would transform the northern movement for workplace equality more than the Reverend Leon H. Sullivan. Appointed pastor of Philadelphia's prestigious Zion Baptist Church at the age of twenty-eight, Sullivan had cut his teeth as a minister and activist in World War II–era Harlem. As a student at the liberal Union Theological Seminary in New York, Sullivan was steeped in the Social Gospel. In Popular Front Harlem, Sullivan's religion and civil rights activism merged seamlessly. As many young black radicals did, Sullivan gravitated toward A. Philip Randolph and worked as a coordinator of New York's March on Washington Movement. Sullivan also attracted the attention of Adam

Clayton Powell, Jr., and won a plum position as assistant pastor at Powell's Abyssinian Baptist Church. After a short stint in East Orange, New Jersey, a suburban black community with a long tradition of militant activism, Sullivan moved to Philadelphia in 1950, where he brought his brand of political Christianity to one of the city's most respectable middle-class congregations. Over the course of the 1950s, Sullivan became particularly interested in the problems of unemployed young black men, with an emphasis on juvenile delinquency and crime. For Sullivan—as for so many black ministers—the church was a base from which to provide social services and to engage in racial uplift. But Sullivan was not, as later critics would charge, a latter-day Booker T. Washington. His experience with direct action and radical politics left an indelible imprint on his political vision. By the late 1950s, Sullivan had concluded that neighborhood-based activism was not enough.

What irked Sullivan most was that white employers were unwilling to hire black workers, regardless of their qualifications. And the gradualist tactics of Philadelphia's racial liberals were just not enough. A trickle of well-paying jobs would not solve the problem of chronic underemployment. Direct action would. By the late 1950s, insurgents throughout the North were reviving the "Don't Buy Where You Can't Work" campaigns of the Depression. In Gary, Indiana, a group of activists created the Fair Share Organization in 1958, picketing department stores, groceries, and manufacturers who failed to hire blacks. That same year, the Chicago NAACP branch boycotted a South Side restaurant that advertised for a "Waitress—white" and the Bronx NAACP branch demonstrated at a local Sears, demanding the hiring of blacks and Puerto Ricans during the Christmas season. But no campaign was more influential than Philadelphia's. Sullivan set his sights on the city's most prominent businesses. Sullivan had also learned that mass movements were not simply the sum of individual acts of resistance: They were most effective when they came out of institutions—and drew on the resources of grassroots activists. In 1959, four years after Pennsylvania passed its weak FEP law, Sullivan drew together a coalition of black ministers from throughout the Philadelphia area—"the 400 Ministers"—and launched a four-year "Selective Patronage" campaign. "We just felt that government wasn't fast enough," stated one campaign supporter. Their goal, recalled Sullivan, was nothing short of "breaking down the company's entire pattern of discriminatory practices."

The 400 Ministers chose a deliciously symbolic first target: the Tasty Baking Company, makers of the sugary Tastykakes, a staple in the diet of Philadelphia schoolchildren. Tasty had a sizeable number of black employees, but mainly in inferior jobs. Rather than demanding the hiring of a token black or two, as had "breakthrough" advocates, the 400 Ministers demanded that sizeable numbers of blacks be hired at every level, including as bakers, delivery people, chemists, and clerical staff. When Tasty's management refused to cooperate, the ministers launched a boycott. The 400 Ministers took to their pulpits and denounced the company for its racist practices. One newspaper estimated that 80 percent of black Philadelphians joined the campaign. Signs reading "We don't sell it and we don't buy it" replaced displays of Tasty's desserts in black neighborhood stores. After six months, the company capitulated and hired two black truck drivers, two clerical workers, and four black women production workers, the first on a racially mixed but gender-segregated shop floor. The victory was small but hard-won. Emboldened by the fall of Tasty Baking, the 400 Ministers launched successful boycotts of twenty-nine other firms, including Pepsi-Cola, Sunoco, Gulf Oil, A&P, Breyers Ice Cream, and the Philadelphia *Bulletin*, the city's largest daily newspaper.

Selective patronage advocates pointedly repudiated gradualism. "TOKENISM IS NOT ENOUGH," read one poster at protests outside the *Bulletin*. One boycotter argued: "We're tired of hearing times are changing. How long is long? And how gradual is gradual?" The campaign led Sullivan and his fellow ministers to advance arguments that would later inform the debate over affirmative action. In their campaign against Sunoco, they demanded a "crash program" for hiring black workers and, stopping just short of a call for quotas, demanded a "minimal acceptable standard" for the number of blacks hired. Sullivan defended what he called "discrimination in reverse," that is, upgrading blacks ahead of whites with seniority. "Black men have been waiting for a hundred years," argued Sullivan; "white men can wait for a few months." In the end, Leon Sullivan estimated that the boycotts had opened two thousand jobs for blacks.

Word of the Philadelphia protests spread nationwide, largely through a loose network of black churches and fraternal organizations. The Prince Hall Masons, one of the largest black fraternal organizations in the country, joined the Sunoco boycott. The National Baptist Sunday School Congress endorsed the selective patronage strategy. Activists from other cities descended on Philadelphia to meet with the 400 Ministers. Sullivan vaulted to national prominence. The Reverend Martin Luther King, Jr., promoted the idea. In 1962, inspired by Sullivan, the Southern Christian Leadership Conference announced the creation of "Operation Breadbasket," which began to deploy the "selective patronage" strategy throughout the South. Congress of Racial Equality chapters in many cities also embraced the strategy as they struggled to be relevant to working-class blacks. The selective patronage campaign also appealed to more radical black activists. For example, Maxwell Stanford, an insurgent who had founded the Revolutionary Action Movement—which combined black nationalism and Maoism—saw selective patronage as "proof that the black masses, not civil rights liberals, were the key to black liberation." By early 1963, activists throughout the North—from Atlantic City to Brooklyn, Cleveland, Detroit, New York, and Pittsburgh—had launched dozens of "selective patronage" campaigns. Perhaps most important, the 400 Ministers' increasingly militant language and confrontational strategy emboldened a younger, more working-class cadre of activists to push even harder for change.

THE STRUGGLE AGAINST employment discrimination had come a long way from the March on Washington Movement. Between the mid-1940s and the early 1960s, most northern states had passed fair employment practices laws, the result of growing black political clout. Antidiscrimination efforts, however limited in their effects, raised the expectations of ordinary blacks. But the growing grassroots sentiment against gradualism and tokenism mounted over the course of the 1950s, spurred a blue-collar rebellion, and would lead to a more militant turn in the 1960s. Workplace discrimination may have been the most important and unfinished battleground of the postwar years, but it was only one place where activists struggled to transform American society. Just as fiercely contested—in countless local skirmishes—was the persistence of Jim Crow public accommodations in the North. It is to that battle we now turn.

CHAPTER 5

"NO PLACE FOR COLORED"

IN JUNE 1950, MARTIN LUTHER KING, JR., THEN A STUDENT AT CROZER THE-
ological Seminary in Chester, Pennsylvania, joined a group of friends for
an evening out. They crossed the Delaware River and ended up in Mary's
Café, a restaurant in Maple Shade, New Jersey, a suburb just outside
Camden. It could have been a scene from a movie—four students in a
roadster headed to a roadside diner. But our neon-tinged images of 1950s
Americana generally leave out Jim Crow. King, a native of Atlanta, had
spent his short time in the North in a cocoon of theological liberalism,
largely protected from the slings and arrows of overt racial prejudice. But
any illusions King might have held about the liberality of northern whites
were dashed when he encountered the diner's white owner, waitstaff, and
customers. When King's party arrived, the atmosphere grew tense. The
waitress refused to serve them. King and his friends refused to budge, citing New Jersey's recently enacted antidiscrimination law. The outraged
proprietor pulled a gun, threatened the students, and chased them into
the parking lot, firing a shot into the air. With the support of the local
NAACP branch, King and his friends filed a complaint against the restaurant. The case fell apart when three white witnesses—students from the
University of Pennsylvania—failed to testify.

King's experience was a reminder of the tenacity of everyday discrimination in the North—and of the countless, largely unheralded acts of resistance, organized and unorganized, against Jim Crow that peaked in the
years during and after World War II. North of the Mason-Dixon Line,
there were no official Jim Crow laws. Blacks could sit at the same lunch
counters with whites without fear of arrest; they could drink from the
same water fountains; they could use the same restrooms; they could ride
at the front of the bus and sit side by side with white passengers. "We can

go anywhere we want," King wrote home incredulously in 1944 from a Connecticut tobacco farm where he held a summer job. But, as with so many aspects of life in the North, the lack of de jure segregation did not guarantee smooth passage. Northern cities were invisibly divided by race. There were colored hotels and white hotels, Negro bars and white bars (with a few "black and tan" clubs where adventuresome whites mixed with blacks, always in black neighborhoods), black restaurants and white restaurants. Places where more "intimate" contact and family outings occurred, such as beaches and pools, remained segregated, as did venues where young people, particularly adolescents, mingled with minimal adult supervision. Most northern amusement parks, bowling alleys, and roller rinks shut their gates to blacks or allowed them to use their facilities only on special days.

Northern Jim Crow was capricious and frustrating. The "very complexity and uncertainty" of segregation, wrote sociologist Charles Johnson, "have become . . . abundant sources of confusion and discontent." Cities had widely varying reputations as hostile or relatively accommodating to black residents and visitors. While Jim Crow was commonplace in Chicago restaurants, fifty dining establishments, most of them chains, served blacks in 1946. Horace Cayton wrote a chatty article on the "best cities for Negroes" in 1947 that captured the range of experiences. Of Philadelphia: "Don't think that because they have the Liberty Bell there you can go into every restaurant—it's tightening up a bit lately." Of New York: "There are frequent infringements of civil liberties," but overall the situation there was better than most. Of "overcrowded, tense and tawdry" Los Angeles, he noted that there were few cues—other than the visible presence of blacks—as to what establishment would be welcoming or hostile, what park would be safe or dangerous, or what restaurant would require blacks to eat in the kitchen or refuse to serve them altogether. "As for sleeping," wrote a sardonic Langston Hughes, "I guess Negro travelers are not expected to sleep. Hotels and tourist camps almost uniformly refuse colored guests. Mind you, I am not asking to sleep with any white man's daughter. I merely want to SLEEP—and be on my way."

The indignities of everyday Jim Crow took a real toll among northern blacks. Kermit Bailer, born in Detroit in 1921, a Tuskegee Airman during World War II, and a civil rights activist in the postwar city, described the exhaustion of living "with racism twenty-four hours a day, seven days a week, thirty days a month, and three hundred and sixty five days a year." Bailer could have been writing about Alabama, but he wasn't. Of mid-twentieth-century Detroit, a place that many called the "northernmost southern city," Bailer's memories were bitter. "In those days, life was dominated by racial discrimination. . . . What I am talking about is living a very narrow life in a large dynamic city with a host of opportunities but for 'whites only.'" The gap between the rhetoric and reality of northern segregation also outraged many black migrants who found themselves ne-gotiating an unpredictable maze of racial proscriptions in the "promised land." Returning veterans were particularly infuriated. William M. Ashby, a longtime Urban League activist in Newark, spoke for his fellow veter-ans: "They said: 'I'm tired of all this goddam crap. Tired of hearing the white man say, "I can serve no niggers in my restaurant," tired of being told "I ain't got no place for colored in my hotel." Why, hell, I've been to Europe. Hitler leveled his bullets at me. Missed. I went to the Pacific. Mr. Hirohito sent his madmen to blow me to hell in their planes. I'm still here. Why don't I tell the white man, "Take your goddam boots off my neck!"'"

To negotiate northern Jim Crow was exhausting, demoralizing, and often dangerous. Travelers faced particular risks. Salesmen and railway workers frequently found rooms in Negro YMCAs, even though, as in New York, the Y's dormitories were usually far from train stations and bus depots. Often travelers relied on conversations with redcaps, the black porters who served white railway passengers. Some relief came with the publication of *The Negro Motorist Green-Book* in 1937, a black Baedeker that gave "the Negro traveler information that will keep him from run-ning into difficulties, embarrassments, and to make his trips more enjoy-able." Black newspapers also ran advertisements for "race" hotels and restaurants. *Ebony* published an annual summer vacation guide begin-ning in 1947, and over the course of the 1950s, several other publishers issued competing guides. In Detroit, those with money stayed at the Gotham; in Chicago, they found rooms at the Pershing on the South Side; in New York, at Harlem's Hotel Theresa. Travelers on a tight budget could usually rely on word of mouth to find someone renting out a room in a black neighborhood. Black vacationers could find cabins or tourist rooms in an archipelago of black resorts throughout the Northeast and Midwest, places from Atlantic City, New Jersey, to Idlewild, Michigan.

Even celebrities such as Josephine Baker, Paul Robeson, Dorothy Dandridge, and Marian Anderson had a hard time finding rooms and faced restaurant Jim Crow when they toured the North. When she arrived in New York from Paris in 1948, Baker and her husband were turned away from thirty-six hotels before they found a room. Paul Robeson was expelled from the lobby of Detroit's posh Book-Cadillac Hotel and refused service in an upscale San Francisco restaurant. Lena Horne was bounced from a Chicago restaurant that adopted a "members only" policy as soon as she asked for a table. An Oakland, California, restaurant made Duke Ellington's band sit at a table behind a curtain where they would not be seen by white customers. And in Minneapolis, where she had a singing engagement, Marian Anderson had to stay in the Phyllis Wheatley House, the local black YWCA, because she could not get a hotel room. In Dayton, Ohio, where hotels practiced "stringent discrimination" against blacks, Anderson found accommodations at a white hotel, but only after its staff worked out advance arrangements so she "didn't register or come anywhere near the desk." Occasionally black travelers engaged in subterfuge to get access to white-run restaurants or hotels. One troupe of actors, tired of eating in "all but the cheapest of restaurants" and staying in the "most fleabitten hotels," donned turbans and spoke in "stage gibberish" to gain entrance into white-run hotels. Those who knew foreign languages could take advantage of the ignorance of white proprietors and pass themselves off as Spanish, Arabic, or even in one case "Hebrew." But most black travelers did not risk the humiliation of being rebuffed at a hotel or treated rudely at a restaurant. Those traveling in the long stretches of the suburban and rural North where there were few if any blacks often slept in their cars. They avoided white-run businesses altogether. A public official in Atlantic City, a resort that attracted large numbers of blacks as well as whites, reported: "It is seldom a sensible colored man will thrust himself in where he is not wanted."

What made northern racial barriers so frustrating was that they were sometimes as hard and fast as they were in the South—but, at the same time, they could also be surprisingly and unpredictably flexible. The rules of racial engagement in the North were seldom posted. And a countervailing set of rules—state civil rights laws, many dating to the nineteenth century—promised blacks that the strong arm of the law would be on their side. By World War II, eighteen northern states had civil rights laws that forbade discrimination or segregation in public accommodations. But the exclusion of blacks from hotels, stores, restaurants, and recreation centers in the North operated in a strange gray zone, blurring distinctions between "private" and "public." Exclusion was the consequence of private actions, sometimes backed by legal sanctions but seldom encoded strictly in the law. As L. D. Reddick complained in 1944, "despite the absence of Jim Crow laws," northern Jim Crow was widespread. Michigan, for example, had a law dating back to 1885, strengthened in 1937, forbidding discrimination by race. But when the Michigan Commission on Civil Rights issued a report in 1948, it noted the "daily humiliation" blacks faced when they were denied access to restaurants, hotels, and even some stores in Michigan. As late as 1960, Carl Fuqua, head of the Chicago NAACP branch, complained that "nobody pays any attention to the laws against discrimination if they don't want to." As long as "local opinion" was "often pro-segregationist," laws were honored in the breach.

Police officers, in particular, played a critical role in enforcing the segregation of public places. Northern protests at bars, restaurants, hotels, and amusement parks did not usually bring down the full wrath of officialdom, because unlike in the South, challenges to Jim Crow were not usually affronts to the state. But regardless of the law, northern police officers were seldom sympathetic to blacks who attempted to cross the color line. Often they stood aside indifferently, unwilling to intervene in what they viewed as disputes between private parties. They regularly discounted black complaints and frequently arrested black complainants for "disorderly conduct." Police-community relations, already tense in the aftermath of wartime riots, worsened with every such incident. What good were laws against racial discrimination if they were not enforced? Still, Reddick and many other activists were optimistic that state civil rights laws could be a powerful tool to challenge segregation. "The law is on the Negro's side in his fight for equal rights." Throughout the North, during the war, ordinary blacks stepped up their challenge to racial barriers in public accommodations—using civil rights law, however weakly enforced, as one tool to force change.

The exclusion of blacks from stores, movie theaters, and public parks made for an obvious, appealing target. What embodied the promise of the American consumer culture more than a restaurant, movie theater, or pool? Why should blacks be treated like pariahs by white waiters or hoteliers? Protests at hotels, amusement parks, and stores were also an expression of an emerging consumerist rights consciousness. One of the promises of mid-twentieth-century America was "the good life," promoted in ubiquitous advertisements, in periodicals, and in political speeches. Access to consumer goods—the right to buy—was a defining characteristic of what it meant to be an American citizen. Did not blacks have the right to partake fully in America's consumer culture? The face might be black, but as the folk saying went, "all money is green." To Cold War–era civil rights activists, the creation of a race-neutral economy was an essential step toward full citizenship.

Civil rights organizations had practical reasons for challenging commercial Jim Crow. Most local activist groups between the Depression and the 1960s were very small. Protests against segregated businesses did not require a mass mobilization. Juanita Nelson, a Cleveland-based activist in the 1940s, noted that "all you had to do was get a few people to sit in a restaurant or stand in front of a theater box office." Her civil rights organization, the Cleveland chapter of the Congress of Racial Equality, was small and had limited resources. To make a splash, her cell of protestors needed clear targets and quick victories. "Public accommodations," she recalled, "was easier than anything else to try to crack. It was a lot easier than employment. Job discrimination was harder to prove. How do you prove that somebody was qualified for a job[?]" By contrast, with carefully devised strategies, activists could prove that commercial establishments had turned them away and use the evidence they gathered to pressure businesses to accept black customers or face legal repercussions.

Protestors found their staunchest allies in the black press, which had expanded in scope and scale to include the national periodicals *Ebony* (1945) and *Jet* (1951). One of *Jet*'s first stories, combining an interest in celebrity and civil rights, reported on efforts to revoke the license of New York's famed Stork Club for rebuffing Josephine Baker. Local papers in particular filled their pages with coverage of efforts to gain access to restaurants and theaters, open up amusement parks, and desegregate swimming pools and roller rinks. "These things," wrote one commentator, "are more tangible evidence of freedom and acceptance to the average Negro than the passage of state civil rights laws." Ordinary blacks felt outrage at coverage of Jim Crow and elation at the accounts of the many triumphs against it. At stake was black dignity. But getting the attention of

the white-dominated news media was much more difficult. White journalists almost completely ignored public accommodations protests, because most protests were on such a small scale, often initiated by a few
activists or by small groups unknown to white journalists. In addition, the
targets of protest were diffuse—after all, not all enterprises discriminated
against blacks. To most whites, even public officials, the northern freedom struggle was often invisible.

Crusading black papers were not alone among the media covering the
freedom struggle, but they were the most important. Beginning in the late
1930s, advocates of better race relations began using the relatively new
medium of radio. Public affairs radio broadcasts on such topics as black
history and the black contribution to the war were part of the battle to
change the "hearts and minds" of white Americans. Radio programs
brought black issues into the public sphere in an unprecedented fashion,
but they had serious limitations. National broadcasts reached wider audiences than the black press, but they remained firmly under the control of
white broadcasters, scriptwriters, and directors. Major network programming on "Negro issues" was, in the words of an astute critic, "tossed . . .
without continuity into the radio flood . . . with the awkward flavor of
conscious 'tolerance.'" Filling in the gap, to some extent, were union-
sponsored radio programs, which used the airwaves to promote antidiscrimination legislation and racial tolerance. But the impact of such
programs on both black and white audiences was limited. Black listeners
found inspiration in broadcast accounts of their history, but, scattered stations excepted, radio did not serve the same mobilizing purposes as did
the print media.

It would not be until the 1950s and 1960s—as radio became more
local, white-run companies began to recognize the commercial potential
of black-oriented programming, and blacks began to gain control of
broadcast licenses—that radio began to complement the press as a resource for organizing. Black ministers found large audiences for their sermons on black-oriented stations. Some, such as Detroit's C. L. Franklin,
who began broadcasting in the early 1950s, powerfully combined Christianity and black liberation. Detroit's WDET, a union-sponsored station,
dramatically expanded its black programming and, along with popular
music, ran programs on housing and workplace discrimination. By the
late 1950s—when there were some six hundred black-oriented stations

around the country—disc jockeys such as Philadelphia's Georgie Woods began to weave together music and political commentary. Woods was an entertainer with a mission. Like many of his counterparts, he advertised products to black consumers, introduced listeners to new music, but also used his forum to announce mass meetings and rallies. Together, black newspapers and radio built local solidarity and shaped a consciousness of civil rights and protest.

The northern battle to open up public accommodations would last a long time and would be fought little by little, place by place, in countless small skirmishes that went largely unnoticed outside a small circle of activists and readers of the black press. The struggles against northern-style Jim Crow were fiercely contested, but grassroots activists gradually expanded blacks' access to public places and, more than that, reminded ordinary blacks of the difficulty and efficacy of protest. It would not be until the late 1950s—and in some places the 1960s—that the struggle to open northern accommodations would be more or less won. Activists chipped away at the customs that separated the races until the sight of blacks at northern lunch counters, hotel lobbies, theaters, and amusement parks was not unusual—at least in big cities.

The motivations in the struggle against Jim Crow were as many as the participants themselves. Communists deliberately flouted racial segregation in their effort to promote "social equality" and pushed particularly hard against whites' deepest fears of racial mixing and interracial intimacy. In the 1940s, the newly founded Congress of Racial Equality viewed integrated public accommodations as a precursor to the creation of a "beloved community," where black and white people could break bread together in peace. Unionists, particularly those in left-led, interracial unions, knew that the process of building union solidarity required fostering ties between workers on the shop floor and in the bars and restaurants where they socialized at the end of the day. Others, particularly racial liberals, decided to test the North's rarely enforced antidiscrimination laws. Many ordinary blacks simply wanted to order a cup of coffee or get a sandwich or stay in a hotel without being harassed.

Most civil rights activists saw their efforts to open up public accommodations as a matter of honor. They chafed against the petty humiliations of Jim Crow. Their battle was based on a simple premise: Blacks had the same right to consume that whites did. But the direction of the battle against segregated institutions revealed a lot about both the changing strategies of civil rights activists—particularly a shift from uplift to direct action and protest—and the deep-seated fears of blacks that pervaded northern popular culture. The battle against Jim Crow exposed white fears of black intimacy and black sexuality. Those fears were intertwined with notions of public and private—distinctions particularly blurry in the public sphere of commerce. The more public the place, that is, the more anonymous, the more likely antisegregation activists would succeed. The more intimate the institution—the closer it got to the family and to taboos against interracial sexuality—the more difficult the fights were.

MOVIE THEATERS WERE AMONG the most extravagant buildings of the early twentieth century, veritable palaces of popular culture, decked out in neo-Egyptian finery or Art Nouveau extravagance, or, in the 1930s, lined with the sleek stainless steel and brass tracery of Art Deco. With their architecture of fantasy and luxury, movie palaces stood apart from the dreary shacks and shoddy tenements blacks often inhabited and the decaying commercial districts where they shopped and socialized. Garnished with neon lights and flashy marquees, plastered with posters, theaters embodied the extravagance of Hollywood, promising patrons entry into a world wholly detached from their own. During the summer, theaters offered an escape from the heat traps of crowded, poorly ventilated inner-city apartments: They were among the first places in America to introduce air-conditioning. No amusement in mid-twentieth-century America was more popular: Between 1930 and 1950, more than eighty million people saw movies every week.

It was fortuitous that movie palaces sprang up in cities just as black migrants flooded northward. Southern blacks were awed by the fantastic world of big-city theaters, which often presented musical performances as well as films. Civil rights groups quickly turned their attention to the silver screen. The NAACP led the way. After all, the NAACP had arisen nearly contemporaneously with Hollywood itself. In one of its earliest crusades, NAACP activists protested the runaway hit *The Birth of a Nation*, whose blackface villains, deferential mammies, and heroic Confederates embodied prevailing racial stereotypes. In the 1930s, NAACP activists targeted *Gone with the Wind* for its wistful portrayal of plantation life. And *Amos 'n' Andy*, whose bowing and scraping protagonists were the latter-day version of the hated minstrel shows, faced black criticism from its first screening in 1930, not to mention its radio broadcasts and its short-lived television run. Civil rights activists did not merely target the image of blacks in popular culture—they demanded the right to watch.

The black experience in movie theaters—as with so much Jim Crow in the North—varied from place to place. "Many theaters in the North," noted Gunnar Myrdal in 1944, "refuse to let a Negro enter, or if they are in a state with a civil rights law, they try to find some excuse to make him stay away voluntarily." In Dayton, Ohio, theater managers "discourage[d] Negro patronage" by inflating ticket prices for black customers. In many cities, black moviegoers were confined to neighborhood movie theaters that often showed second-run movies. In other places, where they had access to downtown movie palaces, they were relegated to the side aisles or balconies—sardonically called "buzzard roosts," "crows' nests," or "nigger heaven." Denver's largest theaters regularly segregated black patrons: One theater rang a bell to beckon ushers to escort black ticket holders to the balcony. Another gave special red tickets to black patrons, good only for upstairs seating. And a third gave blacks tickets stamped "Good only in the upper right balcony." In Springfield, Ohio, still only partially reformed from its Klan days, the ironically named Liberty Theater screened out blacks by posting an "Invitation Only" sign at its entrance in the mid-1940s, which remained in place until a group of Antioch College students led a "stand-in" protest there in 1961. "Who says segregation exists only in the South????" charged one of the demonstrators.

In cinema, as with so many other aspects of northern Jim Crow, the color line seldom buckled or broke on its own. In cities with large, well-established black communities, the battle against Jim Crow in the theaters was largely fought and won in the 1920s. In Great Migration–era Chicago, black patrons were sometimes admitted to downtown movie theaters and occasionally confined to balconies. Most blacks, however, attended movie houses in their own neighborhoods, which few whites patronized. Over the 1920s, local activists targeted the downtown theaters, usually owned by large chains. This proved to be a farsighted strategy. As the chains moved into neighborhoods, gobbling up dozens of small, independent cinemas, they followed corporate policy and opened their doors to blacks. In *Black Metropolis*, Horace Cayton and St. Clair

Drake reported that "discrimination against Negroes in downtown movie theaters was virtually non-existent and only a few neighborhood houses tried to Jim-Crow Negroes."

Philadelphia's battle against theater Jim Crow foreshadowed many later fights. In the mid-1920s, Raymond Pace Alexander, a Harvard-educated lawyer and rising star among the city's black elite, defended a group of schoolteachers who had been rebuffed from the Aldine, a downtown movie palace. The teachers were ideal plaintiffs. Members of respectable black families, they were soft-spoken, professional, light-skinned, and of a better class than many white moviegoers. Alexander highlighted the plaintiffs' educational attainment and high status, winning the sympathy of the judge, who ruled against the theater. Throughout the late 1920s and 1930s, Alexander (whose national influence grew in this period) continued to deploy the most respectable plaintiffs, playing up their class rather than their racial identities, and successfully challenged segregation in other theaters, golf clubs, hotels, and restaurants. But litigation was a scattershot strategy to combat segregation. Opening one hotel or theater to blacks, unless it was part of a chain, did not usually have a domino effect. If they were not directly challenged on a case-by-case basis, the barriers of Jim Crow fell slowly.

By the 1930s, the movie business had become big business. In the heyday of the silver screen, after the introduction of "talkies," major chains largely supplanted local, independent theaters in most cities. A successful protest against a single company could open dozens of theaters to black patrons at once. Around the North, activists took on the chains. In 1940 and 1941, Cincinnati's NAACP chapter pursued a two-pronged strategy of resistance and litigation to desegregate the Queen City's theaters. *The Crisis* promoted it to NAACP branches nationwide. James Smith, a "brilliant student and star athlete" at the University of Cincinnati, approached the ticket window of an RKO theater downtown. Behind him in line—unbeknownst to the theater staff or management—were three white witnesses. "This house does not sell tickets to niggers," snarled a theater staff member. At that point, Smith, "polite, intelligent, controlled, and fearless," walked away.

Smith became a plaintiff in a lawsuit against RKO Midwestern Theatre Corporation. Under Ohio law, he had the right to purchase a ticket and enter the theater unhindered. But RKO and other theater operators usually dodged their legal obligations. In court, a plaintiff had to prove that race was the "sole basis" for refusal of admission. Overt expressions of racial prejudice were taboo, but ticket sellers generally engaged in subterfuge to prevent blacks from buying tickets, to stick within the letter of the law. Ticket sellers informed black customers that machines were out of order or "use[d] any appropriate phrase short of an unequivocal refusal." Other ticket agents engaged in "sit-downs," stopping work while a black was at the counter, angering customers in line, and forcing the black customer to give up his place. But in Smith's case, the presence of white witnesses (presumably blacks would not have been credible) bolstered his legal position.

Smith's "attack" on RKO was part of a larger strategy to target the chain's "fashionable" theaters. After Smith's rebuff, Cincinnati activists elaborately orchestrated "theater excursions," where blacks would attempt to purchase tickets. The key was finding litigants, like Smith, who would be soft-spoken, well dressed, and, in every way, nonthreatening. "Parties who were too argumentative and too belligerent," noted the architects of Cincinnati's theater strategy, "made very poor prospective patrons." Accompanying the suitable black patron were white witnesses, who stood "immediately behind the Negro principals" and were "directed to witness all verbal and physical facts of the refusal, purchase tickets of admission, and to attend the performance." Each "excursion" was carefully rehearsed, to "anticipate and outwit" theater managers.

Excursion parties descended on the city's eight RKO theaters simultaneously. They took places in every ticket line and stood still while flummoxed ticket sellers—mum because of the prohibition against overt racial discrimination—simply refused to speak to the protestors. The actions shut down business at the theaters for anywhere from five minutes to a half hour. While activists gummed up the works at the theaters, launching dozens of excursions, local NAACP attorneys engaged in what they called "vexatious litigation," tying up RKO's lawyers by refusing the company's settlement offers. Finally, on May 24, 1941, after nearly a year of protests and costly legal proceedings, RKO opened its doors to black patrons.

The victory in Cincinnati, like its precursor in Philadelphia, was a triumph of the politics of respectability. Black theatergoers used the wedge of the law and wrapped themselves in the mantle of class status to push open theater doors. The battle to open theaters proved to be relatively easy. Chain theaters were easy targets. Downtown shopping districts in most northern cities were already heterogeneous by the 1940s (much to the chagrin of white businesses that feared that the presence of sizeable numbers of blacks would scare off their white, female clientele). But the victories in the battle against silver screen Jim Crow were more symbolic than real. In the wake of protests, whites often abandoned downtown theaters, leaving them to blacks. And as growing numbers of whites moved to the suburbs, cinemas usually followed. Given the ferocity with which whites defended their turf against blacks, few, if any, blacks ventured into white neighborhoods to watch films. The battle to open theaters would not be fatal to northern Jim Crow.

DURING WORLD WAR II, protestors turned to another obvious target: restaurants and bars. Protests against culinary Jim Crow would be far more diverse—in the types of activists they attracted, their targets, and their strategies—than their cinematic predecessors. "For many years, I have been puzzled as to where and how America expects Negro travelers to eat," lamented Langston Hughes. "At least a hundred times (making a conservative estimate) I have been refused service in public restaurants in strange cities." Horace Cayton and St. Clair Drake found that Chicago's blacks were most likely to be refused service in "exclusive" establishments and in restaurants and bars along the border of black neighborhoods. They were most likely to be served in the "city's popular priced restaurants." Unlike in the South, where dime store lunch counters became the symbol of Jim Crow, in the North, where blacks frequented discount stores in downtown shopping districts, Woolworth's and Kresge's usually welcomed them. The cafeterias in these stores were places of convenience and anonymity, not intimacy. But local customs, even in chain stores, varied. In Topeka, Kansas, for example, blacks were expected to stand at lunch counters even if seats were vacant. And throughout the North, many restaurants consigned blacks to separate seating, especially at rear tables near kitchen doors. Others complied with the letter of the law by admitting black customers, but overcharged them or served them inedible food.

The barriers were firmer in neighborhood restaurants. In many communities, restaurants and bars were part and parcel of the fabric of every-day life. They served food and drink but also provided places for patrons to gather, build networks, and nurture friendships and relationships. What would be the fate of these local establishments in the racially fluid wartime city? Would a white bartender in a transitional neighborhood admit a black customer? If so, would white patrons perceive the place as a "black and tan" or "Negro" bar and stop coming? Should a restaurant remain an all-white outpost amid racial change?

The enormous influx of black migrants northward put unprecedented pressure on racial boundaries. Bars and restaurants—many of which were on the major streets that often served as racial dividing lines—were often the first commercial establishments to confront racial change. In Portland, Oregon, where the black population expanded during World War II, café owners placed signs in their windows reading "We cater to white trade only." Blacks all over the North confronted the color line in bars and restaurants around large factories. Before World War II, the many beer-and-a-shot bars seldom had to face the question of race. But during the war, as black workers found themselves in steel mills, auto plants, and aircraft manufactories for the first time, where would they buy an after-work drink? Shift-change bars served a number of functions other than providing refreshment to workers after a grueling day on the assembly line. It was an axiom among union organizers that working-class taverns were great places to organize—for there, over a drink, work-ers complained about their jobs, traded information, and talked politics. Many bars near factories also served an economic function. On payday, they cashed workers' paychecks, so the workers could take home money for the weekend, when banks were closed. But the appearance of a black person at the wrong bar outside the factory gates could lead to fisticuffs or worse.

To challenge segregation at bars and restaurants, then, had several lay-ers of meaning. Most simply, protestors demanded their consumer rights—the right to eat and drink, to spend their money, where they pleased. It was also a matter of respect. Blacks should be treated just like whites, rather than suffering the hassle that usually came with setting foot in a "white" establishment. And in cities with rapidly growing black populations—of both shoppers and workers—there was a certain prag-matism to challenging restaurant discrimination. It gave blacks access to more choices and, as a result, better quality and fairer prices. Chicago activist Wanda Penny remembered that "the emphasis was on public accommodations because that was where a great need was. If you had ever tried to eat downtown, as I did, and been refused service, you would have seen the need to do something about public accommodations. Even before CORE started there were a few Negroes who would 'sit in' places to try to get service."

Challenging restaurant segregation, protestors believed, would undermine the exclusive sense of community that shaped whites' understandings of everyday life. If you are what you eat, you are also where you eat. The lack of casual racial mixing in taverns and bars reinforced ideas that blacks and whites "naturally" congregated with their own kind, and it made impossible the ordinary interactions—the rubbing of shoulders, the sharing of miseries, the experience of cheering for a team—that broke down the barriers that separated people in other arenas. It would be all the more difficult to create an integrated society, a place where color differences truly did not matter, if blacks and whites were forbidden from socializing in the most routine, everyday ways. For upwardly mobile blacks, segregation jeopardized their still-precarious class status. The indignity of exclusion was particularly acute for blacks on the make who moved to upper-middle-class suburbs such as Plainfield, New Jersey, where few establishments catered to them. A good meal might mean a half-hour drive to Newark because in 1947 blacks were systematically excluded from five of eight downtown restaurants and three hotels.

The most important wartime challenges to commercial segregation came from a handful of radical Christian activists—James Farmer, Bayard Rustin, and George Houser—who wove together many of the strands of 1930s radical activism. Farmer was the son of the dean of Mississippi's Rust College (where Anna Arnold Hedgeman had briefly taught). As a student in religion at Howard, he had imbibed the Social Gospel from one of its most luminous theologians, Howard Thurman. Thurman was both an intellectual mentor and sympathetic to Farmer's growing radicalism. In 1940, Thurman helped place Farmer with the pacifist Fellowship of Reconciliation. Raised a Quaker in West Chester, Pennsylvania, Rustin had briefly moved through the Communist Party and had found his way to the Fellowship of Reconciliation as a pacifist opponent of World War II. Houser had been a student at Union Theological Seminary in New York, another important center of Social Gospel teaching during the Depression. An opponent of World War II, Houser had worked to integrate the federal prison in Danbury, Connecticut, where he served nearly two years for draft resistance, before returning to Chicago as an activist. All had spent time reading and discussing the work of Mohandas K. Gandhi—and began to think systematically about the ways that satyagraha, or nonviolent resistance, could become a vehicle for achieving racial equality.

Rustin, Houser, and Farmer shared a common benefactor, A. J. Muste, the director of the Fellowship of Reconciliation (FOR). Founded at the outset of World War I, the FOR brought together Socialists, pacifists, members of peace churches, and other opponents of war. Muste was a charismatic leader who had ties to nearly every faction of the left. A supporter of Norman Thomas, Muste followed a circular path from the ministry (in the Dutch Reformed Church) to secular leftism (as a unionist, labor educator, Socialist activist, and founder of the small American Workers Party) and back to religion again after a "mystical" experience in a European monastery in the mid-1930s. By the time Muste took the helm of the FOR, its members had fashioned an eclectic organizing strategy that combined Christian communitarianism, the Bolshevik notion of the "vanguard," and Gandhian principles. In Harlem, Newark, and later Chicago, FOR activists formed radical "cells" and "ashrams," racially mixed, egalitarian households where they would live out their vision of an alternative America and, more practically, create base camps for radical organizing. Muste also had close ties to A. Philip Randolph and lent his organizational support to the March on Washington Movement. In 1941, Muste sent two young FOR organizers, Rustin and Farmer, to Randolph's fledgling organization, where they tutored the labor activist in the philosophy and strategy of nonviolent resistance. Rustin became one of Randolph's closest aides. Farmer also traveled throughout the country in early 1942, speaking to FOR chapters in Milwaukee, Madison, Pittsburgh, Cleveland, and Detroit. The network they created covered a large part of America's non-Communist left, including trade unions, the Workers' Defense League, Quakers, Social Gospellers, Socialists, and grassroots antiwar and civil rights activists.

In 1942, Farmer and Houser began laying the groundwork for what would become the Congress of Racial Equality (CORE), again with financial and staff support from the fellowship. Their vision was a holistic one:

They hoped to live the reality of a transformed society by embodying the ideal of nonviolence and Christian brotherhood, without respect to the distinctions of race. CORE activists did not simply seek to overthrow Jim Crow. Interracialism was not solely for the picket line or the meeting. For CORE activists, it was essential to practice what they preached. They set out to create, in their own everyday lives, a model of the ideal interracial society. Many early CORE members formed interracial households, like one in the neighborhood just south of the University of Chicago. At its meetings, black and white CORE members shared dorm or hotel rooms and, in an act redolent with biblical (and Gandhian) symbolism, "broke bread" together. Their lived interracialism collided with white northern customs.

Not surprisingly, activists in the newly formed CORE chose restaurant desegregation for some of their earliest "direct action" protests. In late 1942, they chose two targets: Jack Spratt, near the University of Chicago, and Stoner's, in the Loop. Both restaurants were openly hostile to black customers, with staff engaging in petty forms of harassment. They ignored interracial tables, threatened black customers, and served inedible dishes (one sandwich consisted of "lettuce and tomato cores picked out of the garbage can" on bread). CORE's tactics began with diplomacy and negotiation, moved to protest, and eventually resulted in a "sit-in." James Robinson, an early CORE member, recalled that Chicago activists were "interested in radical politics and sympathetic toward labor." They borrowed their tactics from the famous sit-down strikes in the "early UAW days, when people were using their bodies to occupy something." In May 1943, CORE activists descended en masse on the Jack Spratt restaurant, occupied every table, and refused to leave until their interracial parties were served. Flush from their success at Spratt, activists from CORE's first annual convention descended on Stoner's in June 1943, blockading the restaurant's doors to "interfere with the normal passage of patrons to and from the place," creating a ruckus that forced that establishment to serve blacks.

CORE activists knew that striking a blow at Jim Crow restaurants would not alone remake race relations in the United States. Robinson acknowledged that "the [Jack Spratt] case is minor ... but all such small cases are important—in the aggregate they make up a significant persecution of the Negro race." In the wake of the Chicago protests, A. Philip

Randolph promoted CORE's strategy of nonviolence in articles and speeches. He called for resistance to segregation in public accommodations, to be coordinated by "trained and disciplined groups of leaders, young people and students prepared in advance to contest the practices of segregation and discrimination." Mixed-race teams would test the compliance of a restaurant or shop, followed by "efforts" to convince the manager or proprietor that his actions violated the U.S. Constitution or state laws. If negotiations failed, resistance would escalate to include legal action and finally pickets or a "sit down strike in the place to bring the issue to a head." White retaliation, argued Randolph, was to be "considered as part of the price which must be paid, in sacrifice and suffering, to eliminate an evil which has been acquiesced in and permitted to exist by the inaction and fear of the Negro people." For nonviolent resisters, CORE published a step-by-step guide for challenging restaurant discrimination. Through a process of "investigation, negotiation, public pressure and education, demonstration, and noncooperation," small groups of protestors could break down Jim Crow and offer a practical demonstration of the tactic of "non-violent direct action." The process, especially maintaining "the spirit of non-retaliation and goodwill," was just as important as the outcome itself.

CORE saw the challenge to restaurant segregation, both its techniques and its goals, as the first step toward building the beloved community. But other left-wing activists had more instrumental reasons for trying to undermine Jim Crow. They too had a vision of community—but it differed significantly from CORE's. Black and white solidarity was a necessary precursor to class struggle. The division of the working class by race thwarted potential revolutionary solidarity. As early as 1929, small bands of Communists—following the Party's directive to draw attention to racial inequality—targeted restaurants, parks, and hotels. White party members regularly sponsored racially mixed dances and held racially mixed house parties, often to their neighbors' chagrin. Party members openly flouting "bourgeois" conventions also frequently engaged in interracial sexual relationships and sometimes married across the color line. Not to be outdone by the Communists, the Workers' Defense League engaged in its own protests, challenging segregation at O'Gara's Bar, a popular hangout for labor organizers in New York, and in a series of Manhattan hotels (in conjunction with the United Automobile Workers). The WDL's Milton

Henry (later a CORE Freedom Rider and, after that, a major figure in black power) led a group of fellow Lincoln University students who challenged a segregated restaurant in Oxford, Pennsylvania.

In Detroit, the battle against restaurant Jim Crow was led by the UAW's left-wing caucus, which had attracted the majority of the city's black autoworkers because of its outspoken demands for racial equality. The UAW, which had effectively reached out to blacks in its organizing drives of the late 1930s and early 1940s, confronted Jim Crow in the many bars and restaurants around auto factories. The intense rights consciousness of wartime black workers moved seamlessly from support for public housing, to demands for black union leadership, to efforts to integrate union-sponsored bowling leagues. Over the course of the war, black workers became increasingly confrontational, engaging in walkouts over shop-floor discrimination. Black and white Communists, who made up a small but highly influential minority in the UAW, socialized together after union gatherings, part of a deliberate strategy to build interracial solidarity. Even interracial dancing—which could provoke a lynch mob in the South—was not taboo at UAW events. At a meeting of workers at the Dodge Main plant, just before a union-sponsored dance, a Communist union official pronounced, "If whites and Negroes want to dance together at the social, they will dance. . . . Those who don't want to see this don't have to come."

What better place to address racial inequalities than right outside the factory gates? Opening the bars and restaurants that catered to the city's working class would be one important step toward the construction of a new social order of racial and economic equality. Black autoworkers, in collaboration with the local NAACP chapter and the Civil Rights Congress, led the drive "to break down the restaurants," using Michigan's 1937 Diggs Act, which forbade discrimination by race in restaurants and stores, as their legal wedge. Sometimes their tactics were creative. In one restaurant where waitresses refused to serve black customers, NAACP youth workers went to the cafeteria line instead—getting their way. On the city's East Side, black Chrysler and Hudson workers targeted restaurants around their plants, calling the police and threatening to press charges unless the proprietors signed an agreement to refrain from discrimination. James Boggs and Ernest Dillard, Sr., two autoworkers and leftist activists, led the effort to "break down" restaurant Jim Crow. Dillard rode the streetcar from downtown Detroit out past Grand Boulevard. "I got off and went into every place on the way back to downtown," he recalled. "Didn't a single one serve me. I was getting what you folks now call raw data. If I would ask for coffee, they would say, 'We don't serve coffee.' " Armed with a list of Jim Crow coffee shops, Dillard and Boggs recruited fellow autoworkers and sent them out to challenge them one by one. They too combined outward respectability with the tactic of nonviolence. "You go in there; you comb your hair; you wear your tie; and I don't care what the hell they do to you, don't respond." Their little interracial army picketed, filed complaints, and went back again and again until they would "break it up."

Whether organized by leftist unionists or part of the new Gandhian strategy of CORE and Randolph, protests against restaurant Jim Crow were covered by local black papers and had a snowball effect. Throughout the North, ordinary blacks, often not part of concerted desegregation efforts, took matters into their own hands. By the end of World War II, civil rights organizations were flooded with complaints by individuals who had been denied service in white-run restaurants. Many of them lacked the restraint of nonviolent activists. One customer denied service at Detroit's Kuhn Tea Room challenged a belligerent waitress "to come out from behind that counter" and fight. Another black Detroiter, Lonnie Saunders, sat at a restaurant counter until he was told that "Negroes were served in the kitchen only." Saunders went to a pay phone, called the police to report that he had been refused service, returned to his seat at the counter, and demanded service. The daughter of the restaurant owner flayed Saunders with a rubber hose; he gave her a black eye, and both faced assault and battery charges. Occasionally, attempts to breach restaurant segregation turned fatal. On a winter night in early 1946 in Freeport, Long Island, brothers Charles, Joseph, Richard, and Alphonzo Ferguson argued with a white restaurant owner who refused to serve them coffee. A police officer summoned to handle the "misbehaving Negroes" arrested the brothers, lined them up against a wall, kicked them, and then shot two of them dead and injured a third. A Davenport, Iowa, veteran killed a restaurant owner who threatened him when he demanded service (he was acquitted on grounds of self-defense).

Faced with mounting evidence of a grassroots rebellion against restaurant Jim Crow, the NAACP's *Crisis* printed a "how to" manual for the growing number of ordinary blacks resisting discrimination in public places.

(1) If refused service, ask to see the manager. Ask to be served something which is in stock or in sight such as coffee, pie, etc.

(2) If you have no witness, call the police. . . .

(3) In the presence of the officers, again place your order. . . .

(4) Go to precinct station. . . . Tell the detectives you wish to swear out a warrant for violation of the civil rights law. . . .

(5) Be polite at all times. Avoid creating a disturbance either in the establishment refusing service or the police station.

The key to effective protest, argued the NAACP, was avoiding violence—and simply demanding that local civil rights laws be enforced.

Antisegregation protestors also directly challenged the police, the courts, and the legal system, demanding the enforcement of civil rights laws already on the books. But getting public officials to take discrimination cases seriously was difficult. In Chicago and Detroit, police officers often refused to intervene in discrimination disputes, preferring to let the disputants work things out themselves and getting involved only if violence ensued. Prosecutors were often reluctant to take up cases involving "persons usually regarded in the community as 'responsible businessmen' acting in a way not regarded as wrong by local residents." Many northern courts, even if they ruled on behalf of plaintiffs, did not award damages sufficient to cover court costs. Still, NAACP chapters, local civil rights groups, and individuals filed suits against Jim Crow restaurants throughout the North in the 1930s and 1940s. In places as diverse as Cassopolis, Michigan; Columbus, Ohio; Newark, New Jersey; Chicago; and Detroit, activists demanded the enforcement of civil rights laws already on the books. One of the more creative campaigns involved the Vanguard League, a civil rights group in Columbus that filed fourteen simultaneous lawsuits against restaurants in 1942. Juries were often sympathetic to white defendants. In a 1947 Detroit case, involving discrimination at Greenfield's restaurant, which activists had targeted since 1940, a jury found the restaurant manager innocent after the defense asserted that the plaintiff was party to an NAACP plot to "create a disturbance." In many cases, white juries did not find black complainants credible. Detroit's

Ernest Dillard discovered that "in the process of breaking down restaurants, you just couldn't make a legal case unless you had some white folks with you." Sometimes restaurant discrimination activists found allies in high places, though more out of fears of disorder than any fealty to anti-discrimination laws. In Portland, Oregon, a 1945 campaign to force restaurants to remove their Jim Crow signs won the reluctant support of Mayor Earl Riley. Riley believed (wrongly) that such signs were legal under Oregon law but nonetheless instructed police to "remove the obnoxious placards." Only after five years of agitation did Portland's city council outlaw discrimination in restaurants.

Restaurants became a proving ground for tactics that—when they were successful—shaped other battles against discrimination. One of the most important was "testing." Avoiding outright confrontation, interracial teams visited restaurants, documented Jim Crow, and testified against it. A black tester would demand service in a restaurant; if denied, a white tester would be seated and ask to be served. The evidence would be used to challenge a restaurant, to file a complaint with a civil rights group, or to initiate litigation. In Cincinnati, the Citizen's Committee for Human Rights (a CORE affiliate) sent teams of testers, black and white, to downtown restaurants. At the root of testing was the depressing recognition —as Dillard described—that black complainants would not be taken seriously. It took white witnesses to "prove" segregation.

By the early 1950s, testing strategies grew more elaborate. After a spate of discrimination complaints in New York City in 1951, Olivia Frost, a black sociologist, formed the Committee on Civil Rights in East Manhattan. Building on the experience of previous activists, Frost's committee, with the assistance of psychologist Kenneth Clark, turned restaurant testing into a science. One hundred and fifty-three volunteer testers divided into black teams and white teams, matched by sex and economic status, to visit restaurants on Manhattan's East Side. Assiduously, they gathered data. Their reports were mixed, reflecting the liberality of New York on one hand but the persistence of petty harassment on the other. No restaurants refused service to black customers, but black diners were ill treated—seated in separate areas, served inferior food, rushed along, or overcharged in about 40 percent of the establishments. Frost's publicity efforts were effective. A coalition of restaurateurs' and waiters' unions pledged to eliminate discriminatory practices. When Frost directed a repeat of the survey in 1952, she found that far fewer restaurants mistreated black customers. Between 1953 and 1960, the committee received only seven complaints. The fear of negative publicity, especially in a liberal bastion such as New York, effectively deterred discrimination.

Habits would change, but it took sustained pressure to break down the barriers of Jim Crow in much of the North. Throughout the 1950s, the black press reported local struggles to desegregate public accommodations, from big cities to small towns in places as far-flung as Wyoming, Arizona, Oregon, Illinois, and Ohio. In Canonsburg, Pennsylvania, a small NAACP branch won victories against discrimination in local restaurants and in the community pool, inspiring Father Edward Richards, "a stout-hearted white Catholic priest," to sue the Boykas Tavern in nearby Finleyville, where Richards and a black companion were denied service. Activists in Atlantic City and Los Angeles adopted similar techniques, mostly operating in a scattered, haphazard way throughout the decade. Public pressure and the willingness of activists to take their complaints to state agencies weakened restaurant Jim Crow. By the mid-1950s, state antidiscrimination agencies still heard dozens of individual complaints about discrimination in public accommodations, but the intensity of battles weakened.

In many places, however, Jim Crow went down only after prolonged struggle. In Kansas, local activists had pushed since the 1940s for an ordinance forbidding discrimination in public accommodations. In Wichita and Kansas City, local CORE and NAACP chapters challenged segregated restaurants and hotels but won only piecemeal victories. Most of the state's businesses were untouched by protest and immune from the law. In July 1958, however, a group of students in Wichita, led by Ronald Walters, later a well-known political scientist, staged nearly four weeks of sit-ins at a Rexall drugstore lunch counter, generating sympathy for the cause, opening up some downtown restaurants, and attracting national attention. Walters and fellow members of the local NAACP youth council gathered in a church basement, where they "simulated the environment of the lunch counter and went through the drill of sitting and role-playing what might happen. We took turns playing the white folks with laughter, dishing out the embarrassment that might come our way." The white resistance they faced was no laughing matter. The protests took an ominous turn when members of a local motorcycle gang taunted the protestors and the local police refused to offer protection. "I have orders to keep our hands off of this," whispered a police officer to the store manager. The situation was defused only when carloads of black community members showed up at the drugstore (beckoned by a phone call from Walters). In Wichita, as in much of the North, nonviolent protests and black self-defense were inseparable.

Finally, in 1960, Kansas City activists succeeded in pushing through an antidiscrimination ordinance. But they faced a whirlwind of resistance— much more organized than in places that had long-standing, if unenforced, laws. A group of mostly small businesses, led by tavern owners, fought the ordinance in court, while building a grassroots movement that branded civil rights activists as Communists and offered a libertarian defense of "freedom of choice." Argued one critic, the "ordinance was definitely in harmony with the furtherance of the Communist program to destroy the system of free enterprise." Antidiscrimination activists countered by charging that their critics were in league with white southern racists, a charge that stuck in the early 1960s as televised images of white supremacist violence gave civil rights activists a powerful tool to discredit their foes. In a hard-fought referendum battle—with an especially high black turnout—Kansas City voters upheld the ordinance by a mere 1,614 votes out of nearly 90,000 cast.

Restaurant Jim Crow in the north eventually lost, not because of white goodwill, but rather because of the relentless skirmishes that broke down discrimination. "To a great extent," wrote one black journalist in 1956, "integration, North of the Mason-Dixon Line, has changed the eating habits of many Negro families." That was certainly true of wealthy blacks, such as those he chronicled eating in Chicago's posh Palmer House. But after the barriers broke down, the black masses did not flood into white-run establishments. Poor service and the hostility of white customers remained effective deterrents. If it was difficult to prove outright discrimination, it was even harder to document cold shoulders or cold food. At a Philadelphia gig in the early 1960s, black comedian Jackie "Moms" Mabley turned her experience of the glowering stares of white patrons in a fancy restaurant into a comic indictment of white racism: "I don't want to go to school with any of you. I just want a piece of cheesecake." It took more than the lowering of formal barriers to persuade many northern blacks that the benefits of a meal were worth the risk of harassment or embarrassment. In any case, access to haute cuisine hardly mattered to the majority of northern blacks from working-class backgrounds, who lacked the disposable income to spend in exclusive restaurants. Still, integrating the commercial sphere was a substantial accomplishment. Civil rights activists had broken down one of the most visible manifestations of Jim Crow in the North.

NEVER FAR FROM the heart of white segregationists in the mid–twentieth century were fears of sex. Beaches—places of seminudity, of frolicsome behavior, and often of illicit sexual activity (particularly "under the boardwalk")—were especially threatening to the racial order. Northern whites stubbornly clung to myths about disease, dirt, and black bodies, fearing contamination if they shared the same pools. Those views were instilled in young children and took deep root. A Cincinnati teacher— who was part of a "Brotherhood Week" effort to educate white children to accept blacks as equals—found that few of her sixth-grade students "will deny the principle of fair and equal rights for all human beings," but they "believe in separate swimming pools for colored people, are uncomfortable in playfields where Negroes are playing, and still have not become used to the new law which permits Negroes to attend all theaters in the city." The fear of the promiscuous mixing of black and white bodies led operators of amusement parks, swimming pools, and dance halls to exclude blacks as a matter of course. In the early 1950s, blacks were barred from public pools in cities throughout the North, among them Buffalo, Chicago, Pittsburgh, Denver, Grand Rapids, Omaha, Akron, Cleveland, and Youngstown. In Atlantic City, blacks were confined to the city's gritty Chicken Bone Beach through the 1950s. And Jim Crow stood fully exposed at a New Jersey nudist resort that, despite its uninhibited ambience, turned away a group of blacks.

Some of the most intense racial conflicts in the twentieth-century North were sparked by incidents at beaches. The Chicago riot of 1919, which left thirty-eight dead after white mobs ravaged Chicago's Bronzeville neighborhood, stemmed from an altercation after a black swimmer drifted ashore on the white section of a Jim Crow beach. During World War II, many parks and beaches became interracial battlegrounds. The Detroit riot of 1943 was sparked by rumors of interracial sexual attacks on Detroit's Belle Isle. Racial inequalities of all sorts provided the tinder for beachfront clashes, but sexual fear was an important spark, and enraged masculinity provided more than enough fuel to keep the flames in both Chicago and Detroit burning for days. The violent enforcement of beach-blanket Jim Crow kept blacks away from many lakefront and oceanfront areas altogether. Blacks avoided Buffalo's Crystal Beach throughout the 1940s and 1950s; they stayed clear of the South Boston beaches that were close to the black enclaves of Roxbury and Dorchester; and they found themselves confined to the gritty sand of specially designated black beaches in Atlantic City and Asbury Park, New Jersey. When black youths gathered at Rainbow Beach in southeast Chicago in 1961, they faced a barrage of rocks. In Plainfield, New Jersey, a suburb with a sizeable black population, whites had many swimming options but black residents had none. In 1966, after years of complaints about the lack of pools in the city's mostly black West End, the city made arrangements to bus blacks to nearby Rahway, where they could swim in a majority-black public pool.

The battle for the beaches and parks had both material and symbolic consequences. To blacks, whose neighborhoods throughout the North were usually devoid of adequate recreational facilities, access to a pool or park mattered. Illegally tapped fire hydrants had long cooled urban youths during the summer, but however pleasurable the blast of water might be, dodging traffic, not to mention zealous utility officials or police officers, took away from the fun. And parks were, after all, public spaces, paid for by all citizens from their hard-earned tax dollars. After World War II, access to recreational facilities took on an even greater symbolic importance, as they were emblems of the "good life" promised by postwar consumer culture.

Jim Crow parks, pools, and beaches were the targets of protests before World War II. In Chicago, St. Clair Drake and Horace Cayton grimly reported, blacks avoided "white" pools and beaches because "most Negroes do not wish to risk drowning at the hands of an unfriendly gang. Therefore they swim at all-Negro beaches, or in the Jim-Crow sections of mixed beaches, or in one of the Black Belt parks." In 1929, Chicago blacks protested separate and unequal beaches along Lake Michigan. In 1935, a group of University of Chicago students, branded as "Communists" by their opponents, attempted to breach a fence dividing black and white beaches on the city's South Side. Throughout the late 1930s, pitched battles between black and white youths broke out along the Chicago waterfront. In Cleveland's Garfield Park, where an interracial religious group attempted to desegregate a pool in 1941, four blacks and twelve whites entered the water, prompting small boys to shout "Fight! Fight!" Older swimmers called out "Niggers! Everybody out!" An "antagonistic crowd" of at least one hundred surrounded the interracial group. Through a carefully planned strategy of nonviolence, the steely protestors faced the crowd, "extended their hands in a friendly gesture toward those closest to them," and "threw the leaders off balance." Before leaving the pool unharmed, one protestor lectured the white crowd "on the meaning of democracy." After another "test" of the pool, the protests subsided until 1944, when a group of CORE members engaged in another swim-in at Garfield Park. But their efforts were sporadic. As late as 1948, CORE continued "a series of interracial visitations" with hopes that they would "in time break the pattern of discrimination in the Garfield Park pool."

Despite the obstacles, small bands of activists challenged segregated pools throughout the North. At Palisades Park in Fort Lee, New Jersey, Communists and Workers' Defense League and CORE activists mounted several years of demonstrations against the segregated dance hall and swimming pool, first sending matched couples, one black, one white, to the ballroom to see how "free" the park's "free dancing nights" were. When the park denied blacks tickets to the swimming pool because they were not "members," they protested and filed a lawsuit accusing the park of violating New Jersey law. Stepping up the pressure, protestors conducted "stand-ins" at the pool. Among them was a young James Peck, whose brutal beating during the 1961 Freedom Rides through Alabama would make him famous worldwide. After several years of clashes between protestors and the police and a CORE-initiated lawsuit, the pool finally opened to blacks. CORE activists imported the "stand-in" technique elsewhere. In Los Angeles, they targeted the Bimini Baths, which excluded dark-skinned Mexican Americans and all blacks. In 1947, CORE members stood in line at the Bimini's ticket booth. Pool managers pushed one protestor through a window and twice used fire hoses to disperse the activists. But in face of the protests, Bimini finally opened its gates on a nonsegregated basis. The victory was, however, short-lived. In 1952 the baths closed and were sold to a developer who planned to convert the facility into a gymnasium.

The difficulties in desegregating public pools were particularly clear in a lengthy campaign to desegregate Pittsburgh's pools beginning in 1952. The Urban League, the NAACP's "Swimming Pool Committee," the Pittsburgh Central Labor Union, and the Catholic diocese joined forces to put pressure on the city to abide by a 1950 Pennsylvania superior court ruling that prohibited segregation in swimming facilities. In 1953, Pittsburgh's newly integrated municipal pools hired their first black lifeguards. Flush with victory, activists targeted pools just outside the city limits, but there, without the law behind them, they faced intense opposition. When a group of unionists and Catholic priests threatened to cancel events at suburban Kennywood Park to protest discrimination, park managers converted the swimming area into a "boating lake" to keep would-be Negro bathers away. "We have found our swimming pool was not a particularly profitable operation," claimed the pool manager. "Regardless of our personal feelings," he claimed, "we are not in a position where we can afford to take a chance on a riot or racial disorder. We have to cater to the majority." At Allegheny County's South Park, which had two pools, officials continued to "escort Negroes" away from the main pool to the smaller one, pursuing a "separate but equal" swimming policy. In July, two teenage members of a black youth group demanded that they be allowed into the main pool, but their efforts met with counterattack. A white lifeguard "advised them that if they wanted to avoid bloodshed," they should leave. After the brouhaha, park authorities promised that "Negroes have the same rights and privileges as other persons" and pledged that black swimmers would be treated fairly. At nearby West Park, officials avoided integration altogether by closing the pool, filling it in, and paving it over.

Even when pools, recreation areas, and beaches did open to blacks, the fears of brawls and "race riots" remained paramount. Recreational facilities attracted large numbers of teenagers who often defended their own racial identities and played out turf battles on public space. When an interracial group of CORE members attempted to play baseball in Chicago's Tuley Park in the fall of 1947, they were pummeled by white gang members. Two players suffered broken jaws and one woman bystander got a black eye. A particularly brutal struggle over segregation occurred ten years later in Chicago's Calumet Park, near a changing South Side neighborhood. For nearly three weeks in late July and August 1957, white teens attacked black picnickers. On July 21, members of the Ta-Wa-Si Negro Mothers Club were beaten. When they complained, police chastised them for not having "gone to Jackson Park [in a black neighborhood] in the first place." The following weekend, one hundred and fifty white teens armed with metal rods and bottles rampaged through the park, injuring thirty black picnickers. "Hoodlums" broke the windows of more than twenty-five cars as terrified blacks rushed to escape. What particularly outraged the victims was that police appeared to side with the youths. Officers refused to escort victims into the park to retrieve their belongings, left several black women and children stranded in a park building as the mob attacked, and again rebuked the picnickers for using the "wrong park." In the aftermath of the Calumet Park "riots," black leaders met with the mayor and public officials, a group of victims filed suit against the police department, and in late August, more than two thousand blacks rallied and signed a "Ballot for Freedom" demanding the protection of "the rights of all Chicagoans, regardless of race, to use all parks, beaches, and public facilities."

A close second to beaches as a site of contestation over Jim Crow—and an equally difficult battleground—was urban amusement parks. Like beaches, they were largely playgrounds for the young, with games, rides, restaurants, dance halls, and other attractions. In most cities, they were segregated by race. By comparison to the struggles to open restaurants and movie theaters, the battles against segregated amusement parks were usually prolonged. Park operators sometimes set aside certain days for black admission or, as did those running Bob-Lo Island in the Detroit River, expelled would-be black patrons. A group of black veterans, a black teacher, and a nonwhite group of church women all complained of discrimination by Bob-Lo. They found some sympathy among local courts, but for technical reasons (Bob-Lo Park was in Canada, though the excursion boats to reach the island were based in the United States) it took three years of litigation—and finally a U.S. Supreme Court decision—to open up the park to blacks.

Most older amusement parks were more accessible than Bob-Lo; they were often located on public transit lines close to central-city black neighborhoods. Like beaches, amusement parks were a magnet for teenagers who sought escape from the dullness of their neighborhoods. What was most noteworthy about amusement parks was their youthful ambience.

In a period when teenagers moved freely through city streets with little adult supervision, amusement parks were havens. Thus, as adults grew increasingly fearful of the "epidemic" of juvenile delinquency, amusement parks were places where they imagined all sorts of dangers, including interracial contact and intimacy, but also gang wars and brawls, particularly between antagonistic blacks and whites.

The difficulty in breaking open amusement parks was especially clear in Cincinnati. In 1951, members of the Cincinnati Committee on Human Relations began a nearly ten-year battle against segregation at the Coney Island amusement park. Coney Island's owners tried to hide behind the subterfuge that it was a "members only" club, even though whites entered freely. Activists picketed and handed out leaflets and, in a variation on the stand-in, drove their cars to the park's entrance, blocked the ticket window and park entrance, and were arrested. In 1952, three protestors, jailed for attempting to enter Coney Island, went on a hunger strike. Finally, in 1955, Coney Island's operators agreed to open the park to blacks but excluded them from the swimming pool and dance pavilion. It was one thing for blacks and whites to share roller coasters and carousels but quite another for them to dance or swim together. Not until May 1961, when CORE and NAACP members were arrested at Coney Island's pool, did the last bastion of Jim Crow at that park fall.

THE HARD-FOUGHT STRUGGLES in the North to open public accommodations slipped into historical obscurity, eclipsed by the 1955 Montgomery bus boycott and the southern lunch counter sit-ins of the early 1960s. The countless skirmishes to open restaurants, swimming pools, and amusement parks in the North were forgotten by all but the participants themselves. But northern civil rights protestors had developed and perfected strategies of protest and litigation that would influence activists in the South. Many of those who had led the battle to open northern public accommodations turned southward—where they provided advice and counsel to their southern counterparts through informal networks, publications, and retreats like those held at Tennessee's Highlander Folk School, where Rosa Parks got her start. CORE's James Farmer and James Peck, who had first applied the principles of satyagraha to the struggle against Jim Crow restaurants in Chicago, carried their lessons southward.

Bayard Rustin worked closely with Martin Luther King, Jr., and the Southern Christian Leadership Conference (SCLC). And King's visionary aide C. T. Vivian, who participated in the 1960 Nashville sit-ins, had been involved in restaurant desegregation protests in Peoria, Illinois, in 1947.

CORE also published accounts of its 1940s public accommodations protests in pamphlets distributed to activists in the early 1960s. Building on its tried-and-true tactics, CORE imported the "stand-in" tactic to challenge segregated movie theaters in Miami, Louisville, and other cities south of the Mason-Dixon Line. And in the early and mid-1960s, after their victories at northern amusement parks, CORE and other groups turned their sights on Jim Crow amusement parks in suburban Maryland, Tennessee, and elsewhere in the South, gradually breaking down the color line as they had in the North. The southern battle to open restaurants and pools in places like Birmingham and Atlanta was part of deep-rooted history, with the North at the center, to overcome Jim Crow.

Both north and south, the challenge to open public accommodations was a beginning, not an end. It was a sign of changing times that the venerable *Green-Book* struggled with declining readership in the late 1950s and finally stopped publishing in 1964. But if it was now possible for blacks to travel with less harassment, public accommodation discrimination did not wholly vanish. Well into the 1960s, blacks continued to complain of discriminatory treatment, although the grievances were more sporadic than systemic. When members of the Ann Arbor, Michigan, chapter of CORE tested restaurants in all-white Dearborn, just outside Detroit, in 1961, they found that many of them still practiced discrimination. Even in liberal cities such as San Francisco, a sociologist noted the "covert nature" of discrimination against blacks in hotels and restaurants and the persistence of "evasive devices" to keep blacks out. The last holdouts, where blacks often continued to face hostility, were resort areas and small towns. But even if discrimination faded, the struggle against northern-style Jim Crow had limitations that protests could not address. Opening up the marketplace to blacks did not guarantee access, for that was a fundamentally economic problem. So long as blacks were trapped in poor-paying, insecure jobs, the desegregation of amusement parks and movie theaters, fancy hotels and restaurants would be at best a partial victory, one that mostly benefited better-off blacks.

The desegregation of recreational facilities—especially those that were

inexpensive or free—was also tinged with irony. At restaurants and hotels, the dollar barrier allowed entry to the "right sort" of blacks but deterred the working class and poor. More plebeian amusements could not
so easily screen out "undesirables." Many closed or resegregated. Integrated pools seldom lasted long. To a great extent, whites in northern
cities abandoned public pools for backyard pools and private swim clubs.
In racially tense cities such as Philadelphia, white teens continued to defend nominally integrated pools in white neighborhoods against outsiders. In some places, such as Kansas City, pool operators shut down
altogether to avoid integration. Others found that white patronage plummeted after desegregation. By the late 1950s, New York City's Coney Island and Rockaway beaches, which had been the target of protests in the
1940s, attracted mostly blacks and Puerto Ricans. As blacks moved beyond Atlantic City's once-segregated Chicken Bone Beach, white bathers
decamped for nearby all-white towns.

The battle to open public accommodations occurred at the same time
that larger structural changes were remaking American urban market-
places and resorts. Shops and stores were rapidly suburbanizing, moving
to places where few blacks lived and where they were unfamiliar and unwelcome. Amusement parks closed by the dozens in big cities and their
suburbs, especially in the mid-1960s as their clientele grew increasingly
African American. Newark's Olympic Park closed its gates in 1965. When
black patronage skyrocketed at New York's Coney Island, whites stopped
coming, leading to the shutting down of its famed roller coaster. Chicago's
Riverview Park closed in 1967, just a few years after it tried to boost attendance by holding a special day for children in War on Poverty programs. And a few years later, Cleveland's Euclid Beach Park saw its last
customers. The vast majority of amusement parks that survived were
those inaccessible by public transportation, most in rural areas or small
towns. Likewise, the big urban movie palaces saw a dramatic decline in
attendance as white moviegoers abandoned downtowns. While urban
movie palaces shut their doors, drive-ins and suburban "multiplex" cinemas sprung up to take their place, following the white exodus.

Left behind in the places that blacks frequented were increasingly tat-
tered business districts, ravaged by disinvestment, increasingly run-down.
It was not coincidental that just as black consumers gained access to
urban commerce, it began to decentralize. Real estate developers and

urban planners began to lament the "blackening" of downtowns and tried to devise strategies to lure middle-class white customers back. Increasingly, that process led to the creation of safe, nonpublic, white-dominated spaces outside cities. Racial discrimination did not, after all, begin or end with commercial establishments: It was woven into the fabric of everyday life in the North. The ordinariness of racial separation in metropolitan America's neighborhoods, schools, and workplaces made it even more difficult to challenge. To protest against lunch counter discrimination or exclusion from a pool was relatively easy. To challenge the exclusion of blacks from suburbia or the lack of federal loans for black homebuyers or the partial segregation of workplaces or the segregation of schools would be much more difficult. The early victories for black dignity would not be easily replicated in the urban North.

CHAPTER 6

"GOD HAVE PITY ON SUCH A CITY"

SEPTEMBER 8, 1943, WAS THE FIRST DAY OF THE NEW SCHOOL YEAR IN the village of Hillburn, New York, at the foot of the Ramapo Mountains. The Brook School, a ramshackle, three-room, wood-frame building that served as Hillburn's Negro school, was silent. The school's outdoor privies, boarded up since they had been replaced by indoor plumbing earlier that year, loomed over the schoolyard's untrammeled grass. Across a busy highway, the small American Legion hall that served as a surrogate gym stood dark. Only six of the school's hundred children showed up for classes that morning. The other ninety-four had joined a "general strike" against the school.

A half mile away, in the center of town, the school day was also off to an unusual start at the Main School, a sturdy brick and limestone building constructed in the 1920s. It boasted state-of-the-art classrooms, a library, a clinic, a music room, a gymnasium, and a large playground. As white children shuffled into their classrooms, NAACP attorney Thurgood Marshall escorted five-year-old Allen Morgan, Jr., and his parents into the principal's office and demanded that the boy be enrolled. The outcome was a surprise to no one: Marshall and his young client were rebuffed. Marshall drafted an official letter of complaint to the school board, the first step in a possible lawsuit. Later that morning, a delegation of black parents marched to the school board president's palatial home on a hillside overlooking the village. They demanded that the district allow black students to attend classes in the all-white Main School. The school board, hoping to quell unrest, announced that classes at both the Brook School and the Main School would be suspended for a day.

No outside observer would have pegged Hillburn as a hotbed of protest. Only nineteen miles from New York City, it seemed a world apart.

A little industrial town in Rockland County, Hillburn was dominated by a single factory, the Ramapo Foundry and Wheel Works. Nearly a company town, it was small enough that most faces were familiar. The town's geography marked everyone's place in the rigid social order. On the wooded slopes were large houses occupied by plant managers and other elite families; down below, on the crowded streets near the wheel works, huddled the modest brick and frame houses of factory workers.

Like many older towns in the Hudson Valley, Hillburn had a sizeable black population dating back to the colonial period. The town's most established black families shared the names of many of Rockland County's old white families—van Dunks, van Cotts, and de Groats—a reminder of the days when the Dutch and Anglo elite of early New York owned slaves. Others proudly traced their family heritage to freed blacks, Ramapo Indians, and Hessian mercenaries who had intermingled in nearby mountains in the eighteenth and early nineteenth centuries. Most had less romantic family histories: They were the descendants of black workers recruited beginning in the 1870s to toil in the hot, dangerous foundry. At the outset of World War II, Ramapo Foundry and Wheel Works remained the town's major employer of blacks.

Cutting through Hillburn was State Highway 17, the town's major thoroughfare and a symbolic dividing line. It might as well have been a wall. On one side lived six hundred blacks; on the other fourteen hundred whites and only six black families. Hillburn represented racially divided America in microcosm. The Brook School, not surprisingly, stood on the "colored" side of town, where it had been built nearly forty years earlier as a "separate," racially segregated school. The existence of a colored school was not at all unusual in New York's small towns, older suburbs, and middle-sized cities. Until 1938, the state permitted the construction of single-race or separate schools. Presiding over the local school board was Hillburn's patriarch, J. Edgar Davidson, whose family owned the foundry. Davidson fiercely defended the separation of black and white children in the district's schools, for only "Negro" teachers "understood the peculiarities of the race." Unburdened by racial "peculiarities," it was only natural that Hillburn's white students attended the Main School. The very physical plants of the two schools embodied ideas of racial difference. One was a solid masonry building, the other a sagging wood-frame structure. Black parents derisively called Brook "the dump."

Hillburn's black residents had long resented their town's segregated school system. In 1930, T. N. Alexander, a postal worker who commuted to New York and headed Hillburn's NAACP branch, began to agitate for equal schools. But Alexander led his crusade nearly alone. Amid the Great Depression, Hillburn's blacks feared reprisals at the hands of local employers. In the nearly feudal town, bucking the system came with a potentially high price. Still, the NAACP's national office investigated the complaints and petitioned the state board of education to desegregate Hillburn's schools. The effort came to naught. State education officials refused to intervene: The separate schools were legal under New York law.

By the early 1940s, everything had changed. In 1938, New York eliminated the legal justification for separate schools. Three years later, the economic and political whirlwind of World War II swept through Hillburn. Many of the town's young men—black and white—left to fight overseas. Black women entered local factories, including the wheel works, as defense workers. The combination of economic security—and, more important, the wartime rhetoric of democracy—led Hillburn's residents down the path that T. N. Alexander had blazed more than a decade earlier. In the midst of the war, local activists revived the town's dormant NAACP branch and took on the town's hated "Jim Crow" schools, using the same rhetoric that animated wartime protests from the streets of Harlem to the kitchens of segregated battleships. Hillburn's separate schools were "grist for Hitler," an insult to the nation's pretense of democracy.

When parents struck against Hillburn's separate schools at the beginning of the 1943–44 school year, school officials were compelled to respond to charges that they illegally maintained racially separate schools. The school board tried a subterfuge, to comply nominally with New York law. It redistricted Hillburn into two "neighborhood schools." The "new" boundary separating the Main and Brook schools mostly followed Route 17. It could not draw a legally defensible boundary that excluded all black students from the Main School, so the new enrollment zones brought twenty-six black students into the Main School. But the Brook School remained all black. One act of gerrymandering belied the neighborhood school premise: The school district line jumped across Route 17 at one point to encompass the single white family who lived on the "colored" side of town.

In preparation for the "general strike," Hillburn's NAACP branch invited attorney Thurgood Marshall to visit and begin preparations for liti-

gation against the Ramapo Central School District, which included Hillburn. Marshall, who in 1940 had pledged the NAACP Legal Defense and
Educational Fund to fight school segregation both north and south,
promised to "back the local group to the limit in the fight against segregation." Marshall's presence aroused white suspicions of a conspiracy.
Surely Hillburn's Negroes, if left to their own devices, would not have
risen up against the school district. J. Edgar Davidson charged that "we
have some fine colored people here, but I'm afraid a few are being led
astray by outsiders." Davidson was partially right: Marshall played an invaluable role in helping coordinate the protest. He also helped Hillburn
residents tap into collective memories of successful school desegregation
efforts elsewhere, many initiated by local NAACP branches. While parents boycotted the school, Marshall set into motion legal proceedings that
would eventually bring the state to their side. In Hillburn—as with so
many protests in the North—the local and the national blurred; local
activists quickly learned that their struggles were part of a nationwide
battle. Likewise, Marshall and the NAACP's legal team relied on local
rebellions to develop a strategy for litigation. The two processes—
agitation and litigation—were wholly intertwined.

The two-pronged attack on Hillburn's Jim Crow schools lasted well into
October. More than half the district's black students remained out of school.
"Nobody's going back," proclaimed local NAACP head Marion van Dunk.
For those students who remained out of classes, activists started a "Freedom
School." Two parents volunteered to run classes until the NAACP paid for
the hiring of a professional teacher. School district officials retaliated by
taking legal action against the boycotting parents for violating the state's
mandatory education law. The threat of prosecution did not deter them.
"We'll go to jail if we have to," stated one parent. "We aren't scared and we
won't quit," asserted another. When a judge levied ten-dollar fines (with
suspended jail sentences) to the parents of forty-six boycotting students,
they "trooped across the highway . . . and presented their patient, mystified
tots to Hillburn Main School." Once again they were turned away. Angry
parents roared: "You'll be sorry!" "We won't go back." The NAACP reported that "children shall not return again to the [Brook] school which,
unlike that old time religion, is no longer good enough for them."

Hillburn's black uprising caught the town's whites off guard. They had

had no inkling that the "quiet and industrious Negroes" (in Davidson's words) were so angry. When the delegation of parents marched to the Davidson estate to present their grievances, Davidson's overwrought wife complained: "I've been nice to these people. . . . I've fed them when they're sick and given them money when they needed it. Why should they try to enroll their children in the white school? What do they want to do that for?" To Davidson, the protest was but "a celebrity stunt." School board member Jacob Schenck argued that "we have no feeling against the colored people. We proved that by improving their school building [by replacing the outdoor privies with indoor toilets]." Mayor John Creelman more bluntly expressed his shock at the boycotting parents' high aspirations for their children's education. In his view, "all a Negro wants is a full belly."

However small, Hillburn was not isolated. The tough little town became a powerful symbol of northern Jim Crow. The boycott was covered extensively by the black press, by leftist newspapers, and by New York area dailies and weeklies. Through *The Crisis*, NAACP members nationwide read of the battle. NAACP activists denounced the school board for its "astonishingly 'southern' viewpoint." The American Labor Party and American Civil Liberties Union denounced the "Mississippi Jim Crowism" of Hillburn's school board. A blue-ribbon committee of leftist and liberal Rockland County residents, including playwright Maxwell Anderson, actress Helen Hayes, and composer Kurt Weill, signed a petition in support of the striking students. Hillburn parents, encouraged by the outpouring of support, came to see themselves as part of a movement with national and even international significance, as soldiers in the ongoing, conjoined struggle against Jim Crow at home and fascism abroad. When a group of parents marched to the Main School, they posed for a photograph in front of a wartime propaganda poster headlined "Democracy at Home."

The Hillburn boycott even generated a protest song. In late October 1943, the left-leaning *People's Voice* published Harlem poet Countee Cullen's "Hillburn—The Fair." Folk singers at the Highlander Folk School set the verse to music.

> *God have pity*
> *On such a city*
> *Where parent teaches child to hate*

In early October, more than twenty thousand posters appeared on telephone poles and in bars, stores, and churches throughout Harlem advertising a "mass rally" on behalf of the Hillburn boycott. "JIM CROW BLOCKS SCHOOL HOUSE DOOR IN NEW YORK STATE," read one. "HILLBURN AND HATTIESBURG!" read another. When an NAACP sound truck rolled through the streets announcing the event, crowds of pedestrians broke into spontaneous applause. The Harlem efforts culminated on October 10, when Thurgood Marshall, Adam Clayton Powell, Jr., and a group of striking parents addressed several thousand supporters at the Golden Gate Ballroom. The outpouring of support encouraged Harlem NAACP activists, including Ella Baker, to hold similar mass meetings on issues such as poll taxes and Jim Crow in the military, all with hopes of making the Manhattan branch of the NAACP "an organization for the masses of the people."

By mid-October, the protests and the threat of litigation bore fruit. In response to the NAACP's complaint, the state commissioner of education overruled the district's policy of segregation, shut down the Brook School, and ordered the enrollment of black students at Main. But the Hillburn victory was only partial. On October 18, all but one white student failed to show up for classes at the newly integrated Main School; his schoolmates' parents voted with their feet and enrolled their children in two Catholic schools. Malcolm Stead, a local painter, self-consciously imitated the NAACP's boycott strategy and called for the creation of a "National Association for the Advancement of White People." An undercover NAACP informant found that most white Hillburn parents feared that their children would be exposed to "dirty" and "unhealthy" black children.

The mass white exodus from the Main School remained an enduring problem for the NAACP. Over the course of the next two years, NAACP activists tried and failed to form a biracial committee to bring black and white parents together, to attract white students back to the Main School, and to keep the school district from closing the now all-black school. Hillburn parents and national NAACP officials alike had learned—the hard way—that the fight to break down school segregation would not be quick and easy. But despite the less-than-ideal outcome, the Hillburn boycott had statewide and national implications. In 1944, newly elected New

York assemblyman Hulan Jack, a black West Indian, pushed a "Hillburn Education Bill" through the state assembly, forbidding state funding to segregated schools.

The Hillburn general strike kept alive a long-running grassroots history of school boycotts and inspired protestors elsewhere in the North. Dozens of telegrams and letters of support and donations to the boycotting parents flooded into the national NAACP headquarters, most from leftist activists, black churches, and parent-teacher associations in black schools that had been or would be rocked by school protests of their own. The NAACP, working through its branches, also disseminated information about school boycotts. The fact that the NAACP was a national organization with an institutional memory—and hundreds of local affiliates—was crucial in the spread of boycotts.

The six-week Hillburn boycott was one of more than a score of school protests that erupted throughout the North between the mid-1920s and the mid-1950s. Black parents boycotted inferior, segregated schools in Chicago, New York, and Philadelphia, but the most significant protests occurred in suburbs and industrial towns throughout the North: Berwyn, Abington, Chester, Coatesville, and Willow Grove, Pennsylvania; Springfield, Lockland, Dayton, Hillsboro, and Shaker Heights, Ohio; East Orange, Montclair, Toms River, Long Branch, Fair Haven, and Mount Holly, New Jersey; Hempstead, Malverne, and New Rochelle, New York; and Benton Harbor, Michigan.

The stories of the northern school boycotts are largely forgotten. But together they constituted a vitally important front in the battle against racial inequality in the North. Grassroots boycotts, led largely by mothers, inspired activists around the country to demand equal education. Their efforts also reflected—and sometimes reinforced—divisions within northern black communities, particularly over questions of black separatism and integrationism. In addition, the battles foreshadowed the difficulties that the large-scale efforts to desegregate metropolitan schools in the North would face in the 1960s and 1970s. Perhaps most important, they allow us to reassess the relationship between grassroots social movements and legal strategies. Beginning in the 1960s, many activists and scholars criticized litigation strategies for their "top-down" approach to social problems. But in the school desegregation cases, litigation and protest were never separate. Grassroots activists pushed for social change and enlisted the support of national civil rights organizations such as the NAACP in their cause. Together they reshaped public policy, state by state, school district by school district.

PARENT-LED SCHOOL BOYCOTTS grew from a deep taproot: the desire for equal education and the frustration at the persistence of separate, unequal schools. The black migration to the North in the twentieth century corresponded with the dramatic expansion of American public education. In 1920, only 16.3 percent of Americans graduated from high school; by 1970, the figure had risen to 75.3 percent. Schooling became the crucial credential in the scramble for economic success; over the course of the century a growing number of jobs, even entry-level positions, required high school diplomas. Economists talked of the "growing returns to education," meaning that the more you learned, the more you earned. By the mid–twentieth century, the number of Americans under age eighteen who were in school had skyrocketed; fewer and fewer students dropped out to work. The post–World War II years witnessed an unprecedented boom in school construction, in teacher training, and in public funding for schools. More than ever, ordinary Americans obsessed about schooling and directed energies toward spending more money on schools to keep up with the Soviet competition.

Few Americans appreciated the value of education more than blacks—in large part because they looked at the American educational boom from the outside. In the South, where a majority of blacks lived until 1960, public education for blacks was abysmal. Many southern states spent mere pennies on the dollar for public education, although school spending had risen in the aftermath of World War II. Blacks were confined to some of the worst schools in the country. In rural areas in particular, school buildings were often as ramshackle as the shanties that housed most of the students. With the exception of a few well-funded schools, black school curricula emphasized vocational and agricultural skills, preparing students for jobs at the bottom tier of the economy. Most black children dropped out of school to work, because their impoverished families needed their labor. Many southern counties did not even have high schools for black students, so as not to disrupt a labor market that depended on a ready supply of unskilled workers.

Blacks who migrated northward held high expectations about education. And blacks born in the North had rates of school attendance nearly equal to those of whites. They saw education as a ticket out of poverty, but their hopes were often dashed when they confronted the racial barriers to equal education above the Mason-Dixon Line. Black educator Doxey Wilkerson wrote in 1940 that education "in the North is characterized by tendencies toward structural separateness" and that the "degree of such separateness tends to be most pronounced in areas where the Negro population is relatively most heavily concentrated and where the general social status of the Negro is lower than in the North as a whole." At the end of World War II, when NAACP investigator Noma Jensen visited twenty-two school systems in the Northeast and Midwest, she concluded that "the integration of Negroes, both pupils and teachers, into our public schools in the North is a very spotty affair."

Black students found themselves in deteriorating, usually underfunded schools. While some schools, particularly those on the border of mostly white neighborhoods, were racially mixed, the status was almost always temporary, as whites fled to outlying neighborhoods where schools were still all white. Most teachers in predominantly black schools were white; many had fewer credentials than their counterparts in white-dominated classrooms; and turnover was appallingly high. School districts regularly classified blacks as intellectually inferior. A leading northern educational reformer in the early twentieth century advocated the creation of separate schools "for defective, delinquent . . . or negro" children, and many school districts took heed. Throughout the first third of the twentieth century, Philadelphia used intelligence test results to justify segregated schools. In the 1920s, the Chicago public schools classified three-quarters of southern-born blacks as "retarded" and confined them to special classrooms for the "subnormal," which proliferated in city schools. When these classrooms grew overcrowded, black students were held back, sometimes for years, and taught with a watered-down curriculum that reflected the district's low opinion of their skills. In Detroit, blacks were disproportionately represented in the special education classes, vocational training, and the "general track," which one historian described as a "warehouse for unemployed youth."

Northern school districts not only segregated blacks and whites by tracking them, they also worked mightily to create parallel black and white schools. Where state laws permitted it—New York, Indiana, and Kansas—many districts constructed separate "colored" or "Negro" schools, like Hillburn's Brook School. In the majority of northern states, where laws forbade racial exclusion in public schools, educators devised subterfuges to keep blacks out of white-dominated schools. Ohio law forbade segregated schools, but local districts disregarded the law. "Of course we have separate schools, although we don't call them that," admitted a candid Dayton, Ohio, school administrator. To buy off black discontent, Dayton's officials contended that the creation of "all-Negro" schools opened up more jobs for black teachers—who were forbidden to teach white students. Until 1956, when a federal court ordered desegregation after a two-year school boycott and the arrest of a white integrationist for attempting to burn down the all-black school, nearby Hillsboro, Ohio, had three elementary schools: two large, new buildings with all-white student bodies, and one tiny school with just twenty-four students, all of them black. There, too, some black teachers feared that the abolition of the town's Lincoln School would cost them their jobs.

The solution to the problem of separate and unequal education was by no means simple or agreed upon. From the 1930s through the mid-1960s, most grassroots activists favored integration, but a prominent subset of intellectuals and educators insisted that separate schools could provide good educations to black children. The most prominent and frequently cited skeptic about educational integration was none other than W.E.B. Du Bois. In a forum on "separate schools" published by the *Journal of Negro Education,* the NAACP founder argued that "theoretically, the Negro needs neither segregated schools nor mixed schools." But the record of "mixed" schools offered little promise to Du Bois. "I know that race prejudice in the United States is such today that most Negroes cannot receive proper education in white institutions. . . . There are many school systems in the North where Negroes are admitted and tolerated, but they are not educated, they are crucified." Whites, he argued, would not yield to protest. "Any agitation or action aimed at compelling a rich and powerful majority of citizens to do what they will not do is useless." Advocates of racial separation in school, both black and white, cited Du Bois's article. But his position on unequal education was more complicated than it appeared. He was no advocate of the status quo. He believed that Jim Crow schools were "undemocratic and discriminatory." But as long as segregation persisted—a state that he believed would "continue longer than any of us now living survive"—it was incumbent on reformers to "make the best of a bad situation and take every advantage of that situation." In the end, Du Bois's goal was first-rate education for black students, in integrated schools if possible but in separate schools if necessary.

Joining Du Bois in his skepticism of integration was a vocal contingent of intellectuals, educators, and grassroots activists. Black teachers and administrators, in particular, often strongly supported separate schools. Most were less than satisfied with underprovisioned schools but clung to a belief in racial uplift. Black students would benefit from the moral and educational example of black teachers. Some couched their defense of separate schools in terms of racial essentialism. Black students would be best served by teachers who understood them. All but the most cowed or conservative teachers, however, expressed dissatisfaction at the conditions in most separate schools, even if they supported the idea of segregated education. They demanded better facilities and higher wages as an alternative to the risky and untested proposition of desegregation. Teaching was a high-status profession among blacks. For black women, teaching was a rare job that offered decent pay, security, and prestige. Many black middle-class families were headed by teachers. Black teachers justifiably feared that if separate schools were abolished, they would lose their jobs, for hardly any white-majority schools had black teaching staff. In many segregated districts, white school officials, reluctant to disrupt the status quo, capitalized on those fears.

For most black parents in the postwar years, however, the arguments for and against segregated schools were too abstract. Parents of schoolchildren had to make decisions about their children's education in the short run, and they would take better education in whatever form it came in. That said, between the 1940s and the 1960s, the lion's share of civil rights activists—from intellectuals to national civil rights organizers to grassroots protestors—demanded an end to separate schools. Their reasons for supporting school integration were varied: Some activists simply wanted access to what they saw as better education in white-dominated schools. The decrepit condition of most "colored" schools offered a graphic reminder that separate was unlikely ever to become equal. Many educators, civil rights activists, and protestors saw racially mixed schooling as the first step toward the abolition of racism. Still others focused on what they believed were the pathological consequences of separate education. Drawing from the burgeoning scholarship on the social psychological effects of racism, they argued that segregation lowered black self-worth and reinforced stereotypes of racial inferiority. Perhaps most important was a sense of rising expectations about the possibility of equal citizenship that had been unleashed during the Great Depression and World War II. The result was a push—through protest, litigation, and advocacy—to break down Jim Crow schools.

The places that erupted in conflict over segregated schools were not random. School boycotts occurred most frequently in those places where blacks and whites came into close contact, primarily small cities and suburbs with black populations. Few of the earliest boycotts took place in big cities, where segregation was of such a scale that it seemed inevitable and immutable. If the effects of segregation were keenly felt in big cities, the causes were often distant and relatively invisible. In big cities, as two social scientists noted in the early 1950s, only a "relatively small number" of families living in "'border' or 'transitional zones'" were "directly affected by desegregation." When protests erupted in Gary, Chicago, Detroit, and Philadelphia, they usually involved individual schools in racially changing neighborhoods rather than whole districts. It was not until the aftermath of *Brown v. Board of Education* that big cities joined small towns in the struggle against educational Jim Crow in the North.

That the battle against school segregation started in mostly small places may seem surprising, given that the vast majority of the North's black population was concentrated in the largest cities. But by 1950, nearly 20 percent of northern blacks lived outside central cities. In some older suburbs, such as Berwyn, Pennsylvania; Shaker Heights, Ohio; Freeport, New York; and Princeton, Montclair, and Mount Holly, New Jersey, black day laborers, household servants, gardeners, and chauffeurs had lived in shadows of wealthy white communities since the nineteenth century. In other places, such as Mount Laurel, New Jersey, old settlements of black farmers or laborers, dating to the era of slavery, were swallowed up by postwar suburbanization. Blacks also lived in some small industrial satellites of big cities, such as Pontiac and River Rouge, Michigan, and Chester, Pennsylvania. As millions of blacks migrated northward in the postwar years, a segment of the population was attracted to these black enclaves, which had higher rates of home ownership than the neighboring cities. Like white suburbanites, blacks were attracted by the possibility of owning land, but not always for the same reasons. Many southern blacks looked for parcels of land large enough to cultivate; few city neighborhoods had the space to keep a few chickens or grow some crops. Most of these communities were quite small, and a large number were surrounded by predominantly white areas and incorporated into white-dominated school districts. Others were enveloped by white neighborhoods as suburbia expanded around them.

Why did many of these little black communities become such hotbeds of protest? Above all, their populations were small and tightly knit. Local organizers could speak at one or two churches or fraternal organizations and reach everyone in the community or go door-to-door and canvass a town's entire black population in a few days. Black suburbanites had moved to such outlying places in part because they sought an alternative to the large, predominantly black neighborhoods in central cities; they made the self-conscious choice to move to places where they were a small minority. But however small these towns were, they were umbilically connected to nearby cities. Their residents were part of a translocal black world, linked by work, transportation, and, perhaps most important, by the black and radical presses, which publicized local protests.

Small-town protestors had obvious targets—often just a single Jim Crow school in an overwhelmingly white district. In small towns, Jim Crow was in plain sight. Suburban and small-town blacks almost always lived close to whites. White-dominated schools were often just blocks away, most no more than a mile or two distant. In many towns, black students walked directly past white schools on their way to their own, separate buildings. Empowered by the now-pervasive rhetoric of equality, many black parents saw no good reason why their children should be cordoned off from whites as if they were leprous or retarded. Passing by new campuslike suburban public school complexes hardened suburban blacks' sense that they were being left with white America's educational scraps. Educational inequity was not a distant, abstract concept.

One of the most important battlegrounds over school segregation was New Jersey. Within its boundaries was the most diverse black population in the North. Encompassing gritty mill towns, leafy suburbs, garish resorts, truck farms, and settlements in the vast swamps of the Pine Barrens, the state was a microcosm of America's East Coast. Trenton, Camden, Newark, and Jersey City, the state's largest cities, were home to black industrial and service workers. Clusters of blacks peppered New Jersey's sprawling suburbs outside New York and Philadelphia. Household servants and groundskeepers formed small communities, particularly in railroad suburbs such as Montclair, Englewood, East Orange, and Mount Holly, and in some prosperous older towns such as Princeton. Several coastal resort towns also had old black populations—porters and kitchen workers and hotel employees who catered to tourists in Atlantic City, Cape May, and Asbury Park. Scattered throughout the Garden State, particularly in its southern half—which appeared to observers to be Dixie's northern outpost, complete with scrubby truck farms and tumbledown shacks—were rural and small-town settlements, populated by the descendants of slaves and agricultural laborers. There New Jersey more closely resembled North Carolina than New York.

In the 1920s and 1930s, New Jersey had been a hotbed of protests against segregated schools. In Toms River, where agricultural New Jersey bumped against the touristy Jersey Shore, black parents boycotted a segregated school in 1927 and marched on the school district headquarters. In 1933 and 1934, the black residents of posh Montclair protested the fact that their children were confined to an old, overcrowded school while the district's wealthy white students attended classes in new, well-equipped buildings. In 1936, East Orange parents led a boycott. Throughout the state, residents simmered at the obvious evidence of their children's second-tier status. In the case of one New Jersey town that cordoned off black children with barbed wire in a separate playground, they saw the inequalities of power in their starkest form.

New Jersey's battle against school desegregation would not have been won without the coercive power of the state backing local activists. Beginning in the late 1930s, the NAACP began to organize its chapters to agitate for equal education statewide. Armed with a Teachers College study of unequal education in the Garden State, the NAACP demanded the hiring of more black teachers and worked to improve conditions in schools with large numbers of black students. The NAACP simultaneously put pressure on the state government to strengthen the state's civil rights laws.

New Jersey's protests accelerated during and after World War II, as local activists looked for ways to bring the "Double Victory" campaign to the home front. When the Trenton activists tackled the segregated Lincoln School in 1943, the NAACP quickly drew an analogy to Hillburn. White children in Trenton went to their neighborhood schools, but all black junior high school students in the district attended Lincoln. In a terse opinion, the New Jersey Supreme Court ruled that the segregated school was illegal and that black students had the right, just as whites did, to attend "the school nearest their residences." NAACP attorneys hoped that the victory in Trenton would be "an opening wedge in a drive to break" the practice of separate education in the state.

At war's end, New Jersey's NAACP increased its pressure on the state government. In 1947, it released a grim survey of school segregation in eleven counties. Segregated education was pervasive in the Garden State. In Berlin, black students attended a two-room "colored school in bad condition"; in Rio Grande and Whitesboro, white students were bused past the Negro school to their own segregated building; in West Cape May, black students attended classes in an "annex" to the white elementary school; in Wildwood, black and white students were divided into separate classes in the same building; in Mount Laurel, the "colored school" was within a block of the "white school"; in Moorestown, the black junior high school did not offer Latin, French, or algebra, thus leaving its students ineligible for college preparatory courses in the high school; in Mullica Hill and Marshalltown, black students from first to eighth grade were crammed into a single classroom; in Penns Grove, the Negro kindergarten met in the dark basement of the white elementary school. Altogether sixty communities, as diverse as Hackensack, Princeton, Egg Harbor, Montclair, and Camden, had at least one "colored school." Among its sobering findings was that black teachers in segregated schools had teaching loads that averaged three times those of their white counterparts.

Armed with data, local NAACP activists stepped up protests and lobbied state officials. In 1945, the state created a Division Against Discrimination, and in late 1947 New Jersey amended its state constitution to forbid segregation in schools on grounds of race, creed, or color; in 1948 the state department of education began investigating and forcing segregated school districts to desegregate; and in 1949 the state legislature strengthened antidiscrimination laws, giving the state power to issue "cease and desist" orders involving segregated schools and public accommodations. The complete overhaul of New Jersey's laws was one of the great success stories of the civil rights struggle in the 1940s.

Grassroots activists, however, quickly learned that state laws were not self-enforcing. It often took parental pressure to break down the barriers of segregation. In 1947, black parents in Long Branch, for example, withdrew more than one hundred children from the town's Liberty Street school, a "drab block of red brick overlooking a cinder playground" enveloped in noxious fumes from the neighboring gasworks. While the nearby white elementary school (located upwind from the gas fumes) had empty desks, the colored school was forty students over capacity. Parents marched their children to register in the white school—and with the NAACP's backing and New Jersey law on their side, their boycott succeeded. Similar protests met with success in Toms River, Asbury Park, and Camden. With a strong state law backing them, boycotters were usually able to win quick victories. In Mount Holly, for example, a 1949 boycott instigated by sixty black mothers led to the closure of the city's two-room, all-black Samuel Aaron School and the transfer of black elementary students to formerly all-white schools. Facing pressure to desegregate, some New Jersey districts experimented with voluntary plans to dissolve their separate schools. Desegregation advocates singled out Princeton for its innovative effort. Rather than replacing separate schools with neighborhood schools—a tactic that often replicated patterns of racial segregation—the "Princeton Plan" created a single, townwide school district, reorganizing the town's white and Negro elementary schools into two integrated schools: one serving students up through fifth grade, the other students from sixth through eighth grade. By 1954, New Jersey no longer had officially segregated schools. Local protests and state action proved to be mutually reinforcing.

Throughout the North, school segregation remained a vexingly persistent problem, despite the victories in school boycott cases and the changes in state laws. By the late 1940s, the NAACP had turned most of its energy toward southern school desegregation, but northern activists continued to press for equal education. The victories in Hillburn and Trenton and Long Beach and Mount Holly only whetted the appetite of northern activists for more change. But they faced an obstacle to equality much bigger than the stray, remaining Brook or Lincoln school. That was the poisonous link between housing segregation and school segregation. Most northern school districts were racially homogeneous. Within districts with more than a handful of blacks, there remained overwhelmingly black and overwhelmingly white schools because of housing patterns. By the early 1950s, to anyone who cared about northern education, the problem was no longer Jim Crow schoolhouses, it was the "neighborhood school."

New Jersey's battles against school segregation may have been the most typical of the North's variation in segregation and resistance to it. But the most important school struggles in the postwar period played out in that most atypical of places, metropolitan New York. At the center of the metropolis was the nation's single largest and most important black community, Harlem. On New York's periphery were some of the country's largest and best-established black suburbs. What happened in and around New York was magnified in importance because of the unusual concentration of black media there. New York's daily newspapers also offered better coverage of black issues than most of their white-run counterparts elsewhere. The left-liberal *PM* (which lasted through 1948), the (then) liberal *New York Post,* and even the more conservative *Herald Tribune* offered decent coverage of black issues. And despite charges that it was elitist, *The New York Times* was surprisingly thorough in its coverage of civil rights issues in its home region. New York's leftist press, in particular the *Daily Worker,* brought local civil rights battles to a national audience. And New York events also had international resonance, not inconsequential during the Cold War. New York's activists, in particular, wove the rhetoric of human rights into their protests, knowing that among the witnesses to their local struggles were members of the newly created United Nations. The result was a media-oriented civil rights consciousness unparalleled anywhere in the United States. Extensive news coverage of black events created a heightened expectation of social change, particularly during the war and postwar years. As a result, New York became a ground zero for northern civil rights protests.

Following Hillburn, activists in an archipelago of black communities on New York's periphery began to test New York's law forbidding separate education. But the New York cases, especially in suburban Long Island, quickly revealed the limits of state antidiscrimination laws. In 1949, young NAACP attorney Constance Baker Motley was assigned her first solo case, involving Hempstead's public schools. By the late 1940s, the NAACP was laying the groundwork for its challenge to Jim Crow in the South. With limited resources, NAACP attorneys took on school desegregation cases that they hoped would eventually culminate in a Supreme Court case challenging Jim Crow. Places like Hempstead were on the margins of that strategy, which is probably why a relatively inexperienced attorney like Motley, only three years out of law school, landed the case.

Born in 1921, Motley was the daughter of West Indian immigrants to New Haven, Connecticut. Coming of age in the Great Depression, she found work with the National Youth Administration. With the assistance of a local white philanthropist who heard her speak at a community center, Motley attended Fisk and New York universities, before earning a law degree at Columbia in 1946. As a black woman she faced a double handicap on the job market, despite her stellar credentials. But her talents, unrecognized by the white-dominated bar, were a real gift to the civil rights movement. When she applied for a clerkship at the NAACP, Thurgood Marshall hired her with enthusiasm.

Hempstead lay just east of New York City at the heart of Long Island's postwar sprawl. Home to a small black population, most of whom worked as domestics for wealthy whites, Hempstead witnessed a dramatic expansion of its black population in the 1940s. Black migrants sought the tranquility of suburbia but also access to the booming defense and retail industries in Nassau County, a place that was remade by an infusion of federal housing and military expenditures. Most of Hempstead's blacks lived in a few isolated enclaves, the largest of which surrounded the all-black Prospect Street School. Even blacks who lived in outlying neighborhoods were required to send their children—usually by bus—to Prospect Street. At the beginning of the 1949 school year, black parents called for the district to close Prospect and "distribute the Negro students through all the other Hempstead schools." When the school district ignored their demand, 195 black students—every one at Prospect—walked out for a week. As in Hillburn, protesting parents used a black church as an alternative school for boycotting children. White religious and leftist activists provided financial and logistical support.

Motley and the NAACP legal staff fashioned an argument that dovetailed with their strategy to defeat educational Jim Crow in the South.

Blacks, Motley argued, should have the right to attend their neighbor-hood school. This was a right ensured to white students; thus it should be ensured to blacks as well. Motley won her first victory easily. Under state order, blacks were no longer confined to the Prospect Street School but instead could attend the elementary school closest to their homes. The district was compelled to establish neighborhood school attendance zones. But the state department of education ruled narrowly that "school boards are not under compulsion to bring about an even distribution of races within all the schools of their districts." While the NAACP cele-brated this cautious decision, local whites resisted it fiercely. Parents of white children now assigned to the Prospect Street School demanded the right to voluntarily transfer their children out of their neighborhood school.

It would not be long before northern activists came to see the folly of the neighborhood school strategy in a region where most school segrega-tion resulted from the rigid color line in housing markets. In the racially divided world of suburban America, upholding the neighborhood school principle resulted in a Pyrrhic victory. As long as school district bound-aries followed neighborhood boundaries, it would just be a matter of time before whites took advantage of their freedom to move, exploiting the fact that blacks had few choices about where to live. Hempstead quickly resegregated. Some of the black students who would have gone to the Prospect Street School went to the Jackson and Franklin schools closer to their homes. Within a decade of Motley's victory, these two schools be-came overwhelmingly black as white families moved away. By 1962, two of Hempstead's elementary schools were over 95 percent white, but Franklin and Jackson were nearly 75 percent black. At the nominally de-segregated Prospect Street School, 86 percent of the students were black. Jim Crow had risen again in a new form, this time legitimated by a seem-ingly race-neutral principle that even the NAACP had endorsed.

IN MAY 1954, the U.S. Supreme Court struck down "separate but equal" education in its landmark *Brown v. Board of Education* decision, in a case argued by Thurgood Marshall. The Supreme Court had in mind officially separate schools—the latter-day version of Hillburn's Brook School or Trenton's Lincoln School or Hempstead's Prospect Street School. By

1954, officially separate schools still existed in scattered small towns in the North, but the system of separate education was on the wane nearly everywhere outside the South. No one—neither Marshall and the NAACP's litigation team who developed *Brown* nor the Supreme Court justices who decided it—considered the possible impact of the decision on northern public schools. Commentators on the case, from law journals to mainstream dailies to the black press, assumed that *Brown* would utterly transform the system of state-mandated educational apartheid in the South. Massive white resistance, especially in the Deep South, quickly tempered their optimism. But the story of the reaction to *Brown* is woefully incomplete if told solely from a southern vantage point. Within a year of the decision, activists around the North began to hold meetings and conferences on what implications *Brown* would have for their schools. In the process, they pushed at the boundaries of the Supreme Court's decision. The implications would be far-reaching and controversial.

Brown offered several tools to northern activists, though with many ambiguities. Northern school desegregation advocates quickly latched on to one key phrase in the Supreme Court's decision: "Separate educational facilities are inherently unequal." The phrase was broad. Its implications were open-ended. If separate, unequal education was constitutionally impermissible, could *Brown* lead to the eradication of segregated schools, even when there were no laws mandating the separation of students by race? Another section of the Court's decision, however, potentially limited the impact of *Brown* on northern education. The Court rested its decision on the demonstration of intentional discrimination, or what came to be called de jure segregation, namely state-sanctioned and enforced separation by race. The question for the North would be whether school districts could be held responsible for racial segregation that was the result of housing policies or other official state actions that encouraged racial separation.

Another element of the Court's decision that would have decisive implications—north and south—was the Court's use of social scientific research on the damaging impact of segregation on the black psyche. Of black students, the Court argued that segregation "generates a feeling of inferiority as to their status in the community that may affect their hearts and minds in a way unlikely ever to be undone." The Court built on more than a decade of social scientific and psychological research on race and gave credence to psychological understandings of race and racial difference. The National Association of Intergroup Relations Officials—which vocally advocated school desegregation in the North—argued that the "most fundamental indictment of school segregation" was "the damage that it does to the personalities of minority-group children." Nearly every school desegregation case after *Brown* included psychologists as expert witnesses, testifying that segregated education injured the self-esteem of black children. By the early 1960s, such arguments were commonplace in the countless books and articles that guided activists, school administrators, and litigators on the questions of educational equality.

No sooner had *Brown* been decided than civil rights activists in the North turned their attention to school inequalities. In the remaining northern towns with officially separate schools, *Brown* gave public school officials, many of whom were more liberal than their constituents, legal cover for rapid desegregation. In York, Carlisle, and Steelton, Pennsylvania, school district officials quickly capitulated to pressure to abolish their towns' separate Negro schools in the summer after *Brown* came down. School desegregation on such a small scale met with relatively little white resistance, especially where neighborhood schools provided a sanctuary for whites. But elsewhere in the North, the battle would be prolonged and the victories often more elusive.

Even in the absence of officially separate schools, northern public schools were nearly as segregated as those in the South. But the causes were more complex. What prevailed in the North came to be called, quite misleadingly, de facto segregation. "There is, of course, no official segregation in the city," noted a *New York Times* columnist in 1957. "It is illegal." Using the passive voice, thus making the process of segregation seem the inevitable consequence of impersonal forces beyond control, he argued that segregation "is caused by the residential pattern." At the heart of the analysis of de facto segregation was an erasure of intention: Northern schools were segregated because of the natural forces of the market, of individuals making choices about where to live, ostensibly unaffected by government policy and unshaped by considerations of race. Northern whites, wrote sociologist Alfred McClung Lee, "often take the position that their school is a 'neighborhood' one and that their district 'happens' to be white." The banking practices that denied loans to blacks who wanted to live in white neighborhoods or, vice versa, the federal mort-gage programs that forbade the introduction of "incompatible" groups into neighborhoods, the tactics of real estate agents who steered blacks into black-dominated or racially transitional neighborhoods—all of these were largely invisible. The visible manifestations of Jim Crow—separate drinking fountains and bathrooms, lynch mobs, white-only elections— these were rare in the mid-twentieth-century North. In the land of Dixie, segregation was intentional. Southern whites, from ordinary folks to elected officials, were responsible for Jim Crow. It was their creation, en-acted into law by their duly elected representatives, openly endorsed by fire-eating politicians at election time, defended by lynch mobs and police officers alike. In the North, by contrast, public officials claimed that the separation of races was just a fact of life, not mandated by law or con-trolled by the state. Whites could deny responsibility for racial segrega-tion, for their choices about where to live and where to send their children to school were individualized and ostensibly race-neutral. The logical conclusion of this line of reasoning was that it was the natural order of things that the vast majority of whites lived in all-white commu-nities and that blacks were confined to segregated neighborhoods and mostly minority schools. Like lived with like, birds of a feather flocked to-gether. No one was at fault.

One of the biggest challenges to those who wanted to bring *Brown* north was the distinct nature of school segregation in the region, particu-larly in a period of rapid black migration from the South and massive white suburbanization. In the South, racial segregation before *Brown* was not fundamentally intertwined with residential segregation. In many southern communities, blacks and whites lived in proximity, often across alleys or railroad tracks or even on the same farms and in the same houses. By and large, southern school districts did not use geographic at-tendance zones to separate black and white. Segregation was simple: Col-ored went to colored schools, whites went to white schools. Outside of communities with southern-style separate schools, northern school dis-tricts used geography, not skin color, to preserve racial homogeneity. Re-flecting on the implications of *Brown* for the North, *The Chicago Defender* noted that "the problem [of unequal education] will never be licked as long as the segregated pattern in housing persists and the North-ern device of gerrymandering school districts . . . continues."

The debate over race and education in the North came to hinge on the meaning of "neighborhood schools." The neighborhood school, argued two liberal critics of segregation, "has become as deeply embedded in American tradition as turkey on Thanksgiving" or, as *Time* magazine concluded, "a concept as American as apple pie." But the "neighborhood school," if it was a tradition at all, was a relatively new one, given the high mobility of American urban life. In densely populated cities, schools were often within a few blocks of one another, meaning that several schools might serve a "neighborhood." Outside big cities, students regularly traveled great distances to attend schools. As the nation suburbanized in the postwar years, the distance between home and school grew. The neighborhood school "tradition" took on its greatest salience in racially changing cities. As one observer of northern education noted, "the nearer Negroes get to [the neighborhood school], the more sacred it becomes."

In the rapidly growing twentieth-century city, what constituted a neighborhood was by no means a settled question. In cities with distinctive topographical features, such as hills, rivers, and streams, the boundaries of a neighborhood might be very clear. Nearly every northern city had at least a few neighborhoods that were easily defined because of natural and human-built features—hills or water or highways—that cut them off from the rest of the metropolitan area. Some old neighborhoods were the remnants of separate towns or villages that had been incorporated in the nineteenth or early twentieth centuries, when northern cities expanded dramatically. But by the mid–twentieth century, as populations grew increasingly mobile and as the automobile and public transportation drastically shortened the time to get from one neighborhood to another, these distinctions had become increasingly meaningless. There was little natural or permanent about most urban neighborhoods. Their residents, their boundaries, and even their names changed regularly. And for different ethnic groups, neighborhoods also had different degrees of significance. For Catholics, neighborhood was defined by parish (I live in Saint Cecilia's, you live in Holy Cross). But for members of religious groups who did not define their membership territorially (most Protestants and Jews), their most important social and cultural connections might crisscross an entire metropolitan area. Neighborhoods had greater meaning in the nineteenth century, when most workers lived near their workplaces. But in the decentralizing mid-twentieth-century city, workers scattered across whole metropolitan areas and relied on cars or public transportation to get to work. The separation of work and home further weakened neighborhood attachments. Imagine a series of transparencies, stacked one atop the other. One has school attendance zones, one Catholic parish boundaries, another shows the locations of synagogues and Protestant churches and the residences of their members; another draws lines between where individuals live and where they work; another shows links between where people live and shop. In the twentieth-century city, as the automobile became ubiquitous, those boundaries were less and less likely to overlap. A few places excepted, neighborhoods meant much less in 1940 than they did in 1900, and even less in 1960 than in 1940.

The boundaries that mattered in cities were mostly invisible. On the flat, featureless terrain of Chicago's South Side or Detroit's East Side or North Philadelphia or Queens, two nearby streets might appear virtually identical to an outsider, with similar architecture, streetscapes, and landscaping. But to a local, the differences between those two streets might be profound. In northwest Philadelphia, residents of one side of Mount Pleasant Avenue attended the Houston School; on the other, they attended the Emlen School. That kind of invisible line—particularly when it corresponded to a racial division—became a matter of great importance. It determined your access to one school or another, one future or another, one average real estate value versus another, membership in one set of social networks versus another.

There was nothing fixed, permanent, or natural about most urban boundaries. They were political creations. Some boundaries were inherited: When you moved into a city, you found yourself in one school district or another. What constituted a neighborhood was ultimately a matter of politics. Within school districts, administrators carefully mapped the boundaries of elementary schools and high schools, creating attendance districts where most or all school-age children would attend a single school. The drawing of these lines was, like so many issues of local government, politically fraught, perhaps more so because children were involved. The drawing of a district line down a street could separate friends. The shift of a school boundary might mean that a child would have to cross a busy highway or take a bus rather than walk to school. The construction of a new school often precipitated intense debates about who would be in and who would be out. White parents might squabble about any of these, but most agreed when it came to race. As the northern black population skyrocketed, the easiest way to preserve segregation was to gerrymander school attendance zones. As Gunnar Myrdal observed, "school boundaries . . . are usually set at the boundary of the white and Negro neighborhoods."

Not all school districts gerrymandered. The inherently racial meaning of neighborhood school boundaries became clearest in the case of white students who remained behind, "trapped" in school attendance areas that had become mostly black, or the black student (often the child of live-in domestics) who lived on the "white" side of town. The occasional white student who lived near a Negro school would usually be permitted to attend the closest white-majority school; black students in mostly white sections would be "encouraged and sometimes coerced into going to a Negro school." In Highland Park, Michigan, a suburb of Detroit, with a small but growing black population, officials changed the school attendance policy in 1945 to give parents in the neighborhood adjoining the town's black section the "option" of sending their children to nearby white-dominated schools, rather than districting them into the nearby Thompson School, which was overwhelmingly black. In 1961, when blacks had moved in large numbers into the "optional zone," school district officials again reshuffled school boundaries, mandating that all students in what was now a mostly black section of the city attend the black Thompson School. However, transfer options were not always tools to perpetuate racial segregation. In Philadelphia, school officials gave all students the option to transfer into district schools with vacancies; most whites used their right of transfer to move from predominantly black to mostly white schools. But two-thirds of the students using transfers were black students, most of whom took advantage of the policy to enroll in predominantly white schools.

Preserving racial boundaries came at a high cost, particularly to blacks. Black schools were regularly overcrowded, and because blacks had little choice but to move into the oldest urban neighborhoods, their schools were often aging and decrepit. In Chicago's black belt during the Great Depression and World War II, there were simply too few classrooms to accommodate black students. Principals ran "double and triple shift schools." Halfway through the school day, one group of black students shuffled out while the next shift came in. By 1940, all of Chicago's four-teen double-shift schools were in the black section of the city. As the city's black population dramatically expanded in the postwar years, the num-ber of double-shift schools skyrocketed to forty-eight by 1957. Through-out the 1950s, at least half of black students—and as many as 100 percent in certain years—attended double-shift schools. Overcrowding in black schools remained a chronic problem. As late as 1962, Chicago's white stu-dents had an average class size of thirty-one; Chicago's black-dominated classrooms averaged forty-seven students.

BY THE LATE 1950s and early 1960s, many commentators found, to their surprise, that "the north and west have problems, too" and in the process "discovered" that northern schools were often every bit as segregated as their southern counterparts. That discovery, hailed in article after article in local and national news media, was, of course, old news to blacks. It took the actions of northern black protestors, building on the past gener-ation of grassroots challenges to separate education, to make possible that "discovery." One of the unintended consequences of *Brown* was an accel-eration of northern school protests. Blacks in hundreds of northern cities and towns, beginning in the mid-1950s, pushed school boards to imple-ment *Brown* through boycotts, demonstrations, and litigation. What *Brown* meant—particularly in the North—was legally and politically up for grabs. The battles over northern school desegregation were not, as they are often portrayed, top-down, bureaucratic impositions, forced upon whites by meddling justices, abetted by "limousine liberals" who had the luxury of sending their students to elite private or suburban schools. Judges and white liberals played an important role in the battles over school desegregation, but black activists set the agenda.

The battle over *Brown* played out throughout the North, perhaps most decisively in and around New York City. By the early and mid-1950s, Harlem seemed a natural place to challenge northern segregation. Home to the nation's densest concentration of blacks and Puerto Ricans, its schools were nearly completely segregated by race. By every measure—teacher turnover, physical plant, student test scores—Harlem's schools were among the worst in the city. Typical were junior high schools 120, 136, and 139, where poor students were crowded into run-down buildings. Even before *Brown*, Harlemites began working for desegregated schools in their own community. In February 1954, psychologist Kenneth Clark, whose research on segregation and self-esteem undergirded the NAACP's litigation strategy, lambasted New York school segregation in a speech to the Urban League, and in April he invited representatives of dozens of civil rights and political organizations to a meeting titled "Children Apart" to formulate a plan to integrate New York's schools. A remarkable cadre of civil rights activists joined the effort, among them Ella Baker, who would soon become an advisor to the Reverend Martin Luther King, Jr., and the Reverend Milton Galamison, who had his hand in nearly every New York civil rights protest in the 1950s and 1960s. New York's school officials, who denied that the city's schools were segregated, agreed to cooperate with an independent study of race and ethnicity in the schools. The report's findings, which received extensive press coverage, were damning.

In 1957, the New York Board of Education announced its plans to implement a program of school integration but moved slowly. Civil rights groups and local activists, inspired by *Brown* and impatient at the pace of change, stepped up their pressure, holding mass meetings and rallies. Ella Baker ran parent workshops on equal education. By the beginning of the school year in 1958, the organizing efforts bore fruit. Rumors that the New York schools were transferring a small number of "gifted" middle-class black students from Harlem to a mostly white school nearby angered residents of Harlem's Lincoln housing project, among them Bernice Skipwith and Shirley Rector, whose children were confined to a run-down, overcrowded, and poorly staffed junior high school—one of two in Harlem with no white students. They led a group of mothers who withheld their children from school in early October, demanding transfers to mostly white schools. They were not alone. Another group of Harlem mothers, nicknamed "The Little Rock Nine of Harlem," also withheld their children from the city's public schools. Among the mothers was Mae Mallory, a former Communist who would later become well known as an associate of black self-defense advocate Robert F. Williams. While school officials—and many opinion makers—blamed black women for family dysfunction and pathology, Harlem's school activists wrapped themselves in the mantle of assertive motherhood, contending that the schools, not their parenting, had failed their children.

The case of Skipwith and Rector ended up in front of juvenile court justice Justine Wise Polier, member of a prominent left-liberal Jewish family in New York (her father, Stephen Wise, was one of the key figures in Reform Judaism, and her husband, Shad, was a well-known civil liberties attorney). Justine Polier had a long interest in child welfare, had been a member of the left-leaning National Lawyers Guild as a young attorney, and, as head of the American Jewish Congress Women's Division, had played a key role in spearheading the group's involvement in the black freedom struggle. The boycotting mothers could not have found a more sympathetic judge. In a decision that got international news coverage, Polier ruled that the boycotting parents had the "constitutionally guaranteed right to elect no education for their children rather than to subject them to discriminatorily inferior education." Polier's decision electrified civil rights activists throughout the North, and they flooded her mailbox with letters. Even though her decision set no precedent and did not mandate the desegregation of New York's schools, many saw it as the decisive blow for racial equality. It also energized protestors. In the fall of 1959, Shirley Rector led another wave of boycotts, with the support of New York's NAACP branch. In the aftermath of the case and the boycotts, New York's Board of Education began investigating the possibility of "free choice transfers," that is, allowing black children in segregated schools to transfer to predominantly white schools.

Harlem simmered, its tensions unresolved, when a group of activists in nearby New Rochelle, one of New York's older and more diverse suburbs, targeted their own school district. Built largely between 1890 and 1920, New Rochelle was denser and older and more blue-collar than its tony Westchester County neighbors, although its north side, bordering prosperous Scarsdale, was home to many professionals and executives and grew rapidly in the postwar years. New Rochelle had an established black population, which had gradually expanded outward from a nucleus of domestic and service workers. By 1960, New Rochelle's population of 77,000 was 14 percent black, many of whom lived in the vicinity of the Lincoln School, one of the city's oldest. As the neighborhood's wealthy whites fled for more fashionable outlying neighborhoods, the Lincoln School's black population grew rapidly. In 1930, a quarter of Lincoln's students were black; by 1949, it was nearly all black. In a practice common to many northern school districts, New Rochelle permitted white families who lived in the Lincoln School attendance area to transfer their children to nearby white schools. In 1949, when the school district ended its transfer policy—thus requiring white students who lived near Lincoln to attend the school—white parents opted out, sending their children to private schools or moving out of the Lincoln district. Lincoln remained New Rochelle's "Negro school."

In the aftermath of *Brown*, New Rochelle's NAACP chapter set its sights on the Lincoln School. As with most school controversies, New Rochelle's had a long history. In 1930, NAACP officials had opposed a plan to gerrymander most of the city's black students into the Lincoln School district, but in a state where separate schools were still legal, their protests fell on deaf ears. Over the course of the 1930s and the 1940s, white students opted out of the Lincoln School and most of the white transferees passed Lincoln on their way to their majority-white school.

In the late 1940s, New Rochelle activists—this time led by black and white leftists—again targeted the Lincoln School. They demanded that the district end its policy of granting transfers to white students living in the Lincoln School area. "The existence of a completely Negro school in a community such as New Rochelle is deplorable," wrote members of the interracial Council for Unity, who demanded a redistricting of the city's public schools. The all-black Citizen's Committee for Lincoln School concurred, bemoaning the poor quality of Lincoln's education.

At a lengthy, contentious school board meeting in January 1949, New Rochelle school officials faced a barrage of criticism. An extraordinary range of groups—including the Prince Hall Masons and Elks, as well as the NAACP, the Lincoln School PTA, the Communist Party, and the American Labor Party—denounced New Rochelle's policy of segregation. "Here we have one of the richest cities in the country," charged Lester Lennon, the father of a Lincoln School child, "and yet we have to come here and ask that my boy be given an equal opportunity." Like many of the speakers who demanded "education for democracy," Mrs. Robert Washington, the mother of eleven, most of them Lincoln students, reminded the board of its responsibility for "future citizens of the nation and what they are going to be."

After hours of such criticism (and with little legal alternative), the district abolished its transfer policy. New Rochelle's children were now required to attend the "neighborhood schools" to which they were assigned. But the fate of the Lincoln School was by no means settled by the school board's decision. White parents (about half the population in the school area) led a backlash against the new policy—they resisted being "forced" to send their children to the "neighborhood" school. In late 1949, they filed a lawsuit against the district for requiring their children to attend a demonstrably "inferior" school. When they lost the suit, whites fled en masse from the Lincoln district, leaving the now ostensibly integrated Lincoln School 94 percent black.

Just as in Hempstead, it became clear that the neighborhood school concept was no panacea for the problem of separate, unequal education. The battle over the Lincoln School was a reminder of how shallow and instrumental white commitment to the "neighborhood school" really was. When the neighborhood school was no longer theirs, white parents packed up and moved. By the mid-1950s, New Rochelle's grassroots activists had a new target—the neighborhood school. Their weapon was the still-untested *Brown* decision.

When the New Rochelle school district proposed to rebuild Lincoln as part of a massive school modernization project in 1956 (the seventy-year-old building was encased in scaffolding because of falling bricks and cement), the NAACP and a group of local activists called the Committee Against Segregation in the Public Schools put up a fight. They argued that Lincoln should be closed and its students moved to mostly white schools. In 1957, a citywide referendum on rebuilding the Lincoln School passed by a three-to-one majority, with heavy white support. Most black residents of the Lincoln School area opposed the plan. At the beginning of the 1959 school year, still opposing the rebuilding plan, black parents marched on the Lincoln School for two days, while 200 of the school's 497 students did not attend classes. In late November, Roy Wilkins of the NAACP addressed a four-hundred-person rally opposing the construction of a new Lincoln School. How, in the aftermath of the *Brown* decision, could the district channel money to a Jim Crow school? In the spring of 1960, black parents petitioned the New York state education commission to close the Lincoln School and reassign students throughout the district to achieve racial balance, but the state rebuffed them.

The battle over the Lincoln School came to a showdown at the beginning of the 1960–61 academic year. New Rochelle activists approached Paul Zuber, the young black attorney who had defended the parents of the Harlem school boycotters. Just thirty-five, the son of a postal worker who had migrated from Williamsport, Pennsylvania, to Harlem, Zuber fought in the army, attended Brown University on a football scholarship, and went to Brooklyn Law School. Zuber was always confident and willing to take risks, both in protest and in the courtroom, fearless even when he was breaking new legal ground. "He moves like a Sherman tank into areas where few men dare to tread," noted *The Chicago Defender*. Zuber quickly saw the potential of New Rochelle to test the principles of *Brown* in the North. Building on the successful tactics of the Harlem protests, Zuber encouraged parents to boycott classes at the Lincoln School while he prepared a lawsuit.

As in Harlem, the New Rochelle protests were led by women. Hallie Taylor, the mother of two Lincoln School children, organized a boycott. The parents of fifty other children joined her. Taylor's rationale was straightforward: "I feel that at Lincoln School my child Leslie was not achieving up to her potential, and I want her to have an education at an integrated school." Behind the scenes Taylor and Zuber plotted a further strategem: A group of parents would attempt to enroll their children in a predominantly white school. Fully expecting to be rebuffed, they knew that a confrontation would make a splash. On September 14, a week after classes had started, the parents of twelve black children—ages five through ten—showed up in the principal's office of the brand-new Ward School in Quaker Ridge, a wealthy, all-white section of town near the Scarsdale border. Their choice of targets was calculated: The Ward School was modern, light, and airy, and on spacious grounds, unlike the crumbling, cramped Lincoln School.

Herbert Clish, the superintendent of New Rochelle's schools, was caught off guard by the intensity of the school protest. Interrupted while shaving with news that black parents had invaded the Ward School, Clish hastily washed up and rushed to the scene, where he rebuffed the parents and insisted that the Lincoln School was every bit as good as Quaker Ridge. (Throughout the ensuing court battle, Clish would maintain that position, arguing that there were no significant differences in the quality of education between the town's wealthy white-dominated schools and its poorer majority-black ones.) The parents were out of line: New Rochelle, Clish contended, was sticking to its policy of "neighborhood schools." Intransigent and politically inept, Clish played into the hands of the boycotters.

The New Rochelle protests accelerated over the following month. Throughout the third week of September, a group of black mothers attempted to register their children at every white-dominated elementary school in New Rochelle. They were rejected again and again. Embittered by the inflexibility of the school district, the boycotting parents were also empowered by a flood of media interest in their campaign and by an outpouring of local support for their activism. Inspired by that year's wave of sit-ins at southern lunch counters, a group of boycotting parents planned their own act of civil disobedience on school grounds. On September 22, the NAACP's Reverend M. DeWitt Bullock led seven parents to the grounds of the Ward School, armed with folding chairs. They presented their demands, then gathered in prayer, and when the police approached, they walked into the school, unfolded their chairs, and calmly awaited their arrests for "loitering." Among those hauled off by the police were some of the most respected members of New Rochelle's tight-knit black community, including Bullock, Paul Dennis, a Republican and driver of the New Rochelle Public Library's bookmobile, and Marjorie Williams, Willine Murphy, and Hallie and Wilbert Taylor, all parents of boycotting children. A week later, four mothers, including Hallie Taylor, led twelve children on a march to the majority-white Roosevelt School, where they were served a court order enjoining them from entering the school grounds.

New Rochelle protestors also played the international card, further attracting media attention. Parents enlisted the support of Ghana's prime minister, Kwame Nkrumah, and lobbied two black United Nations envoys, one Ghanaian, the other Liberian (their embassies to the U.N. were located in New Rochelle), to withdraw their children from the New Rochelle schools. But as with many protests, New Rochelle's engendered conflict. Some black New Rochelle residents saw the sit-ins as divisive and disorderly and two of twenty-one NAACP board members quit their posts after an acrimonious debate about the efficacy of protest. Some parents wanted to see the new Lincoln School built and cared little about integration as long as their children were in a modern school.

The protests did not succeed in closing the Lincoln School, but they turned New Rochelle into a cause célèbre. News reporters from around the United States and the world swarmed into the town, attracted by the novelty of what was dubbed the "Little Rock of the North." Of course, the hapless Clish was no Orval Faubus. His continued insistence that the school district was not at fault and that "New Rochelle public schools are not segregated" was no line in the sand: In fact, several of the city's schools, including its high school, had sizeable black student populations, something unthinkable in the segregated South. Clish made no brief for segregation: He claimed to abhor it. Instead, he dodged responsibility. "The schools," argued Clish, "reflect residential neighborhood patterns." The Clish defense—that segregation was the result not of public policy but rather of market forces—became commonplace in the post-*Brown* North. If their schools were not de jure segregated, New Rochelle should not be responsible for finding a remedy.

Meanwhile, New Rochelle activists happily embraced the comparison to Little Rock. The analogy between North and South gave them the moral high ground. That the black press (and much of the northern white press) had treated the "Little Rock Nine," the first black students to break the color line at Central High School, as heroic, gave northern protestors the mantle of legitimacy. In Little Rock, students faced the angry mob and the state militia. Mob and state collaborated to fight for the racial purity of the schools. That the New Rochelle police had arrested eight parents for trespassing was a publicity coup for the protestors, for it made their analogy all the more powerful. Like southern protestors, they had committed civil disobedience in service of their cause.

But the use of such rhetorical hyperbole was less than effective—in fact, it gave white opponents of school desegregation cover, for New Rochelle, like most northern bastions of segregation, was not besieged by angry mobs. There was no need to deploy the 101st Airborne to restore order, as had been done in Little Rock. Sensitive to the charges that they were racist, school district officials developed elaborate, legalistic strategies to defend their position. White New Rochelle residents, the majority of whom supported rebuilding the segregated Lincoln School, insisted that they were liberal, that they had the best interests of their children and of black children in mind. Superintendent Clish argued that the protestors had misinterpreted *Brown:* The Court did not require "enforced integration by abnormal procedures." On the grounds that the school district lines were race-neutral, school board officials warned that the consideration of race for the purposes of school integration would open a "Pandora's box." The Clish defense took racial separation for granted.

That blacks and whites lived apart was natural. Public policy—like the drawing of school boundaries—was race-neutral. Any government intervention in school enrollment patterns, any attempts to achieve "racial balance" represented an unwarranted government intervention in the market, but more than that introduced "race consciousness" into what was ostensibly a color-blind polity. In addition, the shifting of "culturally deprived" black children from Lincoln into other schools would simultaneously disadvantage those children and their better-off classmates.

Above all, New Rochelle whites saw themselves as the opposite of the angry, rock-and-torch-wielding lynch mobs of the South who had become stock figures in northern depictions of the southern civil rights struggle. "Nothing makes my blood boil more," stated New Rochelle's school board president, distancing himself from a leading southern segregationist group, "than a letter from the white citizens' council saying 'keep up the good work.'" The very fact that New Rochelle residents politely defended the ostensibly race-neutral concept of neighborhood schools rather than bombing churches or attacking protestors was a sign of their virtue—and it rationalized their defense of the status quo. By using antidiscrimination rhetoric, white opponents of school desegregation found a powerful tool to legitimate their opposition to integrated schools.

On October 21, after more than five weeks of protests, Paul Zuber filed a lawsuit against the New Rochelle public schools on behalf of eight-year-old Leslie Taylor and several other children. The core of Zuber's complaint was an indictment of the neighborhood school. "It has been well recognized," Zuber argued, "that in many cities of New York state, and elsewhere, ghettos exist in which minority groups . . . are crowded. As a result thereof the public schools in such neighborhoods in such cities are segregated, reflecting the segregated pattern of the neighborhood. The utilization of the 'neighborhood school' policy in such areas must, of necessity, produce segregated schools." Racially separate and unequal, neighborhood schools were unconstitutional. Zuber fashioned a strategy to push *Brown* in a new direction: to delegitimate neighborhood schools, regardless of whether they had been created with segregative intentions.

At trial, however, Zuber modified his argument, like any good attorney looking for an argument that would stick. He presented evidence that the Lincoln School had inferior facilities, overcrowded classrooms, and inexperienced teachers. Inspired by the successful use of social science in *Brown*, Zuber hired experts to testify to the damaging psychological effects of segregation. In addition, Zuber mounted a case that New Rochelle's school board had deliberately gerrymandered the Lincoln School boundaries and tinkered with school attendance rules to allow white students to transfer out of Lincoln to nearby majority-white schools. In the process, Zuber shifted the grounds of the case to proving intentional discrimination—whereas his brief had made the more controversial case that regardless of intention, segregated schools were inherently unequal and thus constitutionally impermissible. For its part, the school district stuck to its position that Lincoln's segregation was unintentional and that the school district was racially integrated (indeed, many of its schools, especially its junior high schools and single high school, reflected the town's racial mix). Still, New Rochelle's attorneys did not strengthen their case when they deployed their own expert, Henry E. Garrett, a prominent conservative psychologist (and past president of the American Psychological Association). Garrett had denounced the *Brown* decision on grounds that segregation was not damaging, a conclusion that grew from his scholarship on the intellectual inferiority of blacks and his distaste for what he called the "equalitarians and moralistic social reformers" who called for "dysgenic and socially disastrous race mixing."

Federal judge Irving Kaufman—who ten years earlier had ordered the execution of alleged Communist spies Ethel and Julius Rosenberg— heard the case and found in favor of the plaintiffs. The segregation of the Lincoln School, he contended, was not "an unfortunate fortuity." It was the result of gerrymandering and the district's refusal to redraw school boundaries when it was presented with evidence of segregation. The heart of Kaufman's opinion was an indictment of school district boundaries that, while purportedly race-neutral, reinforced patterns of segregation. "The neighborhood school policy certainly is not sacrosanct," wrote Kaufman. "It is valid only insofar as it is operated within the confines established by the Constitution. It cannot be used as an instrument to confine Negroes within an area artificially delineated in the first instance by official acts. If it is so used, the Constitution has been violated and the courts must intervene." Kaufman's opinion carefully hedged its legal bets. Ultimately, Kaufman stuck to a close reading of *Brown*—in particular its emphasis on the need to prove that discrimination was the result of intentional school district policies. Kaufman was, however, unwilling to accept Zuber's argument about neighborhood schools: His opinion did not incorporate the plaintiffs' contention that the "de facto" segregation—without evidence of state action—was constitutionally impermissible. That was a question that would be the focus of court battles and wildly divergent opinions for the next fifteen years.

The New Rochelle boycotters were jubilant about their victory. "It's wonderful, it's marvelous, it's grand," cheered Marjorie Williams, a boycotter. "Lincoln School should be torn down." Turning the argument about the educational disadvantages of segregation on its head, another black supporter of the boycotts, Mrs. Walter Murphy, argued that the victory would give white children the benefit of classroom diversity. For Joseph Green, a father of six, it was a triumph against racism: "Every white man who insists on segregated schools should be hanged." But in a foreshadowing of disagreements that would divide advocates of educational equality, not all black New Rochelle residents celebrated. "There should be more talk about the good education [Lincoln] provides," argued Carrie Prockman, "not so much talk about what color people are." But Prockman was in the minority. Black supporters of the desegregation of the Lincoln School denounced parents who wanted to keep their children there as "Uncle Toms" and "Aunt Jemimas." But that summer, the parents of nearly two-thirds of Lincoln students applied for transfers to other schools.

School district officials, on the other hand, decided to appeal the decision. School board president Merryle Rukeyser fumed about the "adverse publicity" and "factual errors" of the court case: "We have been lynched by people who use words loosely." Although the district lost its appeal and the U.S. Supreme Court declined to hear the case, the school board continued to resist by refusing to pay the transportation costs for children transferring from Lincoln. Because many Lincoln parents were poor, the local NAACP chapter created a nonprofit transportation fund, raising nearly sixteen thousand dollars in its first year to subsidize desegregation. Finally, in 1963, the Lincoln School was closed. It was eventually torn down. With New York state funding, all children who had to travel more than a mile and a half to school were transported by bus.

The New Rochelle victory rippled quickly outward, first to other districts in metropolitan New York, then to cities throughout the North and

West. The New Rochelle case, wrote the U.S. Commission on Civil Rights, "challenges many school boards in the North and West which have thought that they were immune from attack because existing segregation did not result from school assignment explicitly by race." Kaufman's ruling, noted a prominent civil rights attorney, "opens the door to a host of other situations, even if they are dissimilar."

Taylor v. Board of Education also launched Paul Zuber into the national limelight. Activists in Englewood, New Jersey, and Chicago recruited him to challenge school segregation in their communities. In addition, *Taylor* forced the NAACP to reorganize its litigation strategy. The NAACP Legal Defense Fund had had little interest in northern cases before New Rochelle but fretted that freelance attorneys like Zuber—who had tense relations with Thurgood Marshall—would take center stage in post-*Brown* school litigation. Marshall and Constance Baker Motley handled the appeals and would be more assertive in future cases. Throughout the early and mid-1960s, NAACP staff attorney Robert L. Carter represented plaintiffs in many of the rapidly proliferating "de facto" cases.

From Hillburn to New Rochelle, the battles for equal education in the small-town and suburban North succeeded in making school desegregation a national, not just a southern, issue. More than that, they served as a reminder of the ways that social movements pushed litigation in unexpected directions and of how court decisions empowered grassroots activists. The postwar legal agenda around racial equality in education was not simply or primarily a top-down imposition but instead grew from local agitation. The results of challenges to unequal education in the North were mixed: Some school districts quickly resegregated; others experienced massive white flight. The process intensified in the early and mid-1960s, as grassroots activists pushed even harder, throughout the North, for civil rights in the schools. The inadequacies and the possibilities of the *Brown* decision sparked an extraordinary wave of grassroots protest, school boycotts, and litigation. Activists and renegade attorneys—and the NAACP itself—began to challenge the boundaries between de facto and de jure segregation. Increasing impatience with the persistence of unequal education, as with employment discrimination, would usher in a period of activism, policy innovation, and experimentation that would have enduring consequences.

CHAPTER 7

"NO RIGHT MORE ELEMENTAL"

NOTHING SYMBOLIZED THE PROMISE OF POSTWAR AMERICA MORE THAN Levittown. Affordable housing for the common man, these massive suburban developments remade America's landscape after World War II. The iconic images of little ranches and Cape Cods, set in spacious yards on curvilinear streets, stood for everything that America celebrated in the Cold War era. The Soviets lived in cramped, communal apartments, but even ordinary Americans could afford a three-bedroom house with a picture window and an attic that could be converted into a playroom or a bedroom for another kid. William Levitt, master builder of Levittown, celebrated the distinctive Americanness of suburbia: "No man who owns his own house and lot can be a Communist. He has too much to do."

Outside Philadelphia, Levitt constructed one of his trademark subdivisions, which he marketed as the "most perfectly planned community in America." On farmlands in lower Bucks County, between Trenton and Philadelphia, Levittown, Pennsylvania, was finished in 1958. It immediately attracted a heterogeneous mix of suburbanites: blue-collar workers employed in a nearby U.S. Steel factory, teachers, clerks, and administrators. As was the case in every Levittown, by Levitt's orders, not a single resident was black. It was not for a shortage of potential black buyers. Black housing demand far exceeded supply. In metropolitan Philadelphia, between 1946 and 1953, only 347 of 120,000 new homes built were open to blacks. Racial exclusion had perverse economic effects: It created a vast gap between supply and demand. As a result, blacks paid more for housing on average than did whites. In nearly every northern city, black newcomers crammed into old and run-down housing, mainly in dense central neighborhoods left behind by upwardly mobile whites. In a bitter reflection on the urban housing market, Langston Hughes described black neighborhoods as the "land of rats and roaches, where a nickel costs a dime."

Levitt was unabashed in defending the racial homogeneity of his planned communities. "We can solve a housing problem or we can try to solve a racial problem," he argued, "but we cannot combine the two." The housing problem and the racial problem were, however, utterly inseparable in the postwar North. As economist Robert Weaver argued, "among the basic consumer goods, only for housing are Negroes traditionally excluded from freely competing in the open market." The struggle to open housing was not just a matter of free access to a market that excluded blacks. Persistent racial segregation in housing had high stakes. In postwar America, where you lived shaped your educational options, your access to jobs, and your quality of life. The housing market also provided most Americans with their only substantial financial asset. Real estate was the most important vehicle for the accumulation of wealth. Breaking open the housing market would provide blacks access to better-funded, higher-quality schools. It would give them the opportunity to live in growing communities—near the shopping malls, office centers, and industrial parks where almost all new job growth happened. And it would narrow the wealth gap between blacks and whites. The battle against housing discrimination—in Levittown and elsewhere—was perhaps the most consequential of the entire northern freedom struggle.

The most characteristic feature of the postwar northern housing market was its nearly complete segregation by race. The whiteness of Levitt's vast developments, and of postwar suburbia in general, was not an accident. By the late 1940s, white Americans had come to take for granted the racial homogeneity of their neighborhoods. But the existence of all-white and all-black neighborhoods was not a fixed, timeless feature of northern life. Rather, rigid housing segregation by race was a relatively new creation. Until the early twentieth century, most northern blacks lived near whites in racially mixed neighborhoods, usually on blocks with many white neighbors. In central cities, blacks usually lived scattered among other working-class and poor urbanites, many of whom were recent immigrants. Many smaller towns and suburbs, most notably in Chicago's North Shore, Philadelphia's Main Line, and New York's lower Westchester County, had black enclaves. The suburban rich depended on black menial labor in their kitchens, gardens, laundries, and garages.

Racial segregation in the northern housing market was achieved—it was not in any respect a natural process. Contrary to the conventional wisdom, the division of metropolitan areas by race was not the sum of millions of individual choices about where to live. Housing segregation northern-style was built on a sturdy foundation of racial restrictions encoded in private regulations and public policy. In the late nineteenth and early twentieth centuries, the Midwest—and especially Indiana and Illinois—were dotted with "sundown towns," places whose residents drove blacks out by force, enacted ordinances to prohibit black occupancy (although such ordinances were struck down by the Supreme Court in 1917), and sometimes posted signs, like that in Wendell Willkie's Elwood, Indiana, warning blacks of the dire consequences of staying around after sunset. Such crude techniques sometimes succeeded in driving blacks out of small towns, but they were less effective in the major northern metropolitan areas that attracted the vast majority of African American migrants beginning in World War I.

Three exclusionary devices, each of which had been perfected in the two decades preceding World War II, gave postwar American metropolitan areas their racially segregated character. First, private but legally enforceable restrictive covenants—attached to nearly every housing development built between 1920 and 1948—forbade the use or sale of a property to anyone other than whites. Second, federal housing policies, enacted during the Depression, mandated racial homogeneity in new developments and created a separate, unequal housing market, underwritten with federal dollars, for blacks and whites. Third, real estate agents staunchly defended the "freedom of association" and the right of home owners and developers to rent or sell to whom they pleased, steering blacks into racially mixed or all-black neighborhoods.

Levitt's huge subdivisions were covered by restrictive covenants. Included in deeds and enforced in civil courts, restrictive covenants controlled how a property could be developed, how it could be used, and who could live there. A device to preserve a neighborhood's homogeneity, covenants often specified minimum lot sizes and forbade multiple-family housing, and by so doing priced out poor and working-class purchasers. Other restrictions further blocked access by low-income residents. In the early twentieth century, when most working-class people, especially rural migrants, kept chickens or pigs as a matter of survival, suburban developers put restrictions on household animals, to keep out not just squealing pigs but their owners, too. By the 1920s, restrictive language grew more specific in categorizing not just undesirable uses but undesirable users. By the 1920s, deeds in nearly every new housing development in the North prevented the use or ownership of houses by people other than "the Caucasian race." Using the racial argot of the day, covenants variously forbade home sales or rentals to "Africans, Negroes, and Ethiopians" and less frequently Asians, Mexicans, and Jews.

The real estate industry held restrictive covenants sacrosanct. From the 1930s through the 1960s, the National Association of Real Estate Boards (which trademarked the word "Realtor") issued ethical guidelines that specified that a Realtor "should never be instrumental in introducing to a neighborhood a character of property or occupancy, members of any race or nationality, or any individual whose presence will be clearly detrimental to property values in a neighborhood." Lest there be any confusion, an industry brochure offered guidance. "The prospective buyer might be a bootlegger who would cause considerable annoyance to his neighbors, a madam who had a number of call girls on her string, a gangster who wants a screen for his activities by living in a better neighborhood, a colored man of means who was giving his children a college education and thought they were entitled to live among whites.... No matter what the motive or character of the would-be purchaser, if the deal would institute a form of blight, then certainly the well-meaning broker must work against its consummation."

Private real estate practices alone did not shape the metropolitan landscape of segregation. Federal housing programs, especially those introduced in the New Deal, mixed the gravel of racism into the mortar of public policy. FDR made the reform of the housing market one of the linchpins of his social policy. To that end, the government created the Home Owners' Loan Corporation (HOLC) in 1933, which provided low-interest loans to home owners at risk of foreclosure. In 1934, Roosevelt signed legislation creating the Federal Housing Administration (FHA), which wholly restructured the American mortgage market. The FHA—and for returning veterans after World War II, the Veterans Administration—guaranteed mortgages from default. These government programs wholly remade America's real estate and banking industries by minimizing the risk of home loans. Federal guarantees allowed lenders to package long-term (usually thirty-year) mortgages at low interest rates. More than that, the FHA provided crucial financial support to the housing industry. Without federal intervention in the housing market, massive suburbanization would have been impossible. In 1930, only 30 percent of Americans owned their own homes; by 1960, more than 60 percent were home owners. Home ownership became an emblem of American citizenship.

Federally backed loans and mortgages were, however, seldom available to residents of racially mixed or "transitional" neighborhoods. The presence of even a single black family rendered a whole neighborhood "actuarially unsound." To assist lenders, the HOLC prepared "neighborhood security maps." The maps were elaborately drawn and backed up with detailed descriptions of a neighborhood's housing stock and racial, ethnic, and class composition. The best neighborhoods, denoted "A" and "B," were colored green and blue; the riskiest neighborhoods were denoted "C" and "D" and colored yellow and red. If "inharmonious racial and ethnic groups" lived in a neighborhood, "stability" would be at risk. Residents in neighborhoods with old housing stock (at risk of "transition to lower class occupancy") or with even a handful of black residents were marked "D" and were usually ineligible for FHA-backed loans. To preserve stability, FHA officials supported the use of restrictive covenants.

Whites often engaged in extralegal actions to enforce restrictive covenants and racially discriminatory lending policies. They fought tenaciously to keep "undesirables" out of their neighborhoods as blacks migrated northward. Whites had economic reasons to resist the "Negro invasion," as they called it. Their ability to secure mortgages and loans was at risk. But their motivations were not solely economic. Intertwined with concerns about property values were fears of black predation. Above all, whites—both north and south—recoiled at the prospect of miscegenation. In the South, those fears were allayed through legal restrictions on intermarriage and racial mixing in public places; in the North, those fears were addressed by the regulation of housing markets.

Rapidly changing neighborhoods in northern cities, particularly those whose white residents could not afford to pick up and move easily, became bloody battlegrounds. In Detroit, between 1945 and 1965, nearly two hundred white neighborhood associations formed—most with the explicit purpose of keeping blacks away. In Chicago, mobs of angry whites beset blacks who had the temerity to cross the city's sharply defined neighborhood color lines. In Philadelphia, blacks who breached neighborhood boundaries were often victims of physical attacks. Cross burnings, arson, window breakings, and mobs greeted black newcomers to white neighborhoods in nearly every major northern city between the 1920s and the 1960s.

While many whites stayed their ground, many more decamped when blacks moved nearby—and many more simply avoided racially mixed cities altogether. The mass migration of whites to suburbia resulted in staggering change. Between 1950 and 1960, 700,000 whites moved to Philadelphia's suburbs, at the same time that the city lost 225,000 whites and gained 153,000 blacks. Suburban Chicago gained more than one million whites, but the city lost 399,000 whites and gained 320,000 blacks. During the same period, the numbers of black suburbanites grew very slowly. Most blacks had no choice but to live in central cities. Those who suburbanized were confined to established black enclaves.

The reasons for white's movement to suburbia were as many and varied as suburban residents themselves. Some moved because they clung to a romantic vision of green space. Others claimed to be fleeing urban "congestion," although by the 1960s, most suburban areas, with their car-choked roads, were just as congested as central cities. Many whites, particularly those with children, went in search of good schools, which, funded by local property taxes, were almost always better equipped and staffed than their urban counterparts. Others fled the fear of crime, which though it seldom affected whites directly, had become a staple of the daily newspapers and, when television arrived on the scene in the 1950s, the evening news. Still others, compelled by the desire for something new, rushed to be the first buyers in the ubiquitous subdivisions springing up on former cornfields and marshlands and woods outside big cities. In the booming postwar economy, rising wages, employment security, and generous federal mortgage programs allowed many whites to afford new housing for the first time and fueled massive suburban growth.

The most salient feature of postwar suburbs was their political isolation from the increasingly heterogeneous central cities. Some cities—most of them in the Sunbelt—encompassed outlying rural and suburban areas in a single regional government, but with few exceptions, northern metropolitan areas were balkanized into fragmented, competing jurisdictions. Suburbs were politically and fiscally separate from central cities. In the late 1950s, political scientist Robert Wood found more than 1,400 governments in metropolitan New York alone. The three-county Detroit metropolitan area had eighty-three separate school districts. This division of metropolitan America had profound racial consequences, since the boundaries between city and suburb were racial—and political. Suburbanites benefited from their proximity to major urban centers. In most metropolitan areas, cities provided their outlying suburbs with essential utilities such as gas, water, and electrical power. The relationship between cities and suburbs was, however, unequal. Urban residents—especially minorities—were hurt when suburbs drained tax dollars, population, and jobs away from their communities.

In modern America, still an intensely localistic society, goods and services were not distributed equally across all political jurisdictions. Some municipalities had better infrastructure, better schools, and better public services than others. Political membership—your residence in a particular municipality—affected the quality of the goods and services you got from local government in exchange for your tax dollars. Because of the persistence of localism, most northern municipalities provided their own services. They built their own roads, maintained their own parks, built their own libraries, staffed their own police and fire departments, and, most important, supported their own school districts. All these services were bankrolled mainly by local property taxes. The systematic exclusion of blacks from most suburbs meant that few (other than scattered residents of suburban black enclaves in white municipalities) benefited from the clustering of wealth, political resources, and capital that characterized postwar suburbia.

Suburbia represented the merger of identity and interest. Group membership—race—shaped where you lived and your self-perception. Whites saw their neighborhoods as the antithesis of the black ghetto— neat, orderly, well funded, and well run. By contrast they viewed black communities as filthy, lawless, run-down, and poorly managed. Whites kept up their properties, Negroes did not. In a society that emphasized housing and real estate as a matter of free choice and explained the movement to suburbia as the consequence of hard work, the commonsensical explanations of racial inequality emphasized individual success and individual failure. The political mechanisms that made possible massive white home ownership and discouraged black home ownership were largely invisible. "In the North," wrote Gunnar Myrdal, "there is actually much unawareness on the part of white people of the extent of social discrimination against Negroes." Whites saw residential segregation not as the result of public policy but rather as a "natural and desirable situation," the result of separation by class and the sum of individual choices about where to live.

Local struggles to open up suburbs were both challenges to assumptions about race and battles over the meaning of citizenship in a period of American history when public goods were largely meted out by local political institutions. Efforts to provide blacks with equal housing opportunities touched a raw nerve not just because whites were fearful of having black neighbors, but because whites were unwilling to share their tax dollars and the benefits those tax dollars bought. The stakes in opening up the suburbs were very high.

TWO DECADES BEFORE the rise of the Levittowns, the NAACP had begun fashioning a legal strategy to combat housing segregation. The cases were few and scattered. Most involved black professionals who aspired to live in predominantly white neighborhoods. In 1925, in an early and much-celebrated victory, the NAACP defended Ossian Sweet, a black Detroit doctor charged with murder after firing into a crowd of angry whites who besieged his newly purchased house in an all-white neighborhood. The Sweet case helped to launch the NAACP's legal department. But the NAACP did not spend much energy litigating housing segregation cases. The key mechanism maintaining housing segregation in the 1920s and 1930s—the restrictive covenant—had been upheld as constitutional in a series of legal challenges. But, as was often the case with the NAACP's litigation strategy, grassroots activists forced the question. Local branches launched a "determined fight" against racial covenants, beginning in the early 1940s, building on the wartime rhetoric of freedom. "There is no right more elemental nor any liberty more fundamental in a democracy than freedom to move where and when you please," wrote the editors of *The Crisis*. The Chicago branch, for example, assisted Carl Hansberry in a challenge to restrictive covenants in a South Side neighborhood in a court battle that his daughter Lorraine would fictionalize in her play *A Raisin in the Sun.* The Detroit branch alone litigated nine restrictive covenant cases during and immediately after World War II, hoping to "wipe out Detroit's ghetto walls." Often local attorneys offered creative legal theories, reflecting shifts in understandings of race. In *Sipes v. McGhee,* a case involving a black Detroit couple barred from buying a house because of a racially restrictive covenant, lawyers brought in a prominent anthropologist who argued that "race" had no valid biological meaning. But the challenge to restrictive covenants also happened outside the NAACP's purview, in part because better-off blacks often hired their own lawyers.

The proliferation of uncoordinated, grassroots challenges to restrictive covenants forced the NAACP legal team to take up the issue. But the battle against restrictive covenants faced a serious obstacle. By the 1940s, the validity of restrictions on the use of property was firmly established in the law. To end-run around the court's unwillingness to interfere with private sales and rentals, NAACP lawyers crafted an ingenious argument. They emphasized "state action," that is, the power of the government to enforce private contracts. In addition, NAACP lawyers developed a social scientific case—drawing from cutting-edge work in urban sociology and economics—about the negative consequences of restrictive covenants, including overcrowding, poor health conditions, and crime. Finally, their efforts to force the Supreme Court to reconsider racial restrictions came to fruition in the 1948 *Shelley v. Kraemer* case, involving covenants in Detroit, St. Louis, and Washington. Behind the scenes, NAACP attorneys were not at all confident that they would win on the merits. Three justices recused because their own properties were covered by racial restrictions. But in its landmark decision, the Supreme Court unanimously ruled that courts could not enforce racially restrictive covenants. The reaction to the case was overwhelmingly positive. "We can live anywhere!" screamed the headlines of *The Pittsburgh Courier.* "Kill Restrictive Covenants!" read the *Defender*'s banner headline. *The New Republic* called it a "momentous decision."

Few black activists placed their bets on *Shelley* transforming race relations in America. Constance Baker Motley later noted that *Shelley* "aided upper-middle-class blacks who were seeking to move from segregated inner-city areas (which even then were deteriorating) to better housing in white neighborhoods or the suburbs." Its impact was more symbolic than real. The Supreme Court had ruled that covenants were unenforceable, but it did not prohibit private individuals from putting restrictions on their own properties. A restriction might not have legal force, but it could still exert moral sway over a home seller or real estate broker—thus ensuring the neighborhood "stability." In the aftermath of *Shelley*, FHA officials unapologetically continued the official policy of encouraging lenders to favor racially restricted developments. Finally, in late 1949, in the face of ongoing pressure from the NAACP—using *Shelley* to condemn official action condoning segregation—the FHA announced that it would no longer underwrite loans to racially restricted properties, although it issued a clarification that it would not invalidate already established restrictive covenants.

The legal victory against restrictive covenants was the beginning, not the end, of the battle against housing segregation. The Court had struck down the most obvious, but in many respects the least effective, tactic to enforce racial segregation. Restrictive covenants covered nearly all housing in the North built between World War I and the late 1940s. But covenants were more often than not honored in the breach. After all, many neighborhoods where housing had been covered by restrictive covenants had turned over quickly after the first blacks had moved in. The enforcement of restrictive covenants before *Shelley* required lengthy, costly civil suits. And vast sections of metropolitan areas remained white regardless of whether they were covered by racial restrictions. The root causes of housing segregation were deeper.

Key to the legal strategy of opening the housing market was defining segregation as the outcome of state action (just as the courts had done in the *Shelley* case). Even though the fingerprints of public policy were all over postwar housing developments, it was extraordinarily difficult to persuade the courts to accept that housing developers were, in effect, creatures of the state. Postwar developers, even as they relied on government programs, depicted themselves as the embodiment of free enterprise. But the northern housing market was anything but laissez-faire. Housing developers depended on progrowth public policies. Municipalities used eminent domain law to condemn land for new construction and zoning codes to regulate what was built. Banks made loans and provided venture capital with mortgages underwritten by federal housing programs. Federal tax policies, notably the home mortgage interest deduction, further subsidized home ownership.

As was the case with restrictive covenants, grassroots activists forced the question of what constituted discriminatory state action. One of the earliest efforts involved New York's Stuyvesant Town, a moderate-income housing development on Manhattan's East Side that was designed to house more than twenty-four thousand people. Government action literally paved the way for the vast project. The city cleared a huge tract of working-class apartments, closed several streets, and provided subsidies for the Metropolitan Life Insurance Company, Stuyvesant Town's developer. From the moment that it announced the project in 1943, Metropolitan Life forbade African Americans (many of whom had lived in the neighborhood before it was cleared) to rent apartments there. MetLife lawyers justified the action on the grounds that landlords had the right to choose their own tenants. Critics denounced the development as a "new style ghetto" and as "an unholy walled city." A coalition of civil rights, leftist, labor, and religious groups fired off letters to public officials denouncing "Jim Crow" Stuyvesant Town. They regularly picketed at the site. The protests sparked litigation—in a case that hinged on the definition of state action. In *Dorsey v. Stuyvesant Town*, Thurgood Marshall argued that the city had condemned the land and that city and state laws had made possible the very development. As a "state undertaking," Stuyvesant Town should not be permitted to discriminate on grounds of race. But New York State and the federal courts did not find the plaintiffs' arguments persuasive, and the Supreme Court did not hear the case.

The ink had barely dried on the *Shelley v. Kraemer* decision and the protests had barely abated at Stuyvesant Town when New York–based activists turned their attention to William Levitt and his new Long Island Levittown—an even more prominent target. In the late winter of 1949, representatives from a number of left-wing organizations—including the Civil Rights Congress, the American Labor Party, and the Great Neck chapter of the NAACP, suspected to be Communist-dominated—met with Thomas Grace, the FHA's New York state director, to push the federal agency to refuse to underwrite mortgages in Levittown unless the developer adopted a nondiscrimination policy. Levitt, the activists argued, "is using federal aid and assistance for an unconstitutional purpose." Grace insisted that racial matters were not in the FHA's purview. The Cold War weakened the effectiveness of the activists who challenged Levitt's "free enterprise." A homegrown group of Levittown integrationists who joined the effort lamented that they were victims of a "McCarthyite attack" led by "bigots and foes of civil liberties."

Unchecked by the FHA, Levitt continued to practice racial segregation. In August 1950, his firm launched eviction proceedings against two families renting homes in the Long Island Levittown. Under the terms of the restrictive covenants that covered Levittown, "the use of these premises by persons other than Caucasians" was forbidden. The Novick and Ross families had committed the unpardonable sin of inviting the children of some black friends to play in their yard. (Most likely the Novicks and Rosses were Communists; in 1949 the Party had taken an unwavering line against restrictive covenants, encouraged its members to defy them, and expelled forty-six New York party members who had signed leases with racial restrictions.) Lawyers from the NAACP intervened, challenging the eviction under the *Shelley* precedent, but their efforts were rendered moot when both families moved from Levittown for reasons unrelated to the case. In 1953, when Levitt evicted a black family as "undesirable" tenants, his lawyers again vehemently defended their right to lease at will. Restrictive covenants may no longer have been in force, but Levitt's attorneys crafted an argument that had deep resonance in the probusiness climate of the early 1950s. They charged that any interference with the right to choose one's tenants was a blow to the very principles of free enterprise and free association.

While local activists were struggling—to little avail—to desegregate Levitt's flagship development, the NAACP shifted its attention to Levitt's newest development, in Bucks County, Pennsylvania. Behind the scenes, in negotiations with government officials, and in the courts, the NAACP sought to open Pennsylvania's Levittown to blacks. In October 1951, a group of civil rights activists, including Constance Baker Motley, held a conference with William Levitt. "Mr. Levitt," the NAACP attorney reported, "made it quite clear that the proposed Levittown will be restricted to whites" because "white people refuse to live in a community to which Negroes will be admitted." Levitt stated that he "could not take a chance on admitting Negroes and then not being able to sell his houses." In the meantime, NAACP president Walter White sent telegrams to the FHA and to Governor John Fine, demanding that the new Levittown be open to buyers regardless of race. Fine summarized the official position on Levittown: He supported the nondiscrimination in principle, but was unwilling "to impose conditions of occupancy on a private builder." When the FHA also refused to intervene, NAACP officials grew so frustrated that they threatened to withdraw the organization's support for all federal housing programs.

As negotiations faltered, the NAACP prepared for yet another lawsuit against Levitt. In late 1952, the local NAACP found an appealing group of plaintiffs when Arthur Johnson and "several Negro veterans" complained that they had been rebuffed by Levitt's sales agents. "On several visits to this project and an inquiry about price, we were told 'This is an all white community.'" Before filing suit on Johnson's behalf, the NAACP exhausted its efforts to win over Levitt and federal officials. Throughout 1952 and 1953, the NAACP lobbied United States Steel officials, whose new Fairless Hills plant was minutes from Levittown, to put pressure on Levitt to open the development to blacks. In Washington, NAACP officials raised their concerns about federal subsidies for Levittown in a meeting with President Eisenhower in January 1954 and continued to push the federal housing agencies to refuse to underwrite "Jim Crow" Levittowns. But their efforts were fruitless.

Finally, in early 1955, the NAACP Legal Defense Fund, fresh off its victory in *Brown*, filed a federal lawsuit on behalf of Johnson and five other black veterans. Thurgood Marshall and Constance Baker Motley argued that Levitt's refusal to sell homes to blacks violated the Fourteenth Amendment and Pennsylvania law. Frustrated with federal inaction, the suit also named FHA and Veterans Administration officials, whose agencies underwrote mortgages in Levitt's developments. The suit, however, went nowhere. In a terse opinion, the court ruled that the federal and state governments could not be held responsible for Levitt's actions. Although government regulations "touch the project at a great many points," that did not make the federal government "the builder of the project." Moreover, the court reasoned that the enforcement of antidiscrimination measures "cannot be forced upon [the FHA and VA] by the courts through the medium of the injunctive process." NAACP attorneys, busy with other cases and certain of defeat, did not appeal the decision.

. . .

LITIGATION TO OPEN the housing market had serious limitations. *Shelley v. Kraemer* had not led the courts to devise a broader theory of state action in the realm of housing segregation. Federal, state, and local courts continued to view developers as private actors, regardless of the fact that they were creatures of public policy and depended on federal largesse. And the "right" of developers or individuals to choose their associates—by discriminating in home rentals and sales—remained sacrosanct. By the early 1950s, integration advocates began to reconsider the litigation strategy. "The right to equality," wrote Charles Abrams, the most prominent white advocate of housing integration, "is not created of law or decree alone." Throughout his career, Abrams emphasized the "moral nature of this fight." The battle against housing segregation would ultimately be one for the hearts and minds of white Americans.

The principles that Gunnar Mydral laid out in *An American Dilemma* undergirded what came to be called the "open housing movement." Housing integration would not come about naturally. To open up the housing market would require an appeal to white Americans' morality. Habit, culture, and emotions—all interacted to perpetuate housing segregation. To break open what Gunnar Myrdal called the "vicious circle" of segregation required systematic "scientific research" in service of "social engineering." Housing integration—more than any other civil rights effort of the postwar years—was an effort shaped by social scientists with hopes that socially engineered interracial contact would deal the death blow to prejudice, discrimination, and inequality.

If, as Myrdal had suggested, racism was irrational and pathological, what better tool than the science of the human psyche to identify the roots of the illness and eradicate them? Myrdal himself had emphasized the incorporation of blacks into the American political system, but postwar social scientists offered a narrower vision, arguing that political change would be facilitated by therapeutic intervention. The transformation of attitudes was a necessary precursor to political change. Psychology provided a compelling but deeply problematic framework for understanding racial prejudice and inequality. Whereas Depression-era and wartime activists had situated racial inequality in the larger context of power relationships and economic inequalities, a growing number of postwar social scientists saw prejudice as the manifestation of individual psychological or emotional deficiencies, as a disease that needed to be eradicated. A burgeoning subdiscipline in postwar psychology—and in related fields, especially survey research in political science—explored the origins of prejudice and "intergroup relations" through a careful examination of individual opinions. The social scientific research agenda on race was profoundly shaped by concerns about the social psychological bases of Nazism and communism—encapsulated in the concept of the "authoritarian personality," which responded to psychic insecurity and the lack of self-worth through expressions of hostility, overt aggression, and ultimately violence. With the analogy of American racism and Nazi fascism at hand, social scientists saw "authoritarian" traits as the root cause of racial inequality in the United States. "It seems that the 'authoritarian personality,'" wrote leading scholar of prejudice Arnold Rose, "hates not only Negroes, Jews, Orientals, and so on, but tends to hate everyone."

If housing segregation was one manifestation of the troubled white psyche, social scientists also saw it as a cause of black pathology. Racial prejudice, they contended, irrevocably damaged self-esteem and unleashed dangerous psychosexual dynamics that deformed Negro culture. Dr. Frederic Wertham (later infamous for leading a national crusade against comic books) opened Harlem's first psychiatric clinic in 1945, with hopes of addressing the "free-floating hostility" that was the result of racial prejudice. Wertham's treatments were unorthodox: He told his patients that it was "far better to be subversive than subservient." Like other psychologists and psychiatrists, Wertham traced black neuroses to feelings of inadequacy and inferiority, the result of internalized white prejudice. Wertham's diagnosis was widely shared. "The Negro child," wrote David Ausubel, a prominent sociologist, "inherits an inferior caste status and almost inevitably acquires the negative self-esteem that is the realistic ego reflection of such status." Oppression, argued Abram Kardiner and Lionel Ovesey, fostered "psychoses" among black youths that led them to express their frustration through delinquent behavior. Crime, family dysfunction, unemployment, and poverty were the tragic results. As long as blacks internalized white views of them as subhuman, unintelligent, lazy, and violence-prone, they would never be equal. Eradicating prejudice was a necessary first step to the liberation of blacks from the "inferiority complex" caused by racism.

Sociologists and psychologists viewed the internalization of oppression, family dysfunction, and ghettoization as three interlocking and mutually reinforcing processes. Black men were emasculated by race prejudice, unable to hold their heads high and provide for their families. Black women ran households, creating a dangerous "matriarchy." The result was a disfigured sense of manhood, one that found an outlet in hypermasculinity and public expressions of rage. Overbearing mothers and angry fathers created what psychologist Thomas Pettigrew called a "ghetto subculture" that compounded the already deep-seated psychological effects of racism. Exacerbating the black pathologies was the lack of "moorings," of institutions to provide social control for urban blacks, or what Pettigrew called the "lack of a sense of community." Living in "disorganized" inner cities, wrote sociologist Guy Johnson, made it "impossible for [blacks] to stabilize, to achieve a moral order or a sense of community *esprit de corps*."

Ghetto pathologies had even more damaging consequences, particularly, as Johnson argued, for "crime causation." In the ghetto, he argued, "social institutions and community controls do not operate with sufficient strength . . . to repress the disorganizing influences." Mozell Hill, summarizing the scholarship, argued that "segregation creates slum behavior." She advocated the "planned relocation" of "tragic individuals," entrapped in "blighted areas" with "socially disorganized population[s]" featuring a preponderance of females over males. Even black radicals described youth criminality in similar terms—a reminder of how ubiquitous the psychological framework had become. "In his own peculiar way," wrote the Detroit militant Albert Cleage, Jr., about a prototypical black, male criminal, "he is fighting for *recognition* and *acceptance*. The basis of his sickness is the total pattern of life into which he was born and in which he has developed." White prejudice, mapped onto the urban landscape, left the black family and especially "ghetto youth" deeply damaged.

Social psychologists provided a powerful rationale for activists who challenged racial inequality. It gave them a diagnosis of the "disease" of prejudice. While the vast majority of civil rights activists did not pore through the *Journal of Social Issues*, the *Journal of Abnormal and Social Psychology*, or the *Journal of Inter-Group Relations*, scholarly ideas filtered out through the publications of official race relations organizations, liberal general interest magazines, church newsletters, and the black press. Indeed, many of the leading researchers on prejudice and psychology did not draw a bright line between academic research, political advocacy, and grassroots activism and published their work in nonacademic journals, contributing to a vast well of public interest in emotions and their public consequences. In the postwar years, there was no taboo against engaged scholarship in the social sciences—as there is in large sections of academia today. Kenneth and Mamie Clark opened the Northside Center in Harlem, to work with black families scarred by racial inequality. Others got involved in protest politics. In 1953, Johns Hopkins University psychologist Herbert Kelman organized a CORE chapter in Baltimore. A recent Ph.D., Kelman was a pioneer in the application of intergroup psychology to international relations and conflict resolution but had also worked on juvenile delinquency, group therapy, and attitudinal change. It was a natural leap from a concern about the psychology of intergroup relations to antiprejudice activism. Like Kelman, Lionel Ovesey, co-author of *The Mark of Oppression,* believed in social science as a vehicle for social change—and combined his scholarship with participation in civil rights protests.

Even more influential than their local activism was that sociologists and psychologists consulted for foundations, religious groups, and civil rights organizations and wrote articles to distill their findings for the general public. The National Conference of Christians and Jews, the National Council of Churches, the National Association of Intergroup Relations Officials, the American Friends Service Committee, and the Anti-Defamation League of B'nai B'rith all underwrote scholarship on prejudice and published pamphlets that popularized it. Liberal foundations, perhaps none more important than the Fund for the Republic, also subsidized work on discrimination. In a climate where social scientists were rewarded for serving as public intellectuals, they felt no stigma in distilling their findings in popular periodicals, with hopes of undermining racial prejudice. They cooperated with journalists who disseminated their findings to a wider public. In all these forms, social science made its way into general circulation.

The most important organization that popularized social scientific studies to justify open housing was the National Committee Against Discrimination in Housing (NCDH), founded by Charles Abrams in 1950. NCDH quickly became a clearinghouse of information and a network to connect open housing activists throughout the country. It held annual conferences on open housing. Through its newsletter, *Trends in Housing*, it summarized scholarly research on housing for its largely nonacademic readers involved in grassroots efforts. It reached an interested public through its well-written and well-illustrated articles and its many pamphlets. NCDH played a particularly important role in reporting open housing success stories from communities around the country.

The popularization of psychological concepts of race and prejudice made its way into a wide variety of periodicals. The *Negro Digest*, for example, summarized the latest research for its readers. "Prejudice," argued one article, "is a symptom of neurosis," the result of "emotional scales . . . gone out of balance." Discrimination, reported Betsy Emmons in a summary of psychological scholarship, is the result of "neurotic people who are hiding from themselves the fact that they need to hate and despise others because of their own emotional weakness." In the pages of *Commentary*, a periodical with a mostly Jewish readership, Jerome Himelhoch identified "factors in prejudice" against Jews and African Americans and emphasized the displacement of childhood frustrations on minorities. Some antidiscrimination activists, less attuned to the nuances of social psychology, offered their own, popular, often derisive explanations of prejudice as madness. In an article for an open housing group, Dr. Benjamin Spock, author of the bestselling child-rearing advice book, offered a popular distillation of recent scholarship. How could a victim of prejudice, asked Spock, "grow up self-respecting, ambitious, and a good citizen"? Spock argued that the "child is hurt" by harboring prejudice and would be "a less adequate person in his dealings with others in childhood and eventually adulthood." In a series of articles intended for use for sermons and church discussion groups, black open housing activist Herman H. Long argued that opposition to housing integration lay in the "realm of fantasy" and was "basically psychological" in origin. Taking a different tack, white religious activist Galen Weaver explained segregation as the consequence of "prejudices, irrational phobias, and fantasies arising out of guilt feelings, as well as ignorance and old wives' tales."

Despite their grim vision of white prejudice and black damage, postwar social scientists were fundamentally optimistic that human behavior could be modified through therapeutic intervention. Syracuse University social psychologist Joseph Masling expressed the optimism of his discipline. "Over and over again, there have been data that show you can change people's prejudices." Social psychologists focused on childhood as the formative moment when tendencies toward prejudice emerged, a vision that led to a growing emphasis on the family and the household as the nexus where prejudice could be fought and overcome. Gordon W. Allport, a Harvard psychologist and author of an influential study of prejudice, argued that the antidote to authoritarianism was the creation of a "tolerant personality" through interracial contact, education, and, if necessary, psychotherapy. Whites, if given the chance to interact with blacks on a daily basis, would jettison their irrational claims of racial superiority. And blacks, if they were removed from their isolation and freed from the inferiority complex that it engendered, could assimilate into mainstream American culture rather than remain entrapped by the "frustration," emotional repression, and pathologies of the ghetto.

The emphasis on housing as a vehicle for overcoming black pathologies had particular resonance among middle-class blacks, especially those who clung to the ideology of racial uplift. Open housers found allies, particularly among Realtists, black real estate brokers who formed their own professional organization because the all-white National Association of Real Estate Boards did not allow black membership and use of the trademark name Realtor. Realtists had a particular economic interest in opening up white neighborhoods and suburbs: Open housing would give them access to lucrative listings in better-off neighborhoods. But many Realtists also saw themselves as part of the "talented tenth." Their role, as members of the small black middle class, was to lift up the black poor. Black realty executive George Harris, a Chicago native, made the point clearly. "The future direction of American cities will be determined by the type of leadership that comes from the growing non-white middle-class of this country.... We must let them know that we the privileged have not deserted them. We must give them the benefit of our knowledge and experience. We must impart hope and inspiration."

The long-term impact of housing integration would be the growth of a black middle class that could serve as a "role model" for the poor. Above all, open housing would mitigate the stigma of being black. Blacks who lived in proximity to whites would be bolstered by their acceptance into mainstream American society. As blacks rubbed shoulders with whites on a daily basis, they would absorb the values of white America and, over time, pass those values down to their poorer relations. Integration was, in other words, part of a long-term process of racial uplift. Dispersing the ghetto was a first—and essential—step toward ridding black communities of their pathologies.

The open housing movement fused liberal religion and social science. Christian and Jewish antidiscrimination organizations popularized and disseminated social scientific findings about race and prejudice, fusing morality and psychology. By the 1940s, liberal theologians were making their peace with psychology, in part because of its emphasis on the power of personal transformation. William McConaghy, pastor of the First Presbyterian Church in Syracuse, New York, and director of the Institute on Racial and Cultural Relations for the Presbyterian Church, U.S.A., explained that "segregation subjects sections of our population to constant humiliation and forces on them moral and psychological handicaps in every relation to life." But "still more devastating is the moral and spiritual effect on the majority." Psychology easily segued into spirituality, since each, in its own way, focused on human redemption. Segregation, argued McConaghy, was "a violation of the gospel of love and human brotherhood."

A small cadre of liberal Protestants—most of them heirs to the Social Gospel tradition—had begun tackling the "race problem" in the 1920s. In 1922, the Federal Council of Churches (later renamed the National Council of Churches) launched Brotherhood Sunday, a yearly event when preachers introduced themes of the common humanity of blacks and whites in Christ. By invitation, black preachers delivered sermons in white churches and vice versa and black choirs sang side by side with their white counterparts. Churchwomen, many of whom had done missionary work in the Third World, met at teas and began holding annual prayer meetings and conferences to promote racial equality. During World War II, however, Brotherhood Sundays expanded rapidly. The National Conference of Christians and Jews sponsored an annual Brotherhood Week with educational efforts to overcome prejudice, with special attention to white schoolchildren.

Over the course of the 1950s, civil rights in the North took on an increasingly therapeutic cast. If whites jettisoned their irrational prejudices, if they had a change of mind or a change of heart, then the problem of racial inequality in America would at last be vanquished. Central to healing the scar of race would be interracial contact—everyday, common-place interactions between blacks and whites, particularly in neighbor-hoods. To win the hearts and minds of whites meant providing concrete evidence that housing integration would not hurt white property values. It also meant justifying housing integration both in religious terms and in the larger context of appeals to the "American Creed." Civil rights activists could knock down barriers, but they knew that their goal of an interracial society required positive examples. It was one thing to challenge the status quo; it was another to create viable alternatives. Successful racial integration required model communities—living examples of "interracial harmony"—to persuade whites that racial segregation should be a thing of the past. "If Negroes are integrated with whites," Charles Abrams wrote, "initial tensions tend to subside, differences are reconciled, and cooperation develops."

Open housing advocates developed a two-pronged strategy to "save" neighborhoods. First was to persuade a critical mass of whites to stay. Second was to recruit blacks who were like whites in every respect other than their skin color. When whites saw that black home owners kept up their houses, maintained their yards, and lived quiet, bourgeois lives, they would see the irrationality of their own prejudice. And they would have little reason to flee. Slowly, incrementally, racial integration would ripple outward from these model communities and eventually reshape American society.

ULTIMATELY, OPEN HOUSING activists came to view the creation of stable, racially integrated communities as the key to breaking down the psychological barriers of race. And that led activists to look for visible symbols—and what better than Levittown? As the NAACP was failing to change federal housing policy in the courts, grassroots activists were working to undermine Levitt's discriminatory policies. As construction began in Bucks County, watching Levitt—unbeknownst to him—was a small band of Quaker activists. Beginning in 1953, the American Friends Service Committee held secret meetings to figure out a way to crack open Levittown. The Quakers had long been committed to civil rights—some would say back to their days spearheading antislavery efforts. In the late nineteenth century, Quakers allied themselves with the settlement house movement, channeling resources and talent into social programs meant to educate and "uplift" the urban poor. The Quakers were also a greatly respected voice on behalf of the disenfranchised. During World War I, the newly formed AFSC won international acclaim for its work with war refugees. At home, it established projects on Indian reservations, in impoverished industrial towns, and in migrant worker camps. As the political climate in the 1930s and 1940s shifted, many Quakers embraced the ideal of "intercultural education." Quaker activist Rachel Davis DuBois (no relation to W.E.B.) led a campaign to bring together black and white children in interracial schools. During World War II, she helped promote the federal government's campaign for tolerance and pluralism. Although the Quakers had a checkered record in integrating their own institutions, by the postwar period they took the goal of "human brotherhood" more seriously than most Americans did. The Quaker *Book of Christian Discipline* instructed that Friends were motivated by the "simple awareness that the human race is one race, that the human family is one family; all are members of one another." The AFSC took the principle further, arguing that one of its major tasks was "replacing segregation with freedom, equality, and mutual trust."

A small, dissenting denomination, the Quakers were out of the American mainstream. More so than any religious group in the mid–twentieth century, they pushed aggressively for racial equality—and for a small group, they were ubiquitous. Their zeal made them the most visible white-dominated group in the civil rights movement besides Communists. The AFSC directed most of its energies southward. There were a few Quaker beachheads in the South, most notably Greensboro, North Carolina, where the Quakers ran Guilford College. There Quakers challenged employment discrimination and segregated education. AFSC activists fanned out throughout the region south of the Mason-Dixon Line, desegregating playgrounds and pools in Washington, D.C., pushing for interracial housing in the packinghouse towns of Louisiana, and working with fledgling civil rights groups in places as far-flung as Dallas, Texas, and Prince Edward County, Virginia. By the late 1940s, they began to turn their attention to the unfinished problem of racial inequality in the North. Members of the AFSC built an integrated cooperative housing project in North Philadelphia, collaborated with the United Automobile Workers to construct racially mixed housing for industrial workers in Milpitas, California, and worked closely with Chicagoans trying to integrate the city's Trumbull Park public housing project. In Syracuse, New York, and Columbus, Ohio, among many other northern places, Quaker activists coordinated efforts to eradicate slum housing and open new suburban developments to blacks. But of all these northern efforts, the most important and influential were in their own backyard—Philadelphia's suburbs.

William Levitt probably did not know that he had chosen to build his newest eponymous development right in the middle of the Quakers' ancestral home, southeastern Pennsylvania. Levittown was only twenty miles outside Philadelphia, nicknamed by some the "Quaker Vatican" for its concentration of venerable Friends schools and meetinghouses—and the AFSC headquarters. As Philadelphia suburbanized, new subdivisions began to encroach on what had been rural Quaker outposts that dotted the countryside of Pennsylvania and southern New Jersey. Two meetinghouses, unadorned and mostly unmodernized, stood in stark simplicity just a short distance from Levittown, their very existence a reproach to the sprawl and tackiness of the suburban frontier that engulfed them.

No sooner did Levittown open its first model house in 1952 than the Quakers, working with other local activists, began plotting against Levitt. Joining the Friends was the newly formed Human Relations Council of Bucks County, whose supporters included novelists James Michener and Pearl Buck, who lived in the nearby countryside. "We attempt by persuasion and convincement," stated housing activist Judith Wicoff, "to bring persons on the opposing side to a place where they will be willing to accept a new neighbor in a spirit of brotherhood and fair play." As Levitt's houses sprang from the soil (the whole development was finished by 1958), a grassroots suburban housing movement rose just as quickly. A victory at Levittown would have national, perhaps international, repercussions.

Jane Reinheimer and Jacques Wilmore, two young Quaker activists, one white, one black, who worked for the AFSC's Community Relations Division, spearheaded the Levittown campaign. Their task was to identify whites who might be willing to sell their homes to blacks—and, more important, to find a black family to be "pioneers" on the suburban frontier. Through connections in the labor and liberal communities, Reinheimer and Wilmore reached out to white activists and gradually built a little network of Levittowners for racial justice. In July 1954, Reinheimer met with Joseph and Minnie Hitov, two local activists who had helped create a nondiscriminatory nursery school. Levittown was a tight-knit community, and the Hitovs knew several neighbors who would be sympathetic to the cause of racial integration. Reinheimer came away "impressed" by the "quality of leadership" and "forthright concern" that they had for the integration of Levittown. By word of mouth, AFSC staffers also found several white home owners who were willing to sell to blacks. Not all of them were idealists—a few suggested high sales prices, perhaps aware that integrationists might pay a premium to break down the barriers of exclusion. After almost two years of one-on-one meetings, a small band of Levittowners held a "confidential meeting" with Quaker activists in December 1955 to plan for a "Levittown move-in."

Throughout 1953, 1954, 1955, and 1956, Reinheimer and Wilmore interviewed several black "prospects," with little success. For one, the Quakers set very high standards: The family who moved in would be the first blacks that most Levittowners had ever met. "Ideal pioneers" needed to be as nonthreatening as possible. The key was finding middle-class blacks with normative families. At the heart of the Levittown integration project was an unacknowledged but obvious class politics: Opening suburbia was not intended to provide new housing opportunities for the poor, it was intended to change the hearts and minds of white Americans. In his classic study of prejudice, published in 1954, Gordon Allport found that interracial contact would not succeed unless the two groups that came into contact were of "equal status" and "seek common goals." In this view, one that open housing activists embraced, any attempt to mix middle-class whites and poor blacks would fail miserably.

Finding blacks to move into Levittown proved to be difficult. One early "very good candidate" had "an attractive manner and is very intelligent and thoughtful" but could not be persuaded to move in. By contrast, another black family lacked "the smoothness, sophistication, or intellectual development which might be desirable in this case." In one of the greatest ironies of the search process, the Quakers—members of a traditional peace church—found some of their most promising recruits among black members of the military, perhaps because of their experience in a newly integrated institution, perhaps because of their uniformed respectability. Fort Dix, New Jersey, the largest military base in the region, was an easy commute to Levittown.

Despite the best efforts of the AFSC and the Human Relations Council of Bucks County, it took several years to find a willing black family. Many of the prospects feared racially motivated violence or hostility. An army sergeant who had survived the integration of the military was "not particularly bothered with being the first" black to move to Levittown but worried about danger to his wife and children. One black woman feared being "isolated from a Negro community." Others had financial worries. Looking back over the efforts to recruit black pioneers, Quaker activists recognized one major problem: "Do members of minority groups feel integration has concrete personal advantage for them?" The implied answer was no. "Those who will act in the absence of concrete personal incentives are the pioneers and there are not many of them in any group."

Finally, in 1957, William and Daisy Myers, residents of a small black enclave in nearby Bristol Township and members of the Bucks County Human Relations Council, came forward. The housing market was slow during the deep recession, and a house at the corner of Daffodil and Deepgreen lanes, owned by a white family willing to sell to a black family, had been on the market for nearly two years. The Myerses were ideal pioneers. Both were in their mid-thirties. He was a World War II veteran and a graduate of the Hampton Institute who worked as a refrigeration technician in nearby Trenton, New Jersey; she was a schoolteacher and a member of the Bristol Township recreation board. Like most Levittown families, the Myerses were baby-boom parents, with a newborn, a three-year-old, and a five-year-old. But however much they resembled their white neighbors, when word got out that they had purchased the Levittown house, a grassroots mobilization against them began. More than two thousand white Levittowners signed petitions opposing the Myerses. In a reflection of the changing postwar rhetoric of race, the petitions claimed that their motives were untainted. "As moral, religious and law-abiding citizens, we feel that we are unprejudiced and undiscriminating in our wish to keep our community a closed community . . . to protect our own."

Several white Levittowners, most of them leftists or Quakers (contra Levitt, suburban home ownership often appealed to radicals), worked to smooth the Myerses' path. Two members of the local Friends meeting, Peter von Blum and Sam Snipes, coordinated welcome efforts and worked out a two-month timetable of scheduled visits from supportive neighbors. A week before the Myerses' "move-in," von Blum invited local ministers to a tea to meet the family. Fearful of being dismissed as "outside agitators," both Snipes and von Blum were careful to emphasize that the move-in "was not in any sense an *organizational* effort." The Myerses' new next-door neighbors, Lewis and Bea Wechsler, former Communists and committed civil rights activists, also played a crucial role, holding meetings in their house and coordinating support efforts. Shortly after the move-in, the Wechslers received one hundred copies of an open housing pamphlet to distribute throughout the neighborhood.

On August 13, 1957, the Myerses moved into their little three-bedroom ranch. Daisy Myers looked forward to having "a little space for flowers" in the yard, but she would have no time to garden. A several-week siege followed the move-in. One typical evening, white protestors formed a "solid wall stretching at least 50 yards long and about five persons deep." Under the cover of darkness, most of the Myerses' windows were broken. Police officers and white residents battled on the streets, leading whites to shout "Gestapo!" and "This is Russia!" as police dispersed the crowd after one officer was knocked unconscious by a rock. Over the next week, opponents of the move-in spray-painted "KKK" and splattered paint on the Wechslers' house and burned a cross on Peter von Blum's lawn. The owner of a vacant house next door to the Myerses let his property be used as an "anti-integration social club," which served as a base of operations for the "war of nerves" against the black family and their supporters. "A lot of terrible things were done to them," recalled Tom Colgan, a Quaker activist who moved in with the Myerses for the first three weeks after the siege. A month after the move-in, Fire Association Insurance canceled the Myerses' policy, leading the outraged Colgan to accuse the company of participating in "an economic boycott" against the family. While NAACP officials in New York negotiated for a new insurance policy on the home, the Myerses continued to live in a state of fear. In mid-September, local police dropped their nightly patrols near the Myers home. William Myers threatened to move out unless police protection were restored. But he also quietly defied the protestors. One nice fall day, he joined in a quintessential suburban ritual, weeding his lawn. But Myers did not use a rake or hoe; he pulled dandelions with a bayonet from his army days.

More than two hundred whites—most of them from outside Levittown—called on the Myerses in their first two months on Deepgreen

Lane. A wide range of white-dominated leftist and liberal organizations, including the Bucks County Council of Churches, local steelworkers' and electrical workers' unions, the Women's International League for Peace and Freedom, and several Jewish organizations spoke out on behalf of the Myerses. Some local religious leaders, including the pastor of a nearby Congregational church, also supported the integration effort. Behind the scenes, the AFSC volunteers negotiated with the police, organized community meetings, and coordinated press coverage. Perhaps the most important Quaker role was providing the Myerses with financial assistance. The family struggled with expenses throughout the fall, running up enormous phone bills, repairing their house, traveling to meet with supporters in New York and Harrisburg, and even "providing coffee and cake" for their flood of well-wishers. As if that were not hard enough, Daisy Myers spent part of the fall sick and William Myers suffered a recession-related cut in his weekly work hours. In addition, Quaker activists and neighbors established a nonviolent "citizens guard" in front of the Myers home after the police left.

A cadre of white neighbors also provided unwavering support to the Myerses. That the Myers family had white supporters in Levittown was evidence of the changing racial climate of the 1950s. In the aftermath of the protests, a local group of about a dozen families called the "Dogwood Hollow Neighbors," with the support of the AFSC and the National Conference of Christians and Jews, prepared a statement denouncing the "terrible incidents that took place in our neighborhood during August and September" and reached out to their neighbors to persuade them of the benefits of integration.

But even if most Levittowners were not breaking windows or protesting, many were cool toward the Myerses and their supporters. Local Republican leader James H. Paul blamed the family for "the violence and disruption in a once peaceful suburban community" and urged them to "go back where you came from." "We feel we have the moral right to protect our property values and rear our children in the best possible surroundings," argued white Levittowner J. P. Walsh. One neighbor candidly told a reporter, Bill Myers was "probably a nice guy, but every time I look at him I see $2000 drop off the value of my house." Others raised concerns about crime—one referred to "these colored kids and men, killing, raping & robbing and making eyes and passes at us white women." One anonymous "Group of Levittowners" placed an advertisement in the local paper arguing that "we favor racial integration, but only at such time the negro shows he is ready for it." The Cold War played its part, too. The pastor of the large local Catholic parish was unsupportive; many parishioners believed that the move-in was part of a Communist plot. Even a group of moderates, organized as the Citizens Committee of Levittown, labeled integrationists as "a group of subversives." That Lewis Wechsler was a well-known leftist only fueled their suspicions; some religious activists, worried about Wechsler's politics, attempted to persuade him to renounce communism publicly.

In addition, several Myers supporters suffered retribution. Irving Mandel lost his job when his employer learned that he had sold his house to the Myers family. When the AFSC attempted to find Mandel another job, they were forced to defend him from charges that he was a subversive. "You should understand that Mandel is not a 'radical,'" wrote a Quaker job counselor to prospective employers. "He was merely seeking a buyer for his home which has been on the market for two years." Peter von Blum saw a hemorrhage of clients from his civil engineering firm and found himself out of work. And Fred Manthey, the Congregationalist minister who supported the Myers, saw an exodus of members from his congregation and was assigned to another post because of the controversy.

In the aftermath of the move-in, the Quakers worked hard to find another black family, but the negative media attention made their task difficult. Philadelphia's leading black newspaper, the *Tribune*, listed homes for sale in Levittown. But their case was not helped when in September, a *Tribune* reporter was warned by a white "to get out of Levittown; you don't want to get hurt" and, the same month, a Levittown house for sale was vandalized after a dark-skinned Indian family visited it. One *Tribune* reader angrily concluded that "the white man can have all of his Levittowns and go hang." The paper denounced white Levittowners as "hate-spreading . . . terrorists." Amid the hostility, it was not surprising that few blacks wanted to retrace the Myerses' footsteps. Finally, by the spring of 1958, the AFSC had identified a second family, Kenneth and Julia Mosby and their school-age children, Carol and Kenneth, Jr. After three months of behind-the-scenes meetings, the Mosbys moved in peacefully in late June 1958. The overt resistance to black move-ins was spent, but white neighbors remained on edge.

Now that Levittown had been nominally integrated, open housing activists faced a potentially more serious challenge: How could they prevent panicky whites from fleeing the community en masse? And what would happen to property values? Observers of the Levittown move-in believed that the key to preserving the community's stability was controlling the number of blacks who moved in; but if only two or three black families lived among tens of thousands of whites in Levittown, it could scarcely be considered integrated. When one of the Mosbys' near neighbors was contemplating selling her home to a black family, the AFSC intervened and quickly found a white buyer for the house, fearful that a sale to blacks "might touch off panic selling and even start the development of a 'Negro' section." They also intervened when another white sought to sell her home to blacks as a "spite sale" after a neighborhood dispute.

Levittown, Pennsylvania, did not attract a flood of black buyers. The Myerses themselves moved from the neighborhood in 1959, tired of their life in a fishbowl. Even when Levittown had quieted down, their experience, covered by local and national news outlets, served as a chilling reminder to blacks of the obstacles they might face if they breached the suburban color line. Opening the suburbs was a fragile, difficult task— one that exacted a high price from both the black "pioneers" and their white supporters. Increasingly, open housers began to ask if the results were worth the extraordinary efforts.

Levittown, Pennsylvania, was only one of dozens of postwar suburbs that threw up obstacles, legal or illegal, to open housing. In Cicero, Illinois, just west of Chicago, a riot broke out in 1951 when thousands of angry whites attacked an apartment complex as a black family attempted to move in. Adding insult to injury, a grand jury indicted the black family and the white agent who had rented the apartment to them on charges of "conspiracy" to lower property values. Their efforts were successful in keeping Cicero all white for decades, despite its proximity to Chicago's increasingly black West Side. In 1980, one-tenth of 1 percent of Cicero residents were black, the vast majority of whom lived part of the year in cinder-block dormitories at a horse-racing track where they worked.

Mayor Orville Hubbard of Dearborn, Michigan, home to Ford Motor Company's headquarters, pledged to keep "Detroit's trash" out, and local residents bragged that theirs was a sundown town. In 1963, open housing activists marched on Dearborn, but to no avail. As a small band of black and white ministers addressed the marchers, they were greeted by a jeering crowd of several thousand angry whites. "Let's do this peacefully, as brothers in Christ," one activist meekly demanded. "The old order changes and must give way to the new." But boos drowned out the prayers and even "The Star-Spangled Banner." The old order prevailed. When Orville Hubbard's extraordinary thirty-six-year term ended in 1978, Dearborn had just a handful of black residents, most of them live-in domestics, even as the black population of contiguous Detroit neighborhoods skyrocketed.

In the heavily segregated suburbs of Columbus, Ohio, a few blacks had attempted to cross the racial divide in the 1950s, but whites sent chilling messages to the would-be suburbanites. When a black family moved to suburban Columbus in 1956, whites greeted them with a burning cross and cut telephone wires. While open housing activists continued to help individuals move to the suburbs, they also challenged housing developers. When the massive Lincoln Village housing development was announced, Columbus open housers saw their chance to change racial housing patterns writ large. Barbee Durham, an activist who had hoped to move to Lincoln Village, fumed, "All our lives we have suffered affronts, we have been told that we can't do this or can't do that, we can't live here or live there because we are Negroes! Local American Negro Citizens!" Columbus integrationists appealed to liberal whites on moral grounds, while reassuring them that only the "best" Negroes would move into their communities. Hoping to persuade Lincoln Village to open on a nondiscriminatory basis, they assured the developer that high prices would ensure that they "will not be deluged by applications from Negroes." But their arguments fell on deaf ears. Lincoln Village's developer expressed sympathy for the plight of excluded blacks but, like Levitt, argued that integration did not make good business sense.

Relatively liberal communities also mounted fierce opposition to open housing, even if it took more polite forms. In Swarthmore, Pennsylvania, a small college town outside Philadelphia dominated by Quakers, fair-housing activists tried with little success to find a white resident willing to rent to blacks. In 1955, when a developer proposed to build a small, exclusive subdivision for "open occupancy," Swarthmore residents filed a petition opposing the construction and won a zoning battle at the borough council. It was not a matter of class. The houses proposed in

Swarthmore would have cost between twenty thousand and thirty-five thousand dollars, significantly higher than the town's average house price. The Swarthmore Property Owners' Association, which represented area residents, argued that "we do not want Swarthmore to become a laboratory in which to try out this or other schemes which have no assurance of success"; 315 of 350 association members opposed the development. In 1958, when Clarence and Margaret Yarrow, two Quaker supporters of integration, listed their house for sale for open occupancy, their neighbors politely but firmly revolted. Twenty-two fellow Quakers challenged the Yarrows, arguing that "regardless of the principles underlying the problem of integration, it is a cold, hard, economic fact that property decreases in value when Negroes move into a neighborhood. We feel that you are deliberately depreciating the value of your neighbors' real estate when you sell your home to colored people."

DESPITE MASSIVE WHITE opposition to the integration of suburbia, open housers remained optimistic. They put their faith in a few experiments in housing integration, none more important than Concord Park, Pennsylvania. Just a few miles away from Levittown, it was carved out of a fifty-acre farm in a rapidly suburbanizing area just northeast of Philadelphia. Concord Park was meant to be an interracial Levittown, with 139 modest-sized single-family houses affordable to middle-class homebuyers, regardless of race. It looked just like any other cookie-cutter suburban development of the 1950s. Its first model house, "the Arizona," had three bedrooms, a living room–dining room combination, and a one-car garage, all for $11,990. There was nothing in the least bit urban about the place.

Concord Park was the vision of Morris Milgram, a most unlikely suburban housing developer. The son of Jewish garment workers from New York's Lower East Side, Milgram had been "weaned on Socialist tracts." His path to Concord Park began with the campus radicalism of the 1930s. An ardent antifascist and peace activist, member of the Student League for Industrial Democracy and Student Strike Against the War, Milgram was expelled from the City College of New York in 1934 after leading protests against a visiting delegation of fascist students. In the late 1930s, Milgram served as New Jersey executive secretary of the

Workers' Defense League, where he battled against Jersey City machine boss Frank Hague's control over New Deal welfare programs and was arrested for handing out antifascist leaflets in suburban New Jersey. During World War II, as a confidant of Socialist Party leader Norman Thomas, Milgram became the national secretary of the WDL. The WDL had a long record of supporting racial equality, which it saw as inseparable from "labor's rights." During the war, the league protested the working conditions of southern farmworkers, "America's refugees." The WDL also vocally criticized the internment of Japanese Americans. Closely allied with CORE and the March on Washington Movement, Milgram advocated nonviolent civil disobedience. Milgram and his lifelong friend Pauli Murray campaigned against the execution of Odell Waller, a southern sharecropper accused of murder, whose case became a cause célèbre in northern civil rights circles. In the aftermath of the Waller case, Milgram pledged to turn the WDL into "a new abolitionist agency to abolish all forms of racial discrimination." Milgram's work brought him into contact with both radical pacifists and civil rights activists, including A. Philip Randolph and Anna Arnold Hedgeman. The WDL's newsletter was edited by CORE's James Peck. And in 1945, Milgram found CORE founder James Farmer a job as an upholsterers' union organizer in Virginia.

After the war, Milgram shifted gears and left the WDL. By 1947, the organization had fallen on hard times, with only a small cadre of members who had hung on through the factional disputes that so divided the left. The Socialist Party, never big, dwindled almost to the vanishing point. Many leftists folded their tents and moved into mainstream party politics. By 1952, Milgram had become a Democrat and a volunteer for Adlai Stevenson's presidential campaign. As the Cold War progressed, Milgram never wholly jettisoned his radicalism, as did many of his erstwhile comrades (although in a widely distributed reprint of a *Fellowship Magazine* article about Concord Park, the words "Workers' Defense League" were blotted out and retyped as "Civil Liberties Organization"). Acknowledging Milgram's Socialist background would do little for the cause of winning the hearts and minds of white suburbanites. But even if the Cold War forced Milgram to downplay his past, he remained deeply committed to the ideals of racial equality that had motivated so many leftists during the 1930s and 1940s. Throughout his career, he found both financial and moral support from Socialists, former Socialists, and antiwar activists, many of whom, whatever their current political affiliations, remained committed to the goal of racial equality.

At the WDL, Milgram had grown increasingly concerned with housing segregation. Many of his closest friends faced the slings and arrows of northern segregation. In 1941, Milgram's Queens landlord had chased Pauli Murray out of the building when she was house-sitting for the vacationing Milgrams. "Go back to Harlem where you belong!" the angry landlord shouted before changing the locks. In 1945, Milgram bought a house in Lynbrook, a Long Island suburb, that he hoped to rent out as "the first interracial house in the town." Milgram's growing interest in housing led him to a career shift. Quitting the WDL in 1947, Milgram joined his father-in-law's construction firm in suburban Philadelphia. Milgram asked his father-in-law if he would "be able to build for any of my friends," regardless of their racial and ethnic background. His father-in-law was both bemused and skeptical: "We builders build for whites; that's just the way it is." Milgram did not have much business experience, but he learned the ropes quickly. Mastering the intricacies of marketing, the tax code, zoning laws, and construction finance, he had moved a long way from his days as a WDL activist. For four and a half years, under his father-in-law's supervision, he built new housing for whites in suburban Philadelphia. "My conscience hurt," he recalled of his short stint as a developer of segregated suburban housing. Gradually, Milgram gained the experience and the capital to begin an experiment in what he called "open occupancy" housing.

When his father-in-law died, Milgram moved forward with a plan for an interracial alternative to Levittown. His goal was to create a community whose demographics reflected the racial mix of Philadelphia—about 80 percent white and 20 percent black. But Milgram was greeted with "dire predictions of violence, financial disaster, and personal ruin." The main problem he faced was financial. Banks and investors were unwilling to take a risk on an integrated housing project. In his first year of fundraising, Milgram collected a mere $14,000. Finally, Milgram found an ally in George Otto, a suburban builder who chaired the Philadelphia Friends Social Order Committee. Together, Milgram and Otto formed a corporation and raised $150,000 in venture capital. Otto was well connected, particularly to wealthy Quakers, whom he reassured that their investment would be sound. Milgram made his sales pitch in moral terms: "Put your money where your heart is." Milgram found that "Quakers and Socialists were the easiest to get as investors"; in fact, more than half of Concord Park's capital came from Quakers. But obtaining mortgage financing for the project turned out to be more difficult. More than twenty financial institutions turned Milgram down. The same zealous style that he used to attract investors turned off many conservative bankers. Most banks had little or no experience with mortgages for blacks. No one had ever heard of a planned interracial community. It was a canon of actuarial science that blacks lowered property values. Finally, one New York–based bank, with experience lending to blacks, broke the ice. Its support pulled Concord Park from the "brink of financial ruin."

Milgram had no intention of creating a left-wing utopia. Although many on the left had advocated interracial cooperatives as an alternative to mainstream America, Milgram set his sights on the broad middle class. The novelty of Concord Park created a buzz. More than twenty-five thousand visitors came through Concord Park's model home—decorated by Levittown's own interior designer—when it opened in 1954. Most of those visitors were white. But what Milgram had not anticipated was that the vast majority of interested purchasers would be African Americans. Blacks had hardly any housing options in the suburbs. Their pent-up demand was simply overwhelming. Of the first sixty applicants for housing in Concord Park, fifty were black. Milgram recalled his trepidation at the prospect of an all-black suburb. "I woke up one night in a cold sweat and said to myself, 'Morris, you s.o.b, you're building a ghetto.'" White buyers were nervous that they would be moving into a majority-black community. "Well, you know how Negroes depreciate the value of property," demurred one white visitor. "It would be like buying an off-brand automobile. Nice, but what would its resale value be?" Others worried about the social risks of living in a racially mixed community. "My parents would never get over it," claimed one white woman, who found the new houses appealing but couldn't imagine living there. A white lawyer worried that he would "lose face with his clients" if word got out that he lived with blacks. Milgram had unwittingly bumped against the limits of racial tolerance. As Milgram recalled, the "hardest task was to secure the first ten or twenty white sales." Concord Park needed a "nucleus" of whites to attract other white buyers.

How could Concord Park succeed as a model integrated community if whites would not buy? The question generated an intense debate among Milgram's handpicked interracial board. Several board members felt obliged to meet the unanticipated black demand for suburban housing, even if that meant putting integration on hold. Should deserving black homebuyers be turned away, left in the ghetto, in service of a well-meaning experiment in racial integration? George Otto, more hard-headed about financial matters than Milgram, feared that the investors would lose money if they waited for whites to move in. Milgram counseled patience.

In mid-1955, Concord Park's board came up with an ingenious—if controversial—solution. After a contentious meeting, on the advice of AFSC housing activist Jane Reinheimer, they decided to establish a "controlled occupancy pattern," namely a quota of home sales to blacks and whites. Forty-five percent of the community's homes would be set aside for blacks, 55 percent for whites. The very notion of quotas rankled many board members. Weren't they just another form of racial discrimination? A prominent black civil rights activist who feared that Concord Park would "just be another ghetto" if it were not deliberately integrated, nonetheless instinctively recoiled at the notion. "I don't believe in quotas," he stated. "They are undemocratic." By a narrow margin, the board approved the plan. George and Eunice Grier, two sociologists who were among the first whites to move to Concord Park, defended the decision. "Liberals and social workers must face up to their ambivalence about quotas and ask themselves whether a little 'discrimination' at first is not better than indefinite continuance of the 'separate but equal' philosophy." So long as whites were prejudiced and blacks had limited options on the "open" market, integration would be difficult to achieve without some drastic intervention. But quotas—which in the case of Concord Park meant singling out blacks and keeping them at bay—sat uneasily with many activists. Some civil rights activists, argued CORE's James Farmer, himself a supporter of open housing, "became discouraged at the solemn spectacle of Negroes chasing whites from suburb to suburb—in quest of integration." The question of quotas would haunt civil rights activists for decades to come.

Attracting whites was hard work—both before and after the board's quota decision. At first, sales agents were given bonuses for recruiting white families. By the spring of 1955, Concord Park hired a white broker who agreed to move into the community and speak from his own experience to reassure nervous whites. Milgram directed nearly all the advertising to the white market. Concord Park brochures went to twenty thousand "liberal" households. Ads appeared in Quaker publications and, later, in liberal magazines with a national circulation. Quaker activists recruited among their own personal contacts—persuading a few whites to move in. Milgram tirelessly traveled around speaking to church groups, synagogues, and liberal organizations—anyone who would give him a platform—in an attempt to build support for the principle of integrated housing. Back in his office, Milgram nervously kept a map of the entire community on a bulletin board, with red and blue pins to represent blacks and whites.

By 1958, the development was completed, all of its houses were sold, and the racial quota had been met. One white resident described her neighbors as "nonconformists, especially on the racial issue." Not surprisingly, a handful of Communist families made Concord Park their home. Several interracial couples bought houses there. Reflecting the racial dynamics of the housing market, black Concord Park residents were disproportionately older than their white counterparts. Many had civil service jobs, a reflection of the limited opportunities for black professionals in the area's labor market. Milgram celebrated the triumph of Concord Park as a "democratic" alternative to the "un-American type of housing" that Levitt built. When Levitt announced plans for his third segregated Levittown, this one in New Jersey, Milgram denounced the project as "another propaganda boost for the Kremlin line that we—who pledge allegiance to a land of liberty and justice for all—don't practice what we pledge."

What was noteworthy about Concord Park and Milgram's subsequent developments around the Northeast was how little overt resistance they generated. Angry whites did not rise up and thwart the developments. "Here is proof," wrote activist Paul Blanshard, "that we Americans can throw off the fears and misunderstandings behind housing segregation. Here is proof that whites will rise to the opportunity of democracy in housing if given a chance." Nearly every journalistic observer of Concord Park celebrated the spirit of cooperation between black and white neighbors. Blacks and whites played bridge together, joined the same bowling, photography, and sewing clubs, and formed a babysitting cooperative.

Every stereotype of the suburban world of joiners was confirmed in Concord Park, with the new twist of black and white faces together. To the news media, hungry for examples of racial cooperation in a world of intensifying conflict, Milgram's story was proof positive of the willingness of whites to drop their irrational prejudices.

But the peace at Concord Park was less the result of northern liberality on race than it was of Milgram's careful planning. Most of Milgram's projects were on sites "carefully chosen to minimize community resistance." Concord Park was in the white-dominated suburbs, yes, but it was bordered by a small black suburban enclave and cut off from nearby white housing by a railroad line, the Pennsylvania Turnpike, and a cemetery. "We've had some mild kicks from people," remarked George Otto, "but they've been much milder than if the development was across the street from them." In Northeast Philadelphia, Milgram's semisuburban Greenbelt Knoll, with nineteen architect-designed modernist houses (where Milgram settled), nearby white neighborhood groups expressed worries about the development, but they were assuaged by the isolation of the site, which was surrounded by a heavily forested park and a train line. To prevent racial clashes at city pools, Milgram constructed a private swim club for Greenbelt Knoll residents. Outside Princeton, New Jersey, which had a century-old black enclave, Milgram's firm, newly rechristened Modern Community Developers (MCD), built two small developments in conjunction with a local interfaith organization committed to racial integration. In Hockessin, Delaware, a racially mixed Wilmington suburb whose Jim Crow schools had been part of the *Brown* decision, MCD built another small subdivision near a black settlement. Milgram's firm also built mixed apartment complexes in Washington, D.C., Providence, Rhode Island, and the Bronx. None of these faced stiff resistance.

Over the next decade, Milgram led a national crusade to build integrated housing developments. It was, as Milgram put it, "a business venture with a social goal." He traveled around the country, speaking to community groups, religious organizations, the Urban League annual conference, and pretty much anyone else who was willing to listen. He enlisted the support of a veritable Who's Who of liberals, black celebrities, and civil rights leaders, among them Jackie Robinson, his old comrade A. Philip Randolph, and the NAACP's Roy Wilkins. In 1957, the irrepressible Milgram turned his energies toward Chicago, where he found real enthusiasm for his vision of interracial suburbs among the city's well-organized open housing movement. Ed Holmgren, a Chicago activist, described the "whirlwind developed by Morris" when he spoke to a group of local civil rights leaders at a living room meeting in suburban Evanston. Inspired by Milgram, local investors formed Progress Development Corporation, a Chicago-based subsidiary of MCD, and launched plans to build an interracial subdivision in the heart of Deerfield, Illinois, an all-white suburb.

There Milgram's "whirlwind" hurtled into a wall. A small village in 1950, Deerfield tripled its population by 1960 with white-collar baby-boom families seeking refuge on the suburban frontier. In the postwar years, the prairie land around the quaint Deerfield village center was ripe for development. Demand for new housing was nearly insatiable. Aluminum-sided colonials and ranches sprung up virtually overnight. Easily accessible to the attractive, well-heeled suburbs of the North Shore, it was a magnet for young families who wanted the prestige of Kenilworth or Lake Forest without having to pay top dollar.

Deerfield's strongest selling point was that it was not Chicago. Twenty miles northwest of the Loop, Deerfield marketed itself as a quaint throwback to the pioneer era. Even if most of its housing stock was newly built, the town had some old farmsteads and a one-room schoolhouse dating to the mid–nineteenth century. Pockets of woodlands and open fields dotted the community. Farther to the north and west was still largely undeveloped prairie. In Deerfield, suburban homebuyers escaped the racially and ethnically heterogeneous metropolis. Although many towns on Chicago's North Shore had long had small black populations, the nearest black community was eight miles away. Some Deerfield residents even compared their town favorably to other suburbs such as Glencoe, a magnet for Jewish exiles from Chicago, which anti-Semitic locals derisively nicknamed "Glencohen."

In Deerfield, as in so much of suburban America in the 1950s, local politics was dominated by three issues: zoning, education, and taxes. Deerfield enacted strict zoning laws to preserve the community's exclusive ambience. No apartments were permitted; all new construction had to be single-family detached homes. Except in the old village center, developers built curvilinear streets, the antithesis of Chicago's relentless grid. By using the tools of suburban planning, Deerfield officials could keep out "undesirables," particularly those who rented rather than bought. Zoning was an essential ingredient of suburban exclusion, but not the only one. Good education was crucial. Much of the village's budget went into the construction of new schools, to meet the needs of baby-boom families. Villagers were sensitive to high property tax assessments and had little interest in spending local funds on anything other than education.

Milgram's Progress Development Corporation played by all of Deerfield's rules. Progress purchased two sites for the construction of fifty-one single-family homes, received zoning approvals, and began construction in the summer of 1959. By the fall, water and sewer connections had been laid for most of the lots and construction on two model homes was nearing completion. To any passerby, it looked like a typical suburban housing development. But unbeknownst to town officials, twelve of the new homes would be set aside for blacks. When word that Progress intended its development to be integrated finally got out in early November, the community exploded. Deerfield officials halted construction on grounds of building code violations the day after the integration plan became public. The partially built homes were vandalized several times during the controversy. Harold Lewis, a prominent local developer, formed the North Shore Residents Association and assembled a blue-ribbon "action committee" of ten leading Chicago lawyers to battle the project. Their goal was to find "a legal and constitutional way out" of what they called—in an unknowing inversion of Gunnar Myrdal—the "Deerfield dilemma." Milgram, Lewis charged, had engaged in "subterfuge" and "unethical" behavior by failing to divulge to local officials that the development would be integrated. Even the town's Episcopal minister, who claimed to support his denomination's open housing position, opposed Milgram's "motives and methods."

At town meetings about the project, tempers flared. Supporters of the housing development were jeered and booed. A local history teacher who announced that he supported integration was heckled. "Resign!" shouted angry audience members. "Fire him!" One young lawyer in a leading Chicago firm lost his job after he spoke out in favor of the development. Deerfield residents suggested that members of Progress Development be investigated for ties to the Communist Party; they charged that Milgram and his associates were involved in a "totalitarian" plan that involved "forcing Negroes and other non-caucasians on the village." Others criticized "interlopers" and "Eastern money interests" who underwrote the proposed development. Above all, residents expressed fear for their property values if blacks moved in, stoked by speculators who "bombarded [Deerfield households] with telephoned offers to purchase their homes" at 50 to 75 percent of their market value. Blacks would turn their village into a suburban ghetto and drive away potential white homebuyers. *The Pittsburgh Courier,* reporting on the events, warned that Milgram's opponents were creating an "upper-middle-class version of Trumbull Park," the Chicago public housing project where whites had violently resisted integration a few years earlier—and that had received extensive coverage in *Ebony* and black weeklies.

Amid the controversy, opponents of the Milgram development hatched a scheme to stop Progress in its tracks. They urged the village Park Board to resuscitate a mothballed proposal to set aside land for public parks, including two to be built on the sites of the Progress development. In early December, the Park Board approved the plan but could not proceed without funding to acquire the sites, a move that required a village wide referendum. Under ordinary circumstances, Deerfield's tax-conscious voters could not be counted on. Twice earlier in 1959, they had handily rejected bond issues for village parks. But Milgram's development changed everything. A hastily called referendum held four days before Christmas attracted the highest voter turnout of any election in village history. Despite the door-to-door lobbying of a newly created Deerfield Committee on Human Rights, which argued that "Negroes have a right to live in Deerfield" and cited scholarly research that blacks did not lower property values, voters overwhelmingly supported the park plan, 2,635 to 1,207. Reflecting on the Deerfield debacle, civil rights attorney Loren Miller argued that it "lays bare the harsh truth that residential segregation depends for its vitality on the exertion of state power."

Milgram and Progress sued Deerfield to prevent the town from stopping construction and seizing the land by eminent domain. Milgram had become a nationally known figure by the late 1950s, and he quickly assembled a platoon of prominent liberal politicians to back his case. Eleanor Roosevelt, who had met Milgram through their mutual friend Pauli Murray (now a New York attorney who provided Milgram with legal advice), was named co-chair of the American Freedom of Residence

Fund to raise money for the Deerfield case. Roosevelt proclaimed that Deerfield was "the Little Rock of Housing." Representing Progress in its lawsuit was Adlai Stevenson's Chicago law firm and a crack team of lawyers including Joseph Rauh, a founder of the liberal Americans for Democratic Action who, as a young New Deal attorney, had drafted Roosevelt's Executive Order 8802; Willard Wirtz, who would become secretary of labor in the Kennedy administration; and Newton Minow, who would later chair the Federal Communications Commission.

The Deerfield brouhaha got national attention. "There is a man in Philadelphia who makes his living by making other people unhappy," wrote *The Alabama Journal*. "His name is Morris Milgram. . . . His practice is to choose a happy, contented community of attractive homes where there has never been a race problem and build a lot of integrated apartments and residences." *The Augusta Courier*, a conservative Georgia paper, gleefully lauded the Yankees of Deerfield for their commitment to the cause of preventing "the amalgamation of the white and Negro races." The article might be dismissed as a southern racist misinterpretation of the events in Deerfield, but it was prompted by a letter to the Association of Citizens' Councils, a confederation of white supremacist groups based in Greenwood, Mississippi, from none other than Deerfield community leader Harold Lewis. "Crushing pressure," wrote Lewis, "is being brought to bear on us by church groups and many other organizations seeking to impose instant and compulsory integration." To his northern audiences, Lewis publicly insisted that he and Milgram's other opponents harbored no racial prejudice; but to his sympathetic southern correspondents, Lewis pledged that a "united" citizenry was "determined to resist at any cost."

However unsavory Deerfield's homegrown activists were, Milgram and his attorneys fought an uphill legal battle. When the suit made its way to court, Deerfield public officials denied any ulterior motive for their selection of Milgram's developments for parks and relied on the expert testimony of a professional park planner who had identified the two sites in a comprehensive plan for the village issued before Milgram's development was launched. Deerfield attorneys also attempted to discredit Milgram for his radical past. The county court found that the Deerfield Park Board had properly exercised its right of eminent domain. On appeal, the Illinois Supreme Court refused to consider "the motives that may have actuated those in authority" in Deerfield and confined its decision to the narrow grounds that the town had demonstrated that "parks are clearly needed in Deerfield and that the land condemned is appropriate for that purpose." Milgram privately lamented that the Deerfield officials were "cocksure of victory" and that "there is no one on their side that seems big enough to arrange a settlement that would give them some park land and use some land on which to build integrated housing."

Milgram also filed a civil rights lawsuit in federal court but met with an equally harsh fate there. In a rambling—but often biting—opinion, federal district judge Sam Perry dismissed Milgram's suit. "No member of the Park Board had shown or indicated any hostility or opposition to Negroes as a race or to Negroes owning property or living in Deerfield." The court even exonerated the building inspector who had halted construction on the development—after he had admitted in court that he was "biased against Negroes" and "had moved to Deerfield to get away from Negroes." To the court his "ill temper" was not sufficient to constitute a civil rights violation. Deerfield officials were simply doing their job: enforcing building codes and building parks, even if, as the court conceded, "had it not been for aroused public opposition" to Milgram's development, the December referendum would have gone the way of the previous park proposals.

Judge Perry reserved particularly harsh judgment for Milgram and his project. In an angry passage, Perry excoriated Milgram's plan for "controlled occupancy," lashing out at what he viewed as "illegal" quotas that would lead to "controlled or forced integration." (To many civil rights groups, this part of Perry's opinion was most threatening: It was, as one legal memorandum contended, the first judicial challenge to the use of "benign quotas.") And in a last indignity to Milgram, the court criticized the longtime activist for "misleading biographical information" about his radical past on his company's prospectus. Deerfield's attempts to tar Milgram's reputation had succeeded. In a candid interview after he dismissed the lawsuit, Perry expressed his skepticism about Milgram's efforts even more bluntly: "If the housing company was really interested in integrated housing, I do not think they would have built $30,000 to $40,000 homes 20 miles from the city. The whole thing smacks of a money-making scheme to me."

Milgram's attorneys appealed the two cases to the Illinois Supreme

Court and to the U.S. Court of Appeals, but privately they were not confident about their chances in the higher courts. A victory on appeal would require a rethinking of the law of eminent domain, and Milgram's attorneys were not confident that the courts would take such sweeping action when there was "an ostensible municipal purpose" for condemning land for parks. More than that, it was difficult to prove that Deerfield's Park Board had engaged in a conspiracy to deprive citizens of their civil rights. Even though Park Board members had met privately with Lewis and opponents of the development, there was no "smoking gun" that proved without a reasonable doubt that the town officials had segregationist motives. Both courts upheld Deerfield's decision to bulldoze the Milgram developments for parklands. The U.S. Court of Appeals distanced itself from Perry's acerbic opinion, rebuking him for his comments on quotas, but did not question the finding that Deerfield's condemnation of Milgram's sites served legitimate municipal purposes.

As the Deerfield cases wended through the courts, black and white activists weighed in on Milgram's behalf. The Reverend Martin Luther King, Jr., and *The Chicago Defender* lauded Milgram's attempt to integrate Deerfield. James Farmer, NAACP board chair Bishop Stephen Spottswood, and Pauli Murray met with Attorney General Robert F. Kennedy in a failed attempt to get the Department of Justice to intervene. The U.S. Supreme Court refused to hear an appeal. The National Committee Against Discrimination in Housing lamented that the Deerfield ruling "gives local officials a blank check to use their powers to maintain racial exclusiveness." Financially devastated by the lengthy suit, Milgram gave up on suburban housing development and turned his attention to developing racially mixed apartment houses in Washington, D.C., and other big cities with large international populations.

Milgram's pioneering efforts to open up America's deeply segregated housing markets had roots in the churches and in mainstream civil rights organizations. The open housing movement brought together an unlikely coalition of middle-class blacks, eager to get their share of the suburban dream, and liberal, predominantly religious whites, most from middle- and upper-class backgrounds, who believed that interracial living was the first step toward the creation of a color-blind society. Milgram may have come from radical roots, but he shared a vision of American society that—minus its black faces—was not so different from William Levitt's.

Unlike the wartime radicals who saw racial segregation as a fundamentally economic problem, who emphasized the role of capitalism in perpetuating racial inequality, Milgram had no intention to redistribute wealth or alter the class structure of American society. He had made his peace with capitalism, with the middle class, and with the values of private home ownership. Where Milgram differed from the mainstream—and where so many of the 1950s-era racial activists concurred—was in his emphasis on "social engineering." Like Myrdal, Milgram appealed to the "American Creed" of freedom, home ownership, and equality. The success of the Concord Parks of America would awaken Americans from their irrational fears of racial mixing and undermine segregation. Milgram knew that the housing market, left to its own devices, would never meet the needs of African Americans or fulfill the vision of an interracial America. Drawing from a mixture of moralism, marketing, and mainstream social science, Milgram hoped to create a just society, where middle-class blacks and whites would freely mingle and, by their very example, challenge deep-rooted assumptions about the inevitability of racial conflict. But as Milgram found out, building an integrated America would be a task no easier for social engineers than for construction engineers. For every Concord Park, there were hundreds of Deerfields. Opening the suburbs proved to be one of the great failures of postwar racial liberalism, for it won neither the support of whites, who had created a suburban world that reflected both their interests and their identity, nor of blacks, who saw white resistance on the suburban frontier as confirmation of their worst suspicions about white America.

THE DEBACLES IN Levittown and Deerfield did not discourage open housing activists. In the late 1950s, they redoubled their efforts to win the hearts and minds of white Americans. Leading the way were mainstream religious groups. By the mid-1950s, most mainstream denominations—Protestant, Catholic, and Jewish—issued general statements supporting "open occupancy" in housing as a moral imperative. "Christians can make their love real when they welcome people as good neighbors regardless of race," wrote the National Council of Churches in 1959. Creating racially inclusive communities, argued Protestant activists, would serve as "practical demonstrations of love which will contribute to overcoming the estrangement and to binding up the broken fellowship which discrimination and segregation have caused in the Christian community." Brotherhood Sundays were held only once a year, but religious periodicals began publishing sermon guides and articles for church discussion groups. Many religious leaders turned their attention to liturgy—providing model prayers encouraging interracial cooperation that were meant to be heard by hard-hearted white congregants as well as the Almighty himself. In a "litany" presented in a Congregational Church publication, worshippers asked for contrition for the sins of racism and for blessings to those who had overcome it. "Our Father, we ask thy mercy upon all of us whose lives are impoverished by racial prejudice. Have pity on us whose friends are restricted to persons who look like us and think as we do. Forgive us if we have rejected the opportunity to know a black-haired, brown-skinned woman dressed in a colorful sari of India; or a gay, golden-hued child from Japan; or a reserved, blue-eyed man of Northern Europe; or a swarthy-cheeked man clothed in flowing robes of Saudi Arabia; or a woman whose brown skin recalls the centuries her ancestors spent in Africa." Such appeals spoke to the conscience of whites in growing numbers. Their misty multicultural appeals were tailor-made to a morality that viewed all men as the same beneath the skin. Sermons and hortatory articles emphasized the righteousness of open housing and desegregation. In the words of Buell Gallagher, a Congregational minister and president of City College of New York, desegregation was "God's task, waiting for human hands to do it."

Jewish organizations funded the lion's share of intergroup advocacy work in the postwar years. The American Jewish Committee conducted and disseminated research on "the basic nature of prejudice as a social and individual maladjustment"; the American Jewish Congress joined challenges against housing segregation. Jews had both pragmatic and principled reasons for supporting open housing. For one, many Jews had been victims of restrictive covenants and "gentleman's agreements" by real estate agents to keep them out of wealthy Protestant suburbs in many northern cities. Jewish groups also worked closely to minimize racial tension, especially in urban neighborhoods undergoing racial change. In Detroit's Twelfth Street area, Jewish groups circulated petitions in Yiddish, discouraging homeowners from panicking. But their efforts were not confined to Jewish neighborhoods. In Chicago, the Anti-Defamation League of B'nai B'rith joined in efforts to curb violent white-led housing protests, mostly in Catholic working-class neighborhoods, over desegregated housing projects. Perhaps most important, the ADL and the American Jewish Committee used their formidable resources to publicize the cause of open housing well beyond the Jewish community.

Moral rhetoric found a growing audience. Americans were among the most God-fearing people in the Western world in the 1950s, and interracial religious activists worked to mold their congregants' opinions. The National Conference of Christians and Jews had more than sixty thousand members concerned with interreligious and interracial affairs. They saw churches and synagogues as important players in the public sphere. "God cares how we think and what we do about great public issues," argued the editors of *Social Action*, one of the leading organs of liberal Protestant activism. "We need communicators who know how to relate eternal principles to specific problems." Preaching to the converted would not suffice. "We cannot confine our communication to the Sunday sermon and to our pitifully inadequate church press. . . . We must speak to the whole world." Religious organizations viewed their mission as forming public opinion—changing the hearts and minds of white Americans and their elected officials.

The 1950s, in many respects, was the age of mass marketing. The fields of public relations and advertising grew exponentially in the postwar years. Thus open housing activists deployed a formidable PR arsenal toward their cause, with church-based activists at the forefront. Part of the "sell" was crafting positive images of racial integration to undermine irrational prejudices. Religious periodicals ran uplifting stories. When Dr. Arthur Falls, a black thoracic surgeon, moved to Western Springs, Illinois, "property values in their neighborhood continued the spectacular rise characteristic of the time." After an interracial Christmas party that "went off handsomely" in St. Louis's Windemere Place, two whites removed the for-sale signs on their houses. Part of the public relations effort was mobilizing the liberal press—not a difficult task given the many connections that the Protestant establishment had to the world of middlebrow print journalism. When a black family moved peacefully into Ashburton, Maryland, in 1959, *The Saturday Evening Post* ran a story, "When a Negro Moves Next Door," touting the fact that property values did not plummet when blacks moved in. Accompanying many articles were carefully composed photographs that replicated stereotypical images of postwar suburban life: the kitchen, the playground, the white picket fence. The only difference between their photos and the insipid commercial photography in real estate brochures was the presence of black faces. Accompanying an article by the NAACP's Walter White on integration were photos of black and white children playing together on a suburban lawn.

Proponents of open housing also turned to film and theatrical productions in more subtle efforts to win over converts. In *Crossroads at Cedarmont*, produced by the Congregational Church's social action committee, the faithful watched a white veteran "remember with pleasure Negro friends of Army days" and a sociologist using "the findings of science to combat the prejudices of his neighbors." *A House for Marvin*, a play written to be performed in church halls, followed the travails of a well-meaning white congregation that provided housing assistance for its black sexton but struggled with conflict when he moved to a white neighborhood. Religious groups collaborated with the NAACP and commissioned filmmaker Nathan Zucker to produce dramas and documentaries to promote open housing efforts. Hoping to appeal to whites without being too controversial, Zucker's films, such as *All the Way Home* (1958), focused on the drama surrounding the movement of the first black family into an all-white suburban neighborhood. To Zucker the key was using film as a vehicle for persuasion but without it becoming "a blatant propaganda piece haranguing one point of view." Zucker offered unflattering depictions of white opponents of integration—one vandalizes his black neighbor's lawn; others make snide comments about blacks in private. But Zucker's films were also redemptive: They featured whites who responded sympathetically to their black neighbors. To undermine white fears of black inferiority, Zucker showed "well-dressed blacks at home and work." Churches and civil rights groups held screenings of the films or lent them to member churches. Some Jewish theater owners arranged screenings in neighborhood cinemas.

The most far-reaching religious effort on behalf of housing desegregation was the open housing pledge or covenant campaign. It is time, argued a Nassau County, Long Island, religious group, for the church to "search its corporate nerve and conscience" and "make every effort to enlist its members in a covenant of open occupancy." To that end, a Huntington group circulated a "Statement of Conscience," seeking one thousand signatures of town residents who would "welcome into their neighborhood any residents of good character, regardless of race, color, religion or national origin." Perhaps the most impressive effort took place in Minneapolis, where, beginning in 1960, the Congregational Church's Committee on Social Action spent nearly sixty thousand dollars to fund an open housing campaign that culminated in the publication of full-page advertisements listing the thousands of area whites who pledged their support for integration. Inspired by such examples, covenant drives spread to places as diverse as Syracuse, New York; Bergen County, New Jersey; and Pasadena, California.

By the end of the 1960s, tens of thousands of northern whites, most of them churchgoers, the majority suburban, had signed open-occupancy pledges. "There have been enough resolutions passed by American church conventions to paper the wall of every courthouse in Dixie," wrote one open housing activist. The popularity of the pledges was a sign that racial attitudes were changing. Some proponents had promised signatories confidentiality. But in wealthy suburban circles by the mid-1960s, there were few stigmas attached to advocating open housing, particularly in communities where integration was a concept rather than a genuine threat. Signing a pledge card was a cost-free way to demonstrate one's liberality on racial issues at a moment when racial violence was making headlines. One could occupy the moral high ground built up by sermons, newsletters, and a swell of public opinion in favor of civil rights. Holding interracial teas and attending Brotherhood Sunday sermons and collecting signatures on pro-housing-integration petitions proved to be easy in the 1960s. Persuading whites to stay in racially changing neighborhoods or creating integrated housing markets in the suburbs proved to be much more difficult.

In 1965, just two years after Milgram exhausted his appeals in the Deerfield case, something quite extraordinary happened. Several thousand churchgoers in the now safely all-white suburb—like their counterparts throughout the suburban North—signed an open-occupancy pledge. The battle for integration in the North had clearly changed northern attitudes about racial matters dramatically. Survey researcher Paul Sheatsley examined responses over more than two decades to the question "If a Negro with the same income and education as you moved into your block, would it make any difference to you?" In 1942, only 42 percent of northern whites would have approved of such a black neighbor; by December 1963, 70 percent of whites claimed they would accept such a neighbor. The shift in attitudes about housing tracked other major changes. By similar figures (40 percent in 1942, 75 percent in 1963), northern whites agreed with the statement that "white students and Negro students should go to the same schools." And in 1963, four-fifths of northern whites agreed that "Negroes are as intelligent as white people." Only on the matter of interracial dating had white attitudes changed very little. A *Newsweek* poll in 1963 found that 90 percent of whites would object to their "own teenage daughter dating a Negro." That interracial intimacy was still a taboo was a reminder that racial fears were still deep-rooted. But in every other respect, white racial attitudes had improved to an extent that seemed to bear out Gunnar Myrdal's optimistic predictions about the power of education. Longtime open housing activist Charles Abrams was thrilled at the "almost complete shift, particularly in the North and West, in the public feeling about discrimination and racial prejudice."

The shift in attitudes, however, was not accompanied by a shift in behavior. The open housing movement had not overcome the forces encouraging racial segregation—federal policy, real estate practices, and the fragmentation of municipal governments. But racial liberalism did bequeath to suburban whites a new language of color blindness that allowed them—despite the long history of deliberate racial exclusion in housing—to claim that they had overcome their racist past and to profess their innocence. In fact, hidden in the very question that survey researchers asked about housing—the "class" of African Americans—was part of a shift in how northern whites talked about race in the postwar years. Expressing concern about "class" had become an increasingly common way for northern whites to express discomfort with integration, based on a widespread but inaccurate assumption that all blacks were blue-collar or poor. Whites could profess their color blindness—they did not move to all-white communities because they were racist but rather because they were simply exercising their free choice to live among people of their "class." But choice was a white freedom, one still systematically denied to most African Americans in the early 1960s. As distinguished demographers Karl and Alma Taeuber noted, "the net effect of economic factors in explaining residential segregation is slight." Blacks were frozen out of white communities, regardless of their ability to pay.

The very geography of postwar metropolitan America reinforced racial differences in education, employment, and access to public goods and services. Whites were able to accumulate advantages as a result of their relative freedom in the housing market. They could choose communities with adequately funded schools, well-run public services, excellent police protection, and a lack of costly social problems, especially those of the poor, ill housed, and unhealthy who remained concentrated in central cities. Ultimately, the problem of housing segregation was one of political and economic power, of coercion, not choice, personal attitudes, or individual morality.

Efforts to change white attitudes had little impact on the reality of northern segregation. Even if a sizeable majority of whites in the North professed their support for racial integration, they moved in overwhelming numbers to all-white communities. By 1960, more whites in the North lived in suburbs than in central cities. In small trickles, here and there, blacks made their way into majority-white enclaves. The peppering of a few white neighborhoods with a handful of prosperous blacks gave the impression that prejudice was eroding while, in the aggregate, racial patterns barely changed. In 1970, northern cities remained nearly as segregated by race as they had been in 1940. The balkanization of postwar metropolitan America into racially separate territories perpetuated—indeed hardened—racial differences at a time when activists worked to undermine notions of racial superiority and inferiority.

Most blacks found themselves confined to ever-expanding central-city ghettoes, places that were afflicted by multiple disadvantages. Nearly every major northeastern and midwestern city—and some West Coast ports, such as Oakland—lost population and jobs over the course of the 1950s. The central-city job loss was only compounded by the fact that blacks remained frozen out of the communities where job growth was most robust. As people and capital fled, tax bases shrank, putting further strain on local infrastructure and public services. Nearly every urban institution that blacks relied upon—schools, welfare offices, hospitals—came under growing strain.

The ongoing racial isolation of blacks and the rapid increase of black population in northern cities had unintended consequences that would play a role in reshaping the struggle for racial equality in the 1960s and 1970s. More and more blacks lived in communities wholly removed from white America. Residents of inner-city communities lived their daily lives with little or no contact with whites except law enforcement authorities, shopkeepers, and schoolteachers, almost all of them outsiders. Racial isolation also created a sense of solidarity among urban blacks. And it gave them greater political power than they had ever before had in the North. The concentration of blacks in central, homogeneous neighborhoods strengthened their influence in city governments.

A growing cadre of black activists began to wonder—with good reason—whether housing integration was worth the bother. Pushing a few blacks through the sieve of white resistance seemed a long, slow, and ineffective way to deal with racial inequality. Were efforts to integrate suburbs a diversion from the pressing problems of survival that confronted inner-city blacks? Should civil rights groups put their energy into pursuing policies that would mostly benefit the black elite? What about the poor and working-class blacks who were left out of open housing campaigns? Were they to wait patiently for the trickle-down benefits of black suburbanization? The struggle for open housing also raised vexatious political questions. Would integration dilute black electoral power just at the moment when it had reached critical mass in many cities? Would it be possible for blacks to take control of municipal institutions if the black population scattered across whole metropolitan areas? These questions—still unresolved—would be raised in high relief in the ongoing debates about housing, civil rights, and racial politics in the 1960s and 1970s.

PART III

FREEDOM NOW

CHAPTER 8

"NEW FRONTIER"

DECADES SERVE AS CONVENIENT BUT PROBLEMATIC SHORTHAND FOR DIVIDING up our past. Social movements seldom occur in ten-year cycles; lives are not structured in ten-year blocks of time; political terms are not measured by tens. But the major statistical apparatus of the United States follows a ten-year calendar. Those years that end in zeros are moments of intensive data gathering. Since 1790, the U.S. Census Bureau has surveyed the American population every ten years, and it did so in 1960. The release of census data prompted national soul-searching on what the nation had been and what it was becoming. While census statisticians made every effort to be comprehensive and neutral in their presentation of data, the interpretation of the census was invariably political. The census provided ammunition for those who hoped to change the direction of American history. Armed with hard statistics, girded with medians and means, activists battled for public policies that would change those statistics. In the cubicles of the Department of Labor, policy analysts combed through employment statistics. In the back rooms of the Capitol, staffers pored over population statistics, preparing for electoral redistricting. Advocacy organizations drafted reports, press releases, and policy briefs. In the two or three years that it took to release the raw data from the decennial census, activists scrambled to interpret the figures to sway public opinion and influence policy makers.

No civil rights organization paid closer attention to census data than the Urban League, whose local affiliates and national office regularly released reports on the state of black America. Most of the Urban League reports were dry, but in the hands of activists, they could come alive. No one knew that better than Whitney M. Young, Jr., who took the helm of the venerable organization just after the release of the first data from the

1960 census. Young's profile was like that of many local Urban League leaders. He was a social worker, deeply committed to using his skills to uplift "the race." Steeped in the professional culture of casework, Young believed that social problems were best solved by gathering as much data as possible, whether at the individual or aggregate level. To Young, who had a head for numbers, statistics documenting employment discrimination and racial disparities in income were a call to arms. As a young Urban League executive, he directed his nearly inexhaustible energy to "vocational services" and "industrial relations"—the league's programs for employment training and placement. In his positions as industrial relations secretary of the league's St. Paul, Minnesota, branch and then as executive secretary of the Omaha branch, Young gained extensive experience negotiating with white business leaders.

Young was not just a technocrat. Unlike many Urban League officers who eschewed confrontational tactics, he did not sit on the sidelines during civil rights protests. While a social work student in Minneapolis in the late 1940s, Young joined CORE-led demonstrations against segregated restaurants in the Twin Cities, and later, as dean of the Atlanta University School of Social Work, he supported lunch counter sit-ins. Young's sympathy for protestors grew out of his growing dissatisfaction with cautious, liberal civil rights strategies. From his leadership positions, Young saw firsthand the limitations of the Urban League's gradualist approach to job creation. He was particularly sympathetic to the mounting impatience among members of the black working class. How can "good, educated, church-going Americans," he asked in a 1961 speech, "tell a well-prepared Negro who had suffered all the indignities and pain of jobs, homes, and other normal needs being closed to him that he must be patient, be philosophical about these denials of civil and human rights."

By the time Young took charge in 1961, the Urban League was under siege as an anachronistic organization. Because it had operated behind the scenes for most of its half-century existence, the league had a low profile. As *Defender* columnist Nat Williams commented in 1960, "the masses of Negroes greet the name 'Urban League' with only a blank stare. They have never heard of it." Radical activists denounced the Urban League's obsequious "Uncle Tom-ism," accusing its leaders of bowing and scraping to white business leaders. "If the Negro accepted the social service tactics of the Urban League as the only way toward freedom," wrote critic Ossie

Sykes, "your freedom should arrive by the year 4064." Urban League staff members, like black race relations experts generally, faced the suspicion of many ordinary blacks because of their detachment from protest, their reliance on expertise, and their political invisibility. Even if such experts helped to "make protest effective protest" by challenging segregation, their association with white elites also rendered them suspect. The Urban League, wrote one critic, was not "truly emancipated from the ideological shackles of 'white is right.'" Of all the criticisms of the league, charges of "tokenism" hit particularly close to home. Such symbolic victories as the hiring of the first black airline stewardesses and bank tellers hardly struck fatal blows to pervasive workplace discrimination. Despite years of painstaking work, the Urban League's job placement efforts had scarcely made a dent into northern job markets.

Much to the surprise of observers—and some of the Urban League's old guard—Young took his critics seriously and set out on an activist course. More than any other black organization, the Urban League believed in the power of social science, and its local affiliates gathered scads of hard data on black employment, housing, and educational status. Most of the league's reports ended up in the hands of social welfare agencies and other civil rights organizations that could put them to use, but their findings—thorough, careful, and unfailingly accurate—were seldom well publicized. Young dusted off the reports and breathed life into them in nearly every speech and interview he gave. For Young, census data were weapons to be used for the advancement of the race. "On an economic level," warned Young, "the hard but simple fact—borne out by comparative statistics on unemployment, income, mortality rates, substandard housing and education—is that the past of the Negro exists in the present."

The 1960 census made clear that black America was at a turning point. A greater percentage of blacks than ever, 40 percent, lived outside the South. And for the first time since census records had been kept, a greater percentage of blacks than whites lived in urban centers. The massive migration of blacks from the underdeveloped South to the urban, industrial North had fundamentally changed blacks' economic fortunes. Black workers had made inroads into white-dominated occupations, particularly in unionized manufacturing employment and in the public sector. Blacks' personal and household income rose steadily—as did all Americans'—in the twenty years following entrance into World War II. America was a rich country, and blacks shared in that wealth. More blacks than ever were home owners in 1960. White suburbanization opened up large sections of cities to blacks for the first time and broke the logjam in housing, reducing overcrowding over the course of the 1950s.

In nearly every other realm, the census showed mixed gains. Compared to 1940, blacks had made some inroads in semiskilled employment and in white-collar work. But the statistics were chastening to those who believed that blacks were being carried upward in the affluent society. Gains are relative as well as absolute. Throughout the 1950s, blacks remained several steps behind whites. Despite the growth in black income, black men in the North earned only three-quarters the income of white men, and the black-white income ratio fell between 1949 and 1959 in the Northeast, Midwest, and West. Brighter news was that the income gap between black and white women had narrowed to the vanishing point, although this reflected the fact that more black women were in the workforce and worked more hours than their white counterparts. Labor statistics painted a grimmer picture. Every year after 1953, blacks suffered unemployment rates more than double those of whites—a pattern that would stubbornly hold throughout the following decade. In 1960, 10.2 percent of blacks, compared to only 4.9 percent of whites, were unemployed. It was, in other words, close to a full-employment economy for whites, but a deep recession for blacks.

The state of black America—in the long view—gave grounds for hope. The Great Depression and World War II had witnessed real gains in black economic attainment. Over the course of the 1950s, even in the face of widespread white indifference, civil rights activists had kept equal employment opportunity, educational equality, and open housing on the political agenda. Even if the cumulative impact of local and state antidiscrimination laws was more symbolic than real, they nonetheless held out the possibility that formal racial equality was no longer a distant dream. The southern freedom struggle, in particular, had moved black issues out of the political shadows to the center of the national political agenda. And northern blacks had joined the consumer society of postwar America. Piecemeal they had won access to restaurants, hotels, amusement parks, and pools, even if there were still deep pockets of resistance to integration in many smaller towns and in resort areas.

But most black Americans in the early 1960s did not look at their everyday lives and compare their lot to that of the slaves freed one hundred years earlier or even to that of their counterparts who had marched for social change during World War II. Their perceptions of progress and possibility were shaped by the current political, social, and economic climate and especially by their still profoundly unequal position in American society. Above all, northern blacks could not help but notice the enormous gap in affluence, status, and power between themselves and whites. The gains of the postwar period gave them a sense of the possibility of change, but the magnitude of change—small—engendered bitterness.

Despite improvements in the aggregate, the economic reality for most northern blacks was starkly unequal. The industrial cities of the Northeast and the Midwest and the port cities of the West Coast offered grim examples of economic decline. These places had attracted the lion's share of southern black migrants because of their vibrant economies, and they were rusting fast. The heavy industries that had opened their doors to black workers during World War II were shuttering their urban plants and relocating production to suburbs and small, rural towns, most of them all-white. Detroit lost 140,000 manufacturing jobs between 1947 and 1963, most in unskilled and semiskilled positions that had provided an avenue of opportunity for black workers. New York City underwent a massive economic restructuring. The finance and real estate sectors were expanding, but they employed few minorities. By contrast, the city lost more than 70,000 garment industry jobs in the 1950s, at just the time when blacks and Puerto Ricans found work there. Garment workers—struggling against the competition of cheap labor in the upper South and overseas—took significant wage cuts. Chicago's meatpacking district, a major magnet for black workers, atrophied as the industry opened new plants in Rochester, Minnesota; Waterloo, Iowa; and other small towns. Port cities such as Oakland, Newark, Philadelphia, and Baltimore, which had provided longshore, shipbuilding, and warehouse employment, saw their wharves emptied as shippers turned to containers and trucking.

The railroads, which had provided employment for tens of thousands of African Americans as porters and redcaps, struggled financially as wealthy travelers gave up the comfort of the dining car for the convenience of the personal automobile. In one of the greatest ironies for those blacks who went north in search of opportunity, major northern firms were engaged in their own out-migration, heading southward in search of low wages in the largely nonunionized region. Camden's RCA moved to rural Indiana for a short stay before fleeing to Memphis and, eventually, Ciudad Juárez, Mexico. General Motors and Ford opened plants in Atlanta and Memphis. Major defense contractors, which had provided tens of thousands of jobs to northern blacks during and after World War II, decentralized to an industrial archipelago across the Sunbelt.

The combination of persistent employment discrimination, the flight of capital from northern cities, the lack of residential mobility, and the deficiencies of unequal education were devastating. By every economic measure, blacks were worse off than whites. Not surprisingly, public opinion reflected a sense of pessimism among northern blacks. In a May 1962 Gallup Poll, 54 percent of black respondents agreed that Negroes would have a "hard time . . . finding steady work in areas outside the South." Only 17 percent thought that finding such work would be easy.

The economic restructuring of northern cities was to some extent color-blind, but whites had some significant economic advantages that mitigated its effects. The most important was residential mobility. Housing segregation severely restricted blacks' choices as to where to live, whereas whites could follow fleeing industry, whether to lily-white suburbs or to small towns. For most northern blacks in the early 1960s, moving to the new mecca for industry—the South—was an absurd option. In the last, desperate days of Jim Crow, few were tempted to follow employers to the land of cross burnings, massive resistance, and murder. Blacks faced another major disadvantage. The employers who stayed in the North increasingly demanded better skills and more education. In the aggregate, whites were better educated than blacks. In northern states, blacks were one to two years behind whites in educational attainment. Even those with comparable educational levels—say, high school graduates—were not on the same educational playing field because of the disadvantages of separate and unequal northern schools.

A few well-to-do black families lived in white neighborhoods in the North. However, the euphoria that had accompanied the Supreme Court decision that struck down racially restrictive covenants was a distant memory. Northern metropolitan areas were as segregated in 1960 as they had been in 1940, despite twenty years of sustained activism and despite polls that showed that whites were more willing than ever to accept black neighbors. By 1960, cities contained larger, more homogeneous, and more racially isolated black communities than ever before. Whites fled central cities in record numbers in the decades following World War II, most of them to suburbs where blacks did not live. Real estate agents still steered whites away from racially mixed or "transitional" neighborhoods. Federal housing policy and bank lending practices channeled mortgages, loans, and insurance toward "desirable" white neighborhoods and away from "risky" mixed and black neighborhoods. The situation of northern cities was worsening, with the flight of commerce to suburbia and with the destruction of black neighborhoods and business districts for urban renewal projects and highways. In nearly every northern city, the new federally funded expressways that whisked whites to their suburban homes passed over the remnants of former black commercial districts and residential neighborhoods, places that fell to the wrecking ball and bulldozer for the sake of easy commuting. Not only did expressways obliterate much of black urban America, but to the majority of commuters, the grassy embankments and concrete walls rendered most of the remaining black community invisible.

As urban areas in the Northeast and Midwest hemorrhaged their white population—and with it white capital—the physical impact of disinvestment and depopulation grew more visible to those driving along surface streets. By the early 1960s, most black urban shopping districts were tawdry affairs, pockmarked with vacant storefronts, cluttered with liquor stores, bars, pawnshops, and cheap clothing emporia, and graced with billboards, some mounted on the sides of buildings, others looming over rooftops. Dominating many major intersections were the stalwart neoclassical façades of banks now boarded up or converted into other, lesser businesses. Many surviving shops appeared to be fortresses, with their plate-glass display windows covered with bars or bricked over. Black neighborhoods were well stocked with stores selling malt liquor, but they lacked many of the businesses that could be found in most nearby white suburbs: supermarkets, full-scale pharmacies, bookshops, car dealerships, and chain stores of nearly every kind.

Many of the nation's most vital black commercial districts had been obliterated by massive public works projects. Detroit's Paradise Valley, once the center of the city's black cultural and economic life, was entombed by an expressway. Philadelphia's Black Bottom, a neighborhood of choice for many first-generation southern migrants, was bulldozed to create a science and research center attached to the University of Pennsylvania. What remained of Chicago's famed Bronzeville neighborhood was sandwiched in by an interstate and high-rise public housing projects that drained the streets of commerce and vitality. And by 1963, Newark, once a thriving regional shopping destination, had "one of the nation's most depressed downtown areas." As factories in northern cities downsized or shut their doors, the once-bustling shopping districts where workers cashed checks, bought sandwiches, and gathered for beer at shift change atrophied. Railway corridors were lined with abandoned industrial buildings, their windows open to the elements, their parking lots overgrown with weeds. The cities that had been a promised land for black migrants metamorphosed into the Rust Belt over the course of the 1950s and 1960s.

In big cities and small towns, blacks inhabited secondhand neighborhoods left behind by whites following the relentless march of suburban sprawl outward. Throughout the North, blacks could be found "on the wrong side of the tracks" in the shabby, mostly wood-frame housing that huddled along train tracks and in the shadows of factories. In cities large enough to have inner-city apartment districts, cramped tenements and once-luxurious 1920s-era apartment buildings alike were disproportionately inhabited by blacks. And in the countless neighborhoods of grand nineteenth-century row houses and turn-of-the-century manses, especially on the outskirts of downtowns, poor and working-class blacks laid claim to the once-fashionable homes of white industrialists and merchants, while landlords and investors, both black and white, often divided spacious mansions into boardinghouses and apartments, visible by the telltale sign of a rack of doorbells next to inglenook windows, faux Gothic doorways, and elaborately carved pilasters and moldings. There were some advantages to white flight—over the course of the 1950s, blacks escaped the overcrowding that had been the norm in the World War II years. By 1960, the average housing stock in black sections of northern cities, while still likely to be older and in greater disrepair than white housing, was better than the cramped tenements of the 1940s or the shotgun shacks and log cabins of the South.

The only new housing inhabited by blacks—a few private developments like Concord Park exempted—was public housing projects. Most big cities and many smaller towns with black populations had some low-rise subsidized housing, often built during World War II to accommodate defense workers. The largest cities also had high-rise projects, arrayed on windswept, muddy lawns, usually the tallest buildings in their neighborhoods. In nearly every city, the projects were physically isolated from the surrounding neighborhoods. Because of intense white opposition to the construction of public housing, most cities took the path of least resistance, constructing projects in the heart of long-established black neighborhoods or on marginal land where they would generate little controversy. Chicago's infamous Robert Taylor Homes and Stateway Gardens were cut off from the rest of the city by a major expressway and rail yards. Boston's Columbia Point project was constructed on a dump site on a peninsula that isolated it from nearby white neighborhoods and from public transportation. Philadelphia's Passyunk Homes sat on a former wetland bounded by oil refineries. During rainstorms, oily rainbows formed in puddles on the site, caused by contaminants seeping from leaky underground tanks over which the project had been built.

The costs of economic marginalization were particularly visible on the street corners of inner cities, where, day and night, young black men hung out. By the early 1960s, observers began to write of the emergence of "the hard-core unemployed," a group that consisted of poorly educated, working-class black men who had simply given up on the workforce altogether. In Detroit, what locals derisively called the "slave market" sprang up in a black neighborhood along Eight Mile Road, the street that separated the city from the nearly all-white suburbs, where contractors picked up black men to work as day laborers on suburban construction sites. Sociologists and anthropologists noted the rise of "street corner society," where disaffected, unemployed men hung out, gambling, drinking, and dodging the police. And around the North, some young men with an entrepreneurial bent began to discover the lures of an illegal consumer economy—one that ranged from numbers running to selling moonshine alcohol to dealing narcotics. Social workers interviewing black teenagers on Detroit's West Side about their job aspirations in the early 1960s found that none mentioned "skilled trades, office, clerical or technical occupations." Aspiring to such middling jobs was not realistic, given the persistence of discrimination and their educational handicaps. Instead, they mentioned a "whole range of deviant

occupations—prostitution, numbers, malicing, corn whiskey, theft, etc."
The underground world was insecure and dangerous, but it offered a degree of independence and the promise, if seldom met, of rewards greater
than entry-level jobs or meager unemployment checks.

But however decrepit the environment in most northern cities, the
fruits of almost a half century of black migration and community building
were visible. Black neighborhoods were institutionally rich. Dotting black
neighborhoods, and easily the most vital institutions there, were
churches—little storefronts marked with a crucifix and handwritten
signs, recycled synagogues abandoned by their suburbanizing congregations and now home to Protestant sects, and ostentatious Gothic edifices,
once home to well-endowed white congregations, now home to their
black counterparts. Black ministers were among the most prominent
community leaders in many northern cities. Their churches received extensive coverage in the social pages of the black press. And some, such as
Detroit's Reverend C. L. Franklin, took advantage of the proliferation of
black radio stations to carry their sermons to a nationwide audience.
Their politics ranged widely—from those who were resolutely apolitical
to those who used their pulpits to advocate racial equality. Churches often
served as social service organizations, providing food, counseling, job
training, and shelter for their members, especially in working-class and
poor neighborhoods.

Northern cities were also the home to increasingly visible prophets of
radical change. The Nation of Islam, and most notably its spokesman Malcolm X, came to national attention in a 1959 documentary, *The Hate That
Hate Produced*. A former street hustler known as Detroit Red for his
auburn hair, Malcolm Little had joined the Lost-Found Nation of Islam,
a small black sect, while he was in prison in the early 1950s. The Nation's
philosophy of uplift and race pride found a particularly receptive audience among young black men in northern jails, where it aggressively recruited. The Nation provided Malcolm, like many of its jail-cell converts,
with a blueprint for rehabilitation: a life of military-like discipline and
hard work, a strict dietary regimen that included abstinence from alcohol
and pork, and a theology that called for self-emancipation by breaking
the shackles of white-imposed economic and psychological "slavery."
Most of all, it gave young men like Malcolm—those "bottom of the pile
Negroes, the Negroes who through their entire lives have been kicked

about, treated like children"—a way to channel their rage away from themselves, their families, and their neighborhoods. " 'The white man is the devil,' " noted Malcolm, "is a perfect echo of the black convict's life-long experience." As part of their conversion, most "Black Muslims," as they were called, gave up their surnames or took new Muslim names altogether. Malcolm gave up his "white slavemaster name," Little, and took the surname X, to stand in for the identity that had been stolen generations earlier by slaveholders. "I have no last name," he claimed. "Just a name some white man gave one of my ancestors a long time ago. I'd rather be called nigger."

The Nation of Islam had small outposts in several northern cities, and, though small, had grown rapidly through the 1950s, in large part because of the powerful witness of its new converts, who stood out in northern ghettos because of their austere dress, somber manner, and compelling conversion narratives. Of the Nation's many ministers, none had refashioned himself more compellingly than Malcolm. A powerful orator, he wrapped his personal story of redemption—the petty criminal made good—with acerbic denunciations of white supremacy. Through word of mouth and media attention, which he astutely cultivated, Malcolm attracted growing audiences in northern cities. He succeeded in converting some of those who heard him, but even when he failed to win over followers, Malcolm gave voice to the outrage of the ghetto in a way that few other ministers, even the most compelling and radical, did.

The Lost-Found Nation of Islam was founded in Detroit in 1930 by W. D. Fard (also known as Wali Farad and Fard Muhammad), a peripatetic prophet who mysteriously disappeared in 1934, never to be seen again. Fard's Temple No. 1 remained in a dreary storefront on Detroit's East Side, but the Nation moved its headquarters to Chicago's South Side, where Fard's successor, Elijah Muhammad, built a mosque, a school, and a cluster of Nation-organized businesses. Fard and Muhammad's theology combined numerology, elements of Islamic tradition, and its hallmark, a quirky creation tale of a mad scientist named Jacub who had fashioned a race of white-skinned, blue-eyed devils who systematically oppressed blacks. At the core of the Jacub myth, however bizarre, was a larger and more popular argument about the terminal corruption of white America. In one of his columns in *The Afro-American*, Muhammad argued that "today's world is floating in corruption; its complete disintegration is both imminent and inescapable. Any man who integrates with the world must share in its disintegration and destruction. If the Black Man would but listen, he need not be a part of this certain doom."

Muhammad's followers embraced a philosophy of racial separation and self-determination, and to that end created a series of Black Muslim—run institutions, including butcher shops, clothing stores, bookstores, and, eventually, the newspaper *Muhammad Speaks*. The Nation's philosophy of self-help was neither distinctively Islamic nor African American, although its community-run businesses had much in common with earlier nationalist and separatist organizations such as Marcus Garvey's Universal Negro Improvement Association and the black cooperative movement of the Great Depression. The Nation did not rely—as did many black Christian congregations—on the beneficence of white patrons. It was wholly self-sufficient. Members of the Nation were required to tithe a sizeable portion of their income to the organization.

Northern black migrants and their children had also created a rich cultural infrastructure. Along Detroit's Twelfth Street and Chicago's Grand Boulevard and New York's 125th Street were jazz clubs. Motown musicians attracted throngs to their city's Greystone Ballroom; bebop bands packed them into the Apollo in Harlem; and blues musicians created an artistic enclave around Philadelphia's Royal Theater. Even more important were the quasi-public spaces that brought like-minded blacks together for socialization and, often, political organizing. Countless fraternal and sororal organizations, from Elks Clubs to women's union auxiliaries, provided gathering places and networks for a city's residents. The "Negro Ys" sponsored recreational activities but also hosted political speakers and rallies. And perhaps the most important thread connecting northern blacks, regardless of whether or not they belonged to a sorority or went to a blues club, was the ubiquitous black press, supplemented in the early 1960s by a slew of pamphlets, broadsides, and magazines, ranging from the slick, mainstream *Ebony* and *Jet* to the countercultural *Liberator* and *Freedomways*. Part of the cacophonous, richly diverse cultural life of northern cities, they helped shape a race consciousness that informed the social movements of the early 1960s.

By 1960, community building had come to fruition in another very important way. In most northern cities between the Great Depression and

the late 1950s, blacks were not a large enough segment of the urban electorate to play a crucial role in local political races. Henry Lee Moon's argument about blacks' role as swing voters in hotly contested northern
states gave civil rights activists clout in state legislatures, but the black
vote did not hit critical mass in most northern cities until sometime in
the late 1950s or early 1960s. In 1960, four northern cities (New York,
Chicago, Philadelphia, and Detroit) had black populations ranging from
nearly 500,000 to over a million. By 1970, one in every five New Yorkers,
one in every three Philadelphians and Chicagoans, and more than four of
ten Detroiters were black. Other major cities, among them Newark and
Gary, had majority-black populations by 1970. The growth in black population meant a growth in the number of black elected officials. Just as
important, the new political demography meant that local white elected
officials ignored black votes at their peril. Increasingly, blacks could not
be bought off with low-end municipal jobs and symbolic appointments to
city agencies.

In the early 1960s, most northern activists were guardedly optimistic
about the prospects for change. Perhaps the most significant reason was
the regime change in Washington. With the exception of radical nationalists and the rapidly dwindling rank of black Republicans, most black activists looked to the new Kennedy administration with hope, even if it was
not at all clear that northern inner cities, black poverty, and unemployment would be anywhere near the top of John F. Kennedy's "to do" list.
On the campaign trail, Kennedy had endorsed the civil rights movement,
although his record in the House and Senate had been spotty. He had
been a late and reluctant supporter of the rather toothless Civil Rights Act
of 1957 and had not joined the swelling ranks of liberal northern Democrats who called for sweeping civil rights legislation. Like most Democrats
with national political aspirations in the postwar years, Kennedy tiptoed
carefully around issues of race and rights, for fear of alienating his party's
powerful southern wing. Kennedy's position on poverty offered more
grounds for optimism. Kennedy made celebrated campaign stops in the
left-behind, mostly white towns of Appalachia, signaling that he cared
about the down-and-out, even if most of the hands he shook were white.
But Kennedy gave few indications that the problems of the northern
inner cities would be part of his program. Other than blanketing vote-rich

black neighborhoods with more than a million pamphlets touting his support for then-imprisoned Reverend Martin Luther King, Jr., Kennedy did not spend much time reaching out to northern blacks.

Presidents, however, do not govern alone. The Democratic Party had adopted a civil rights plank in its 1960 platform that was far to the left of Kennedy, not to mention the party's southern wing. *The Pittsburgh Courier* lauded it as "the strongest pronunciation of principles ever adopted by any party." The platform mattered relatively little compared to the Democratic Party's quarter century of support for a generous welfare state. New Deal social programs were crucial to the well-being of northern blacks, and Democrats, even with the limitations imposed by the party's powerful southern wing, were more likely to ally themselves with black rights than the GOP was. Progress was halting—sometimes frustratingly slow—but the executive branch and the Supreme Court were responsive to black demands. Roosevelt had implemented the Fair Employment Practices Committee, and Truman had desegregated the military. None of these breakthroughs had come easily; all were incomplete. But their very existence was a reminder of the efficacy of black protest, litigation, and lobbying.

After eight years of Republican control in Washington, liberals and leftists were guardedly optimistic about the Kennedy administration. Kennedy's domestic policy staff, drawn heavily from the ranks of foundation executives and social scientists, believed in the application of scholarship to pressing social problems and to race relations. The administration's economic advisors and domestic policy staff shared no consensus: Some called for tax policies to stimulate growth, arguing that a rising tide would lift all boats; others called for investment in "manpower" or skills training; and still others offered more redistributionist solutions, including the expansion of public works. But diverging opinions fostered a climate of policy experimentation in the New Frontier, especially regarding poverty, youth issues, and employment policy. Working closely with liberal foundations, especially the Ford Foundation, which had begun to expand funding to anti-juvenile-delinquency and job training programs in urban "gray areas," the Kennedy administration channeled new resources into social service organizations in northern cities. Administration officials, along with liberals in Congress, breathed new life into a program to target federal economic development funds to "depressed areas," disproportionately northern industrial cities and towns. Although Kennedy did not develop a full-fledged "war on poverty," his administration was scoping out the battlegrounds and beginning to gather the troops.

At the same time the Kennedy administration encouraged innovation in poverty and urban policy making, it took tentative first steps toward extending civil rights. On March 6, 1961, Kennedy issued Executive Order 10925, creating the President's Committee on Equal Employment Opportunity (PCEEO), charged with eliminating discrimination in government and federally contracted employment. The order mandated a still vaguely defined "affirmative action" by employers to eliminate discrimination. By the standards of presidential action, this was no bold move. Eisenhower had created the President's Committee on Government Contracts, a largely do-nothing body that gathered information on race in government contracting but did little to enforce antidiscrimination measures. Kennedy's PCEEO, a minor interagency committee that would oversee government contracts and hear complaints about discrimination in hiring and upgrading in federal jobs, looked like a dreary reprise of previous efforts. When it first met, on April 11, President Kennedy defined the committee's mandate as one of "high moral purpose." In his own remarks, the committee's chair, Vice President Lyndon Johnson, argued that "the genuineness of our democracy will be largely gauged by the extent of our progress" in the effort for equal employment opportunity.

The PCEEO had neither enforcement powers nor its own budget. Its small staff regularly complained that it was swamped with work and strapped for time, but it proved to be far more effective than anyone predicted. The federal government alone employed 2.5 million and government contractors over 15.5 million more. The sheer number of workers who came under the committee's purview meant that any antidiscrimination efforts would have far-reaching consequences. The PCEEO's first task was to gather hard data on the racial composition of government offices and contractors to determine whether employers were in "compliance" with the president's antidiscrimination order. Without data, it would be impossible to tackle the problem of workplace discrimination systematically. The federal government had been collecting racial data from government contractors since 1956, but without the rigor that it would under Kennedy's executive order. PCEEO data offered a comprehensive picture of discriminatory practices for the first time. In a survey of contractors—whose workforce totaled more than half a million—the committee found that "nowhere (north, south, east, or west) did Negroes hold a significant number of their better jobs." The conclusion was grim: "The problem of the Negro in employment today is serious and . . . in 25 to 50 years it will be worse unless steps, calculated toward large and lasting improvement, are soon taken."

Even though the PCEEO lacked enforcement powers, black workers and civil rights groups alike used its grievance procedure to great benefit. The committee was flooded with complaints of workplace discrimination. In its first year of operation, it received more complaints than had Eisenhower's weak predecessor committee in its first seven and a half years. Like state FEPCs, the PCEEO acted on individual reports of discrimination. Unlike most state FEPCs, however, the committee allowed for what it called "complex group complaint situations," which involved many workers in a single job classification. Those complaints could not be handled easily: rather, they required what PCEEO executive director John Feild called "comprehensive investigations and, in most instances, public hearings." When four hundred black workers in the Bureau of Engraving and Printing charged discrimination, columnist Lynn Williams hailed the "grass roots stirrings" that forced the administration to "go beyond the image projected by page one strategic high-level appointments, and to prove in depth the substance and promise of New Frontier pronouncements."

While federal employees were filing grievances, established civil rights organizations also took advantage of the Kennedy administration's policy shifts. The NAACP's labor secretary, Herbert Hill, had long battled against discrimination in trade unions and workplaces. Using the PCEEO as a weapon, the NAACP filed more than five hundred complaints in its first year, targeting such prominent firms as Republic Aviation, which ran a large, mostly white plant on Long Island, and General Motors, which had $347 million in sales to the military in 1960 but had few black apprentices. At the same time, the NAACP lambasted the agency itself as ineffectual. The PCEEO, charged Hill in early 1962, yielded "high returns in press notices and only superficial and token results in job opportunities." It was a calculated strategy to take advantage of the PCEEO and simultaneously put pressure on the government to strengthen it.

The President's Committee introduced another policy innovation with far-reaching consequences. It demanded that employers fill out "compliance reports," which shifted the burden of proof away from individual complainants. The very lack of black workers could be prima facie evidence of discrimination. Prospective government contractors and subcontractors needed to file these reports as part of their bids or contract negotiations, thus giving the government the potential to exercise maximum leverage over employers: They would have to prove that they were not discriminating, or else they might be ruled ineligible for a government contract. Employers—subject to investigations, either because of individual workers' grievances or because of the demands of compliance—responded to the PCEEO by altering the composition of their workforces, sometimes dramatically. In one Richmond, Indiana, plant, an individual complaint led to the discovery that the contractor had "employed no Negroes in its 20-year history." The hearing resulted in "pattern-changing results": The firm hired eighty-five blacks. Fearful that it would lose government contracts, the Danly Machine Company in Cicero, Illinois—a firm that had separate black and white "employment groups" with unequal wages—engaged in an "aggressive program of affirmative action" and hired a black accountant and its first black machinists. And in San Pedro, California, the President's Committee forced the eradication of separate seniority lines for black and white shipyard workers. The PCEEO also opened up thousands of new government jobs: In its first year, federal agencies hired almost eleven thousand black workers, more than 17 percent of their new employees nationwide.

While the PCEEO was unleashing a wave of antidiscrimination efforts, another underfunded arm of the government, the U.S. Commission on Civil Rights, was also goading the administration and providing ammunition for grassroots activists and journalists throughout the North. Created as part of the 1957 Civil Rights Act, the Commission on Civil Rights had a vague mandate to "study and collect information" on "denials of equal protection of the laws" and to "evaluate" federal civil rights policies. No one expected much of the commission. In bureaucratese, to "study" something usually meant to spend a lot of time gathering information that no one would ever read. From its first year, critics regularly lambasted the commission as a do-nothing agency. An independent body, made up of well-meaning liberals with little political clout, it had a miserly budget and no powers other than investigation and education. The commission could not compel witnesses to testify, nor did it have any mechanisms to enforce existing, weak civil rights laws. Even less promising were its fifty state advisory committees, consisting of "citizens of standing"—not necessarily experts—all of them uncompensated for their work, deputized to prepare reports on local conditions.

Given its limitations, the Commission on Civil Rights was surprisingly effective. It held hearings throughout the country, including a series of visits to major northern cities in 1960 and 1961. In the South, white public officials stonewalled the commission, usually refusing to participate in hearings. But in the North, the commission took testimony from long lists of witnesses and attracted large crowds. The commission had a master publicist: the ambitious and charismatic University of Notre Dame president Father Theodore Hesburgh. From his office in South Bend, Indiana, Hesburgh had worked tirelessly to raise Notre Dame's academic reputation by recruiting talented faculty members, raising admissions standards, and publicizing Notre Dame's turnaround (it had long been well known as a second-tier school with first-tier sports teams). Hesburgh was not just a reforming administrator: He believed that academic leaders should engage the problems of society. Hesburgh's intense commitment to racial equality and his media-savvy personality made him the commission's public face and, by the early 1960s, one of the nation's most prominent white advocates of racial equality. In February 1962, he was the subject of a *Time* cover story, but he also gained favorable attention in the black press. Hesburgh used his prominence—and his close ties to the Catholic president—to press the case for civil rights forcefully. "Personally," wrote Hesburgh, alluding to one of the Kennedy administration's pet programs, "I don't care if the United States gets the first man on the moon if, while this is happening on a crash basis, we dawdle along here on our corner of the earth, nursing our prejudices, flouting our magnificent Constitution, ignoring the central moral problem of our times, and appearing hypocrites to all the world."

What Hesburgh and his colleagues found, especially in the North, shocked them. In its first extensive reports—five crisply written volumes, released during Kennedy's first year in office—the commission offered scathing depictions of the persistence of racial segregation in nearly every arena of American life, both north and south. Its findings for northern cities and towns were particularly eye-opening. Hesburgh noted with surprise that "there may be more residential segregation in large Northern cities than in most Southern cities" and put special emphasis on policies targeted toward those who "live in blighted neighborhoods with no hope of the most elemental physical well-being without which human dignity and decent lives become impossible." Providing ammunition for the PCEEO, the commission also documented widespread workplace discrimination, especially in the skilled trades, and found that complaints were particularly numerous in ostensibly liberal California, New York, and Michigan. Its public airing of widespread police harassment of blacks in the North brought a long-simmering issue into the public eye. The commission also denounced separate and unequal education in the North, which it saw as a problem every bit as serious as that in the South. In 1962, in a series of reports, the commission reported "token gains" in school integration in the North. The commission's conclusions were chastening: "Discrimination in one context is apt to be interlinked to discrimination in other contexts." As a result, "no single, limited approach will bring an end to discrimination."

The Kennedy administration continued to hope that its civil rights initiatives—as small-scale as they were—would diffuse black discontent. Like many policies, they had unintended consequences. The shift in administration priorities, however gradual, provided an opening that civil rights leaders exploited. On the national level and at the grassroots, they pushed for more aggressive policies. Attentive to the growing plight of the urban poor and attuned to the growing sense of unrest in northern cities, black leaders began to highlight the intertwined problems of race, unemployment, ghettoization, and inadequate education. More than that, they acted with the hope that they would be heard—if not by the president himself, then at least in the corridors of the West Wing and in various government agencies. Trade unionists who had pushed for full-employment policies since World War II renewed their demand for federal job creation programs, confident that they had a sympathetic ear in the White House. Behind them were activists in the streets, who stepped up protests and marches throughout the early 1960s.

A slew of black leaders, encouraged by the fact that government agencies were headed by a phalanx of liberals, began to push the Kennedy administration for more. To an extent unknown since the Truman years, they received a hearing in the White House, even if the president was prone to symbolic gestures rather than substantive action. Leading the efforts to force racial issues onto the White House agenda was Whitney Young, who established an Urban League lobbying office in Washington. Playing on the league's image as a respectable organization that would not threaten the status quo, Young worked closely with White House aides. In January 1962, Kennedy granted Young an hour-and-fifteen-minute meeting. Young used the occasion to push for a collaborative relationship between the Urban League and the executive branch, an arrangement that Kennedy supported. Urban League staffers began to advise Health, Education, and Welfare, Labor, and Housing and Home Finance administrators. From his prominent position, Young pushed the White House to expand job creation and training programs, increase federal education and welfare spending, and draft civil rights legislation.

Young also had a more ambitious vision. From almost his first day in office, armed with statistics, he began to push for what he called "compensatory" programs, "special inclusion," and "indemnification" for the long oppression of African Americans. These were all controversial ideas that had enjoyed little support outside the black left. The best-known advocate of reparations in the early 1960s was Audley "Queen Mother" Moore, an activist whose career was extraordinarily eclectic. A former Garveyite turned Communist who left the Party in 1950, she was as comfortable with clubwomen as with leftist seafarers. Moore was a lifelong member of the National Council of Negro Women, briefly one of the only women in the National Maritime Union, and a tireless crusader against police brutality and workplace discrimination. On a political odyssey that would eventually lead her to the nationalist Republic of New Africa, Moore founded the Reparations Committee for United States Slaves Descendants, a group that filed incorporation papers in California in 1962. Whitney Young had probably never run into the "tall, regal woman who wore spectacularly colored African robes and was every inch the queen," speaking on the ladder that served as a street corner soapbox at the corner of 125th Street and Seventh Avenue in Harlem. And Moore was decidedly not the Urban League type. In 1963, the centennial of the Emancipation Proclamation, her committee petitioned the Kennedy administration for compensation. "Without Reparations, our people can never be on equal terms with the white sons of our former slavemasters who continue to reap the abundant benefits of the wealth created by our foreparents through their centuries of unrequited labor." Moore's committee couched the demands in universalistic terms—"for the sake of dignity which all men strive"—but also linked their cause to the "unquenchable revolutionary fervor" of liberation movements in Africa.

Young did not share Moore's radical views or pitch his demands using anti-imperialistic rhetoric. His approach was more rigorous and more cautious. He relied on the Urban League's mountain of carefully documented research and his assessment of the weaknesses of the previous twenty years of civil rights activism. In his view, data and history led to one overarching conclusion: Formal political rights and dignity were not enough. Employment counseling and job placement efforts were necessary but insufficient to undo centuries of racial inequality. Finally, in spring 1963—with the swell of grassroots protests serving as a compelling backdrop—Young went public with his demand for a "Marshall Plan for the Negro." Young's argument was pointed: to achieve racial equality would require massive federal expenditures on jobs, training, housing, and quality education for African Americans.

Young continued to defend the league's efforts to place blacks in white-dominated industries, but he addressed his left-leaning critics head-on. "Token integration and pilot placement in business, industry and government are not enough," he admitted. Equality for the Negro required recognition that American economic and political institutions systematically benefited whites and disadvantaged blacks. "For more than 300 years," argued Young, "the white American has received special consideration or 'preferential treatment,' if you will, over the Negro." It was now time to turn the tables. "Indemnification," he told journalists at a press conference in August 1963, "means realistic reparations for past injuries and wrongs." To that end, he argued for what would later be called affirmative action. "Industry must employ Negroes because they are Negroes." To clinch his argument, Young offered an ominous warning. Racial conflict in the South, he contended, was "mild in comparison with that which is on the verge of taking flame in the tinder-box of racial unrest in Northern cities."

Young took heat for his demand for "preferential" treatment—indeed, his own board debated it intensely before endorsing the concept. Critics of the "Marshall Plan" argued that it was "in conflict with the principle of equal treatment for all," even if that was a principle seldom upheld. By an overwhelming majority, whites opposed Young's plan. But Young stuck to his guns and defended "special help" as part of the American political tradition. "We have generously—and with justification—given special consideration in employment, education, and welfare to Hungarian and Cuban refugees fleeting oppression. We have given preferential treatment to the G.I. after World War II—in the form of free education, reduced interest loans for homes and businesses, a ten-point advantage on civil service examinations and other benefits—because he had been out of the mainstream for four or five years. Even now we designate certain geographic areas as depressed and disaster centers, and their people entitled to special help because of joblessness and acts of god. . . . Apart from historical equity, a massive compensatory effort may well be the only means of overcoming the present results of past neglect." Young's shift in emphasis resounded with ordinary blacks. A survey taken in 1963 showed that 64 percent of northern blacks viewed the Urban League positively, about the same as those who had favorable opinions of CORE and King's SCLC.

YOUNG WAS NOT alone in his urgent emphasis on racial equality and his hope that the Kennedy administration could be pressured into addressing the deep-seated problems of racial inequality, unemployment, and poverty. After more than a decade in the political wilderness, the social democratic left—which included A. Philip Randolph, Bayard Rustin, Martin Luther King, Jr., and a slew of local unionists—renewed its push for a full-employment economy and for robust antidiscrimination measures. Randolph still clung to an unfashionable socialism—he refused to endorse Kennedy's bid for the presidency in 1960 and called for "nonviolent assault on reactionary institutions" to accomplish civil rights. But he was enough of a pragmatist to realize that the climate of discontent, both south and north, combined with the new liberal administration, gave him and his allies as much leverage as they had possessed in the mid-1940s, when they had successfully pressured Truman to endorse a far-reaching civil rights agenda.

Behind Randolph was a small cadre of Socialist intellectuals and activists who had not lost sight of the problems of unemployment, poverty, and inequality, even during the chilliest days of the Cold War, when those issues had fallen almost completely off the national political agenda. In small journals such as *Dissent* and *New America*, they reported on problems of technological change, warned of unemployment, and chronicled poverty. The democratic left had more than its fair share of talented writers, but none better than Michael Harrington. From his berth in the cramped quarters of the Catholic Worker house on New York's Lower East Side, where volunteers served the homeless and agitated against capitalism and war, Harrington experienced firsthand the ravages of urban poverty in the early 1950s. As he moved from Catholic to secular radicalism, Harrington did not jettison his concerns with the "least of his brethren." In the mid-1950s, Harrington joined the Manhattan NAACP branch and worked with Bayard Rustin supporting Martin Luther King, Jr., and the southern freedom struggle. In 1960, he joined protests outside the Democratic National Convention, demanding a strong civil rights plank. Like many on the left, Harrington came to see questions of economic and racial justice as fundamentally intertwined. His ideas exploded into the public eye in 1962, with the publication of his unlikely bestseller *The Other America*. In an evocative combination of reportage, social scientific analysis, and exhortation, Harrington focused on the economic restructuring that remade whole sections of postwar America, from the coal hollows of West Virginia to the small farms of the Deep South. Drawing from the latest work of social scientists such as Oscar Lewis, Harrington emphasized the persistence of a "culture of poverty," a sense of hopelessness and despair that plagued those who had been left behind. But for Harrington—unlike others who embraced the culture of poverty argument—nihilism and self-destructive behaviors were the consequence, not the cause, of poverty. Efforts to reform the behavior of the poor—to instill in them a work ethic—were doomed to failure. Harrington argued for policies that addressed the root causes of poverty: joblessness, substandard housing, and poor education.

For Harrington and his comrades, poverty knew no race or color. His book focused extensively on the white, rural poor and raised the plight of Hispanic migrant farmworkers to national attention. But Harrington was clear in emphasizing the distinctive hardships that African Americans faced. Blacks suffered disproportionately from the introduction of automated machinery and the loss of unskilled factory jobs. He also emphasized the high costs to blacks of their confinement to nonunionized, poorly paying, insecure jobs. Harrington's *Other America* found its most prominent audience in President John F. Kennedy's inner circle of advisors. Kennedy himself read a lengthy review of the book published in *The New Yorker*. But Harrington's book, and its positive reception in the highest ranks of Washington, had a galvanic effect on the black democratic left and its white allies.

The Other America gave Randolph and his trade union supporters even more ammunition in their struggle to turn policy makers' attention to the intersection of race, unemployment, and poverty. They pushed for a full-employment economy, building on a campaign that organized labor had waged since the end of World War II. Randolph and Harrington shared a common view that technological change was the key to understanding black unemployment. "The crisis confronting the Negro worker today," wrote Randolph, echoing Harrington, "can be summed up in one word: automation." But Randolph also made a case for the aggressive pursuit of antidiscrimination laws and for "a massive job retraining program . . . on a scale infinitely more ambitious than anything now envisioned." The only solution to African American poverty would be addressing structural unemployment, job training, and workplace discrimination simultaneously. It was a tall order—but in the heady years of the New Frontier, Randolph's ideas had adherents in the White House.

How to balance fair employment and full employment became a matter of intense debate among labor and civil rights activists. Democratic leftists, particularly those who hoped to keep alive interracial solidarity in the working class, worried that Young's call for racial preferences would benefit the black middle class at the expense of the poor. Tom Kahn, a close associate of both Randolph and Harrington and a key advisor in CORE's national office, argued that under a system of racial preferences black and white workers would squabble over a shrinking pie, especially in cities with declining economies. Randolph took the middle ground. "It has become increasingly obvious that the absence of race bias is not to be equated with equal job opportunity . . . non-discrimination and equal opportunity are not the same." If preferential treatment "is interpreted as a program to end poverty and unemployment, [it] is an extremely narrow and hopeless approach indeed." But it had other valid purposes, in Randolph's view. "It can be used as an approach to undo or correct a pattern of discrimination in a particular company or even industry." In building trades, "to require that Negro applicant[s] go to the end of the long waiting list or to be barred by father-son referral systems is to make a mockery of the equal employment opportunity principle."

At the same time that activists put unemployment, racial preferences, and equal opportunity onto their agendas, they began to think about the third string that tied together the Gordian knot of black unemployment and poverty. Not only did black workers face systematic workplace discrimination, not only were they concentrated in declining sectors of the industrial economy, they were also disadvantaged by poor education and training. Since the 1950s, a whole school of labor economists had put an emphasis on "manpower development" and "human capital," arguing that the key to lifting blacks into the economic mainstream was individual skills. In this view, poverty could be remedied only through programs to modify the dysfunctional behavior of poor people. Many manpower theorists emphasized "soft skills," such as personal grooming, dress, and language. Poor people, manpower advocates contended, lacked the work ethic and "future orientation" necessary for them to succeed in the job market. President Kennedy's blue-ribbon Committee on Youth Employment contended that children who grew up in "slum families" in "congested city areas, surrounded by social disorganization, poverty, and despair" and lacking "successful examples among their elders to guide them . . . are not likely to succeed." Other manpower economists advocated the expansion of programs to provide workers with "hard skills" necessary for success in the labor market, including advanced mathematics and literacy.

Of all the civil rights organizations that embraced "manpower" ideas, none was more important than the Urban League, which conducted skills-training programs and workshops on how to succeed in job interviews. But such efforts were no substitute for large-scale job-training programs. On the need for the federal government to make job training a major initiative, the Urban League, black trade unionists, and liberal policy makers found common ground. In 1962, the Kennedy administration launched the first of what would be a series of job training initiatives that culminated in the 1964 War on Poverty. The Manpower Development and Training Act (MDTA) had strong bipartisan support, in large part because it both represented an expansion of government spending on unemployment and was steeped in an "up by the bootstraps" mentality that appealed to probusiness Republicans. Politically unassailable, job-training funding expanded rapidly. Between 1962 and 1968, the MDTA spent $1.5 billion to train nearly one million workers. In 1964 alone, MDTA funds went to agencies that trained 110,000 young people, more than half of them black. The Department of Labor, which had funded apprenticeship programs since the 1930s, also expanded its own job-training programs with further appropriations, although many racially exclusive unions, especially in the building trades, were unwilling to open their programs to blacks. Private foundations—eager to make a dent in "hard-core unemployment"—jumped onto the bandwagon and channeled millions of dollars more into skills-enhancement programs.

Flush with funds—and increasingly uneasy about the inner-city poor and their economic prospects—local civil rights activists took up job training with the zeal of converts. The Urban League expanded its vocational training and launched a job bank program to provide skills and match prospective workers with eager employers. Even those who had been skeptical of the "uplift" rhetoric of the Urban League eagerly started their own job-training programs. In 1963, a coalition of New York trade unionists and civil rights activists, led by A. Philip Randolph and the Workers' Defense League, created skills-training programs to prepare blacks for work in the construction industry and to dissipate "the turmoil and frustration" that had resulted in an "explosive summer." A wide range of civil rights activists from liberal to radical, among them actor Ossie Davis, supported the WDL's job training efforts. In Chicago, the Woodlawn Organization, which combined an emphasis on grassroots organizing with an increasingly militant rhetoric of "self-determination," received several hundred thousand dollars for vocational training. Old-line organizations such as Boys and Girls Clubs and the YMCA established job-training programs, and hundreds of small, locally run organizations such as Milwaukee's Youthpower sprung up nearly overnight to take advantage of federal job-training dollars. The MDTA trained workers for a wide range of jobs, from the menial (typist and short-order cook) to the skilled (nurse and electrician) and for jobs in expanding fields such as retail sales and hospital record keeping.

Proponents of job training argued that the programs had low dropout rates and high placement rates; their critics charged that many of the resulting jobs were poorly paid and that there was little evidence of long-term benefits to the "hard-core" jobless. Given the heterogeneity of job-training programs, both claims were true. But whatever the deficiencies of these efforts, federal funds—in combination with foundation support and corporate grants—bankrolled the dramatic expansion of social services and community nonprofits throughout the North. One of the largest sectors of job growth for blacks in the 1960s was in social services—a reminder that job-training programs were, for at least some workers, job creation programs, too.

The most zealous proponent of job training as the solution to black unrest was Philadelphia's Reverend Leon H. Sullivan. Just at the moment when his "selective patronage" campaigns took fire nationwide, Sullivan shifted gears, eschewing protest for vocational training. In his youth ministry, Sullivan saw the difficulties that young blacks faced on the job market, largely because of their lack of skills. He was familiar with the Urban League's vocational services approach, and as a student of social psychology he had certainly encountered the work of manpower theorists. Even at the height of his militancy, Sullivan clung to the uplift ideology that had long motivated middle-class black activists. Sullivan fused together these impulses in a new, ambitious project. In late 1963, he launched the Opportunities Industrialization Centers (OIC) to train black youth for skilled and high-tech jobs. OIC attracted national attention almost from the outset and quickly garnered funding from the Ford Foundation. *The Pittsburgh Courier* hailed the project as "radical." *Ebony*—a voice of racial uplift attuned to its middle-class readership—celebrated Sullivan as a hero. And the mainstream white press ran glowing reports about Sullivan's new project. Sullivan's turn from militant protest to job training and black entrepreneurship aroused a lot of suspicion on the part of black activists to his left, who argued that OIC was a revival of Booker T. Washington's strategies of self-help. Even the Reverend Martin Luther King, Jr., who maintained superficially cordial relations with Sullivan, privately worried that "Sullivan has just almost turned into a conservative." But Sullivan also attracted favorable attention from federal antipoverty officials, in large part because his militant history gave him legitimacy among urban black activists and his call for public-private job creation programs dovetailed so well with the liberal manpower agenda.

. . .

WHILE THE KENNEDY administration was experimenting with social policy, civil rights remained a low priority in the White House. But events in the South—and increasingly in the North—forced questions of race and inequality onto the national agenda in ways that the president could not ignore. The Kennedy administration had dodged the question of civil rights in large part because of its fear of alienating the Democratic Party's still potent southern wing. Anticipating the 1964 campaign, Kennedy and his advisors were mortally afraid that any substantial civil rights efforts would lose southern votes. But from 1960 to 1963, activists in the South stepped up their protests in ways that the president could not ignore. Nineteen sixty witnessed a remarkable wave of sit-ins, as high school and college students in Greensboro, North Carolina; Nashville, Tennessee; and Atlanta, Georgia, refused to budge from their seats at lunch counters in their demand for equal service. In 1961, CORE sponsored a series of Freedom Rides to desegregate interstate bus transportation in the South. Some of the older protestors—the seasoned veterans of the movement such as CORE's James Peck and James Farmer—had come out of the northern movement to open up public accommodations. High school and college students, with the aid of Ella Baker, then working for King and SCLC, formed the Student Nonviolent Coordinating Committee and began efforts to organize black voters in the rural Black Belt. In 1962 and 1963, Martin Luther King, Jr., led a series of marches, culminating in the brutal repression of the protests by Birmingham, Alabama, police in April 1963. Increasingly, the Kennedy administration worried—justifiably—that the protests were fueling Soviet propaganda and undermining the nation's carefully crafted Cold War image.

If the White House was drawn reluctantly into the southern battleground for racial equality, until the spring of 1963 the Kennedy administration paid little heed to northern protestors. But the northern movements for racial equality were galvanized by the southern freedom struggles—and encouraged by the sense that change was possible in the new Kennedy administration. In northern and western cities, CORE, which had done more than any organization to introduce Gandhian nonviolence to the freedom struggle, had shrunk to only a handful of active chapters by the mid-1950s. In most northern cities, it was nearly invisible. Many lapsed CORE activists who had started with the organization during its World War II heyday had moved on, joining other civil rights, labor, and religious groups. The South, particularly after the Montgomery bus boycott, lured activists who sought a place where Gandhian tactics could have real impact. Some of the most charismatic CORE members, among them James Farmer and Bayard Rustin, headed southward, joining with Reverend King and providing vital behind-the-scenes assistance to SCLC. But in most northern cities, by the end of the 1950s, CORE was a distant memory, recalled by only a handful of stalwarts. Nationwide, it had no more than four hundred members.

In 1960, CORE suddenly awoke. Nothing was more important in the revitalization of CORE chapters than the lunch counter sit-ins in the South. The sit-ins, reported Lerone Bennett, Jr., in *Ebony*, "released waves of dammed-up energy that flowed to every section of the country." CORE benefited from a sudden rise in interest in civil rights, particularly among students who "trooped from cloistered campuses and set up picket lines" to show their solidarity with the southern freedom struggle. "If southern Negro students can brave death to fight for democracy," advocated a protestor on a bitterly cold day in front of a Woolworth's in Harlem, "we can brave the cold to show them that we are on their side." "With the success of the sit-ins," recalled a longtime CORE activist, "there was an unreal conviction that National CORE was a big deal—we weren't as big as we seemed in the press. But people read the newspapers and believed we were really big and powerful." Membership in CORE chapters skyrocketed more than tenfold, and millions of dollars in donations resuscitated the organization. CORE chapters found themselves once again at the cutting edge of northern protests—bringing the strategy of "direct action" back to where they had pioneered it two decades earlier.

Inspired by the southern sit-ins, northern activists planned sympathy protests and launched regional boycotts of the chain stores that had refused service to blacks at southern lunch counters. Typical of this trajectory were the Ann Arbor and Detroit chapters of CORE. A spirited group of high school and college students, they led a nearly yearlong series of pickets at the suburban Detroit headquarters of dime store giant S. S. Kresge. When CORE launched its southern Freedom Rides to desegregate interstate transportation, Detroit CORE sponsored a "Freedom Sing" with the Reverend Albert Cleage, soon to be famous for his black nationalism, as the featured speaker. But solidarity with the southern movement was not enough for youthful CORE protestors, who wanted to turn to "more pressing issues" that "demand immediate attention." Staging what they called their own "Freedom Ride," a group of black and white CORE activists descended on suburban Dearborn and "tested for racial discrimination" in twenty-one restaurants and two bowling alleys. Later that summer, CORE "Freedom Swimmers" challenged segregation at a suburban Detroit pool.

There was nothing new about CORE's strategies. But in the 1960s, activists had one tool not available to their counterparts in the 1940s: an attentive mass media, which increasingly portrayed sit-ins and demonstrations, north and south, as part of a black revolution. News reports had an electric effect on the movement. What was most exciting—but ultimately problematic for CORE—was that its membership became more heterogeneous. Direct action protests brought many first-time activists, especially young blacks, into what had been for most of its history a majority-white organization. The infusion of young protestors gave CORE an increasingly militant edge. In Brooklyn, for example, the CORE chapter began cautiously, supporting pickets at Woolworth's in solidarity with southern protestors. But like their Detroit and Ann Arbor counterparts, Brooklyn CORE did not stop there. Over the next few years, it led militant, not always nonviolent, demonstrations at stores, schools, corporate headquarters, and construction sites, and in one dramatic protest dumped tons of trash at New York's City Hall.

The inspiration of the southern freedom struggle and the sense of a new liberalism in the White House also breathed new life into the open-housing movement. The National Committee Against Discrimination in Housing, the lobbying group founded in 1950 by Charles Abrams, moved from obscurity to national prominence during the Kennedy administration. During the 1960 election, NCDH had persuaded the platform committees of both parties to insert language calling for an end to discrimination in federally subsidized housing projects. On the campaign trail, when pressed by open housing activists about persistent segregation, Kennedy had promised to "eliminate segregation with the stroke of a pen." After the election, facing the monolithic power of southern Democrats, Kennedy prevaricated. NCDH refused to let the issue go. Its lobbyists, who had extensive connections in the federal housing bureaucracy, pushed for a nondiscrimination order. In a letter-writing campaign, open housers flooded the White House with pens. Joining with NCDH were editorialists at a number of liberal newspapers, including *The New York Times*, *The Denver Post*, and *The Milwaukee Journal*. The *Amsterdam News* reminded the president that "Negroes listened to and believed in Mr. Kennedy's pledges and promises and sent him to the White House. And we think he owes it to them to keep his word." Empowered by Kennedy's delay, anti-open-housing groups began to counterlobby. The National Association of Home Builders argued that any open housing executive order would slow housing starts and have a negative economic impact. Joining the efforts were the Realtors, who forcefully argued that any prohibition on housing discrimination would violate the constitutional right of freedom of association.

Finally, in November 1962, just after the midterm elections were safely behind him, Kennedy signed an executive order prohibiting discrimination in federally subsidized housing developments. He sent NCDH a pen that he used to sign the order. But Kennedy's executive order met with skepticism from open housers. Critics accused the president of signing a symbolic order; they noted that it applied only to newly constructed housing, and they lamented the lack of enforcement mechanisms. By the spring of 1963, NCDH complained of "glacial movement" on the open housing front; by the summer of 1963, it called for a "broader 'stroke of the pen.'" NCDH's head, Frances Levenson, argued that "limited measures will simply not do the job." Nothing in the order prevented housing developers from steering potential black homebuyers away even while professing their commitment to equal opportunity in housing. NCDH had pushed for a broad regulation that would affect the entire private real estate sector, but because Kennedy's order was not retroactive, it affected only a tiny fragment of the nation's housing market. Open housers argued that the executive order would never solve the problem. Even members of the President's Committee for Equal Opportunity in Housing, created to monitor compliance with the executive order, called Kennedy's open housing policy "ineffective and inadequate."

Open-occupancy pledge drives spread throughout the 1960s. Over five hundred open housing groups existed nationwide by 1965, but seasoned civil rights activists worried that their voluntary housing integration efforts would never be sufficient. Efforts to change the hearts and minds of whites had yielded little by way of real change, argued black economist Robert S. Browne. "Futile would be the traditional discussion groups addressed by a prominent Negro doctor who would emit platitudes to a gathering of supposedly liberal old ladies who would nod in vigorous agreement at everything he said and just as promptly forget it all." In 1963, Herman H. Long, a black United Church of Christ minister and a longtime open houser, came to a conclusion that many religious integrationists found unsettling. "Voluntarism," he argued, "is not enough." The movement of a token black family or two into a suburb or congregation would assuage the consciences of some guilty whites but would not solve the problem of racial inequality in housing.

Long was in the vanguard of the open housing movement—those who called for coercive action to force open the doors of segregation. Even groups that had long favored quiet persuasion began to adopt confrontational tactics, including civil disobedience. "Words and declarations are no longer useful in this struggle unless accompanied by sacrifice and commitment," stated the National Council of Churches in a summer 1963 statement. In "places of particular crisis," it was time for "immediate action," including "demonstrations and direct action." Northern civil rights groups, particularly CORE chapters, took up the call. New Haven and Chicago CORE led sit-ins demanding housing integration; Brooklyn CORE staged "sleep-ins" at rental agencies that had notoriously discriminated against blacks. In San Francisco, the NAACP picketed a housing developer that turned away attorney Willie Brown and his family; and in suburban Monterey Park, California, CORE sat in for thirty-five days at a housing development that excluded blacks. On Long Island, white activists challenged the long-segregated Levittown by renting homes to blacks. And in Evanston, Illinois, not too far from Deerfield, CORE activists were arrested after they illegally occupied the office of a real estate broker who had vocally opposed "forced housing."

The largest-scale CORE efforts began in Philadelphia. There CORE initiated "Operation Windowshop," sending small groups of black homebuyers to view model homes in new suburban developments. Publicized in CORE's bimonthly magazine, Operation Windowshop was duplicated throughout the North. Detroit CORE members shopped for houses in some of the city's most exclusive suburbs. Los Angeles activists descended on white-run real estate offices. In Cleveland, a busload of black CORE members headed to the sales office in a new suburban development, accompanied by camera crews and reporters. The sight of two dozen black homebuyers confronting a "shook-up" white Realtor made for dramatic press.

ACTIVISTS HAD PUT open housing on the table and had forced concessions from the Kennedy administration, however symbolic. They had taken the Kennedy administration's executive order on affirmative action and run with it. And they had used the administration's emphasis on job training and job creation to launch grassroots antipoverty efforts. Kennedy's cautious innovation had created a feedback loop effect, empowering civil rights activists, who, frustrated at the gradual pace of change but emboldened by their victories, put more pressure on the White House. The White House responded with a little more. But by early 1963, Kennedy's efforts to deal with the combined problems of poverty, racial inequality, and urban problems had barely begun. And, to an extent that he and his advisors could not have anticipated, those efforts proved to be too little, too late for a growing number of blacks, especially in the North. The course of public policy, and of civil rights activism, would be altered fundamentally in 1963, in a year that witnessed an unprecedented outburst of protests nationwide, a new current of black militancy at the grass roots, and furious policy innovation as political leaders scrambled to respond to a situation that was rapidly spinning out of their control. It was the year of the "Negro Revolt," a year when the pressures of reform unleashed revolutionary expectations. Nothing would be the same afterward.

CHAPTER 9

"FIRES OF FRUSTRATION AND DISCORD"

JANUARY 1, 1963, MARKED THE CENTENNIAL OF THE EMANCIPATION PROCLA-mation. Ringing in the New Year from Lithuania to Kamchatka was the baritone voice of NAACP head Roy Wilkins, addressing listeners of Radio Liberty, an American-government-sponsored station heard around the clock in Russian and sixteen other languages spoken in the Soviet Union. Wilkins's speech was a rejoinder to "Soviet propaganda" that depicted the "U.S. Negro citizen as a terrified, helpless being, driven without recourse and respite through a morass of discriminatory laws and organized perse-cution." Negroes, Wilkins sunnily reported, had higher incomes than the British, French, or West Germans and "have amassed billions of dollars of property, contributed measurably to the economic growth of the country, and to its cultural enrichment." Wilkins and black conservative columnist George Schuyler—who seldom agreed on anything—concurred on this point. "One of the greatest positive revolutions in world history," wrote Schuyler in his own reflections on one hundred years of freedom, "has been the social, cultural, and economic progress of the American Ne-groes, in just one short century." Unlike Wilkins, who told the Soviets that the NAACP would "vigorously" challenge the "vestiges" of racial discrim-ination in American life, Schuyler drew a different lesson from his ac-count of racial progress. "Sometimes we are a little impatient," he chided, "demanding immediate solutions of problems which are not expected to be solved elsewhere in the world in centuries. But we should on such oc-casions think back soberly on what we were a century ago, and what we are today, and that further progress will be made in growing cooperation with other races and groups that make up America."

Not everyone shared the optimism of Wilkins and Schuyler. Beneath the celebratory atmosphere at the New Year was a deepening sense of impatience—one that Schuyler himself had recognized even as he dismissed it. Reflecting on the Emancipation Proclamation for *Liberator* magazine—an upstart periodical that had become the leading voice of black radicalism by 1963—novelist James Baldwin offered a pessimistic assessment. "Let us, for once, leave in the filing cabinet all those pathetic statistics proving Negro gains and changes," he wrote. "We talk endlessly about progress and chatter about the future because we are afraid to pay the price of change in the present." Baldwin captured the growing sense of impatience and a tone of frustration that was especially audible at the grass roots. So did Lincoln Lynch, who headed Long Island's CORE chapter. At an early January commemoration of the Emancipation Proclamation, Lynch departed from the usual script of dull after-dinner speeches and instead offered an unsparing call for a "revolt" in the suburban North. "I urge that this first day of the 101st year should see, beginning now, a massive and sustained assault on the bastions of segregation and debasement of Negroes and Puerto Ricans." At the end of the centennial year, he hoped that "we can all look back with pride that here in this little corner of America the bonfire of human dignity will be burning bright." Lynch's fellow speakers seconded his call for militant activism. Louis E. Lomax, a black journalist and author of the 1962 landmark study *Negro Revolt*, denounced northern white hypocrisy. "The white liberal tone of the North, although they do not recognize it, is in keeping with the white tone of the South—gradualism." Gladys Harrington, another CORE activist, concurred. "The Negro is like a man being strangled. We say stop the choking now, at once. You can't afford to be gradual about stopping a strangulation."

Just a few months after the centennial celebrations, the optimism of Roy Wilkins would seem hopelessly anachronistic. George Schuyler's rosy portrait of black progress and his counsel of patience would seem utterly unrealistic. Baldwin's gloomy prognostication better captured the simmering anger throughout the black North. Over the centennial year, the militancy of Lincoln Lynch, Gladys Harrington, and Louis Lomax would move to the mainstream of the northern freedom struggle. In fact, by the end of the year, even their brand of protest would come under sustained challenge by a newly empowered black left, which demanded more immediate, revolutionary change.

The shift in mood—and what *The Chicago Defender* called the "frightening suddenness" of it—caught most observers by surprise, even sea-soned activists. Herbert Hill, the NAACP labor secretary and a veteran of more than fifteen years of organizing, had a hard time explaining the sense of tension that pervaded the North in 1963. In June, Hill told an interviewer that he was "rethinking through all his theories about the civil rights movement—old theories don't hold." The freedom struggle seemed to be "taking [a] revolutionary turn." Testifying before the New York State legislature in June 1963, Louis Lomax and longtime political activist Reverend Gardner Taylor warned of impending riots in Harlem. "The mood of the Negro, particularly in New York City, is very, very bit-ter," argued Lomax. "He is losing faith. The Negro on the streets of Harlem is tired of platitudes from white liberals." Norman Hill (no rela-tion to Herbert), one of the most prominent black activists in CORE, agreed that there was a "good chance that the movement will become more violent." The struggle for racial equality, he contended, "is in a po-sition of conflict and disequilibrium in part caused by the dispossessed el-ement. This group wants to move, regardless of what Kennedy or their own leaders say." In Chicago, Edwin Berry, head of the city's Urban League, warned of the "impatience and uneasiness" in black neighbor-hoods, an "evil brew" that "could easily lead to violence." But where Berry saw danger, other observers saw opportunity. "From Tuscaloosa to Cambridge, from Oxford to Philadelphia, from Danville to Los Angeles, ours is a nation in which revolution has been forged," editorialized *The Afro-American* in June. "We do not shrink from the use of the term 'rev-olution,' for how else can the social upheaval that has shaken our nation be honestly described?"

By summer, moderate voices quavered with concern. At its annual convention in July, the NAACP warned that a "permanently unemployed mass of Negroes" could soon rebel and endanger "the American social order." By August, the mainstream media—black and white—noted the changing mood in the North. "In this one hundredth year of *de jure* free-dom," *Ebony* editorialized, "today's Negro is not too impressed with how far he has come from bondage." In place of a "ghetto mentality" was a new attitude of defiance and racial unity. "Suddenly it seems that the Negro is mad at everybody," reported *The New York Times*, with more than a little incredulity and a great deal of concern. In September, NBC ran a three-hour documentary (unprecedented at the time) on the

"American Revolution of '63," which included lengthy segments filmed in Harlem and Chicago, reminding viewers that the black freedom struggle was national in scope.

Northern black activists in the centennial year encouraged a growing strain of black discontent, one that had been visible to well-informed observers well before 1963 but took unprecedented public form that year. What activists and pundits alike began calling the "Negro Revolt of 1963" would have seismic effects on national politics. Northern activists banded together in protests prompted by the atrocities in the Deep South, where white supremacist resistance to civil rights was reaching its zenith. But they also turned their attention to their own region and took up perennial grievances, most notably workplace discrimination, educational inequality, and police brutality. Over the course of the year, their protests grew increasingly impatient—in rhetoric and in strategy. A revivified black left—driven underground by McCarthyism but never wholly silenced—emerged as an increasingly influential political force. Black radicals had never disappeared from the urban scene in the postwar years. Small cells of black Marxists continued to teach, publish insurgent pamphlets, and organize among blue-collar workers. Amid the Negro Revolt, their audience expanded dramatically. More than that, a new generation of insurgents looked for inspiration among black groups that had struggled in the postwar years. Nationalist bookstores, black separatist religious sects (such as the Nation of Islam and the Moorish Science Temple), and remnant Garveyites seemed relevant again.

At northern protests throughout 1963, advocates of nonviolence and integration marched side by side with proponents of black nationalism, self-defense, and revolution. At the time—and since—many observers drew a sharp distinction between integration and separation, between nonviolence and self-defense. But for a growing number of northern activists, the two impulses were never so sharply distinct. They existed in creative tension as two prongs of a strategy for black freedom, as a growing number of activists worked for equality but adopted increasingly militant strategies and rhetoric. The leading established civil rights organizations, especially the NAACP and CORE, went through wrenching internal debates about their politics, strategies, and goals. By the end of the year, groups such as the Nation of Islam, the Revolutionary Action Movement, and the Freedom Now Party—all with deep roots in northern urban centers—emerged as increasingly prominent voices of black protest. Policy makers in the Capitol and in northern city halls searched desperately for ways to stifle black discontent. Lincoln Lynch's much-hoped-for "bonfire" had become a wildfire of rage.

THE NEGRO REVOLT, like most rebellions, was a fusion of hope, frustration, and solidarity. Rebellion depends on frustration at the status quo but a belief in the possibility of change. Above all, it requires the summoning of collective energies and resources and the development of shared consciousness and identity. In northern cities in the early 1960s, all these ingredients were present, but to different degrees. Frustration was abundant. The fruits of twenty years of activism made change seem possible—though northern blacks had a wide range of opinions on what type of transformations they wanted to see. The Kennedy administration's policy innovations, however incomplete, inspired activists to push harder for more sweeping programs to eradicate racial inequality. And the concentration of blacks in northern cities and towns—and their isolation—fostered a sense of common identity. Over the course of the 1960s, these ingredients would continue to combine, but frustration remained the predominant ingredient, the sense of hope waxed and waned, and the very conditions that fostered a sense of common identity also powerfully militated against it.

The first three months of 1963 were relatively quiet in the North. Early spring brought the first serious rumblings of discontent. Although northern grievances ran deep, the first stirrings of mass protest were provoked by events hundreds of miles to the south. Televised images of Birmingham police officers attacking nonviolent demonstrators—many of them children—with police dogs and fire hoses functioned as a metaphorical outside agitator in northern black communities, outraging ordinary blacks and whites, stirring pastors to rework their sermons, inflaming editorialists, and mobilizing activists. Civil rights groups throughout the North staged rallies to express solidarity with the Birmingham protestors and their outrage at the police violence. Thousands took to the streets. In late April, CORE and NAACP chapters in major cities throughout the North once again established picket lines outside chain stores—among them Woolworth's and Kress—to support the efforts of King and the

SCLC to open Birmingham's lunch counters to blacks. And northern activists held mass meetings to raise bail money and other funds for the Birmingham protestors. In May and early June, emissaries from the southern movement addressed churchgoers and demonstrators in places as diverse as Chicago, Harlem, and Atlantic City. They portrayed Birmingham as a triumph of nonviolence against naked brutality and urged northern crowds to push for the passage of federal civil rights legislation.

But many northerners took home altogether different lessons, seeing Birmingham as evidence of the failure of nonviolence. Birmingham commissioner Bull Connor's atrocities demanded self-defense, not passive resistance. In many cities, Birmingham solidarity rallies became shows of black defiance. Northern protests usually did not follow the script that the media had made familiar in its coverage of southern protests. The southern freedom struggle, circa 1963, took the form of a televised morality play, pitting suffering, nonviolent protestors against raging white counter-protestors, whether they were Connor and his police dogs, vicious white mobs, or snarling politicians such as Alabama's George Wallace or Mississippi's Ross Barnett. Northern protestors in 1963, however, increasingly broke that mold. They targeted institutions like construction sites and schools—places that embodied white power and exacerbated racial inequality but where whites seldom displayed their power nakedly. With a few exceptions, northern activists that year met few angry whites. Northern politics was full of petty racists, but only a few reacted publicly with the venom of Wallace or Barnett. Unlike their southern counterparts, most white politicians in northern cities vacillated in the face of protest. Only the police played their predictable roles—arresting demonstrators, wielding billy clubs, and sneering at protestors.

At a May rally in Harlem to support "the valiant fighters in Birmingham," a cadre of protestors started loudly chanting, "We want Malcolm X," by then famous for his rhetoric blasting Martin Luther King, Jr., and John F. Kennedy. When a moderate black minister rose to the podium and told the two-thousand-strong crowd that "I did not come here to inflame you," an angry voice shouted out, "We want to be inflamed!" Others joined in, shouting their approval. Increasingly, pro-Birmingham protestors in the North urged self-defense, self-determination, and militancy. In Chicago on May 13, nearly three thousand black teenagers pelted the police with bricks and bottles to express their outrage at police brutality in Birmingham and in their own city. A week later, a group of blacks beat Chicago mayor Richard J. Daley's nephew, shouting "This is for Birmingham!" as they pummeled him. "Reality for the slum kid," wrote one Detroit activist, "has always been in the street. Why not let him use the streets to help make a new reality for himself like the kids in Birmingham did?" Not only did northern protestors change tactics, they also shifted targets. Solidarity with Birmingham was not enough. By late spring and early summer, northern black activists—organized and unorganized—turned their attention away from the atrocities of the South to battles on their home front, particularly workplace discrimination and educational inequality. They also highlighted issues that had long been the source of simmering grievances, particularly urban renewal, police brutality, and welfare.

Just as King and his allies were opening their nonviolent siege of Birmingham, an extraordinary wave of protests shook Philadelphia—protests that drew energy from the outrages of Bull Connor but took a direction that would reshape the northern freedom struggle. Philadelphia's branches of CORE and the NAACP launched a campaign demanding the inclusion of black workers in city-sponsored construction projects. Beginning in early April, protestors blocked the street in front of Mayor James Tate's modest North Philadelphia row house and staged regular protests at City Hall, at the Liberty Bell, and at building sites. In May, an NAACP-sponsored march in solidarity with Birmingham became a forum for challenging the city's segregated municipal construction projects. Demonstrators held an overnight sit-in at the mayor's office, shut down construction on the city's Municipal Services Building, battled with police and white unionists at the site of a partially built school in a black neighborhood north of downtown, and unleashed an intense debate on racial politics, discrimination, and employment.

The most visible leader of the Philadelphia protests was attorney Cecil B. Moore. A criminal defense lawyer with a special passion for representing victims of police brutality, Moore had long set his sights on Philadelphia's hidebound NAACP chapter. In January 1963, running as an insurgent candidate for the branch presidency, he was victorious. A rebel against his bourgeois roots, Moore chafed at well-to-do black folks, "the 20 percent or so who don't want to be Negroes." As North Philadelphia grew rougher and poorer, Moore stayed in his aging row house at Seventeenth and Jefferson. He was committed to living and working with those he affectionately called his "barbecue, porkchops, collard green eating people." Moore rebuked his old-guard critics: "I run a grass-roots group, not a cocktail-party, tea-sipping, fashion-show attending group of exhibitionists." Moore's streetwise demeanor brought him considerable support in poor and working-class neighborhoods. One fervent Moore supporter from North Philadelphia frankly acknowledged that the NAACP president was "an arrogant foul mouth radical" but praised him for his interest in the "rank and file Negro," an approach "much needed . . . among a restless people."

Moore's outspokenness won the support of blacks whose grievances had remained unaddressed after World War II and who were alienated from the cautious racial liberalism of the 1950s and the frustrated promises of the early 1960s. "His method," argued one prominent minister, was "to get in touch with the people who are not being reached too effectively by the moral, religious leadership." Moore brought NAACP recruiting to where it had never been before: Under his leadership, the NAACP solicited members in over four hundred bars and taprooms in black Philadelphia. Like other insurgents in the NAACP, he attempted to turn his branch into a militant protest organization. Within months at the helm, Moore spearheaded a campaign of direct action and civil disobedience. And in the process, he attracted a growing number of followers who jettisoned the NAACP's emphasis on integration and moderation.

Part of Moore's appeal was his brashness. At his inauguration, he came out fighting against the status quo. "We are serving notice that no longer will the plantation system of white men appointing our leaders exist in Philadelphia," he raged. "We expect to be consulted on all community issues which affect our people." He would be satisfied with nothing short of black "self determination." Some moderate civil rights leaders worried that under Moore, the "NAACP will move out of the camp of the integrationists, where it was a leader, to some unknown hitching post in militancy." Their fears were well founded. Moore eschewed the politics of respectability: He used profanity at public events, made deliberately provocative antiwhite comments, and denounced black integrationists as "Uncle Toms" and "Judases" who operated from a "lofty perch midway between the integration they long for and the segregation from which they have profited."

The Philadelphia protests were more improvisational, cacophonous, and menacing than most southern ones. Throughout the two-month siege, local protestors experimented with different strategies. Members of the NAACP and CORE deployed the tactics of nonviolent direct action. NAACP members, flaunting their respectability, showed up at protests in their Sunday best, even as their leader Moore denounced white construction workers and black and white liberals alike as racists. But they were joined by other, less patient activists: workers who showed up in their oil-stained overalls, teenage gang members, and black militants, each less polite than the other. In mid-May, after demonstrations forced the temporary shutdown of a city-funded construction site near City Hall, protestors surrounded the partially built Strawberry Mansion High School and formed a blockade at the delivery gate. Arrested at a North Philadelphia school site for scuffling with police and white trade unionists were two members of the fledgling Revolutionary Action Movement, a small black insurgent group that viewed Philadelphia (and other northern industrial cities) as key battlegrounds for black self-determination. In a theatrical inversion of the infamous televised images of police brutality in Birmingham, a group of youthful protestors signaled that they would not be intimidated by the police. They showed up at the protests with their own "fierce-looking mastiffs." Marching on the North Philadelphia construction site, demonstrators rhythmically chanted a militaristic version of the old southern freedom anthem: "WE . . . SHALL . . . OVER . . . COME," while beating rolled-up newspapers against the palms of their hands. The military cadence was a marked contrast to the choral version made famous in southern demonstrations. With some hyperbole, *The Pittsburgh Courier* reported: "Significant is the fact that the Martin Luther King philosophy of non-violence was totally discarded."

The Philadelphia protests had an impact well beyond the City of Brotherly Love. Kennedy administration officials, still struggling with the fallout from Birmingham, grew increasingly fretful as northern cities such as Philadelphia grew restless. In a May 20 meeting in the Oval Office caught on the White House recording system, Attorney General Robert F. Kennedy recounted a conversation with Chicago-based activist and comedian Dick Gregory, whom he asked to explain the shifting mood in the urban North. "They're all getting tough," reported Bobby. "Negroes?" asked President Kennedy. "They're awful tough to deal with now," his brother replied. "He says you can't have a moderate Negro anymore." A week later, concerned about the "radical and forceful" protests that shattered the ostensible racial peace of the urban North, the attorney general held a private meeting with a group of influential northern blacks in his New York City apartment. Participants tried to explain to Kennedy that the "festering hostility in New York, Chicago, and Los Angeles—as well as Birmingham—is rooted not in segregation of public accommodations or even in segregation by neighborhoods, but in resentment at being so long and so hopelessly at the bottom." The meeting did not go as Kennedy had planned. "Communication broke down," and the meeting spun out of control. "If *you* are so proud of your record, Mr. Attorney General," Lena Horne lashed out, "you go up to Harlem into those churches and barber shops and pool halls, and *you* tell the people. We ain't going to do it because *we* don't want to get shot." The room was tense as others offered equally harsh opinions. "Suddenly I looked at the Attorney General," recounted psychologist Kenneth Clark, "and understood that he did not understand us and for just a minute I felt for him. We were, after all, saying something quite un-American. We were talking against tinkering. We were saying that even the most effective political manipulation is basically unacceptable to most Negroes."

The causes of the Negro Revolt befuddled the White House, but its consequences were obvious and alarming. Worried that the "successes of Birmingham, Philadelphia, and elsewhere" would fuel an incipient black uprising, Kennedy administration officials moved decisively. On June 4, just as the first wave of Philadelphia construction site protests was subsiding, Kennedy announced his opposition to discrimination on federally funded construction projects, singling out "economic distress and unrest." Unnamed administration sources suggested that the president's statement was "partly in response to violence in Philadelphia." On June 11, the president addressed the nation on the "fires of frustration and discord that are burning in every city, North and South, where legal remedies are not at hand. Redress is sought in the streets, in demonstrations, parades and protests which create tensions and threaten violence and threaten lives." Although the president's address was, in part, a response to the battle to integrate the University of Alabama, what was most noteworthy about the speech was the president's emphasis on the nonsectional nature of the civil rights problem and issues such as black unemployment. It was, the president stated, "a time of domestic crisis." Speaking to his hope that social problems could be solved without protest, he made the point baldly: "It is better to settle these matters in the courts than on the streets."

Scrambling to put out the fires of frustration, the president also dispatched Secretary of Labor Willard Wirtz to conduct a hasty investigation of workplace discrimination in twenty cities—several of which Wirtz identified as "danger spots," most of them outside the South. Other Kennedy advisors prepared troubling reports on growing black discontent in northern cities. G. Mennen Williams, former Michigan governor, warned that "large segments of the Negro population are losing confidence in interracial approaches to the problems of gaining full civil rights. The dialogue between Negro leaders and white liberals clearly runs a danger of being broken." The White House stepped up its efforts to contain the growing unrest. In mid-June, Kennedy met with union leaders to discuss workplace discrimination and dispatched cabinet officials to several cities to meet with black leaders to examine ways to create "greater employment opportunities for Negroes." On June 22, the president issued Executive Order 11114, prohibiting discrimination against minorities on government-contracted construction projects, an extension of his 1961 "affirmative action" program. Two days later, Kennedy publicly announced plans to draft a civil rights bill. The combination of mounting southern protest and northern rebellion—and most of all, the unflattering news coverage of both—gave the Kennedy administration impetus to move quickly.

While the administration was preparing civil rights legislation, it collaborated with Time-Life Broadcast, Inc., to prepare a series of public service advertisements for radio and television. With the support of Lee White, the president's special assistant on civil rights, and White House advisor Pierre Salinger, who pitched the plan to the president for his approval, Time-Life prepared more than a dozen "Civil Rights Spots," featuring politicians such as Hubert Humphrey, celebrities such as Lena Horne and Jackie Robinson, and Catholic, Jewish, and Protestant leaders. Five ads featuring the president himself were targeted to the North as much as the South. Each contained excerpts from his June 11 address. Urging whites to accept their "responsibility" for civil rights, Kennedy spoke more indirectly to blacks. In an acknowledgment of the growing unrest, in the one advertisement that seemed to be targeted especially to blacks, he argued that "we have a right to expect that the Negro community will be responsible, will uphold the law."

But northern blacks would not be assuaged by a few advertisements. As the White House attempted to put a lid on construction site protests, other demonstrations were breaking out by the day. Between May 19 and July 1, demonstrations erupted in 153 cities, most along the eastern seaboard. Northern protestors—more and more of them angrily defiant—targeted unequal education. In Englewood, New Jersey, a two-year battle to desegregate public schools took an unexpected turn in the spring of 1963. Black parents had demanded that the school district open majority-white schools to the black children stuck in the city's run-down Lincoln and Liberty elementary schools, both nearly all black. Initially they framed their arguments for integration in the terms of racial liberalism, but over time they grew embittered and impatient. In April and May, twenty elementary school children in Englewood committed civil disobedience and sat in at the majority-white Cleveland School. Their parents and dozens of classmates picketed in support of the sit-ins. School district officials, hoping to avoid a reprise of Birmingham, let the children alone while fining their parents for encouraging truancy in a vain attempt to stem the protest. As the school board procrastinated, boycotting parents began to jettison their integrationist rhetoric, even as they continued to demand integrated schools. The school boycott committee invited Malcolm X to their community (he eventually declined) and "whooped" when Adam Clayton Powell, Jr., told them that because of black protests, "the white man is afraid."

In school districts large and small, protestors took to the streets, impatient with the polite strategies of petitioning school boards and participating in hearings. In Boston, demonstrators picketed a June school board hearing, while eight thousand students boycotted classes and attended classes in temporary "Freedom Schools," where they took courses in civil rights law and black history. Empowered by the protests, Boston's education activists began coordinating a "Stay Out for Freedom" boycott of high schools in the fall, which involved tens of thousands of students and their parents. In Twin Oaks, Pennsylvania, a small town near the Delaware border, picketers targeted the all-black Thaddeus Stevens School with signs like "Jim Crow Must Go" and "We've Stopped Talking and Started Walking." In St. Louis, a group of protestors blockaded buses and marched on the school board. "The point of the demonstration," argued one protestor, "is that we want action now and not talks—we have had hearings and talks off and on for three years." St. Louis activists perceived negotiation and hearings as a substitute for action.

The most extensive protests against unequal education rocked Chicago—and they marked a grassroots rebellion against both white power and accommodationist black leadership. A growing insurgency in Chicago had risen up against the city's separate, unequal schools and targeted two figures: Benjamin Willis, the white school superintendent, and Edith Green, the sole black member of the Chicago Board of Education. Green came in for particular derision. In late June, nine thousand demonstrators, most of them black, surrounded the all-black Paul Laurence Dunbar Vocational High School, where Green was to give the commencement address. Leading the angry crowd was Charles H. Jones, Jr., head of the Chicago Friends of the Student Nonviolent Coordinating Committee. "We are sick at heart that this public protest is necessary," argued Jones, "but in the last half of the twentieth century—one hundred years after Emancipation—when this nation's children, generation after generation, have been marred and maimed by second-class treatment, we can no longer allow false representation of Negroes to be challenged." The protestors targeted Green's authenticity and her capacity to speak for Chicago's black children. Jones put a point on it: Green "has no psychological or emotional identity with the Negro community."

On June 23, while President Kennedy's speechwriters were adding the final flourishes to his civil rights speech, between 125,000 and 200,000 activists joined together in Detroit's "Walk to Freedom March," the largest demonstration for racial equality in the United States up to that date. The crowd, reported *Business Week*, was "restrained in action although determined in mood." Leading the throng of professionals, poor people, trade unionists, and schoolchildren, some in overalls, others in their Sunday best, was Martin Luther King, Jr., walking side by side with Walter P. Reuther, the head of the United Automobile Workers, who for his union's steadfast support of the southern freedom struggle had earned the moniker "the white Martin Luther King, Jr." Despite Reuther's presence, few whites joined the march. An estimated 90 percent of the marchers were black. "This is just like being in Africa. I don't see any white faces, only black ones," commented one participant. "The view was of a black sea, a mighty sea of black faces," reported the Reverend Malcolm Boyd, a marcher. In his speech to the assembled masses in Detroit's Cobo Hall, King celebrated the "magnificent new militancy" that brought huge crowds to Detroit's streets. Reprising themes common to his speeches, King highlighted the need for voting rights and the abolition of Jim Crow in the South, but he also urged Detroiters to deal with the problems of inequality in their own city, with an emphasis on jobs, housing, and schools. "We must come to see," exhorted King, "that the *de facto* segregation in the North is just as injurious as the actual segregation in the South."

What form that "magnificent new militancy" would take would not be under King's control. In many respects, the "Great March," as local activists called it, was a dress rehearsal for the even larger March on Washington in August, then being organized by Bayard Rustin, A. Philip Randolph, and Anna Arnold Hedgeman. But it also heralded major political changes in the civil rights landscape of the North. Beneath the façade of unity among the marchers on Woodward Avenue were deep divisions over politics and strategy. Detroit's NAACP branch, still one of the largest and most powerful in the country, threatened to withhold support from the Great March unless white liberals, including Reuther and Detroit mayor Jerome Cavanagh, were given prominent billing. The march's coordinator, the Reverend C. L. Franklin (father of singer Aretha), labeled the NAACP a "bunch of Toms," although he was sympathetic to the goals of Reverend King. Franklin hoped to build momentum from the march to create the Northern Christian Leadership Conference, a corollary to King's southern organization. But Franklin was outflanked on the left. The Reverend Albert Cleage, Jr., saw the march as a vehicle for creating black solidarity and cared little for King's rhetoric of integration and nonviolence. "I do not identify myself with those interracial groups who issue statements promising open occupancy in Michigan," announced Cleage a few months before the Great March. "I do not identify with those Negroes who are so identified with the white community that they would die if it collapsed." For Cleage, the black freedom struggle was not about incremental change, nor was it about assimilation to the white majority. "Negroes," he argued, "are struggling against a total white society, a total white civilization."

In many respects, Detroit's insurgents overshadowed King. Cleage ascended to the stage just before King delivered his stirring address. At fifty-two, Cleage was a rising star among Detroit's black radicals and a formidable preacher. His base of operations was Central Congregational Church, whose staid, redbrick neoclassical façade contrasted with Cleage's increasingly radical politics. Like many inner-city churches, Central Congregational had been largely abandoned by its suburb-bound white members when Cleage took the pulpit in 1956. An outspoken advocate of racial justice, Cleage used his "analytical and agitational" sermons to demand workplace equality, educational equity, and an end to police brutality. On these issues, Cleage shared a common agenda with most of Detroit's civil rights leaders. But intertwined with Cleage's demands for racial equality was his skepticism about postwar white liberalism and racial gradualism.

From relative obscurity, Cleage became well known to Detroit blacks in 1961, as the publisher of the *Illustrated News*, a radical counterpart to Detroit's three black newsweeklies. In the distinctive salmon-colored pages of the biweekly paper, Cleage promoted black self-determination and self-defense and excoriated "Uncle Toms" and accommodationists. Like Philadelphia's Cecil Moore, Cleage viewed the civil rights establishment with disdain. The NAACP, lamented Cleage, "spends too much time trying to keep white 'Liberals' happy for the $100 a plate Freedom Dinner." A legitimate "Negro leadership" could not be dependent on the sustenance of white liberals; rather, it "must secure its strength from the masses of Negro people." He also challenged Detroit's liberal-led institutions. Arguing that the public schools had failed black students, Cleage led a campaign against a referendum to increase school taxes. Colorfully written and informative *Illustrated News* articles highlighted the deplorable conditions in Detroit's schools. Cleage also used the pages of his paper to argue for black bullet voting. Of Detroit's at-large political races, where the top vote getters won seats, he argued that blacks should vote as a bloc for black candidates and withhold their support for whites. Even the most well-meaning white liberals, he contended, could not adequately represent their black constituents.

Despite his skepticism about King and his supporters, Cleage backed the Walk to Freedom and used his newspaper to rally participants. But he envisioned the event in more radical terms. More moderate leaders celebrated the "brotherhood" of blacks and whites on the day of the march; others used the podium to advocate for liberal civil rights legislation. Cleage, by contrast, argued that blacks needed to join forces and deploy militant tactics. He used his time at the podium to call for a boycott of Detroit supermarkets. Cleage's very presence at the Detroit event was a reminder of the heterogeneity of the northern freedom struggle and the recognition by organizers that the Great March would not be legitimate if it did not include militant voices.

Just a few months after the Great March, Cleage came out more forcefully against what he considered the polite and ultimately ineffective nonviolent tactics of civil rights protest. Black political victories, Cleage argued at an October 1963 meeting of radical leaders, would not come from peaceful demonstrations or collaboration with the white power structure. Moral suasion would not result in racial equality. What was needed instead was a "strategy of chaos." Whites, he contended, would not give up their privileges unless they were forced to pay a high price. If necessary, black activists would have to follow through with acts of retaliation. "Either we get all our rights," argued Cleage, "or we are going to tear it up." Cleage tried out the strategy at protests demanding the inclusion of blacks in apprentice training programs in Detroit. Protestors carried signs reading "SCHOOL FOR ALL OR SCHOOL FOR NONE. EQUALITY OR CHAOS." Cleage's "strategy of chaos" failed to open up Detroit's apprentice programs, but it succeeded in giving young black militants a powerful alternative—mass disruption—to a strategy of nonviolence that many saw as hopelessly ineffective.

The increasingly aggressive tone of activists in Detroit and Philadelphia was not unique. Over the summer, civil rights activists faced off hard hats and government officials in a string of demonstrations throughout the Northeast that drew their inspiration from the springtime protests in Philadelphia. Demonstrators did not simply picket peacefully: They were deliberately disruptive and increasingly devised strategies to attract the attention of the local news media. Activists in Newark and Trenton blockaded construction sites. In Brooklyn, nearly 650 people were arrested for civil disobedience at the site of the Downstate Medical Center, most for lying down in front of construction vehicles. Other protestors held sit-ins and "sleep-ins" at Nelson Rockefeller's New York City office, hoping to force the governor to integrate the building trades. In July, some twenty-five thousand protestors in Cleveland, members of the United Freedom Movement, a coalition of more than thirty civil rights and community groups, marched downtown for civil rights. At each of these protests, demonstrators stepped up their militant rhetoric. In August, ongoing pickets in New York at the Downstate Medical Center turned ugly as protestors and police clashed. "This nation is going to hell!" shouted the Reverend William Jones. "This proves there's no difference between New York and Alabama, no difference between the United States and South Africa."

Over the summer of 1963, the U.S. Department of Justice catalogued a total of 1,412 separate civil rights demonstrations around the country. It was the most sustained wave of protests for black equality ever. The protests were not just noteworthy for their frequency. Even the best-choreographed events took unexpected turns, as sizeable numbers of protestors experimented with more disruptive and coercive tactics, pushing at the boundaries of direct action. All over the North, black nationalists, separatists, and radicals joined demonstrations, sometimes clashing—but also cooperating—with advocates of nonviolent change. On the Fourth of July, thirty thousand people joined an NAACP-organized march through Chicago's Loop demanding racial equality. The NAACP found itself unable to control the heterogeneous crowd. Members of the Revolutionary Action Movement, fresh from their arrests at the Philadelphia construction site protests, stoked the crowd's anger. When Mayor Richard J. Daley took the stage to address a postmarch rally, he was booed off, leaving "red-faced and embarrassed, with tears streaming down his cheeks." The Reverend Joseph H. Jackson, head of the five-million-member National Baptist Convention and the most vocal black critic of direct action, stormed off the podium when the volatile crowd jeered "Uncle Tom Go Home!" The *Chicago Tribune* called the protests an "act of intolerance and bigotry." But militants did not let up. Olivet Baptist, Jackson's home church in Chicago, became the target of protestors throughout the summer.

Even the icons of the southern freedom struggle faced rough treatment by skeptical northern crowds. In Chicago, black activists catcalled James Meredith, on a speaking tour after desegregating the University of Mississippi, when he denounced the "childish" tactics and lack of "discipline" of some younger activists. And radicals began to harass the Reverend

Martin Luther King, Jr., or, as some black detractors called him, "Martin Loser King." At a July appearance at Harlem's Salem Baptist Church, King was attacked by egg-throwing protestors, suspected to be followers of Malcolm X. It was particularly unsettling for King to discover that the egg throwers were not adherents of the Nation of Islam—they were followers of a Harlem Christian minister who advocated "fighting back" against segregationist violence.

Perhaps the most portentous development in 1963 was growing discontent about police harassment and brutality, an issue that the U.S. Commission on Civil Rights had warned about in its 1961 report. Many civil rights protests—over long-simmering issues such as discrimination in public accommodations, workplaces, and schools—became antipolice demonstrations, with a growing number of them turning violent. When the police beat and arrested protestors at Philadelphia's construction sites, local activists led by the Revolutionary Action Movement directed their anger toward the city's unpopular police force. In June, rioting broke out on the streets of Cambridge, Maryland, a town of 12,000, where police clashed with civil rights activists who had been challenging segregation in restaurants and movie theaters. At the end of the month in New York City, demonstrators and the police squared off in an angry confrontation at the construction site of the new Harlem Hospital in a protest that "jolted" the city. In early August, activists protesting the lack of black construction workers at Rochdale Village in Queens demonstrated against police misconduct. Long Island CORE's Lincoln Lynch and another activist were arrested after they charged the police with administering "rough treatment" to women taken into custody for committing civil disobedience at the site. Later that month, a construction site protest in Elizabeth, New Jersey, spun into a "screaming, fist-swinging melee" between seventy-five activists and the police. A mid-August protest against school overcrowding on Chicago's South Side in August spun out of control as demonstrators pelted police officers with "stones, bricks, and chunks of concrete." Even a CORE-led demonstration in Chicago led to a "shoving battle" between ostensibly nonviolent protestors and the police.

Often, advocates of nonviolence and their critics found common cause in their distrust of law enforcement officials. In Rochester, New York, a broad spectrum of civil rights activists and nationalists, including Malcolm X, joined forces in protesting the city's police, who had arrested twelve members of the Nation of Islam in January. At Harlem's Speakers' Corner, police patrolled uneasily and listened carefully to militant addresses, poised to make arrests if the crowds grew unruly. One hot summer day, when police officers attempted to disperse a large crowd gathered on 125th Street to listen to a vocal argument between members of CORE and the Nation of Islam, Blyden Jackson of CORE stood atop his car and confronted the police. The nationalists and CORE, he argued, "were entitled to discuss their differences on the corner." Participants on both sides roared in approval, and the police, unwilling to make mass arrests, left the feuding activists alone, momentarily unified by their shared suspicion of the police.

Nineteen sixty-three was also frequently punctuated by tense confrontations between young black men and the police over allegations of police misconduct. Hardly any city seemed immune to what observers termed "near riots." In mid-June, a protest following the arrest of an unlicensed ice-cream vendor in Harlem led to clashes between an increasingly angry thousand-person crowd and the police. Twenty-seven were arrested after an evening of sporadic window breaking and arson. Insurance companies, fearful of a larger riot, increased commercial rates throughout Harlem. In Detroit, seven hundred protestors—including Malcolm X's brother Wilfred—led demonstrations in early July after the city's police gunned down Cynthia Scott, a black prostitute, killing her instantly with shots to the back. Fifteen black militants staged a sit-in at the police commissioner's office in memory of "Saint Cynthia," demanding that the city crack down on police brutality and hire a black police chief.

The situation was even tenser in Philadelphia, where in October police shot to death twenty-four-year-old Willie Philyaw. In response, black youths looted stores and hurled bricks at police cars. Inspired by the spontaneous protests, North Philadelphia's RAM chapter made the Philyaw case the centerpiece of its efforts to organize a grassroots rebellion. In New Rochelle—another city whose established NAACP leadership had been challenged in the winter of 1963 by an insurgency—angry marchers took to the street in November after police bloodied a gas station attendant wrongly accused of a crime. In New Rochelle, and elsewhere in the North, observers quickly drew analogies between the police brutality north and south. "Looks as if we have Birmingham in Westchester County," wrote Inez Henderson, the suburban New York correspondent for the *Courier*, commenting on allegations of police violence in New Rochelle.

The growing militancy of northern protests—and the frequency of violence—frightened white public officials. Around the country, police departments began preparing for what many viewed as the inevitable racial apocalypse. During the summer of 1963, police departments throughout the North held special "mob violence" training sessions to prepare for demonstrations and riots. The Pittsburgh and Seattle forces instituted "riot work" courses. Minneapolis authorized the purchase of metal riot helmets for its officers; in Chicago, police prepared rapid response teams to intervene in protests and defuse incipient riots. Federal Enterprises, the nation's leading producer of tear gas, reported a spike in sales during the 1963 fiscal year, as police departments girded themselves for race war. "If we get through the summer without any severe mass violence," stated a Pittsburgh official, "I will thank God."

Even blacks who were not active in protests or clashes with the police vented their anger. "White folks ain't going to give you nothing," said Junius Brown, a New York factory worker. "You've got to go out and take it." After a wave of protests in Pittsburgh in late July, ordinary blacks in the Iron City expressed their growing impatience. "Violence seems to be the only way of making the integration problems known," Henry Clay Smith, a Pittsburgh construction worker, told a reporter. Another Pittsburgh resident, Emma Lee Jones, put it pointedly: "I'm a peace-loving woman and I don't like violence, but sometimes you just got to fight." Longtime CORE activist James Robinson saw 1963 as a turning point. From that point on, he said, "new people . . . had radical expectations."

THE ICONIC EVENT in the rebellious year of 1963 was the March on Washington for Jobs and Freedom. Lead organizer Bayard Rustin hoped it would reinvigorate the alliance between civil rights and labor. Some 250,000 strong, "the throngs were orderly and the voices of their speakers temperate," reported *Newsweek*. Martin Luther King, Jr., consummated the event with the most celebrated speech of his career. Northerners were probably the majority of those gathered on the Mall on August 28. Union Station staff counted 17,791 marchers arriving in Washington by special train and at least another 4,500 on regular trains. Many marchers flew to Washington. Thousands more arrived by car. Still others made their way to the nation's capital on one of 1,514 chartered buses. A caravan of fifteen buses and a special eighteen-car "Freedom Train" carried thousands of Pittsburgh residents to Washington. Hundreds of buses came from Detroit, Chicago, and Philadelphia. Some demonstrators even arrived on roller skates. Unlike Detroit's Great March, there were no radicals like Cleage on the stage at the Mall. (Cleage, in fact, had discouraged his followers from joining what he called a "symbolic protest" and a "tame demonstration of Negro docility.") The day's most militant speech, by Georgia's John Lewis, had been purged of its biting references to the Kennedy administration's inefficacy. Black militants largely joined in Cleage's denunciation. Malcolm X denounced what he called the "Farce on Washington." Michael Thelwell, later known as a black power activist and pioneering figure in African American studies, described "an overhanging atmosphere of complete political irrelevance" at the march. SNCC's James Forman saw the demonstration as a "victory celebration for the Kennedy administration" rather than a representative gathering of the people.

Like most events in 1963, however, the March on Washington defied such simple characterizations. The mass protests and street rebellions of the year of the Negro Revolt called into question the very institutions that had defined the black freedom struggle since World War II. Insurgencies roiled established groups like the NAACP and CORE. New radical organizations took new form on the political left, hoping to capture the allegiance of the rank and file. A rising cadre of radicals attacked established civil rights leaders, provoking a crisis of purpose and identity in older civil rights organizations and unleashing a period of intense political experimentation and contestation. Advocates of racial equality—from liberals to self-proclaimed revolutionaries—debated the goals of political change, the means to achieve it, and the very meaning of freedom, rights, and equality. Policy makers and political leaders embarked on a period of innovation in an attempt to respond to the crisis of widespread rebellion. Above all, the Negro Revolt threw up for grabs conventional categories like integration and separation, radical and conservative, personal and political, in ways that would have far-reaching consequences by the end of the 1960s.

For those who paid close attention, the March on Washington was a much more heterogeneous affair than its detractors contended. *Courier* columnist Hazel Garland described the diversity of the crowd: "Doctors, lawyers, and people of all professional fields marched together with little folk and the unemployed men and women of all races, creeds, and colors. Perhaps the largest delegation was composed of labor groups." Trade unionists were perhaps the most visible contingent at the march, in part because for all of their difficulties with race issues, many local unions were among the few truly integrated institutions in northern cities. A few weeks before the march, A. Philip Randolph had pulled together more than eight hundred union and civil leaders and gained the support of the ubiquitous United Automobile Workers, the Drug and Hospital Workers, the Fur and Leather Workers, the Seafarers, and several unions representing municipal and government employees. For their part, the Retail Workers pressed employers to give its members a paid holiday to attend the march. Activists made special efforts to include the jobless, to make the point that civil rights and economic justice were fundamentally intertwined. The United Packinghouse Workers, a major financial supporter of Martin Luther King, Jr., and one of the only left-led unions in the CIO to survive the anti-Communist purges, subsidized transportation for unemployed workers, as well as its members.

Many of the speakers reiterated themes that harked back to the struggles of the Depression and World War II, to highlight the need for measures to combat both discrimination and persistent unemployment. But the economic climate of the previous ten years gave the demands particular urgency. Many unions whose rank and file marched on Washington had seen their membership plummet as manufacturers introduced automation and relocated production to low-wage regions. The Packinghouse Workers, for example, had lost nearly one-quarter of its members between 1954 and 1960. Detroit, the bastion of the autoworkers, had lost 140,000 jobs between 1947 and 1963. And the retail industry—which had just begun to open its doors to blacks—was rapidly suburbanizing. The loss of jobs was devastating for black workers. In his speech on the Mall, A. Philip Randolph denounced "profits geared to automation" that "destroy the jobs of millions of workers" and called for measures to address unemployment, raise the minimum wage, and increase federal aid to education. After two decades, he remained unflinchingly committed to the principle that economic justice and racial justice were necessary to each other. Walter Reuther also rallied the crowd with the call for jobs and freedom. "The job question is crucial," he argued, "because we will not solve education, or housing, or public accommodations as long as millions of Americans, Negroes, are treated as second-class citizens." For Reuther, as for Randolph, the key was "fair employment within the framework of full employment." Labor activists were, however, bitter that the mainstream news media spilled "millions of words" about the march but "conspicuously downplayed economic demands . . . [that] may prove ultimately more significant than the eloquent speeches."

Joining the throng were other marchers whose views were not as "temperate" as those coming from the podium, whose anger and frustration had—and would—lead them to reject "orderly" demonstrations. The *Liberator*, the leading organ of black radicalism, encouraged its readers to join the march to "challenge" the "Uncle Tom leaders" and "move far beyond the narrow issues" of civil rights legislation. Many militants answered the call. New York's Umbra group, a collective of radical poets, artists, and writers, joined the marchers and were armed with pistols in case things went bad. Another delegation of black radicals carried signs with a more threatening message than King's: "FREEDOM NOW—OR THE FIRE NEXT TIME!" The tensions of 1963 sometimes surfaced in collisions between black and white demonstrators. A *Village Voice* reporter described a clash aboard a bus to Washington between black marchers and a white Peace Corps volunteer. "If this thing comes to violence," a young black protestor declared to the idealistic volunteer, "yours will be the first throat we slit. We don't need your kind." The white reacted defensively: "What's he talking about? What did I say?" Soon, other black passengers piped up: "We don't trust you." "We don't believe you are sincere." "We have been stabbed in the back too many times."

Activists who disdained the Reverend Martin Luther King, Jr., and his allies as hopelessly moderate used the occasion of the march to pitch their own, more radical demands. One figure who worked the crowd was Conrad Lynn, a radical black lawyer based in New York who had made a career representing civil rights activists and leftists. During World War II, had Lynn created a cause célèbre by defending his brother's refusal to join the "Jim Crow" military. In 1947, Lynn had joined CORE in its "Journey of Reconciliation," the first systematic challenge to segregation on interstate transportation and the precursor of the celebrated Freedom

Rides of 1961. A fervent critic of McCarthyism, Lynn represented black radicals accused of affiliation with the Communist Party. The Cold War did not dampen Lynn's militancy and his affinity for unpopular cases. In the late 1950s, Lynn had taken on the case of Robert F. Williams, who had been expelled from the NAACP for his advocacy of armed self-defense and who had gone into exile in Cuba after being framed on kidnapping charges in Monroe, North Carolina. A perennial fly in the milk, Lynn used the march to launch the Freedom Now Party, a separate, black-run third party. While King was delivering his "I Have a Dream" speech, Lynn and his comrades circulated copies of the "Declaration of Washington"— a handbill that outlined the Freedom Now Party's alternative vision for America. Its language was uncompromising. "We have to *take* our freedom; no one will hand it to us," proclaimed the declaration. The Freedom Now Party "will concentrate the voting power of black America in a single organization that can deliver knock-out punches to the enemies of equality." The party's proponents knew that it would face an uphill battle. "Only a party with no illusions about winning immediate and sweeping electoral victories," wrote William Worthy, "is likely to take a principled position when heat is applied." The Freedom Now Party had little good to say about the Republicans, but its spokespeople took off their gloves when it came to the Democrats. "If our revolt means anything," wrote party activist LeMar Barron a few weeks after the march, "it is our rejection and repudiation of the white liberals whom we have permitted for too long to dictate what we ask for, when, where, and how."

The most influential black radical in Washington that day was Malcolm X. "I observed that circus," he recalled in his autobiography. After the march was over, Malcolm held court in the lobby of Washington's posh Statler Hilton hotel, greeting well-wishers, among them James Forman, and offering his own, cynical take on the day's events. Labeled a "Negro extremist" by the white-dominated media (and much of the black press), he articulated a powerful undercurrent of black discontent that few whites understood. By late 1963, Malcolm and the Nation of Islam still faced real suspicion among African Americans but were growing in prominence and popularity. A 1963 *Newsweek* poll found "massive negative feeling" toward the Nation of Islam: Only 13 percent of northern blacks expressed a positive view of the Nation, and only 10 percent approved of Elijah Muhammad. (Malcolm X was not yet enough of a celebrity to make the questionnaire's list of Negro leaders.) For many northern blacks, the Nation of Islam was a hard sell. The poll's results outraged many black radicals, though they were surely not far off from the truth. But the *Newsweek* surveyors, mostly black professionals, did not interview anyone under eighteen years old and most likely avoided (and were avoided by) the ex-cons and younger people who made up much of the Nation's following. The influence of the Nation could not, however, be measured simply by its poll data or even by the group's still-small membership. By 1963, Malcolm's appeal had spread well beyond the small circle of Elijah Muhammad's acolytes. Like a magnet, Malcolm attracted a committed band of followers, disproportionately men, who found that his message offered a compelling alternative to the mild, accommodationist politics of so many northern black leaders. Charlie L. Russell, a black radical who was critical of the Nation, recognized its appeal. "At one time, the Muslims were like a breath of fresh air on the civil rights scene; there was an intriguing boldness about them—they dared express publicly what many Negroes uttered in private."

Malcolm became a particularly popular headliner at gatherings of black radicals. In November 1963, when the Reverend Albert Cleage pulled together the Northern Negro Grassroots Leadership Conference, he secured Malcolm X as the keynote speaker. Malcolm's "Message to the Grassroots," released as a Motown record, spoke to black internationalism in its celebration of African and Asian revolutionaries; it captured the growing discontent of black radicals against the civil rights establishment in its denunciation of the "House Negroes" and "Uncle Toms" who "keep us passive and peaceful and non-violent." Malcolm captured the growing discontent of black activists in 1963: "There's no such thing as a nonviolent revolution. The only kind of revolution that is nonviolent is the Negro revolution. The only revolution in which the goal is loving your enemy is the Negro revolution. It's the only revolution in which the goal is a desegregated lunch counter, a desegregated theater, a desegregated park, and a desegregated public toilet; you can sit down next to white folks—on the toilet. That's no revolution."

Malcolm's fiery speeches attracted the growing interest of a group of activists whom James and Grace Lee Boggs called "80 percent Muslims," those who were skeptical about the Nation's religious teachings and its strict regulations but who agreed with the "prophecy of the inevitable doom of white society and the need of every black man, woman, and child to emancipate himself or herself from identification with it." Malcolm's public denunciation of white treachery brought into public discourse ideas that had long been circulating at the black grass roots but that had been muted during the era of interracial, liberal organizing. Perhaps most important, just as mainstream black organizations were going through a period of internal tumult, Malcolm's rhetoric empowered black dissidents. "The Black Muslims have been overplayed by the press," argued CORE activist Marvin Rich in 1963. *"But the nationalism which the Black Muslims represent is a powerful force.* Psychologically perhaps, Black Muslims force other groups into more militant action."

Black grassroots activists with "radical expectations" would ultimately convulse the North in a wave of protests—increasingly violent—over the next several years. The combination of grassroots insurgencies and a roiling debate among civil rights leaders over political goals and strategies would give the northern freedom struggle a new orientation from 1963 forward. In a series of articles published as the Emancipation centennial year came to a close, the Reverend Albert Cleage reflected on the "much publicized 'Black Revolt' of 1963." With approval, he noted that "upon occasion it has shocked and terrified the white man out of his customary complacency." Like many popular observers, Cleage noted that the northern insurgents had "departed radically" from Martin Luther King, Jr., and the southern freedom struggle. "In northern urban centers," noted Cleage, "a new kind of 'Black Nationalism' began to emerge. The Negro, disillusioned with 'integration' began to look for another way." Cleage saw the revolt as the beginning of a struggle between two visions of black leadership and political change and strategy—a "prelude to revolution." Reiterating an argument that he shared with a mostly younger generation of militants, Cleage contended that the "Old Guard in the North has no answers to the basic questions which confront the Negro people."

Cleage's arguments were prophetic. Nineteen sixty-three marked the beginning of an intense contest over the future direction of the black freedom struggle. Advocates of black power such as Cleage and Malcolm X would become increasingly vocal over the next several years; grassroots insurgencies would proliferate; but the "Old Guard," along with integrationist liberals, also grew increasingly vocal and influential.

The longtime activists, and their younger counterparts who demanded "Jobs and Freedom," would pressure the government for civil rights, antipoverty, and employment programs. The question "Who speaks for the people?"—who would represent the aspirations of African Americans in the next stage of their struggle for freedom—would remain unresolved for the next ten years.

CHAPTER 10

"LONG HOT SUMMERS"

JAMAICA, QUEENS, WAS AS UNLIKELY A SPRINGBOARD FOR REVOLUTION AS any of the places that exploded in protest in 1963. And Herman Ferguson, a New York City teacher and school administrator who spearheaded the Jamaica protests, was an unlikely revolutionary. Described by a colleague as "one of those mild-mannered, slow-burning but very dedicated kind of guys," Ferguson embarked on an odyssey of protest in the early 1960s that began with liberal optimism but became increasingly militant. In the spring of 1963, Ferguson led protests against a Jamaica bank for its "Billy Banjo" mural, which depicted a happy, strumming Negro with a plantation house as his backdrop. It was a demand for respect but hardly revolutionary. In late July, Ferguson joined NAACP and CORE in demonstrations demanding the employment of black workers in skilled construction jobs at Rochdale Village, a six-thousand-unit cooperative apartment project under construction in Queens. This was part of the wave of antidiscrimination protests in the North targeting the building trades. On July 23, two hundred demonstrators joined a picket line and twenty-three were arrested for obstructing an entrance to the construction site. Six days later, after a fund-raising rally, protests resumed. For the remainder of the summer and throughout the fall, demonstrators converged on Rochdale several times a week, with the protests growing increasingly vociferous. In early August, protestors were arrested for lying down in a roadway and blocking traffic. In early September, Ferguson and eight other activists broke into the construction site, chained and locked themselves to the top of a crane, and threw away the keys.

The Rochdale Movement, headed by Ferguson, gained national attention. In October, SNCC leader John Lewis joined the protestors and advised them that it was "time to put the movement back into the streets" and that "the Negro must revolt against not only the white power structure but also against the Negro leadership that would slow the Negro march to a slow shuffle." Expanding their targets in October, Rochdale protestors launched a selective patronage campaign against neighborhood stores, part of an all-out challenge to labor market segregation. Ferguson argued that "we are calling for economic militancy. More and better jobs for Negroes. Our weapons are boycotts, sit-ins, mass demonstrations, not moderation. Our forum is in the streets, not in the courts." In their handwritten banners—"This is a SELF-DEFENSE Demonstration. UNITE or PERISH"—Ferguson and his fellow marchers made it clear that nonviolence was but one of the weapons in their arsenal.

By the end of 1963, many Rochdale Movement activists repudiated the liberalism that had galvanized their initial protests. They welcomed radical activists, among them members of the Nation of Islam. Malcolm X addressed a December rally, leading many protestors to endorse his call to "buy black." Ferguson's colleague Merle Stewart called for the revival of Garveyism. "The civil rights efforts of 1963," argued Stewart, "are being viewed by a steadily increasing number of people with frustration and dissatisfaction." The lesson that Stewart learned from Rochdale was the need for a "psychological and spiritual awakening of all Black people," along with "race consciousness, unity and solidarity" and "independence and self-reliance." Ferguson went even further. One of his neighbors described Ferguson's trajectory: "You could almost watch him growing more and more bitter." In early 1964, Ferguson allied with Malcolm X, joined the fledgling Revolutionary Action Movement, and began a long march to the left that would lead to his eventual trial and conviction for allegedly masterminding a plot to assassinate moderate civil rights leaders.

The story of the rise of black power in the North is the story of hundreds of protests like those at Rochdale Village and thousands of activists like Herman Ferguson, impatient with the pace of change and willing to experiment with new, more militant forms of protest. Increasingly they emphasized a political street theater of disruption and couched their demands in revolutionary rhetoric. Only a minority of black activists in 1963 and beyond would embrace Ferguson's radicalism, but they would have an impact far beyond their numbers. They would become the public face of the black rebellion—inspired by grassroots protests and drawn toward violence as a tactic for forcing systematic change.

By the end of 1963, a growing number of radicals like Ferguson had fashioned a critique of the postwar civil rights movement that would, in various forms, shape the freedom struggle for the rest of the 1960s. The insurgencies that rose up in the mid-1960s were fractious, fragmented, and intensely local in their orientation. Even at their peak of influence, they did not constitute anything resembling a coherent movement, but rather were a series of impulses, bound together by a common critique of postwar racial liberalism. First, they lashed out against moderation or "gradualism." Second, they repudiated liberal integrationism—in particular, its emphasis on changing white attitudes and assimilating blacks into mainstream American culture. Third, and related, they framed their insurgencies in populist terms—they, not established civil rights organizations and their leaders, were the authentic representatives of the black masses. Fourth, they situated their arguments in an internationalist framework, drawing from a deep current of anti-imperialism in black radical thought, linking the black freedom struggle in the United States with anticolonial freedom struggles in Asia and, especially, Africa. Finally, to one degree or another, even as they repudiated postwar racial liberalism, they drew heavily from postwar social scientific understandings of psychology and culture, arguing that self-esteem and racial pride were essential to black liberation. But if they shared a common critique of postwar America, they diverged widely on the means to transform it. And their differences were most pronounced over that which was most distant and unattainable: the sort of society they hoped to achieve.

HERMAN FERGUSON AND the Rochdale Movement—and their counterparts throughout the North—sought to create a movement that would supplant the nonviolent freedom struggle. The quest for radical alternatives led Ferguson toward the Revolutionary Action Movement, a group of young activists, led by Maxwell Stanford, Donald Freeman, and Wanda Marshall, that first gathered in Cleveland in 1961. Cleveland had long been a bastion of civil rights activism and home to militant, all-black organizations such as the Future Outlook League, whose strategies defied easy categorization as either nationalist or integrationist. Cleveland also had a thriving, revitalized CORE chapter and a strong NAACP branch. It was also one of the nation's centers of open housing activism. Over the course of the 1960s, Cleveland became a crucible of racial conflict over segregated education, persistent workplace discrimination, and poverty.

In this heady environment, Freeman, a Case Western Reserve student, and Stanford and Marshall, activists at historically black Central State University, convened a group of young black intellectuals to discuss politics and social change. After running insurgent candidates for student councils on their respective campuses (under the name Reform Action Movement), Stanford and Freeman moved to a larger stage. Renaming their group the Revolutionary Action Movement, they were inspired by the anticolonial movements in Africa and Asia. Part of a black intellectual and political current that ran deep to the popular internationalism of the Great Depression and World War II, the young RAM activists envisioned American blacks as key to the worldwide struggle against Western imperialism. Their interest in Third World revolutions led them to the works of Frantz Fanon, Che Guevara, and especially Mao Zedong. But they also found a homegrown revolutionary—someone whose activism bridged the civil rights movement and revolutionary internationalism. He was Robert F. Williams, Jr., who, by the early 1960s, was the most celebrated American black radical besides Malcolm X.

Observers in the 1960s painted black nationalism and black power as a departure from the past, a new historical moment. But so many of the key figures in black power, including Williams and Malcolm X, were products of the previous generation of activism. A World War II veteran from Monroe, North Carolina, Williams moved to the booming industrial North after the war, working for a time in an auto factory in Detroit and an aircraft plant in New Jersey. Although Williams was not a union leader, he was inspired by the labor movement. "Without knowing it," he recalled, "I had picked up some of the ideas of organizing from the activities around me." When he returned to Monroe, he quickly rose to be chair of the local NAACP—and it was from there that he had a national impact. In 1957, Williams and his fellow NAACP members took up arms to protect themselves against white supremacists. A fierce advocate of blacks' right to self-defense, Williams found himself cast as the anti–Martin Luther King, Jr. Mainstream civil rights leaders denounced Williams as an extremist, and, in 1959, the NAACP expelled him. "However understandable these emotional outbursts may be in terms of gross injustice to Negroes in the United States," intoned the NAACP board in an official statement, "the NAACP cannot support any sentiment calling for the use of violence to correct injustice." The larger debate about nonviolence versus self-defense that continued to swirl around Williams hinged on a false dichotomy between the two strategies. Most of Williams's harshest critics, including the NAACP and King himself, acknowledged that self-defense was justifiable in some circumstances. In fact, many ostensibly nonviolent protestors carried weapons. Given the threat of retaliatory white violence, it was not unusual for protestors at CORE, SNCC, and SCLC events to "pack heat." Where nonviolent activists diverged with Williams was in their deep fear that the sight of "Negroes with guns," bearing arms publicly and squaring off with white supremacists, would incite even more violent reprisals by whites.

The NAACP debate over Williams's fate brought a discussion of black self-defense out of living rooms, barbershops, and bars into the open. To a young generation of militant northern blacks, Williams was a hero, the embodiment of a black man who stood up for his family and his people, rather than allowing himself to be abused and scorned by white suprema-cists. "If anyone thinks that Robert F. Williams' creed on the race ques-tion is way out of this world, let him talk around with little Negroes," wrote a *Pittsburgh Courier* reporter. "He'll soon find that every one of them is willing to slug any white guy who first slugs them." Self-defense, assertive masculinity, and race pride had a widespread appeal at the grass roots. Williams also became a celebrity in the small world of black radical intellectuals. In 1961, after being framed for kidnapping and terroristic threats during a series of racial clashes that accompanied CORE's Free-dom Rides to Monroe (the charges were later dismissed), Williams fled the United States for Cuba and later, after a falling-out with Cuban au-thorities, to China. There Williams added a layer of Marxist revolutionary politics onto the politics of self-defense.

Chairman Rob, a term of endearment that many of his followers used, made a splash in 1962 with the publication of his short manifesto, *Negroes with Guns*, which Max Stanford and his Cleveland comrades devoured. He also launched *The Crusader*, a newsletter that by the mid-1960s reached about forty thousand readers, most of them in northern cities. On his regular broadcast from Cuba, Radio Free Dixie, heard on clear evenings as far north as New York, Williams argued that American blacks were part of a global struggle against white-led capitalist oppression.

Williams elaborated three long-running strains of black activism: the necessity of self-defense, black dignity, and racial pride and, perhaps most important, the argument that American blacks were a colonized people who needed to liberate themselves from the corrupt American empire. To black intellectuals and grassroots activists who had followed the Ethiopian struggle against Italian fascism in the 1930s; the Indian independence movement of the 1940s; Nigerian, Ghanaian, and Kenyan battles against European imperialism in the 1950s; and revolutions in China, Vietnam, and Cuba, Williams placed them in the heart of a freedom struggle, led by people of color, that transcended national boundaries.

Williams was not a movement builder—the practical constraints of being in exile were too great. But from Cuba, Williams corresponded with Stanford and agreed to serve as RAM's official chairman. Williams used RAM's newsletters to spread his gospel of self-defense and third-world Marxism. Williams's endorsement brought RAM immediate credibility in black radical circles—and also brought the new organization to the attention of law enforcement officials, who closely followed its every move.

No more than a small cell, RAM had influence far exceeding its numbers, largely because of Stanford's indefatigable efforts. RAM's charismatic leader was a natural networker, someone who managed to build bridges with nearly every leading black activist and organization in the early and mid-1960s. Stanford spent extended periods in four major centers of northern civil rights activism: Cleveland, Philadelphia, Detroit, and New York. In Cleveland, Stanford attended CORE meetings and pushed that chapter to organize in defense of Mae Mallory, a close associate of Robert F. Williams and former Harlem school boycott leader, who faced criminal charges in North Carolina. In Philadelphia, which became RAM's primary base, Stanford assisted the Reverend Leon Sullivan's selective patronage campaign. He also worked briefly and tumultuously for Cecil B. Moore and the NAACP. While in Philadelphia, he became a student of Audley "Queen Mother" Moore, during the period she was advocating reparations. In Detroit, Stanford forged an alliance with James and Grace Lee Boggs, longtime socialist theorists and labor activists who had been close associates of C.L.R. James and, later, the Reverend Albert Cleage. Stanford's interest in creating a united black radical movement propelled him toward the Nation of Islam. Though he argued that RAM "remained to be convinced" of the merit of Elijah Muhammad's principles, Stanford saw untapped revolutionary potential in the nationalist sect and contributed to *Muhammad Speaks*.

The line between civil rights and black revolutionary politics was blurry for RAM, especially in the organization's first two years. RAM members worked with both mainstream civil rights organizers and black radicals and joined antidiscrimination demonstrations. But from the outset, RAM members had little interest in nonviolence and expressed an impatience that disturbed many established civil rights activists. In 1963, RAM emerged into the public eye when Stanford and a colleague were arrested for clashing with the police during Philadelphia's construction site protests. Even Cecil B. Moore—who regularly used inflammatory language—distanced himself from RAM. For its part, RAM denounced Moore as a "sell out" and broke decisively with "Slick Cecil" by late 1963. Rapidly shifting leftward, Stanford issued a series of manifestos, began publishing the radical newsletter *Black America*, and started organizing among high school and college students. RAM publications relentlessly criticized integrationism. "The Negro cannot integrate into this anti-negro machine," argued one contributor to *Black America*. "We've already integrated into a 'no-citizenship' position of subhuman, super-exploited beasts of burden."

RAM's rhetoric was syncretic. Stanford and his comrades borrowed Nation of Islam phrases such as "white devils." They offered a critique of exploitation that drew from Mao and Fanon and offered an analysis— which would become commonplace on the left—that described American blacks as "semi-colonized" or "colonized" peoples. Endorsing the creation of an all-black political party, they called for blacks to take control of the White House. They also fashioned a critique of "mainstream" civil rights protests. Stanford jabbed at what he saw as the futility of protests to open public accommodations. "The core of the black man's problem is not that of eating at a restaurant. His plight is much more than discrimination. The word that is most expressive of our situation is exploitation." Stanford went on to criticize an emphasis on "racism" that he saw as diverting attention from larger problems. "What we must understand is that the Afro-Americans are not discriminated against by the oligarchy simply because it doesn't like us." For Stanford, the problem was one of inequitable economic power. "Greedy pigs," he argued, profited from exploiting blacks. His associate Wanda Marshall described the fundamental problem: "the survival of the black race in an automated economy."

Inspired by Williams's Maoism, RAM hailed China as a utopian alternative to America. RAM was not alone in its infatuation with the People's Republic. Most prominently, Malcolm X idealized Chinese revolutionaries as leaders in the global struggle of people of color against white domination. But RAM activists did not just look eastward for inspiration. They also embraced a romantic view of African culture as an alternative to the "materialism" and "decadence" of the United States. Later radicals would draw a sharp distinction between "cultural" and "economic" nationalists, but in the case of RAM, as with most black power groups, the cultural was political and the cultural was economic. RAM cofounder Donald Freeman wrote that the "prerequisite to a *genuine* Black Revolution" was the "'ReAfricanization' of Black People in America. 'ReAfricanization' repudiates decadent bourgeois, materialistic values, and the 'rat-race' or 'pathological' egoism and individualism inherent in American society. It embraces a humanism derivative from the African Heritage which exalts aesthetic, intellectual, and spiritual development, and 'Communalism' or cooperation rather than exploitation." To undo American "indoctrination," blacks must "know their *authentic* history in Africa and America." Max Stanford also saw artistic endeavors as liberatory. An artist and sometime Yoruba drummer, Stanford was powerfully drawn to the Black Arts movement—a group of poets and writers, dramatists, painters, sculptors, and musicians who believed that a common black culture was necessary to forge a revolutionary consciousness. In Newark and New York, he worked closely with LeRoi Jones (later Amiri Baraka), the most prominent black literary radical. Poet Larry Neal's apartment became RAM's unofficial Manhattan headquarters—a place where revolutionaries gathered to read verse, talk politics, and plan the revolution.

A cultural transformation was, however, only the first step toward the larger goal of the revolutionary overthrow of the American government. That required a systematic challenge to existing civil rights organizations—and their white liberal allies. To create a revolutionary cadre, RAM would have to discredit "bourgeois" black leaders who provided white racists with "the façade of a new and modern Uncle Tom front office." The first stage of revolution was purification: creating black unity by making common cause against the enemies of black liberation. Lumping together two enemies, a typical RAM cartoon read "Killer Cops Must GO! Sell Outs Must Go!" Moderate blacks were just as problematic as the "sadistic animals . . . robed in a blue uniform" who patrolled inner cities. "We are afraid to walk the streets at night, afraid for our children, afraid of losing our jobs, houses, cars," wrote William Woodley, one of Stanford's close associates. "How much longer can we live in such fear? We can't take our problems to the 'Uncle Tom' leaders. They only get rich off our misery and suffering and tell us about the dreams that they've had."

RAM's animus toward sellouts and Uncle Toms, the police, and white political leaders led its members to gird for battle. As early as 1965, FBI informants reported that "STANFORD told of having an 'assassination list' which includes leaders of the 'non-violent' civil rights groups and leaders of the 'far right.'" By 1967, Stanford's rhetoric had grown increasingly apocalyptic. A key goal of RAM, he argued, was to "get rid of traitors (uncle toms) and collaborators," otherwise known as "the white-man's secret weapon." As a step toward revolution, the "Toms" who ran civil rights organizations would have to be overthrown. But neither would happen without a revolutionary army.

To that end, RAM began the process of recruiting, particularly among black youth. To build a "guerilla youth force," RAM established the Black Guards, a paramilitary cadre. Recruiting young people who would be willing to die for the cause of black revolution was not easy. RAM activists trolled college campuses, seeking would-be revolutionists. In Chicago, RAM reached out to South and West Side gangs, hopeful that these "freedom fighters" would join the front line of struggle. But Chicago's gang leaders were volatile and lacked the discipline and revolutionary commitment that RAM desired. Attuned to the emerging black power sentiment in the Deep South, in 1965, Stanford spearheaded ill-fated efforts to establish northern chapters of the Deacons for Defense, a militant black patrol organization based in Bogalusa, Louisiana. Although the Deacons never established more than a few chapters northward, even baseball star Jackie Robinson, a moderate, expressed "real empathy for these brave and committed men of the South who have decided that the brutalities and killings of the Negro have gone unpunished too long." Still, RAM kept looking for soldiers. Stanford himself was arrested in May 1967 when Philadelphia police caught him spray-painting "Join the Black Guard" on the side of a building in a gang-ridden section of North Philadelphia.

RAM, like most black power organizations, found its most committed revolutionaries among disaffected members of the black middle class, those who had the time to attend its lengthy meetings, the discipline to follow its strictures, and the single-minded and intellectual commitment to its increasingly complex radical ideology. One of those revolutionaries was Herman Ferguson. By early 1964, Ferguson had grown increasingly frustrated at the failure of the Rochdale Movement to transform even his small corner of Queens. After months of protests and mass arrests at Rochdale Village, workplace discrimination persisted in New York's building trades. Even "Billy Banjo" remained untouched, his toothy grin, straw hat, and bare feet an ongoing affront to Ferguson. Ferguson also took heat from fellow civil rights activists who thought that his civil disobedience—including chaining himself to the crane—was too extreme. Ferguson felt that moderate civil rights organizations like the NAACP and CORE had let him down. By early 1964, however, more radical leaders and new organizations provided the Herman Fergusons of the North with alternatives to liberal integrationism.

Herman Ferguson and other members of the Revolutionary Action Movement were drawn powerfully to Malcolm X and by early 1964 had become key players in his inner circle. In early December 1963, Malcolm addressed the Rochdale Movement. The meeting came at a propitious time. It was one of his last speeches before he was silenced by the Nation of Islam. Over the course of the early 1960s, Elijah Muhammad had grown increasingly jealous of his charismatic protégé and his growing appeal among northern blacks. The dislike was mutual. Malcolm X grew disaffected with "the Messenger," who was plagued by a series of financial and personal scandals. Chafing at the Nation's proscription against participation in organized politics, Malcolm spoke out on civil rights— and in particular distanced himself vocally from Reverend King. Elijah Muhammad used the uproar surrounding Malcolm's statement that Kennedy's assassination was a matter of "the chickens coming home to roost" to suspend him from the Nation. In March 1964, Malcolm left the Nation, forming the Muslim Mosque in New York. After his trip to Mecca on hajj—the traditional Islamic pilgrimage to the holy city—Malcolm returned, his ideology in flux. Still a committed nationalist, he also began to distance himself from the antiwhite rhetoric that had infused Nation of Islam teachings. Working closely with other black radicals, in particular RAM, Malcolm formed the Organization of Afro-American Unity (OAAU) in June 1964.

Ferguson was never attracted to Islam, but he was drawn to Malcolm's assertive anti-integrationism and his rejection of nonviolence. Ferguson's militancy and his skills as an educator and administrator were useful to Malcolm. Ferguson became the chair of the OAAU's Education Committee and worked for Malcolm helping to develop a black curriculum with "original educational methods and procedures which will liberate the minds of our children from the vicious lies and distortions that are fed to us from the cradle to keep us mentally enslaved." The OAAU was still a fledgling organization with no more than a few dozen members when, on February 21, 1965, Malcolm addressed a gathering of activists at the Audubon Ballroom in upper Manhattan. Ferguson was sitting in the audience just a few rows from the stage when Malcolm, just beginning his speech, was shot dead. The assassination pushed Ferguson even further to the left. Convinced that Malcolm had been murdered by the federal government—not by the Nation of Islam members who were convicted of the crime—Ferguson hardened himself for the racial apocalypse. If white authorities had murdered Malcolm X, there was no guessing whom they might attack next.

Malcolm's assassination—coming at a moment when his political views were changing—led a wide variety of groups to lay claim to his memory. Len Holt, a radical black author, argued, "Black people must use Him. Black people need their heroes as desperately as white Americans needed the myth of a non-lying George Washington and a god in John F. Kennedy." No one took on a greater mythic status among black radicals. Activists of nearly every variety projected their vision of black America onto Malcolm's memory. Those most faithful to Malcolm's message repeated his call for black self-defense and made famous his "by any means necessary" argument for black liberation. However much Malcolm's politics shifted in 1964, he remained to the death a steadfast critic of nonviolence. Had he survived, they believed that he would have led blacks on a march toward revolution. Others interpreted Malcolm X as an apostle of black self-help. Had he survived, he would have led blacks from servitude to "their own salvation." Malcolm had left the Nation of Islam but never jettisoned its goal of creating black-run institutions, uncorrupted by white influence. Even integrationists, largely inspired by a few passages in Alex Haley's bestselling *The Autobiography of Malcolm X*, found a useful Malcolm. They focused on the Muslim leader's pilgrimage to Mecca in early

1964 and his discovery that not all white men were devils. Had he survived, he would have become the architect of an interracial movement of the poor. Leftists—most notably the Socialist Workers' Party, which played a more important role in publicizing Malcolm X's speeches than any other organization in the mid-1960s—held out the possibility that he would have been on the front lines of a black-led revolution against American capitalism that would have transcended traditional racial divisions. The very cacophony of memories of Malcolm, and the inchoate nature of his ideas, meant that there was no single "Malcolmist" movement. Malcolm's followers fragmented. His OAAU was too new and disorganized. It lacked a charismatic leader to fill Malcolm's shoes. As a result, Malcolm's uncompromising style—his ability to channel black rage—became his greatest legacy.

To a great extent, Malcolm was a blank screen on which activists of all varieties projected their visions of a new society. That was his power. It is doubtful that Malcolm was on the path toward integrationism. He had certainly not jettisoned his contempt for white power and its excesses, and however his views of whites might have changed, he was unlikely to find much of an interracial following. And about socialism, Malcolm remained cagey, even if he spoke regularly at the Socialist Workers' Pathfinder Forum and met with black leftists of all varieties. In an interview in the spring of 1964, when asked about socialism by a leftist-nationalist interviewer, he responded enigmatically. "Why speak of it? If you want someone to drink from a bottle, you never put the skull and crossbones on the label, for they won't drink. The same is true here." Of all the Malcolms who lived on, perhaps the most influential was the one eulogized by actor Ossie Davis. "Malcolm was our manhood, our living, black manhood." He was "a Prince—our own black shining Prince." The Malcolm who inhabited the imagination of countless black youths was not the strict preacher of the Nation of Islam or the cryptic socialist or the pilgrim to Mecca. He was Malcolm the man who unflinchingly stood up to whitey, refusing to turn his cheek. He was Malcolm the patron saint of the "long hot summers."

MALCOLM MAY HAVE been the most powerful icon of the black insurgency, but nothing gave the black radicals of the mid-1960s more hope than the escalation of unrest in northern cities, particularly clashes between young black men and the police. The proliferation of urban uprisings provided seemingly irrefutable evidence that the revolution was at hand. In the summer of 1964, black residents of Harlem; Rochester, New York; and Philadelphia took to the streets, looting and burning stores and battling their cities' mostly white police forces. The Harlem riot—the largest uprising in the North since World War II—grew out of protests after police shot James Powell, a black junior high school student. Civil rights groups, including the NAACP and CORE, led marches demanding that New York City investigate the shooting and reform the police department. But the protests moved fluidly from peaceful picketing to violent retaliation. On July 16, hundreds of "screaming youths" pelted police officers with bottles and cans in Manhattan's Yorkville neighborhood. The following day, two hundred teenagers took to the streets carrying signs that read "Save Us from Our Protectors" and "Stop Killer Cops." Two days later a demonstration over Powell's murder turned violent as thousands of angry teenagers took to the streets of Harlem, looting, burning, and attacking police officers. Over the next week, roving bands of youths and the police clashed throughout the city. The uprising followed a pattern that would become commonplace during the mid-1960s—beginning with a police incident, ending with angry crowds in the streets. No sooner did Harlem cool down than another riot erupted in Rochester, an escalation of the protests that had simmered throughout 1963. There, after police cracked down on civil rights protests at a local Kodak plant, angry demonstrators clashed with police on the streets, looted stores, and burned buildings. And at the end of August, the neighborhood around RAM headquarters in North Philadelphia erupted into three days of disorder after the arrest of a driver and rumors that police had killed a pregnant black woman.

Harlem, Philadelphia, and Rochester foreshadowed a series of long hot summers. In 1965, black residents of the Watts section of Los Angeles, and of Chicago, rioted; in 1966, black youths rose up in Cleveland and Chicago. Nineteen sixty-seven was the most combustible, with 163 uprisings, capped by deadly clashes between black residents of Newark and Detroit and the police, the National Guard, and the U.S. Army. In Newark, thirty-four people died in a weeklong uprising that laid waste to large parts of the city's Central Ward; in Detroit, forty-three people, three-quarters of them rioters, were killed. Millions of dollars of property was damaged by arson and looting. The following year, riots broke out again in dozens of cities in the aftermath of the assassination of Martin Luther King, Jr., on April 4. Sporadic uprisings marked the summers of 1968, 1969, and 1970. Particularly noteworthy was how widespread the riots were. The most visible were in big cities, but upheavals shook leafy suburbs, industrial towns, and small cities alike. Of the 163 uprisings in the summer of 1967, 45 percent occurred in cities with populations under 100,000 and 28 percent in cities with populations under 50,000. During July—the same month as the Newark and Detroit uprisings—riots broke out in places as diverse as Wyandanch and Nyack, New York; Massillon and Sandusky, Ohio; and Plainfield, Rahway, Livingston, Elizabeth, East Orange, Paterson, Irvington, Jersey City, and Montclair, New Jersey.

The form, scale, and duration of urban riots varied from place to place. Most of them did not result in fatalities. Only a handful of cities—notably Detroit, Newark, and Los Angeles—accounted for nearly all the deaths. And most of the casualties were the result of law enforcement actions against blacks, not black violence against the police or white bystanders. Although reports of rooftop snipers were pervasive, most black rioters were unarmed and most reports of sniping were greatly exaggerated. Most of the riots lasted for just an evening or a few days and resulted primarily in property damage or destruction.

For all their differences, 1960s riots had crucial commonalities. Rioters chose their targets carefully, and had just two: the police and shopkeepers. They seldom ventured into white neighborhoods and left most white-dominated institutions alone. They rarely looted segregated schools or attacked white churches. They did not march on corporate headquarters or break into office buildings, even though most northern downtowns were within easy reach. And they did not torch the factories that loomed over inner-city neighborhoods. They did not pillage sports arenas or stadiums, even when they abutted black business or residential districts. They left urban university buildings and hospitals—many of which had been built on the bulldozed ruins of black neighborhoods—intact. The offices of white-dominated trade unions, even those infamous for discrimination against blacks, stood mostly untouched. Terrified white urbanites barricaded their houses, stockpiled weapons, and girded for race war, but it did not come. Rioters seldom attacked private homes and, with few exceptions, left individual whites (other than law enforcement officials and shopkeepers) alone, even those who had the temerity to enter riot zones. In larger cities such as Detroit, some whites actually joined in looting, though they were greatly outnumbered by blacks. In every riot-torn city and town, the targets of violence were limited to stores and the police, although some private residences and institutions were destroyed through the collateral damage of arson.

Of all the underlying causes of rioting, nothing mattered more than police-community conflict. Nearly every riot in the 1960s—other than those following King's assassination—was sparked by a police incident, usually the arrest, injury, or alleged harassment of a black person by a police officer. Police brutality and the capriciousness of the criminal justice system had been a long-running complaint among blacks. From slave patrols to lynchings, from the framing of the Scottsboro Boys for rape in the 1930s to the police dog attacks on civil rights protestors in Birmingham in 1963, American blacks have had a deeply vexed relationship with law enforcement officials.

By the early 1960s, complaints about the police had reached crisis proportions. Much to the surprise of members of the U.S. Commission on Civil Rights, which conducted hearings in northern cities between 1959 and 1961, black complaints about police conduct were as frequent as or more than those about unemployment, housing, and education. The combination of personal experience and media images fueled a deep sense of outrage at the police. Since World War II and the "We Charge Genocide" manifesto, civil rights activists had targeted police brutality, but they stepped up their scrutiny when protestors in northern cities clashed with police officers at construction sites, schools, and city halls. Black orators and writers from Malcolm X (speaking from experience) to James Baldwin denounced police tactics. In 1962, Baldwin described the tensions that pervaded police-community relations. "The only way to police a ghetto is oppressive. None of the Police Commissioner's men, even with the best will in the world, have any way of understanding the lives led by the people; they swagger about in twos and threes patrolling. Their very presence is an insult, and it would be, even if they spent their entire day feeding gumdrops to children." The National Advisory Commission on Civil Disorders (also known as the Kerner Commission for its chair, Illinois governor Otto Kerner), established by President Lyndon Johnson to investigate urban unrest, described the intense animosity between blacks and the police. "To many Negroes police have come to symbolize white power, white racism, and white repression."

The black press played an important role in highlighting the problem of police brutality. "Without such cases to report," wrote Louis Lomax, "Negro newspapers would have considerable blank space." When police arrested and beat Guinea's deputy ambassador to the United Nations after a routine traffic stop in 1961, *The Pittsburgh Courier* covered the incident on its front page. Members of the African diplomatic corps complained about being stopped and searched by the police as they tried to enter their "white" apartment buildings. New York, they charged, was a "Jim Crow town." In 1962, the *Amsterdam News* offered a chilling report about the beating of Marshall Whitehead, a "prominent designing engineer" who had just been photographed for a magazine story on the Emancipation Proclamation centennial. After he was stopped, searched, and "slugged" by four police officers when he was out for a run, Whitehead went to his local precinct on New York's Upper West Side to file a complaint. After a fruitless meeting with the head detective, Whitehead encountered the four officers coming in from duty. "We'll give you something to complain about," one of the officers shouted before taking Whitehead to the station basement, beating him, and charging him with resisting arrest. The charges were later dropped. The lesson was clear: If the police harassed black diplomats and celebrities, they would have no compunctions about busting the heads of ordinary black folks. In 1965, *The Chicago Defender* ran a front-page story reporting that the city police department routinely strip-searched all women in police custody. The mother of three high school girls arrested at a civil rights demonstration complained that during their strip search, the investigating officer called them "tramps" and "junkies." The moral of the story was that the police even lacked the sensitivity to treat women with respect.

But of all the well-publicized cases of police brutality, nothing compared to the extensive coverage, both in newspapers and on television, of the role of southern law enforcement officials in resisting civil rights. The arrests of Martin Luther King, Jr., and other black ministers received extensive coverage in both the black and white press, as did arrests, beatings, and police malfeasance involving southern civil rights protestors. Northern black editorialists denounced the mockery of law and order throughout the South, where police officers actively defended Jim Crow.

In 1960, blacks reacted with outrage when white police officers hauled peaceful sit-in protestors in Greensboro, Nashville, and Atlanta into paddy wagons—while their white assailants walked away free. They were appalled by the horrific news from Anniston, Alabama, in 1961, when a state police escort left unattended the Trailways bus that carried the interracial Freedom Riders just in time for an angry white mob to surround the bus, light it on fire, and savagely beat them as they fled the smoke and flames. And they rallied against the Birmingham police's vicious attacks on children marching for civil rights in 1963. Assistant U.S. attorney general Burke Marshall worried about the cumulative impact of media coverage of southern atrocities. "The Negro mass in the North doesn't see anything but the dogs and hoses. It's all the white cops."

Televised images of brutality in the South resonated with northern blacks because they confirmed already deeply rooted and well-grounded suspicions of the police. As northern black populations skyrocketed and urban police departments remained nearly all white, collisions between young black men and the police became commonplace. At the end of World War II, most northern police departments had few, if any, black officers. Most northern urban police officers came from working-class backgrounds, lived in central cities because of residency requirements, and often lived in neighborhoods threatened by black migration. Most police officers shared white resentment toward black newcomers. Fueling the resentment—especially for those who patrolled black neighborhoods—was their encounter with black criminals. Throughout the North, black neighborhoods were often coterminous with "vice" districts. Marginalized in urban economies, many poor and working-class blacks depended on illicit activities as a matter of survival. Gambling, numbers running, and prostitution—all vices that drew a white clientele, as well as blacks—flourished in black business districts. And in the North, violent clashes between white police officers and black men accounted for a large percentage of interracial homicides. For many white police officers whose only significant encounters with blacks were those involved in the illegal economy, it was easy to assume that all blacks had criminal proclivities. "In the mind of the 'quick trigger' policeman is the fear of the 'bad nigger.'"

The scarcity of black police officers played a crucial role in shaping white officers' attitudes and in delegitimating law enforcement authority in the eyes of blacks. Perhaps the biggest problem facing northern police departments, especially in cities with large black populations, was the paucity of black police officers. The fact that northern police departments were nearly all white through the early 1960s did little to inspire blacks' confidence in their unbiased enforcement of the law. For much of the twentieth century, police departments had operated like a guild. They tended to hire through personal references or, in cities with political machines, on the recommendation of ward bosses. By the 1950s and 1960s, many police departments professionalized, eliminated residency requirements, and recruited in suburbs and small towns, attracting mostly white applicants. The result was a racial gap. Whites policed black neighborhoods, but few, if any, socialized with blacks, lived in their neighborhoods, or attended their churches and schools.

Police departments remained white bastions throughout the 1960s. When rioting erupted in Los Angeles in 1965, only 3.5 percent of the police force was black in a city whose population was 16.5 percent black. In New York City, where police-community tensions were high, nearly one in four city residents but only one in twenty police officers was black. Detroit, a city that was close to 40 percent black, had a force that was only 5 percent black. Even in Chicago, where black machine politicians had helped open the city's police force, only 17 percent of officers were black, compared to 27 percent of the population. Racial integration of northern police departments proceeded painfully slowly. "Colored citizens cannot be expected to be treated fairly by the average white policeman," wrote a columnist for *The Afro-American.* "If the policeman has a background that is all lily-white and anti-black, he should not be allowed to stalk up and down the streets in colored neighborhoods."

In a male-dominated, all-white culture, police officers felt few checks on their overt expression of racist sentiments. In Plainfield, New Jersey, where more than a third of the population was black by 1967, only five of the town's eighty-one law enforcement officers were black. Clashes between white police officers and angry black youths were commonplace in the town's black West End by the mid-1960s. In 1966, Plainfield's police department came under investigation after reports that police officers and radio dispatchers regularly used the word "nigger" to describe suspects over the police radio. In the eyes of many white police officers, the line between "nigger" and criminal was a thin one. In Detroit, where police-community relations were particularly tense, a federal study conducted just before the riot discovered that 45 percent of white police officers who patrolled in the city's black neighborhoods were "extremely anti-Negro" and another 34 percent were "prejudiced."

Only a minority of blacks had directly experienced harassment by the police, but many more believed that it was a problem in their communities. Police violence was the least common, if most publicized, of events: Only 7 percent of black men surveyed by the Kerner Commission reported that they had been "rough[ed] up unnecessarily" by police officers, but more than a third believed that it happened to people in their neighborhoods. Police "stop and frisk" tactics were more common. More than one in five black men reported they had been stopped and searched "without good reason." And about one in five claimed that police officers had used "insulting language" toward them. Young people were particularly prone to believe that police harassment was common in their communities and were more likely than older people to have had negative experiences with police officers. The omnipresent fear of police violence and harassment—even if it did not affect a majority of blacks—had a corrosive effect. Young black men regularly complained that police scrutinized them closely without cause, even if they were not stopped, searched, or beaten. "Police? They bugs me," black San Franciscan Larry Dillard told an interviewer in 1968. "Like if you standing on a corner, they'll slow down and look at you a long time. I'm not doing a thing. Just standing there. He might hang a U-turn and come back up. It ain't their job to look at me." The distrust of police was widespread. Louis Lomax, who lived in a racially mixed section of Queens, reported that he had been pulled over four times in 1960 and 1961. He used his press card to deflect the police. "I don't know of a single Negro who doesn't get a flutter in his stomach when approached by a white policeman. Anything can happen; sometimes it does."

Young men were also the most likely to congregate in the public places that made them targets for police action. Unemployed urban black men, who often moved fluidly into and out of the illegal urban economy, held the deepest grievances against the police. The Kerner Commission wrote that "ghetto youths, often without work, and with homes that may be nearly uninhabitable, particularly in the summer, commonly spend much time on the street." A common police practice was to break up street corner gatherings of young black people, day or night. The clash of young men and police officers became occasions for both sides to exchange insults and, often, blows. Even the most routine encounters were tinged with masculine put-downs. Police officers regularly referred to black men as "boys," denying their masculinity by using a derogatory term dating to slavery. Police officers chafed at the "attitude" of young black men and often struck back with epithets like *nigger, monkey,* and *punk* (a term that, in the 1960s, had homosexual connotations). Blacks regularly complained that police used "foul language." Such affronts could not go unmet by the code of the streets. "Right now," Cleveland activist Harold Sampson told an interviewer in 1968, "the younger black is equating defiance of authority with a show of masculinity. And the authority is best represented by the police." Sampson reported that "if this cat [a police officer] pushes him, he's gonna let him know, 'I'm a man.'"

Rumors played a crucial role in sparking and spreading riots, as they had in uprisings and rebellions in the past. In situations of imperfect information, profound distrust, and an asymmetry of power, rumors provided seemingly plausible explanations of troubling events. Rumors traveled quickly. "Everywhere the telephone provided a direct link to the scenes of violence," reported the Kerner Commission. "The telephoned messages frequently were at variance with reports transmitted by the mass media." Phones carried accurate, frontline accounts of rioting, but in the heat of the moment, it was difficult to distinguish between eyewitness reports and secondhand stories, between experience, hearsay, and falsehood. Rumors served several purposes: They gave meaning to otherwise inexplicable events, they justified anger and rage, and they served as a call to arms. What made rumors particularly effective was their relationship to plausible fears, mainly of police brutality. Especially common were rumors about police mistreatment of women or children—a seeming confirmation of the outrageousness of police behavior and a justification to take to the streets. Allegations of police harassment of women challenged black manhood: Men should—indeed must—protect their women.

In every city where riots broke out, looting was widespread. Rioters raided and burned shops, stores, and restaurants, especially those with a reputation of gouging their black customers. In the view of many rioters, looting was a combination of retribution and redistribution. In Philadelphia, one looter shouted out to Cecil Moore (who futilely attempted to stop the riot): "Listen, man, this is the only time in my life I've got a chance to get these things." In Los Angeles, a teenage rioter described his motivation: "We just wanted to make the white man suffer as we have." In Newark, one witness to the riots (speaking to a reporter in a local bar) argued, "I don't understand all this talk about 'looting.' They rob us every day. They rob us on the rent! They rob us on food, on the job! They rob our kids on education! *Everything!* What in hell do they expect?" In Plainfield, New Jersey, a journalist reported a conversation between two looters carrying a purloined TV: "That set had a tag on it for a thousand dollars / Yeah, but you know the white man always jacks up the price." To be sure, some rioters were opportunistic: One Plainfield teenager confessed that he and his friends were "just a group of kids who liked to steal if they wanted something and they did and that was the cause of the problem." Indeed, the most conspicuously looted item in Plainfield was liquor—more than three hundred pints of alcohol were stolen during the riot.

Rioters targeted nearly every type of store. A list of looted Detroit businesses, compiled by the police department, made the range clear. Hardest hit were grocery stores—262 were looted. Establishments that sold alcoholic beverages were also prominent targets: eighty-five bars, liquor stores, and party stores were pillaged. A panoply of small neighborhood businesses were gutted: eighty-five drug stores; seventy-one dry cleaners and laundries; seventy-one clothing stores; and forty-nine furniture and department stores.

Even opportunistic rioters generally left black-owned businesses alone. In the two largest riots, Newark and Detroit, businesses posted "Soul Brother" signs on storefronts to deter looters—and for the most part succeeded, although in both cities and elsewhere, prominent black-owned businesses were not unscathed. In Detroit, looters ransacked Barthwell's Drug Store, one of the city's most prominent black-owned businesses; firebombed the Drome Show Bar (forcing singer Diahann Carroll to cancel her gig there); and stole fifty thousand dollars in clothing, musical instruments, and cash from the Motown group the Temptations. Newark looters pillaged a well-known black real estate agency. In Cambridge, Maryland, black businessman Hensel Green committed suicide after arsonists destroyed his motel, bar, and nightclub. Still, the overwhelming majority of businesses attacked during the northern riots were white-owned.

The riots flummoxed liberals, outraged conservatives, and thrilled radicals. The terms that commentators chose—"civil disorder," "disturbance," "riot," "rebellion," "uprising"—signaled their position on the meaning of the events. "Civil disorder" suggested a breakdown of civil society, and was a social scientific term, ostensibly neutral, to describe the lack of law and order on urban streets. "Disturbance" suggested a disruption of an otherwise tranquil state of affairs, like a thunderclap in the middle of the night or a barroom brawl, something anomalous and troubling. "Riot" was the most commonly used, an ancient word describing a seemingly senseless, inarticulate expression of violence or rage—one that observers continued to use because of its imprecision and its association with mobs and irrationality. "Uprising" was the least used but perhaps most accurate term: It suggested a spontaneous upsurge of protest or violent expression of discontent, something with political content, but short of a full-fledged revolutionary act. At the left end of the political spectrum, "rebellion" described a deliberate insurgency against an illegitimate regime, an act of political resistance with the intent of destabilizing or overturning the status quo. Depending on the observer and the participant all these terms captured elements of what was going on in the urban North—and probably more about the vantage point of the person using the term. But whatever term they used, nearly every observer—black and white; conservative, liberal or leftist; grassroots participant or law enforcement official; civil rights leader or alienated youth—believed that the long hot summers were, to some extent, acts of resistance. They disagreed on how to interpret them.

MANY BLACK LEFTISTS interpreted the urban riots as protorevolutionary or revolutionary struggles. For their part, many whites, particularly law enforcement officers and elected officials, took black radicals at their word. They viewed the riots as products of a conspiracy, hatched by cells of black militants who hoped for nothing short of overthrowing the white power structure. But there was little evidence that the urban rebellions of the 1960s were planned, coordinated, and controlled. What was most striking about the long hot summers was not their coordination or coherence. Their very spontaneity convinced many leftists that they were man-ifestations of a popular—if still undeveloped—revolutionary conscious-ness. As Watts burned in August 1965, Max Stanford declared that "a guerilla war" had erupted. Thrilled at the revolutionary moment, he wrote: "One group of Freedom Fighters would drive through the liber-ated areas hurling objects through plate glass windows, and then they would set the stores afire. A Reparations Detachment would usually be on hand to claim any material goods which could be carried to the homes of the revolutionaries." Not all leftists shared the purposive interpretation. Richard Price and Rob Stewart, community activists in Watts, argued that the "masses were rebelling *against* something (i.e. police brutality, unem-ployment, and white domination in general) but it was not a rebellion *for* something." In the aftermath of violence in Detroit and Newark, H. Rap Brown (who was charged for inciting a riot in Cambridge, Maryland) de-clared that the "rebellions are but a dress rehearsal for real revolution." Revolutionists of many stripes saw the uprisings as evidence that blacks were prepared to stand up to "the Man," a sign of "revolutionary con-sciousness," but argued that it would take disciplined leadership to lead the masses into an all-out war on racist, imperialist "Ameri-KKK-a."

As the cities burned, would-be revolutionaries hunkered down for what they believed was the inevitable war between the races. In Queens, Herman Ferguson helped established the Jamaica Rifle and Pistol Club and trained young blacks in the art of self-defense while honing their skills for the impending black revolution. (Similar rifle clubs, which RAM saw as revolutionary cells and which Malcolm X had prominently sup-ported, sprang up through the North; some, like Ferguson's, were char-tered by the National Rifle Association.) "'We have to learn to fight,'" fellow activist Yuri Kochiyama recalled Ferguson arguing. "'I don't mean just with words.'" Sometimes the recourse to weapons was symbolic. In postriot Detroit, members of the radical City-Wide Citizens' Action Com-mittee wore "50mm rifle bullets attached to leather thongs around their necks," which they called "devil chasers." But just as often they were real.

RAM's revolutionary rhetoric—and its clandestine preparations for race war—attracted the attention of the FBI and local police depart-ments, which monitored it closely. FBI offices in New York, Chicago, De-troit, Philadelphia, and Cincinnati all gathered extensive information about Stanford and his associates, through surveillance, the reports of unnamed informants, and interviews with RAM activists, including Stanford himself. The FBI files on RAM are a reminder of the limitations of federal surveillance: Agents relied on rumors, unsubstantiated claims, and widely available published sources, particularly newspaper accounts. Covert operators often parroted back information that was part of the public record or proffered ludicrous, unverifiable opinions. One informant, reporting on a small RAM meeting in May 1965, recounted that Stanford "played a leading role in this conference," hardly news to anyone familiar with the organization, and went on to offer the insupportable opinion that Stanford "believed himself to be some kind of a God." Many reports simply stated the obvious: "RAM is entirely non-white in membership, clandestine in nature," and so on.

Even if FBI memos were often uninformative and tedious, they gave life to rumors, which spread as quickly among credulous police officers as had stories of police malfeasance among rioters. In the ears of law enforcement officials, rumors often had devastating, even deadly consequences. Unattuned to the black rage simmering in inner cities and provoked by radicals who took credit for the violence, executive branch officials viewed urban riots as part of a coordinated effort—aided by Communists, racial separatists, and maybe even America's international enemies—to start a revolution. FBI director J. Edgar Hoover argued that the American Communist Party and its "tailor made" partners in the black power movement "created a climate of unrest and has come to mean to many Negroes the 'power' to riot, burn, loot and kill." Stemming urban unrest meant curbing dangerous radical organizations such as RAM. A July 1965 memo reported that "STANFORD told of having an 'assassination list' which includes leaders of the 'non-violent' civil rights groups and leaders of the 'far right.'" Whether such a list actually existed (or whether it was the product of agents provocateurs or faulty intelligence, as were many such plots), it fueled law enforcement officials' sense of urgency. For his part, Cleveland police chief Richard Wagner publicly warned that RAM planned to "overthrow the Government of the United States and, incidentally, shoot all the Caucasians." Law enforcement officials were every bit as convinced as black revolutionaries themselves that the apocalypse was imminent.

.   .   .

ONE YOUNG ACTIVIST who found inspiration in RAM was Stokely Carmichael. A Jamaican-born New Yorker, the young Carmichael had participated with CORE in the 1961 Freedom Rides and had quickly risen to a leadership position in the SNCC. Working in the Deep South, Carmichael and fellow SNCC members grew increasingly disaffected at persistent white resistance, critical of the tactics of nonviolence, and skeptical about the possibility of interracialism. The passage of the Civil Rights Act of 1964 had weakened some of the underpinnings of Jim Crow, particularly segregated public accommodations, but blacks remained trapped in mediocre jobs, run-down housing, and second-class schools. Since 1964, RAM activists had worked with the SNCC in the South and found there a receptive audience for their call for self-defense and their denunciation of imperialism. And young SNCC members debated articles on self-defense by Stanford and Williams.

By 1966, some SNCC activists had started using the phrase "black power" as they searched for alternatives to the nonviolent freedom struggle. In June 1966, at a rally in Greenwood, Mississippi, Carmichael uttered the two words that named the swirling, inchoate impulses that animated the black rebellions of the mid-1960s. "The only way we are gonna stop them white men from whuppin' us is to take over. We been saying freedom for six years and we got nothing. What we are gonna start saying," he shouted, "is Black Power." No phrase seemed to better capture the insurgency that was roiling through black America. Carmichael provided a potent catchphrase to describe the increasingly militant combination of self-defense, self-determination, and separatism that was reshaping the black freedom struggle. Reflecting on the firestorm that his speech fueled, Carmichael was modest. "We certainly did not change the entire direction of the black movement or the attitudes of black America merely by combining two simple words at a rally in Greenwood, Mississippi. That's silly and absurd." Indeed, no one who had spent any time at Harlem's Speakers' Corner or in the pews at Detroit's Central Congregational Church or on picket lines in front of Chicago's public schools or Rochdale Village would have found Carmichael's speech exceptional.

Carmichael's two words captured both the thrill and the terror that many observers felt in 1966. Whether it was organized revolutionary groups like RAM or unorganized rioters and looters, insurgencies seemed to be subverting the civil rights movement, undermining liberalism, and remaking the North. The term "black power" was certainly more compelling than "Negro Revolt," which seemed terribly dated by 1966. By the mid-1960s, radicals were jettisoning the term *Negro*—which Malcolm X and others mocked as an emblem of white supremacy—in favor of *black*. And the word *power* suggested that the struggle in the mid-1960s was more than just a reformist effort to tinker with the status quo; it was a battle for control of key American political and economic institutions.

Black power was not a new phenomenon; it named an impulse that reflected the richness, complexity, and contradictions of black political thought. Overlooked in the sensationalistic accounts of black power were its roots in a long-running black self-help tradition, its relationship to the deep current of black anti-imperialism that dated to the 1930s and 1940s, and its appropriation of elements of postwar racial liberalism, particularly psychological understandings of racial inequality. Black power lumped together widely disparate social movements and ideologies and, as a descriptive term, effaced the profound political, social, and cultural differences among black activists. In popular parlance, black power became a synonym for all varieties of black militancy, even when they varied enormously. Finally, news coverage of black power exaggerated its institutional strength while downplaying some of its most influential manifestations.

The news media "frame" stories—they choose what to cover, what is worthy of emphasis, and how to present it. Novelty and conflict, particularly violence, are powerful factors in the framing of news stories. Black power, however complicated, ideologically diverse, and inchoate, provided a powerful new narrative. It gave new meaning to some of the oldest stereotypes about black male violence. It played to whites' deepest fears. It provided titillating headlines at a moment in American history when observers across the political spectrum believed that revolution or civil war was imminent. What better copy than vocal denunciations of "honkies" and of "the pigs" and of "racist, imperialist" America? What better film footage than black men in black leather jackets and berets marching to chants of "Get whitey"? Some commentators were cynical about the media's fixation on black power. *Afro-American* columnist Ralph Matthews argued that black power was a creation of the white press, necessary to "scare the daylights out of the white world." Matthews downplayed the indigenous origins of black power and the fact that many activists welcomed the publicity, and the more inflammatory the better. But he was right that black power was irresistible to the mainstream media. Gil Jonas, a publicist for the NAACP, struggled mightily to book talk show gigs for NAACP executive Roy Wilkins, but TV producers had little interest in reasonable-sounding, respectable black "moderates" when they could interview black militants instead. Black revolutionaries made for "good TV." Conflict sold.

In the summer of 1966, *black power* became a flashpoint for debate, because of its evocative challenge to nonviolence, but even more because of its theoretical imprecision. Black activists, both locally and nationally, struggled to define the term. Was black power a movement? Was it a political party? Was it a tendency? Was it a mood? Was it revolutionary? Was it racist? Was it a cultural expression? What did it mean? What implications would it have for the black freedom struggle? In the mid-1960s, *black power* had nearly as many definitions as it did adherents.

Leading civil rights activists—already fearful that their work for racial equality would be undermined by groups that spouted Marxist rhetoric, rejected integrationism, and called for violence—swiftly denounced black power. Railing against Carmichael, Roy Wilkins sneered that "SNCC has formally chosen a racist course, that is, black racist." "Black separatism is black group suicide," he continued. At its 1966 annual meeting, the National Baptist Convention, the largest black religious conclave in the country, denounced black power as "the other side of the old coin of segregation," which "renders the people who use it guilty of the same type of prejudicial thinking and feeling that they have so long condemned in white segregationists alone." In a "manifesto" titled "Crisis and Commitment," prominently published in *The New York Times* in October 1966, a diverse group of established black leaders, among them Dorothy Height, A. Philip Randolph, Bayard Rustin, Roy Wilkins, Whitney Young, Amos Hall (executive secretary of the Prince Hall Masons), and Hobson Reynolds (head of the black Elks Club), defended the ideal of racial integration and repudiated violence as a vehicle for social change. One notable name missing from the list was Martin Luther King, Jr., who agreed with much of the statement but who did not want to "excommunicate" anyone from the civil rights movement.

Not all civil rights activists were sour on black power. James Farmer, long an advocate of interracial activism, had resigned from CORE in

March 1966, in the midst of that organization's turn to black separatism, but nonetheless saw the utility of the new militancy. The rhetoric of black power, he believed, could "force the nation to see the sensitivity of the poor." New York's Adam Clayton Powell, Jr., one of six black members of Congress, issued "My Black Position Paper" in June 1966. In it, Powell offered a pluralistic definition of black power—one that would, in various forms, find a large number of adherents. "Other ethnic groups lead their own organizations. We must do the same." To that end, blacks needed to demand a "proportionate share of political jobs and appointments . . . equal to their proportion in the electorate." And "black communities must insist on black leaders living amongst them, knowing and sharing the harsh truths of the ghetto." In September, Powell convened a black power summit, calling together more than one hundred leaders from around the country, to bring "this new breed of cats" into a movement. Powell supported self-defense but repudiated revolutionary violence.

Floyd McKissick, who led CORE away from its pacifist roots, made the case powerfully at CORE's 1966 annual meeting. "The cup is running over in the ghetto, and when it runs over, we're not going to start condemning anyone. We're tired of condemning our own people when they start to fight back." Self-defense supplanted peaceful protest. "There is no possible return to non-violence," he argued. "It is inevitable that violence will occur." James Williams, an *Afro-American* columnist, lauded black power advocates like McKissick for "turning away from a slavish dedication to non-violence at all costs," and celebrated CORE for having "accurately placed its finger on the throbbing pulse of many colored persons. . . . The non-violent movement, while it held the admiration of the masses, never held their hearts enthralled."

Coming, as it did, after a several-year resurgence of black organizational militancy in the North, black power set off a scramble among black activists. Established black militant groups and a staggering array of new organizations that burst onto the scene throughout 1966 and 1967 claimed the mantle of "black power" and struggled to be its spokesmen locally, nationally, and internationally. Local organizations jockeyed to establish themselves as "the" black power group. Ambitious local leaders tried to position themselves as the authentic voice of the new movement. Black radicalism in the North, recalled Carmichael, had "no clear, solid center . . . no single accepted community of leadership and resistance you could identify." Rushing to fill the gap were "all kinds and varieties of militant groups, frequently armed and competing . . . popping up like mushrooms."

An instant celebrity, Carmichael spent most of the summer and fall of 1966 on a speaking tour as the prophet of black power. He found particularly attentive audiences in the urban North—and quickly came to realize that the future of his movement was in the inner cities. In August, he met with both RAM and the Nation of Islam and, with Max Stanford, announced the creation of the North's first—and short-lived—Black Panther Party (taking its name from one that SNCC helped establish in Lowndes County, Alabama). At a September meeting at the Devil's Inn, a dance hall on 158th Street in Harlem (just a few blocks from the Audubon Ballroom), Stanford and a panel of five activists presented the party's platform (Carmichael, languishing in an Atlanta jail, could not attend). The somber audience, coiffed in "the Afro hair style" and dressed in "African-inspired clothing," listened to Stanford while men "clad in black uniforms bearing shoulder patches containing the party's clawing black panther" stood guard. The party challenged the "racist political system," called for the creation of "liberation schools" (one of Ferguson's pet projects), and urged members to take up arms in self-defense.

Stanford and Carmichael's New York party never really gelled. Stanford remained committed to RAM's strategy of organizing underground. Carmichael, by contrast, moved into the camera's glare on a four-month overseas trip, following Robert Williams to Havana and China. He then visited Vietnam and Guinea, positioning his version of black power in an international context. However, Carmichael remained ambivalent about communism and socialism, unlike RAM. Increasingly, he embraced a black internationalism, shorn of its Marxism, which emphasized the common denominator of blackness. Derisively nicknamed "Stokely Starmichael" by his grassroots critics, Carmichael did not transfer his charisma into grassroots organizing. He became black power's best-known publicist, but not its most important practitioner. Regardless of its leaders' travails, activists in places as diverse as Oakland, Chicago, Indianapolis, and Detroit, as well as Paterson, New Jersey; Des Moines, Iowa; and Wichita, Kansas, formed their own Black Panther organizations.

Of the post-1966 black power groups, the most influential was the Black Panther Party for Self-Defense, founded in October 1966 in Oakland by Bobby Seale and Huey Newton. Drawing from the same Marxist fount that had sustained Williams and RAM (Seale had been affiliated with RAM for two years by 1966) and deeply influenced by the example of Malcolm X, the Panthers announced a "ten point program":

1. WE WANT FREEDOM. WE WANT POWER TO DETERMINE THE DESTINY OF OUR BLACK COMMUNITY.
2. WE WANT FULL EMPLOYMENT FOR OUR PEOPLE.
3. WE WANT AN END TO THE ROBBERY BY THE CAPITALISTS OF OUR BLACK COMMUNITY.
4. WE WANT DECENT HOUSING FIT FOR SHELTER OF HUMAN BEINGS.
5. WE WANT EDUCATION FOR OUR PEOPLE THAT EXPOSES THE NATURE OF THIS DECADENT SOCIETY. . . .
6. WE WANT ALL BLACK MEN EXEMPT FROM MILITARY SERVICE.
7. WE WANT AN IMMEDIATE END TO POLICE BRUTALITY AND MURDER OF BLACK PEOPLE.
8. WE WANT FREEDOM FOR ALL BLACK MEN HELD IN FEDERAL, STATE, COUNTY AND CITY PRISONS OR JAILS.
9. WE WANT ALL BLACK MEN . . . TO BE TRIED BY A JURY OF THEIR PEER GROUP OR PEOPLE FROM THEIR BLACK COMMU- NITIES AS DEFINED BY THE CONSTITUTION OF THE U.S.
10. WE WANT LAND, BREAD, HOUSING, EDUCATION, CLOTHING, JUSTICE AND PEACE; AS OUR MAJOR POLITICAL OBJECTIVE WE WANT A UNITED NATIONS–SUPERVISED PLEBISCITE TO BE HELD THROUGHOUT THE BLACK COLONY IN WHICH ONLY BLACK COLONIAL SUBJECTS WILL BE ALLOWED TO PARTICI- PATE FOR THE PURPOSE OF DETERMINING THE WILL OF BLACK PEOPLE AS OF THEIR NATIONAL DESTINY.

Much of the Panther platform recycled ideas that were widely held among black liberals and leftists. The call for "full employment" had been part of the labor–civil rights agenda of the 1940s and remained a key el- ement of Democratic Party politics. The demand for "decent housing" echoed FDR's Second Bill of Rights. And the nod to the U.S. Constitu- tion and to the United Nations was a reminder that for all their revolution- ary rhetoric, the Panthers were affiliating themselves with mainstream political institutions. But when the Panthers demanded black self-determination and identified their location in a "black colony," they drew from the tradition of black anticolonialism that hearkened back to the National Negro Congress. In denouncing "this decadent society," they riffed off themes that Malcolm X had articulated so forcefully. And by demanding an end to the "robbery" of black communities by "capitalists," they echoed RAM's critique of exploitation.

What was new about the Panthers, however, was their singular focus on the criminal justice system. To be sure, black activists had long protested police brutality. But the Panthers offered the most systematic critique of police power and the legal system since the authors of *We Charge Genocide.* They saw the police as agents of racial oppression, demanded the immediate release of black men in prison, and pushed conventional notions of trial by a jury of peers to specify the selection of jurors from "the black community." While capitalism and the "decadent society" remained the Panthers' rhetorical targets, in practice they chose to focus on "police brutality" and the "murder of black people." By drawing attention to the "pigs" in a way that no other activist group had, the Panthers struck a raw nerve in black America at a moment of rebellion in the streets.

"What is a pig?" wrote an anonymous writer in *The Black Panther,* the party's incendiary newspaper. The answer summarized the power of the metaphor: "A low natured beast that has no regard for law, justice or the rights of the people; a creature that bites the hand that feeds it; a foul depraved traducer, usually found masquerading as the victim of an unprovoked attack." Filthy, bloated, alternatively snarling and weeping, and always swarming with flies, pigs appeared in Panther prose, poetry, illustrations, and even a children's coloring book. Minister of Culture Emory Douglas, a soft-spoken revolutionary whose pen was sharper than his tongue, drew graphic cartoons in nearly every issue of *The Black Panther* depicting pigs being shot, beaten, stabbed, dynamited, strangled, and hanged. "This is revolutionary art," he wrote, "pigs lying in the alleyways of the colony, dead with their eyes gouged out—autopsy showing cause of death: 'They fail to see that majority rules.'" For the Panthers, the category of pig was capacious—it did not simply include police officers but rather encompassed the "power structure" broadly defined. What made the metaphor of the pig so powerful was its play on long-running cultural ambivalences about pigs. Poor blacks had long relied on pigs as food—

rooting pigs were a commonplace feature in the landscape of southern farms and northern urban backyards alike. As ubiquitous a feature as they were in black vernacular landscapes, pigs lived in unsanitary conditions, making them a symbol of filth and depravity. Their pinkish pigment—so much like the skin coloration of "whites"—gave visual resonance to the image. And, given the taboo against pork in the Nation of Islam, the Panthers' anthropomorphic pigs resonated even more widely.

Panther cartoons depicted such powerful political figures as Richard Nixon, Hubert Humphrey, and George Wallace as pigs. In one cartoon, liberal Democrat Eugene McCarthy removed a mask to reveal his porcine visage. They showed the Soviet Union and the United States as pigs. The pig could also stand in for abstract concepts such as "thug capitalism" and "political thievery." "Imperialism" appeared as an enormous pig. Black "Uncle Toms" appeared as sycophants groveling at the feet of pigs, quivering in their presence, and licking their feet. And the "avaricious" black bourgeoisie appeared with a porcine mien. Even Santa Claus appeared as a red-clad pig coming out of the chimney to be greeted by a mother ready to club him with a Christmas tree and a father and his young son with their guns pointed at his head.

Of all the Panther slogans, the most viscerally appealing was "Off the pigs"—a term that came to refer mainly to the police. Law enforcement officials were a natural and appealing target for the Panthers and their young male recruits. In a dramatic act of protest that launched the obscure Oakland group into international prominence, the Panthers, bearing rifles, marched into the California capitol in a May 1967 confrontation with authorities cloaked as the Second Amendment's "well-regulated militia" with its "right to bear arms." Throughout the late 1960s, heavily armed Panthers carried out police patrols in Oakland. Huey Newton, David Hilliard, and other Panthers piled into their cars and trailed the "pigs," ready to defend blacks against police brutality. The Panthers' emphasis on armed resistance, with a strong emphasis on masculine power through violence, became their trademark.

French writer Jean Genet, reflecting on his several-week sojourn with the Panthers in 1970, aptly described their power. "Wherever they went, the Americans were the masters, so the Panthers would do their best to terrorize the masters by the only means available to them. Spectacle." A cadre of black power activists realized that the local and national news outlets, both black and white, could be a powerful ally in conveying their spectacular message to a wide audience. Without deprecating the seriousness of the issues that they addressed—police brutality, American intervention in the third world, black poverty—the pages of *The Black Panther,* particularly in the organization's first two years, were full of hyperbole. Cartoons depicting small children learning to use firearms appeared beside outrageously inflammatory articles intended to provoke more than to inform. In many respects, Panther publications were the journalistic equivalent of the "dozens," a game of ever-escalating insults—but in this case, insults directed with the implication of deadly violence toward whites and their black "sycophants." At the peak of the black power movement, linguist William Stewart, a sympathetic observer, argued that militant language "is a dramatization," a "type of rhetoric" deeply rooted in black culture. "When they tell a crowd to go burn the honkies out," argued Stewart, "they don't expect the threat to be taken literally and are surprised when it is." *The Black Panther*'s editor offered a similar view of the anti-pig language as "rhetorical" for the purposes of "letting off steam."

Black Panther politics were tailor-made for the mass media. The television news was the ideal stage for the performance of black power—and it gave viewers the impression that the Panthers were more numerous and influential than they actually were. Panther police patrols purveyed images of dangerous black masculinity that stood in sharp contrast to the prayerful, nonviolent civil rights protests that had, for a decade, dominated news coverage of the southern freedom struggle. The Panthers were not alone in their use of spectacle as a vehicle for conveying their message—indeed, the nonviolent tactics of the Southern Christian Leadership Conference were often carefully staged events intended to reveal the brutality that undergirded Jim Crow. But nonviolent protests were at heart morality plays—the direct confrontation of brutality and nonviolence, the oppressive arm of the state squashing peaceful protestors. Black power–influenced protests, by contrast, took the form of shouting "fire" in a crowded movie theater. Like their nonviolent counterparts, they relied on confrontation: not the sort of clashes that were intended to generate sympathy but rather collisions that gave the impression that the entire political and social system was unstable, at the brink of apocalypse.

Their goal was to terrify whites while giving blacks a sense of taking power into their own hands.

BY 1967 AND 1968, black power and the riots fueled each other, even if most black power organizations were too small and too ineffectual to play any role in fomenting urban unrest and most urban rioters were not members of radical organizations. Law enforcement officials, convinced that the riots had to be purposeful, looked high and low for evidence that black power groups had sparked the riots. They pursued every rumor that black radicals had played even bit roles: giving inflammatory speeches or distributing rifles or forming brigades of rooftop snipers. The shards of evidence that they dug up were unpersuasive. The riots were not part of a conspiracy. But it is impossible to make sense of the urban riots—the form that they took, the meanings that they assumed for both black and white Americans, and, especially, the language and self-perception of their participants—without placing them in the context of black radical-ism. Whether riot or disorder or uprising or rebellion or guerrilla warfare based in the slums or the newest front in an international struggle against racist, imperialist AmeriKKKa, most Americans saw something purposive, deliberate, and intentional at work in the "long hot summers" of the mid- and late 1960s. For critics and supporters, rioters and counterrioters, rev-olutionaries and counterrevolutionaries, the riots were inseparable from black political demands; to many they became synonymous with "black power" itself. The association of rioters with black demands for racial equality was, however, a two-edged sword.

If black power activists were not behind riots, black rioters—during the riots and afterward—described their experience looting, burning, and clashing with the police as exhilarating and liberating, and increasingly described events in terms of race pride and black power. "I was feeling proud, man, at the fact I was a Negro," proclaimed a Detroit rioter. "For a change, we're all thinking together," recounted a black teenage ob-server of the Detroit uprising. "For a change, we have one voice saying that black people are not satisfied with the way that they have to live." Many black residents in Plainfield, New Jersey (where rioters looted stores, burned cars, and killed a white police officer), interpreted the events as an expression of black power. Mounting the barricades that closed off streets in Plainfield's West End to whites, young protestors re-named their neighborhood "Soulville." One looter remarked on the Sat-urday of the outburst, "The state troopers are coming tonight, but that's okay, because Stokely [Carmichael] will be here tomorrow." Plainfield activist Linward Cathcart interpreted the riot as a necessary first step to-ward black pride and unity. "Since the riot, we're not niggers anymore," he claimed. "We're black men, and most of the people in the community have learned this. We are no longer jealous of one another and are work-ing together and respecting the neighborhood." Plainfield's rioters viewed their town's uprising as one small part of a nationwide black re-bellion.

What was more striking was how many ordinary blacks shared black radicals' views of the riots. In surveys and in interviews, black observers of the riots described the events in political terms. David Sears, a UCLA political scientist who led a team that interviewed blacks in Los Angeles and elsewhere, wrote that "the black community has generally inter-preted the riots as being revolutionary in nature." Surveys taken during and after the riots offered many surprising findings. The majority of riot-ers were males ages fifteen to twenty-four. Researchers demolished the widely held theory that rioters were an "underclass" or a criminal riffraff—and they also undermined black revolutionaries' belief that the rebellions were led by the urban "lumpenproletariat." Those arrested for looting, arson, and other riot-related crimes were not the poorest of urban residents. They were better educated than most northern blacks but despite their education were disproportionately confined to low-end jobs. One-third of rioters were unemployed. Some hypothesized that southern migrants—maladjusted to life in northern cities—were behind the riots. But the vast majority of rioters, even in cities with large num-bers of newcomers, were northern-born. "A significant consequence of growing up in the South," the Kerner Commission reported, was "nonin-volvement" in riots.

Survey researchers made another discovery that confirmed the politi-cal motivation of rioters. Rioters were far more likely than nonrioters to hold strong political views about whites, civil rights, and race relations, even if they were seldom members of formal political, civil rights, or mil-itant organizations. Their lack of institutional affiliation was not, however, a sign of their lack of political consciousness. Black rioters, as a whole, held deeper antiwhite sentiments than nonrioters, they were more likely than nonrioters to be knowledgeable about civil rights and black politics, and they were far more likely to distrust authority. By a sizeable margin, rioters were suspicious of government—local, state, and federal. And by large majorities, they opposed U.S. involvement in the Vietnam War. Most important, they were more likely than nonrioters to express their racial pride.

Why did young, northern-born, nonpoor black men join the crowds on the streets of northern cities? The most influential explanation came from the Kerner Commission. Using the moral vernacular of the civil rights movement, the commission interpreted the riots as the consequence of pervasive racial separation. In the preface to its bestselling report, the Kerner Commission memorably proclaimed that America was becoming "two societies, one black, one white—separate and unequal." There was much to this theory—given the pervasive separation of blacks and whites institutionally, economically, and residentially. However, while such a theory might explain the deep underlying causes of the riots, it did not explain their timing, their location, and their manifestation.

Social scientists offered a more refined view of the riots and their causes. One influential theory held that blacks rebelled against their "relative deprivation": That is, even if they were not poor, they were closed out of the well-advertised American dream. Television carried the promise of the "good life," beaming pictures of new suburban houses, modern appliances, and fancy cars into the living room of every black American. Yet blacks were excluded from suburbia, they lived in neighborhoods poorly served by shops and stores, and they saw clearly the gap between white wealth and black poverty. Blacks, in this view, fought desperately for inclusion in the postwar American consumer culture. Relative deprivation offered a convincing explanation for looting—rioters simply appropriated the consumer durables that had been denied them. Images of looters hauling away furniture, clothes, and appliances gave credence to the theory. In one particularly postmodern moment, a Detroit news team taped a black couple in their living room watching the images of themselves looting a television on the flickering screen of the looted television itself.

A second, related theory emphasized "frustrated expectations." In this view, the riots were a reaction to the unmet promises of postwar liberalism and of the civil rights movement, both of which had held out the hope that centuries of inequality and impoverishment were unraveling. From the view of the street, segregation, black poverty, and unemployment showed few signs of abating—even after decades of grassroots civil rights organizing and liberal victories in the courts and legislatures. That most rioters were northern-born gives credence to the theory. Newcomers from the South marveled at the relative liberties in northern cities: Compared to the everyday violence of Jim Crow, the indignities of northern life were minor. For longtime residents of the North, however, racial change seemed excruciatingly slow. And the fact that rioters tended to be more aware of civil rights politics than nonrioters were suggests that they could see the movement's limitations clearly.

Not all social scientists agreed with these theories. The most prominent dissenter, conservative political scientist Edward Banfield, interpreted the riots as "outbreaks of animal spirits and of stealing by slum dwellers." Banfield's theory, which discounted the political motivation of rioters, gave social scientific credence to the sense of moral outrage that many Americans, particularly whites, felt toward rioters. What right did they have to loot and pillage? How would burning down stores or stealing liquor and electronics accomplish political change? Weren't rioters just in need of a good disciplining? In Banfield's view, "efforts to end racial injustice and to eliminate poverty, slums, and unemployment" were naïve at best. Only the imposition of law and order would bring peace to inner cities.

Whatever their interpretation of the riots' causes, few commentators spilled much ink on the fact that rioters were disproportionately male. The widely held assumption—beyond questioning—was that men were more prone to violence and more likely to express their anger publicly. But there was nothing timeless or biological or predetermined about the masculinity of rioters. Urban, working-class men, those who made up the majority of rioters, were also those hit hardest by the tidal wave of economic restructuring that swept through urban America after World War II. To a generation of northern black men who had come of age in the decaying cities and the stagnant urban economies of the 1950s and 1960s, the economic outlook was not hopeful. Their fathers and brothers may have looked wistfully on the wartime boom. But for men coming of age in the 1960s, that was remote history.

One observer astutely saw the riots as a form of political theater.

"Those cats [the rioters] were playing the dozens with live ammunition." The clashes between young black men and white authorities were political dramas with deadly consequences. As destructive as they were, the riots had at their core something else—a demand, however destructive, for dignity. It was that sense of masculinity aggrieved that became a central driving force in black politics and activism throughout the 1960s and well beyond. That the majority of rioters were men provides a starting point. To describe the urban uprisings as uncoordinated or spontaneous is not, however, to drain them of political content. Those who looted, tossed Molotov cocktails, and engaged in pitched battles with the police might have been motivated, as Banfield charged, by a desire for "fun and profit." But the timing, the form, and the rhetoric of urban uprisings suggests that more was at stake than uncontrollable youthful impulses.

Urban riots were part of the black insurgency of the 1960s—an insurgency that tapped deep roots of discontent but also manifested the particular political and cultural sensibilities of the era. They grew from simmering discontent at the continued subordination of African Americans. The urban riots were, above all, about turf and control. They reflected a popular consciousness that black communities were insensitively ruled by white outsiders—a consciousness that drew sustenance from international anticolonialism. Facing what they saw as illegitimate white rule, young people throughout the country began to fashion an alternative politics of resistance and rebellion. Without access to government and with no viable outlet for their newfound racial consciousness, they created a grassroots, youth-based set of black politics that saw violence as a viable alternative to legitimate action. Competing with the largely ineffectual city governments were loosely structured groups (some called them gangs) of black teenagers who began to arm themselves and turn to violence in order to maintain physical control of the ghetto. Taking to the streets, looting, and burning were, literally, attempts to purge communities of white control. A related impulse was a deeply rooted (but to whites largely invisible) black popular belief in the redemptive power of self-defense. And finally, the urban uprisings manifested a sense of the importance of honor, of respect that permeated black culture and politics—with a particular masculine sensibility. To be sure, the very fact that riots were uncoordinated and inchoate in their political vision made their outcomes ambiguous at best and tragic at worst.

ACTS OF RESISTANCE and rebellion usually have unintended consequences. Black revolutionaries hoped that they would destabilize the political system; black rioters hoped to stick it to "the Man," whether brutal police officers or white shopkeepers. The fear of rioting led white elected officials, from the Johnson administration on down to local mayors, to fashion policies to try to buy off black discontent, what sardonic observers called "riot insurance." But riots also fueled urgent demands for law and order and enhanced police power. No one took the performance of black power and street rebellion more seriously than law enforcement officials. Many observers described the disorders on urban streets in the mid-1960s as "police riots," where armed law enforcement officials retaliated against those who challenged their authority, often with brutal force. The Kerner Commission warned of the "indiscriminate use of force against wholly innocent elements of the Negro community" during riots. The vast majority of riot-related deaths came at the hands of law enforcement officials. The combination of adrenaline and fear—along with racial animosity— led white police officers to take out their aggression on black rioters. On occasion, particularly brutal police practices made international news. In Detroit, four white police officers raided the Algiers Motel on fears that it was a haven for snipers, even though most of the gunfire during the Detroit riots emanated from the police and National Guard. There, they executed three unarmed black men.

The FBI and local police forces took black radicals' revolutionary politics and militant posturing at face value. In a climate of growing concern about the revolutionary potential of the black power movement, law enforcement officials in both New York and Philadelphia stepped up their scrutiny of RAM. In Philadelphia, the police, with the cooperation of the FBI, surveyed RAM meetings, took the license plate numbers of those who attended, and arrested and often rearrested RAM supporters on minor charges. A July 1967 FBI memo reported that "any possibility of neutralizing a RAM activist was exercised." The previous month, sixteen RAM members, including Herman Ferguson and Max Stanford, had been arrested. New York police raided the Jamaica Rifle and Pistol Club, confiscating thousands of rounds of ammunition, rifles, and directions to the homes of Roy Wilkins and Whitney Young. RAM members fiercely denied what they called the "jive assed charges" of conspiracy. From exile, Robert Williams described the arrestees as "victims of fascist kangarooism." Insisting on his innocence, Stanford wrote Wilkins after the arrests, pleading for his support and arguing that the arrests had been part of a "deliberate frame-up attempt" designed to crush RAM. For his part, Wilkins was unsettled by the alleged plot, though he saw it as "farfetched." Ferguson and his comrades continued to claim they had been set up, a position that was, to some extent, borne out by the trial when undercover police officer Edward Howlette testified that he had purchased the maps of Wilkins's and Young's neighborhoods, written the directions, and helped RAM members case out Wilkins's home. Stanford was not convicted, but Ferguson was tried and found guilty by an all-white, all-male jury under an obscure New York state law that forbade "anarchistic" conspiracies.

While the conspiracy case against Ferguson was wending its way through New York's courts, he stepped up his calls for black separatism. A leading advocate of community control of schools, Ferguson parlayed his educational experience into advisory positions in Ocean Hill–Brownsville and Harlem, where the New York school district was engaged in controversial community control experiments. At a rally at Harlem's P.S. 120 to commemorate the anniversary of Malcolm X's assassination, Ferguson urged blacks to "obtain weapons and practice using them in preparation for 'the hunting season,'" when, he feared, white police officers and extremists would attack blacks for their involvement in urban riots. (For his "inflammatory remarks," a New York judge raised Ferguson's bail to one hundred thousand dollars.)

Ferguson also joined forces with other black power and separatist organizations. After his conviction, he ran in New York for the U.S. Senate as a member of the black power–oriented Peace and Freedom Party. Breaking bail, he traveled to Detroit, where he was arrested at a rally in support of the creation of the Republic of New Africa (RNA), a black-controlled independent nation to be built on confiscated land in the southern plantation belt. The RNA—headed by the Reverend Albert Cleage's longtime friends Milton and Richard Henry (now Gaidi and

Imari Obadele)—appointed Ferguson its "minister of education." Ferguson, however, disappeared as quickly as he had emerged. Unwilling to do time in jail for a crime he claimed he had not committed, Ferguson joined a small number of black radicals in exile overseas. He spent nineteen years living under an assumed name in Guyana, still firmly committed to the goals of black revolution.

RAM WAS NOT the FBI's only target. Readers of *The Black Panther* may have perceived its graphic images of decapitated and bloodied pigs as metaphorical, but law enforcement officials took them literally. J. Edgar Hoover, who only a few years earlier had declared Martin Luther King, Jr., the most dangerous man in America, found black power an even more ominous threat. In August 1967, just after the arrests of Stanford and Ferguson, the FBI refined its "Counterintelligence Program" (nicknamed COINTELPRO), which sought "to expose, disrupt, misdirect, discredit, or otherwise neutralize the activities of black nationalist, hate-type organizations and groupings, their leadership, spokesmen, and supporters, and to counter their propensity for violence and civil disorder." The FBI's tactics included "cooperation of established local news media contacts . . . to insure the targeted group is disrupted, ridiculed, or discredited through the publicity and not merely publicized." The FBI had long infiltrated a wide range of liberal and radical organizations, including the SCLC and the SNCC, but under the new COINTELPRO, the FBI planted informants in nearly every major and minor black power organization. Working closely with the FBI, local police officials pursued black activists doggedly, both overtly and covertly, often with devastating long-term consequences.

The Panthers faced especially intense scrutiny because of their militancy and their direct confrontations with the police. Over the last three years of the 1960s, the Panthers escalated the war of rhetoric and law enforcement officials sometimes retaliated violently. In Chicago, where police had a long-standing feud with the Black Panthers, two Panthers were slain in an early morning raid in December 1969. Local leader Fred Hampton, in bed and unarmed, was killed by a barrage of bullets. The FBI and local police departments also infiltrated Panther chapters with undercover officers who posed as black militants. Many were agents provocateurs who used their cover to create or exploit factional disputes. The very suspicion of the presence of an undercover informant (true or false) led to recriminations, factional struggles, and expulsions from black power cells, further weakening their coherence. New Haven's Panther chapter, already prone to factionalism, was riven asunder when an FBI informant inflamed organizational rivalries. Undercover agents also pushed black power activists to extremes of rhetoric and action, thus justifying police raids and reprisals. The presence of agents provocateurs explains some of the violent excesses of the black power movement—but it cannot explain everything, for it was only in the climate of escalating revolutionary rhetoric that those provocateurs were credible. Black power's romanticization of violence became a self-fulfilling prophecy—and the retribution that authorities exacted was the tragic consequence.

THE CHILIASTIC EMBRACE of revolutionary rhetoric and the performative politics of clashes with the police preoccupied black radicals and their critics in the mid- and late 1960s. But black power was more than just a display of revolutionary bravado. Many black power organizations developed elaborate intellectual analyses of urban problems—even if their ideological positions were often reduced to sound bites. Here, the media were not wholly responsible. Activists and the press reinforced each other's tendencies toward hyperbole. In the perfervid climate of media-fueled sensationalism, many black power activists, not surprisingly, succumbed to the temptation of letting simple slogans stand in for more complex ideas. What was profound in black power—and what was problematic—disappeared in the profusion of sloganeering and symbolism. The nuances of black radical ideology were lost to those who boiled the struggle down to the simple dichotomies of integration versus separation, of nonviolence versus violence, of conks versus Afros. As black journalist William Worthy lamented in a prescient 1967 article, "the media will not report more than a fraction of what's being said in radical and black power circles." What made it to the news media tended to be the simplest ideas, usually framed in the most exaggerated ways.

Lost in the flattened accounts of black radicalism and its performance was the rich, contradictory, and often problematic set of ideas that animated the movement. Above all, black power was a series of experiments, attempts to envision a political alternative to the racial liberalism that had prevailed through most of the postwar years. It is difficult to reduce black power to its essence, but nearly every major and minor organization developed a series of interwoven ideologies. First, black power thought globally and acted locally. In its various strands, black power advocates viewed black America in an international context that included Africa (or idealized images of Africa) and, more broadly, third-world struggles against imperialism. Despite their keen internationalism, black power advocates were essentially localist in their politics—even as they constantly framed local struggles in the broadest international context. Second, black power advocates widely embraced a psychological understanding of racism and its effects. At the core of this psychological framework was a distinct mid-twentieth-century understanding of gender and sexuality that privileged masculinity. Third, they embraced a cultural politics, one that rested on an understanding of blackness and that created a set of cultural practices that articulated blackness, celebrated it, reinforced it, and marginalized those who questioned or rejected it. At the core of black power was cultural essentialism—the notion that there was a true, identifiable, authentic form of black racial expression and that movement energies should be directed toward the production and reproduction of it. On these three broad themes there was much commonality—even if the fragmented, decentralized groups that made up the black power movement disagreed on the particulars. From the mid-1960s to the early 1970s, black power would become an increasingly influential force in black urban politics. Even if no black radical organization gained a mass following, black power ideas profoundly shaped the politics of racial equality in housing, community economic development, and education. It is to those movements that we now turn.

CHAPTER 11

"UNCONDITIONAL WAR"

PRESIDENT LYNDON JOHNSON TOOK THE OATH OF OFFICE AS THE NEGRO RE-
volt was intensifying, a moment of crisis and opportunity. He seized that
moment, pledging to create a Great Society where poverty, inequality,
and racial discrimination would be eliminated. "Unfortunately, many
Americans live on the outskirts of hope—some because of their poverty,
and some because of their color, and all too many because of both. Our
task is to help replace their despair with opportunity." So Johnson introduced the intertwined problems of race and inequality in his first State of
the Union address, delivered to Congress on January 8, 1964. He followed
boldly: "The administration today, here and now, declares unconditional
war on poverty in America." Johnson's war was to be fought on many
fronts—but above all, it was to be "a joint Federal-local effort" that would
"pursue poverty, pursue it wherever it exists—in city slums and small
towns, in sharecropper shacks or in migrant worker camps, on Indian
reservations, among whites as well as Negroes, among the young as well
as the aged, in the boom towns and in the depressed areas." Johnson and
his aides were careful to pitch the antipoverty effort in universalistic
terms (it was "in no sense a help-the-blacks program," recalled aide
Adam Yarmolinsky), but coming, as it did, in the midst of the "Negro Revolt," Johnson clearly had black urban America first in mind.

Johnson's War on Poverty was not the result of a lobbying effort by
civil rights organizations, nor was it an effort to win black votes. It grew
out of the Kennedy administration's economic and urban policy experiments. But whatever its origins, black Americans—all except for the small
(but rapidly growing) fringe of nationalists and radicals—greeted Johnson's declaration of war with enthusiasm, even if they quibbled with
many of its specifics and would grow increasingly critical of its implemen-

tation. When Johnson took office on November 22, 1963, African Americans were still disproportionately represented in the ranks of the poor and unemployed. Despite a two-year-long economic boom, 10.8 percent of blacks but only 5 percent of whites were out of work. Blacks earned a mere fifty-three cents to every dollar made by whites. And 55 percent of blacks, compared to only 18 percent of whites, lived below the poverty line. With more than half the black population on the brink of subsistence, poverty was an inescapable daily reality, even for those who had the good fortune to move into the slowly growing black middle class. Persistent housing and school segregation meant wealthy and poor blacks lived in proximity. Most extended families included poor people. Well-to-do and poor blacks shopped in the same stores, attended the same schools, and often worshipped in the same congregations. Any federal efforts to alleviate poverty would affect the quality of life of nearly all black Americans, poor or not.

Blacks' enthusiasm for the Great Society was not only the result of their disproportionate representation in the ranks of the poor. It was also evidence of their real faith in government, especially liberal government, as an agent of positive social change. Even if the Kennedy administration's civil rights and antipoverty efforts had been halting, experimental, and incomplete, blacks held great expectations for the Democratic White House. In 1963, a remarkable 83 percent of blacks saw the federal government as "helpful" to them. Their support softened a bit by 1966, but still 74 percent expressed faith in the federal government. The smaller the government, the more black support for it eroded. A minority of northern blacks (40 percent in 1963 and 46 percent in 1966) saw state governments as "helpful." Only about one-third of northern blacks in both 1963 and 1966 saw local governments as their allies, and between one-fifth and one-third saw local governments as "harmful to Negro rights." The grounds for distrust of state and local governments were many. States' rights had been a subterfuge for maintaining Jim Crow. Even in liberal northern states, civil rights legislation had been more symbolic than effective. And municipal governments were the key architects of racial inequality. Local control had kept housing segregated, steered blacks into inferior schools, bulldozed black neighborhoods in the name of urban renewal, and punished welfare recipients with harsh regulations and widely varying benefit payments. Capping it off, blacks were underrepresented in the most visible municipal jobs, especially construction, law enforcement, firefighting, and public education.

To a great extent, these statistics shaped the direction that black politics would take in the 1960s. Black activists directed their energies toward the federal government, out of real optimism that it could be the agent of racial progress. The irony of the War on Poverty was that the federal government did not, for the most part, address the economic problems that were the root cause of poverty. Even though they had staunch advocates among civil rights activists and in the White House, job creation and full employment remained distant dreams. Likewise, federal antidiscrimination efforts were halting and incomplete. But, unexpectedly, the federal government allied itself with local activists who challenged the very legitimacy of local government and used the War on Poverty as a wedge to shift the balance of power in local governments and to increase black participation in policy making. In many localities, black activists attempted—with the assistance of federal antipoverty programs—to create alternative institutions to unresponsive local governments. Even when those efforts failed, they gave black activists leverage to demand greater representation on the local level. The Johnson administration unleashed and legitimated an insurgent movement for "community control" that dovetailed with the growing demand for black power. The consequence of the Great Society was to wholly recast the terrain of debate over race, rights, and equality in the United States—from the federal to the local. Everyone's horizon shrunk by the end of the 1960s, as blocks, wards, and city governments, not Congress and the White House, became the primary battlegrounds for the future of black America.

NO MOMENT WAS more formative in shaping northern blacks' expectations of the federal government than the passage of the Civil Rights Act of 1964. Civil rights legislation was the most important piece of unfinished business that the Kennedy administration had bequeathed to Lyndon Johnson. During the tumultuous summer of 1963, Kennedy began to lay the groundwork for a far-reaching civil rights law. Kennedy was a reluctant warrior, forced against his political instincts to fashion civil rights legislation in response to the Negro Revolt. After Kennedy's assassination, Lyndon Johnson put it at the top of his agenda. In the early months of

1964, Johnson administration officials and members of Congress worked through draft after excruciating draft of the proposed legislation, tinkering with language, struggling to come up with a bill that would satisfy northern liberals and their black allies, probusiness Republicans, and at least a fraction of southern Democrats.

The two civil rights issues that mattered most in the North were housing and employment. Housing was, however, too hot an issue for Johnson and Congress in 1963 and 1964. Legislation that guaranteed civil rights in housing met with unanimous southern opposition—but it also faced deep skepticism among northerners across party lines. House minority leader Everett Dirksen, a key figure in the passage of the Civil Rights Act, hailed from Illinois, where white opposition to housing integration was particularly intense. As it had done for decades, the National Association of Real Estate Boards spearheaded opposition to civil rights in housing. Over the course of the 1950s, in response to the growing delegitimation of overt racial prejudice, NAREB had modified its code of ethics, removing race-specific language. But the Realtors left the determination of what constituted an incompatible "character or use" of a property up to "local determination in accordance with local practice." By the early 1960s, Realtors were implacable foes of open housing legislation. Cloaked in the mantle of race neutrality, NAREB mounted a city-by-city and state-by-state campaign against open housing laws. Building on postwar understandings of "free enterprise" and embracing the rhetoric of Americanism, Realtors argued that open housing laws were a violation of individual rights, particularly the "right of association." Efforts to mandate nondiscrimination amounted to "forced housing," which would abrogate individual choice in service of social engineering.

Opponents of fair-housing laws made inroads everywhere. Most alarming to civil rights activists was their appeal in Democratic strongholds outside the South. In California, where Governor Pat Brown, a Johnson ally, staunchly supported open housing legislation, Realtors and white homeowners led a statewide counterrevolution against open housing. Voters in liberal Berkeley defeated a local anti-housing-discrimination ordinance in 1963. A year later, real estate groups bankrolled Proposition 14, a referendum to repeal California's newly enacted open housing law. While Californians voted overwhelmingly for Johnson, they also supported Proposition 14 by a two-to-one ratio. In Democratic enclaves in the Midwest, open housing also took a political beating. In heavily blue-collar Detroit and Akron, white voters rejected local ordinances that prohibited racial discrimination in home sales. For many northern elected officials, open housing became a political "third rail" (touch it and you are electrocuted). Despite the pressure of liberal civil rights groups, a federal open housing provision would not survive the drafting process.

A measure forbidding employment discrimination, on the other hand, squeezed through Congress like a camel through the eye of a needle. When the Kennedy administration prepared the first draft of the civil rights bill in June 1963, it did not include fair employment practices. Administration officials were worried that a debate about workplace antidiscrimination would undermine the bill. But civil rights groups kept pressure on the administration until it capitulated. After nearly two decades of pushing for a permanent Fair Employment Practices Committee, mainstream civil rights organizations and their labor allies were well practiced. The NAACP, the Urban League, and the AFL-CIO lobbied the White House. Adding to their clout was the fact that most of the disruptive demonstrations in northern cities in 1963 had focused on workplace discrimination.

To draft a section of the bill that neutralized Dixie-GOP opposition to anything resembling a permanent Fair Employment Practices Committee required Herculean efforts. The proposed civil rights bill's Title VII, which covered employment, generated intense debate and complex behind-the-scenes negotiations. Probusiness Republicans resuscitated arguments that banning employment discrimination would cramp "managerial prerogative" to hire and fire at will. Title VII was, in the view of the National Association of Manufacturers, an affront to free enterprise. Southern Democrats—for decades hostile to organized labor—suddenly embraced conservative unionists' arguments that a robust antidiscrimination law would undermine seniority. Particularly upsetting to Republicans and many Democrats was the fear that the law would include some form of "compensatory" policy—the requirement that employers offer preferences to workers by race like those advocated by selective patronage protestors, the Urban League, and CORE. The result of contentious debate about Title VII was a compromise. The bill's supporters explicitly disavowed "benign quotas" or "reverse discrimination" to open jobs to black workers. Title VII ultimately specified that "it shall be an unlawful employment practice for an employer to fail or refuse to hire or to discharge any individual, or otherwise discriminate against any individual" based on "race, color, religion, sex, or national origin." It accomplished what two decades of fair employment practices advocates had demanded—the removal of discriminatory barriers to employment.

Many northern activists worried that Title VII would be just as toothless as many state fair employment practices laws. Enactment did not ensure enforcement or implementation. "Now the responsibility for translating [Title VII] from a paper law into a working tool lies not only with federal officials . . . but with Negroes themselves," argued *The Pittsburgh Courier.* Like most state FEPs, Title VII required evidence that discrimination was intentional—it could not be inferred from statistics about the racial composition of workforces. And like most FEPs, it relied on aggrieved individuals coming forward with complaints. In addition, as part of a deal brokered by Dirksen, Title VII did not give the newly created Equal Employment Opportunity Commission (EEOC) the power to file suits against discriminatory employers. Instead, like most state FEPCs, the EEOC was to resolve disputes through "informal methods of conference, conciliation, and persuasion." If such efforts failed, the EEOC could send complaints to the U.S. Department of Justice for litigation, but only "if the case is of general public importance." The EEOC did not have the power to issue "cease and desist" orders if employers were found to be practicing discrimination. And there were no provisions in the law for measuring results, something that many local activists had insisted upon. "We sort of gummed them to death if we could," noted Johnson aide Clifford Alexander of the EEOC, "but we had no enforcement powers."

Black opinion on the Civil Rights Act of 1964 was mixed. Syndicated columnist Chuck Stone was scathing. "If there's anything the Senate-passed civil rights bill does for Negroes in the North, it's cocooned in one simple word: nothing." Many editorialists celebrated the legislation as a landmark, but noted that without political pressure, the act would be more symbolic than real. Congressman Adam Clayton Powell, Jr., warned that the act was not a "cure all" for the problems of racial inequality and that, at least in the North, the "anti-poverty bill is more important than the Civil Rights Act." Martin Luther King, Jr., argued that the act was inadequate to "deal with the magnitude" of joblessness and "sub-standard housing conditions" across the country, and he called for a massive public works program.

Whatever they thought of its limitations, civil rights organizations aggressively demanded the Civil Rights Act's enforcement. As soon as the ink dried on the act, NAACP labor chief Herbert Hill began collecting evidence of discrimination (using his web of connections among black trade unionists) and pledged the organization's resources to use Title VII to challenge discriminatory employers. The NAACP labor department provided assistance to workers who filed grievances against employers and unions accused of discriminatory behavior. The Urban League joined the enforcement effort. In August, it provided the Justice Department with a list of federally aided programs that discriminated against blacks, most in the South but including some northern hospitals and apprentice training programs. CORE chapters also joined the battle to "pressure the federal government" to enforce antidiscrimination laws. Still, many black commentators worried that federal civil rights legislation was irrelevant to the North. "Equal opportunity is essential, but not enough, not enough," wrote *The Pittsburgh Courier*. The Civil Rights Act was designed to unravel the last vestiges of southern-style Jim Crow—which, for the most part, it effectively abolished. But a year after Johnson signed the landmark law, the North did not cool down. Riots in Harlem, Rochester, and Philadelphia and protests at construction sites, schools, and police stations highlighted ongoing black grievances. The passage of the Civil Rights Act was a beginning, not an end.

Throughout the North, activists kept the heat on the federal government. In 1964, 1965, 1966, and 1967, construction site protests erupted in Philadelphia, Newark, New York, New Rochelle, Cleveland, Cincinnati, Oakland, and St. Louis, where, in a dramatic act of civil disobedience, a protestor chained himself to the top of the Gateway Arch. In 1967, the NAACP announced a national campaign to open up the building trades. The threat of disruption had its intended effect. Federal officials took note of the protests. "The absence of non-whites among construction trades workers," wrote a Labor Department official in 1967, "has been a focal point for racial unrest" and "a prime symbol of the lack of equal employment opportunity." Civil rights activists found allies in the ranks of the equal employment bureaucracy. Officials in the newly created EEOC gathered volumes of statistics to document workplace discrimination. Armed with data, Labor Department officials singled out certain sectors for close scrutiny. In Philadelphia, for example, they accused construction unions of "dragging their feet" on minority employment. Cecil B. Moore noted that, if it wanted to enforce Title VII, the "Federal government can do it with ease . . . just withhold the money until they employ."

Protests and policy innovations reinforced one another. In 1965, President Johnson issued Executive Order 11246, which gave the newly created Office of Federal Contract Compliance the power to terminate government contracts to firms that did not practice "affirmative action" in employment. What "affirmative action" and "compliance" meant would be defined in 1966 and 1967 in a series of policy experiments in four metropolitan areas rocked by construction site protests. In the aftermath of the Gateway Arch demonstrations, federal officials fashioned a "St. Louis Plan" that required "pre-award" evidence of contractors' efforts to hire minorities—the awarding of a federal contract was contingent on the recruitment of underrepresented minorities. When a St. Louis contractor hired three blacks, white workers walked out, leading to years of litigation. In California, in the wake of protests against the Bay Area Rapid Transit system, the 1966 "San Francisco Plan" obliged contractors to document their efforts to train, hire, and place minority construction workers. The plan led to nominal changes: Labor Department officials criticized Bay Area contractors for their "paper compliance." But San Francisco's troubles provided lessons for other "city plans" to combat workplace discrimination. In 1967, federal officials mandated a "Cleveland Plan" (in response to huge antidiscrimination protests) that required pre-award "manning tables," which specified how many minority workers would be hired on federally funded job sites and what positions they would hold. Finally, in March 1967, administration officials announced a "Philadelphia Plan" requiring "affirmative action" in hiring on all federal contracts in that city, with pre-award manning tables to be enforced by a compliance committee of federal officials who would visit job sites and conduct head counts of minority workers.

The Johnson administration had two goals: to stem growing black discontent and, somehow, to fashion a proposal that would not alienate building trade unionists who had been Democratic Party stalwarts. Straddling the fence proved difficult. Defending the Philadelphia and Cleveland plans to skeptics at the AFL-CIO, Labor Secretary Willard Wirtz stated that the government had singled out the two cities for their intense racial tension—and suggested that it would not impose such plans on other cities. The Philadelphia Plan, in particular, became a flash point of controversy. Construction unions staunchly opposed it, and the Johnson administration was divided on its constitutionality. In its 1967 incarnation, the Philadelphia Plan did not survive. But the prospect of a federal affirmative action program with teeth sparked a new wave of demonstrations. Demanding immediate remedies, not gradual change, Philadelphia's activists protested at local hospitals, the University of Pennsylvania, the Philadelphia School Board, and the U.S. Mint. When Richard Nixon took office, they pushed again—and used the threat of racial unrest as a bargaining chip. In April and May 1969, a delegation of Philadelphia civil rights activists lobbied Nixon officials with the grim prediction of a new outbreak of riots if the administration did not revive the plan. Finally, in June, Nixon issued a revised Philadelphia Plan—one that gave definition to the vague phrase "affirmative action" by requiring "goals" and "timetables" to be met by federal contractors if they were to remain eligible for funding.

WHILE CIVIL RIGHTS groups and local activists pushed for aggressive affirmative action in the workplace, they also turned their attention to the combined problems of unemployment and poverty. Few believed that, alone, the Civil Rights Act of 1964 would transform the economic status of urban blacks. But they held out hope that Johnson would enact a comprehensive antipoverty program. Bolstering that hope was the fact that many prominent civil rights leaders gained a hearing in the White House. Whitney Young, even more a White House fixture during the Johnson administration than he had been under Kennedy, continued to push his Marshall Plan for the Negro.

CORE's James Farmer and the NAACP's Roy Wilkins also got privileged access to the White House. A. Philip Randolph and Bayard Rustin, bolstered by the success of the March on Washington, occupied positions of influence in Washington that they could not have imagined just a few years earlier, although their channels to power were less direct. In 1964, Randolph made his first Democratic Party endorsement—for Lyndon Johnson. Through trade union circles, where Randolph still had pull, the idea of full employment found its way into the Department of Labor. Even though Hubert Humphrey and Randolph were not close, the vice president had long advocated policies that linked full employment and fair employment. Echoing the arguments of left-labor activists such as Rustin, Humphrey argued that "the problems require much more than simply eliminating overt racial discrimination."

How much more—and what form that "much more" would take—were the fundamental questions that shaped Johnson's War on Poverty. The idea of an all-out assault on poverty, like the Civil Rights Act, was yet another piece of Kennedy's unfinished business that Johnson inherited. The Kennedy administration had greatly expanded job-training programs—garnering the approval of civil rights leaders and grassroots activists alike. Under Kennedy's Committee on Juvenile Delinquency, the federal government had channeled resources to antipoverty programs that served mostly blacks in a number of large cities, among them New York, Detroit, and Philadelphia. And under the president's direction, Walter Heller, head of the Council of Economic Advisers, had been putting together an antipoverty plan since May 1963, even if his project was still woefully incomplete when Kennedy was assassinated. Johnson, however, moved the project to the top of his agenda. An all-out attack on poverty appealed to both Johnson's vaunting ambition and his deepest aspirations. The very first day that Johnson occupied the White House, he met with Heller and gave him the order to "move full speed ahead" with the antipoverty initiative. "That's my kind of program," Johnson told the economist. "It will help people." And it would allow him to step out of Kennedy's shadow with a program not identified with the martyred president.

By March, Heller and his team had hastily drafted the Economic Opportunity Act of 1964, which offered a hodgepodge of programs to eradicate poverty, most notably federally funded job training programs (Job Corps and Neighborhood Youth Corps) and the still-to-be-defined Community Action Program. Johnson held out particular hope for the Job Corps and Neighborhood Youth Corps. Targeting "young men . . . whose background, health, and education make them least fit for useful work," the Job Corps would send them to rural conservation projects and urban job-training centers. Johnson and his aides looked wistfully backward to the New Deal's jobs programs—especially the Civilian Conservation Corps and the Works Progress Administration. But unlike the New Deal programs, which actually created jobs, the Job Corps provided skills training but only promised placement in the private sector to successful graduates. The lack of full employment provisions concerned Rustin, Randolph, and members of their circle. "A multi-billion dollar federal public-works program," argued Rustin, "is required to reabsorb unskilled and semi-skilled workers into the labor market—and this must be done if Negro workers in these categories are to be employed." But Johnson administration officials were optimistic that training alone would mitigate unemployment. In their view, the problem was that poor people, especially blacks, lacked skills, not that jobs were wanting. Also, Johnson believed that creating New Deal–style public works employment was simply too expensive. Sargent Shriver, Johnson's key antipoverty aide (and Kennedy's brother-in-law), pledged to Congress that Johnson's antipoverty bill would "not raise the national budget by a single dollar." Above all, Johnson hoped to solve poverty on the cheap.

Like the New Deal works agencies, the Job Corps established camps— often in remote places—where trainees would participate in conservation projects. The program's rationale rested on the romantic idea that exposure to the outdoors was character-building. Interior Secretary Stewart Udall made the case that the Job Corps would uplift "urban kids and ghetto kids and deprived kids" by giving them a sense of "pride" from working with their hands in the fresh air of national parks. With characteristic bravado, Johnson and his advisors oversold the Job Corps. "These are not simply camps for the underprivileged," pledged the president in a flurry of hyperbole. "They are new educational institutions comparable in innovation to the land grant colleges." To make sure that everyone got the point, the Johnson administration engaged in what one wag called "maximum feasible public relations." The Office of Economic Opportunity (OEO) bombarded black neighborhoods with Job Corps recruitment materials, produced a promotional film, and placed dozens of favorable articles in the black press. More than three hundred thousand people applied for about ten thousand training slots in the first months of the program. Johnson aides scrambled to get the Job Corps up and running, and in the haste, many of the first recruits got a lot less than they had hoped for.

Above all, Job Corps boosters played on the old themes of uplift. At Camp Kilmer, New Jersey, "a combination educational institution, trade school, military camp, and counseling center," the director promised to provide "these young people with marketable skills and make good citizens of them." Camp Kilmer was one of the better-run camps—unlike the Kalamazoo, Michigan, center, where a group of restless corpsmen looted downtown stores and clashed with police officers in November 1965, just a few hours after Shriver had spoken there. But life at Camp Kilmer—as in many camps and training centers—was disorganized. Hastily launched programs often lacked instructional materials and qualified teachers. Trainees complained, with justification, that the camps were overcrowded and served bad food. "This is the biggest damn runaround I've ever seen," griped a Camp Kilmer corpsman. Young participants, bored by their menial labor and trapped in single-sex camps, often fought, gambled, and drank. And although Camp Kilmer's director raved that the program had a 70 percent placement rate, follow-up studies were less sanguine. A 1969 survey of 9,463 Jobs Corps graduates and 1,815 employers found that 75 percent had jobs six months after graduation. But the long-term results were discouraging. "After three years," the survey found, "the advantages are blotted out" because "graduates were submerged again in the same quagmire of discrimination and disadvantage."

While the Johnson administration experimented, mostly unsuccessfully, with job training, another War on Poverty initiative, the Community Action Program (CAP), fundamentally reoriented the northern struggle for racial equality. Unlike Job Corps, CAP was not one of Johnson's pet projects, and it was unpopular among White House aides from the very start. Never well funded, the entire Office of Economic Opportunity, which administered CAP, drew only 1.5 percent of the entire federal budget between 1965 and 1970. But its political effects far exceeded its minor budgetary impact. Community Action was the first stage in what would be a forty-year devolution of antipoverty policy to community organizations, nonprofits, and local governments, ultimately giving poor people and their representatives the responsibility of solving unemployment, inferior housing, and economic disinvestment.

CAP started with a simple, radical idea. Community Action Agencies (CAAs) would be "developed, conducted, and administered with the maximum feasible participation of residents of the areas and members of the groups involved." Rather than being administered top-down from Washington, CAAs were to be local creations. Although the law allowed for local government input, it was possible for CAAs to operate largely independently of municipal and state governments. Community Action had its genesis in foundation-sponsored urban revitalization projects in the late 1950s and early 1960s, most notably the Ford Foundation's Gray Areas Program, which funded small-scale projects to combat juvenile delinquency and foster the civic participation of the poor. Community Action rested on the assumption that engagement in policy making and implementation would give the poor a stake in the system and, ultimately, empower them to break the psychological chains of poverty. But Community Action's appeal extended well beyond the world of philanthropy and social science. For many black activists who were suspicious of white-controlled city governments, the call for "maximum feasible participation" was the single most exciting provision in the Economic Opportunity Act of 1964. The War on Poverty opened up new possibilities for grassroots activism and channeled black urban politics in one direction to the exclusion of others.

Community Action's fate was intertwined with a new black urban populism that fused elements of civil rights and black power and emphasized the importance of local politics for the liberation of black America. At the heart of this populism was the argument that urban policy should be controlled by "the people," not by mayors, city councils, or political machines. Burned by locally administered public policies—urban renewal, unequal education, punitive welfare regulations, and police brutality—a growing cadre of activists offered an alternative vision: neighborhoods taking control of their own destiny, through grassroots organization and bottom-up political mobilization. One of the earliest and most articulate proponents of black community organization was C. E. Wilson. In a 1964 *Liberator* article, Wilson laid out the rationale and strategy for "community development and improvement through community organization." Small was beautiful. Wilson advocated a "block-by-block effort around specific issues" as an alternative to "tackling entire ghettoes at one fell swoop." Poor people should organize themselves—not be the passive objects of urban public policy.

The impulse toward community control and community participation was deeply rooted in traditions of local governance in the United States. But even if black urban populism tapped into deep-rooted American understandings of localism, the demand for community control took a distinctive form in inner cities in the mid-1960s. Activists drew from the long tradition of black self-help and uplift, which emphasized the importance of self-improvement in service of community betterment. They grafted it onto an increasingly vocal critique of "white power"—a category that included well-meaning but condescending white liberals and conservative white racists alike. And they fused it together with black power's demand for self-determination.

Whatever black power meant to the small band of intellectuals and radicals who embraced it, its abstract claims took on real meaning in the struggle over urban public policy. Urban populists increasingly rejected claims that whites could represent black interests or that the nonpoor could speak on behalf of the poor. The key to ameliorating urban poverty and inequality was putting power in the hands of the people themselves, to give them the tools to take on urban problems on their own. In a letter to *The Chicago Defender* in early 1965, one Jean Latimore chastised the "paternalism" of "outside saviours" who worked in the black community. "The time has come for communities to insist upon choosing their own leaders as it is their right to do." Community participation required, in the words of left activist W. H. Ferry, "minimum participation" by whites. "Let blacks do it themselves," Ferry wrote to his white readers. "Let them choose their own leaders. Don't try to run things. Stay away until you are invited, and go away when you have provided whatever it is you can offer blacktown." A New York Black Panther pamphlet succinctly described community control. "BLACK POWER MEANS ... where we are in the majority, in a place like Harlem or Bedford-Stuyvesant, we use our majority to win political and economic power—We run things."

Countless neighborhood groups, most of them ephemeral, sprung up in northern cities, fusing conventional volunteerism with more radical demands. A group of Harlem women founded the "Citizens Committee to Keep New York City Clean." Citizens Committee activists organized efforts to remove litter and pressured city officials to improve trash pickup, but also joined more radical anti–police brutality campaigns. In Los Angeles, NOW (the Neighborhood Organization of Watts) campaigned against grocery stores that overcharged blacks for mediocre goods. "These are the small, unpublicized organizations," wrote *Liberator* magazine, "that undertake the glamorless tasks that are necessary if the exploitation and wretched living conditions existing in the ghetto are to end." Community control could become the practical application of black power itself. Indeed, black power advocates celebrated "cement-roots" organizations in inner cities, and many community organizers couched their demands in black power rhetoric.

CORE led the way in bridging community organizing and black power. By 1964, as many CORE chapters experimented with black separatism, they also shifted targets. If integration was impossible or undesirable or both, why bother to open suburban housing or challenge the color line in white-dominated workplaces? In Boston, a racially and politically divided CORE chapter debated "whether we should continue to work on big corporations" such as Howard Johnson's restaurants or instead challenge "small, local neighborhood stores." Those who argued for locally oriented struggles prevailed. In 1965 and 1966, Boston CORE led a "Black Saturday Project" that boycotted small neighborhood stores and demanded the hiring of blacks. Detroit CORE followed a similar course, turning away from major employers such as the American Automobile Association and toward neighborhood grocers who sold inedible food (the "no green meat" campaign) and inner-city slumlords. Detroit activist Tommie Moore argued that CORE had a "definite responsibility to the Negro community in general and to the people of the 'inner city' in particular." Above all, a new generation of activists began to emphasize community organizing as an end in itself. One Boston CORE activist described what would become the preeminent goal for many community groups: It was "getting the people involved in the struggle, feel some strength, to learn something about using power." The problem that poor people faced was anomie and powerlessness, a psychological state of helplessness and inaction. Whether or not they prevailed against the "system"—and most of the time their victories were few—they would gain the psychic satisfaction of having joined a collective struggle.

The impulse toward community organization was not limited to radicals. Established civil rights organizations such as the NAACP and the Urban League were swept up by the growing emphasis on community organizing. In the fall of 1964, the NAACP encouraged the creation of local "economic advancement committees" to assist with the implementation of the War on Poverty nationwide, shifting emphasis to "initiating, developing, and monitoring" youth employment and training programs. The NAACP encouraged its local branches to push for inclusion on Community Action Program boards, taking advantage of "maximum feasible participation." The shift in priorities toward community organizing was a decisive reorientation of the NAACP. "Branches are becoming more a service operation—little Urban Leagues," noted the NAACP's John Morsell in 1969.

As activists called for "power to the people," the very meaning of the War on Poverty came up for grabs. Nothing generated more controversy than the meaning of maximum feasible participation. In the first year of the War on Poverty, over one thousand Community Action Agencies throughout the country received federal funding. Many of these organizations opened offices in predominantly black neighborhoods and drew their staff from neighborhood residents, and by 1968, four-fifths of them were run by private, nonprofit organizations directly funded by OEO. Some Community Action Agencies started up with little difficulty and were well organized. Sargent Shriver hailed Pittsburgh's carefully coordinated program as "the pilot program for the entire United States." In less than a year, with OEO funding, Pittsburgh established seven community offices, which provided job training, child care, social services, and Head Start classes. Some of the programs—such as the one that instructed neighborhood women in "the rudiments of homemaking"—were of little use to poor people's survival, but the Pittsburgh program also provided housing services, welfare consultants, legal services, and health care.

For many urban activists and politicians, the effective provision of social services was not the point of Community Action. What mattered instead was democratic participation and community self-determination. Many offered black power–influenced arguments about racial authenticity. Only blacks could speak for the poor. Adam Clayton Powell, Jr., for one, lambasted Sargent Shriver for surrounding himself with white advisers. Shriver, he argued, "has rejected as policy makers those who know the most about poverty and lack of opportunity." In New York City, Congressman Powell joined activists who complained that "neighborhood and voluntary groups" were "not being given enough say" in antipoverty programs. Protestors forced Mayor Robert Wagner to create an unwieldy sixty-two-member council to oversee the city's antipoverty efforts. In Philadelphia, a group of black leaders, including Cecil Moore, insisted that the city appoint a black antipoverty head and provided a short list of names. The venerable *Philadelphia Tribune* editorialized that "a non-white person should have the duty of carrying out" Philadelphia's antipoverty program because "qualified colored executives have a better understanding of the needs of their brothers."

Conspiracy theories about wealthy whites profiteering from federal antipoverty spending were widespread. "Folks across, up and downtown," wrote a Philadelphia-based columnist, suspected that "the rich are draining the poor." When Mayor James Tate appointed black businessman and Democratic activist Samuel Evans to head the city's War on Poverty, satisfying demands that the agency be black-run, he sparked objections that Evans was not an authentic representative of the poor and that antipoverty programs would become patronage mills for party hacks. Under Evans, most community board members got city or poverty agency jobs. By 1968, Philadelphia's War on Poverty had come under such suspicion that seventeen area civil rights, religious, and labor organizations called for a cessation of federal funding until the city expanded "grassroots participation as required by the Anti-Poverty Act." But by that point, the federal government was already drastically cutting funding for Community Action Programs. Philadelphia's erstwhile poverty warriors were hobbled by the loss of nearly two million dollars in federal funding in 1968 and 1969.

One of the central questions in Philadelphia—and elsewhere—was how representative antipoverty agencies were. Federal officials initially hailed Philadelphia as a model of maximum feasible participation, even though only 2.5 percent of eligible voters participated in elections for community board members. (Turnout rates were highest, about 20 percent, in parts of predominantly black North Philadelphia.) The call for community involvement raised an even more serious question: What constitutes effective representation? In Boston, thirteen black activists in Roxbury leveled "an all-out attack" on the city's ABCD (Action for Boston Community Development) agency because it was not "representative of the community." Their demand—for "a program by which the people can plan for themselves"—was met with the ouster of the organization's "elite board" and its replacement with twenty-two new members, including ten public housing residents. But it was not clear that the new board was any more representative or responsive than the old. In Cleveland, where only one of twenty-five members of the city's Council of Economic Opportunity lived in a poor neighborhood, a group demanding greater inclusion of poor people in the city's antipoverty agencies deposited a bushel of dead rats outside City Hall. Eventually, Cleveland city officials appointed five poor people to an expanded thirty-person council, scarcely the "maximum" participation that activists had demanded.

War on Poverty agencies faced challenges to their legitimacy right from the get-go. In Norwalk, Connecticut, a city "gripped by explosive tensions" in the summer of 1965, eight black groups founded the Norwalk Economic Opportunity Committee to challenge the city-run War on Poverty agency for being out of touch with the city's poor. In Chester, Pennsylvania, the mayor and all his appointees to the board of the Greater Chester Movement, funded by War on Poverty dollars, resigned in the face of criticism by black militants, putting the whole program into jeopardy. And in Plainfield, New Jersey, the Community Action Program faced complaints that it did nothing other than provide a few social workers with jobs. Funding it, argued a critic, was "like throwing money down a rat hole."

It was also unclear whether maximum feasible participation actually improved services to the poor. Detroit and Chicago served as studies in contrast. In Detroit, liberal city officials created an inclusive antipoverty board that included representatives of the UAW, the NAACP, and the Urban League as well as radical grassroots organizers in a West Side tenants organization, CORE, and the now black power–oriented SNCC. Detroit was second only to New York City in the amount of federal antipoverty spending it attracted. Just behind Detroit in funding was Chicago, where Richard J. Daley's machine was at its zenith. Community Action involved what two observers called "minimum feasible participation." There, Daley tamped down the involvement of radical organizations, neighborhood groups, and poor people themselves, instead leaving Community Action in the hands of machine supporters who used it to dispense patronage. Critics lashed out at Daley's "welfare state colonialism." But Chicago's antipoverty agencies were up and running quickly: The machine was well organized to deliver services. In Detroit, by contrast, community boards were consumed with debates about how best to organize themselves.

The relationship of CAP to city governments was especially controversial. Big-city mayors were suspicious of Community Action groups that threatened traditional urban political arrangements. In cities with strong political machines, such as Chicago, local elected officials feared that independent antipoverty agencies would dilute their ability to reward and retain voters with patronage jobs and contracts. Mayor Daley quickly co-opted Chicago's CAA, packing its board with machine hacks and using War on Poverty money to hire community organizers whose best credentials were their connections to ward heelers. Even in cities without political machines or with greatly weakened patronage systems, mayors and city councils feared that the diversion of federal dollars to community-based organizations would cut into the federal urban spending that had become such an important part of their budgets in the postwar years.

At the same time that Community Action faced black challenges to its legitimacy, it came under more sustained—ultimately devastating—criticism from the right. Almost from its inception, conservatives viewed maximum feasible participation as a vehicle for radicals to take over the War on Poverty. Accusations that Johnson's programs were aiding and abetting black radicalism plagued Community Action almost from the start. When LeRoi Jones received an OEO grant in the fall of 1965, New York Republican Paul Fino argued that "the federal government has taken complete leave of its senses to bankroll black segregationists." Syracuse's Community Action Agency became a center for protests against the city housing authority. In San Francisco, where black power and more moderate civil rights leaders clashed over the War on Poverty, some community programs were run by gang members. To Johnson's right-wing critics, the lesson was clear: The federal government was subsidizing nationalism, separatism, and antiwhite politics. Johnson aide Daniel Patrick Moynihan, by this time disaffected, denounced Community Action for "denying the legitimacy of those institutions of electoral representation that had developed over the years—indeed the centuries—and which nominally did provide community control."

AS THE WAR on Poverty struggled along, President Johnson continued to rally the troops. Urban unrest in the summers of 1964 and especially 1965, when riots broke out in Los Angeles, heightened Johnson's sense of urgency. As Watts burned, Johnson had lengthy conversations with the Reverend Martin Luther King, Jr., and former CIA chief John McCone, who would soon lead a commission to examine the riot's causes. As different as King and McCone were, LBJ made the same point to each: Antipoverty programs—particularly job training—would prevent future rioting. On the phone to King a few days after Watts quieted, Johnson sounded like a preacher: "Let's get busy and let's get into this housing. Let's get into this unemployment. Let's get into this social security situation. Let's get into this education. . . . I've spent the biggest part of my life the last four years on civil rights bills, but . . . all of it comes to naught if you have a situation like war in the world or a situation in Los Angeles." To McCone, Johnson was no less forceful: "We've just got to find some way to wipe out these ghettoes. . . . And find some place . . . housing . . . and put them to work. We trained 12,000 last month and found jobs for them." For Johnson, the War on Poverty was riot insurance.

But many civil rights activists thought otherwise. They blamed the inadequacy of civil rights and antipoverty legislation for rising discontent in the streets. Herbert Hill argued that "we must shed ourselves of the illusion that there is a war on poverty. There is only a BB shot against poverty." Others further to the left agreed. "With its titanic rhetoric and piddling appropriations," wrote activist Penn Kemble, an associate of Randolph, Rustin, and Michael Harrington, "it has raised the hopes of many of the poor people whom it has reached without significantly affecting their living standards." Black activists also denounced the Johnson administration for failing to create jobs and deal with the structural underpinnings of poverty. In Chicago, ACT (not an acronym) and its political arm, the Organization for Black Power, claiming to represent the "indigenous leadership of the ghetto," called for poor people to "halt all cooperation" with antipoverty agencies because the War on Poverty "does not and cannot deal with the immediate needs of the poor." Daniel H. Watts, the editor of *Liberator*, lamented that the War on Poverty consisted of "so-called unskilled poor people . . . participating in training and retraining projects such as picking up 3 leaves with a pointed stick, sweeping sidewalks, jockeying cars around in parking lots and receiving certificates of merit for proficiency in their new found 'skills.'"

Even as the Johnson administration promoted the Job Corps and Community Action as antidotes to urban unrest, a growing number of activists—particularly in A. Philip Randolph's circle—saw the riots as a call to action. In November 1965, more than two hundred activists gathered at a White House–sponsored conference on civil rights. Unlike many official Washington assemblies, the event was not stacked with administration sycophants. Many delegates expressed their frustration at the slow rate of progress. CORE denounced the Johnson administration's policies as "advanced tokenism." Delegates discussed the problems of enforcement of the new federal civil rights legislation, but they spent most of their time discussing the problems facing northern cities. In the keynote address, Randolph highlighted persistent urban poverty and unemployment. There was "only one remedy" to defuse the "increasingly explosive socio-racial dynamite in the black ghettos," he warned. That was "the creation of a vast 'freedom budget,' a nationwide plan for the abolition of the ghetto jungles in every city, even at the cost of a hundred billion dollars." Randolph's proposal generated a real buzz. Over the next several months, under Rustin's supervision, a blue-ribbon committee including Harrington, sociologist Herbert Gans, and economist Leon Keyserling, a veteran of the Roosevelt and Truman administrations, hashed out the details.

Released in October 1966, with the endorsement of hundreds of civil rights, labor, and Democratic groups, "A Freedom Budget for All Americans" called for a job creation program; a guaranteed annual income for poor families; and increased federal spending to eradicate slums, improve schools, and build public works. The budget reprised political language that dated back to Roosevelt's Four Freedoms and Second Bill of Rights. It argued that "freedom from economic want and oppression . . . is the necessary complement to freedom from political and civil oppression." The budget offered an implicit critique of what Randolph called the "haphazard, piecemeal efforts" of the War on Poverty. Whitney Young concurred that the Freedom Budget was a necessary "master plan" that would allow the federal antipoverty effort "to make a maximum impact." But neither Rustin nor Keyserling was eager to alienate Johnson or liberal members of Congress. Eager to build a bipartisan, interracial coalition to support the Freedom Budget, Rustin reached out to New York's two senators, liberal Republican Jacob Javits and former attorney general Robert F. Kennedy, who pledged to help promote it on Capitol Hill. To disarm critics who saw the Freedom Budget as an urban black program, Rustin and Keyserling sold it as an effort that would benefit all poor people, regardless of race or region. And playing to worries that the budget was fiscally irresponsible, Keyserling argued that the program could be funded "without robbing anyone," contending that it would pay for itself by generating additional tax revenues by putting more people to work. And both dodged the "guns and butter" question—too optimistically, as it turned out. Keyserling asserted that the $185 billion antipoverty plan would not interfere with the increase in military spending as the United States escalated the Vietnam War.

Even with its temporizing language, the Freedom Budget provided common ground in the increasingly fractious black freedom struggle. The NAACP and Urban League rallied around the plan; both CORE and SNCC, which had recently embraced racial separatism, promised their enthusiastic support, even if they denounced Randolph for failing to include poor people in the planning meetings. And white-led church groups and labor unions joined in support. Advocates of the Freedom Budget, most notably Bayard Rustin, who traveled around the country promoting it, argued that economic independence was the key to eradicating racial inequality. It appeared, for a moment, to be a revival of the proletarian turn of the Depression and World War II years, when a broad swath of activists found common ground challenging the intertwined problems of racial and economic inequality.

The Freedom Budget, even if it brought together a broad coalition of civil rights groups, faced serious obstacles in the rapidly changing political climate of the mid-1960s. In the midterm elections, just a few weeks after the announcement of the Freedom Budget, House Democrats suffered serious losses; several key liberal senators were defeated; and conservatives made major inroads, particularly in California, where Ronald Reagan was elected governor. It was not a propitious moment. A guaranteed national income, a massive public works program, and large-scale investments in the inner cities seemed even more remote. As the Freedom Budget sank into obscurity, the common ground between liberals and radicals vanished. By 1967, many radical black activists jettisoned the budget's universalistic rhetoric and instead pushed for race-targeted reparations and a separate black economy.

The political shifts of 1966 and 1967, combined with the steady increase of federal funds to the war in Vietnam, doomed the prospects for the Freedom Budget and also boded ill for Johnson's antipoverty programs. Community Action Agencies were lighting rods of controversy. The administration began to trim its budget, battered by criticisms of CAP by urban mayors and a spate of negative news stories about the program. An increasingly conservative Congress was loath to rescue a program that was unpopular among big-city mayors and reviled by conservatives, and whose primary constituency—urban African Americans—had little power. Still, government programs were harder to terminate than create. Severely cut by 1968, Community Action struggled through the Nixon and Ford administrations. Nixon restructured the Office of Economic Opportunity to provide grants-in-aid to city and state governments, which then disbursed funds to the job-training, social welfare, and youth-training programs. Funding decisions were safely back in the hands of local public officials, who distributed them to agencies that were far less controversial than their 1960s counterparts.

The Job Corps also suffered from growing skepticism about the War on Poverty. From the outset, its defenders worried that the "rapidly accelerating trend toward an all-Negro Job Corps" would undermine its political support. Their fears were well grounded. A majority of Job Corps participants were black, and they were unwelcome in many of the small towns that were home to the camps. Accounts of rioting corpsmen outraged skeptics already critical of Johnson's antipoverty efforts. "Has the program become a high-cost haven for coddled young hoodlums?" asked *Reader's Digest* in February 1967. The OEO published its own glowing accounts of the program in a vain attempt to deflect criticism. When the Job Corps came up for reauthorization in late 1967, it barely survived serious funding cuts. With less funding, the troubled program foundered. By 1969, a reporter visiting Camp Kilmer charged that the "kids are just sitting around vegetating." The Nixon administration restructured Job Corps in 1969, steadily cut its funding, and finally axed it in 1973. It was mourned by few.

THE JOHNSON ADMINISTRATION's job creation programs had disproportionately targeted black men. Although the Job Corps and Neighborhood Youth Corps did offer programs in clerical and secretarial skills, as well as "training in family life responsibilities" for women, Johnson's antipoverty aides had given little thought to the problems facing poor women. But the issue came to the fore in 1965, with the publication of *The Negro Family: A Case for National Action*, a controversial report by Johnson aide Daniel Patrick Moynihan. A leading social scientist who moved from Harvard to the Department of Labor, Moynihan synthesized the latest scholarship on race and poverty. Building on postwar psychology that emphasized the perils of "maternal smothering" and that saw black culture as fundamentally deformed because of its "matriarchal" orientation, Moynihan brought gender issues to the forefront of public policy. Moynihan offered a devastating critique of black family breakdown as both a cause and consequence of urban poverty. For Moynihan, black women were the key to the "tangle of pathology" that marginalized black men, crippled black children, contributed to the rise of illegitimacy, and perpetuated the "cycle of poverty and disadvantage." By the 1960s, the critique of the "matriarchal" black family and the "emasculated" black man had moved to the mainstream of social policy.

Black opinion on the Moynihan report was mixed. Liberals and radicals were quick to denounce it. CORE's Floyd McKissick railed at Moynihan's assumption that "middle class American values are the correct ones for everyone in America." *The Chicago Defender* criticized Moynihan's "sophomoric treatment of illegitimacy." James Farmer contended that the report blamed the victim and offered a "massive academic cop-out for the white conscience." But the Moynihan report also generated positive press. Black columnist G. C. Oden, for example, argued that it "pretty well verified what we knew about ourselves." An Associated Negro Press writer took the lesson from the report that "swift, uncompromising national action in favor of Negro family structures is imperative."

Many grassroots activists proffered a gender politics that was strikingly similar to Moynihan's, even if shorn of some of his social scientific language and its assumption that white middle-class family life was normative. In particular, black radical activists railed against matriarchy. Alvin Brooks, head of the black power insurgency that captured Kansas City's CORE chapter, lamented that "from Rosa Parks to Harriet Tubman to [Daisy] Bates, women had been pretty much running the show." In his view it was time to "move beyond the matriarchal." Brooks, like many other male black power advocates, argued that women should be in subservient roles. "Black Power means Black Pride, Black Identity and Black Manhood, and Black Manhood means that black men should be leaders, should be assisted in every way by women, but the leadership roles should be male . . . the decision makers were to be male."

Around the country, CORE activists pushed for a new masculine leadership. A New Haven activist lamented that "the black male has been consistently subjugated to a less influential role in the larger society and even in his own family." The solution was to elevate black men into leadership positions. Roy Innis, a leading black power advocate in CORE, offered a scathing description of Harlem's CORE chapter, which he saw as dominated by "feminine, reformist" elements. Under his leadership, black insurgents set up a "black male caucus . . . to bolster [the] self-image of black guys." The confluence of black power and male power alienated many women activists. Gloria Brown, a longtime Detroit CORE member who left the organization in 1967, angry at its "male chauvinism," lamented that "one of the biggest problems was that in beginning to think black, many men felt that to be black meant to be male."

CORE activists were not alone in linking black power and masculinity. Gender essentialism—the belief that differences in sex roles were natural and authentically black—infused many nationalist organizations. The Nation of Islam and Malcolm X advocated a politics of "protection," as Farah Jasmine Griffin has argued. "All women by their nature are fragile and weak," wrote Malcolm; "they are attracted to the male in whom they see strength." Elijah Muhammad lauded the Moynihan report's findings. The Revolutionary Action Movement also embraced notions of assertive masculinity. In a poem published in *Black America*, RAM organizer Ronald Snellings painted an image of a mother figure, suffering without the protection of men: "Where are the warriors, the young men? / Who guards the women's quarters?" Taking up arms would redeem young men: "It is better to live just 30 seconds in the full and beautiful dignity of manhood than to live a thousand years crawling and dragging our chains at the feet of our brutal oppressors."

Leading the way in the essentializing of gender roles was US, Maulana Karenga's cultural nationalist organization, based in Los Angeles. Karenga's mission was to forge a common black identity through the rediscovery of an Afro-American heritage. An advocate of a national holiday to commemorate Malcolm X, a staunch critic of the Vietnam War, and a proponent of the study of African history and language, Karenga is best known as the creator of Kwanzaa—the wintertime holiday that celebrates black unity, commonality, and solidarity as an alternative to Christmas and Hanukkah. Karenga demanded a return to "traditional" gender roles as part of his vision of creating an authentic black society. "What makes a woman appealing is femininity and she can't be feminine without being submissive. A man has to be a leader. . . . The role of the woman is to inspire her man, educate her children and participate in social development." At the heart of Karenga's understanding of gender roles was the concept of "complementarity," that "you complete or make perfect that which is imperfect."

The black power movement was not alone among radical organizations in its embrace of traditional gender roles in the 1960s. Women in civil rights organizations and in white-dominated leftist groups faced harassment and regularly found themselves shut out of leadership positions as men unreflectively followed in their fathers' footsteps. And on the right, grassroots activists and leaders demanded a return to the "traditional" family and challenged feminism on grounds that it abrogated supposedly natural differences between men and women. Ironically, it was the right wing's gender essentialism that had most in common with that of black nationalists; both (for their own reasons) treated gender differences as essential, natural, and normative. "It was but a short step" from the black power politics of masculinity, wrote feminist Paula Giddings, "to advocate that women remain politically barefoot and literally pregnant." An important strain of black nationalists joined a culturally conservative politics of gender and family that continued to shape public policy well after the Moynihan report gathered dust.

The gender essentialism of the mid-1960s came under siege by an increasingly assertive movement of black feminists, many of whom were sympathetic to the goals of black power, self-defense, and self-determination but rejected its pervasive male superiority. "The Black man," wrote Betty Lomax, "frustrated by white America turns inwards to a perverted form of male supremacy in his relationship with the Black woman." Lomax had harsh words for the "Black 'experts'" who accused "women of maintaining a matriarchial household and emasculating her man." Louise Moore, a longtime organizer of domestic workers, was equally critical. "This society is anti-woman," wrote Moore. "We are tired of being cheated of our womanhood by Black men, white men, white women, and a whole capitalist-military system." Black feminists Jean Carey Bond and Pat Peery denounced members of the "avant garde" who were mesmerized by the "popular and dangerous fiction: the myth of black male emasculation, and its descendent concept, the myth of the black female matriarchy."

By 1970, a growing number of black women embraced a feminist politics that at once repudiated the myth of matriarchy and insisted on the "double jeopardy" of racial and sexual oppression. Some black power organizations, among them the Black Panthers, had a change of heart and crusaded against "sexual fascism" in the party. But change was slow to come and intensely fought. Lomax, Moore, and other critics of black sexual politics took heat. Evelyn Rodgers accused her "sisters" of participating in "castrating discussions and articles," rather than recognizing that "we are reflections of the strength of our men." The debate over women's roles raged into the 1970s.

At the grass roots, however, many black women resisted traditional assumptions about gender, challenged the notion of a self-perpetuating "culture of poverty," and pushed for an expansion of the liberal state in ways that challenged simple assumptions about women's role in national politics and in radical social movements. Leading one of the largest and most influential insurgencies of the mid-1960s were black women—those who faced criticism for being part of the "tangle of pathology" and who had been marginalized by many in the rising black insurgency for their role in "emasculating" black men. They pushed for a redefinition of the War on Poverty, to put the issues of single women and their families at the center of public policy. In the process, they both challenged Great Society liberalism and added a new dimension to black radicalism. Eventually, they would win over a minority of black power activists to their position.

In cities throughout the North, black women activists took a program that had been a key part of the American welfare state since the New Deal—but which Johnson and his advisers had downplayed—and moved it to the front and center of the debate about poverty and social policy. Their target was the most controversial liberal social program of the twentieth century: Aid to Families with Dependent Children (named Aid to Dependent Children up through 1962), known colloquially as "welfare." AFDC was one of a series of wealth transfers in the form of grants to the poor, elderly, and disabled that had been created through the Social Security Act of 1935. AFDC was at the bottom of America's two-tiered welfare state, underfunded and politically fragile. Assistance targeted to the poor took second place to the ostensibly universal program of Social Security, which rewarded male breadwinners and stigmatized those outside the paid labor force as undeserving "dependents."

AFDC was a relatively stingy program that provided grants-in-aid for unemployed, single parents, the vast majority of them women, who had children under eighteen. Welfare, like most federal social programs, was managed by states and localities, which had discretion over eligibility rules, the amount of grants, and conditions for continued support. Welfare payments varied widely from state to state, although they tended to be significantly larger in northern states than in the South. Still, for most families, welfare provided insufficient funds to get by, even in the most generous northern states. To supplement meager welfare checks, women regularly worked under the table and got financial assistance from family members and sometimes the fathers of their children. Many relied on extended kin networks to support their children or served as informal day-care providers for their relatives and neighbors. Not infrequently, they found work in the "informal" or underground economy that ranged from taking in boarders to engaging in illegal activities such as numbers running, prostitution, and theft.

Despite the fact that its payments were meager, AFDC was an enormously important program for African Americans in the North. In 1961, in the six northern states with the largest black populations (New York, Pennsylvania, New Jersey, Illinois, Michigan, and Ohio), the percentage of welfare recipients who were black ranged from 40 percent (Pennsylvania) to 73 percent (Illinois). Poor women had a love-hate relationship with welfare. Stingy though it was, welfare support often allowed women to escape abusive relationships. It enabled them to raise their own children rather than pursue strategies common in prewelfare years—putting children up for adoption, placing them with relatives, or sending them to orphanages. Monthly checks also saved many families from hunger and homelessness. Many states even provided welfare recipients with coupons that allowed them to purchase coats and shoes, ensuring a decent minimum standard of living.

Local officials, worried about the budgetary implications of welfare—and responding to the growing unpopularity of the program as its rolls became increasingly black—began to crack down on "chiseling" in the postwar years. Leading the way was Detroit, where the black population had more than tripled between 1940 and 1960 but was devastated by un-employment during the serial recessions of the 1950s. In the early 1950s, amid a panic about welfare "chiseling," some states, including Illinois and Indiana, passed laws requiring the publication of the names of families receiving relief. Some politicians worried that their communities were becoming "welfare magnets" that attracted poor black migrants in search of high benefits. And in the Cold War climate of a celebration of individ-ual initiative and free enterprise, welfare receipt grew controversial.

In 1961, welfare moved from the local to the national stage in New-burgh, New York, a declining industrial town along the Hudson River. Newburgh had a sizeable minority population and, as its economy tanked, growing welfare rolls. When its town manager proposed cutting all unmarried women with children from the rolls and instituting resi-dency requirements, journalists from throughout the country descended on Newburgh. State welfare officials fought the city in court, eventually leading to the restoration of welfare payments in Newburgh. At the same time, the brouhaha raised the specter of unworthy poor people living off the largesse of the state. The city's welfare mothers became a flashpoint for an intense national debate.

Around the country, state legislatures and local officials battled over competing visions of welfare. In Illinois, the state halted welfare payments for more than two weeks in May 1963 because of a dispute involving Re-publicans who called for "more intensive casework," a benefits cap on welfare recipients, and "efficient prosecution of frauds." Democrat Arnold Maremont, the feisty and short-lived head of the state welfare commission, denounced Republican critics as "definitely anti-Negro" and charged that their position "smacks of Hitlerism." Stingy welfare payments in Illinois, argued Maremont, did not facilitate the movement from "rags to riches" but from "rags to rags." In the fury over his intemperate language, Mare-mont lost his job, but the debate about welfare continued. Similar argu-ments over welfare roiled other states and localities. In New York City, critics of rising welfare rolls demanded a residency requirement; in Con-necticut, where only 5 percent of the population but nearly 50 percent of welfare recipients were black, debates swirled around eligibility standards. And in California, Alameda County and Los Angeles County officials im-plemented a "no work, no dole" program in 1964, forcing welfare recipi-ents to take jobs as farmworkers. Even in states with generous benefits, welfare officials faced pressure to keep rolls down and were secretive about what factors counted in determining eligibility and, if a family were declared eligible, how much support it would be provided.

As welfare authorities cracked down on "chiseling," they and recipients engaged in a sort of cat-and-mouse game around questions of outside income and eligibility. AFDC recipients needed outside income to get by, but they had to conceal extra income from authorities. Welfare authorities policed welfare recipients—penalizing them or cutting them off if they showed signs of having outside support. Most states and localities demanded that welfare recipients maintain "suitable homes," a vague category that could be used to deprive unmarried mothers of support and penalize women who did not keep their houses to high standards or who had family members involved in criminal activity. Welfare recipients reported to caseworkers who ascertained their eligibility and often had to open their doors to investigators looking for evidence of outside income or the presence of a man in the household. Welfare inspectors relied on anonymous tips from snoopy neighbors or suspicious social workers and often appeared at welfare recipients' homes when they were least expected, at dinnertime or late in the evening.

What made AFDC particularly frustrating was that it was often administered capriciously. City and state welfare officials had great discretion in determining a woman's eligibility. Around the country, the application process was lengthy, often requiring hours of waiting in welfare offices only to be rudely dismissed for the lack of acceptable documentation. Social workers might cut off a recipient because she had a television set or because a pair of men's shoes peeked out from beneath a bed. Investigators could go to a house on the whiff of a rumor, usually that a welfare recipient had a live-in boyfriend. E.T.F., an anonymous Chicagoan writing to the *Defender*, expressed a typical grievance. "Just because they suspect some poor welfare mother may have a man on the premises," she wrote, "doesn't give them the right to invade the privacy of the poor woman's apartment. It's wrong to have one law for the rich and another for the poor, to respect the privacy of the rich and flout that of the poor." Barbara Harris, another Chicagoan, lashed out against the premise that welfare agencies should investigate the character of recipients. "The Poverty Program, to my knowledge, was not instituted to investigate the moral principles of the poverty stricken, but to establish a means whereby the poverty stricken would not be." But moral regulation and public assistance went hand in hand.

By the early 1960s, welfare mothers joined the debate about poverty and public policy. Discontented with the administration of welfare programs and frustrated at the meagerness of their support checks, small groups of women began to mobilize for welfare reform. Sociologist Belinda Robnett calls these women "bridge leaders," those with the skills to draw community members into larger social movements. In Oakland, California, a group of women formed a "welfare rights" movement in 1964, to challenge the "slave labor" of the "no work, no dole" program. In Los Angeles, antipoverty activists "grounded in militancy and conflict" struggled to "capture control of welfare programs." Inspired by black radicalism, they demanded "welfare power." Fifty groups representing welfare recipients sprung up in New York City in the spring and early summer of 1966 alone. When the fledgling Poverty/Rights Action Center (PRAC) held its first meeting in the summer of 1966, it drew delegates from similar grassroots groups in twenty-five cities.

A typical grassroots welfare rights group was Boston's MAW (Mothers for Adequate Welfare), founded in 1965. Doris Bland, a welfare recipient in the Roxbury neighborhood, began by gathering a small group of women and publicizing their complaints. "Being on Aid to Dependent Children (ADC) is nothing to be ashamed of," Bland told a reporter. "Things happen in a person's life that she cannot always control." No issue outraged welfare recipients more than judgmental social workers and punitive eligibility rules. Bland's organization, like similar groups throughout the North, pushed for an end to snooping to determine whether a recipient had other sources of support. "You're watched all the time," she complained. "You're spied upon and talked about." MAW wanted to create a more humane welfare system, one that respected the "dignity" of welfare recipients. "When we have enough [members], we will begin to think about ways of protesting to bring pressure on the city officials who won't treat us as human beings." But dignity was not enough. MAW also pushed for larger welfare checks. Given Boston's high rents and weak economy, AFDC checks were insufficient.

Bland's call to protest drew more women into her circle. By the summer of 1966, MAW had enough members to stage a march on the Massachusetts State House. Over the next few years, MAW regularly protested there, at local welfare offices, and with other welfare mothers in Washington, D.C. MAW's demonstrations were usually peaceful, but MAW members sometimes threatened rioting and disruption. In the summer of 1967, a MAW demonstration outside a Roxbury welfare office turned ugly when the group clashed with police. But unlike many radical groups in the mid- and late 1960s, MAW kept channels of negotiation open with local and state officials. Their first march on the State House was followed by a meeting with Governor John Volpe and Lieutenant Governor Elliot Richardson, who was particularly sympathetic to their demands. That a few hundred welfare recipients found a hearing in high places was testimony both to the growing fears of black discontent in the urban North and to the openness of liberal state officials around the country who, inspired by the War on Poverty, were rethinking welfare. State welfare officials supported MAW when they joined a national protest demanding an increase in federal welfare aid to the states. Social workers threatened a sit-in to support MAW's demand for better clothing allowances for poor children. And the state government responded to MAW's demands by restructuring the Massachusetts welfare system, simplifying its regulations, and appointing poor women to its advisory board.

MAW's experience with state welfare officials was not atypical. While some social workers excelled at being gatekeepers to the welfare system, others were deeply sympathetic to the poor. Many social workers chose their profession because of their commitment to social change, and many social work educators came from the religious or political left, combining their pedagogy with a commitment to economic equality, fairness, and civil rights. Social workers on the front lines of the welfare system saw that AFDC was often unfair, capricious, and punitive. A cadre of social workers—many of them sympathetic to the larger civil rights movement—began to challenge the welfare system from within. In Chicago in 1966, a social workers' union issued a "Manifesto for a More Humane Welfare System," which denounced "paternalism" and called for more generous benefits. Around the country, inside agitators in welfare offices began to leak out copies of eligibility requirements. Armed with these internal documents, welfare activists began to fight welfare authorities on their own terms, challenging eligibility rulings. However Byzantine their bureaucracy seemed, welfare offices were publicly accountable. Questions of eligibility became the wedge for grassroots organizations to challenge the welfare system.

More so than battles over open housing or education, the welfare rights movement brought together the local and the national. That welfare rights moved from small cells of local activists such as MAW onto the national stage was the result of the extraordinary organizing efforts of George Wiley, a Syracuse University professor who left his post to become a full-time organizer, and Johnnie Tillmon, a former laundry worker in Los Angeles who depended on AFDC to support her family after chronic arthritis made it impossible for her to continue working. Wiley and Tillmon came from totally different places. Raised in a middle-class black family in mostly white Warwick, Rhode Island, Wiley grew up with a strong sense of privilege and social responsibility. One of the first African Americans to earn a Ph.D. in chemistry, Wiley seemed destined for a prominent academic career. But he was not content with running a laboratory and publishing scholarly articles. In the early 1960s, his interest in the burgeoning civil rights movement brought him to CORE. For a small city, Syracuse had a long history of civil rights activism, drawing its energy largely from liberal faculty and students and from Social Gospel–influenced churches. In the early 1950s, Syracuse activists challenged housing segregation and pushed public officials to improve living conditions in the notorious fifteenth ward. When CORE chapters throughout the North sprang back to life, Syracuse had a strong infrastructure already in place. Wiley built on Syracuse's energy and, through his charisma and vision, turned the city's CORE chapter into one of the most active in the country.

Wiley's successes in Syracuse—most notably negotiating a school desegregation plan with the Syracuse school district and leading protests at segregated construction sites—quickly brought him to the attention of CORE's national headquarters. A charismatic speaker as comfortable with foundation heads and business executives as he was with public housing tenants, Wiley rose in prominence in CORE and strongly supported efforts to push it in a new direction, toward grassroots organizing among the poor. In 1965, Wiley and national CORE pushed for an expansion of the War on Poverty—emphasizing the need for far-reaching programs to address the root causes of economic inequality, among them an

Anna Arnold Hedgeman,
lifelong civil rights activist,
1965. *(AP Photo)*

A. Philip Randolph, head of
the Brotherhood of Sleeping
Car Porters, former president
of the National Negro Congress,
and strategist of the March on
Washington Movement, 1943.
*(Walter Reuther Library,
Wayne State University)*

Flyer for the
March on Wash-
ington Movement,
1943. *(Library of
Congress)*

What Are Our Immediate Goals?

1. To mobilize five million Negroes into one militant mass for pressure.

2. To assemble in Chicago the last week in May, 1943, for the celebration of

"WE ARE AMERICANS – TOO" WEEK

And to ponder the question of Non-Violent Civil Disobedience and Non-Cooperation, and a Mass March On Washington.

WHY SHOULD WE MARCH?

15,000 Negroes Assembled at St. Louis, Missouri
20,000 Negroes Assembled at Chicago, Illinois
23,500 Negroes Assembled at New York City
Millions of Negro Americans all Over This Great
Land Claim the Right to be Free!

FREE FROM WANT!
FREE FROM FEAR!
FREE FROM JIM CROW!

"Winning Democracy for the Negro is Winning the War
for Democracy!" — A. Philip Randolph

Gunnar Myrdal, author of *An American Dilemma*. *(The Granger Collection, New York)*

Jim Crow's pall-bearers at the NAACP Parade for Victory, Detroit, 1944. *(Library of Congress)*

Packinghouse workers leading a demonstration linking the issues of racial equality and wages in Chicago, probably mid-1940s. *(Walter Reuther Library, Wayne State University)*

Activist, writer, and lawyer Pauli Murray, about 1950. *(The Schlesinger Library, Radcliffe Institute, Harvard University)*

Workers' Defense League activists Layle Lane and Morris Milgram at the funeral of sharecropper Odell Waller, July 1942. *(Walter Reuther Library, Wayne State University)*

NAACP New York branch storefront headquarters, 1945. *(The Granger Collection, New York)*

Henry Lee Moon, NAACP publicist and advocate of black electoral and political power, standing, with (left to right) NAACP leaders Roy Wilkins, Walter White, and Thurgood Marshall, circa 1951. *(Library of Congress)*

NAACP attorney Thurgood Marshall (center, next to woman with flowers) with parent leaders of the Hillburn, New York, school boycott, 1943. *(Library of Congress)*

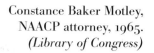

Constance Baker Motley,
NAACP attorney, 1965.
(Library of Congress)

Whites gather in front of the home of Daisy and William Myers, the first black family to move into Levittown, Pennsylvania, August 1957. *(Temple University Libraries, Urban Archives)*

Open housing advocate Morris Milgram outside his home at Greenbelt Knoll, a planned, racially integrated subdivision in Northeast Philadelphia. *(Temple University Libraries, Urban Archives)*

CORE members leading an open housing protest in suburban Detroit, July 27, 1963. *(Walter Reuther Library, Wayne State University)*

CORE members picketing the Detroit headquarters of dime store chain S. S. Kresge in solidarity with southern sit-in protestors, 1961. *(Walter Reuther Library, Wayne State University)*

Whitney Young, president of the National Urban League, circa 1960. *(Walter Reuther Library, Wayne State University)*

The Great Walk to Freedom, Detroit, June 23, 1963. *(Walter Reuther Library, Wayne State University)*

The Reverend Albert Cleage fires up the crowd at Detroit's Cobo Hall,
taking the stage just minutes before Martin Luther King, Jr., June 23, 1963.
(Walter Reuther Library, Wayne State University)

The Reverend Martin Luther King, Jr., addressing
the June 23, 1963, rally in Detroit. *(Walter Reuther
Library, Wayne State University)*

Protestors challenging discrimination in the building trades chained themselves to a crane at the construction site of the Rochdale Village housing project in Queens, New York, September 20, 1963. *(AP Photo)*

Maxwell Stanford, Revolutionary Action Movement founder, 1967. *(AP Photo)*

RALLY AND DANCE

Herman Ferguson, educator and black power activist, March 1968. *(AP Photo)*

Firefighters and rioters on the streets of Newark, New Jersey, during the uprising that shook the city in mid-July 1967. *(Temple University Libraries, Urban Archives)*

Black power graffiti painted on a debris-strewn Detroit street on July 23, 1967, the first day of the uprising. *(Walter Reuther Library, Wayne State University)*

A. Philip Randolph meeting with President Lyndon Baines Johnson, circa 1966. *(Library of Congress)*

Doris Bland, of Mothers for Adequate Welfare, leading a protest in Boston, 1966. *(Courtesy of Boston Public Library, Print Department)*

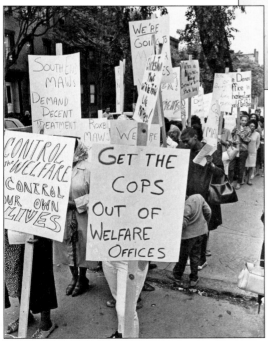

Mothers for Adequate Welfare demonstrating for welfare rights in Boston's South End, 1966. *(Courtesy of Boston Public Library, Print Department)*

Two of the nation's most prominent black power leaders, the Reverend Albert Cleage (left) and Stokely Carmichael, meet in Detroit, July 30, 1966. *(Walter Reuther Library, Wayne State University)*

Tenants' rights activist Jesse Gray outside the Harlem headquarters of his Community Council on Housing, May 1965. *(AP Photo)*

Open housing activist Clarence Funnyé, 1967. *(National Committee Against Discrimination in Housing Collection, Amistad Research Center at Tulane University, New Orleans, Louisiana)*

The Reverend Leon Sullivan promoting black economic power at the opening of Progress Plaza mall in North Philadelphia, October 27, 1968. *(Temple University Libraries, Urban Archives)*

Republic of New Africa press conference, September 12, 1969. Robert F. Williams is seated at the microphones, and to his left is Gaidi Obadele (Milton Henry). Immediately behind him, standing, is reparations advocate Audley "Queen Mother" Moore. To her left is Imari Obadele (Richard Henry). *(Walter Reuther Library, Wayne State University)*

James Forman, author of the Black Manifesto, addressing the National Black Economic Development Conference, December 10, 1969. *(Walter Reuther Library, Wayne State University)*

Protestors against separate and unequal education, Englewood, New Jersey, February 1962. *(AP Photo)*

Militant attorney Paul Zuber in the 1970s. *(Institute Archives and Special Collections, Rensselaer Polytechnic Institute, Troy, New York)*

June Shagaloff, NAACP staff member and architect of the organization's northern school boycott and litigation strategy, August 17, 1962. *(Bancroft Library, University of California, Berkeley)*

Ronald Bradley, the elementary school student who was one of the named plaintiffs in the landmark school desegregation case *Bradley v. Milliken*, January 20, 1976. *(Walter Reuther Library, Wayne State University)*

Richard Hatcher at the podium addressing the National Black Political Convention, March 10, 1973. Standing to his right are Amiri Baraka and Jesse Jackson. *(AP Photo)*

Activist and future Pennsylvania state senator Roxanne Jones meets with Governor Richard Thornburgh, 1981. *(Temple University Libraries, Urban Archives)*

increased minimum wage, a public works program, and a guaranteed annual income for the jobless. But Wiley's close alliance with integrationists in CORE became a liability as the organization moved toward racial separatism. After he was passed over to be CORE's national director by the black power insurgency that backed Floyd McKissick, Wiley left the organization and carried with him a commitment to creating an interracial movement of the poor.

Until 1963, when she started receiving AFDC, Johnnie Tillmon—like the majority of black women—had held a variety of paid jobs, none of them very good, to support her family. A migrant from Arkansas, she found that work in Los Angeles was a bare step upward from the tough life that her sharecropper parents had led. During World War II, she had worked as an inspector in a munitions plant, the best-paid job she would ever hold. But as a mother with five children and few skills, she did not have many choices. She worked as a maid, a dishwasher, and, after she divorced her husband in 1960, in a commercial laundry. Tillmon had been elected a shop steward for her local of the Laundry Workers Union, but her stint as an organizer was short. Disabled by arthritis, she found herself unemployed in 1963. To support her family, she applied for welfare. The process was degrading. In her Watts housing project, Tillmon brought together a group of women who shared her frustrations with the welfare system, especially since California was experimenting with tighter eligibility requirements. Over the next few years, Tillmon held meetings, many of them surreptitious, to begin challenging California's punitive and penurious ANC (Aid to Needy Children) program. Tillmon's group, ANC Mothers Anonymous, circulated information, helped women maneuver through the welfare bureaucracy, and began to organize protests. By 1966, Tillmon was part of a statewide effort to organize welfare recipients and had begun making connections with similar groups in other states.

More so than most grassroots activists, Wiley and Tillmon had eyes on both the local and the national. Through his nationwide connections, Wiley knew of efforts to reform AFDC in cities from San Francisco to Chicago to Detroit to Boston, led by welfare recipients. In April 1966, Wiley founded the Poverty/Rights Action Center to serve as a bridge between fragmented welfare rights efforts around the country and bring their agenda to the corridors of power in Washington. Events in the summer and fall of 1966 demonstrated the energy of local activists who marched by the thousands to demand a humane, better-paying welfare system, but also pushing for economic reforms, including the expansion of job-training programs for poor women and subsidized day care. In June, welfare rights activists marched across Ohio and demonstrated peacefully at the statehouse in Columbus, in a reprise of the southern freedom marches. In September, in Hartford, Connecticut, 150 demonstrators, most of them women, chanted the newly minted slogan "Black Power" and clashed with police in a "fist-swinging" demonstration demanding increased welfare benefits. Also that month, welfare mothers led more militant protests in New York, where seventeen protestors were arrested for committing civil disobedience, CORE-style, at the city's central welfare office. New York welfare commissioner Jack R. Goldberg (who was sympathetic to calls for welfare reform) realized that the protests were part of something bigger. "This is part of a national movement to organize welfare recipients to smash welfare departments," he observed, "so that Congress will be forced to pass legislation for a guaranteed minimum income."

Many local activists in the North in the mid-1960s lost sight of national politics because of their emphasis on the daily rigors of grassroots community organizing. The welfare rights movement was a noteworthy exception. Tillmon and Wiley believed that on-the-ground organizing was necessary but not sufficient for policy change. They would not be content winning a string of local battles. Instead their goal was to harness the remarkable energy of hundreds of grassroots welfare groups and use their combined clout to push for changes in federal public policy. The National Welfare Rights Organization (NWRO)—as Wiley and Tillmon rechristened PRAC in 1967—fought the battle on several fronts at once, using every tactic at their disposal, from protest to lobbying to litigation. Welfare mothers continued to march, using the threat of disruption as a lever for change. But they also worked the "system" to their advantage, forging alliances with liberal welfare administrators and social workers. It simply would not be possible for welfare reform to be implemented quickly or decisively without the support of welfare bureaucrats—the movement needed allies in government if it were going to be more than just another prophetic voice calling for change. Community action agencies—created by the War on Poverty—were serving, at least in some cities, as cauldrons of activism. Academics, many on the political left, argued that the eradication of poverty required mobilizing the poor. Two New York–based academics, Frances Fox Piven and Richard Cloward, advised the NWRO as part of their broader vision of empowering the poor to be the agents of social change. And, increasingly, a cadre of young attorneys, infused with the hope that they could make litigation into a vehicle for societal transformation, joined the struggle for welfare rights.

The architects of the War on Poverty did not envision the creation of legal services for the poor, but a handful of local antipoverty organizations, most with funding from the Ford Foundation, began experimenting with legal programs. The most influential model was the bureaucratically named "Neighborhood Socio-Legal Team" developed in New Haven by Edgar and Jean Cahn, an interracial couple who had recently graduated from Yale Law School. The Cahns viewed legal services as a vehicle to give voice to the poor. The New Haven model, which they spelled out in an influential *Yale Law Journal* article, attracted the attention of War on Poverty czar Sargent Shriver. For Shriver, reading the Cahns' article was like "Columbus discovering America . . . something that captured my mind and imagination." Enamored with the idea of a legal component to Community Action, Shriver brought the Cahns to Washington.

In late 1964 and early 1965, the Cahns laid the groundwork for experimental neighborhood legal services projects under the aegis of the Office of Economic Opportunity. At first, OEO's legal services initiative—like many War on Poverty experiments—was a disorganized affair. But even as the program struggled to establish an office and hire a staff, its first director, lawyer Clinton Bamberger, offered a clear vision of the program as an instrument of social change. Under the OEO, legal services would "provide the means" to break "the bonds which imprison people in poverty, to marshal the forces of law to combat the cause and effects of poverty." Under the vaguely written language of the War on Poverty legislation, Community Action grants, awarded on an ad hoc basis, created legal services programs. By 1966, legal services had gained the support of the legal and political establishment. When the Equal Opportunity Act came up for reauthorization, Congress allocated $22 million to fund a Legal Services program that would "further the cause of justice among persons living in poverty by mobilizing the assistance of lawyers and legal institutions and by providing legal advice, representation, counseling, education, and other appropriate services."

Much OEO funding went to traditional charitable organizations that provided legal aid to poor people, but a sizeable cadre of legal activists shared Bamberger's broad vision of the law as a vehicle for political change. Legal Services became a magnet for bright, left-leaning law students—of whom there were many by the mid-1960s. Many started their legal training with hopes of using the law to better the world, but before the creation of Legal Services, few found real opportunities to do so and, at best, represented indigent clients through pro bono work. By 1971, the Legal Services program had two thousand attorneys nationwide and handled more than one million cases per year. Legal Services attorneys took on all sorts of cases that larger firms would seldom touch, including landlord-tenant disagreements, family disputes, and credit problems. But they also viewed themselves as the legal arm of grassroots civil rights, black power, and community organizing efforts. Under the supervision of state and local bar associations, Legal Services had an establishment rationale. Its defenders were "committed to the proposition that the 'system' will serve the poor as well as the rich," or, as President Nixon put it, "to secure justice within the system and not on the streets." But most of the young attorneys drawn to Legal Services had a more expansive view of the law as a vehicle for social change. And their clients, many of whom gained competent counsel for the first time, staunchly defended the program.

Other activist attorneys—many attached to law school clinics and civil rights groups—joined Legal Services in taking on an array of cases intended to bolster grassroots struggles against police brutality, educational inequalities, and housing discrimination. Critics of advocacy lawyers on the left saw their use of litigation as a top-down strategy that placed faith in an elite institution and sapped energy from grassroots organizing efforts. Empowering lawyers, they contended, was an indirect way to empower the poor. Other critics put their faith in lobbying, legislation, and electoral politics. Real change would not come through judicial fiat; it would result only from efforts to rewrite existing laws through the democratic process. But few welfare rights organizers drew a bright line between the "march on the courts," legislation, and protests in the streets. In the realm of poverty policy—as with education, housing, and public accommodations—litigation efforts were fundamentally intertwined with grassroots organizing efforts.

The most important welfare rights cases showed the power of the synergy between protest and law. Activists had expanded the rights rhetoric that had been a staple of American politics since the New Deal. But for the right to welfare to become a reality, not just an abstraction, required changing the law. In *King v. Smith* (1968) and *Lewis v. Martin* (1970), the Supreme Court struck down "man in the house" rules. And in a 1969 case, *Shapiro v. Thompson*, it ruled that state residency requirements were unconstitutional. Welfare might still be administered on the state level, but the Court firmly ruled that it was a national concern. Still, welfare attorneys pushed further. In *Goldberg v. Kelly*, they achieved their greatest victory of the generation. John Kelly, the named plaintiff, was a homeless black man who had been denied benefits on a technicality. A group of lawyers, including members of New York's Mobilization for Youth, a War on Poverty–funded community agency, represented Kelly and a group of similarly situated welfare recipients. In its landmark 1970 ruling, the Burger Court ruled that welfare was "not a gratuity" but an entitlement. Under *Goldberg*, welfare recipients won the right to due process, namely to get a hearing before their relief payments were cut off. But the courts were also fickle allies. Later that year, the Supreme Court upheld Maryland's cap on welfare benefits, a blow to those who advocated welfare payments sufficient for survival.

Welfare rights activists relied on litigation, but they continued to protest in the streets. While many black-dominated radical organizations embraced the strategy of separatism, the NWRO eagerly sought allies across racial lines. The NWRO continued to organize locally, but also forged links with other civil rights groups, religious organizations, and trade unions. At a moment when many radicals—especially in male-dominated groups—viewed the federal government as the enemy, welfare rights activists reached out to prominent black and white leaders in the nation's capital. In May 1968, just five weeks after Martin Luther King, Jr., was assassinated, Johnnie Tillmon led 1,700 welfare recipients and their supporters on a march through riot-ravaged Washington, D.C. Several thousand more joined a rally where Coretta Scott King, still in mourning black, gave a twenty-minute speech. What was noteworthy about the rally was the number of high-profile supporters it attracted. Ethel Kennedy, the wife of Senator Robert F. Kennedy, joined several prominent women on the stage. Johnson administration officials, including a high-ranking member of the EEOC and the assistant attorney general for civil rights, were spotted "mingling with the crowd."

While NWRO protestors demonstrated in Washington, they also continued to battle for rights in state capitols and in the localities, where social workers stood between recipients and the benefits to which they believed they were entitled. The Pennsylvania Welfare Rights Organization—led by single mother Roxanne Jones—was one of the most creative and influential. A migrant from North Carolina, Jones worked as a dancer and waitress before being abandoned by her alcoholic husband. A young mother with two daughters, she moved to Southwark Plaza, a windswept public housing project whose towers stood sentry over a riverfront neighborhood that had been home to Philadelphia's working class and poor since the eighteenth century. Life in Southwark Plaza politicized Jones. There, she found herself at the center of a network of young, unmarried mothers—a rapidly increasing segment of the population in Philadelphia's public housing. They were frustrated at the indignities of life in the projects. Public housing never lived up to its promise. The buildings were badly managed. Cheap construction caused all sorts of problems: ill-fitting windows, cold cement floors, thin walls. The elevators frequently failed. The corridors were dimly lit and dangerous. The lawns surrounding the towers were muddy and trash strewn. The dark corners, stairwells, and corridors provided children all sorts of places to play with little or no adult supervision. Bored teenagers hung out in the playgrounds at night, and the police seldom patrolled.

Like Doris Bland and Johnnie Tillmon, Jones and her neighbors lived under the constant scrutiny of social workers and housing officials. Jones recalled the humiliation of applying for welfare. "The social worker made me feel like I had committed murder when I first asked for help." Welfare authorities gathered information on their familial status, always on the lookout for those who violated "man in the house" rules. Women who took jobs in the underground economy—sewing, taking in boarders, watching their relatives' or neighbors' children—were subject to eviction for their unreported income. The intrusive inspections were galling. And even though Pennsylvania offered some of the more generous AFDC benefits in the country, welfare checks provided barely enough for survival.

Things got very tight by the end of the month, especially for those without under-the-table income. In 1968, Jones and her children received only $232 per month.

Swept up by the movement for social change in the mid-1960s, Jones joined the Pennsylvania Welfare Rights Organization in 1967. A charismatic leader, a forceful and witty speaker, and a fearless protestor, she quickly rose to head the organization. Under Jones's leadership, PWRO took on an ambitious agenda. The battle for security for poor women needed to be fought on several fronts simultaneously—and the tactics varied on each. Like other welfare rights groups, PWRO challenged capricious eligibility requirements. The welfare system was not, however, their only target. In 1968, Jones led a campaign—one that welfare activists nationwide subsequently adopted—to demand credit for welfare recipients at local department stores. Armed with leaflets and banners, Jones and her "sisters" picketed, joined by mostly white, middle-class allies (the Friends of Welfare Rights) at Lit Brothers and Gimbels stores. Poor people, she contended, deserved the right to consume. A year later, she mastered the obscure rules of the Pennsylvania welfare system and, empowered by the call for "maximum feasible participation," successfully lobbied the state to place a welfare rights representative in every state public assistance office—a program that simultaneously provided welfare recipients with sympathetic ears and created jobs for poor women. In addition, Jones and her fellow activists took on quality-of-life issues, pressuring public utilities to offer discounts to people living below the poverty line, challenging the local phone company's practice of charging welfare recipients higher installation fees for their phones, demanding better police protection in poor neighborhoods, and pressuring state officials to expand job training and literacy programs.

Under Jones, the PWRO fused civil rights and black power tactics, sometimes challenging the system through disruptive protest and at other times working within the system to effect change. Welfare rights activists picketed and leafleted public offices, wearing thrift-store dresses and pushing baby carriages. At other events, they chanted black power slogans and threatened violence. In 1970, Jones was arrested for throwing a shoe through a window of the Pennsylvania state capitol in Harrisburg during a demonstration against proposed state cuts in assistance to the elderly. But protest—peaceful or disruptive—was just one of Jones's weapons. Like many activists before her, Jones did not see litigation and community organizing as antithetical. She worked closely with Philadelphia's Community Legal Services program, filing lawsuits on behalf of welfare recipients and challenging the state's punitive welfare laws. And Jones found allies in the federal government, winning a grant in 1969 to employ VISTA (Volunteers in Service to America) workers. Jones celebrated more victories than defeats. Pennsylvania, like many states, expanded its welfare rolls and adopted less punitive regulations. Many department stores offered welfare mothers credit. The city's gas and electrical companies gave poor people extensions to pay their bills before the utilities turned off their heat and lights. Not surprisingly, in 1971, George Wiley singled out Jones as one of the movement's most charismatic and effective leaders.

The welfare rights movement played a crucial role in transforming poverty policy, though its precise impact proved difficult to quantify. Undoubtedly, its major accomplishment was modifying eligibility rules and, simultaneously, raising the consciousness of potential welfare recipients that they indeed had a right to welfare. By 1971, nearly 90 percent of eligible families received AFDC—a startling increase from ten years earlier, when restrictions kept nearly two-thirds of eligible families away. The results were reflected in the dramatic increase in welfare rolls. In 1960, 3.1 million people received Aid to Dependent Children. The figure was 4.3 million in 1965 and 6.1 million in 1969, and 10.1 million in 1974. Most of the increase in the caseload came in the North—40 percent in New York and California. Both states had large welfare rights movements, but both—like Bland's Massachusetts and Jones's Pennsylvania—also had state and local welfare bureaucracies that grew increasingly sympathetic to welfare recipients. Whatever the alchemy between bureaucratic innovation and protest, the results were striking. Studies showed that transfer payments from the government to the poor were essential to the reduction in poverty in the 1960s and early 1970s, especially among households headed by African Americans, among whom rates of poverty would have remained stagnant without federal support.

By the early 1970s, however, conservatives stepped up the siege on the Great Society. When President Nixon proposed a complete overhaul of welfare—creating a lump-sum Family Assistance Plan (FAP) to replace AFDC—welfare rights activists joined a broad coalition of liberals and leftists who fought the program. Welfare rights activists supported the concept of a guaranteed annual income, but they worried that Nixon's proposed annual allowance of $1,600 per family would be significantly lower than many state welfare payments, especially in the North. In Jones's Pennsylvania, a family of four barely survived on the average annual payment of $3,600. "Nixon couldn't live like this," charged a PWRO member. "If this bill passes," Jones threatened, "all hell is going to break loose." Their worries were well founded. In 1970, while the Nixon administration lobbied for FAP, the Philadelphia Housing Authority raised rents to as much as ninety-six dollars per month for a four-room apartment. Market-rent apartments, even in run-down buildings, were usually more expensive. How could people survive? Another element of FAP was just as controversial. Nixon's plan required welfare recipients to work. But in the rapidly shrinking labor markets in northern cities, jobs, especially for unskilled women with children, were scarce. The FAP also did not include provisions for day care.

Nixon's FAP, under siege by welfare rights advocates and their allies, as well as by conservatives who opposed the concept of a guaranteed annual income for the poor, failed in Congress. However, the debate over welfare turned more sharply to the right in the aftermath of FAP's demise. In the months leading to the election of 1972, Nixon jettisoned the idea of a guaranteed income altogether and launched a broader campaign against welfare, now endorsing the call for mandatory "workfare." Amid the hostile political climate, the NWRO broke into factions. George Wiley resigned from the organization and died in a tragic accident in 1973, having just begun to plan for the creation of a Movement for Economic Justice, to bring working-class people and the poor together across racial and ethnic divides. The movement, however, remained an unrealized dream, a utopian idea that largely died with Wiley. By the mid-1970s, grassroots organizations continued to struggle for social justice, but in an increasingly hostile political environment.

Welfare rights, more than any grassroots movement of the late 1960s, rose and fell with Great Society liberalism. As Johnson's War on Poverty came under siege by the right and as Republicans began to exploit deep-rooted antiwelfare sentiments held by whites, the very concept of a right to welfare also came under attack. To a great extent, welfare rights was a victim of its own success. Average payments per capita reached a peak in

1972. But the very expansion of welfare seemed—at least to its critics on the right—evidence of big-government liberalism run amok.

HOWEVER SHORT-LIVED, THE War on Poverty and the welfare rights movement reshaped the struggle for racial equality. In many cities—whether antipoverty agencies were machine-controlled or independently run—maximum feasible participation brought a whole new generation of black political activists to the table. If community control meant "the people" controlling their own fate, the legitimacy of social welfare agencies and community development organizations depended on having black faces dealing with black constituents. The number of black social workers, preschool teachers, welfare caseworkers, and government clerical workers skyrocketed. In addition, Community Action Agencies became a training ground for a whole generation of black political leaders in the North. Most striking was the significant increase of women in positions of responsibility in antipoverty organizations and in government writ large. The emphasis on community organization tapped a deep current of black women's community activism in northern cities, especially around issues of welfare, childhood education, and housing. Their efforts were largely overlooked by journalists and scholars at the time but were far-reaching. In Philadelphia, more than 70 percent of the elected Community Action board members were women.

In addition, the War on Poverty solidified a trend that had been under way since the New Deal and had accelerated during the Kennedy administration. Over the course of the 1960s, government became the single most important employer of African Americans in northern cities. By 1970, 20 percent of blacks were employed in government positions. A staggering 72 percent of college-educated black women in 1970 were on government payrolls, as were 57 percent of black college-educated men. Government jobs were relatively stable and offered generous benefits. At a time when many private-sector employers looked askance at black workers, government became the most important vehicle for the expansion of the black middle class. At the peak of the Great Society, longtime NAACP activist Gloster Current considered the "federal government the largest civil rights organization today."

Community Action had another unanticipated long-term effect. It crystallized the notions that the struggle for racial justice must fundamentally be local and community-based and that urban problems are best dealt with on a piece-by-piece, neighborhood-by-neighborhood basis. A few longtime activists, such as A. Philip Randolph, worried about the "very localized neighborhood uplift and retraining programs of the War on Poverty." Randolph, still committed to coalition building, worried that "the plethora of programs and scarcity of funds balkanizes the community internally." Tillmon, Wiley, and Jones had a broader vision of a social movement that drew its strength from the grass roots but that mobilized otherwise scattered local activists into a nationwide movement to transform public policy. But they were all swimming against powerful currents. Foundations and grassroots organizers had already begun to shift their attention to the local playing field. Community Action ensured that for most of the next forty years—even as the War on Poverty receded into distant memories—the battle against poverty and inequality would be fought largely at the local level. The Great Society left in its wake a whole generation of local politicians and activists who believed in the importance of community control and place-based public policies that targeted inner cities and their poor residents. Community Action also played an important role in discrediting large-scale, integrationist, regionwide solutions to racial inequality, including open housing, school desegregation, and mobility strategies. The welfare rights movement's short-term victories but long-term defeat led many activists to redouble their local efforts. Over the next several years, empowered in their own way by the Johnson administration's climate of experimentation, a range of antidiscrimination activists would challenge and be challenged by advocates of black political power, community control, and political autonomy.

CHAPTER 12

"THE BLACK MAN'S LAND"

"MELTING POT HARLEM—HARLEM OF HONEY AND CHOCOLATE AND CARAMEL and rum and vinegar and lemon and lime and gall." So the venerable Langston Hughes recalled his adopted neighborhood in 1963. To most black Americans, Harlem—the Mecca for black artists, intellectuals, and entertainers—evoked intense, contradictory feelings. Its tenements continued to fill with migrants from the South who were seeking the promise of jobs, pleasure, and politics. But Harlem was also one of New York's most run-down and dangerous neighborhoods, a symbol of "ghettoization." Its decrepit, overcrowded buildings were mostly owned by unscrupulous slumlords, its streets the contested terrain of vicious gangs and brutal cops, its commercial district a mix of black-owned businesses, mostly in the shadows of white, absentee-owned shops. "Harlem is a prison," argued Noel Marder, head of Back-Our-Brothers, a community organization, in the spring of 1963. Marder's neighbors shared his complaint. A 1966 survey of Harlem residents offered a sobering reflection on the neighborhood's woes: Poor housing, drugs and crime, and the lack of police protection were high on the list. Infant mortality in Harlem was twice that of New York City as a whole. Forty percent of Harlem's housing was classified as uninhabitable or dilapidated. Six out of ten area high school students did not graduate. Despite the romance of Harlem, only 17 percent of its residents stated they would stay in Harlem if they could find housing options elsewhere; only 6 percent hoped that their children would grow up there. It was a place of promise and peril—one that generated everyday political activism and a sense of communal pride and identity unmatched anywhere else in black North America—and, at the same time, a place of wrenching poverty and powerlessness.

Harlem stood out for its size and for its national symbolic importance.

But it was not unique. Every big northern city had its own Harlem, its own vibrant equivalent of 125th Street, and its own neighborhoods whose residents lived in unspeakable squalor. Black Detroiters congregated in the Twelfth Street district; Newark had its Central Ward; to black Clevelanders, Hough was a household name; Chicago's Bronzeville was second only to Harlem as a center of black music and culture; North Philadelphia's Jump Street lived up to its name. Each of these neighborhoods was a center of black political power by the 1960s. Each had powerful churches and mosques. Each had formidable black nationalist groups and civil rights organizations competing for the allegiance of area residents; each had business districts that were contested terrains of economic power; each had dangerous streets, underfunded and overcrowded schools, escalating crime rates, and troubled police-community relations. Each became, in the words of Detroit activists Grace and James Boggs, "the Black Man's Land," territory that reflected the aspirations and the oppression whose intertwined effects gave 1960s-era black America its distinctive politics. Each was a landscape created by more than two generations of public policies that marginalized blacks and steered whites and their investments away from central cities; each was a terrain whose very existence was the consequence of exploitation. The very dual nature of Harlem—and of other black neighborhoods—raised fundamental questions over which activists and policy makers struggled mightily in the mid and late 1960s. Should such places be eliminated in the name of racial equality? Or were they what one activist called "wellsprings of future progress" that should be nurtured in the name of self-determination and community empowerment? Or should activists fashion a middle-ground policy, temporarily reinvigorating the "ghetto" while pushing for its long-term eradication?

Two New York activists—Jesse Gray and Clarence Funnyé—grappled with these questions and reached significantly different conclusions. Both drew energy from the extraordinary concentration of civil rights and black power activists based in their city. Both were profoundly dissatisfied with the quality of life in the neighborhood they loved. Both were energetic speakers, forceful thinkers, and savvy grassroots organizers. Their work brought them into some of the same circles, mostly in and around New York CORE, which one ran and the other never joined but deeply influenced. Jesse Gray was a tireless tenant organizer and sometime political candidate. Clarence Funnyé rose to lead New York's fractious CORE chapter. Both Gray and Funnyé made urban housing their issue and rose to national prominence as the result of their grassroots organizing. They shared an ability to articulate their visions of the city clearly and forcefully.

But Gray and Funnyé had radically different ideas about how to solve the problems of concentrated urban poverty in New York and in black America. Gray became the inspiration for a whole generation of community-based activists, those who argued that the solution to the problems of the inner city lay in tapping the power of the poor and directing it into a movement to improve their everyday living conditions. Gray and his supporters, disproportionately women, accepted the concentration of poor blacks in inner cities as a given—an unalterable reality of modern American life. Funnyé, on the other hand, joined forces with the open housing movement, pushing for what he called the "deghettoization" of America's Harlems as the first step toward full economic and racial equality. In his view, blacks needed to be liberated from the segregation that perpetuated their status as second-class citizens. The approaches were not necessarily incompatible—one could improve living conditions in the inner city in the short run while working for the eradication of segregation. But by the end of the 1960s, the two paths diverged, with enduring consequences. Neither open housing nor community-based economic redevelopment and empowerment fulfilled their potential. By the 1970s, the dream of housing integration had largely collapsed as a result of white resistance and black fatigue. Liberal political leaders who had supported integration in the 1960s found themselves marginalized. Community-based economic development, by contrast, attracted an unusually broad coalition of supporters, including black power advocates, white liberals, self-help conservatives, and even the Nixon administration. But it barely made a dent in the problems of the inner city, hampered by the fact that small, underfunded neighborhood organizations were held responsible for problems they ultimately did not have the capacity or resources to solve.

DESCRIBED BY A critic as "a blend of nine parts crafty street brawler and one part Marxist-Leninist," Jesse Gray was a tough survivor of the anti-

Communist purges of the 1950s who remained a tireless grassroots activist after most of his comrades had gone underground or moved on. A native Louisianan and a merchant marine during World War II, Gray cut his teeth as an organizer with the National Maritime Union but was caught up in its factional battles and expelled for his radicalism. After moving to New York City, Gray joined the American Labor Party (ALP), worked for the campaign of Benjamin Davis (a Communist elected to New York's City Council), and joined in ALP-led civil rights, rent control, and labor campaigns. Gray's radicalism brought him to the attention of HUAC, which subpoenaed him to testify in its New York hearings. Gray took the Fifth Amendment, refusing to answer charges that he was a Communist. In 1952, the twenty-eight-year-old Gray joined the ALP's Harlem Tenants' Union and found the issue that shaped the rest of his career. Building on a long history of left-led activism on behalf of rent control in New York, the ALP attempted to build a base among the city's large population of renters. After the ALP folded, Gray founded a series of similar tenant organizations. Although the ALP had fearlessly promoted residential integration (it joined battles to integrate Stuyvesant Town, Levittown, and several housing projects in the outer boroughs), Gray had little interest in open housing. He directed his energy into improving the quality of life for poor and working-class Harlemites. A "formidable bundle of energy," Gray regularly put in twenty-hour days, going door-to-door in run-down apartment buildings. While many left-wing activists spent their time on shop floors, organizing industrial workers, Gray saw the inner city as a terrain for political change. Gray's long hours paid off. He became a confidant of and counselor to many of the neighborhood's poorest residents. "There were buildings in Central Harlem," wrote one activist, "where the name 'Jesse Gray' would open any door."

Gray was a charismatic leader, but one who knew that his efforts would come to naught without a committed group of supporters. Most civil rights and radical organizations in the postwar years had male heads but depended on the energy of a large female rank and file. Tenants' movements and housing organizations in New York—and in many other cities—relied on women as the social glue that held together fragile, transient communities of renters. In Philadelphia, as in New York, women spearheaded efforts to organize tenants' associations and community betterment projects in public housing. In Detroit, many community conservation efforts in black neighborhoods were female-headed. And in Baltimore, women residents of public housing forged communal networks to share information, put pressure on municipal officials, and create safe spaces for their children in the oft-dangerous public spaces in surrounding neighborhoods. Few of these efforts made headlines. Even the African American press paid them relatively little heed. Civil rights organizations, especially those concerned with legislation and litigation, considered neighborhood-based "quality of life" politics marginal. But Jesse Gray saw them as the vanguard of racial liberation.

Gray's turf was one of the grimmest sections of Harlem, where residents complained "of frequent fires from electrical short circuits, of rooms without adequate heat, and bathroom commodes that haven't worked in months," and rats "as big as greyhounds." To appeal to poor women, Gray fashioned a militant, maternalist rhetoric that emphasized the special grievances of poor families. Ideologically committed to empowering the poor, Gray defined a tenants' rights movement as necessary to protect children from the dangers and indignities of slum housing and mobilized angry mothers to demand that government protect their families. After the death of a boy in a Harlem tenement in 1959 and officials' discovery of ninety-nine building code violations at the site, Gray organized tenants on Harlem's 116th Street to picket and engage in a rent strike until the conditions were corrected. By getting groups of tenants to withhold rents, they tried to hit landlords where it hurt the most—their pocketbooks.

Gray's little army of tenants also demanded that the city enforce building codes, sanitation regulations, and rent control laws. The city agencies that inspected buildings and regulated landlords were both understaffed and unmotivated. Landlords faced few penalties for letting their buildings fall into disrepair. And Harlem's streets were filthy because of irregular garbage pickup. In the fall of 1959, Gray led rallies demanding that the city abate Harlem's persistent rat problem, highlighting stories of children who suffered rat bites. Gray carefully chose moments to stage protests—often after disasters that made the evening news, but sometimes preemptively. During the summer of 1963, anticipating the harsh winter to come, Gray led a group of tenants chanting "No Heat, No Rent!" They threatened disruption unless their demands were met, giving landlords ample warning of their intentions and city regulators more than enough time to inspect boilers. Their protests often got results.

New York's tenant protests peaked in late 1963 and early 1964, when residents in over two hundred buildings (organized in part by the local CORE chapter and Gray's new Community Council on Housing) picketed, withheld their rents, and marched on City Hall. Gray often exaggerated the size of the tenants' movement. Usually just a handful of tenants in any building actually joined protests. But he was a brilliant publicist. Gray brought TV crews into run-down tenements to stage photo shoots of tenants "wrapped in overcoats and seated around gas stoves in their kitchens." His deliberately confrontational strategies were ready-made for media consumption. Aggrieved tenants deposited piles of dead rats in courtrooms to provide evidence that their buildings were vermin-infested. Protestors mailed plastic rats (and the occasional real one) to New York governor Nelson Rockefeller and mayor John V. Lindsay. "Every week," Gray argued, "we have some child bitten by a rat. This must stop." In February 1964, he rained on the parade of New York boosters preparing for the summer's influx of tourists to the World's Fair. He announced that he would open a booth outside the fairgrounds, selling tickets for tours of Harlem. "We want the whole world to see what we're talking about—to see why we have rent strikes." When the fair opened, Gray held "opening ceremonies" for the "Worst Fair" at his 117th Street headquarters, handing out rubber rats to visitors.

Gray's media strategy paid off. The tenants' rights movement got extensive coverage in the New York dailies, in black weeklies, and in national periodicals including *Newsweek, The New Yorker,* and *Ebony.* Gray was also featured in a prime-time CBS documentary, *The Harlem Temper,* broadcast nationwide in early December 1963. The wave of media attention put pressure on city officials to step up building code enforcement and bring actions against offending landlords. To great fanfare, Mayor Lindsay announced a citywide rat eradication campaign. Favorable coverage of the New York protests inspired activists in other cities to take up inner-city housing issues. Rent strikes, inspired by Gray, swept through Cleveland and Chicago in January and February 1964. Gray himself traveled widely, encouraging the formation of tenants groups in other cities, and led a thirty-two-city "National Housing Action Day" of pickets and protests in June 1964.

Gray saw the tenants' rights movement as the first step in a mass mobilization of the poor, not as an end in itself. "People unite in struggle," argued Gray, "not in talk." Gray ambitiously hoped that a tenants' movement would "force a mass rehabilitation of the slums" but also provide the basis of nationwide challenge to white power. "People ask me why I spend all my time on heat and hot water and I say heat and hot water is the biggest organizing tool we have; it may even kick off the revolution in the ghetto." Gray also aspired to political office—and embraced the color-conscious populism increasingly common on the black left. In a 1963 campaign for city council, Gray campaigned on a "racial basis," arguing that "regardless of how good a white man is, he cannot speak for us." Gray denounced his black critics as "Toms." His dreams of revolution drew Gray into the circle of Malcolm X, who cheered him as an authentic nationalist. Gray continued to organize tenants, but by late spring of 1964 he was drawn into other community issues, especially protests against police brutality.

Gray was never a peacemaker. When Harlem exploded in riot in August 1964, he ramped up his militant rhetoric. "There's only one thing that can correct" the "police brutality situation in Harlem," he argued, "and that's guerilla warfare." He called for "100 skilled black revolutionaries who are ready to die." Gray's fighting words embroiled him in controversy. A late July court order enjoined him from holding demonstrations between 110th and 155th streets for nearly two months. (Gray responded by gathering protestors on 109th Street and Fifth Avenue and marching through the East Side.) Gray sympathized with the impatience of many black radicals. Throughout the mid-1960s, he built alliances with nationalists and black Marxists, among them Max Stanford and RAM. But Gray was a pragmatic revolutionary. At a November 1964 rally with Malcolm X at the Audubon Ballroom, Gray chastened those who had unrealistic visions of social change. "It's always very easy for us to be ready to move and ready to talk and ready to act, but unless we truly get down into the heart of the ghetto and begin to deal with the problem of jobs, schools and the other basic questions, we are going to be unable to deal with any revolutionary perspective, or with any revolution for that matter."

Gray was the most public face of a grassroots community organizing effort that spread throughout the North in the mid-1960s. Tenant organizing and other community-based efforts to improve the quality of life in inner cities proliferated. Established civil rights groups, under siege by black militants, struggled to remain "relevant" by creating their own

Gray-like housing campaigns. And the burgeoning student left joined the effort. In Newark and Chicago, Students for a Democratic Society, the leading campus radical organization of the 1960s, sent cells of organizers out of their ivory towers into black and white communities, where they joined efforts to create an "interracial movement of the poor." The Socialist periodical *New America* hailed rent strikes as an alternative to civil rights protests that it considered "peripheral to the needs of the vast majority of Negro people who live in poverty."

No group put more stock in tenant organizing than the Congress of Racial Equality. By the mid-1960s, CORE chapters, once in the vanguard of open housing protests, largely jettisoned integrationism in favor of campaigns to empower the black poor. Doris Innis, a New York CORE activist (she was also Clarence Funnyé's sister and Roy Innis's wife), expressed an increasingly common sentiment that pro-integration protests would do little for ordinary blacks. Recalling a CORE-led effort to integrate a Queens apartment building, she recalled "picketing all day to get a black couple into a building and thinking how irrelevant it was.... Here we were in the capital of Black America and going out to Queens for demonstrations." Boston activist Frank Merande, who had joined CORE because of his own experience with housing discrimination, soon gave up on "picketing for integrated housing." As he recalled, "what was really needed was better housing and most Negroes would not move into the integrated areas in any case." Detroit CORE had revived in the early 1960s with a focus on integrating the suburbs but quickly threw aside its open housing efforts. Motor City activists Ralph and Janice Rosenfeld recounted that by 1964, CORE's "suburban housing projects" seemed "passé." CORE moved its headquarters to the heart of Detroit's Twelfth Street ghetto and launched "Operation Cleanup," an effort to target slumlords on Detroit's West Side. It created a Community Housing and Planning Review Board consisting of poor people who demanded the construction of new, affordable housing in the inner city. Like Gray, CORE activists saw tenant organizing as a vehicle for community empowerment. One Cleveland activist put it clearly: "We knew from the start that we would not solve the problem of housing. But from the start we felt we had this other purpose in mind"—specifically, "getting the people involved in the struggle, feel some strength, to learn something about using power."

Tenant organizing was difficult and time-consuming. Renters moved frequently because of the terrible conditions of their apartments, financial insecurity, or some combination of the two. In the mid-1960s, fewer than half of Harlem's residents had lived at the same address for more than five years. It was hard to get people with few community ties, distrustful of their neighbors, struggling to make ends meet, and fearful of eviction and homelessness involved in political efforts. Even the charismatic Gray had a difficult time getting more than a handful of tenants in even the most decrepit buildings to withhold rents and join pickets. Even when they were organized, tenants faced formidable obstacles thrown up by property owners, city agencies, and the legal system. In Detroit and Boston, rent strikes were frequently unsuccessful: Landlords evicted tenant activists just as they were making headway (and in the process intimidated other tenants who feared losing their apartments). Rent strikers found few legal remedies in the courts. Tenant organizers, most of whom were amateurs, often did not have staying power. Many burned out. As a Detroit CORE organizer recalled, "Tenant organizing needs skills and plenty of time. People simply have to be available a great deal for this kind of work." In Philadelphia, most CORE members held full-time jobs and had little time to organize. All in all, most CORE tenant campaigns were short-lived and unsuccessful.

In the late 1960s, some black power groups launched their own tenant-organizing campaigns. But few radicals had the discipline or the broad base of community support necessary for effective grassroots organizing. One black radical worried about his organization's "small numbers and the doubt that the general Negro community would join them in battle." Many militants were too impatient to engage in the tedious work of door-to-door canvassing—they "just want to run out and take heads." And those who imitated Gray's media-oriented strategy were usually disappointed. Journalists were fickle. As protests against slumlords became commonplace, they ceased being "newsworthy."

One activist, Carolyn Foster, a member of the New York Black Panthers, spent thankless hours going door-to-door in Harlem tenements. Her diary, a spiral-bound notebook adorned with Panther slogans and radical poetry, brimmed with enthusiasm for the black revolution. She described her fearless encounters with "pigs" who tried to stop her from distributing *The Black Panther*. And, in her most revealing entries, she wrote of her hopes and frustrations as an organizer in some of Harlem's worst buildings. She aspired to unite "the tenants against these 'pig' landlords" by organizing petition drives, protests, and rent strikes. "I have gotten hoarse twice from relating to the masses," she penned in 1970. What was most troubling to Foster was how few of her comrades were willing to lose their voices and wear out their shoes for the sake of movement building. "The cadre," she lamented, "doesn't relate to door-to-door section work."

Foster's lament reflected a serious problem. To be sure, the Panthers did some community organizing, particularly through their "Survival Programs." They distributed free breakfasts to schoolchildren in many cities, under the motto "Feed the Youth and the Youth Will Feed the Revolution." Although male Panther leaders took credit for these programs—and were sometimes photographed dishing out meals to children—most of the Survival Programs were run by uncelebrated women members. Perhaps the Panthers' most important contribution was organizing protests, inspired by rent strikes, around inequitable health care. At a time when black health problems were at the bottom of medical research agendas (if they were there at all) and blacks still faced systematic discrimination in many hospitals, the Panthers created free medical clinics in a number of cities and publicized diseases that disproportionately afflicted blacks. In pamphlets and newsletters, they highlighted lead poisoning, an epidemic among children who lived in run-down houses in the once-grand neighborhoods of inner cities where sweet-tasting paint chips were a major health hazard. And they brought attention to sickle-cell anemia, the debilitating blood condition that afflicted many people of West African descent. But shorn of their revolutionary rhetoric, the Panthers were doing what so many other community organizations and churches—many of which black radicals denounced as "bourgeois" and hopelessly "respectable"—were doing in inner cities throughout the country. Claims that there was something new and revolutionary about the establishment of free breakfast programs and health clinics revealed a willful ignorance of the extraordinary array of black-led and interracial social service agencies, meal programs, and health clinics, most of which operated off camera.

Much of the story of the transformation of social movements in the late 1960s is that of the professionalization of protest, a response to the limitations of grassroots organizing. Despite the hurdles that it faced, the tenants' rights movement did not die off. Tenant organizing took on a new life in the hands of foundation-funded social service organizations and, in some cities, the War on Poverty. In place of volunteer activists emerged a new generation of professional organizers and attorneys, who mastered the intricacies of landlord-tenant law and were paid for their services. Gray's hopes for a mass movement of tenants did not come to fruition, but his hopes that landlords and city regulators would be held accountable did. New York's Mobilization for Youth, an antidelinquency program with significant foundation and War on Poverty funding, deployed full-time organizers in New York's tenements and hired Jesse Gray as a consultant. Federally funded legal services programs provided tenants groups with legal representation and, in many states, won cases that protected the rights of tenants to withhold rent in escrow without fear of eviction. In many major cities, professional tenants' rights organizations created in the late 1960s or early 1970s—or at least a cluster of public interest attorneys and social workers—still survive, working with public officials and challenging landlords.

WHILE GRAY WAS organizing in Harlem's tenements, Clarence Funnyé was rising through the ranks of New York CORE. A good ten years younger than Gray, Funnyé was an engineer who served during the mid-1950s as a navigator and officer in the newly desegregated U.S. Air Force. The son of a minister in Georgetown, South Carolina, he graduated from historically black North Carolina A&T. But it was not until his stint in the military, when he traveled around the country, that he "had the chance to see and feel" what he called "some of the harsh inequalities of our so-called 'democratic' way of life." Funnyé's encounter with discrimination, both north and south, did not, however, lead him to embrace Gray's leftist politics. He was a product of Cold War America, even as he eschewed the knee-jerk patriotism of the era. In 1958, he wrote: "I do not have a flag, and if I did I don't know if I would be seen waving it on a Fourth of July. But this country is my country. I love America and have great hopes that she can yet become the democracy which the founding fathers intended." Funnyé's faith in the promise of democracy put him in company with the religious activists and social engineers who advocated integration. But

Funnyé's optimism was always tempered by a bitterness that grew out of experience. He knew that goodwill alone would not eradicate segregation. As he confronted the combined social problems of Harlem and white indifference to them in the 1960s, Funnyé, like many activists, grew increasingly impatient. He called for "freedom fighters" and "shock troops" to undo racial inequality. "Negroes cannot indefinitely absorb the blows and brutality of racists without retaliation," he wrote in the summer of 1963. He saw the struggle for racial equality as a struggle for power—power that would have to be wrested from the hands of whites and white-controlled institutions.

After his discharge from the air force, Funnyé moved to New York, where he earned a degree in city planning at the Pratt Institute. There he gravitated toward New York's newly revitalized CORE chapter. In 1961, Funnyé led CORE in eighty hours of protests at an 1,800-unit apartment complex in Brooklyn's Clinton Hill after he was denied a lease. Finally, CORE activists staged a twelve-hour sit-in at the rental office, leaving only when the landlord agreed to rent to Funnyé and open the building on a nondiscriminatory basis. In 1963, the New York CORE chapter grew increasingly militant. It targeted employment discrimination in grocery stores, organized protests at Harlem Hospital and other construction sites, and occupied Governor Rockefeller's New York office demanding equal opportunity in the building trades.

Funnyé had a knack for creative protests—a skill that quickly raised his profile. In the summer of 1963, he led CORE demonstrations challenging the exclusion of blacks in the media. "Wouldn't it be nice," asked Funnyé, "if now and then on television a little Negro girl came running in shouting 'Look Ma, no cavities'? That's all we want, just ordinary things. We are not asking for anything revolutionary." To make the point, he set up seven television sets at Speakers' Corner in Harlem, kept a scoreboard counting how many black faces appeared, and promised passersby a silver dollar for every Negro who flickered across the screen. Funnyé did not lose much money. Armed with data from his unscientific survey—and wielding the threat of consumer boycotts of offending advertisers—Funnyé won pledges from several Madison Avenue ad agencies and from CBS to show more black faces and eschew racial stereotyping.

Turning his attention to the lack of black representation in skilled and white-collar jobs in major corporations, Funnyé led protests at the New

York headquarters of General Motors, demanding that the nation's largest employer engage in an "action program" to open up more jobs to blacks across the country. Unwilling to court a public relations disaster, GM executives met with Funnyé, CORE's James Farmer, and the NAACP's Madison Jones and pledged to take aggressive antidiscrimination measures. Funnyé also joined demonstrations in Albany to demand an increase in the state minimum wage and to push for "appropriations for integrated housing for working people." Increasingly, he saw the questions of housing, education, and economics as inseparable—with segregated housing as the nub of the problem. Just as black radicals began to celebrate the liberatory possibilities of the "black man's land" of the inner cities, Funnyé argued that the concentration of poor and working-class blacks in neglected "ghettos" was the fundamental cause of racial inequality. He became a militant integrationist, but he eschewed the patronizing arguments that blacks would be uplifted by their association with whites. Integration was not a matter of culture, it was a matter of power. So long as blacks were isolated and marginalized in their own separate communities, they would not get access to the economic resources—jobs, well-funded public schools, and decent housing—that whites had hoarded for themselves in racially segregated communities.

Funnyé's militant integrationism put him at odds with CORE's newfound black nationalism. In the increasingly fractious world of black radical politics, Funnyé found himself labeled "middle-class," a charge that stung. When a group of insurgents critical of the "small isolated group of people intent on bearing personal witness against evil" broke from New York CORE, Funnyé moved into a position of leadership. Funnyé was no "bourgeois" moral perfectionist, but he had serious disagreements with those who argued for ghetto-based community organization tactics. After election as CORE chapter head in October 1964, he took two controversial steps that grew from his experience as a protestor and from his understanding of the root causes of racial inequality. Protests, he argued, were no longer enough. He called for CORE to move "away from the 'sit in' approach in favor of a program of 'down to earth' political, social and economic action." The civil rights movement, he contended, needed more responsible planning. "No more sloppy yelling. 'Hey now—Freedom now' and that's it." Responding to the rising tide of black nationalism, he also argued that CORE should reject separatism and find "common cause . . .

between the white majority and the colored minority." At CORE's 1965 national convention, Funnyé stated his position most bluntly. "It is my hope that this convention will grapple with what seems to me to be a basic conflict of aims. There are those among us who feel strongly that we must now turn our energies toward rebuilding and strengthening the ghetto to enhance black political power. There are those, on the other hand, who feel that our major thrust must be toward eliminating the ghetto, with all its attendant ills of slums, inadequate schools, high crime rates, poor police protection, inadequate services, and a feeling of hopelessness on the part of the inhabitants."

It was clear where he stood. Funnyé advocated what he called "deghettoization." For its part, CORE firmly repudiated Funnyé's vision and moved in an increasingly separatist direction. "Black Power," stated CORE in a resolution adopted at its 1966 convention, "is effective control and self-determination by men of color in their own areas. Power is total control of the economic, political, educational, and social life of our community from the top to the bottom. The exercise of power at the local level is simply what all other groups in American society have done to acquire their share of total American life." Jesse Gray, a plenary speaker at the convention, argued that the black freedom struggle must be fought in the "back streets and alleys" of urban America.

While CORE endorsed black power, Funnyé marched in a different direction. He joined forces with the open housing movement just as it reached its pinnacle of influence. Eclipsed in the mainstream news media by accounts of black militancy, the open housing movement was larger, better organized, and far more ambitious than it had been in the 1950s. In 1959, the National Committee Against Discrimination in Housing found only eighteen open housing committees in the entire country. By early 1964, there were nearly four hundred. By the end of 1965, over one thousand fair-housing groups existed nationwide, the greatest number of them in the North. NCDH harnessed the energy of open housers, raised money, and staged protests and lobbying efforts at the local, state, and federal levels. Fired up by the possibilities of open housing, Funnyé served on NCDH's board, joined a cadre of young, idealistic planners working for the newly formed federal Department of Housing and Urban Development, and in 1968 took the position of NCDH's director of planning and research.

The climate of crisis in the mid-1960s breathed new life into the open housing movement. The black rebellions—in the North as well as the South—served as a wake-up call. In 1964, animated by a growing sense of urgency, NCDH launched a "massive nationwide effort to break down racial ghettoes," including "informing and mobilizing groups of non-white and white citizens to take their own affirmative actions at the local level" but also working with federal, state, and local housing agencies to promote integration. NCDH's efforts were more ambitious than anything open housers had tried in the 1940s and 1950s. With the support of the National Urban League and with War on Poverty funding, NCDH launched Operation Open City, a pilot plan to deghettoize New York City through efforts to "entice whites back to the cities" and to "tackle the vested interests" of slumlords by demanding the strict enforcement of building codes. As a corollary, NCDH called for the development of scattered-site public housing in the suburbs and a "massive educational program" to "convince Negroes that good housing is also integrated housing."

Operation Open City appealed to Funnyé. A vocal critic of small-scale neighborhood development plans and Community Action, Funnyé had particular contempt for efforts to rehabilitate slum housing for blacks. He and other integrationists derisively called it "gilding the ghetto." In 1965, when New York used federal funds to reclaim thirty-six tenement buildings on West 114th Street, Funnyé could not hold his tongue. "Do the planners believe that a mere flick of paint and plaster is sufficient to eradicate or even offset the deficiencies inherent in the pathetically bad neighborhood schools to which the children of 114th Street, and all the children in Harlem, would still be confined?" Funnyé saw such programs as part of the "traditional containment practice" of confining blacks to run-down neighborhoods where they would suffer from the disadvantages of political and economic marginality. "Creating and maintaining a little oasis in the midst of one of the most dense ghettos in the world," argued Funnyé, wearing his hat as a city planner, "goes against all sound planning theories."

WHILE FUNNYÉ WAS promoting deghettoization in New York, the open housing movement vaulted onto the international stage, largely because of the intervention of the Reverend Martin Luther King, Jr. In the aftermath of the passage of the Civil Rights Act of 1964, King began searching for an opportunity to "bring the movement" to what he called the "unled Negro communities" of the North. King was not always greeted warmly in northern cities. What he found was that they were not leaderless, even if black activists seldom spoke with one voice. There were many leaders— not too few. To his surprise, King discovered that grassroots leaders often viewed him as a competitor, not as a collaborator.

Still, the grim realities of segregation, poverty, and unemployment compelled King to find a northern stage in 1965. Beginning in the late spring and extending through early September, King began testing the waters and found most of them too cold. Detroit was too left-dominated and fractious. New York was equally daunting, both for its size and for the strength and heterogeneity of its existing organizations. The irascible Adam Clayton Powell, Jr., fulminated that "no leader outside Harlem should come into this community and tell us what to do." Harlem's radicals, among them Malcolm X's disciples and Gray, would resent King there. Cleveland, Newark, and Boston were briefly contenders, but all were smaller than other northern cities. Each had its advantages, but none of them seemed to possess the symbolic cachet of Montgomery or Birmingham. From King's perspective, Philadelphia looked ideal. As home to the American Friends Service Committee, whose members had long advocated nonviolent social change, it had witnessed some of the North's most innovative protests. Leon Sullivan's selective patronage campaign had inspired SCLC's Operation Breadbasket. Philadelphia's relatively strong CORE and NAACP chapters had come to national attention with their challenges to construction industry discrimination in 1963. And from 1963 to 1965, a group of protestors had marched regularly on Girard College, a whites-only, city-run orphanage, challenging its Jim Crow admissions policy. But King had not counted on the mercurial Cecil B. Moore, who had little patience for "outside" agitators and who made it clear—in any number of ways—that King and the SCLC were not welcome. "I don't go for that non-violent bullshit of King's," Moore told an interviewer in 1967.

That led King to turn to Chicago and to open housing. Chicago was a major center of housing activism. By the early 1960s, the Chicago movement was full of grassroots organizers who had cut their teeth on some of the North's most difficult housing integration battles, including massive white resistance to efforts to open up suburban Cicero in the late 1940s, the Trumbull Park housing project in the mid-1950s, and, of course, Morris Milgram's prolonged Deerfield battle. And in the early 1960s, incomparable organizer Saul Alinsky had created the Woodlawn Organization, dedicated to housing integration, job training, and community empowerment. King had many allies in the Windy City and made it a key stop on a whirlwind six-city tour through the North in the summer of 1965. In an exhausting week of activities, King met with dozens of activists, marched to Chicago's City Hall, joined a mass rally in Grant Park, addressed a large crowd at the Robert Taylor Homes, and delivered sermons at several churches. On July 26, King's visit culminated with a thirty-thousand-person march for "quality integrated education."

The Windy City's vibrant civil rights community impressed King. The Chicago-based meatpackers' union had long provided SCLC with vital financial support. Open housers greeted him with enthusiasm. And beginning in the early 1960s, Chicago had also become one of the nation's hotbeds of grassroots organizing against unequal education. From 1962 through 1965, protestors regularly demonstrated against Chicago's segregated schools and demanded the resignation of school superintendent Benjamin Willis. The Chicago school protests peaked in the spring of 1965, just before King's visit, when hundreds of protestors were arrested at the Board of Education and Willis finally resigned his post. What made Chicago particularly promising for King was that it was large (nearly one million blacks lived there) but lacked a turf-conscious civil rights leader—a plus for King, who did not want to play second fiddle to a local leader or watch his efforts get bogged down in local factional politics.

The second-largest city in the United States, Chicago was also one of the most racially segregated and polarized. A sharp, ever-shifting, invisible Maginot Line divided Chicago into huge territories of race. Blacks lived on the vast South Side, extending from the Loop for more than sixty blocks down the lakefront, and in the old, run-down working-class neighborhoods of the West Side. Whites inhabited vast tracts of the North Side and Far South and Southwest Sides. Since the infamous race riot of 1919, the neighborhoods on the frontier between white Chicago and its ever-expanding black population had been racked by bloody conflict. After

World War II, white Chicagoans had organized a neighborhood-based movement, second only to Detroit's, that pledged to use any means necessary—political or extrapolitical—to keep "the colored" out. Overseeing the balkanized city was Chicago's mighty political machine, the last great machine left, led by the formidable Richard J. Daley, whose own Bridgeport neighborhood, which bordered mostly black sections of the city, was protected from the "Negro invasion" by gangs of vigilante white youths. As a Democratic boss in a swing state, Daley had great influence in the national Democratic Party but had a reputation for granting only token opportunities to blacks. If King could break Chicago, he would have a real foothold in the North. And a victory in Chicago—particularly on the political front—would redound through national Democratic politics because of Daley's power.

Throughout late 1965 and early 1966, King and local activists prepared the Chicago campaign. In the fall and winter, Jesse L. Jackson, a young minister, coordinated Operation Breadbasket, inspired by Leon Sullivan's selective patronage campaign. But, as King stated at a January 1966 news conference, "our primary objective will be to bring about the unconditional surrender of forces dedicated to the creation and maintenance of slums." King took a middle ground between the positions held by Funnyé and Gray. The anti-slum battle would have three fronts: improving existing conditions in Chicago's ghettos, challenging pervasive housing segregation, and working to "arouse Washington" to create inner-city jobs and pass open housing legislation. To that end, King rented an apartment on Chicago's West Side. A shabby dwelling with a broken boiler (the landlord hastily painted the apartment when he found out King was moving in), it was a tangible reminder of the price of housing segregation in the North. For King, living in the tenement was "the only dignified, sincere and effective method of communicating with the poor." Like CORE's inner-city organizers, King believed that change required mobilizing the poor. "You cannot work over them. You cannot work around them. You cannot work for them. You must work with them."

Although he lived among the poor, King was not of them. It was impossible for a celebrity like King to live the life of a poor black Chicagoan, even if he now dwelled in a dreary apartment with the stench of urine emanating from its lobby and a heating system that regularly failed.

King's encounters with West Siders were mostly superficial. Children waved at him, one elderly man "nearly fell onto the slick pavement, apparently overcome with shock" at the sight of King, and others shook his hand as he walked down the street. In late January, six members of a black power–inspired gang, the Young Lords, paid a call on King and toured the neighborhood with him. King and his aides encouraged the gang members to disarm and embrace nonviolence, but his message went unheard. The West Side was not only the contested turf of the Young Lords but also home to a northern branch of the Deacons for Defense. Over the summer of 1966, the Lords sometimes provided protection for King and civil rights marchers, but not out of a sudden embrace of King's political theology. Instead, using baseball mitts, they caught bricks and stones hurled by angry whites and threw them right back.

Working with Chicago's poor was daunting. King and his advisers struggled against widespread indifference to his goals. "All clear-thinking Negroes," wrote one correspondent to the *Defender*, "have to agree with me on this one thing, getting one's brains knocked out for the sake of integrating with another race, vehemently against mixing, is first-class insanity." King and his fellow civil rights leaders were often disappointed at the small size of the protests: They had not generated a mass movement. More than that, King could not dampen the anger and violence in Chicago's black neighborhoods. He hoped that well-planned marches would defuse anger among the city's restive youths, but found out through hard experience that protests were not a very effective form of riot control. On July 9, 1966, the *Defender* reported King's optimism that Chicago's summer would remain cool. The following day, King, comedian Dick Gregory, James Meredith, Mahalia Jackson, and a bevy of black and white liberals addressed an audience of tens of thousands (though far fewer than the hundred thousand that King had hoped for) at a "Freedom Rally" at Soldier Field. A crowd of gang members carrying a large red flag disrupted the event with black power chants. On July 11, things took a turn for the worse when a clash between the Chicago police and a group of black youths playing near an open fire hydrant led to several days of unrest. Angry black men battled the police in front of King's apartment as his wife and children huddled inside. In a futile effort to curb the violence, civil rights activists descended into the riot area "to try to get the [rioting] kids to march away and sing freedom songs." Several days of looting, rock throwing, arson, and occasional sniping ravaged the West Side; 533 people were arrested and three people died of gunshot wounds.

King faced even more serious obstacles from Chicago's political leadership. Mayor Daley and his machine were decidedly unsympathetic, and black ward leaders and party regulars made themselves scarce during King-led rallies. Daley—and those blacks with close ties to his machine—took every occasion to lambaste King as ineffectual and meddling. When he played a role in taking a slum building into "trusteeship," a common tactic among tenant organizers, he faced the wrath of a federal judge who called the action "theft." After the West Side uprising, King took heat from the head of the Urban League for encouraging the riot.

Even more fearsome was the intense resistance that King faced among Chicago's whites. From mid-July to late August, King led open housing protestors in a nonviolent siege of white working-class neighborhoods. Nothing prepared him for the bricks, stones, and angry shouts that greeted the interracial band of marchers in Marquette Park, Gage Park, and Belmont Cragin, three blue-collar neighborhoods. Chicago police deployed nearly half the force to cover the marches. Thousands of angry whites attacked the band of priests, nuns, black and white ministers, and open housers accompanying King. They screamed out racial epithets and threw rocks, stones, and cinder blocks. On August 5, in Marquette Park, King himself fell to the ground, his forehead gashed by a rock. At a protest a week later, a group of white teenagers taunted the protestors with a song to the tune of a TV commercial for Oscar Mayer wieners: "I wish I were an Alabama trooper / that is what I would truly like to be / for if I were an Alabama trooper / I could kill the niggers legally."

King compared Chicago, unfavorably, to Mississippi. But Chicago's violence was thoroughly homegrown. Northern Jim Crow—especially in housing—was more deeply entrenched and more difficult to uproot than King had ever imagined. But to Chicago whites who had terrorized blacks for crossing the city's invisible racial boundaries for nearly fifty years, King was just the latest and most prominent outsider encroaching on their turf. King's experience was chastening. After reaching an agreement with Daley and local real estate leaders in late August, he beat a hasty retreat from Chicago. But Chicago's grassroots activists continued both open housing and tenant-organizing campaigns, though on a smaller scale, mostly outside the media spotlight.

"The phrase open housing," wrote a black journalist in 1965, "is hurling a pack of dynamite with the fuse sizzling." The bloody grassroots battles over housing in Chicago were not atypical of the urban North: Whites in Philadelphia, Boston, Detroit, and Cincinnati regularly attacked blacks who "invaded" white neighborhoods. When blacks had the temerity to move into inner-ring suburbs—and not many did over the course of the 1960s—they also faced intense resistance. When a black family moved into a house in Folcroft, Pennsylvania, just outside Philadelphia, in 1963, outraged whites protested, broke windows, harassed their supporters, and eventually drove out the family. White Folcrofters vented their rage at both the integrationists and the federal government. At a thousand-person meeting at the Folcroft Swim Club, white activists issued their manifesto. "Perhaps this small borough can show this great nation that the Federal government cannot force integration on the population." And in 1968, when the Buffalo Catholic diocese sold a large parcel of land in blue-collar Lackawanna to a black developer, more than a quarter of the parishioners in a nearby parish put empty envelopes in the collection basket. Two years later, huge crowds of protestors gathered in Warren, Michigan, just outside Detroit, to protest a proposed integrated apartment complex.

The intensity of white resistance led some activists to argue that the cost of open housing was too great and its benefit too small. "White inaction has turned the Negroes' hopes away from integration," editorialized *The Bay State Banner*, Boston's black weekly. Why should blacks continue the quixotic quest to break open the housing market if they were going to be treated indifferently at best or physically attacked at worst? Other activists began to argue that open housing was a red herring that alienated whites while diverting energy from the most pressing problems of the poor. Scholar-activists Frances Fox Piven and Richard Cloward argued that "if reformers can be persuaded to forfeit for a time the ideal of desegregation, there might be a chance of mustering political support and money for low-income housing. This would be no small achievement."

The vast majority of northern whites did not march, protest, or attack black newcomers. They did not have to. As suburbs sprawled in the postwar years, more and more whites lived in communities remote from black neighborhoods, unthreatened by the "Negro invasion." It was in these communities where, ironically, open housing found some of its most vocal white proponents. Whites in many wealthy, segregated communities spearheaded local open housing campaigns. Birmingham, Michigan, one of Detroit's wealthiest suburbs, became the first all-white municipality in the United States to pass an open housing ordinance. The margin was narrow, but Birmingham residents had little to lose. Their town's real estate was pricey, its zoning laws were strict, and it had no public or subsidized housing and few apartment buildings. But white suburbanites could assure themselves that they were now color-blind. So long as it was the "right kind of Negro" and only one or two moved in, everything would be fine. Philip Powers, who edited a chain of suburban Detroit newspapers, described the change in attitude among his readers: "The guy who said, if you asked him two years ago, would he want a Negro living next door, would have said 'God no!,' now would say 'How much does he make?' Or 'How well does he keep his lawn?'"

A small number of countercultural whites—part of a burgeoning "back-to-the-city" movement in the early 1960s—took their commitment to integration a step further. They embraced the ideal of diversity, seeking out "authentic" communities that stood as a counterpoint to bland, conformist suburbia. By the late 1950s, heterogeneous urban neighborhoods with appealing housing began to attract liberals in many northern cities. Philadelphia's Mount Airy, New York's Brooklyn Heights, Chicago's Hyde Park, and Denver's Park Hill all began to market themselves to artists, old-house buffs, and political activists. One pro-integration organization summarized the anticonformist sensibility of the movement: "Growing up in communities where everyone seems to fit in the same mold—same age, same dress, same speech, same kind of house, same income, same skin color—too many suburban children are being deprived of the invaluable enriching experience of day-to-day contact with different kinds of people and places." Back-to-the-city integrationists had internalized the message of the postwar open housers: Interracial contact would change their consciousness and thus change the world.

Back-to-the-city movements were, however, riddled with contradictions. At the root of urban cosmopolitanism was an unacknowledged class politics. Urban open housers spoke about "stability," a buzzword for economic homogeneity. To keep a neighborhood "stable" required attracting whites or keeping them from fleeing by restricting the in-migration of working-class and poor blacks who might alienate them. Stability required the strict enforcement of zoning laws to keep out "undesirable" uses such as the conversion of single-family homes into apartments that might attract the wrong sort of people. "Stabilization" campaigns became a central component of open housing activism. Key to "stable" racial integration was keeping away poor blacks and their boisterous barbecues, loud music, and late-night parties. Even the presence of beat-up old cars on the streets would make whites jittery and threaten the precarious status of middle-class blacks trying to escape their humble origins. The integrationist melting pot would not accommodate those whose culture was too far out of the mainstream. One of the greatest ironies of stabilization was that it rested on an unspoken premise: In the words of prominent housing activists George and Eunice Grier of Concord Park, stemming white flight succeeded only by "limiting the amount of decent living space available to minorities." If whites stayed, blacks would have few alternatives except to remain in their own neighborhoods or try to gain entry into nearby, less well organized white neighborhoods.

CLARENCE FUNNYÉ JOINED an open housing movement that, for all its difficulties, was better organized and more effective than ever. In the mid-1960s, NCDH launched an all-out campaign to include housing in civil rights laws. "The Great Society," it argued, "could never become a reality until fair housing was effected." Methodically, NCDH supporters pressured state after state and city after city to pass fair-housing laws. By 1967, twenty-four states had enacted laws against housing discrimination. At the grassroots, NCDH mobilized a battalion of open housers, mostly well-educated, civic-minded, and moralistic whites, who flooded legislative offices with petitions and letters. It also deployed lobbyists—along with prominent unionists, liberal business leaders, clerics, movie stars, and athletes—to meet with legislators. Capping their achievements was the passage of the Civil Rights Act of 1968, which Lyndon Johnson signed into law just a week after the assassination of the Reverend Martin Luther King, Jr.

Passing the 1968 bill was an unexpected victory. Fair housing had been left out of the landmark 1964 Civil Rights Act, and over the next three years after that, Johnson's famed legislative wizardry had failed him. Open housing legislation flew through the House, which had a safe Democratic majority, though some white Democrats from racially changing districts joined southerners and conservative Republicans in the opposition. The bill did not, however, survive a southern filibuster in the Senate. Undaunted, open housers and religious groups continued to lobby for the law—and put pressure on swing voters in the Senate, all of them liberal Republicans, exactly the sort of people the religious integrationists had targeted. In a 1968 bipartisan deal, the bill made it past the filibuster. But the Fair Housing Act (officially known as Title VIII of the Civil Rights Act) was largely a symbolic gesture. While it forbade discrimination in housing by race, creed, national origin, or sex, there was one hitch. To win Republican support, the bill's authors had defanged it. Title VIII left it to private individuals or advocacy groups to file suit against housing discrimination.

The fate of the federal law was foreshadowed in the fate of most local and state open housing laws, which also lacked strong enforcement mechanisms. The process of resolving complaints was difficult and time-consuming. "The practice of closed housing has been in effect so long that it has become a way of life," wrote Philadelphia journalist Bob Queen, and "ineffective state and local laws have failed to stem the tide." Title VIII faced similar problems. The enforcement of open housing was left in the hands of well-intentioned but largely underfunded open housing groups. A few activist lawyers took up open housing cases, but they were few and scattered. Although the courts were generally sympathetic to fair-housing claims over the next several decades, damages were usually low. If whites had never accepted the goal of racial integration and if the battle to win enforcement was difficult, why should blacks continue the fight?

Efforts to open up the suburbs were an uphill battle—despite open housing laws. Throughout the 1960s, local church and open housing groups set up private listing services to market homes in white communities to black buyers. But they usually lacked connections in black neighborhoods. In 1965, *The Wall Street Journal* skeptically reported a "Fair Housing Flop," namely that as open housing efforts proliferated, there were few black takers. Open housers universally complained—as did one group in suburban Boston—that "Negroes don't come out to jobs and open housing" in their community. In Chicago, HOME (Home Opportunities Made Equal) grew out of Unitarian church efforts to integrate the suburbs. But most of its suburban listings were in expensive communities on the North Shore. When the group sent eight hundred letters to black organizations, no one replied. Another mailing to five hundred black groups with return-addressed postcards attracted only two favorable responses. In light of HOME's difficulties, a spin-off group named HOUSE (Help Open Up Suburbia to Everyone) refined its strategies to target middle-class blacks. Through face-to-face meetings with black church groups and clubs, HOUSE played up "both the advantages of living in suburbia and also the changed climate in these suburbs, which are now most receptive to minority group families." HOUSE activists were "enthusiastic about life in the suburbs—except for its lack of integration." Black audiences, however, were more likely to focus on the lack than the enthusiasm.

Even more serious hurdles to open housing were strict zoning and land-use regulations that froze out blacks, as well as other poor and working-class groups. Most twentieth-century suburbs controlled lot size. Throughout the metropolitan North, suburban communities resisted the construction of inexpensive houses, apartment complexes, and public housing—usually through the application of ostensibly race-neutral local ordinances. Communities with established black enclaves frequently used antinuisance and antiblight laws to condemn properties for demolition or redevelopment. The result was that few blacks could afford to live in outlying communities and those already living there were sometimes forced out. Ironically, many of the towns with the most vocal open housing organizations—Chappaqua, New York; Grosse Pointe, Michigan; and Greenwich, Connecticut, to name three—had little affordable housing stock. Gerta Friedheim, an open housing activist in Cleveland's prosperous Shaker Heights—more successful than most suburbs in attracting blacks—lamented that "there is no political force for [the poor] at all." Anything more than "the peppering of white suburbia, if it's going to come at all . . . has to come from federal leverage." As one open housing advocate contended, "low income housing certainly does more for blacks than allowing one Ralph Bunche in." But for all except the most zealous open housers, a Ralph Bunche or two was more than enough. Attracting working-class or poor blacks to their communities was simply out of the question.

Black power advocates also issued a vocal challenge to open housing. They railed against the moralism and paternalism of the white-dominated movement. To integrate suburbia was, in effect, to repudiate one's black identity. The only way to cross the black-white boundary was to adopt "white" attitudes, lifestyles, and culture. That open housing activists had searched long and hard for nonthreatening blacks to be the pioneers in all-white neighborhoods laid bare the liberal assumptions that many race-conscious activists in the 1960s found so troubling. The Reverend Albert Cleage rejected the "sterile, futile struggle for 'assimilation' or the subjective 'acceptance' of the black man by the white man." Northern blacks, he argued, "are coming to realize that even though they must fight for 'open occupancy' or the right to live any place they choose, once this right is secured for cultural, political and economic reasons it is desirable that the great majority of black men choose to live together in separate Negro communities." Why should blacks give up everything distinctive or, in that 1960s buzzword, "authentic" about their culture? "Integration up to this point meant blacks have to act like whites," noted political scientist and black power advocate Charles V. Hamilton. "That's a lot of nonsense."

Black anti-integrationism had another crucial component. The majority of black radicals saw power in territorial terms. Groups such as the Nation of Islam and the Republic of New Africa called for the creation of a separate black nation-state in the Deep South. Only a small minority of northern blacks hankered for their own Black Belt nation, but many more began to describe their neighborhoods as "the black man's land." The control of local political institutions was an essential step toward self-determination. In their bestselling 1967 book, *Black Power*, Stokely Carmichael and Charles V. Hamilton envisioned black liberation through the takeover of urban institutions from ward offices to city halls. In this view, integration would destroy the prospects of black control by diluting black political power. "I'm for the black communities remaining intact," argued Jesse Gray. "If they disperse the communities, they'll only create smaller ghettos subservient to the white middle class. If they remain intact, they'll have some power."

The challenge of black power led many integrationists to rethink their strategies. Like many younger activists, Clarence Funnyé found assertions of black pride and self-determination appealing. Black power offered a powerful critique of white power—one that Funnyé tried to appropriate to justify deghettoization. Funnyé shared black radicals' distaste for assimilationism: For him, black liberation was not a matter of changing white hearts and minds or uplifting Negroes through exposure to white, middle-class "role models." But he challenged the radical notion that separatism could be empowering. Funnyé saw segregation as the political, economic, and spatial manifestation of white power, something that needed to be overturned if blacks were ever to gain self-determination. Still, Funnyé had some sympathy with "brothers who, faced with the realities of domestic racist intransigence, turn to mouthing ill-conceived clichés about preserving the ghetto."

Funnyé did not reject the emphasis on black community, culture, or identity that drove much of the black power movement; he simply suggested that it was not enough. He drew from the rhetoric of self-defense that was so common in black power circles but argued that integration was a matter of pride and self-determination. Responding to a report that a black soldier had refused to challenge off-base segregation, Funnyé was scathing: "A soldier afraid to confront a white merchant, to protect his family from domestic humiliation and denial of freedom is a fraud as a freedom fighter. The fact that such persons don't recognize they are frauds is ample testimony to the depth of the brainwashing to which they have been subjected." Funnyé also adopted the rhetoric of anticolonialism. The opening of black-owned Freedom National Bank in Harlem, he argued, made the community look "less like a colony, less like an area for exploitation." He also argued that many War on Poverty initiatives "only reinforce the ghetto, making it a latter-day plantation. Those programs," he argued, "while involving militant separatists, often divert black leaders from the real sources of power. The ghetto is not a breeding ground for political power. If there were any relationship between blacks per square foot and power enjoyed, ghetto people would be the most powerful people in the world." Eradicating racial inequality required "a new form of militancy" that "keeps an eye on the big ball where the power is, and that's not in a model neighborhood headquarters." So long as black power advocates directed their energy to small-scale, neighborhood-based projects, they would get nothing more than "a division of crumbs from the tables of power."

Funnyé found some allies who endorsed "deghettoization" as a form of black liberation. Four black revolutionaries in *Liberator* compared "the ultimate logic of 'community control'" with South Africa's Bantustans, apartheid-era territories created by the ruling white regime, and contended that it would "have the net effect of strengthening and preserving the present system of American government/economics." Funnyé was heartened by a robust debate on the virtues of separatism that broke out at the Third International Conference on Black Power in Philadelphia in 1968. A vocal minority of conference participants thought of black power in nonterritorial terms. "We don't all have to be in the ghetto just to be brothers," argued one. "Calling a prison a community doesn't make it so." Funnyé contended that his goals of eradicating segregated slums were compatible with efforts to forge a black identity. Adopting the black power call for a "community of culture and spirit," Funnyé argued that "the traditional urban ghetto ('our community') is fast becoming the western white man's instant concentration camp." The creation of a common black identity, he argued, "does not depend on geographical confines—especially if those confines facilitate physical destruction." Funnyé struggled to respect those who advocated black power, while pointing to the limits of separatism. "Control your own communities—but don't just stop there. You're not just citizens of the ghetto. Watch what the man is doing in economic, national, and regional affairs. Watch where the subsidies are going."

By the late 1960s, Funnyé's position was unpopular, especially among members of the black power movement. Even Funnyé's brother-in-law, CORE nationalist Roy Innis, called him a "conservative, reformist, integrationist." A growing number of black activists, with the support of policy makers, stopped watching "the Man" and turned inward instead. A broad spectrum of nationalists and separatists and advocates of racial uplift and self-help looked hopefully onto the bleak commercial landscapes of inner cities. While some lamented the devastation wrought by the urban riots, others saw once white-dominated business districts as "liberated zones." In the ashes of burned-out shopping districts, they envisioned a new, self-contained black economy, where blacks would spend black dollars at black-owned stores, enriching their own communities rather than watching whites leach off their earnings. They embraced a politics of "community nationalism."

Self-determination, self-sufficiency, and economic separatism were old concepts but gained new adherents in the mid- and late 1960s. For decades, groups such as the Nation of Islam and remnants of Marcus Garvey's Universal Negro Improvement Association had run specialized "race" businesses in black communities. In sermons and speeches, Nation of Islam leaders staunchly promoted buying black. "The white man spends money with his own kind," argued Elijah Muhammad. "You too must do this." Although the Nation of Islam had only between 50,000 and 100,000 members nationwide throughout the 1960s, it used its formidable treasury (estimated to be twenty million dollars in 1970) to subsidize small businesses throughout the country. On Chicago's South Side, Elijah Muhammad created a little empire around the Nation's leading mosque, including a catering business, restaurants, a halal butcher, a bakery, a department store, doctors' offices, and a banquet hall. Meat and produce came from Nation-owned farms. In other cities, the Nation provided seed money for stores that provided goods and services to Black Muslims, including theological tracts, artwork, food, suits, veils, and robes. Success in these niche businesses provided powerful examples of the economic benefits of separatism. Impeccably maintained and brightly lit, Nation enterprises were oases in commercial deserts.

Malcolm X, more than anyone else, popularized the concept of black economic and political separatism. "Why should white people be running all the stores in our community?" he asked. "Why should white people be running the banks in our community? Why should the economy of our community be in the hands of the white man?" The key to black liberation was taking control of black territory and establishing black-controlled institutions. "We must take pride in the Afro-American community," he argued, "for it is our home and it is our power, the base of our power."

Other black nationalists followed suit. Activists at the Third International Conference on Black Power demanded the creation of a "Black Economic Front," an effort "to control the cash flow and the wealth within the Black community." Among its goals was the "Black take-over of all existing businesses in the Black community by whatever means necessary." In Detroit, Edward Vaughn, whose African-themed bookstore had been firebombed by the police during the 1967 riot, attempted to reinvigorate the black cooperative movement in his city's riot-torn neighborhoods. In early 1968, Vaughn opened the Black Star (Ashanti) super-market and Black Star gas station, funded by selling membership shares to area residents. Still, Vaughn faced an uphill battle. He lamented that it was "hard to get much support from the community at first; it is hard to break the old community habit of shopping at the A & P." Vaughn's enterprises, like most black businesses, operated at the economic margins, unable to create many new jobs and limited by the lack of capital. In fact, in 1969, only 5 percent of black-owned businesses employed more than ten people and only one-third of minority businesses earned more than fifty thousand dollars per year.

Not all advocates of black economic empowerment were nationalists or radicals, although the lines between them were blurry. Few radicals at the time acknowledged the conservative currents that shaped community control and self-help. Throughout the twentieth century, versions of economic nationalism and separatism often drew together unlikely allies. The "Don't Buy Where You Can't Work" and cooperative movements in the 1930s and 1940s had attracted many members of the black bourgeoisie as well as Communists and other political radicals. In the postwar years, a steady current of "race" business leaders worked through groups such as the Booker T. Washington Business Association to promote buy-black campaigns. Their heirs in the 1960s saw "black enterprise" as a mélange of self-interest and group empowerment. One of the most celebrated organizations advocating black capitalism was the National Economic Growth and Reconstruction Organization—with its wonderfully anachronistic acronym. By the late 1960s, NEGRO had about seven hundred employees, mostly in Watts and Harlem, working in textiles, paint manufacturing, construction, and transportation.

Critics of black economic separatism—whether of the bourgeois or radical variety—offered a scathing rejoinder. CORE founder James Farmer asked, "Will a [black nation] have a General Motors, a General Electric, a separate interstate bus line? Will it be a rival economy?" Farmer's questions were good ones. The demand for black capitalism was essentially conservative. Arguments for black capitalism rested on an interlocking set of assumptions, each of which was more problematic than the last. It included a romance with small, family-run businesses and a celebration of the independent entrepreneur. The belief in the power of small business had great resonance in American popular culture generally and deep roots among blacks, at least back to Booker T. Washington. It was celebrated in the pages of magazines like *Ebony* and *Jet*. In addition, black capitalism rested on the premise that black entrepreneurs would somehow be less self-interested, less exploitative, and more community-minded than their white counterparts. If blacks spent money in their own community, the argument went, it would end up in the hands of black elites, who would reinvest in "the race." Black businessmen might be more likely to create jobs and reinvest in their communities than whites. Given the high rate of membership in civic organizations, fraternal groups, and churches by black business owners, this assumption was not without grounding (although many white business owners who served a largely black clientele advertised their contributions to civil rights organizations and black community groups). But such thinking amounted to a form of trickle-down economics, even in the unlikely scenario that black business owners were selfless, altruistic, and wholly community-minded.

For all the problems with community-controlled economic development, it proved to be immensely popular with the black masses and, to a surprising extent, with white business leaders and policy makers. The notion of black-controlled community economic development was the single most important contribution of black power to American urban policy in the 1960s and beyond. By the end of the 1960s, calls for maximum feasible participation and community action fused with black power–oriented calls for self-determination and self-help. An increasingly influential movement rose in inner cities, led by grassroots black activists but funded mostly by white business leaders and the federal government, that called for community-controlled economic development and began to organize community development corporations, or CDCs. The idea behind CDCs was to rebuild inner-city neighborhoods from within. CDCs insisted that planning initiatives should come from the grass roots. CDCs were businesses, but rather than operating on behalf of private owners or shareholders, they were not-for-profit organizations that were nominally responsible to neighborhood residents themselves.

CDCs appealed to an extraordinarily broad segment of blacks, including racial separatists, machine politicians, and Republican advocates of self-help and small government. They also built on the anticolonial rhetoric of black radicals, for at their best, they would become vehicles of black community self-determination. Robert S. Browne, a prominent black economist and advocate of racial separatism, argued in favor of CDCs as "strongly based community development organizations which would attempt to galvanize the collective resources and energies of black communities for their self-development, using government provided resources to supplement community resources but with maximal control remaining within the community." CDCs would allow blacks to form economically viable institutions, unmonopolized by whites. They would keep black jobs in the inner cities, rather than forcing the ghetto to "export" its labor to white-dominated firms. Local black political activists saw CDCs not only as a vehicle for rebuilding inner-city neighborhoods but also as a way to solidify black political power. CDCs, the argument went, would stabilize black neighborhoods, preventing population loss just as blacks were gaining a foothold in urban electoral politics. If the black population dispersed across city lines—becoming ink spots in a sea of whiteness—they would lose their political clout. Animating CDCs was a profound suspicion of the benefits of "dispersal," that is, economic development policies premised on the opening of residential opportunities for African Americans in rapidly growing suburban areas. If the city was to be the "black man's land," black suburbanization was anathema. Rebuilding the inner city was a prerequisite for the consolidation of black political power.

As black activists experimented with community economic development, they faced one serious issue: Black communities did not have enough capital to rebuild urban economies in their image. Throughout the postwar period, urban small businesses had been battered by the economy. The inner city was one of the last redoubts of small, family-run businesses, in large part because chain stores generally ignored inner cities in their rush to expand their empire in the new shopping malls of suburbia. But by the 1960s, family-run stores were withering. "There has been a gradual and steady erosion of the position of the Negro business community," lamented *The Negro Handbook* in 1966. In the inner city, noted a writer for *Ebony*, "Black dollars buy less, are harder to acquire, and are eaten up faster and in larger bits by usurious and fraudulent practices than 'white' dollars." Marketing surveys showed that blacks were at least as likely as whites to prefer department stores and discount stores over neighborhood "mom and pops," especially as larger stores gained the reputation of being at least somewhat hospitable to black customers (one of the victories of the postwar civil rights movement)—even if blacks were more likely to be followed by store detectives and less likely to be approved for store credit. Blacks still shopped in neighborhood stores that provided locally based services (dry cleaners, shoe repair shops). And despite economic fluctuations, they continued to patronize traditional "race" businesses in inner cities (bars, hairdressers, and funeral homes—all of which provided services seldom delivered by whites). But whether a neighborhood grocery store was black- or white-owned did not have much of an impact on urban residents; those stores were places of last resort. To woo black shoppers to small, understocked, often overpriced inner-city stores proved to be enormously difficult.

If black-run businesses were larger, better funded, and able to expand, they could succeed. But the lack of capital proved to be a very high barrier to black capitalism. Robert S. Browne noted the burdens that faced nascent black capitalists: "Blacks, entering as novices into the massive industrial and commercial world without contacts and with only miserly sums of equity and loan funds, are almost certain to be non-competitive producers, even were there no racial discrimination against them, which there is." Theora Makeda, a nationalist and advocate of black cooperatives, put it bluntly: "Owning and operating a small, independent business is no longer a viable alternative." White-dominated banks were reluctant to give loans to black-run businesses. Black-owned savings and loan associations simply did not have the resources to provide large-scale funding to black entrepreneurs, however successful their projects might be.

Further limiting black access to capital was twenty-five years of urban renewal, highway construction, and redevelopment. "Negro removal," as blacks derisively termed urban renewal, exacted a high price. Around the country, black business districts disappeared beneath the federal bulldozer. Landowners whose property was condemned for urban renewal and highway construction got compensation for their losses, but most black shopkeepers were renters and so got, at best, relocation assistance. Small stores that relied on neighborhood patronage could not simply up and relocate elsewhere and expect that their clients would follow. The process of urban transformation gutted black capital, with long-term ramifications for urban development.

Moreover, small businesses seldom jump-started the urban economy. When they weathered competition, small shop owners, with a handful of employees, could not individually or in the aggregate have much impact on the economic fortunes of inner-city blacks. Retail jobs, by and large, paid poorly. Many small shopkeepers relied on the undercompensated labor of family members to remain viable. Those who hired outsiders usually could not afford high wages and good benefits. At best, a successful small, family-run business might pass on the advantages of wealth to the next generation.

The question of who would fund indigenous community development in the black man's land troubled black activists. It was unrealistic to expect struggling black businesses to do it for themselves on a shoestring budget. And it was simply not enough to expect poor and working-class black people to come up with the funds. The most militant activists looked to redistributive fiscal policies to ignite black economic development. In a period when black self-sufficiency became a mantra, it was ironic that the most successful black enterprises relied heavily on white economic support. Just as black activists called for separation, white banks, foundations, and politicians bankrolled the next generation of race businesses, through programs that *The Chicago Defender* called "compensatory capitalism." Some black activists demanded that white money come with no strings attached and sometimes outright refused white philanthropy. Many activists cheered when the Reverend Albert Cleage turned down a hundred-thousand-dollar grant with "white strings" attached, for the act of resistance "provided millions of dollars worth of pride and self-confidence" to blacks. But given the paucity of black capital, most community developers and black-run nonprofits were happy to accept white money, even as they demanded full control over how it would be used.

Cleage aside, by 1968 the fundamental question for many urban activists was not how to stanch the flow of white dollars into the inner city, but how to get more. Civil rights organizations had long relied on the support of wealthy liberal and leftist whites, and they benefited from white fears of growing urban disorder in the 1960s. While some black power groups refused white financial support as a matter of principle, others, notably the Black Panthers, played to the guilt and fear of wealthy whites in a process that writer Tom Wolfe cynically described as "Mau-Mauing." Even more important than liberal whites, whose support of black radical causes was fickle at best, were liberal foundations. The two philanthropic giants, the Ford and Rockefeller foundations, channeled money to inner-city organizations. By 1969, Ford was bankrolling community-controlled education and community economic development projects throughout the North. Foundations also provided tens of millions of dollars to community development organizations. But as essential as their support was, alone they could not provide enough. Rebuilding the inner city required a greater infusion of capital. Black activists increasingly began to look for deeper pockets—those of white-dominated businesses and churches.

The search for money and justice led a growing number of black activists on the left to demand that whites pay reparations for the long history of slavery and black subordination. Calls for reparations were not new. In the late nineteenth century, Callie House founded the Ex-Slave Mutual Relief, Bounty and Pension Association. In the early 1960s, the notion of "compensatory" programs for African Americans took hold among a range of civil rights activists, including James Farmer, who called for "special treatment of a positive sort"; Whitney Young, whose Marshall Plan for the Negro was a sort of "indemnification, reparation" for the "historical deprivation" of blacks; and Floyd McKissick, who called for the development of a "legal theory of reparation" to pay for the "castration" of black men. The Black Panthers likewise demanded "payment in currency" for the "overdue debt" that the federal government owed blacks for their uncompensated labor.

No one was more closely associated with the call for reparations than Audley "Queen Mother" Moore. The black power movement only enhanced Moore's visibility among black radicals—and gave her new language to justify reparations. At a 1968 black power conference, Moore led calls for reparations, or "what the white man owes us . . . for the damages committed against our families, our homes, and our people." Moore argued that "unless we have reparations, we will never be able to do anything." She had a particularly broad vision of reparations. "The idea," she told an interviewer in the late 1970s, "was not to make one or two or three or ten little people a little wealthier. The idea was to give some form of recompense even unto our fourth generation to come, because we've been four generations injured and it's going to take four generations in order to heal, you see." Moore steeped her call for reparations in the therapeutic rhetoric that had pervaded the black power movement, blaming whites for committing "psychological genocide" and spreading the disease of "Negro-itis." Whites had to pay for the damage they had done to blacks' self-image.

Joining Moore in the demand for reparations was Brother Imari Obadele (born Richard B. Henry), the founder of the Republic of New Africa. A World War II veteran and former journalist, Henry had been a close associate of Albert Cleage. By 1968, Obadele (and his attorney brother Milton Henry, known as Gaidi Obadele) called for an independent black nation to be carved out of black-majority counties in the Deep South and funded through reparations in the form of both money and land. In May 1968, Imari flew to Washington, took a taxi to the State Department, and hand-delivered a note to Secretary of State Dean Rusk, requesting $200 billion in reparations. Within weeks, he had doubled the demand to $400 billion. His gesture was the expression of a radical utopianism that led him to continue to push for the creation of a separate black nation well into the 1970s. But the Republic of New Africa never had more than a few adherents and not a chance of success, even if it generated much press attention and captivated the imaginations of many black radicals.

If Queen Mother Moore and Brother Imari laid the groundwork for reparations demands, their gestures were largely symbolic. They did not have the organizational clout to force the question and were not taken seriously outside black power circles—with the exception of law enforcement officials. Not so with James Forman of SNCC fame. Forman brought reparations to national attention in April 1969, when he penned the "Black Manifesto." Forman directed his call for reparations to a smaller, but perhaps more pliable, target than the U.S. government: "the white Christian churches and Jewish synagogues which are part and parcel of the system of capitalism." Forman demanded $500 million or, as he put it, "$15 per nigger." ("That's a cheap price to pay," commented one Chicago teenager. "Even tiny black slaves sold for much more than that.") The Manifesto did not call for a direct transfer of wealth from whites to blacks; rather, Forman envisioned the funds supporting a range of endeavors, including the creation of a southern land bank to provide farmland for dispossessed blacks, black-run TV networks, job-training programs, welfare rights groups, and cooperatives in the United States and Africa. Forman argued that the demand was "not an idle resolution or empty words" and lambasted religious leaders for their complicity in the "exploitation of colored people around the world." But he also knew that liberal white religious organizations had funded civil rights groups and that many, especially in the North, were sympathetic to black radical demands.

Forman chose a prominent venue to bring the Manifesto to a national audience. On May 4, he interrupted services at New York City's Riverside Church to read it aloud. Riverside's grand Gothic revival tower, built with Rockefeller family money, stood prominently atop Morningside Heights, overlooking the Hudson River. The congregation—a mix of New York blue bloods and Social Gospel Protestants from nearby Union Theological Seminary and Columbia University—was rich and liberal. Many members were active in the antiwar movement (Martin Luther King, Jr., had given one of his most famous sermons there in 1967, denouncing the war in Vietnam). Riverside congregants had also helped bankroll the southern freedom struggle. If any congregation was ready to hear the Manifesto and take it seriously, it was Riverside. But Forman met with hostility. When he appeared, unscheduled, at the pulpit, Riverside's pastor ordered the church organist to start playing. Unflappable, Forman stood defiantly waiting for the right moment to resume. When the pastor canceled the remainder of the service and as most congregants left the church, Forman read the Manifesto. "It was one of the few truly beautiful moments in the Black man's dismal captivity in America," wrote Cleage. The minister and board of Riverside Church reacted angrily by getting an injunction preventing Forman from further disrupting services. Forman complied with the court order technically but showed up at Riverside Church again the following week, one of the few black faces in the audience. In his full-length, robin's-egg-blue African robe, Forman stood out in the gray sea of churchgoers in their Sunday best. As church members tensely waited for another eruption, he remained silent. During the twenty-minute sermon, he stood motionless. Still, many white Riverside church members were outraged. "It was just a plain hold-up," argued a deacon.

Just as Forman had anticipated, many white church leaders took the arguments of the Manifesto seriously, including Riverside's pastor, who at once described the demands as "absurd and fanciful" and at the same time pledged to set aside funds earmarked for the "disadvantaged" (but not Forman's group) as "restitution" and "penance" for white supremacy. "Judgment day was at hand," intoned a prominent member of the National Council of Churches, the umbrella organization of liberal Protestants. Although some officers had privately voiced support for the Manifesto, the council took a position of neutrality, calling its thirty-three member denominations to "study" the document. Forman and Muhammad Kenyatta, a Baptist minister from Chester, Pennsylvania, who became the Manifesto's other leading evangelist, decided to force the question. Throughout the late spring and summer of 1969, they took to the road, protesting at the Roman Catholic chancery in New York and addressing the national meetings of the Presbyterian Church, the American Baptist Convention, and the United Church of Christ. Other Manifesto supporters spoke in dozens of congregations, nearly all of them liberal, mainstream Protestant churches throughout the North. Occasionally, Manifesto supporters staged sit-ins at white churches or used the threat of protest to pressure congregations to "pay up." By July, the Manifesto got its first pledge, from a liberal Methodist congregation in Manhattan.

Forman's in-your-face style and militant rhetoric alienated many religious activists. The Manifesto's preamble, particularly its call for "sustained guerilla warfare" in the United States, riled even the most liberal churchgoers. The head of the American Lutheran Church, the most liberal branch of the denomination, reported that he was besieged with calls from the white faithful urging him to reject the Manifesto. A Gallup poll taken in May 1969 found that only 2 percent of churchgoers supported reparations. More conservative church leaders railed against Forman and his supporters. New York's Episcopal bishop demanded law and order and threatened to call the police if Manifesto advocates disrupted his congregation's services. The Roman Catholic Archdiocese of New York rejected the Manifesto as "closely joined to political concepts which are completely contrary to our way of life."

Still, the Manifesto's play to white liberal guilt appealed to some white church leaders. When Forman denounced participants in the annual meeting of the Presbyterian Church as members of a "white racist institution," they responded with applause. Many white church leaders encouraged their reluctant congregants to give the Manifesto a hearing. *The Christian Century* repudiated the document's "Marxist ideology" but argued that white churches had the responsibility to provide "special help" to blacks. The Manifesto "should be taken literally and should be allowed to do its traumatizing but necessary work on the white body of the established church." Liberal Presbyterian leaders tried, unsuccessfully, to stem a "backlash" against Forman and his demands by issuing a statement that contended that the "existence of the Black Manifesto adds to the frightful evidence of intolerable inequalities in American society" and encouraged its members not to respond "out of fear or anger."

The Manifesto also generated intense debate among blacks. Former SNCC chair and future congressman John Lewis, one of the most respected advocates of nonviolence, hailed the Manifesto as "a bold, dramatic move." Many members of black caucuses in the mainstream Protestant denominations encouraged their white brethren to support the Manifesto. Still, the Manifesto also met with suspicion in many black churches, particularly from those embittered by Forman's thinly veiled attack on those blacks "who have uncritically accepted Christianity." (Just a few years later, Forman wrote bitterly about his childhood experiences with the blond, white Jesus. "Religion and so-called Christianity fucked up my young life in terrible ways," he recalled.) Conservative black churchmen, such as the National Baptist Convention's Joseph H. Jackson, denounced the Manifesto as "Communist." Bishop S. E. Williams, head of the hundred-thousand-member Bible Way Churches, supported the idea of massive government-funded reparations but opposed the Manifesto as "atheistic." Bishop Stephen Spottswood, head of the million-member AME Zion Church and chair of the NAACP's national board, while less conservative, denounced reparations as "easy and emotionally appealing" but "not the fairest way" to address racial inequality. Still, the AME Zion's council, like many black church groups, resolved to support reparations, even if they repudiated the separatism and Marxism that informed the Manifesto.

Forman also took a hit from the left. Imari Obadele argued that the Manifesto went after the wrong target and was nothing but "counter-revolutionary idiocy." Queen Mother Moore "resented the fact that the brothers caught a little piece of the idea for reparations and went and got two or three hundred thousand dollars." Their demands were too small, she contended, and their beneficiaries too few. Other black leaders, particularly skeptics of black power, lashed out against the Manifesto as a misguided attempt to solve the problem of black inequality. The Manifesto would only sharpen black-white hostility and result in few, if any, gains. Reparations, argued Bayard Rustin, are "a ridiculous idea." Forman was "hustling, begging." The NAACP's Roy Wilkins predictably joined the camp of Manifesto critics: "Isn't it just plain old panhandling? It may be raised to the billionth power, but is it not begging just the same?" Overall, blacks were much more likely to support reparations than whites— nearly 21 percent in a 1969 survey. But that was hardly a resounding popular endorsement.

As a test case for reparations, the Manifesto failed. By 1972, it had raised just over three thousand dollars, most of which went to Detroit's radical Black Star Press. But as a starting point for discussions—more often heated arguments—about what whites owed to blacks, it was a smashing success. The Manifesto generated intense discussions in white-dominated churches, even when it failed to win over converts. Most of all, it revealed rifts among liberal whites over how best to respond to black economic demands. In Philadelphia, the Episcopal Church divided badly over the Manifesto. Bishop Robert L. DeWitt, a strong supporter of racial equality, an antiwar activist, and (a few years later) the first Episcopal bishop to ordain women, encouraged "creative dialogue" with the advocates of the Manifesto. When Muhammad Kenyatta disrupted services at Philadelphia's Holy Trinity Church, flinging the church's alms basin onto the floor and scattering money everywhere, DeWitt did not see a breakdown of law and order. Instead he interpreted the protest as "religious poetry . . . worthy of a Jeremiah." In response to the Manifesto, in 1970 the Episcopal diocese of Philadelphia created a "Restitution Fund," which channeled over half a million dollars to black community development organizations and provided scholarships to black students. Still, many white parishioners, particularly in conservative suburban congregations, were outraged and withheld their donations to the diocese. Where their bishop heard prophecy, they heard blackmail.

But the Manifesto had other effects. Many white churches dramatically increased their spending on black community economic development and on outreach to African Americans. The National Catholic Conference for Interracial Justice began to raise funds to compensate blacks. The General Conference of the Episcopal Church added its endorsement of reparations "by whatever name—domestic Marshall Plan, compensatory capital development, freedom budget" and donated two hundred thousand dollars to support economic development. The United Methodists allocated $1.3 million for "economic empowerment of black people," but insisted that the funds be administered by black Methodist Church leaders. Forman, for his part, denounced "greedy" and "opportunistic" black members of mainstream churches for "pimp[ing] off our efforts." The very fact that many white congregations felt compelled to support black causes—even if those causes did not meet with Forman's approval—was a reminder of the power of protest in reshaping institutional priorities, however incrementally.

While leftists continued to demand reparations, more moderate black activists sought white support for black enterprise, particularly in the aftermath of the 1960s riots. The paradigmatic project was Progress Plaza, an inner-city shopping mall that replaced an abandoned textile mill in North Philadelphia. Home to the first new supermarket opened in a black neighborhood in decades, Progress Plaza was the product of negotiations between the Reverend Leon Sullivan and local white power brokers. "You are looking at Black Power," Sullivan proclaimed at the project's 1968 opening: "black economic power." But despite the efforts of Progress to attract black-owned and black-run businesses, the only financially viable tenants were white-owned chains. As small, undercapitalized black businesses such as a black-owned stationery store went out of business, they were invariably replaced by regional or national stores. The result, writes shopping center historian Stephanie Dyer, was that the center became "a symbol of communal pride—proof that the capitalist engine of the postwar economy churned in the ghetto too." But at the same time, it "displaced African American tenants and vendors, and increased African American patronage of white-owned businesses." North Philadelphia's blacks did get access to stores that had for the most part fled the inner city, but that access did not unleash "black economic power," as Sullivan had hoped.

Sullivan pioneered what would become an increasingly common development strategy in black inner cities: the creation of an alliance between white business elites and black activists. Between 1965 and 1970, 201 of the nation's 250 largest corporations created "urban affairs" programs that channeled funds to civil rights groups, economic development projects, and job-training efforts. Only five companies had such programs before 1965. When business writer Jules Cohn interviewed corporate leaders, he found that their motivations varied: Many mentioned "social responsibility," but 40 percent hoped to demonstrate their compliance with equal opportunity programs and a third saw their efforts as "insurance" against boycotts, protest, and rioting. In August 1967, after the Detroit and Newark riots, executives of Alcoa, General Electric, Ford, and Chase Manhattan Bank joined with a thousand corporate executives, civic leaders, and elected officials to found the Urban Coalition. New York's Mayor Lindsay gushed: "Never before in our nation's past has such a broad and powerful group of private citizens joined cause on an issue of public concern." As its first act, the coalition pledged an "all-out attack on urban unemployment." Joining the efforts was the National Alliance of Businessmen, whose program for the "hard-core unemployed" provided job training and employment for 125,000 men and women in fifty cities in 1967. In September 1967, the Life Insurance Committee on Urban Problems, with 155 corporate members, pledged to invest in inner-city housing, job creation, and community service programs. Over the first two years, the committee channeled more than $800 million into low-income home mortgages. Most of the remaining funds provided capital for inner-city commercial redevelopments, such as a $1.5 million loan to allow Harlem's Canaan Baptist Church and the Harlem Freedom Associates to purchase a Woolworth's on 125th Street.

Local business leaders also launched urban redevelopment efforts. In Detroit, department store magnate J. L. Hudson, Chrysler chairman Lynn Townsend, and suburban mall developer Max Fisher founded New Detroit, a group that provided millions of dollars to inner-city business and community organizations. New Detroit channeled substantial funds to black power groups, not out of ideological affinity for separatism but for fear of alienating radicals. In Philadelphia, white business leaders gave more than a million dollars to the Black Coalition, which created twenty-five businesses and social service organizations. Rebuilding the inner city would protect white investments, create a new, skilled black workforce, and assuage the guilty consciences of liberal business leaders who had long been taken to task for ignoring the rapidly growing minority populations in their home cities. But it also generated criticism. "I for one am not knocking anyone who can beat whitey out of some bread," commented New York radical Ollie Leeds about business-funded redevelopment schemes like that conducted by the 125th Street Woolworth's. "But this is not community take-over. This is a hustle pure and simple. . . . It is jive wrapped in militant black rhetoric."

The rhetoric of free enterprise brought some black separatists, corporate executives, and conservatives into an unlikely alliance cemented by none other than Richard M. Nixon. During a radio broadcast in his 1968 campaign, Nixon lauded the antiliberalism of black power, noting that "much of the black militant talk these days is actually in terms far closer to the doctrines of free enterprise than to those of the welfarist '30s." After a conversation with CORE's Roy Innis (on a strange odyssey from black separatism to becoming a Republican advisor, libertarian, and National Rifle Association board member), Nixon promised a "new approach" toward black urban problems. "What most of the militants are asking is to be included as owners, as entrepreneurs, to have a share of the wealth and a piece of the action." Nixon aide John McClaughry recounted that the Republican candidate feared that he would "get skinned for this in the South." Much to his surprise, Nixon's speech generated a lot of favorable press. *Time* reprinted most of it. Conservative editorialists applauded Nixon's new emphasis on what they quickly branded "black capitalism." Buoyed by the favorable attention, Nixon reiterated the theme in his acceptance address at the Republican National Convention in August. "Black Americans—no more than white Americans—do not want more government programs which perpetuate dependency. They don't want to be a colony in a nation. They want the pride and the self-respect and the dignity that can only come if they have an equal chance to own their own homes, to own their own businesses, to be managers and executives as well as workers, to have a piece of the action in the exciting ventures of private enterprise." Nixon's adoption of the rhetoric of internal colonialism and his use of it to denounce the welfare state was nothing short of political genius. It appeared progressive, but, unlike liberal antipoverty programs, it was inexpensive; it showed sympathy to black power rhetoric without yielding to its radical challenge to the legitimacy of the American capitalist economy; it reframed a traditional Republican probusiness argument in terms that made it seem au courant.

When Nixon entered the White House in 1969, he combined an aversion to the welfare programs of the Great Society with the rhetoric of racial uplift. In March 1969, Nixon created the Office of Minority Business Enterprise (OMBE) to expand federal contracts to black- and Hispanic-owned firms. Domestic policy advisor John Ehrlichman argued that the OMBE would "put the administration in a good light with the

Blacks without carrying a severe negative impact on the majority community." Nixon had won election in large part by capitalizing on the racial resentments of southern whites and northern urban ethnics, but the president and many of his advisors remained committed to the gradualist racial liberalism of the 1950s and early 1960s. Many of Nixon's aides came from the ranks of the so-called Rockefeller Republicans, who supported civil rights out of a sense of noblesse oblige toward the impoverished Negro. Some even clung to the party's fading image as the "party of Lincoln." By the late 1960s, that had been trumped by a greater sense of urgency. Nixon and his aides hoped to avoid a replay of the long hot summers of the mid-1960s. Through a careful political calculus, Nixon administration officials embraced the rhetoric of black self-help as riot insurance, a means to win the support of minority voters, and a way of supplanting costly welfare programs with less expensive probusiness policies. Speaking to all of his constituents at once, Nixon wrapped the program in the mantle of free enterprise.

Nixon's embrace of black enterprise brought him some prominent black allies. Jackie Robinson and football hero Jim Brown endorsed Nixon's election bid. The Urban League's Whitney Young never wholeheartedly supported Nixon, but became an informal advisor to the president on black issues. Nixon greeted the Reverend Leon Sullivan like a hero, lavishly praising his job-training and economic development programs. Jesse Jackson, former aide-de-camp of Martin Luther King, Jr., flirted with the Republican Party in part because of his disillusionment with Chicago Democratic boss Richard J. Daley, in part because of GOP support for his program to open corporate America to blacks. And CORE's James Farmer joined the Nixon administration as an undersecretary of housing and urban development. Nixon even found supporters on the black power left, who found common cause with his antiliberalism. On the eve of the 1968 presidential election, *Liberator* magazine published an article arguing that "the conservative is the natural ally *of the moment* for the black man." Daniel Watts, the *Liberator*'s usually firebrand editor, came close to endorsing Nixon for "at least *talking* about Black Power and economics while Vice-President Humphrey is still ritualistically mouthing the old welfare-state trick bag of soul-destroying handouts." In 1972, CORE's Floyd McKissick—who had cultivated close ties with Republican policy makers and had been rewarded with substantial federal grants—joined a group of black Republicans celebrating Nixon's reelection.

To be sure, African American public opinion on Nixon was fiercely divided. *The Philadelphia Tribune,* a black paper with a venerable history of attachment to the Republican Party, charged that "Red Necks Get Green Light" in the Nixon administration. Black unionists fiercely denounced Nixon's labor policy. "His chief weapon is racism, to pit white against black, brown, and other minority groups," argued black electrical worker Jack Hart. Black integrationists and black militants had their own reasons for disliking Nixon's economic strategy. Bayard Rustin argued that the "economic impact of black capitalism has been—and can only be—marginal at best." From certain quarters on the left, critics were even harsher. Looking cynically on Nixon's adoption of black power rhetoric, *The Black Panther* commented that Nixon "sees nothing dangerous in the upsurge of a black militancy, provided that it seeks a traditional kind of economic mobility as its end, even if it wears Afro costumes and preaches a fiery race pride." Black Panther Party minister of information Eldridge Cleaver denounced "Richard the Pig-Hearted Nixon" for his "war of aggression" abroad and suppression of "aggrieved and misused people at home in the name of Law and Order." Panther David Hilliard spared no hyperbole: "We will kill Richard Nixon. We will kill any motherfucker that stands in the way of our freedom." Not surprisingly, Nixon enthusiastically supported ongoing FBI efforts to undermine the Black Panthers, even as he continued to forge alliances with other race rebels.

Of all Nixon's critics, Clarence Funnyé was one of the sharpest. He lashed out against Nixon's "diversionary programs" that left blacks with "crumbs from the tables of power." While Nixon supported black enterprise, he announced his opposition to the "forced integration of the suburbs" but quickly qualified his comment to emphasize that he meant "the economic integration of neighborhoods." Nixon, in other words, opposed exactly the sort of integration by both race and class that Funnyé advocated. "I think what the law does require," stated Nixon, "is that there be open neighborhoods. The law does not require that the Federal Government step in and provide in a neighborhood the type of housing that an individual could afford to move into." Racial diversity was, in other words, fine, so long as it did not disrupt economic exclusivity. The U.S. Commission on Civil Rights harshly denounced the Nixon adminis-

tration's interpretation of the law. "The harsh facts of housing economics," stated the commission, "suggest that racial integration cannot be
achieved unless economic integration is also achieved." The Nixon administration's withdrawal of support for dispersed, affordable housing
had a decisive impact in maintaining the racial and economic homogeneity of suburbs.

Still, in the federal system, states could step in and offer their own low-
income housing plans. Over the course of the early 1970s, New York and
Massachusetts experimented with programs to subsidize affordable housing in the suburbs. But even in liberal white communities, low-income
housing projects met with fierce opposition. Activists in Newton and Concord, Massachusetts, used land-use regulations to squeeze out affordable
housing that might be open to minorities. New Jersey took the most aggressive steps toward opening the suburbs, the result of the 1975 *Mount
Laurel* decision, a challenge to restrictive zoning brought by local legal
aid attorneys and the Camden NAACP. Under *Mount Laurel*, New Jersey
municipalities were required to alter zoning laws to allow for the construction of affordable ("fair share") housing. But opponents fought the
decision tooth and nail. Municipalities filed dozens of lawsuits challenging the order, the New Jersey state legislature intervened to prevent the
implementation of the decision, and after two more state Supreme Court
rulings, *Mount Laurel* was a dead letter. Around the North, critics of affordable housing, finding it politically unpalatable to play the race card,
instead resorted to ostensibly race-neutral rhetoric to express their opposition to new housing projects. They decried congestion, the lack of parking, or a strain on public school enrollments. They also put into place
zoning laws that forbade multiple-family housing, to preserve the "character" of their communities. And they used environmental regulations to
tie up proposed housing developments in a tangle of litigation. The result
was a sieve through which few blacks could move. "In the upper income
areas of the outer city," reported *The New York Times*, "there is salt-and-
pepper integration, a sprinkling of Negroes here and there, but it is in-
significant."

There were some glimmers of hope for open housing activists in the
1970s. A few elite suburbs implemented plans to encourage housing integration, with some success. Oak Park, Illinois, the leafy Chicago suburb
known for its collection of Frank Lloyd Wright houses, responded to the

influx of black suburbanites by encouraging real estate agents to steer white homebuyers to sections of the city that were attracting blacks and vice versa. To counter fears that black newcomers would lower property values, the town offered an insurance policy that would compensate home owners if their property on a racially mixed block lost more than 10 percent of its value. Shaker Heights, Ohio, regularly reorganized school attendance boundaries to prevent racial segregation and white flight from "black" sections of town. Both voluntary efforts worked, and the two towns attracted white liberals and upwardly mobile blacks. But integration required constant vigilance. Only a handful of other communities anywhere had the resources or the desire to create "managed" racial integration.

The most promising of the post-1960s integration programs resulted from a Chicago housing discrimination lawsuit. *Hills v. Gautreaux* concerned persistent segregation in Chicago's public housing projects. The Court's remedy was simple—to provide vouchers to public housing residents for rental in suburban communities. *Gautreaux* affected a relatively small population, but the results were heartening. These public housing residents who used their vouchers to move to Chicago's suburbs were better off than their counterparts who remained in segregated central-city neighborhoods. They were more likely to hold secure, well-paying jobs. Their children were more likely to succeed in school. And their incomes were higher. *Gautreaux* offered the best statistical evidence for the benefits of housing integration, but because it was the result of a court order, it did not become a model for similar efforts elsewhere.

By the early 1970s, overt white resistance to black suburbanization had waned: The violent resistance of Cicero and Levittown grew less common; the opposition to integration in places like Deerfield went underground; and suburban politicians like Dearborn's Orville Hubbard would be fewer and farther between. But the open housing movement succeeded on only one front: breaking down resistance to the movement of a handful of middle-class and wealthy blacks to the suburbs. It did not break down the ghetto, as Clarence Funnyé had so fervently hoped. It did not lead to the creation of many racially mixed urban neighborhoods; and it did not open the suburbs to the poor and working-class blacks who would have benefited most from access to the educational and economic resources that remained concentrated in white suburbs.

Black suburbanization accelerated in the post-1970 years, but it largely replicated well-established patterns of segregation. Steered to second-hand suburbs by real estate agents, blacks found themselves disproportionately concentrated in a band of deteriorating inner-ring suburbs and well-established black enclaves. When blacks moved into all-white suburbs, they quickly resegregated. In metropolitan Chicago, one of the most segregated metropolitan areas in the United States, blacks found themselves in run-down places that scarcely resembled the *Leave It to Beaver* suburbs of the postwar imagination: places like Maywood, a decaying blue-collar town, or Ford City, one of the poorest suburbs in the country. Only a handful of upper-middle-class, white-dominated suburbs, which prided themselves on their liberality—notably Evanston and Oak Park—integrated. But the percentage of Chicago area blacks who found themselves in such enclaves was minuscule. In 1990, metropolitan Chicago was barely less segregated than it had been fifty years earlier.

CLARENCE FUNNYÉ DIED in a plane crash in 1970. To the end, he remained optimistic about open housing. But his successors had little reason to share that optimism. By the late 1960s, the fastest job growth was occurring in outlying, overwhelmingly white suburbs. Suburban school districts were spending more per student while property owners often paid less in taxes. In an open housing market, blacks would have access to housing that was convenient to jobs and to well-funded schools. Persistent housing segregation reinforced economic and educational inequalities. The open housing movement had notable successes, but ultimately it would crash apart on the shoals of white indifference and growing black skepticism. The failure of open housing efforts had profound long-term consequences, most importantly giving credence to black power arguments about the intractability of white racism and, over time, eroding blacks' willingness to spend energy on the goal of racial integration. The result was that between 1960 and 1990, there was precious little change in the racial geography of the North. Clarence Funnyé would not have been pleased at the fate of his dream of a metropolitan America that was color-blind in practice, not just in rhetoric.

Jesse Gray, on the other hand, set a course that would be increasingly common for black politicians in hypersegregated cities. Taking advantage of the growing concentration of blacks in inner cities, they turned to electoral politics. Gray ran for city council in 1969 and, in 1970, attempted to unseat Adam Clayton Powell, Jr. Both bids were unsuccessful. Finally, in 1972, Gray was elected to the New York State Assembly from Harlem. He was never as successful a politician as he was a community organizer, however, and served only one term. While holding office, Gray remained active in tenants' rights politics nationwide. He fought Nixon administration efforts to reduce spending on subsidized housing but, consistent with his position on integration, did not support the construction of low-income housing on scattered suburban sites. Although Gray continued to support grassroots community economic development for the remainder of his life, he withdrew from the public sphere in the mid-1970s. From his weekend retreat in the Catskills, where he spent much time, he kept up with the work of the hundreds of local tenant organizations that he had inspired around the country. But the energy and commitment that he and others put into housing was fading. In 1974, longtime housing advocate Robert Weaver commented on the malaise that had descended on grassroots housing activists, the result of steady cutbacks in federal funding for housing. "Citizens feel a sense of helplessness and hopelessness," he stated. "Even blacks and other minorities are saying 'nothing works.'" By 1977, *The New York Times* characterized Gray as one of many "once powerful protest leaders" who had become "minor actors in smaller dramas." Off the stage, Gray's health deteriorated and he died in 1988. The tenants' advocacy movement that he spearheaded thrived in dozens of cities, but in the aggregate, black inner cities suffered massive disinvestment and depopulation in the 1970s and 1980s. Jesse Gray's lifelong vision of the empowered, thriving inner city remained only partially realized.

CHAPTER 13

"IT'S NOT THE BUS, IT'S US"

IN 1970, A STRONG-WILLED BUT UNASSUMING BLACK WOMAN, VERDA BRAD-
ley, sat in a Flint, Michigan, courtroom, listening to arguments before
Judge Stephen Roth on behalf of her sons, Ronald and Richard, students
in Detroit's DeWitt Clinton School. Bradley was not well known in Detroit's civil rights or black power circles, although she shared with them a
deep discontent at the status quo. Her profound religious faith instilled in
her a strong sense of justice. She engaged in what she called "mission
work," not proselytizing but instead putting her morality into action by
assisting her neediest neighbors. Fired by the spirit and inspired by Detroit's long history of grassroots activism, Bradley hoped to be an agent of
change. "Momma Bradley was always fighting something," recalled a
family friend. She was a "beautiful lady who knew her rights."

Verda Bradley migrated to Detroit from Knoxville, Tennessee, in 1942,
as a young woman looking for work in the booming auto industry. Like
many aspiring black newcomers, Bradley put her hopes on education as
a way for her children to escape the difficult working-class life that had
been her lot. To her disappointment, the schools failed her children—a
disastrous consequence at a time when employers used educational credentials as the first tool for screening prospective employees. By the time
Ronald and Richard entered grade school, Detroit's public schools were
in crisis. DeWitt Clinton represented the problems of the district in microcosm. It reminded Verda Bradley of the schools of her southern childhood. DeWitt Clinton served a neighborhood ravaged by white flight and
disinvestment in the 1960s. Whereas only one in ten DeWitt Clinton students had been black in 1960, 97 percent were black by 1970. As whites
fled, conditions in the schools deteriorated sharply. The loss of white population and jobs dealt the public schools a double whammy. Detroit's

schools served a growing population of children from poor and working-class homes, many of whom needed extra resources. By the 1967–68 school year, 84.5 percent of black students in the Detroit public schools were from low-income backgrounds. The city's property tax base was plummeting, forcing the school district to trim its budgets and principals to scrimp. Textbooks were out of date; school buildings, especially those like Clinton that were decades old, were in constant need of repair. By 1970, Clinton was, like most inner-city schools, "hopelessly overcrowded." Students attended classes in shabby portable trailers in the school yard. Many teachers were demoralized, concerned more with maintaining order in classrooms of forty or fifty students than in providing a first-rate education.

Like many northern blacks in the 1960s, Verda Bradley saw school integration as one means to the end of quality education. Unlike integrationists, she did not believe that association with white students would help children like Ronald and Richard overcome their educational or "cultural" deficiencies. She did not argue, as had the NAACP in its *Brown* case, that her sons' self-esteem was at stake in Detroit's segregated educational system (although some of her advocates did). She cared simply about quality. "We were upset because they weren't getting as many materials as some other schools," Bradley recalled. "We figured if it was desegregated, we would get the same." Her experience as a black person in Detroit made it clear that good education would not come without a struggle. "If you don't know anything about asking or demanding," she stated, "you don't get anything." Detroit provided a strong case for the NAACP, which filed a lawsuit on behalf of the Bradleys and several other black children in August 1970. In *Bradley v. Milliken*, the NAACP offered its most sweeping challenge to northern segregation to date, making the case that the Michigan state government (in the person of Governor William Milliken), its board of education, and the Detroit school system were all culpable for segregating black and white students.

BRADLEY V. MILLIKEN was the fruit of decades of grassroots organizing—led mostly by mothers—against unequal education in the North. Every major current in civil rights and black power politics in the 1960s came into play in the battle for equality in education. The very messiness and intractability of the school issue—the fact that it was intertwined with and inseparable from the housing issue—made it a difficult target for protestors. And the flurry of lower court decisions that came down during the 1960s and 1970s further confused the matter. Federal school desegregation litigation, wrote one commentator, is "marked by uncertainty and ambiguity." That the Supreme Court did not hear a northern school case until the early 1970s added to the confusion. With the law up for grabs, grassroots activists stepped up protest, and litigators tested the meaning of *Brown v. Board of Education* throughout the North, taking advantage of gaps in the case law. The coalition of groups and parents challenging unequal education was constantly shifting and diverse. Local activists experimented creatively, and sometimes inconsistently, in search of solutions to reform or transform the region's failing schools.

No forum was more important for the battle over inequality in education than the courts. Activists had widely varying opinions about the efficacy of using the judicial system to accomplish social change, but whatever their views, two cases loomed large: the still-unresolved *Brown* decision and, more immediately, the much-heralded but inconclusive 1961 *Taylor v. Board of Education of New Rochelle* decision. The New Rochelle case, in particular, excited activists for its powerful combination of protest and litigation. Local branches of the NAACP and CORE, along with some church groups—most with little guidance and usually without the blessing of national civil rights organizations—began to put pressure on local school boards, demanding equal education.

Flush with his victory in New Rochelle—and filling a void left by mainstream civil rights leaders—attorney Paul Zuber became, for a few years, the nation's leading prophet of educational equality. *The Pittsburgh Courier* described Zuber's appeal: "Parents with a segregation grouse, and mad at the fact that their children have to attend segregated schools because of gerrymandering by school boards, have taken up the cry which is gaining currency: 'Get Zuber.'" Although he was an officer in the NAACP's New York branch, Zuber was a gadfly in the organization, challenging Thurgood Marshall and the Legal Defense Fund for their reluctance to litigate northern cases. Zuber argued fiercely against what he saw as the spurious distinction between North and South. "The truth is that what is alleged to be de facto segregation in the North is really de jure segregation." The very notion of "de facto" segregation—that racially separate schools were the consequence of impersonal, race-neutral market forces—was, in Zuber's words, "a hoax." "The Negro is now becoming more and more aware of what is being done to his child in the segregated school in the North. He knows that people whose salary he helps to pay are intentionally discriminating against his child. This is not going to be tolerated any longer."

In the aftermath of the New Rochelle victory, Zuber set his sights on a huge target: Chicago, the nation's second-largest school district. Local activists there had grumbled about unequal education for decades, particularly the infamous double-shift schools that housed most of the city's black students. The *Brown* decision gave impetus to Chicago's activists. In 1956 and 1957, Chicago's NAACP compiled evidence of overcrowding, inferior teaching, and widespread segregation in the city's schools. "The Board," complained the NAACP, "has thus far declined to take any positive stand on a policy of racial integration." But the national NAACP office, preoccupied with the South, did not take action on the Chicago branch's grievances. As in New Rochelle, it took grassroots activism, most of it from parents in small neighborhood organizations, to force the question.

The push for school desegregation in Chicago came from the aggrieved parents. Women activists, working through groups such as the Citizens' School Committee, founded in the early 1930s, had long challenged classroom overcrowding and inferior education in the city's public schools. Activists from South Side neighborhoods became a fixture at school board meetings and in principals' offices, protesting double-shift and segregated schools and demanding black history curricula. As conditions in public schools worsened, Chicago activists grew increasingly impatient. In the late summer of 1961, several South and West Side neighborhood organizations—none of them affiliated with the NAACP or Urban League—invited Zuber to assist them. Even with students split into double shifts, South Side schools regularly crammed fifty students into classrooms, while nearby all-white schools had empty seats. Many South Side schools had hastily erected portable classrooms that local residents derisively called "Willis Wagons" after school superintendent Benjamin Willis. Zuber was shocked. "I've been in Chicago less than one day," he told members of the Chatham-Avalon Community Council, "and I have one question I'd like to ask all you people gathered here tonight. What is taking everyone in Chicago so much time getting started? You've got a segregated school system. . . . What are you waiting for?" With the support of several community groups, Zuber filed suit in late September. He argued that Chicago's "neighborhood school policy" was "illegal and unconstitutional." The NAACP, worried about Zuber's "freelancing," sent two advisors to Chicago in an effort to influence the direction of the protests and litigation.

Zuber owed his support to an army of South Side mothers who took their activism to the streets. Chicago activists pursued the New Rochelle strategy of widespread protests and civil disobedience. In January 1962, dozens of mothers—along with local NAACP members and ministers— engaged in "sit-ins," "walk-ins," and "study-ins" at South Side schools. When seventeen protestors, most of them women, were arrested for disorderly conduct, local blacks were outraged. Even "Ol' Nosey," *The Chicago Defender*'s pseudonymous gossip columnist, weighed in, arguing that "the cops should be doin' some real work in catchin' criminals instead of lockin' up preachers, parents, children and taxpayers."

While Zuber's case made its way through the courts, Chicago school protests took on a life of their own, increasingly unlinked from the pending lawsuit. Advocates of equal education launched a campaign to unseat Willis, disrupting school board meetings and staging theatrical protests. Members of the Woodlawn Organization dressed in black and set up a "death watch" at board of education meetings. A group of black mothers formed a "Truth Squad" that went into mostly white schools and found empty classrooms that could accommodate their children. Another group of women formed the "71st and Stewart Committee" to protest the conversion of a warehouse to a school that would serve the segregated South Side. Chicago's very active CORE chapter also made educational reform one of its key initiatives. CORE activists pushed for "open enrollment for integration," led boycotts of mobile classrooms, and set up "freedom schools." Activists staged protests at high school graduations, marched on school board meetings, and packed public hearings. Over the summer of 1963, CORE held pickets and a weeklong sit-in at the board of education, and "lay downs" to block the installation of new "Willis Wagons." More than two hundred were arrested.

Zuber's lawsuit skidded to a halt in fall 1963, when the U.S. District Court found that the plaintiffs had not provided evidence of "intentional design . . . to maintain segregation in the public schools." The court held that "de facto segregation resulting from the implementation of a neighborhood school policy, or residential segregation is not enough." The court left one opening for future litigation in its conclusion that "there must be some affirmative action of 'segregating' to violate the Fourteenth Amendment, even if it is only the passive refusal to redistrict unreasonable boundaries." Civil rights attorneys would focus on the question of what constituted "passive refusal." Zuber did not appeal the case, but the failure of litigation spurred Chicago's protestors to even more militant action. In a massive citywide school boycott in October 1963, nearly 225,000 students skipped classes, while several thousand protestors took to the streets.

At the same time that Zuber was preparing the Chicago lawsuit, a group of Englewood, New Jersey, activists retained him to challenge their city's segregated schools. Englewood's whites, most of them wealthy, lived in the town's "Hill" neighborhood. Clustered in the small, run-down houses of the "Valley" were blacks, some of them descendants of household servants and groundskeepers who had served the town's white elite, others migrants looking for a suburban alternative to Harlem or the Bronx. Englewood's public school boundaries reflected the town's racial divisions. Local civil rights groups targeted the 98 percent black Lincoln School, demanding that it be desegregated or dismantled. By 1961, local activists had grown impatient. "Let's stop talking about integration—let's do something about it," charged the Bergen County NAACP. They challenged "the concept of the neighborhood school as an instrument of segregated education."

That Zuber surfaced in Englewood outraged national NAACP officials. They viewed him as a smooth-talking demagogue who could derail their southern-focused desegregation strategy. Gloster Current, director of branches, acknowledged Zuber's talent in delivering "crowd-pleasing" speeches "in the style reminiscent of Thurgood Marshall." But in Current's view, the renegade attorney offered no systematic legal theory other than his "Zuberisms," which "violate all the laws of logic." The NAACP prepared a report on Englewood's schools, but the local branch wanted to move more aggressively. Zuber's combination of militant rhetoric and his track record in New Rochelle convinced the local branch that he was the right attorney to lead its struggle.

In early 1962, Zuber, parent activists, and NAACP and CORE members began organizing the "Englewood Movement." Their immodest goal was to turn the town into the "the focal point" of the northern battle against unequal education. Beginning in early February, activists began a series of demonstrations that would continue, more or less unabated, through the spring of 1963. Several dozen women, most of them mothers of schoolchildren, held protests nearly every day during the first three weeks of February. One hundred activists staged a sit-in at city hall, and eleven were arrested, including two Freedom Riders recently returned from their effort to desegregate interstate transportation in the South. CORE also staged a short-lived and not particularly successful boycott of white-owned downtown stores and set up carpools to take black shoppers to nearby communities. Stepping up the pressure on elected officials, the Englewood Movement organized a "phone-in" in August, when hundreds of callers flooded the switchboard of Governor Richard Hughes, who had equivocated on the Englewood case and generally supported the neighborhood school concept. Finally, in September, parents led a three-day school boycott. "This is the showdown!!!" stated an Englewood Movement flyer. "Will the Englewood city fathers be allowed to continue to enforce apartheid in the public schools?" On September 7, Hughes succumbed to the pressure and issued a public statement, demanding that Englewood address racial imbalance in the district "without delay."

As the protests escalated, the Englewood Movement's spokespeople highlighted the hypocrisy of white suburbanites. "Down home," argued Zuber, "our bigots come in white sheets. Up here, they come in Brooks Brothers suits and ties." Englewood, contended Zuber, was a "model suburb," dominated by "the Madison Avenue type of segregationist," who felt "privileged to treat the public schools as his private school." For their part, most Englewood whites played into Zuber's hand: An overwhelming majority expressed support for the status quo. The town's mayor enthusiastically backed them. More than a thousand joined SONS—Save Our Neighborhood Schools. Zuber challenged their logic: "Residents of expensive homes are not entitled to a public school attended only by children whose parents own expensive homes." He scoffed that "the only difference between the North and the South is the Mason-Dixon line." And he laid down a gauntlet. "The North has a choice. They can desegregate voluntarily or they will be forced to do so."

The Englewood Movement's increasing militancy attracted black radicals to suburban New Jersey. Zuber forged alliances with outspoken New York–based desegregation advocate Milton Galamison and Malcolm X. Galamison denounced the Englewood "plantation" and rebuffed charges that the protests were corroding the town's supposedly harmonious race relations: "The truth is Englewood, like many areas of these United States, has never been a community." Galamison's presence as an "outside agitator" was upsetting enough to Englewood's school officials, but the prospect of an alliance between Malcolm X and Zuber outraged local white officials and moderate civil rights leaders. In July, several members of the Nation of Islam joined an Englewood Movement picket line. The growing militancy of school protestors generated intense debate. "Zuber's approach," argued the Reverend Walter Taylor, a black moderate who also supported school desegregation, "is deeply rooted in the philosophy of racism and violence of the Black Muslims." Some moderate whites also railed against what they saw as the "misguided, bitter social irresponsibility" of Englewood's protestors. Although Malcolm decided at the last minute to skip an August 1962 rally, the very fact that he supported the school boycott signaled a new, militant direction. Zuber was unapologetic: "We're not looking for a peaceful, passive non-resistant angle." Englewood, he argued, would be "an armed camp" until city officials gave in. After months of pickets in the spring of 1963, culminating in a semester-long "study-in" at Englewood's schools, the New Jersey commissioner of education ordered the Englewood School Board to desegregate the Lincoln School. Zuber and local activists were exultant: "We stand now in the middle of the black man's revolution."

Zuber celebrated the increasingly impatient, militant tone of northern school protests, although like so many civil rights leaders, he did not acknowledge that the rank and file of the movement to desegregate schools was largely female. "This is a new Negro," argued Zuber. "He is proud and tough and he wants what is his by law and by right. He wants it now, not later." The women who led protests in Chicago and Englewood were not new Negroes. But their protests were more theatrical and less peaceful than the boycotts of the 1940s and 1950s. In Chicago, Englewood, and many other northern cities, women and men turned to disruption and civil disobedience. More and more protests grew violent, as angry parents and militant activists hurled themselves in front of bulldozers, blocked traffic, flung epithets at white school officials, clashed with local police departments, and often resisted arrest.

The NAACP legal team worried greatly about Zuber, the Englewood Movement, and other northern insurgents. A "new cadre of civil rights lawyers," wrote Constance Baker Motley, had taken the lead, not always with the approval of NAACP lawyers, who "tried to control" the agenda by "bring[ing] only those cases that would help implement *Brown* and to speed up the de jure desegregation process." For his part, Zuber accused the NAACP leadership of "a fundamental desire to suppress any movement by new people in the area of civil rights." In 1963, Zuber led an insurgency in the New York branch. By flanking the NAACP from the left, Zuber forced the venerable civil rights organization to direct more legal resources to northern communities. Gloster Current, responding to Zuber's efforts in Englewood, argued that "there is one lesson to be learned from this and that is that we in the National Office must find a way to accelerate our assistance to communities such as this. . . . The people are restive and want to move more rapidly than we realize at times." By pushing at the boundaries of *Brown*, Zuber and other northern attorneys and activists—with or without the cooperation of the NAACP—remade civil rights law.

NAACP Legal Defense Fund (LDF) attorneys Thurgood Marshall, Constance Motley, and Jack Greenberg—three of the key litigators in *Brown*—had little interest in northern cases. But two NAACP staff members did. One was Robert L. Carter. A graduate of Lincoln University and Howard Law School, Carter had collaborated with Marshall on the NAACP's school litigation cases up through *Brown*. Probably the most militant member of the NAACP legal team, Carter had strong opinions about the post-*Brown* direction of NAACP litigation and feuded with Marshall. For his part, Marshall perceived Carter as a rival and they differed on significant questions of strategy and emphasis. In 1961, Marshall anointed the LDF's senior white attorney, Jack Greenberg, as his successor. Carter was bitter that he had been passed over to run the LDF, but took advantage of his position in the NAACP's legal office (separate from LDF) to push in new directions. While the LDF continued to work for the implemention of *Brown* in the South, Carter turned northward.

Working closely with Carter was June Shagaloff, a sociologist who joined the NAACP staff in June 1951, just a year after she graduated from college. One of her first assignments was to assist local NAACP activists challenging segregated public schools in southern Illinois. The "Land of Lincoln" was one of the most racially divided states in the North, its countryside dotted with "sundown towns" infamous for their history of racial exclusion. Illinois had forbidden school segregation since 1877, but as throughout the North, antidiscrimination laws were seldom enforced. Shagaloff ventured into an archipelago of small towns between Cairo and East St. Louis, among them Alton, Mount Vernon, Ullin, Sparta, and Carbondale, all of which had long histories of grassroots black activism and stiff white resistance. Alton, for example, had been the site of black-led school boycotts in the late 1890s and early 1900s; East St. Louis had been ravaged by one of the bloodiest race riots in American history in 1917. Most of these towns had separate "colored" schools or bused black children to nearby towns with black-only schools.

Shagaloff's first stop was Cairo, a tough little town closer to Memphis than Chicago, notorious for its history of racial violence. Cairo proved a particularly difficult place to organize. But local activists challenged segregated schools head-on. In January 1952, a group of one hundred black parents attempted to enroll their children in one of Cairo's all-white schools. Chaos ensued as whites rose up to resist the desegregation efforts. Angry mobs gathered in the streets. Prominent blacks became the targets of violence, cross burnings, and a bombing. Local public officials used the law to thwart the NAACP's efforts. In February, Shagaloff, another NAACP official, and a group of parents were arrested and charged with "conspiracy" to force black children to transfer schools. Still, Cairo's civil rights activists remained resolute, in part because they had Illinois law on their side. Wielding the threat that the state might cut off money to deliberately segregated schools, the NAACP succeeded in breaking down Cairo's color line. The first black students attended classes in formerly all-white schools in the fall of 1952. Flush with victory, Shagaloff headed to nearby Ullin and Sparta and helped local NAACP branches win two more victories against separate, unequal education. Shagaloff's experience in southern Illinois sensitized her to the problems of racial inequality north of the Mason-Dixon Line—a cause that she pursued with zeal over the next decade and a half. Shagaloff also joined in the NAACP's efforts to prepare for the *Brown* case. A committed integrationist who believed in applying the tools of social science to racial problems, she assisted Kenneth Clark in preparing his expert report on the psychological effects of school segregation.

By the early 1960s, Carter and Shagaloff shared a passion for northern school desegregation cases. Shagaloff had an eye for those "local cases that had, in one way or another, national significance." She hoped that northern cases would "establish a legal precedent that would have meaning in scores of communities with the same kind of problems." More so than most of the NAACP's national staff, Shagaloff was sensitive to the growing restiveness in northern black communities. She saw an extraordinary opportunity to mobilize NAACP branches for an all-out assault on unequal education in the North. Her green light came in the summer of 1961, when delegates to the NAACP annual convention—many of them northerners—passed a resolution inspired by the New Rochelle case. "Segregation in education is to be ferreted out, challenged and eliminated wherever it is found in our public school systems," resolved the NAACP. "Schools segregated in fact are as harmful to our youth as are schools segregated by law."

Beginning in 1961, Shagaloff traveled extensively throughout the North, gathering information on segregation. She became a sort of Johnny Appleseed of northern school desegregation, in community after community, particularly in places where parents had not previously organized protests, joined school boycotts, or filed lawsuits. Her intimate knowledge of the NAACP's history of school boycotts and her familiarity with legal strategies was a real asset to local activists. Even in school districts such as Milwaukee, with a long history of protests about racial discrimination in teacher assignments but little grassroots interest in challenging racially segregated schools, local activists responded to Shagaloff. Much to her surprise, she discovered that the "response of Negro parents to this issue [unequal education] was far greater than anything we had anticipated. The response was immediate and overwhelming."

By late 1962, the NAACP was assisting challenges to segregated schools in sixty-nine cities in fifteen northern and western states. Roy Wilkins enthusiastically promoted the NAACP's campaign in language that echoed Zuber's challenge to neighborhood schools. "It is our intention," stated Wilkins forcefully, "to destroy this fiction, this myth—the neighborhood excuse." With NAACP support, parents filed twenty-one suits against segregated school districts including Rochester, New York City, and San

Francisco. But litigation was a last-ditch option: Lawsuits were time-consuming, costly, and divisive. And litigation was inherently risky. In the early 1960s, it was by no means clear how federal courts would apply the *Brown* decision to northern settings. Rather than face uncertain victory in the courts, Shagaloff advised many NAACP branches to use the threat of disruption to force school boards to the bargaining table. In Montclair, New Jersey, NAACP activists forced the school board to close a segregated junior high school and disperse its black students. In Portsmouth, Ohio, school district officials announced a plan to rezone elementary schools, rescinding it when white parents protested, and agreeing again to the rezoning only after an NAACP-led school boycott. Similar boycotts pressured school district officials to desegregate public schools without lawsuits in Coatesville and Twin Oaks, Pennsylvania.

While civil rights groups protested in dozens of northern cities, Carter and his legal team pressed forward with litigation, hoping to expand the body of favorable case law. Above all, they raised the question of how to define what constituted "de jure" segregation. Throughout the 1960s, legal scholars, lawyers, and jurists struggled with the question of "de facto"—that is, whether school segregation was the result of demographic or economic forces beyond the control of school boards or public officials. On one extreme were advocates like Zuber who contended that "what is alleged to be de facto segregation in the North is really de jure segregation." Others, like Shagaloff, argued that school districts "had the responsibility to correct . . . segregation, even if they did not deliberately create it." Some education officials, among them New York's Board of Education head, contended that school boards had the obligation to redress racial "imbalance" whatever its causes were. But the courts, with a few exceptions, insisted on proof that education officials had taken actions with segregative intent. Racial separation alone was not sufficient. School districts could not be coerced into imposing desegregation plans by the courts if they were not responsible for segregation.

With that standard as a baseline, courts varied widely on their interpretation of what constituted intent. Were neighborhood schools with boundaries that divided black and white communities constitutionally impermissible? What constituted "state action" in the case of residential segregation? Could a school district's failure to act constitute intentional segregation? The results of lawsuits in northern districts were decidedly mixed. Federal courts varied widely in their handling of northern cases, and, to the great frustration of integration activists, the Supreme Court, under Chief Justice Earl Warren, did not hear any of the cases. New Rochelle offered the most promising precedent—but it did not stand alone. Between 1961 and 1973, lower courts issued a welter of contradictory decisions. In the narrowest of rulings, courts found that northern school districts could not be held culpable for patterns of racial "imbalance" in schools that resulted from segregated housing patterns. In the broadest of rulings, courts ruled that districts needed to devise far-reaching plans to achieve a desegregated student body.

One of the earliest post–New Rochelle cases, *Bell v. School City of Gary*, put the neighborhood school concept to the test. When the Gary, Indiana, school district proposed the construction of an all-black inner-city high school, Odessa Bell (whose daughter Rachel would attend it) led parents in protest. Gary's NAACP called in June Shagaloff, who encouraged the parents to demand that the district transfer their children into predominantly white schools. In June 1962, Robert Carter announced that he would file suit against the Gary schools, which he called "as Jim Crow as Jackson, Miss." Joining Carter was Richard M. Hatcher, a young Gary attorney who would soon be one of the nation's first black mayors. Carter and the NAACP had a clear goal: "to get the court to declare it the duty of the school board . . . to alleviate and remedy existing racial imbalance in attendance at schools throughout the school system regardless of admittedly existing segregated housing patterns."

Gary was a natural site for one of the NAACP's first high-profile northern cases. On the face of it, the grounds for ordering desegregation were crystal clear. Indiana did not outlaw racially separate schools until 1949—the last state outside the South to do so. And Gary's schools had been a racial battleground since World War II. In 1943, black parents led a protest against the high school's segregation of black and white swimming classes. In 1945 and 1947, white students went on strike to protest the admission of the first blacks to all-white schools. Throughout the 1950s, civil rights activists battled the Gary school district to pick up the pace of dismantling the city's now illegal separate schools. Black parents regularly complained of overcrowded classrooms in run-down schools.

The city used the two-shift system in many of its black schools and even rented space in churches, community centers, and halls to handle over-crowding.

By 1962, when the NAACP filed suit on Rachel Bell's behalf, Gary's public schools were 54 percent African American, but twelve schools were 99 to 100 percent black and another five were more than three-quarters black. By contrast, five schools were 1 to 5 percent black and under capacity. Gary school officials denied responsibility for segregation. The schools' boundaries, they contended, had been "innocently arrived at." Froebel High School, for example, had served an all-white neighbor-hood through the 1940s; it had become all black only as the result of black movement into the neighborhood, a process that the school district contended was out of its control. The key issue of the case was whether the school district had a constitutional duty to desegregate schools that it had not deliberately segregated. Judge F. Ryan Duffy ruled that Gary's district boundaries "were determined without any consideration of race or color." Even if the city's schools were racially segregated, the school system was not compelled "to recast or realign school districts or areas for the purpose of mixing or blending Negroes and whites in a particular school." The court made two related points, both of which drew from de-fenses of the neighborhood school concept. First, arguments for school integration gave "little, if any, consideration to the safety of the children, convenience of pupils and their parents, and costs of the operation of the school system." Second, the existence of segregated schools was the con-sequence of "colored people, on their own volition," moving into a for-merly white neighborhood. The court held that the district did not have the "affirmative duty" to redress school patterns that were the result of a "voluntary Negro influx." Gary activists were disappointed. *The Chicago Defender* denounced the judge as "too biased and too incompetent to ar-rive at an equitable and impartial decision." Duffy's decision may have reflected bias, but it was solidly grounded in precedent. Even in the New Rochelle case, which challenged the notion that neighborhood schools were sacrosanct, the court required proof of intentional discrimination. Other judges would later challenge the de facto–de jure distinction, but Duffy stayed within the narrow bounds of settled law.

Gary was but one battleground in the NAACP's struggle to desegregate northern schools. "The NAACP," June Shagaloff stated bluntly in August

1963, "is not for one moment relaxing or lessening in any way whatsoever demands for immediate and meaningful actions to end discriminatory practices and de facto school segregation wherever it exists." The NAACP threatened to "intensify protest demonstrations of all kinds directed against school authorities and city officials" in every "city where school officials are doing nothing or dragging their feet." Despite their differences with Zuber, Shagaloff and Carter shared his view of litigation and protest as mutually reinforcing.

At the same time, however, the NAACP also turned to a more promising forum for its desegregation efforts: state courts and, in states with strong departments of education, administrative hearings. Facing stiff opposition to desegregation by local school boards, Carter and his team persuaded New York and New Jersey's commissioners of education, through administrative proceedings, that racially imbalanced schools were "educationally inadequate." At the state level, the NAACP was not burdened with having to prove intentional segregation. Rather, litigators emphasized the negative academic effects of racial imbalance—from lower test scores to classroom overcrowding—regardless of its causes. The issue was outcome, not intention. Both states' high courts upheld the power of state administrators to override local school districts and order school integration plans.

Regardless of the status of litigation and administrative action, grassroots activists, more and more impatient, stepped up their protests. Litigation was an abstraction for many black parents; the results of the first wave of court hearings were mixed at best; and the quality of education, especially in major cities, seemed to be deteriorating rather than improving. In Boston, where civil rights activists had been agitating for equality in education since the early 1950s, twenty thousand students and activists boycotted schools in February 1964. The same month in New York, massive boycotts paralyzed many schools in black neighborhoods: 77 percent of students in Bedford-Stuyvesant, 80 percent of students on the Lower East Side, and 92 percent of Harlem students stayed out of school. In response to demands for integration, New York school officials had created a voluntary transfer program, allowing small numbers of blacks and Puerto Ricans to take places in mostly white schools. But New York's CORE and NAACP branches demanded nothing less than the "complete desegregation of all schools." Protestors rejected "the tokenism of transfers and open enrollment, devices which parallel those used by southern school boards asking to slow down or evade the Supreme Court decision." Later that year, black students in Cleveland led a citywide walkout after the death of a white CORE member who was crushed by a truck while protesting at a school construction site.

Growing pressure to desegregate schools—even in the absence of litigation—yielded results. By 1969, fourteen northern and western states had created offices to "encourage school integration." All but one had been created in the previous five years. Several states also enacted regulations mandating that school districts achieve "racial balance" in public schools—although they seldom specified how school districts should do so. Many school districts, facing external pressure or fearful of litigation, launched their own desegregation efforts. Between 1962 and 1966, forty-nine northern public school districts took what June Shagaloff called "substantial steps toward desegregation." School districts as diverse as Berkeley, California; Stamford, Connecticut; Norristown and Lower Merion, Pennsylvania; and White Plains, New York, took affirmative steps to desegregate their schools. Many small districts implemented the Princeton Plan—merging black and white elementary schools. Others closed down all-black schools and dispersed their students throughout the district, usually by bus. Still others implemented "choice" programs, allowing black students (and sometimes whites) to transfer out of "imbalanced" schools. Some districts redrew attendance boundaries to remix the student population in neighborhood schools.

None of these solutions was perfect. Most busing programs took black students into hostile white neighborhoods, generating resentment among black parents who believed that their children were bearing the brunt of desegregation. "Increasing numbers of young Negroes," reported *The New York Times* in 1969, "are tiring of the steady abuse that comes with integrating white schools. Many . . . believe that integration has been too nearly a one-way street with Negroes always leaving their schools to go to white schools." Black and white parents alike complained of classroom and playground brawls. White parents often withdrew their children from schools undergoing integration, and many protested vehemently when neighborhood schools came under siege. Moreover, in some districts integration was a process in name only: Black students in ostensibly integrated schools found themselves confined to special education, vocational, or remedial classes with few white classmates. Fifteen years after the *Brown* decision, Ruby Martin, who headed the civil rights office in the federal Department of Health, Education and Welfare, argued that the "North has slipped backward" while the South had "groped reluctantly forward" in breaking down the barriers of race in its schools.

Many districts struggled with desegregation. A typical one was Plainfield, New Jersey, a suburb of 45,000 people, which reorganized its schools under a 1964 state order. Racism persisted among students; in 1966, the words "nigger steps" and "nigger entrance" were painted on various parts of Plainfield High School. Black and white students regularly clashed, and, at one point, school officials barely averted a riot between hundreds of brawling white and black students. Black students charged white teachers with abusive disciplinary policies. And many critics accused the district of evading desegregation by implementing a rigid tracking system, grouping students by "ability" in grades seven through twelve. Black students were generally denied admission into the higher tracks. Only 5 percent of black Plainfield students were in the upper level of the three-track system in 1966. And 80 percent of Plainfield's lower-track high school graduates attained only ninth- or tenth-grade performance levels in reading and math. Desegregation also spurred white flight from Plainfield's schools. By 1967, Plainfield High School was 52 percent black. The school's black population ballooned to 69 percent in 1970. By 1990, only 2.3 percent of all students in the Plainfield school district were white.

The struggle over equality in education had paradoxical effects on whites. On one hand, white attitudes toward school integration changed dramatically in the years following World War II. In 1942, a Gallup poll showed that 40 percent of northern whites approved of school integration; by 1956, two years after the *Brown* decision, the figure had risen to 60 percent; by 1963, another polling firm discovered that 75 percent of northern whites approved of *Brown*. But even if they approved of desegregation in principle, most northern whites opposed it in practice. In the post-*Brown* world, as southern racism and brutality made the daily news, northern whites were quick to insist on the purity of their motives and on their victimhood. Just as school districts had contended that they were not legally culpable for "de facto" segregation, so too did many white parents argue that it was not their fault that schools remained sharply divided by race. In their telling, they did not harbor racist principles: They approved of the principle of educational integration. In their self-fashioning, they were not "southern style" bigots; they exercised their freedom of choice to select the best schooling options for their children. Blacks were left out either because of their personal, behavioral deficiencies or because of their own "free choice" to live in black neighborhoods. In this version of events, the whole postwar history of residential segregation vanished. Once whites stopped overtly professing their opposition to the ideal of integration, the housing market automatically became race-neutral and the causes of racial separation in schooling became the inevitable consequence of the sum of individual decisions.

Whites' insistence on their own color blindness led them, in many places, to denounce those who were trying to "force" integration. Plans to remedy racial imbalance in schools required taking race into account, gathering data on the racial composition of schools, and using those data to fashion desegregation policies. The perpetrators of racism, in this view, were civil rights activists—and the meddling school officials who allied with them—who took account of race. In March and June 1963, thousands of white parents in East Flatbush, Brooklyn, withdrew their children from school to protest "reverse discrimination," because the New York City school district redrew school attendance areas to increase the enrollment of black and Puerto Rican students in "their" school. Perry Gillery, a leader of the East Flatbush protests, complained that "we want to do right and help the Negro children. But we don't want our rights to be trampled." In Jackson Heights, a Queens neighborhood where the school district deployed the Princeton Plan to consolidate two elementary schools, one overwhelmingly white, the other nearly all black, whites formed Parents and Taxpayers (PAT), a group that would soon claim several hundred thousand members citywide, to oppose integration. In Montclair, New Jersey, parents complained about "discrimination against the majority" when school officials disbanded a black-majority elementary school and allowed black children the option of attending one of several white-dominated schools in the district. In an ingenious lawsuit, a group of white parents complained that the school district had violated the "equal protection" clause of the Fourteenth Amendment by allowing black children the right to choose which elementary school to attend, while not giving whites a similar choice. In all three communities, white opponents of school desegregation embraced the goals of procedural antidiscrimination in service of maintaining a racially segregated status quo. School desegregation advocates, by contrast, focused on results and had no qualms about taking race into account to break down single-race education.

The slow pace of integration—even as whites seemed more accepting of the principle of racial equality than ever—led many northern civil rights activists to rethink the whole integrationist project. "When 10,000 Queens white mothers showed up to picket at city hall against integration," recalled Doris Innis, it was "obvious we had to look for other solutions." June Shagaloff and the NAACP kept the faith, but a growing number of activists grew agnostic about the value of desegregation or even skeptical about the value of racial mixing in public schools. The confusing muddle of court rulings on segregation and the fact that the Supreme Court did not hear a single northern school case in the 1960s did not help matters. Moreover, the fact that much litigation was prolonged and inconclusive tested the patience of civil rights advocates. If integration was, in the words of one black commentator, a "high impact, low probability remedy," then it was time to seek other, more feasible solutions. So long as schooling remained "the black local and the white express," parents and reformers demanded more. In the increasingly impatient post-1963 years, as activists continued to put pressure on school districts, and especially those in large cities, educators, public officials, and grassroots activists proposed all sorts of experiments in education, some practical and others far-fetched. The two most prominent were calls for increased funding for schools that served the urban poor and calls for reform in the governance of urban school districts.

Efforts to desegregate schools—by whatever means—faced one major obstacle. With the exception of the poorest whites, who were generally not concentrated in single neighborhoods, most white parents had the flexibility to withdraw from public schools or to move across district lines. Suburbanization in particular provided skittish white parents a way to avoid desegregation. Throughout the North, most suburban districts were overwhelmingly or completely white. The fixity and impermeability of school district boundaries meant that most outlying communities were completely unaffected by calls for educational integration. As long as housing markets remained segmented by race, white parents could move across district lines and rest assured that their school districts would remain homogeneous.

The localistic nature of public education and the resulting inequity of funding between school districts had long been one of the most distinctive features of American society. School districts largely relied on local tax revenue, usually property taxes, to fund education. The reliance on local taxes to fund schools greatly increased the disparities between wealthy districts, usually protected by zoning restrictions that kept poor and working-class people out, and urban districts, which faced declining tax revenues as the result of population loss and disinvestment. The wealthiest districts had, on average, significantly more resources to assist a student population that had few needy children; urban districts usually had fewer dollars per capita to educate children who came to school from disproportionately poor families with multiple educational disadvantages. By the 1950s, liberal reformers, most of them unconcerned with civil rights issues, had begun to make a case against the localized nature of American public education and government, arguing for more efficient forms of statewide taxation to smooth out local inequities and shift the burden of the provision of services such as education to the state level. Such calls for efficiency dovetailed with the demands of civil rights activists for educational equality. By the early 1960s, amid growing concern about race, poverty, and schooling, the school-funding issue took on greater salience.

Of all the issues that galvanized educational reformers, a wide range of activists found common ground in criticizing the failure of urban school systems to meet the needs of "culturally deprived" students, a category that included juvenile delinquents, children from broken homes, households with unemployed heads, and minority groups. Many educational reformers in the 1960s argued that students from deprived and minority backgrounds lacked the cultural capital to succeed in a modern, technologically advanced society. Theorists of "cultural deprivation" made the case that schools had a special responsibility to undo the psychologically damaging effects of racial marginalization, to provide alternatives to the "disorganized" household, and to imbue in students both the skills and the self-esteem necessary to make them into productive citizens.

Cultural deprivation became a wedge for reformers to push for new school-funding mechanisms. New York and California adopted legislation in the early 1960s that channeled state funds to "compensatory education" programs in districts with large numbers of "culturally deprived" students. The Ford Foundation pumped some of its "Gray Areas" program funds into urban education initiatives targeted toward poor children. New York and Pennsylvania educators experimented with "school readiness" programs—most with Ford Foundation grants—to prepare disadvantaged three- and four-year-olds for elementary school. Grassroots groups created a plethora of programs, most of them small-scale and experimental, to provide alternatives to failing urban schools. The Northern Student Movement, a grassroots organization of college students committed to interracial organizing, established tutorial programs in big-city high schools beginning in 1962. In Boston, civil rights groups that had boycotted the city's segregated schools in 1963 expanded the temporary "Freedom Schools" into year-round educational centers for underprivileged youths. And in Chicago, the Boys Club, a long-established settlement house, set up programs for at-risk high school dropouts. Compensatory education programs, however, generated intense debate among civil rights activists, particularly when northern school districts adopted them as a way to stifle demands for school integration or "to get lower-class Negro children 'ready' for integration." Doxey Wilkerson, a longtime advocate of equal education, worried that compensatory education programs "represented the Northern version of 'separate but equal.'" He argued that "merely to enroll white and Negro pupils in common schools by no means constitutes an adequate approach to equality." Wilkerson sensibly argued for both.

Compensatory education programs, tutorials, and school readiness efforts foreshadowed three key Johnson administration educational initiatives. The loose language of the War on Poverty encouraged the use of federal funds in local compensatory education programs. One of the most visible and successful Community Action Program demonstration projects was Head Start, which provided preschool children with skills. Federal dollars also funded programs that targeted "at-risk" high school students and dropouts and set up extensive training programs for the "hard-core" unemployed. But of all the Great Society's educational initiatives, none held out more promise than the Elementary and Secondary Education Act of 1965 (ESEA), which brought unprecedented federal support to public schools. A key provision in the act targeted "educationally deprived children" with a billion dollars of federal funding for school districts throughout the country. Conservatives griped about the federal "intrusion" into local education, but ESEA enjoyed a broad, bipartisan base of support.

Adam Clayton Powell, Jr., who had long campaigned for better funding for impoverished children, was exuberant. "This is the precise moment in history for which we have waited," he cheered. "Let us ring our bells of liberty and freedom throughout the land." But Congressman Powell's enthusiasm was quickly dashed. Federal educational funding ballooned nearly tenfold per year by the end of 1968, but most of it did not go to help the poorest children or the poorest school districts. Ninety-four percent of school districts in the United States—most of them with few poor students—got ESEA funds. Even when targeted to impoverished communities, federal educational dollars went to a wide range of programs, some educational, but many not—including school nutrition, social services, and health. Congress, reluctant to tread on the local control of education, left spending decisions to school boards, which sometimes expanded "special education" programs for children but seldom used federal funds to reduce class size in impoverished schools, to desegregate districts, or to bolster weak curricula in inner-city schools. More often, they offset property taxes, expanded programs that were not specifically targeted to disadvantaged students, and constructed new school buildings, sometimes in impoverished neighborhoods, but more often in rapidly growing suburbs and outlying neighborhoods. ESEA was a boondoggle that benefited suburban whites, not the urban poor.

The infusion of federal funds into public schools had the unintended effect of intensifying the debate about school integration. Many of the North's oldest and most run-down schools—those to be rebuilt or replaced with new federal funding—served neighborhoods with large minority populations. School reformers struggled over the relationship between new school construction and the goals of desegregation. Should segregated, inner-city schools be replaced by new buildings that would still entrap minority students in segregated classes? Or should school districts use the influx of federal funds to fundamentally alter school patterns? In nearly every major northern city, school reformers called for the creation of "educational parks," clusters of schools that would serve thousands, even tens of thousands, of students on central campuses. New York integrationists proposed recycling the site of the 1964 World's Fair in Queens as a 25,000-student complex. Pittsburgh considered a $111 million plan to build educational parks. In Newark and Buffalo, CORE chapters endorsed the concept. And in Chicago, the Urban League supported the creation of five educational parks serving 10,000 to 20,000 students each. But educational parks were a short-lived fad. Neighborhood school advocates raised concerns about sending students long distances; seasoned educators were skeptical about the management problems of huge, clustered schools; and many school districts worried that transportation and construction costs would be prohibitive. Only a handful of cities actually implemented the concept, most on a very small scale.

While some civil rights activists demanded educational parks, a growing number, especially on the black left, embraced the concept of "community control" of education. The call for community control was the natural outgrowth of black power. Already by 1964, *Liberator*, whose contributors included Paul Zuber and Milton Galamison, began to publish articles by advocates of community control as an alternative to both integration and compensatory education. To be sure, skepticism about racial integration in schools was nothing new in the 1960s—black teachers and intellectuals had long debated the virtues of separate education. In nearly every northern district rocked by school boycotts, a minority of black parents had refused to participate, many because they supported the concept of all-black schools. Black teachers, especially in districts with a long history of confining them to black-only schools, also feared losing their jobs if school districts were integrated. Many black opponents of integration also rejected the paternalism inherent in the idea that proximity to white students would help blacks enter the American mainstream.

S.A.L., a contributor to *Liberator*, was blunt: "Now, about this school integration business—I couldn't care less. I don't believe that just because my kids are sitting next to some old white kids they're going to learn." Like many skeptics, S.A.L. rejected the argument that integration could help black students overcome their "cultural deprivation." Unequal education was not the result of the deficiencies that black children carried with them to the classroom; it was the result of ineffective teaching and low expectations. "I want them to stop finding excuses why they can't get to work and teach my kids—something about 'cultural deprivation' and 'no family structure.' Who they kidding?" Still others launched an attack on integration from the vantage point of black nationalism. C. E. Wilson, a strong advocate of community control and racial separatism, argued that "Negroes as a group . . . cannot serve two masters: themselves and the cultural value system of the oppressive white society." Stokely Carmichael was characteristically sharp-tongued: "I tell you, we don't need their integrated schools in the suburbs if they give us the money that belongs to us for our own schools."

One of the major arguments on behalf of community-controlled schools was that they would encourage the development of a distinctive black culture by teaching black history, music, and art. Psychiatrist Alvin Poussaint made the point forcefully: "Only by strong assertive action by blacks to restructure racist educational processes in America will young blacks today be able to build a positive self-image that will lead Afro-Americans to greater growth, power and achievement." In this view, black students were the victims of a different form of "cultural deprivation": White educators had deprived black students of their own past. Examples of a "whitewashed" education were easy to find. Textbooks depicted white America as normative. Black first graders learned to read through the ubiquitous stories of "Dick and Jane," two blond, suburban young-sters. They read textbooks that depicted the happy "Sambos" of planta-tion slavery and described Reconstruction as a period of black corruption and misrule. They learned about the Boston Tea Party, but not about black patriot Crispus Attucks. In Wichita, Kansas, black parents rose up against the classroom assignment of Laura Ingalls Wilder's *Little Town on the Prairie*, which contained the epithets "niggers" and "coons." New York teacher Richard Turner railed against the "blue-eyed, blond ap-proach" in most schoolbooks. "The Negroes, the Puerto Ricans, these kids are left out," he argued. "They are left out of the books, they are left out of television, they're left out of the movies, except in a distorted way. They are angry."

Civil rights activists had long campaigned for the accurate depiction of black history in American textbooks. "The thought of the inferiority of the Negro is drilled into him in almost every textbook he studies," lamented historian Carter Woodson in 1931. As a corrective, Woodson launched Black History Week (later Month), founded *The Journal of Negro History*, and campaigned for the revision of textbooks and school curricula. The intercultural education movement of the 1930s, led by Rachel Davis DuBois, posited that teaching children to respect different cultures would cure "the alienation, rootlessness, and emotional disorders" that plagued members of marginal racial and ethnic minorities. But the efforts had little impact on school curricula. Finally, in the 1960s, the NAACP and CORE led a nationwide campaign to rectify the faulty representation of blacks in school textbooks. Leading the effort was Berkeley history professor Kenneth Stampp, author of one of the most important histories of slavery. With the assistance of graduate student Richard Tyler, Stampp worked with the NAACP and CORE to design a model school curriculum that incorporated the most up-to-date work in black history. By the mid-1960s, the campaign had begun to bear fruit: School districts and teachers' unions began to devise course plans on black history and culture.

Black radicals took the call for black history a step further. A successful curriculum meant going beyond George Washington Carver and the peanut or even the latest work of Kenneth Stampp. Rather, students needed to be steeped in African culture and history. In New York, Herman Ferguson proposed a "Survival Curriculum" for black-controlled schools. Ferguson's ideal school day would begin with a pledge of allegiance to the "red, black and green flag"—the colors of Africa. Students would participate in a core curriculum of "weaponry and self-defense," including daily target practice. The school would celebrate blackness and militancy. "As our black student moves around the building," wrote Ferguson, "loudspeakers . . . continually bathe him with the quiet sound of Malcolm X speaking, LeRoi Jones reading one of his poems, Aretha Franklin singing a soul song." Black education was a fusion of power, politics, and pride.

Ferguson may have been on the extreme, but in a watered-down version, his ideas took hold in many inner-city schools. It became commonplace to argue that only black teachers—steeped in an authentic black culture—should teach black history. Teachers would serve both as "role models" and as "griots" or storytellers, using their skills to pass on oral traditions that no white person could comprehend. At the core of the new African-focused curriculum was a belief that an exposure to black culture would empower students to reject the "inferiority complex" that came from a curriculum that took white power and privilege for granted. If only the school system, through a celebration of authentic black culture, could restore black students' sense of dignity and self-worth, they would move onto the path of educational success.

Efforts to "Africanize" school curricula were hard-fought in many large urban school districts. Black parents and community groups lobbied for the inclusion of black themes in the classroom, and school district officials and teachers, hoping to buy off discontent, began to realize that weaving African culture into social studies and literature courses came at a small price. But the assumption that culture would enhance group self-esteem and lead to better educational outcomes proved to be dubious. Curricular reforms, at their best, accomplished one important pedagogical goal: to present a better-rounded, more accurate view of the past. But the assumption that good history would have powerful psychological effects, and that those effects would undo the combined disadvantages of family, neighborhood, school overcrowding, and educational underfunding, was unfounded. Kenneth Clark, who had long emphasized the corrosive effects of negative self-esteem on black children, offered a scathing critique of the assumptions of educational uplift. "You cannot give pride to an adolescent," he wrote, "who is four or five years retarded in reading and understanding and using English by trying to teach him . . . racial heritage or racial identification."

For many activists, questions of curriculum and culture were bound up with questions of control. If black radicalism provided the intellectual underpinning for community control, the War on Poverty provided a model of how it could be done. Community control of schools was the natural corollary of maximum feasible participation. Black activists shared in the rising antibureaucratic sentiment of the 1960s. Just as the Community Action Program had promised to put welfare and job training in the hands of local activists and poor people themselves, so too would community control liberate schools from out-of-touch administrators. Schools were run by careerist principals, staffed by teachers with no roots in the "community," held accountable to distant bureaucrats, and managed by paternalistic technocrats. Advocates of community control gave antibureaucratic sentiment a racial gloss: White teachers were insensitive to black students; white principals were disrespectful to black parents; and white administrators were beholden to their white constituents. All of them were racists; all of them had it in their interest to keep black students down. After all, white-dominated school boards had overseen the creation of an educational system that was systematically unequal; white principals had steered black students into remedial classes; and white teachers treated black students as inferior beings. But if schools were taken over by parents or by elected community councils, they would be accountable to "the people." Above all, community control advocates shared a faith that the educational inequities could be overcome by administrative reorganization.

The most intense battles for community control played out in New York City. The first target of protest was the newly constructed I.S. (Intermediate School) 201, a grim, windowless fortress in the heart of Harlem. As soon as it opened in September 1966, civil rights groups set up picket lines, demanding that the district bus white students to the new school to create "racial balance." Both integrationists and black nationalists marched at the school—a reminder of the thin line that separated demands for integration and calls for black power. Burned from the failures of the nearly ten-year struggle against school segregation, the I.S. 201 protestors offered the school district an alternative: If the district did not integrate the school, it should be turned over to the community and assigned a black principal and an all-black staff. Black radicals, among them Herman Ferguson, saw I.S. 201 as an opportunity for black self-determination. The Harlem school became the proving ground for the still-untested concept of "community controlled" education.

The battle over I.S. 201 foreshadowed what would be the most publicized, though by no means the most important, school battle of the 1960s—the struggle over community control in New York's Ocean Hill–Brownsville neighborhood. A black and Hispanic section of Brooklyn with some of the city's worst schools, Ocean Hill–Brownsville was also a well-organized neighborhood, with well-funded antipoverty groups, tenants' organizations, and a strong labor movement. In 1966, activists from Brownsville joined a sit-in at the New York school district headquarters and, demanding black self-determination in public education, anointed themselves the "People's Board of Education." In April 1967, the Ford Foundation, with the backing of the New York school district, designated the neighborhood one of three "demonstration districts" for an experiment in school decentralization. Much as advocates of the War on Poverty had argued that community control would empower the poor by giving them a stake in the system, so too did community control proponents see the Ocean Hill–Brownsville experiment as a way to give the poor a voice in an educational system that had long excluded them. It would be democracy in action.

The Ocean Hill–Brownsville experiment erupted into a crisis in the spring of 1968, when the newly elected local school board demanded the reassignment of nineteen white schoolteachers. The ensuing struggle—pitting the powerful United Federation of Teachers against advocates of community control—culminated in a 55,000-teacher walkout in New York's schools in the fall of 1968, the first of three strikes that year. The predominantly Jewish teachers union accused community control proponents of union busting and anti-Semitism. Black power advocates accused the teachers of racism. Racial hostilities were already deep in postwar New York City, especially in the outer boroughs, where blacks and whites collided over schools and housing. The Ocean Hill–Brownsville controversy hardened those divisions. But New York did not jettison the experiment in decentralization entirely. In the end, a version of community control remained in place. The city took the power to appoint principals and assign teachers out of the hands of local school councils but created thirty-two separate school boards, each locally elected. By the 1970s, some of the local boards were led by advocates of African-themed curricula, but others fell into the hands of whites who used community control to protect the homogeneity of their neighborhood schools. The experiment in public participation in educational governance had defenders (who argued that decentralization was democratic and empowering) and critics (who saw the local school boards as prone to corruption and needless bureaucracy). But the shifts in governance did not address New York's deeper problems. Over the 1970s, New York lost population, saw its tax base dwindle, and went into bankruptcy. Whites continued to flee the schools in huge numbers. By 1980, New York was one of the most distressed school districts in the country—and it was unlikely that community control or its tempered version could have done anything about it. The problem was not one of governance, it was one of resources.

While community control of education dominated many of the debates about schools in the 1960s, very few school districts other than New York actually implemented it. School district bureaucracies—racist or not—

were too deeply entrenched to give up power to parents' groups or community organizations without a fight. More common were experiments in decentralization, usually the devolution of some school district functions to the subdistrict or neighborhood level as an effort to foster greater local participation in educational affairs. Such arrangements seldom altered the balance of power in public school districts.

But for all the attention that went to community control, the vast majority of African Americans continued to support racial integration in schools. Depending on the wording of survey questions, between three-quarters and four-fifths of northern blacks surveyed in 1969 supported integrated schools, while only 16 percent believed that community control would allow blacks to "get ahead better in this country." It was noteworthy that blacks under age thirty were more likely to support community control (30 percent) than older blacks, but a majority (59 percent) still supported integration. The NAACP—still the largest mass-membership black organization in the country—took a middle-ground position, reflecting the growing appeal for community control among black activists and the widespread popularity of integration. "We strongly support the concept of community control of public schools, particularly in the big-city school systems of the North and West, as a means of achieving fundamental changes in the schools and insuring accountability," stated the NAACP in a resolution adopted at its 1969 convention. "We do not believe that community control and desegregation are inherently incompatible or in conflict unless they are made to be by the advocates, white or black, of racial separatism."

The NAACP resolution reflected the realpolitik that shaped most grassroots struggles for quality education, even in the polarized climate of the late 1960s. Many of the same activists who called for integrated schools demanded that school officials recognize and respect black history and black culture and hire teachers from "the community." By the end of the 1960s, few saw racial mixing in the classroom as an end in itself. But to many activists—and black parents such as Verda Bradley—integration still seemed to be the most feasible solution to educational inequality.

Over the course of the 1960s, the NAACP refined its litigation strategy. The courts continued to generate a welter of inconsistent rulings on school desegregation. In *Deal v. Cincinnati Board of Education* (1966), the Sixth Circuit U.S. Court of Appeals ruled that "there is no constitutional duty on the part of the Board to bus Negro or white students out of their neighborhoods or to transfer classes for the sole purpose of alleviating racial imbalance that it did not cause, nor is there a like duty to select new school sites solely in furtherance of such a purpose." At the core of the *Deal* decision was the court's finding that "it is freedom of choice that is to be protected." Only if the school district itself put an unnecessary restriction on the freedom of choice for the individual, based on "the fortuitous, uncontrollable, arbitrary factor of his race," could the court impose a remedy. Even with "a showing of harm" that segregation hindered the education of black students, the district could not be held responsible. Making an argument that betrayed ignorance of the fact that the housing market was riddled with racial discrimination and exclusion, the court ruled that black parents had "the choice of attending a mixed school" and that any imbalance in the racial composition of schools was the result of "population mobility."

But not all decisions supported the de facto–de jure distinction. In Washington, D.C., Julius Hobson, a member of the black power–oriented group ACT, filed suit against the public school district for violating the rights of black children by maintaining a strict neighborhood school system. In *Hobson v. Hansen*, Judge J. Skelley Wright ruled that regardless of the cause of racial separation in schools, whether the school district was culpable was not the point. Instead, "equal educational opportunity" was impossible in a racially imbalanced district. Just as the Supreme Court in *Brown* had drawn extensively from sociological evidence of unequal education, so too did Wright draw heavily from studies of the negative impact of racial separation on educational outcomes. So long as "Negro schools provide their Negro students with an education inferior to that which others, white and Negro alike, receive in integrated or predominantly white education settings," segregation was constitutionally impermissible.

A similar ruling came down in *Davis v. School District of Pontiac*. A racially diverse, industrial city about twenty miles north of Detroit, Pontiac had been a battleground over school desegregation since the 1950s, when local activist—and later black revolutionary—Milton Henry charged the city with segregation when it built a new elementary school in the heart of an all-black neighborhood. In 1958, a federal judge dismissed arguments that Pontiac segregated its schools and upheld the concept of neighborhood-based attendance areas. But Pontiac's activists did not let the case rest. As the city's black population grew and the city built or renovated schools that served all-black neighborhoods, activists began to protest again. In 1970, the local NAACP mounted another, more successful challenge to the city's segregated neighborhood schools. Plaintiffs contended that the school district engaged in unlawful discrimination and denial of equal opportunity under the Fourteenth Amendment. In this case, Judge Damon Keith (one of several African Americans appointed to the federal bench by President Lyndon Johnson) ruled that Pontiac school officials had "intentionally utilized the power at their disposal to locate new schools and arrange boundaries in such a way as to perpetuate the pattern of segregation within the City." By failing to "take the necessary steps so as to negate or alleviate" racial imbalance, the school district had committed a "sin of omission" that was "as serious as sins of commission" and constituted de jure segregation. Keith took direct aim at the reasoning in the Cincinnati case. Districts could not just tell black students, "If you want integration, just move to another neighborhood." Such an argument, he concluded, is "blinded to the realities of adult life with its prejudices and opposition to integrated housing." When the school district lost its appeal, Keith imposed a districtwide desegregation plan that required the busing of about six thousand black and white students.

White Pontiac exploded in reaction to Keith's order. The 1971 school year opened with the bombing of ten Pontiac school buses, followed by mass protests by the newly formed National Action Group (NAG), an antibusing organization led by a local white mother, Irene McCabe. Just as pro-integration protests were women-led, so too did Pontiac's anti-busers wrap themselves in the mantle of militant motherhood. NAG members pushed baby strollers in front of school buses, blockaded a General Motors plant in Pontiac that manufactured parts for school buses (shutting down most of the auto giant's international operations as a result), and opened up "freedom schools" for white students. Nine antibusing activists were arrested for chaining themselves to the gates at the city school bus depot. Other demonstrators picketed schools in white neighborhoods, jeering and catcalling black students as they arrived. Still others vandalized school buses, puncturing radiators with sharpened broomsticks, breaking windows with stones and bricks, and forcing the district to create a high-security parking lot, complete with a bulletproof watchtower, to protect its fleet from further vandalism. NAG also filed a suit against the Pontiac school district, alleging that its school buses were unsafe. While some whites fought, others fled. Enrollment in the district fell by nearly 2,500—more than 10 percent of Pontiac's students—at the beginning of the 1971 school year. Nearly all of the loss was due to the withdrawal of white students. By the end of the 1972–73 school year, Pontiac had calmed considerably, but NAG remained a powerful local organization that lent its support to broader legislative challenges to school busing.

Advocates of integration were particularly cheered by the outcome of a 1973 Supreme Court decision involving the Denver public schools. *Keyes v. Denver School District #1* was the first major decision with the potential to clarify the meaning of *Brown* in the North. For those who wanted to break down the legal distinction between de facto and de jure segregation, *Keyes* offered a strong case. Denver had not deployed any of the traditional techniques to deliberately segregate schools. It did not have a record of gerrymandering or a history of officially separate schools. By northern standards, Denver had the reputation of being a liberal community. Its population was only 14 percent black, and by northern standards it was relatively well off. The city was also home to some of the more aggressive open housing organizations in the North. Its Park Hill neighborhood was celebrated as a model of successful housing integration. Still, conditions in the city's majority-black schools were less than ideal. Forty percent of Denver's black students attended mostly black schools, which were generally overcrowded. Several schools had erected portable trailers to mitigate overcrowding. But many students attended schools that were, by any standard, well mixed. The plaintiffs in *Keyes* argued that Denver's school district had created what was, in effect, a dual school system.

Keyes had potentially far-reaching consequences for northern school desegregation efforts. In a complex decision, the Supreme Court held that "proof of state-imposed segregation in a substantial portion of the district will suffice to support a finding by the trial court of the existence of a dual system." The "Keyes Presumption"—that if part of a district was deliberately segregated, even if other schools were all white as the result of ostensibly race-neutral decisions, then the district was responsible for remedying racial imbalance in all of its schools—gave civil rights lawyers a new tool. It put the burden on school districts, not plaintiffs, to prove that segregation was not the result of "unlawful segregative design on the part of school authorities."

Keyes was overshadowed by the most important post-*Brown* civil rights case, the one involving Ronald and Richard Bradley. Since the 1950s, Detroit's NAACP branch charged that the city had gerrymandered elementary school attendance areas. But even the slightest move toward desegregation sparked white protest. In 1960, when the Detroit schools shifted 314 black third and fourth graders from two overcrowded all-black schools to three nearby all-white schools, white parents in the receiving schools led a three-day strike, keeping 1,200 children at home. Despite white opposition, black activists continued to protest unequal education in Detroit's segregated schools. Beginning in the early 1960s, the Reverend Albert Cleage led a successful campaign to persuade black voters to reject a proposed property tax hike for public education on the grounds that it would subsidize separate, unequal education. In response to mounting protests, the Detroit public schools announced a modest program of desegregation, prompting another white revolt.

Detroit activists, both black and white, also launched one of the country's largest experiments in decentralization. In 1969, the Michigan state legislature split Detroit's public school system into eight relatively autonomous community-controlled boards. Enacted with relatively little controversy, decentralization had three diverse groups of supporters: advocates of a black-controlled educational system, liberal and leftist critics of bureaucracy, and white critics of desegregation. Detroit's decentralization plan had some unintended effects. Even though the city's school district was majority African American, whites controlled six of the eight boards. Anti-busers and social conservatives captured community boards in Detroit's white, outlying districts, embracing the antibureaucratic, populist rhetoric of community control proponents. If parents did not want sex education, the state should not impose it on them. If they wanted their children to walk to school, they should not have distant bureaucrats and judges "force" busing on them.

While the decentralization experiment raged, the NAACP began preparations for a lawsuit challenging segregation in Detroit. A small

number of white Detroiters supported the ideal of school integration—
some of them added their children's names to the NAACP lawsuit. But
they were the exception. White public opinion in both city and suburbs
was staunchly opposed to any "forced" mixing of schools—and city
whites led a successful effort to recall four pro-integration school board
members in 1970. Black Detroiters, by contrast, took a range of positions,
some advocating racial separatism and black-themed education, others
supporting integration, the majority taking a middle-ground position,
looking for anything to improve the quality of schooling in the city's rapidly growing black neighborhoods. One of the middle grounders was
Verda Bradley.

Bradley and the NAACP worried greatly when their case ended up in
the chambers of federal district judge Stephen J. Roth, a former prosecu-
tor, known to be quite conservative, who had been appointed by President Kennedy in 1962. The plaintiffs' attorneys were undaunted. They
mounted a formidable challenge to the de facto–de jure distinction, providing extensive evidence that state action had created a racially segregated housing market in Detroit. NAACP attorneys argued that regardless
of the intention of individual school boards, state action was at the root of
racial segregation in metropolitan Detroit. Federal and state policies, they
argued, were responsible for the "containment" of black students in
schools in the central city and for the subsidization of massive construction of schools for white children in all-white suburban communities. In
addition, they contended that racial restrictions in federal home ownership programs, the state real estate code, and the actions of home owners'
organizations and Realtors had perpetuated a systemic pattern of racial
segregation. Much to the attorneys' surprise, Roth accepted their argument: "Governmental actions and inaction at all levels, federal, state and
local, have combined, with those of private organizations" to maintain
housing and educational segregation.

Roth found evidence that the Detroit public schools had used transfer
programs and racial gerrymanders to separate black and white students,
and so determined that the city had engaged in intentional discrimination. But in March 1972, Roth rejected three proposals for intradistrict
desegregation and ordered the drawing of a metropolitanwide school desegregation plan. "School district lines," argued Roth, "are simply matters
of political convenience and may not be used to deny constitutional

rights." In June 1972, after several months of hearings, Roth held Detroit and fifty-three surrounding school districts responsible for remedying desegregation and ordered a comprehensive plan to bus city students to the suburbs and vice versa.

Of all the education rulings in the early 1970s, none was more controversial than Roth's. He offered a solution to segregation that provided no escape hatch—other than private education—for the majority of whites in metropolitan Detroit. Roth's fifty-four-district desegregation order would leave most whites no choice but to send their children to racially mixed schools. The reaction of suburban whites, wrote *The Wall Street Journal,* "can be summed up in one word—panic." Many white parents argued vehemently for neighborhood schools. "Why ship the kids someplace else when we got a school right here?" asked one white mother. "That's why you bought a house. So you could be near the school for the kids." Others couched their concerns in terms of a fear of crime. A white father said of his children: "I don't want them coming home with their brains beat in and their lunch money stolen." A police officer railed against Roth and the ruling. "What the hell right do these social engineers have using our kids as guinea pigs?" Because the expression of overt racial sentiments—at least in public settings—was taboo, the majority of white opponents fixated on school buses, what Mothers Alert Detroit, a leading antibusing group, called the "Yellow Distractor." Even though by 1970 nearly half of all American public school students rode buses to school (only about 2 to 4 percent as part of desegregation plans), anti-busers defended the "tradition" of children walking or riding their bicycles to school, again avoiding racial language. In the clash of images—buses, forced on innocent students by meddling bureaucrats, versus playful children strolling a block or two to school—the buses lost. SNCC founding member and Georgia congressman Julian Bond acidly commented, "It's not the bus, it's us."

Opponents of busing also repudiated the key premise of the plaintiffs' argument in *Bradley v. Milliken,* namely that school segregation was a matter of public policy, not the sum of thousands of individual decisions. Using rhetoric similar to that which the courts used in the Gary and Cincinnati cases, anti-busers argued that school attendance patterns were the result of the inexorable workings of the market and that any attempt to desegregate schools violated the sacrosanct principle of "choice." "We believe 'forced busing' is depriving us of our Constitutional Rights and our Freedom of Choice," proclaimed a writer in *"Hi" Neighbor,* a northeast Detroit neighborhood newsletter. In the realm of race and education, the term "choice" obscured more than it revealed. For the vast majority of African Americans in the postwar city, the right to choose schools or neighborhoods was nonexistent. That whites, even those with modest incomes, could choose to send their children to well-provisioned schools in white suburbs or in white-dominated neighborhoods was the consequence of racial privilege. The language of choice masked white privilege: It rested on the false assumption that blacks and whites were equal players in a market that was deeply structured by race.

The volatility of the white electorate on the busing issue led many northern elected officials to jump on the antibusing bandwagon. Nearly every white Democratic congressman from Michigan joined the antibusing crusade. Republican senator Robert Griffin proposed an antibusing amendment to the U.S. Constitution. In 1972, the Michigan state legislature passed a law forbidding the use of state money for busing. "It will be interesting," wrote Democratic state representative John Bennett of Redford, "to see where Judge Roth will get funds to implement his forced busing decisions." The reaction against busing resonated nationally. In May 1972, amid the busing dispute, Alabama governor George Wallace won the Michigan Democratic presidential primary, sweeping all of the majority-white precincts in Detroit and many of its suburbs. He railed against busing—the "most asinine and cruel thing I've ever heard of."

Those who continued to support desegregation stood out. Liberals "are all scared out of their wits," argued Congressman Abner Mikva, who represented a Chicago Democratic district where "no one supports me on busing ... except a few intellectuals." Michigan senator Philip Hart was another of the few northern Democrats who stuck to his desegregationist guns. "When the courts found deliberate segregation in the South, I supported desegregation, even if that occasionally included busing. Now the issue has come home and the courts are finding deliberate school segregation in the North. My logic and my conscience do not allow me to change positions." Mikva lost his seat to redistricting in 1972 but clawed his way back to Congress in 1974, riding the anti-Watergate wave, and served for three terms before being appointed to the federal bench in

1979. Hart survived a recall battle, but the busing dispute left him exhausted and he died of cancer before his term ran out.

If all but a few prominent white politicians joined the antibusing crusade, black opinion on busing was complex and fractured. Most black power groups reflexively opposed busing. The Black Panthers, for example, opposed sending black students to schools where they would be "indoctrinated with lies." The 1972 National Black Political Convention, in Gary, Indiana, split over the issue of busing. The draft version of the National Black Political Agenda adopted by the convention contended that the "real educational issue for the Black community is how to get supreme quality education for Black youngsters" but opposed the "disintegration of our children into white dominated school boards, budgets, curricula." However, integrated education still had prominent supporters. Gary mayor Richard Hatcher (who had been involved in the *Bell* case and whose politics fused civil rights and black power) and Detroit congressman Charles Diggs spoke against the anti-integration position. "The delegates," reported Roger Wilkins, nephew of the NAACP executive Roy and an assistant attorney general in the Johnson administration, "were in the mood to vote for anything Black and so they fell prey to [the] plan for perpetual separation of the school systems in the country . . . and now the country thinks that blacks everywhere don't want integrated education. But they are wrong." Taking a middle ground—probably closest to reflecting black public opinion—were activists Earl Ofari and Walter Fauntroy, then the District of Columbia's delegate to Congress. Ofari captured blacks' ambivalence toward desegregation: "Black parents' first concern is that their children get the best possible education. If it can be gotten in ghetto schools—which it can't—then blacks would go along" with busing. But like many black power–influenced activists, Ofari argued that school integration did not address the fundamental "need for an educational revolution." Fauntroy was a realist. "Black parents have had all kinds of different experience with busing," he contended, "some good and some bad. They want good educations for their children. If busing will get it for them, that's what they want."

Black Detroiters were equally conflicted about the *Bradley* decision. Juanita Miles worried about the impact of busing on her daughter. "My seven-year-old baby, she'd be all alone. She'll be away from all her playmates. Who knows how that will affect her psychologically." But Miles still supported integration: "I think children should get to know children of different cultures." Other black parents feared that white teachers would not provide mentorship to black students. Charles Sands put it bluntly: "You take a little black kid in school who can't understand. Someone has got to take an interest in him and show him the way. Otherwise he's just a lost ball in high weeds." Like many blacks, Sands suspected that whites would remain intransigent and hostile. In his words, "You cannot by no way make the white man love you. He's got it in him to hate you and he's going to keep it there." Others expressed skepticism about the premise that integration would uplift black children. One young black mother stated that she did not want her children "to think that they have to leave the black community to get better in the world." Black police officer Fred Williams made a similar argument: "Integrated education doesn't necessarily make better education. I'd rather see the money and energy spent to make inner-city schools—which are almost all-black—better."

Since *Brown*, the courts had divided on whether "de facto" segregation was constitutionally impermissible. Roth rejected the very concept. In his opinion, Roth never used the controversial phrase "institutional racism," but he unequivocally demonstrated that the deep divide between black Detroit and its white suburbs was the result of segregated housing. In his view, discriminatory public policy and real estate brokers' practices were culpable. In answering the question of whether suburban districts should be held responsible for remedying deeply entrenched segregation in Detroit, Roth popped the bubble of racial innocence. But suburban elected officials railed against Roth's "judicial activism." The state and forty-four suburban school districts appealed Roth's decision. The state contended that it should not be held responsible for past acts of segregation; the suburban districts contended that they had played no role whatsoever in perpetuating racial segregation and that under the standards of the law, they should not be compelled to remedy a problem that they had not created.

Roth's opinion did not stand. In its controversial 5–4 decision in *Milliken v. Bradley*, the Supreme Court struck down Roth's plan for interdistrict busing, leaving local school district boundaries and administrative fragmentation wholly unchallenged. Three of the five votes were by Nixon appointees: Chief Justice Warren Burger and associate justices William Rehnquist and Lewis Powell. The Court agreed with the forty-four suburban school boards and the white parents who had elected them that they were innocent. Detroit's problems were its own. Burger also defended the balkanization of Detroit area schools as a public good. He utterly rejected Roth's argument that school districts were creatures of the state and that their boundaries could be redrawn in service of larger educational goals. "No single tradition in public education," wrote Burger, "is more deeply rooted than local control over the operation of schools; local autonomy has long been thought essential both to the maintenance of community concern and support for public schools and to the quality of the educational process." Associate Justice Thurgood Marshall, who had been appointed to the Supreme Court by Lyndon Johnson, issued a blistering dissent: "It may seem the easier course to allow our great metropolitan areas to be divided up into two cities—one white, the other black—but it is a course, I predict, our people will ultimately regret."

The *Milliken* decision spelled the end of the battle for educational integration. For the next twenty years, many northern school districts remained under court orders to desegregate, but the *Milliken* escape hatch allowed most whites to jump across district boundaries and avoid integration. But in an ironic twist, unanticipated by antibusing activists, *Milliken* exempted most suburban whites from the responsibility for desegregation, while leaving inner-city whites and blacks to solve the problem themselves. As a result, in blue-collar and poor white neighborhoods in some northern cities, resistance to desegregation orders was sometimes fierce.

Boston became the most infamous battleground over court-ordered desegregation. Boston was an extreme case—not typical of northern school desegregation battles, but one that attracted massive media attention. Boston had a large, relatively poor white population, many the descendants of Irish and Italian immigrants. The city was a patchwork of deeply segregated neighborhoods, whose boundaries often coincided exactly with Catholic parish lines. Boston's white Catholics defended their neighborhoods fiercely. Exacerbating that turf consciousness was the fact that in the 1970s Boston ranked with Cleveland, Detroit, Newark, and Trenton as one of the nation's most economically "distressed" cities. Through the 1960s, Boston's whites had ferociously opposed even modest school desegregation efforts. (During a 1964 Saint Patrick's Day parade, white Bostonians threw eggs and stones at an NAACP float bedecked with a sign that read "From the fight for Irish freedom to the fight for American Equality—NAACP Boston.") And they elected school board and city council members who represented their turf consciousness.

Boston's school desegregation lawsuit was the result of years of grassroots activism for school equality, even though critics portrayed it as the work of "limousine liberals"—racially liberal white suburbanites. When Judge Arthur Garrity ordered the city to implement a busing program to desegregate its schools in 1974, the city exploded in violence. Observers were quick to draw parallels between Boston and the Deep South, noting—belatedly—that opposition to civil rights was as powerful in the "cradle of liberty" as it was in the land of Dixie. Angry white mobs shut down high schools, pelted buses with bricks and stones, and besieged city council meetings. In 1976, the bicentennial year, a photograph of a group of white protestors attacking a black attorney with an American flag captured the intensity of white resistance. To some observers, the horrific events in Boston were confirmation of the intractability of white racism, but to others the busing crisis was the expression of white rage at elitists like Garrity who attempted to impose their vision of an integrated society on white, working-class Bostonians, without having to bear the costs of desegregation. Neither view was right.

Boston's antibusing activists lost their immediate battle against court-ordered desegregation. But in Boston, as in most of the North, the battle over desegregation was not ultimately a defeat for working-class whites—even if it was usually portrayed that way by white journalists. It was, instead, a defeat for black activists who had spent decades clamoring for equality in public schools. The Boston school desegregation battle played out on the balkanized turf that had been legitimated by the Burger Court in *Milliken v. Bradley*, decided just months before Boston's busing plan went into place. Whites in Boston, as in most northern metropolitan areas, had an exit strategy unavailable to most blacks. They could move to segregated suburbs and hunker down behind the still-intact boundaries of suburban school districts, untouched by court desegregation orders. Not surprisingly, as protests subsided, whites withdrew in droves from Boston's public schools. A few magnet schools aside, school segregation intensified in Boston. The firmness of city-suburban boundaries ensured that the vast majority of whites would never be substantively affected by school integration. The result was that by 1980, fewer and fewer whites cared about segregation or desegregation. And, whether they believed in integration or not, many blacks looked out onto the big cities like Detroit and Boston that remained deeply segregated, despite decades of struggle, and began to turn to other solutions. "Substantial desegregation in many northern metropolitan areas did not fail," wrote political scientists Jennifer L. Hochschild and Nathan Scovronick, "it was never tried."

By the mid-1970s, grassroots black activism on behalf of school integration waned. Many prominent civil rights activists announced their defection from the integrationist project, including law professor and former NAACP staff attorney Derrick Bell. In 1977, Bell reiterated arguments that black power advocates had made in the late 1960s: "The insistence on integrating every public school that is black perpetuates the demeaning and unproven assumption that blacks must have a majority white presence in order to either teach or learn effectively." Bell's lament about the assumptions of liberal integrationists was surely correct. But he ignored the long history of grassroots challenges to unequal education. What had motivated the majority of black activists from the Hillburn boycotts through the *Milliken* case was not the mistaken belief that contact with whites would somehow transform blacks for the better. Grassroots black activists wanted smaller classrooms, better funding, and qualified and committed teachers. Many blacks still shared those aspirations—by every measure, the majority of northern blacks continued to believe that racially diverse schools offered their children the best opportunities for quality education, and that integrated schools were the best, if not necessarily the most feasible, option. Many who could afford to move to integrated communities or send their children to integrated schools often did. The NAACP continued to file school desegregation cases and pushed for the administrative enforcement of school integration, but their efforts lacked the enthusiasm that had shaped nearly half a century of litigation. With integration—especially metropolitan-wide integration—off the table, black activists turned toward other strategies to try to level the educational playing field.

With most black and white students confined to segregated school districts for the foreseeable future, advocates of equal education embarked on a series of experiments, all of them controversial and inconclusive. Advocates of community control continued to shape big-city public education for the next thirty years. In New York City, parent activists in black and rapidly growing Hispanic neighborhoods continued to insist on community participation in local school governance, even if participation in local school board elections was abysmally low. In Chicago, neighborhood activists led protests that eventually resulted in the creation of school-based governing councils as an alternative to bureaucratic centralization. In many cities, community control metamorphosed into a movement to create experimental schools—and, by the 1990s, charter schools, which enjoyed a degree of independence from central school bureaucracies and regulations. Many urban charter schools adopted Afrocentric curricula. In Milwaukee and Cleveland, some local black activists (along with Catholics and free-market conservatives) even joined a call for school vouchers that would allow the use of public funds to send children to private or religious schools of their choice. The results of all of these experiments are still unresolved. What remained deeply entrenched for decades after the *Milliken* decision was the continued segregation of northern and western schools by race.

Some school reformers took their protests to a larger stage. They demanded the equalization of funding between school districts. Their argument was simple: If the poorest students were to be clustered together in the most disadvantaged school districts, then equal funding would help overcome racial disparities. Educational researchers differed in their opinions of the effectiveness of school funding on academic outcomes, but most believed that it mattered. The best school districts were invariably those with large per capita expenditures, which allowed them to purchase cutting-edge equipment and new textbooks and to build state-of-the-art schools. Generous funding also made it easier to pay teachers well and reduce class size. Did it make sense to pay less for schools that educated children who came to school needing more? But equal funding faced political obstacles that were every bit as intractable as desegregation efforts. The most significant was legal. Just as *Milliken* was wending its way through the judicial system, the Burger Court issued a ruling in a Texas case that few noticed at the time. *San Antonio v. Rodriguez* involved the arcane but enormously important issue of school financing. Texas schools were locally controlled and funded by local property taxes. The result was a patchwork of school districts with widely varying budgets. The case had particular implications for northern metropolitan areas, where city-suburban lines artificially separated some of the nation's poorest public schools from some of the richest. *Rodriguez*'s advocates contended that inequitable school financing violated the equal protection clause. The Supreme Court, by one vote, disagreed. In its 1973 decision, five justices (led by the conservatives appointed by Richard Nixon) upheld the localized system of school funding. The decision in *San Antonio v. Rodriguez* ensured that racially separate schools— especially in economically divided northern metropolitan areas—would remain unequal. So long as blacks (and other poor and working-class people) lived in districts that suffered depopulation and disinvestment, they would suffer the consequences of disparate funding. Not surprisingly, during the 1970s and 1980s the gaps in wealth between black and white communities widened and, with devastating consequences, the gap in the quality of education between schools attended by whites and blacks grew.

No place better demonstrated the failure of school reform than metropolitan Detroit. Twenty years after the *Milliken* decision, more than four-fifths of African American students attended school in just three of eighty-three area school districts. All but a handful of the remaining eighty districts remained overwhelmingly white. The wealthiest districts in Detroit's suburbs spent more than twice as much per capita as did Detroit's public schools. Dropout rates in the Detroit public schools are staggeringly high: In 2004, only 53 percent of the city's public high school students graduated in four years. Many of those who did had passed through the system because of their good behavior, not their academic skills. Only one-quarter of 5,624 upper-grade high school students who took the Michigan Educational Assessment Program test in 2004 met or exceeded Michigan "state standards" for mathematics. More than half the students tested in mathematics, social science, and science ranked below "basic level." The only comparatively bright spot was that 58 percent of Detroit public high school students met or exceeded state standards in reading. Even accounting for testing biases, these basic measures were abysmal. But they are typical of segregated, big-city school districts around the country.

Verda Bradley's son Ronald was one of the casualties of the failure of urban education. He dropped out of high school in tenth grade and has struggled for much of his adult life trying to find stable employment. In an economy that relies on workers with more than basic literacy and numeracy, those with less than a high school education find themselves at the very bottom. Looking out onto the troubled Detroit public schools, just over two decades after her sons' case had gone to trial, Verda Bradley weighed in on the state of public education: "I think we're in trouble."

CHAPTER 14

"FIGHTING FOR OUR LIVES"

IN MAY 1996, A STANDING-ROOM-ONLY CROWD GATHERED AT NORTH PHILA-delphia's United House of Prayer for the funeral of state senator Roxanne Jones. Hundreds more crammed into the church basement to listen to the service on loud speakers. Outside, five hundred mourners, unable to find seats, held vigil for the first black woman elected to the Pennsylvania Senate. Nearly every prominent politician in the state rose to offer witness to Jones's remarkable career. Not all were greeted warmly. When Governor Tom Ridge arrived to pay his respects to a woman who seldom agreed with him, he faced catcalls and boos. "Baby killer!" jeered an opponent of the welfare and health insurance cutbacks that had brought Ridge national acclaim as a rising star in the Republican Party. "Go away!" screamed another protestor. The dissonant voices outside the church were as fitting a tribute to Roxanne Jones as the brass band and full gospel choir assembled inside. Jones had spent much of her career on the fringes of power, challenging the political establishment. Coming of age as a brash welfare rights leader, she had had her share of impolite confrontations with public officials like Ridge. But over the years, Jones had also built a remarkable coalition of supporters—people who, before meeting her, had seldom been in the same room together. They were well represented at her funeral. White legislative staffers from Harrisburg who had never been to North Philadelphia awkwardly swayed to the music next to welfare recipients who waved their hands in the air thanking Jesus for the gift of Roxanne Jones's life. Corporate attorneys who had provided pro bono representation for poor women shared the pews with ex-cons. It was an elaborate funeral for a woman who had spent nearly half of her adult life on welfare, did not own a car, and, even as a state senator, preferred to buy her clothes in thrift shops.

In 1967, when Roxanne Jones first entered the political fray at welfare rights protests, she would have laughed at a prediction that she, of all people, would someday be mourned by mayors, state legislators, and a governor. But like many activists who began their careers outside the "system," Jones moved from protest to politics. One of a remarkable generation of grassroots activists who came of age in the 1960s, her subsequent political career owed its trajectory to her experiences with civil rights, the War on Poverty, and black power.

Jones's ascension from the dimly lit hallways of the Southwark Plaza housing project to the corridors of power in Harrisburg was evidence of how much had changed since the mid-1960s. In the three-decade span of Jones's public career, the achievements and the limitations of the postwar black freedom struggle became clear. It was a period when blacks achieved real political gains—evidenced by Jones's election to the state senate in 1983. It was a period that witnessed the rise of a sizeable black middle class, of which Jones was a part. The postwar struggles against workplace discrimination had succeeded in opening new opportunities for African Americans, especially women. But those gains, as Jones knew, were fragile. The last three decades of the twentieth century witnessed real setbacks for African Americans, especially people like Jones's constituents. More than anyone, she knew that the black freedom struggle was unfinished. Increasingly, civil rights activists lost the sense of hope, the great expectations that had shaped their struggle since the New Deal. Jones—and her counterparts around the country—attempted to preserve and maintain the modest gains of her generation. It was not easy.

"THE MARCHING HAS stopped," lamented a 1973 collection of essays by leading black activists and intellectuals. "In less than a decade America has deaccelerated from a March on Washington, where hopes for the future were as high as the brilliant August sun . . . to the shadows of the '70s and the depths of despair where the bright dreams of yesterday strangled on the bitter gall of rising indifference toward efforts to solve America's racial dilemma." The prose was purple, but its meaning was clear. "For black people especially, the years since 1963 have been ones of great expectations shattered on the rocks of bitter disappointment." Countering the gloom were those—mostly white—who believed that the racial gap had narrowed or disappeared altogether. Racial optimists cheered the fact that Congress had enacted the most sweeping civil rights legislation since Reconstruction. Polls showed that many whites believed that, in the aftermath of the 1960s, blacks were more advantaged than they were. But for many blacks—especially the northern working class and poor—the victories were hollow. "Untouched by the civil rights movement," wrote two Urban League officials, "are millions of blacks whose days begin and end with one goal—Survival!"

It was unclear in the early 1970s exactly what direction the freedom struggle would take. Pessimists found plenty of evidence that the "movement was over," that America had entered a "post–civil rights era." Black organizations suffered from the societywide decline in civic participation in the last decades of the twentieth century. Long-established groups such as the National Council of Negro Women shrank as their members grew older and grayer. Church attendance declined. The Congress of Racial Equality saw its membership plummet between the mid-1960s and the early 1970s, as it jettisoned its integrationism for black separatism and then veered rightward, allying with the Nixon administration. The NAACP also hemorrhaged supporters in the 1970s. For decades, as the nation's premier civil rights organization, the NAACP had helped bring together grassroots activists, offering them the assistance of seasoned organizers and savvy attorneys. Even when relations between branches and the national office were tense—as they had been during the battles over northern school segregation—the NAACP brought local struggles to a regional and national audience. It was, for all its faults, a mass-membership organization, and one that had, more often than not, shifted its priorities in response to pressure from below. But no mass protest organization arose to fill the gap left by the NAACP. Even at their peak of influence, black power organizations were small. By the mid-1970s, the Black Panthers had retreated to Oakland, their chapters eviscerated by internecine battles and police infiltration. The Revolutionary Action Movement, never more than a cell, faded away. The Panthers' Huey Newton and US's Maulana Karenga remained popular speakers, especially on campuses, but they were not movement builders. Other longtime activists, among them attorney Paul Zuber, RAM's Maxwell Stanford, and radical economist Robert S. Browne, found careers in burgeoning black studies departments and think tanks.

The waning influence of the black press deprived civil rights activists of another thread in the fraying web that had long connected them. For most of the twentieth century, black newspapers had provided the only reliable reporting on everyday racial indignities and the struggles against them. Many black papers, among them the once-mighty *Chicago Defender* and *Pittsburgh Courier,* struggled for survival. Nearly every paper suffered plummeting readership. The loss was incalculable. Replacing them were the major news dailies, which offered only spotty coverage of black grass-roots politics. Black radio, especially AM talk stations, filled in some of the gap. Independent and black-run stations offered listeners everything from fundamentalist Christian to black nationalist programming. Black-run public affairs programs also proliferated in major cities, although they usually found their way onto lesser UHF stations or public television outlets. Some, like Detroit's *Colored People's Time,* later named *American Black Journal,* offered lengthy interviews with black political leaders, authors, and activists. But apart from such shows, television was more of a curse than a blessing to black activists.

Most problematic was televised evening news, which offered superficial and usually sensationalistic depictions of black urban life. Studies of public opinion showed direct correlations between the amount of television watched and viewers' perceptions of crime and disorder. Media images of blacks and poverty also reinforced negative stereotypes of blacks and welfare. As for civil rights organizations, many succumbed to the lure of TV, but few benefited. In the celebrity-obsessed post-1960s culture, most black community activists were invisible. Only a small number of media-savvy blacks, most of them men without large social movements behind them, vaulted to celebrity status as spokesmen for the black community. Journalists and pundits conducted an obsessive search for a new Martin Luther King, Jr., or Malcolm X—what some critics dubbed the "Head Negro in Charge" syndrome. Minister Louis Farrakhan, head of the Nation of Islam, gained a ready national audience because of his uncompromising separatist rhetoric, but he lacked a sizeable following. Local leaders with small bases, such as New York's Reverend Al Sharpton, became experts in public relations, crafting deliberately provocative speeches to gain the attention of a jaded press corps. Perhaps the most entrepreneurial and successful activist was the protean Reverend Jesse L. Jackson, who had gained prominence as an aide to Martin Luther King, Jr., flirted with Chicago Republicans in the early 1970s, embraced the rhetoric of black nationalism and called for the creation of an all-black political party, and became the most prominent black Democrat in the 1980s. But efforts to anoint a single black leader diverted attention from the less media-worthy activists who continued to toil away, mostly ignored or forgotten. The northern freedom struggle had long been a movement with many bodies and many heads. That did not change in the 1970s.

Arguments that the movement was over, that activism was dead, that America had entered a "post–civil rights era" were decidedly premature. The impulse for racial equality did not die in the 1970s. It thrived in the activities of thousands of grassroots organizations, community development corporations, churches, and protest groups—some delivering social services, some acting as gadflies to state and local governments, others still working against the odds for a revolution that seemed more and more distant by the day. But there were fewer and fewer conduits of information connecting these groups. Community organizations, usually underfunded and understaffed, engaged in parallel organizing activities, sometimes even in the same cities, often with little or no contact with one another. Most grassroots organizations did not have the time or the resources to share information, to combine their efforts, or to look beyond the immediate crises that they faced toward the larger, still unresolved underlying problems that they all shared in common. The tendency toward localization and fragmentation—one that had been encouraged by Community Action and black power—came at a high price.

If the march for racial equality did not screech to a halt in the 1970s, it did take new forms. The most consequential shift was the rise of black electoral politics, the consequence of a strategic alliance between blacks and government that had been building since the 1930s. Blacks cast their lot, for better or for worse, with the liberal state. The question of the relationship of social movements to the government was still unresolved in the early 1970s. Poverty warriors, advocates of desegregated housing and schools, antidiscrimination activists, and community developers had all, to one degree or another, built strategic alliances with legislators and local elected officials. They had often attracted federal funding for their programs. And they used their organizational clout to push government agencies to implement antidiscrimination laws—through behind-the-scenes lobbying, protest, and litigation. But some of the most vocal activists, particularly on the left, continued to see government as an enemy rather than as an ally. A deep strain of antistatism pervaded black radical organizations. Participation in mainstream political institutions, they argued, would inevitably lead to co-optation, complicity with white power, or corruption. The system needed to be overthrown, not reformed. Black radical Rahman Kishiwa Milinik denounced "black imitators who deal in the illusion of power within the game of power set up by white folks. No good!" Milinik's brand of politics appealed to the still-widespread black distrust of white-dominated institutions. But a growing number of activists, even on the left, came to terms with government, with hopes of reconstructing it on their own terms.

The competing strains in black politics came to the fore at the National Black Political Convention, which met in Gary in March 1972. Convening the event were Amiri Baraka, the Newark-based poet, playwright, and community activist formerly known as LeRoi Jones, and Gary mayor Richard M. Hatcher. More than four thousand delegates from forty-seven states joined in the proceedings that resulted in the controversial National Black Political Agenda. Massachusetts delegate Saundra Graham (a welfare recipient and mother of five who had recently been elected to the Cambridge city council) marveled at the diversity of the participants. "From the very low income to the very high income, from the Black Muslims to the National Welfare Rights Organization to the very elitist unions—just about every black interest you could think of was represented." Longtime activists such as Audley "Queen Mother" Moore (whom Hatcher incorrectly introduced as Queen Mary), Dorothy Height, Jesse Gray, and Roy Innis joined black elected officials including New York congresswoman and presidential candidate Shirley Chisholm, Michigan congressman Charles Diggs, and Cleveland congressman Louis Stokes. Even black Republicans, including Nixon aides Samuel C. Jackson and Arthur Fletcher, participated. Louis Martin, an old hand in the civil rights movement and a mainstream Democrat, called the event "one of the most impressive, exciting and exhilarating black events of our time." Black Marxist William Strickland was even more ebullient. "Gary leaped past the limits and concepts of its conceivers," he argued. The convention, "in its broadest aspects, represented a repudiation of existing American politics."

The proceedings in Gary were predictably cacophonous. Diggs, who served as parliamentarian, faced charges that he rigged the rules to curb debate. The Michigan delegation, led by future Detroit mayor Coleman Young, walked out over disagreements with racial separatists. The NAACP, suspicious of Baraka and worried that black nationalists would prevail, sent delegates and observers to Gary and loudly denounced resolutions supporting the Palestine Liberation Organization and opposing school busing. The convention's antibusing resolution, drafted by CORE's Roy Innis and passed at a moment when the hall was two-thirds empty, was particularly controversial. Innis's resolution generated an intense debate about integration and segregation, winning him the support of *The Wall Street Journal's* conservative editorial page, even as it fiercely divided black columnists, politicians, and activists. Much to the surprise of commentators (and to the dismay of some black nationalists), Baraka served as a conciliator, calling for "unity without uniformity," and to that end brokered compromises between radicals and moderates, smoothing ruffled feathers and leavening the events with a self-deprecating humor that few associated with him.

The call to the convention, the Gary Declaration, offered a bleak reflection on the state of black America. "Our cities are crime-haunted dying grounds. Huge sectors of our youth—and countless others—face permanent unemployment. Those of us who work find our paychecks able to purchase less and less. Neither the courts nor the prisons contribute to anything resembling justice or reformation. The schools are unable—or unwilling—to educate our children for the real world of our struggles." But rather than capitulating to hopelessness, the convention's organizers drafted the National Black Political Agenda, a lengthy and controversial blueprint for social, economic, and political change. The final product of the convention, released in May 1972, the agenda represented a compromise among the mainstream black politicians, who made up about a fifth of the delegates, the black nationalists, who were the convention's most vocal participants, and the longtime civil rights activists, who took a middle-ground position between separation and integration.

Of major civil rights groups, the NAACP rejected the National Black Political Agenda outright. Roy Wilkins fumed about the busing and Israeli resolutions, which even watered down were unacceptable to him. His deputy John Morsell lamented that "at almost no point does the agenda also demand an equitable share of control in the institutions and agencies now controlled by whites. . . . Yet these are the real repositories of American wealth and power. In foregoing a share in them Negro Americans would sell themselves short; in focusing all its concerns upon controlling the meager, poverty-ridden institutions of the ghetto, the agenda would fetter black America forever into the poorest and least influential sectors of the national life." To the NAACP's left, Earl Ofari denounced the "elitism and conservativism" of the "usual prominent 'name' black leaders" who headlined the convention. But for Ofari, the biggest sin of the convention was that it "totally obscured the class question. Most participants accepted the false premise that an all-class unity of everyone from the black millionaire to the black milkman can be effected." Ofari, drawing from the vein of economic radicalism that was fading rapidly in the early 1970s, offered a prescient criticism of the agenda's racial essentialism. But it was not shared by a majority of commentators, who celebrated the "unity" they believed was the convention's major contribution.

The National Black Political Agenda was supposed to serve as a blueprint for the next generation of activists. Copies circulated widely to black politicians and community organizations alike. Some read its call for black self-determination as a mandate for creating separate political parties. Others used it as a political litmus test to judge candidates' commitment to black issues during the Democratic primaries and in the election of 1972. But after Nixon's overwhelming reelection in November, many of the agenda's drafters were dispirited. The brief coalition of black leftists, Democratic politicians, and nationalists frayed in a flurry of mutual recriminations. For the next few years, activists convened follow-up conventions, but none had the impact of the Gary meeting. The National Black Political Agenda, as a document, was quickly forgotten. What it reflected, however, remained very much alive.

Gary marked a turning point in the politics of civil rights, namely the shift to electoral politics as the primary strategy of black empowerment. In his keynote address to the convention, Richard Hatcher had sounded the theme: "Political action is an essential part of our ultimate liberation." Hatcher, though he remained a staunch Democrat, offered a balance of power argument about the fluid affiliation of black voters. "If we are to support any political party," he proclaimed, "the price will now run high—very high." Civil rights leaders, a growing number of black nationalists, and welfare rights organizers alike put their hope in the ballot box—even if there were serious disagreements about what strategies to pursue. Some black leaders, among them Jesse Jackson, called for the formation of an independent black political party. Jackson made an argument familiar to those who had advocated the Freedom Now Party in 1963. "Without the option of a black political party," he contended, "we are doomed to remain in the hip pocket of the Democratic Party and the rumble seat of the Republican Party."

As late as 1984, the National Black Election Study, the most respected survey of black public opinion, found that 24 percent of blacks favored the creation of a separate black party. But efforts to create race-conscious parties on the local level invariably failed. In Oakland, the Black Panthers ran slates of candidates for city offices but met with crushing defeats. Remnant leftist sects, for example the Socialist Workers' Party and the Communist Party, selected black candidates for many offices and mounted local and national campaigns, but their efforts were quixotic. Some black independents won office, usually in nonpartisan races. In Detroit, Kenneth Cockrel, an open Marxist, won election to the nominally nonpartisan Common Council in 1977. But in most cities, blacks cast their lot with the Democratic Party and worked to pull it leftward or opted out of the electoral process altogether. In presidential races, for which the best data were available, black turnout in the North and West fell from 72 percent in 1964 to 65 percent in 1968 to 57 percent in 1972. Younger and poorer blacks and those with nationalist sentiments had significantly lower turnout rates.

The 1970s witnessed a stunning increase in the number of black elected officials nationwide. In 1941, there were only thirty-three black elected officials in the entire United States, 31 of them in the North and West. By 1965, 193 blacks held elective offices nationwide. The numbers rose almost fourfold by 1970 to 764. By 1980, the figure had more than doubled to 1,909. The biggest gains came in cities with black majorities or pluralities. The rapid growth of segregated neighborhoods was a crucial factor in the rise of black political representation. Many councilmanic wards and state legislative seats and a growing number of congressional districts had black majorities—the consequence of racial segregation and of black pressure for black representation in areas where minorities were in the majority.

The vast majority of black elected officials were Democrats, reflecting the fact that blacks had become the Democratic Party's most loyal supporters. In national elections, black voters served as the electorate's left flank. But the Republicans, especially Nixon, attempted to reach black voters. One black New Jersey entrepreneur led a twenty-two-state "Black Silent Majority" campaign to pitch Nixon's reelection. But by 1972, Nixon's aides had largely written off the black vote. Gerald Ford—one of the last Rockefeller Republicans—made some gestures toward inclusion but also spent little energy cultivating black voters. Reagan proved to the most unpopular Republican in black electoral history, the defection of a handful of black intellectuals and politicians to his camp notwithstanding. In the 1980 campaign, he picked up only 12 percent of black voters; in his reelection bid in 1984, only 8 percent of blacks supported him. (Strikingly, black voter turnout, especially among the poor, rose significantly in the 1984 election.) By contrast, Democrats with national aspirations relied on black support. Thirty years before the 1976 election, Henry Lee Moon had made the case that blacks could be a balance of power in national politics. That year, black votes were decisive in Jimmy Carter's election, and they would be crucial in Bill Clinton's victories in 1992 and 1996. In each election, only a minority of whites supported the winning Democratic candidate. The large margins among blacks put the two candidates over the top.

Black Democrats brought a distinctive cast to liberal politics. On nearly every issue, the majority of black state legislators and members of Congress were left of center. In 1972, in a nod to the growing influence of black voters, the Democratic Party changed its rules to permit the seating of many more black delegates. Some mainstream white Democrats began to decry their party's capture by "special interest groups," chief among them blacks, whose uncompromising liberalism they blamed for the rightward drift of working- and middle-class whites. It was true that in the aftermath of the 1960s, many black elected officials discovered the usefulness of black power rhetoric in mobilizing their constituents, especially in black majority districts. However, few endorsed the creation of a separate black nation or called for the revolutionary overthrow of American government. Instead, they adopted the cultural trappings of black power and emphasized group pride and identity, particularly if they did not have to worry about winning over white voters. Detroit's Coleman Young, elected mayor in a racially charged election in 1973, made racial appeals to his core constituents. He assured black supporters that he was "a Negro first and a Democrat second." Everywhere, black politicians, even those who had no past involvement in black power groups, donned dashikis and printed posters in the red, green, and black colors popularized by black nationalists. But the negative impact of such political postures on whites was greatly exaggerated. By the 1950s, white voters in northern suburbs were already casting their lot with Republicans. Even if black politicians traded in their dashikis for suits and tempered their rhetoric with calls for interracialism, they were unlikely to win the support of rightward-turning whites.

But interracial politics did not entirely die off. It had its greatest successes in cities where blacks were a relatively small segment of the electorate and where whites were liberal. More than half of the country's black mayors were elected to office in cities where blacks were not the majority. Black candidates in racially and ethnically heterogeneous cities forged broad coalitions, with hopes of winning at least some white voters in elections that were usually intensely polarized by race. Black mayoral candidates, in particular, reached out to white leftists and liberals. In 1983, Wilson Goode, who, like many black politicians of his generation had learned the art of governance during the War on Poverty, was elected mayor of majority-white Philadelphia with the support of white business leaders and 22 percent of the city's white population. Goode eschewed racially polarized language and positioned himself as a reformer who would professionalize city government. That same year in Chicago, Harold Washington reached out to antimachine whites, whose votes were just enough to push him over the top, while he won overwhelmingly among blacks. In Los Angeles, where blacks made up only about 17 percent of the population, Tom Bradley downplayed his history as a civil rights activist and trumpeted his commitment to good government and political reform when he was first elected in 1973. In smaller, white-majority cities such as New Haven and Denver, interracial coalitions also put black mayors into office.

With few exceptions, black mayors proved to be little different from their white counterparts, especially when it came to urban redevelopment. Big-city mayors, black and white alike, placed their bets with "growth politics"—efforts to attract high-visibility investment to downtowns—in the 1970s, 1980s, and 1990s. A new mall, a skyscraper, a convention center, or a stadium would serve as bricks-and-mortar (or glass-and-steel) evidence that a city was "on the move again." Growth politics entailed forging close relationships with white business leaders and responding to their demands for tax abatements and other subsidies. It meant, for many mayors who had once been involved in grassroots protests, building alliances with business leaders whom they had picketed just a few years earlier. Mayors faced real pressure to show results, particularly as cities competed with one another for high-profile development projects. Corporate leaders played on cities' fears that they would pick up and relocate. No mayor wanted to see the loss of a major corporate taxpayer on his or her watch. Corporate leaders quickly learned to pit municipalities and states against one another to their great advantage.

Old industrial cities were particularly desperate to retain or attract investment. Coleman Young may have alienated suburban Detroit's whites and won the support of his black constituents for his brash language, but he had no problem accommodating the power of white-led corporations. Young worked closely with the chief executives of the Big Three automotive companies, with hopes of keeping their investments local. Young presided over the construction of the much-touted Renaissance Center, a high-rise office, hotel, and shopping complex designed to attract white conventioneers and tourists and their dollars downtown. In 1981, Young approved the condemnation of the still-thriving, racially diverse Poletown neighborhood for the construction of a new Cadillac factory complex that covered more than a half square mile and cost more than $200 million in subsidies and tax abatements. More than a thousand houses and several churches were bulldozed. "That one plant," cheered Young, "makes up for every goddamned thing that went to the suburbs in the last twenty years." But the reality was not so bright. Detroit had lost several hundred thousand jobs in the decades before the new plant opened. Poletown employed only a few thousand workers, most of whom had been transferred from other downsizing plants.

Philadelphia's Wilson Goode, who had a larger base of white support than Young, rose to power through his work in community economic development. As the head of a community development corporation in the 1970s, he steered federal and foundation dollars into rebuilding his West Philadelphia neighborhood and gained the reputation of being an astute manager. As mayor, however, Goode turned his attention to large-scale downtown redevelopment. He put much of his political stock in the construction of new office towers, the upscale Liberty Place Mall, and a convention center as ways to revitalize the city. Few of these projects provided any direct benefits to black constituents—in fact, through tax breaks, they arguably redistributed scarce city resources away from poor and working-class neighborhoods to developers and major corporations. (When, in 1985, the Philadelphia police firebombed the headquarters of MOVE, a black radical sect, killing eleven people and destroying a whole city block, Goode faced even greater challenges to his legitimacy.) Like many mayors in declining Rust Belt cities, Goode was desperate for tangible evidence that his city was on the mend. That meant favoring high-visibility projects over less prominent investments in neighborhood infrastructure.

If downtown redevelopment dollars did not trickle down to most urban residents, black political power still had some noteworthy successes, especially in narrowing the economic gap between blacks and whites. Public-sector and government-related employment became the most important niche for black workers in the last third of the twentieth century. By 1980, more than 40 percent of black working women and nearly 20 percent of black working men were employed in the public sector. For the most part, these jobs were secure and offered decent wages (most northern municipal workers were unionized) and generous benefits. Black accountants, social workers, teachers, and lawyers relied especially heavily on government employment. By 1995, more than half of all black professionals worked in the public sector. Black elected officials used the power of their offices to distribute patronage jobs to their supporters. Black mayors aggressively pried open formerly white-dominated bastions, including police and fire departments. Moreover, big-city mayors (black and white) implemented set-aside programs that gave preference to minority-owned businesses seeking city contracts. The rise of blacks in government employment also transformed the culture of government agencies—especially those providing social services. Blacks were disproportionately represented in housing, social welfare, and public health offices at the state and local levels. As historians Michael Katz and Mark Stern have argued, black government employees "encouraged local welfare bureaucracies to respond more generously to black need," with measurably positive benefits. No institution played a greater role than government in breaking the grip of poverty and creating a black middle class.

To a great extent, black economic fortunes were hitched to the new and still-controversial policy of affirmative action, which was most aggressively enforced in the public sector and in government contracts. The first nonpresidential nondiscrimination efforts had opened up government jobs to black workers. Kennedy's Executive Orders 10925 and 11114 and Johnson's Executive Order 11246 had extended the principle of affirmative action to federal contractors. Nixon's Philadelphia Plan further refined and expanded affirmative action, in the form of numerical "targets" and "goals," to government-contracted construction. When federal courts upheld the constitutionality of the Philadelphia Plan, the Nixon administration, in the words of aide Laurence Silberman, sowed Philadelphia Plans "across the country like Johnny Appleseed." In January 1970, Order 4 extended the principles of the Philadelphia Plan to all government contracts of fifty thousand dollars or more; in December 1971, it was amended to incorporate women. Affirmative action, Philadelphia Plan–style, now covered a large swath of the American economy. In addition, state and city governments instituted their own affirmative action plans, usually modeled on federal regulations.

Economists and scholars debated the extent to which affirmative action opened doors to African Americans. Elite universities, under pressure to admit African Americans and other minorities, introduced racial preferences. And private firms, led by large multinational corporations, began to implement voluntary affirmative action plans, in part to avoid costly discrimination lawsuits, in part because they came to believe that workforce diversity—especially in the increasingly fragmented and multinational marketplace—brought competitive advantages. Blacks also made real inroads into large private-sector firms that relied on government contracts, which greatly stepped up affirmative action compliance efforts in the 1970s. Some of the largest gains for minority workers came in personnel and government relations offices that dealt with state and federal agencies that enforced antidiscrimination laws.

From its inception, affirmative action came under siege, in large part because of divergent black and white opinions about the past and present of civil rights struggles. By the late 1960s, surveys showed that whites believed that there was little discrimination in American life and that what little remained was rapidly diminishing. In their view, the struggle for racial equality was over—blacks had won decisively. If indeed blacks and whites were now equal, then racial preferences were unfair and unneces-sary. In contrast, by every measure, blacks saw the victories of the civil rights era as partial, incomplete, and unfinished. In the 1970s, 1980s, and 1990s, many believed that discrimination by race persisted and hardened. Large numbers of minority respondents to surveys reported that they or people they knew were affected personally by racial discrimination and claimed that their race affected their hiring prospects or promotion or treatment in the workplace. In 1988, 87 percent of whites believed that "in the past twenty five years, the country has moved closer to equal op-portunity among the races," whereas the number of blacks who believed the same steadily declined between the 1960s and the 1980s from be-tween 50 and 80 percent to 20 to 45 percent. By the early 1990s, whites generally believed that "compared with whites," blacks had "equal or greater educational opportunity," "equal or greater job opportunity," and "equal or greater opportunity for promotion to supervisory or managerial jobs."

Affirmative action became the touchstone of debates over race, fair-ness, and equality. In a series of court battles in the 1970s and 1980s, af-firmative action in education and employment came under siege. In 1978, the Supreme Court split badly on the question of whether universities could use racial preferences in admissions. In *California Regents v. Bakke*, four justices held that affirmative action was unconstitutional; four held that the use of race in admissions was permissible, if it remedied past discrimination and was narrowly tailored; and one, Justice Lewis Powell, cast the deciding vote, upholding the use of race in admissions, but only as one factor and, crucially, on the grounds that "diversity" was a compelling public interest. The diversity rationale became the most powerful basis for defending affirmative action in the next twenty-five years, but it turned the political discussion away from a consideration of economic disadvantage. *Bakke* was, in many respects, the culmination of postwar racial liberals' belief that interracial contact and pluralism would have positive social benefits in their own right. Powell and the four more conservative justices rejected the minority argument that affirmative ac-tion was a necessary remedy to the past and ongoing disadvantages of racial discrimination. Powell continued to write skeptically about the concept of "societal discrimination," which he considered "insufficient and over-expansive." "With the emergence of the diversity rationale," wrote sociologist John Skrentny, "affirmative action has become separated from *discrimination*."

The diversity rationale had old roots. Postwar racial liberals had defended antidiscrimination on the grounds that the exposure of blacks and whites to one another would have mutually beneficial effects. Powell's argument for diversity echoed past claims for the benefits of interracial contact. It was an argument that was, at core, Myrdalian. In his stand-alone opinion, Powell wrote that "the 'nation's future depends upon leaders trained through wide exposure' to the ideas and mores of students as diverse as this Nation of many peoples." For Powell, race was a "single though important element" of the educational diversity that he sought. Diversity, in his view, was a form of benign social engineering. Students in racially diverse institutions would find their education enriched by the presence of people unlike themselves.

The growing emphasis on the value of diversity was a sign of how much had changed as a result of decades of civil rights activism. The sight of black, white, and brown faces in universities, in corporate offices, and on television would have pleased postwar activists like Clarence Funnyé. But Funnyé did not believe that diversity, whatever benefits it might bring, should be the primary goal of activism. Racial inequality was not a matter of the lack of exposure to difference, it was the result of power dynamics that had resulted in the institutionalization of inequality in housing, employment, and education. By contrast, from the 1970s onward, diversity became a goal in its own right. A whole industry of diversity consultants arose to help businesses "manage diversity." On the micro level, diversity training programs, usually in the form of corporate retreats, could mitigate interoffice conflicts that grew out of racial slights and misunderstandings. But on the macro level, diversity trainers clung to the postwar assumptions that racial inequalities were primarily the consequence of individuals' prejudiced thoughts. Racial sensitivity trainers dug deep into the psyches of whites to root out their hidden, unconscious racism. Just as it was anathema to criticize the market or political institutions for the ways that they structured racial inequality, it became fashionable to emphasize an individualistic, therapeutic model of racial healing. But at the end of the day, persistent racial inequalities were more deeply entrenched than individual feelings. Despite the gains of the postwar freedom struggle, whites—whatever they personally thought of blacks—returned home to white neighborhoods, continued to send their children to segregated schools, and fought to maintain local control over taxation, education, and land use in ways that were far more damaging to the cause of racial equality than any negative feelings they might harbor toward black people.

The emphasis on diversity and racial healing was not restricted to programs that targeted whites. The growing demand for multicultural education—as a vehicle for enhancing students' "self-esteem"—also grew from the taproot of postwar psychology. Calls for self-esteem and group pride, however, rested on the fallacy that racial inequality was the consequence of a damaged black psyche. But educational researchers found no correlations between self-esteem and educational success. There were undeniable pedagogical benefits to school curricula that included underrepresented groups and their histories, but the problems facing inner-city schools—underfunding, high teacher turnover, overcrowded classes, outdated facilities and equipment, troubled families, and persistent poverty—would not be overcome by curricular reform. The problem of unequal education was ultimately one of unequal power. So long as schools remained part of a metropolitan system that distributed tax dollars and social benefits unevenly, the impact of multicultural education and diversity would be minimal.

The most controversial affirmative action programs—and, because they affected a small class of minority business owners, the least efficacious—were set-asides that reserved a certain percentage of federal, state, or local contracts for minority-led firms. In a series of cases, federal courts considered the legality of set-asides. In the 1980 case, *Fullilove v. Klutznick*, the Supreme Court upheld legislation that required the awarding of 10 percent of federal public works contracts to minority-owned businesses on the grounds that set-aside programs were a remedy to past discrimination in government contracting. But as the Court moved to the right, set-asides came under challenge. By the end of the 1980s, they were greatly weakened. In *Richmond v. J. A. Croson* (1989), the Court struck down a program in the Virginia capital that set aside 30 percent of government-contracted construction work to minority business enterprises. The Court held that affirmative action in contracting must be "strictly reserved for remedial settings," defined in increasingly narrow terms. The majority argued that claims of historic discrimination were "inherently immeasurable"; remedy was reserved for measurable current and ongoing discriminatory acts that disadvantaged minorities. Here, the Supreme Court singlehandedly ruled out the consideration of past discrimination, assuming that, unless proved otherwise, blacks and whites competed on a level playing field. In the 1995 decision *Adarand v. Pena*, the Court further narrowed the definition of permissible affirmative action. Striking down a federal contract set-aside program, the Court ruled that any use of race in the awarding of contracts required a compelling government interest and narrow tailoring. The Court set the bar of proof so high that many long-running affirmative action programs were now legally indefensible.

If affirmative action weakened, however, it did not disappear. During his 1980 campaign, Ronald Reagan criticized affirmative action as anathema to civil rights. "We must not allow the noble concept of equal opportunity to be distorted into federal guidelines or quotas which require race, ethnicity or sex—rather than ability and qualifications—to be the principal factor in hiring or education." But Reagan and his congressional allies did not dismantle affirmative action, despite its unpopularity among their constituents. By the time Reagan assumed office, a "contract compliance" and antidiscrimination bureaucracy had been established in nearly every federal agency. Federal bureaucrats ensured that the requirements of the Civil Rights Act were met, enforced minority set-asides in contracting, and gathered data on employers' hiring practices. Rather than engaging in a head-on assault on affirmative action through the legislature, the Reagan administration weakened enforcement efforts within government agencies. Civil rights organizations, working with congressional allies, successfully lobbied Congress to continue to appropriate funds to government offices that enforced affirmative action and other civil rights regulations. Affirmative action survived, even if it was administratively hobbled.

The expanding black middle class—disproportionately public sector employees—reshaped the geography of the postwar metropolis. As whites continued to flee for the suburbs, African Americans moved into outlying middle-class neighborhoods in nearly every city. Typical was southeast Queens, once a redoubt of whites opposed to housing integration. It became the neighborhood of choice for New York's well-paid black municipal employees. Even more striking was the rise in black suburbanization. Suburban locales such as Prince George's County, Maryland (outside Washington, D.C.), Mount Vernon, New York (just north of the Bronx), Southfield, Michigan (outside Detroit), and Yeadon and Cheltenham, Pennsylvania (outside Philadelphia) generated much press coverage for their growing African American populations. The movement of blacks to suburbs was hailed by many as a sign of the success of the civil rights movement. And indeed, for the small number of blacks who moved into formerly all-white communities, the end of officially sanctioned housing segregation with the Civil Rights Act of 1968 made a difference. But the process of black suburbanization gave the lie to optimistic assumptions about the shift in racial practices. With a few exceptions, mostly in rapidly growing Sunbelt cities with small black populations, residential segregation persisted in black suburbia. In most northern metropolitan areas, black suburbanites were greeted with white flight and the white abandonment of public schools.

One of the country's most celebrated black suburbs, Southfield, Michigan, is a case in point. The community's black population skyrocketed between 1970 and the end of the century. Its spacious 1950s- and 1960s-era ranch houses, colonials, and trilevels were unavailable to blacks during the segregated era in which they were built. Only 102 blacks lived in Southfield in 1970; nearly 7,000 lived there in 1980; about 29,000 lived there in 1990, making the black population about one-third of Southfield's total. But Southfield did not become a beacon of racial integration, despite the city's aggressive efforts to market the community to white families. The southern half of the city—south of Ten Mile Road—became overwhelmingly African American. In addition, the Southfield public schools grew increasingly black.

Segregated suburbs were the consequence of three patterns. First was the failure of the open housing movement to persuade whites to choose racially heterogeneous communities. Whites professed color blindness but in polls and surveys they still considered the color of their neighbors. Their tolerance for black neighbors—at least in terms of what they told researchers—rose, but most whites still expressed discomfort at living in neighborhoods with more than a small percentage of black residents. Second was the unwillingness of many blacks to take the risk of moving into mostly white communities. The history of racial hostility in housing was a deterrent to some. And, while a majority of blacks preferred racially integrated neighborhoods, a sizeable and growing minority expressed preference for all-black or mostly black neighborhoods, in part because of their embrace of black separatist ideals. It remained a common myth—but with no real empirical basis—that blacks remained in segregated neighborhoods because they could not afford suburbia. It was true that some of the wealthiest suburbs were out of reach for most potential black homebuyers. But in the last three decades of the twentieth century, suburban housing stock grew more diverse and many working-class suburbs and lower-middle-class suburbs were well within the financial reach of blacks.

In most metropolitan areas, blacks inherited secondhand central-city neighborhoods or inner-ring suburbs with aging housing stock and declining tax bases. Because of persistent housing segregation, middle-class blacks were not, by and large, able to distance themselves from the poor as their white counterparts did. Middle-class black neighborhoods, a prominent sociologist found, are often "nestled between areas that are less economically stable," meaning that poverty and its consequences are seldom distant realities. In addition, middle-class blacks are very likely to live in neighborhoods with large numbers of blue-collar workers, a trend much less common among whites. The proximity to poverty has many other consequences for middle-class African Americans. Blacks of all classes are more likely to be victims of crime; indeed, as a team of sociologists discovered, "the most affluent blacks are not able to escape from crime, for they reside in communities as crime-prone as those housing the poorest whites."

In the last three decades of the twentieth century, the patterns of segregation remained most deeply entrenched in the major metropolitan areas of the Northeast and the Midwest. Metropolitan Chicago consistently ranked among the top two or three most segregated metropolitan areas in the United States. Seventy percent of Chicago blacks lived in the city proper, and a majority of suburban blacks lived in old industrial towns or in long-established black suburban enclaves with underfunded schools, deteriorating public services, and rates of racial segregation that rivaled the poor inner-city neighborhoods. The black suburbs of Long Island, New York, that were battlegrounds over school desegregation between the 1940s and 1960s also grew blacker and poorer in the last three decades of the twentieth century. Some of the country's most troubled school districts—Roosevelt, Hempstead, and Freeport—were abandoned by whites altogether. Roosevelt, for one, had a growing population of impoverished students in 1970, but per capita school expenditures that were a third of those of nearby wealthy white communities. By century's end, five out of every six Hempstead residents were nonwhite and its school system had resegregated. By contrast, the next town over, Garden City, where more than nine out of ten residents were white, had schools that were among the best funded and highest achieving in the country.

The creation of black suburbs was, in part, the result of "steering," the practice of directing white home buyers to all-white neighborhoods and black home buyers to predominantly black or racially transitional neighborhoods. In the 1980s and 1990s, studies of housing discrimination conducted by the Department of Housing and Urban Development and by local housing and nonprofit agencies—matched pairs of black and white "testers" were sent to randomly selected real estate offices—consistently demonstrated the persistence of discriminatory treatment of black home seekers and renters. Similar studies showed that blacks faced discrimination when they applied for mortgages and home loans. Despite the rhetoric of free choice in the housing market, blacks faced all sorts of restrictions on their choices.

Still, few could gainsay the enormous shift in black fortunes in the aftermath of the civil rights struggle. Yet again, whatever optimism there was about the rise of the black middle class and black suburbanization was muted by the problems facing urban blacks, most of which worsened in the last three decades of the twentieth century. If there were ever a golden age in the history of American cities, it was certainly not the 1970s and 1980s. Deep pessimism prevailed about the future of urban America. In 1971, the journal *The Public Interest* asked, "Is the Inner City Doomed?" The widespread answer was yes. Cities had become "dumping grounds for poor people" and "cemeteries" of the American dream. Many agreed with *Time*'s pessimistic prognosis that urban problems were "terminal." Bleak cityscapes offered observers little ground for hope. Since the 1950s, every major industrial center in the Northeast and Midwest and the older port cities of the West had lost population and jobs. Blue-collar workers bore the disproportionate burden of economic restructuring, a process that left city centers increasingly bereft of the well-paying, unionized jobs that had been the bulwark of the postwar economy. At the same time, city governments lumbered through financial crises of a magnitude not seen since the Great Depression. New York was bankrupt; Cleveland, Boston, Newark, and Detroit teetered on the brink of insolvency. Philadelphia's city budget was so strapped by the mid-1970s that the mayor put signs on major thoroughfares encouraging drivers to call the state highway department to make repairs. Throughout the country, crime rates rose by nearly a third in the early 1970s, disproportionately affecting black urban neighborhoods. Millions of Americans, most of them white, continued their massive exodus to sprawling suburbs, where they looked with increasing alienation and hostility toward the cities they had abandoned.

The combination of depopulation and disinvestment was difficult enough. Countering public-sector employment gains—which disproportionately benefited women—was the stark decline in labor force participation rates among black men, especially those between the ages of eighteen and thirty-five. By 1980, a quarter of all black men were wholly unattached to the formal labor market. In some northern cities, especially those ravaged by disinvestment, the figures were even worse. To some extent, unemployed black men were absorbed by one rapidly growing sector of the economy, what observers called the "prison-industrial complex." The period between 1970 and 2000 witnessed a dramatic increase in the population of incarcerated Americans, disproportionately men of color. Blacks, 13 percent of the population, make up more than half of America's prison population. Police-community relations, still burning hot in the aftermath of the riots, remained hostile, exacerbated by the fact that crime rates rose sharply in every major city. Demands for law and order led to increasingly stiff punishments, particularly for the possession of drugs and drug-related crimes—and a corresponding increase in the number of prisoners. For men seeking work, a prison sentence was often tantamount to permanent unemployment. Few employers were willing to take the risk of hiring ex-convicts.

Further exacerbating labor market woes was persistent workplace discrimination. When sociologists and economists interviewed employers in Chicago, Detroit, and Los Angeles, they discovered that negative stereotypes of blacks—especially black men—were pervasive. Others found evidence that ostensibly race-blind employers used workers' home addresses as screening devices. Given the combination of racial segregation and poverty, residents of mostly black neighborhoods found themselves excluded from the hiring process because employers assumed that they could make generalizations about workers' motivations and discipline based on where they lived. It was perverse that while poor people were chastised for not "pulling themselves up by their bootstraps," those who tried faced hostile employers. A black man from a poor community faced nearly insuperable obstacles in the personnel office, regardless of his qualifications, experience, and skills.

No issue offered a more graphic reminder of the half-won victories of the struggle for black equality than the problem of persistent, concentrated urban poverty. Black poverty rates fell sharply in the North between 1960 and 1970 but stagnated from the 1970s through the 1990s. Journalists and social scientists began to write, usually in pejorative terms, about an emerging urban "underclass" whose poverty was the result of antisocial attitudes and maladaptive behavior. The term "underclass" was imprecise and controversial. As the United States grew more conservative in the 1970s and 1980s, cultural and behavioral explanations of poverty proliferated. Poverty could be traced to family breakdown, out-of-wedlock childbearing (observers in the 1970s lamented an "epidemic" of teen pregnancy), and welfare dependency. These dysfunctional behaviors, argued conservatives, were the perverse legacy of the War on Poverty. The most influential critic of the welfare state, conservative economist Charles Murray, argued that the perverse incentives of welfare fostered fecklessness, dependency, and promiscuity among the poor and—worse than that—rewarded such behaviors by fleecing hardworking taxpayers.

Arguments about the underclass invariably downplayed the devastation of inner cities, the travails of the education system, and the persistence of segregation. Above all, they overlooked the effects of dramatic transformations that had been remaking inner cities—with devastating impact on the poor. In cities with volatile, mostly declining economies, holding on to a job was difficult. The most rapid job growth from the 1970s onward was in part-time, contingent work, usually poorly paying and with few if any benefits. Poor people, especially African Americans, lived more concentrated together than ever before, one of the consequences of the failure of housing integration. And a growing fraction of the population, particularly young black men, moved in and out of the formal labor market and battled chronic joblessness.

ROXANNE JONES HAD front-row seats to observe the human costs of poverty and disinvestment in her adopted hometown. In 1976, Jones cofounded Philadelphia Citizens in Action (PCA), an organization that expanded the mandate of the welfare rights movement, working to improve health care and education as well as fighting for the poor, disabled, and elderly. Although the National Welfare Rights Organization was defunct in all but name, women around the country like Jones did not jettison their commitment to improving the lives of poor people. PCA operated out of a storefront office at Columbia Avenue and 20th Street, ground zero of Philadelphia's urban crisis. Of the forty-five thousand people who lived in the surrounding neighborhood in 1980, 98 percent were black. More than half lived beneath the poverty line. Twenty-six percent of the adults were unemployed. Despite those grim statistics, it was not the most depressed section of North Philadelphia; it was the tenth-poorest of thirty-seven neighborhoods surveyed by the Philadelphia City Planning Commission.

Jones's office looked out onto one of North Philadelphia's main streets, lined with stores, restaurants, and music clubs. "Jump Street" (as Columbia Avenue was nicknamed) had been the epicenter of Philadelphia's 1964 riot. Many of the burned-out stores had reopened, but poverty's toll crippled many local businesses. Crime was high. Clusters of men gathered to socialize, to throw dice, and increasingly to deal drugs in front of the neighborhood's ubiquitous "stop and go" stores—places that sold forty-ounce bottles of beer and blunt cigars, which were often emptied of their tobacco and reused to roll marijuana cigarettes. By the mid-1980s, many residents found themselves swept up in an epidemic of crack cocaine, both highly addictive and inexpensive. Little Chinese restaurants stood brightly lit on corners, their fluorescent lights glimmering off the Plexiglas that barricaded the counters to thwart armed robbers. The sidewalks were littered with broken glass, crack vials, and trash.

Not all was grim along Columbia Avenue. On Sunday mornings, families in their Sunday best flocked to the neighborhood's many churches

—august Gothic chapels inherited from fleeing white congregations, Moorish-revival former synagogues housing Churches of God in Christ churches and storefront churches marked with simple hand-painted signs and led by self-ordained preachers. The Nation of Islam had a presence in North Philadelphia, evidenced by the women in hijabs and men in suits walking to Muhammad's Mosque No. 12 on North Broad Street. Many of these religious groups played a vital role in the community, providing hot meals, counseling, social services, and job training. Some of North Philadelphia's largest congregations, such as the Reverend Leon Sullivan's Zion Baptist Church, involved themselves in community economic development projects. With the support of its members—and with large grants from foundations—Zion started an aerospace manufacturing company, hoping to create jobs and win government contracts through minority set-aside programs. Deliverance Baptist Church developed a small shopping center, trying to fill the gap left by businesses that fled the community. The Church of the Advocate, led by Father Paul M. Washington, had hosted the Black Panthers during their 1969 annual convention and had supported the Black Manifesto. The Advocate Community Development Corporation, a nonprofit that spun off from the church, won federal grants to build new housing and train black construction workers. During the 1970s and 1980s, Father Washington continued to support welfare rights activists, community development groups, and advocates of prison reform.

Community economic development projects did not stanch the flow of people and investment from North Philadelphia. Many of the drab, red-brick row houses that filled the neighborhoods around Jones's office stood abandoned, exposed to the elements, their roofs collapsing, their façades blackened by fire. North Philadelphia had lost 25 percent of its population in the 1970s, mostly because working-class blacks moved into neighborhoods to the northwest that were rapidly losing their white populations. Adding to the grim vista were thousands of rubble-filled vacant lots where houses had once stood, punctuating the streetscape like knocked-out teeth. Community development advocates hoped that a "land bank" of vacant lots would appeal to outside developers, but instead they lay fallow. A tangle of rail lines, overgrown and trash-strewn, wove through the neighborhood. Along the tracks lay the rotting hulks of long-abandoned factory buildings, their walls painted bright with graffiti.

Every major northeastern and midwestern city lost jobs—both with the closing of factories and with commercial disinvestment. Between 1947 and 1977, twelve of the largest northeastern and midwestern cities lost a total of 2.1 million manufacturing, wholesale, and retail jobs, while gaining only 316,000 service jobs in their place. Philadelphia was not atypical. Between 1970 and 1980, Philadelphia lost more than 150,000 jobs, one-sixth of its total employment base.

As jobs disappeared from black neighborhoods in North Philadelphia—and from the city as a whole—many area residents found new opportunities in the thriving underground or informal economy. At the bottom rung, young men rummaged through garbage cans and Dumpsters. If they had access to cars or, better yet, trucks, they could expand their forays into middle- and upper-class neighborhoods. Thriving markets in used goods sprung up in front of old factory buildings and in vacant lots, many of the objects scavenged from wealthy neighborhoods on trash day. Men and women alike participated in all sorts of off-the-books work. Some cleaned people's homes. Others ran unlicensed day-care centers. Enterprising men used vacant lots to repair cars. Many such activities crossed a line into criminal enterprise. More and more old houses were abandoned each year. Working at night, teams of young men stripped vacant houses of everything useful. Copper wiring made its way to the metal recyclers that sprung up in old industrial brownfields. Mantels, brass doorknobs, and wrought-iron fences found their way into the hands of antiques stores and junk shops that proliferated on the edge of the ghetto, where they would be resold to contractors and wealthy home renovators. At night, many street corners teemed with life. Gambling, prostitution, and drug dealing provided a few with fast money but many others with dangerous, insecure, only sometimes remunerative work.

The collapse of the urban economy came at a moment when welfare recipients came under attack. By the mid-1970s, white conservative critics of welfare created a powerful and enduring (even if completely fictional) image of "welfare queens"—black single mothers who supposedly bankrolled decadent lives with their AFDC checks. During the 1976 Republican primaries, former California governor Ronald Reagan, aspiring to the White House, had popularized the image. "There is a woman in Chicago," proclaimed Reagan in a story that he would often repeat on the stump. "She has 80 names, 30 addresses, 12 Social Security cards, and is collecting veterans' benefits on four non-existing deceased husbands." Piling on the salacious details, he continued. "And she's collecting Social Security on her cards. She's got Medicaid, getting food stamps, and she is collecting welfare under each of her names. Her tax-free cash income alone is over $150,000." Other versions of the story had her driving a white Cadillac. Reagan's story brought audiences to their feet, but it was a fabrication. He had spun his tale from a rather pedestrian case of welfare cheating: a Chicago woman using four aliases who had fraudulently taken in about eight thousand dollars.

Jones knew full well that Reagan's tale was outrageous. It was nearly impossible to survive, much less pay for a new luxury car, on a meager welfare check or even four. What made the "welfare queen" stereotype so dubious was that poor blacks were far less likely to own cars than any other segment of the population. Jones knew acutely the difficulties of surviving in the city without an automobile. She never got a driver's license. Like many poor people, she could not afford a car—a reliable one, anyway. For most of her life, she could not qualify for a loan to buy one (it had taken months of noisy protests by the Pennsylvania Welfare Rights Organization to get major department stores to offer even token credit to their poor customers). In lower North Philadelphia more than half of all households had no cars. In the neighborhood surrounding Jones's office, only a quarter of all residents had access to a car. Those poor urban residents who cobbled together enough money to buy a car faced high insurance rates, a by-product of the epidemic of auto theft in inner-city neighborhoods and the discriminatory attitudes of actuaries. Without a car, Jones spent countless hours riding the buses and trolleys.

The burdens of being poor grew heavier as revenue-strained public transportation agencies faced the budgetary ax. By the 1970s, the majority of new employment opportunities, especially at the entry level, were in outlying areas, remote from the neighborhoods that housed most of the region's black population. Writing in 1968, economist John Kain coined the phrase "spatial mismatch" to describe the fact that most new jobs were being created in suburban areas—accessible only by car—while the minority population was concentrated in inner cities, often distant from workplaces. Suburban employers who sought low-wage minority employees (such as janitors, shopping center stockroom workers, and kitchen staff) faced a dilemma. A 1971 Philadelphia study made the costs of travel starkly clear. Only one in ten trips to suburban industrial parks could be made in under forty-nine minutes. Overcoming that spatial mismatch was one of the many challenges that Jones's North Philadelphia neighbors faced.

The spatial mismatch was one of the most pernicious consequences of the persistence of housing segregation in the urban North. Despite more white Americans than ever professing their commitment to housing integration, the reality was that northern metropolitan areas remained rigidly segregated by race in the 1970s and 1980s. By 1990, twenty-four of the twenty-five most segregated metropolitan areas in the United States were in the North. Rates of housing segregation rose in most of the North between 1970 and 1990. The most rapid job growth was occurring in the whitest sections of metropolitan areas, places where restrictive zoning laws, real estate steering practices, and a climate of hostility kept most blacks out.

To most policy makers, and to the general public, the spatial mismatch was invisible. Suburbanites seldom passed by the crowded inner-city bus terminals, busy in the predawn hours, where people huddled in the semi-darkness waiting for their buses. By contrast, the "welfare queen"—bearing children only to pick up an additional welfare check—remained a pervasive stereotype. As a welfare recipient for much of her life, Jones was particularly sensitive to charges that welfare recipients were living a decadent lifestyle subsidized by federal largesse. Particularly galling to her was the way that assumptions about poor people's values and behavior steered the welfare debate.

While suburban sprawl and segregation continued unchecked—underwritten by federal tax policies—blacks found themselves overwhelmingly concentrated in central cities. And even more perniciously, poor people found themselves increasingly isolated in neighborhoods that were not just racially segregated but also home to alarmingly high concentrations of poor people. The period from 1970 to 1990 witnessed the proliferation of deeply impoverished neighborhoods—places where 40 percent or more of the residents lived beneath the poverty line. The vast majority were in the Northeast and Midwest. In Philadelphia, twenty-eight census tracts (areas usually encompassing several thousand people) were deeply impoverished in 1970; by 1980, there were sixty-nine such tracts. That year, slightly less than half of all black men between the ages of twenty-five and forty-four in those hyperimpoverished neighborhoods had paying jobs. One-third were not in the labor force at all—meaning that they were either incarcerated, institutionalized, or no longer actively seeking work. Just under half the households—most of them female-headed—depended on public assistance.

By contrast, outlying parts of the metropolitan area grew richer. Suburbs continued to expand, aided by federally funded highway construction, home mortgage tax deductions, and tax incentives to developers of shopping malls, industrial parks, and office centers in outlying greenfields. In the meantime, federal support for central cities began to dry up. Since the New Deal, cities came to rely increasingly on federal assistance. During the Great Society and into the 1970s, federal urban expenditures had risen steadily. However, inflation, unemployment, and economic stagnation sapped support for large-scale government spending. By 1980, the United States had a suburban majority. Residents of those communities—which relied on mostly their own tax bases to support schools and public services—were loath to see their tax dollars "drained" into central cities.

The concentration of poverty in central cities and the loss of population and jobs (and with them tax revenue) devastated urban public schools. Philadelphia was not the worst urban public school system in the country, but it struggled with budget cuts, high teacher turnover, and aging school buildings—at the same time that the number of impoverished schoolchildren grew. Racial and economic segregation, combined with revenue crises, proved devastating throughout the North. Surrounding Philadelphia were some of the richest and highest-performing school districts in the country. Lower Merion, which lay just northwest of the city, had one of the best-funded school districts in the state. Across City Avenue, Philadelphia's school buildings were overcrowded and run-down. Even as more black students completed high school (the black-white gap in years of school completed narrowed substantially in the 1970s and 1980s), the quality of education varied widely. Experts began talking of an "educational mismatch," one that was every bit as sizeable a barrier to remunerative employment as the fact that the most robust job growth happened in places far removed from the central city.

Cities struggled mightily with declining tax revenue at the same time that poverty was rising and infrastructure was decaying. One important stopgap had been the infusion of federal funding to city governments between the New Deal and the early 1970s. But beginning in the 1970s, as central cities grew blacker and poorer, the federal government began a steady withdrawal of urban funding. The Nixon administration took the first steps by launching a "new federalism" that called for a strengthening of the power of the states and grants to localities that would afford them "wide administrative leeway." William Safire, writing for Nixon and his domestic policy advisors, advocated the creation of a "national localism" that "says to communities, 'Do it your way.'" Nixon dismantled much of the Great Society but did not jettison its emphasis on funding local community development organizations even as he cut spending. Nixon's "revenue sharing" policy provided grants to local governments with relatively few strings attached. As War on Poverty programs atrophied, the Nixon administration created the Community Development Block Grant program, which funded local community development corporations.

The growing emphasis on public-private partnerships was not solely a Republican initiative. Jimmy Carter, elected in 1976 with strong support from black voters, pledged to adopt an ambitious urban initiative. Civil rights organizations, hopeful that a Democratic president would revive the Great Society and the War on Poverty, demanded an "urban Marshall Plan" and insisted that Carter reward them for their loyalty. They quickly grew impatient. In July 1977, National Urban League president Vernon Jordan accused Carter (who was in attendance at the Urban League's annual convention) of ignoring black America. Joining Jordan were civil rights leaders and mayors, who charged the administration with "callous neglect" and "falling short on programs, policies, and people." When New York City erupted in riots during the summer of 1977 in a grim reprise of the long hot summers of the late 1960s, Carter faced even more criticism. As the political costs of inaction mounted, Carter promised to develop a "comprehensive" urban policy and engaged in an extensive "outreach" program to solicit the input of civil rights groups. In 1977, Carter signed the Public Works Employment Act, which set aside 10 percent of federal contracts to minority-owned firms. In 1978, he pushed through the Comprehensive Education and Training Act (CETA), a federally funded job-training program. And that same year, he instructed federal agencies to give preference to central cities when opening new offices. Together they helped stabilize black employment gains in the public sector.

Jimmy Carter's urban agenda, however, foundered on the shoals of stagflation—the combination of high unemployment and runaway inflation that devastated the economy in the mid- and late 1970s. Carter shared his Republican critics' animosity toward the Great Society and embraced an alternative vision of community empowerment and local self-help. When he visited New York's devastated South Bronx, Carter took home a lesson in the futility of government spending: A "massive multi-billion dollar infusion of federal funds into the area" would not solve the problems of the South Bronx. Indeed, local activists seemingly endorsed Carter's vision of small government: "The community people," wrote a Carter aide, "do not want such federal intrusions of money, but rather the tools to help themselves and reliable, longer-term commitments of incremental assistance."

When Carter finally announced an urban policy in 1978, one that relied heavily on voluntary, community-based efforts, it was roundly denounced by black critics. Drawing from the rhetoric of decentralization that enjoyed support from both free marketers on the right and community-based activists on the left, the Carter administration advocated the "empowerment" of "mediating institutions" that would, it was believed, provide an antidote to impersonal, distant bureaucracy. The *Amsterdam News* lambasted "Carter's feeble urban policy." Jordan labeled it "disheartening." Whatever the merits of Carter's urban agenda, it quickly fell to the wayside as the economy soured. By the winter of 1978–79, Carter began the process of trimming urban expenditures in his austerity budget. The administration's anti-inflation advisor, Alfred E. Kahn, bluntly told urban officials that the government could not afford to rebuild troubled cities and that "the prescribed medicine is restraint." One urban activist responded that "we are heading into a completely new era and we don't know what to make of it."

That new era continued in the Reagan administration, which cut urban expenditures even more steeply, without the fear of political retribution that had held the Carter administration back. The Republican base was white, disproportionately suburban and rural, and wholly indifferent to urban problems. Not surprisingly, Reagan took the budgetary ax to programs that benefited central cities and minorities. Under the rubric of the "New Federalism"—a more aggressive version of Nixon's plan— the Republican White House proposed a series of programs to devolve governmental decision making to localities, and that coincided with a dramatic reduction in federal urban spending. Reagan winnowed public housing programs; reduced Community Development Block Grants; and cut aid to mass transit. Carter's CETA program lost all its funding. Between 1980 and 1990, the federal share of local government expenditures fell dramatically, from nearly 12 percent to just over 3 percent. The result was that at the very moment that cities were reeling with disinvestment, growing poverty, population loss, and a collapse in tax revenue, the federal government withdrew much of its support. Historian Carl Abbott estimated that city governments bore two-thirds of the cost of Reagan-era budget cuts.

At the top of the Reagan administration's domestic agenda was cutting welfare. In 1982, Reagan cut social programs by $35 billion, most from welfare and health benefits for the poor. The following year, the administration cut $7 billion in job training and other service programs dating to the War on Poverty. While cutting back on federal social spending, the Reagan administration also gave the states more discretion to experiment with welfare reforms. Around the country, state legislators pushed for cuts in general assistance, the aid provided to single poor people without children. Over the 1970s, rising unemployment rates had spurred a significant increase in general assistance payments, especially in the old industrial states. Coming at a time when state legislatures were struggling with declining tax revenues, and amid the growing cultural criticism of the poor, general assistance became an easy target. Why should taxpayers provide support for the able-bodied unemployed? At the same time, many states cut their share of spending for Aid to Families with Dependent Children.

Roxanne Jones's home state hopped onto the welfare reform bandwagon. Republican governor Richard Thornburgh stiffened eligibility requirements for general assistance; reduced the rolls of those eligible for state-funded health insurance; and experimented with work requirements for welfare recipients in an increasingly popular program dubbed "workfare." Coming amid the serious recession of the early 1980s, "Thornfare," as Pennsylvanians called it, had perverse consequences. It increased the ranks of those looking for work at a time when few jobs were available, it led to a spike in homelessness, and it exacerbated a serious health care crisis among the urban poor.

Roxanne Jones reacted with outrage at welfare cuts. "Oh my God!" she exclaimed, when asked in early 1982 about the Reagan administration's proposals to roll back AFDC. "After this cold winter we went through, people freezing to death, not having enough money to pay their fuel bills, I call it human genocide. It is inhumane for (Reagan) to talk of cutting any of the programs any more." Those who supported welfare cuts had "no sense of compassion, no sense of fairness and no sense of justice." In 1983, Jones's organization filed a lawsuit challenging Thornfare. That year, the average single general assistance recipient received only $172 a month; a woman with five children received $460 a month—lower benefits in real dollars than before the welfare rights movement had taken off. Rents for small apartments along Columbia Avenue cost nearly $150 a month. A welfare check simply did not go very far. Jones saw the cuts as punitive.

The climate of welfare cuts was deeply dispiriting. By the early 1980s, Jones found it more and more difficult to mobilize protests. The welfare rights movement in the late 1960s, when she joined it, was one of hope. It was possible to pull together rallies of several hundred welfare recipients at a moment's notice—in large part because activists had every reason to believe that the government would respond to pressure. The War on Poverty and the civil rights legislation of the mid-1960s created high expectations among Jones and her compatriots. By contrast, during the Reagan era, Jones found that the poor were disheartened. Fewer and fewer believed that their actions mattered. Still, indefatigable, she organized protests. In June 1983, she led a sit-in at the Philadelphia Gas Works offices, protesting utility cutoffs of those who could not pay their bills. In September and October, she led a two-week occupation of the Pennsylvania capitol rotunda to protest Thornfare. But these were defensive campaigns, desperate attempts to stem the conservative tide.

Jones never gave up protesting; it was in her political blood. But in the fall of 1983, she decided that demonstrations were not enough. She launched what seemed at first to be a quixotic campaign for the state senate, starting with a primary challenge of incumbent Democrat T. Milton Street, Sr. A former sidewalk vendor, Street was one of Philadelphia's better-known civil rights activists in the 1970s. An aggressive proponent of black economic power, Street denounced city leaders and corporate developers as racist, accused the city of misusing Community Development Block Grants, and led demonstrations that shut down Philadelphia's city council for nearly two months. When Philadelphia public officials cut the ribbon on a new downtown shopping mall, Street disrupted the event with protests demanding that black-run businesses be included. After his election to the state senate in 1980, Street proved to be a mercurial public official. He remained a Democrat in name only, joining the Republican caucus in Harrisburg. In the process, he drifted from his constituents and lost the support of the city's Democratic Party. Street's apostasy gave Jones an opening. After a bruising primary campaign (in which Street and the Republicans engaged in a prolonged and unsuccessful court battle to disqualify Jones), Jones won the nomination by a wide margin. She went on to a decisive victory in November and, after fending off a challenge by state Republicans to unseat her, took office in January 1985. She was one of 6,016 blacks—1,358 of them women—who held elected office in the United States that year.

Over the next eleven years, Roxanne Jones continued to fight valiantly for legislation that would assist the urban poor. But like so many black legislators, she served more as a prophet howling in the void. For most of the time she was in office, a Republican majority controlled the state senate. Still, she pushed for legislation that attempted to address the multiple, tangled issues of welfare, jobs, education, transportation, and poverty. Jones won a fight to procure state funds for rehabilitation programs for drug-addicted mothers. In 1991, she designed a state plan to provide health care to AIDS patients. But her fights to expand heating aid for the poor and to prevent cuts in state assistance to the elderly, and her long-time battle for improved health care for the poor, all ended in defeat.

By the late 1980s and early 1990s, Jones and activists like her were generals without armies. The social movements that had long sustained the black freedom struggle were weaker than ever. The most active leaders—whether community organizers or elected officials—were engaged in a struggle to preserve welfare, fend off challenges to affirmative action, and maintain funding for strapped urban public schools. Their efforts were largely defensive. Many of the most visible antiracist campaigns of the 1970s, 1980s, and 1990s built on a strategy that the left had deployed in the postwar years—namely, focusing on a handful of high-profile cases. In the 1940s and 1950s, leftists had used prominent police brutality cases to highlight the issue of discrimination in the justice system. Beginning in the 1960s, they rallied around imprisoned radicals such as Huey Newton, Assata Shakur, and George Jackson. One of the most prominent national campaigns (and one that had the sympathy of Roxanne Jones) was the campaign to free Mumia Abu-Jamal, a black nationalist accused and convicted of killing a white police officer in Philadelphia. Whatever the merits of Mumia's case (it generated intense debate about the death penalty, police brutality, and criminal justice), it represented the power of embodying social grievances in one individual but also the limitations of social movement building in a time of political reaction. Such cases shed light on the atrocious conditions in many prisons but all too often became unhitched from the larger efforts to transform the criminal justice system. It was more difficult to forge the unlikely political coalitions necessary to challenge federal cutbacks in welfare or to restructure the prison-industrial complex than it was to mobilize outrage around prominent individuals.

One of the ironic legacies of the long march from the late 1960s to the turn of the century was the mismatch between social movements and the huge social problems they faced. Grassroots civil rights movements, many of them small and beleaguered, fought locally on a terrain that was increasingly shaped by dramatic national and global changes. Three interrelated trends reshaped post-1960s America, each reinforcing the others. The first was the hypermobility of capital, foreshadowed by the flight of industry away from central cities beginning in the post–World War II years. As capital moved increasingly outside the United States, many African Americans, especially those with relatively few skills and poor educations, found themselves even more economically marginal. The second was the growing gap between rich and poor as a combination of tax policies and a boom in high-skill service and technological industries yielded extraordinary wealth for a very small segment of the population. The third was the triumph of the market, particularly in the public sector, which led to demands for the reduction of the size of government, individual initiative, and market discipline in lieu of a more generous welfare state. All of these changes disproportionately affected African Americans because of their interconnection with the government.

As the Reagan administration and Jones's own state legislature further cut welfare, the effects were striking. Nationwide, the proportion of female household heads with children receiving AFDC declined from 63 percent in 1972 to 45 percent in 1988. The real value of welfare benefits fell even more dramatically because AFDC, unlike Social Security, was not indexed to inflation. Thus, median AFDC payments in 1992 were 43 percent lower than they were in 1970. The problem for poor women on AFDC was not dependency, it was income insufficiency. In most big cities, it was impossible to make ends meet on welfare alone.

By the 1990s, Jones found herself increasingly marginalized in her own party. After spending nearly two decades in the political wilderness, key Democrats latched on to the argument that the party's future depended on turning to the right, particularly on divisive social issues. Prominent liberal intellectuals argued that the Republicans had become the majority party because of the disaffection of white working- and middle-class voters over the issues of civil rights, race, welfare, and crime. "The special status of blacks," wrote pollster Stanley Greenberg, summarizing a series of interviews he conducted with white ex-Democrats outside Detroit, "is viewed by almost all these individuals as a serious obstacle to their personal advancement." Northern whites professed their racial innocence. "There is no sense of personal or collective responsibility that would support government antidiscrimination or civil rights policies." While some pundits argued for the necessity of cross-race coalition building—building on the Depression-era precedents of simultaneously demanding racial equality and economic opportunity for all—Democratic analysts in the early 1990s drew a different lesson altogether. Democrats would succeed only if they jettisoned their long-standing commitment to civil rights and distanced themselves from policies that were perceived as advancing black interests over whites. They accepted the erroneous assumption that racial equality was a "zero sum game" that advanced blacks at whites' expense.

The lesson translated into policy initiatives. The Democratic Leadership Council, a group of moderate and conservative members of the party, railed against "special interests" that controlled the policy agenda, among them civil rights groups. Some analysts, such as Michael Tomasky and Thomas Edsall, called on the Democrats to distance themselves from race-based programs like affirmative action and instead embrace "class-based" programs that would appeal to white voters, especially the blue-collar and lower-middle-class men who had become "Reagan Democrats." Others suggested that Democrats mimic Reagan's acerbic language about welfare dependency and black irresponsibility. All agreed that the future of liberalism meant reaching out to disaffected white men. So long as the Democrats were perceived as captive to black interests, they would not achieve a national majority.

The Democrats' rightward tack had particularly grave consequences for Roxanne Jones's constituents. Welfare reform was conceived by the Republicans but birthed by the Democrats. President Bill Clinton launched an effort to "end welfare as we know it." Building on the work of social scientists who had written about "welfare dependency" and "underclass behaviors," Clinton's domestic policy team fashioned a set of proposals to reduce the ranks of welfare by "making work pay." But what Clinton and his advisors had not anticipated was that, as they moved to the right on welfare reform, they opened up room for the Republicans to pull the debate even further rightward. The Democrats were outflanked. In 1994, the Republican Party's "Contract with America" included a far more draconian version of welfare reform than Clinton had advocated. When the Republicans took control of the House and Senate after the midterm election, they used their mandate to put the rollback of welfare at the top of their political agenda.

The impulse to reform welfare was deeply rooted in the politics of the 1980s and 1990s. State governors and urban mayors, less bound by federal regulations because of the triumph of the New Federalism, turned localities into laboratories for experimentation on the weakened body of the welfare state. Led by the governors of Michigan, Wisconsin, and Massachusetts, states reduced welfare assistance, expanded work requirements, and put strictures on parental behavior. Many states eliminated general assistance altogether. Pennsylvania's newly elected Republican governor, Tom Ridge, joined the anti-welfare bandwagon in 1994, cutting general assistance from its already low levels from Thornfare days and stiffening eligibility rules for Medicaid. Ridge, like his counterparts in other states, was empowered by a provision in the 1962 welfare law that allowed states to obtain "waivers" from federal welfare regulations to experiment with social service delivery. The popularity of these state and local reforms, particularly among Republicans and conservative Democrats, became the basis of demands for greater devolution of federal social programs. When Republicans gained control of the House and Senate in 1994, they made local experiments the basis of their proposal to dismantle AFDC in 1996 welfare reform legislation.

Roxanne Jones—never much of a fan of AFDC, especially after twenty-five years of benefit reductions and tightening eligibility rules—spent most of her last few years fighting welfare reform. "There is a need for the system to be changed, but it shouldn't be changed by penalizing poor people at a time when jobs are scarce," she argued. "We don't have jobs for them even after they have been through job training. We are too often trying to satisfy people who perhaps do not understand the root causes of poverty and welfare." Indeed in 1995, anthropologist Katherine Newman, who studied low-wage labor markets, discovered that in Harlem, fourteen people applied for every job at McDonald's. It was, in other words, more difficult to get a minimum-wage, fast-food job in a major city than it was to get into an elite university. The problem was not that poor people were unwilling to work. There were simply not enough secure, well-paying jobs. Frustrated at the direction that welfare reform was taking, Jones reverted to the time-honored tactic of protest. She led a statewide coalition of community groups in a demonstration against welfare cuts. "The fight for fairness and justice can be won if we stand shoulder to shoulder, as we have many times before," Jones proclaimed. "We must make them understand that we will not stand by quietly while they throw us out onto the streets. We are fighting for our lives and we will not be denied."

Jones continued fighting until her untimely death after suffering a heart attack in May 1996. In her last weeks, Jones led an unsuccessful effort on the state senate floor to defeat Republican legislation to cut off Medicaid benefits to about 220,000 state residents unless they found jobs. Jones worried about the impact of cuts "in the current era of downsizing" but also expressed concern that urban hospitals would have to cut their workforces if Medicaid cuts were enacted. Urban hospitals—most of them sustained by Medicaid and other public funds—were not just essential to the health care of the poor, they were also among the most important employers of African Americans, from kitchen workers, janitors, and orderlies to nurses, office staff, social workers, and doctors.

While she challenged Medicaid cuts, Jones also turned her attention to a smaller but no less important program. Just days before she died, Jones introduced legislation to reimburse poor families for bus fares to send their children to school. "Nine dollars [the weekly cost of public transportation for schoolchildren] may not sound like a lot to most people," said Jones. "But when you are on a budget that is fixed, that nine dollars often means going without food or missing school. A mother with two children on welfare gets $403 a month to provide for her family. But $80 a month goes for busing to school." It was a sensible argument, but in a climate of fiscal austerity and antiwelfare sentiment, many of Jones's senatorial colleagues saw it as another unwarranted giveaway to the undeserving poor. The proposal went down to defeat.

At the time of her death, Jones was working with local activists to engage in a three-pronged strategy of protest, litigation, and legislation. But these remained—numerically and politically—minority issues in Pennsylvania and in the nation in the mid-1990s. Two months after Roxanne Jones died, President Bill Clinton signed the Personal Responsibility and Work Opportunity Reconciliation Act. With the stroke of a pen, he established welfare as a temporary program, ending the concept of welfare as an entitlement. No adult could receive more than five years of public assistance. The law also mandated strict work requirements to maintain eligibility, but it did not guarantee job training or child care assistance, although it set aside grants to states to provide either, if they chose to do so. Finally, the 1996 welfare reform gave states the leeway to implement stiffer eligibility requirements and shorter time limits.

In its first ten years, welfare reform had two noteworthy effects. First, the rolls of recipients plummeted. Some observers celebrated "the end of welfare." But second, rates of poverty did not budge. Former welfare recipients took jobs, but many continued on as they had before, relying on the informal economy to get by. During the long recession at the beginning of the next decade, poverty rates rose. Welfare reform shuffled the deck a bit, but with little impact on poverty itself. The North Philadelphia welfare recipients who had been Jones's constituents continued to live hand to mouth. More poor people than ever relied on the underground economy or on poorly paying service-sector jobs to scrape together a meager existence. No doubt Jones would have offered a scathing speech on the Pennsylvania senate floor and gathered a group of demonstrators to challenge the law.

EPILOGUE

IN FEBRUARY 1999, SEVERAL HUNDRED RESIDENTS IN WEST MOUNT AIRY, A northwest Philadelphia neighborhood just a few miles from Roxanne Jones's former legislative district, gathered to celebrate the fortieth anniversary of West Mount Airy Neighbors (WMAN). Founded in the late 1950s by a group of religious and secular civil rights activists, black and white, WMAN set itself a seemingly impossible task: to create a deliberately racially integrated community. The odds were stiff. Blockbusting real estate agents went door-to-door, fanning whites' fears that their property values would plummet. Whites in nearby neighborhoods—and their churches and synagogues—had bolted for the suburbs when the first black families moved in. The city's schools were struggling with disinvestment. Even though West Mount Airy attracted the city's black elite—among them congressman Robert Nix, Sadie Tanner Mossell Alexander, who had helped draft President Truman's report *To Secure These Rights,* and jazz musician Grover Washington, Jr.—whites still feared that their neighborhood was "going down."

WMAN drew its energy from the burgeoning civil rights movement of the late 1950s and 1960s. A tireless band of local activists pushed city officials to stiffen the city's enforcement of antidiscrimination laws and to curb unscrupulous real estate agents. Its members collaborated to improve the neighborhood's public schools. To build institutional support for its agenda, WMAN leaders met with local pastors and rabbis, school principals, and businesspeople. They sponsored block parties to introduce newcomers to their often-suspicious white neighbors. Their efforts paid off. West Mount Airy remains, a half century later, a model of racial diversity. The community's population is nearly evenly divided between blacks and whites. Like most thriving neighborhoods, it has lively local institutions—some of them, like one of the country's longest-running food cooperatives, racially diverse; others, like an Afrocentric charter school and a Jewish day-care center, racially homogeneous.

The tone at the fortieth anniversary event was celebratory. Many of the participants, like me, had moved to Mount Airy because of its history as an island of racial diversity in one of the nation's most racially segregated metropolitan areas. Those of us who worked as community activists—trying to better the neighborhood's schools, to challenge slumlords, and to spark community economic development—were inspired by the politics and activism of the previous generation of grassroots activists and proud of our modest accomplishments. When I addressed the crowd, I rather sanctimoniously called West Mount Airy "a rebuke to the nation's long and sordid history of racial separation and segregation." At least in our neighborhood—and in the few places like it around the United States—it seems that we have indeed overcome.

But have we overcome? On that question, blacks and whites do not agree. Public opinion surveys reflect real ambivalence about the state of race relations in the United States. Since the 1960s, blacks and whites have diverged widely in their perceptions of the extent of inequality and discrimination in American life and of the desirability of civil rights policies. Political scientist Jennifer Hochschild, who has written extensively on race and public opinion, found that whites believe that the "American dream" of equality and opportunity "works for everyone," but, by contrast, "blacks believe it works only for those not of their race. Whites are angry that blacks refuse to see the fairness and openness of the system; blacks are angry that whites refuse to see the biases and blockage of the system."

For white Americans, the civil rights movement is old history, past its prime now that the sin of racism has been eradicated from American society. Whites are far more optimistic about the pace of racial change than blacks. Since the passage of landmark civil rights legislation in 1964, they believe that what little discrimination remains in American life is rapidly disappearing. In their view, blacks and whites are now formally equal. Any remaining economic disparities are the result of individual failings, not segregation, unequal education, or discrimination. Most whites would recoil at the charge of racism; indeed, the vast majority (a statistically improbable 87 percent in a 2007 survey) claim to have black friends. To shore up their argument about the transformation of American society, they regularly cite the prominence of blacks such as Oprah Winfrey, Condoleezza Rice, Bill Cosby, and Barack Obama. America has come a long way, in their view, since the grim days of Jim Crow. Whites and blacks alike value "diversity" and "inclusion" as desirable—goals that even a conservative Supreme Court recently upheld as a compelling interest in the University of Michigan affirmative action cases.

By contrast, blacks are generally gloomy about the state of race relations in the United States. Their pessimism has deepened considerably since the 1960s. In 1969, nearly 80 percent of blacks reported that their status had improved dramatically over the previous five years. But subsequent surveys were much less heartening. By 1984, only 37 percent of blacks believed that their status had improved over the previous five years. By 2007, only 20 percent shared that optimism. Whereas 43 percent of blacks believed that the gap in standard of living between blacks and whites had widened between 1997 and 2007, only 19 percent of whites believed the same.

Perhaps the starkest disparity between blacks and whites involves perceptions of discrimination. By sizeable numbers, blacks report that they or people they know have been affected personally by racial discrimination and claim that their race affected their hiring prospects or promotion or treatment in the workplace. Here the gap is quite remarkable. In 2007—more than forty years after the enactment of the Civil Rights Act—two-thirds of blacks but only one in five whites stated that blacks "almost always" or "frequently" faced workplace discrimination. In housing, the results were similar. Sixty-five percent of blacks but only 27 percent of whites reported that blacks faced discrimination when renting or buying. And more than 50 percent of blacks reported discrimination in retail and restaurants, a phenomenon visible to only 12 percent of whites.

Blacks and whites diverge on many other issues, trivial and significant. One of the most notable variations involves matters of law and order and criminal justice. Blacks have long been more suspicious of the police than whites, in part a consequence of the long history of disproportionate white representation on police forces, in part a consequence of deep-rooted memories of the role that police played—both north and south—in reinforcing racial segregation, in brutalizing black suspects, and in thwarting civil rights protests. National survey data shows that blacks are less likely than whites to approve of police use of force against suspects, and they consistently show that blacks are more likely to distrust law enforcement authorities. The furor over the trial of O. J. Simpson offered stark evidence of the black-white gap on legal matters. In the aftermath of Simpson's acquittal, *The Washington Post* found that 85 percent of blacks and only 34 percent of whites agreed with the jury's decision.

Given the racial divide on what problems persist, it is not surprising that blacks and whites disagree over remedies. A 2007 survey found that 62 percent of blacks but fewer than one-quarter of whites believe that it is more important for children to attend racially mixed schools than local community schools. And even though in the abstract whites support the ideal of having black neighbors, only about 40 percent favor "more" neighborhood integration, compared to more than 60 percent of blacks. A plurality of whites—44 percent—believe that the degree of residential integration today is "about right," even though few whites have black neighbors. Not surprisingly, over the last forty years, blacks and whites have diverged widely on what constitutes appropriate public policy on matters such as education, the economy, poverty, and housing. By large margins, blacks consistently support government programs to address discrimination in schools and the workplace.

Whatever the validity of the beliefs expressed in polls and surveys, they are stark reminders of persistent racial differences despite decades of activism. But public opinion is not the only measure of change and continuity. The long twentieth century witnessed some extraordinary gains for African Americans and, at the same time, stubborn continuities. Blacks, especially women, have made substantial gains in employment, particularly in the public sector. But the blacks who report frequent discrimination are not deluded. Data from the Russell Sage Foundation's Multi-City Study of Urban Inequality shows that in Detroit, Boston, Atlanta, and Los Angeles, many employers make hiring decisions based on stereotypes about minorities and use race or ethnicity as "signals" of desirable or undesirable work characteristics. Economists have documented employers discriminating against job applicants with comparable credentials when one has a "black" name. Many employers fear that minority workers will be less reliable, prone to crime, and unwilling to work hard.

Change has also occurred haltingly for middle-class blacks. Fifty years ago, there was a small black middle class, mostly owners of what were called "race" businesses, such as funeral homes, restaurants and clubs, barbershops, and small stores that served a largely black clientele. Black businesspeople, with few exceptions, operated in a segregated world. For example, before the open housing movement forced open the real estate industry, there were no black Realtors. Today there are thousands. In 1963, when Ford Motor Company was asked to list its white-collar occupations open to blacks, it included valets, porters, security guards, messengers, barbers, mail clerks, and telephone operators. That such a list is unimaginable today offers evidence of how much has changed.

The growth of the black middle class is the most obvious result of the civil rights movement. It occurred most dramatically in the period after 1970. A glance at black professions in one northern state makes this clear. In 1960, the entire state of Michigan had only 324 black physicians, 142 black lawyers, 201 black engineers, and 95 black college teachers. The number of black physicians actually fell during the 1960s, and the number of black lawyers increased by only 51 in that decade. But between 1970 and 1990, the number of black professionals rose significantly. By 1990, Michigan had 1,076 black doctors, 1,178 black lawyers, 2,658 black engineers, and 1,509 black college teachers. By any measure, the gains over just twenty years were remarkable. The number of black professionals rose most steadily in the aftermath of the 1960s struggles, as the first sizeable generation of black students graduated from law schools, medical schools, and other institutions of higher education.

The second major change occurred in private- and public-sector hiring practices, particularly for white-collar positions. Government became one of the most important avenues for minority opportunity. And beginning in the 1970s, many employers began to reach out to minority workers out of fear of litigation. Some of the largest minority white-collar gains came in personnel offices that deal with state and federal agencies that enforce antidiscrimination laws. Many employers also began to create more diverse workforces when they realized that multicultural workplaces offered many competitive advantages. In some firms, minorities have made gains in positions that required contact with minority customers or clients in Africa, Latin America, or the Caribbean. Others have hired minority executives in sales and marketing to reach lucrative ethnic niches in the market. In a 1996 *Harvard Business Review* article that surveyed employers about racial and ethnic diversity, David Thomas and Robin Ely noted that a growing number of managers argue that a "more diverse workforce will . . . increase organizational effectiveness. It will lift morale, bring greater access to new segments of the marketplace and enhance productivity." In addition, predictions about demographic change over the next half century have provided a compelling rationale that workplace diversity is crucial to firms' growth and survival.

But the rise of the black middle class is only one measure of change. African Americans are far more likely than whites to be economically insecure. The statistics are grim. In 2006, the median household income of blacks only was 62 percent of that of whites. Blacks were more than twice as likely to be unemployed as whites, in part because of workplace discrimination, in part because they are still more likely to live in areas that have been left behind by the profound restructuring of the national and international economy, notably the major cities in the Northeast and Midwest. Nearly one quarter of all blacks, but only one in ten whites, lived beneath the poverty line.

The most persistent feature of life in the North has been racial segregation in housing and education. Here, too, black public opinion is closer to describing the reality than white. While patterns of black-white segregation are deeply entrenched throughout the country, racial segregation rates are particularly high in large metropolitan areas in the Northeast and Midwest. After the 1968 Fair Housing Act, real estate agents developed more furtive tactics to preserve the racial homogeneity of neighborhoods. The most significant was "steering," that is, the practice of directing white homebuyers to all-white communities and black homebuyers to predominantly black or racially transitional neighborhoods. Real estate brokers catered to what they believed were the prejudices of their white customers. Audit studies of housing discrimination conducted by the Department of Housing and Urban Development and by local housing and nonprofit agencies consistently show the persistence of discriminatory treatment of black home seekers and renters. Discrimination continues to play a significant role in dividing housing markets by race. Blacks simply do not have the same degree of choice when house hunting as do whites.

It is important to note that residential segregation by race is not a natural consequence of disparities in income between blacks and whites. Middle-class and wealthy blacks are no more likely to live near whites than poor blacks are. In an examination of the thirty metropolitan areas with the largest black populations in the United States, sociologists Douglas Massey and Nancy Denton found no significant difference in the segregation rates of poor, middle-class, and well-to-do African Americans. "Even if black incomes continued to rise," write Massey and Denton, "segregation would not have declined: no matter how much blacks earned, they remained racially separated from whites."

The starkest racial disparities in the United States are in wealth (a category that includes such assets as stocks, bonds, and especially real estate). Census surveys and social scientific studies have documented an enormous gap in asset holdings between blacks and whites, largely because of differences in holdings in real estate, the only significant asset that most Americans own. Blacks are still less likely to own their own homes (only about 45 percent, compared to 74 percent of whites). And because of persistent racial segregation, the value of homes that blacks own is significantly lower than that of whites. Using the most recent census data, the U.S. Census Bureau calculated that white households had a median net worth of $74,900, whereas black households had a median net worth of only $7,500. Whereas many whites can expect financial support at crucial junctures in their lives (going to college, getting married, buying a home) and inheritances as the result of their parents' accumulated wealth, few blacks can expect such good fortune.

Another important indicator of quality of life is health. One's long-term expectations are shaped in fundamental ways by one's experience with illness, injury, and death, including the care of a sick child or adult, the economic impact of disease and disability, and the devastation of seeing a family member die, particularly in an untimely fashion. The racial and ethnic gaps in health and life expectancy are significant. The life expectancy of whites in 2004 was 78.3 years; for blacks, it was 73.1. The life expectancy difference between black men and white men was particularly large: White men can expect to live 75.7 years; black men can expect to live only 69.5 years.

Racial gaps in health—closely correlated with poverty—are significant throughout the life course. In 2003, infant mortality rates were nearly two and one-half times as high for blacks as for whites. The rates were highest in impoverished central cities. Blacks have significantly higher death rates than whites for most of the top ten leading causes of death in the United States. Throughout the life course, blacks are more likely than whites to die of homicide, residential fires, drowning, and pedestrian accidents. The gap in homicide rates is enormous. Black men have a rate of death by homicide nearly ten times that of white men; the homicide rate for black women is more than three times that of white women. The gap between black and white homicide death rates is greatest among young men. Homicide is the leading cause of death for black men ages 15–24. The grim reality of violence affects large segments of black America, not merely the poor. A recent study found that a remarkable 70 percent of blacks surveyed stated that they knew someone who had been shot in the last five years, more than double the rate of whites.

IT IS TEMPTING—but risky—to use the past to predict the future. Historians have excellent hindsight but very cloudy crystal balls. Still, there are several lessons worth heeding from the history of the African American freedom struggle over the course of the long twentieth century. First, there is no straight line from a transformation of attitudes and public discourse to an increase in racial equality. The postwar effort to change the hearts and minds of white Americans worked: White Americans still express overtly racist sentiments but seldom prominently and publicly. But the softening of racial language did not dramatically change the patterns of racial inequality in the North. Whites do not live near minorities, and they do not attend school together. They seldom intermarry, although intermarriage rates have risen in recent years. The stark disparities between blacks and whites by every measure—economic attainment, health, education, and employment—are the results. The high degree of separation by race reinforces and hardens perceptions of racial difference. It creates racially homogeneous public institutions that are geographically defined, limits the access of many minorities to employment opportunities, and leads to racial polarization in politics. Residential segregation has led to a concentration of poverty in urban areas and means that even those who are considered middle-class have direct experience with poverty and its consequences.

The changes that took place—the destruction of Jim Crow in public accommodations; the opening of employment, especially in the public sector; the growth in black political power—none of these was solely or primarily the result of a shift in white attitudes. Rather, they were a result of decades of activism and policy making—boycotts, pickets, agitation, riots, lobbying, litigation, and legislation. The most sweeping political changes resulted from disruption or the threat of it, whether the March on Washington, the "Negro Revolt" of 1963, or the urban uprisings of the mid- and late 1960s. Perhaps the most astute observer of power and politics in modern America was theologian Reinhold Niebuhr, who noted that "the white race in America will not admit the Negro to equal rights if it is not forced to do so." That was the second lesson, taught and learned by activists as diverse as Anna Arnold Hedgeman, A. Philip Randolph, Paul Zuber, Herman Ferguson, and Roxanne Jones; the boycotting mothers of Hillburn and Chicago; and the rioters of Detroit and Plainfield.

Third, the most successful social movements have been broad-based, the result of coalition building across racial, religious, and economic divisions. Social movements have benefited most when they have organized locally but networked regionally and nationally and thought globally. The National Negro Congress, the NAACP, and the National Welfare Rights Organization were powerful precisely because they bridged the local and the national. They provided resources and information to grassroots activists—who in turn set the direction for lobbyists, legislators, bureaucrats, litigators, and jurists. Too many current-day scholars and activists draw a false dichotomy between "top-down" and "bottom-up" organizing strategies. Many grassroots activists in Hillburn and New Rochelle, in Gary and Chicago thought otherwise. By contrast, those activists who kept their sights small, squabbled among themselves, and failed to break out of their localities often had little enduring impact. Their struggles were often creative—and sometimes influential—but often fizzled out. Many activists had the will but not the capacity to alter fundamental problems such as mass unemployment, inferior housing, poverty, and an inadequate safety net.

Fourth, networks matter. Northern advocates of civil rights were enmeshed in webs of information; personal and familial ties that crossed regions; and organizations that operated on the local, regional, and national levels. Readers of *The Crisis* could find all sorts of inspiring examples of grassroots resistance to racial inequality. Readers of *The Pittsburgh Courier*, with its correspondents in Detroit, Philadelphia, and Harlem, could share outrage at incidents of police brutality in cities hundreds of miles away. When the white-dominated news media began to cover civil rights issues extensively (not until the late 1950s, and in some places not until the 1960s), they provided activists yet more information. At the same time, religious groups disseminated information about civil rights issues to their congregants through films and pamphlets.

Fifth, government matters. There was no glorious history of federal or local efforts to deal with racial inequality. Even the most progressive white political leaders seldom made black demands a priority. The New Deal was riddled with programs that worsened racial inequality; presidential civil rights initiatives were more often symbolic than real; and War on Poverty experiments were small in scale and often ineffectual. Nevertheless, civil rights activists took advantage of the openings that government provided them and, at propitious moments when they perceived that they had allies in government, used pressure to force political change. The Roosevelt and Truman administrations moved forward because of their concern about blacks and the balance of power, and Kennedy had little interest in the question of civil rights until grassroots protestors forced the question. The Nixon administration's "new federalism," Reagan's attack on welfare and affirmative action, and the Clinton administration's repeal of welfare all had decisive political impacts. When political leaders, jurists, and policy-makers rolled back civil rights gains, activists turned defensive, narrowed their horizons, and pushed for the maintenance of hard-won gains, often against the odds. Finally, even if civil rights victories are partial, black representation in the political process mattered—and matters. Blacks gained a significant voice in northern politics only after the mid-1960s. Without the War on Poverty and the rise of black elected officials, black economic gains would be even fewer.

ALL THE TRENDS that have reshaped the experience of blacks and whites in the North are visible in microcosm in West Mount Airy. The latest census data offers grounds for optimism. The neighborhood is 45.7 percent white and 51.3 percent black. And, drawing from the new census category, 2.8 percent of neighborhood residents considered themselves to be "multiracial." It is also relatively prosperous. Its black residents, disproportionately middle-class, are concentrated in public-sector and public-related employment, reflecting the centrality of government to black upward mobility. But other, less hopeful trends are visible. The income gap between blacks and whites in the neighborhood is widening, and sections of the neighborhood, mostly those lined with small row houses and apartment buildings, are home to a sizeable population of poor people and working-class families who barely have the means to survive. The neighborhood's wealthiest sections are the whitest. It took four decades of organizing to turn West Mount Airy into a neighborhood singled out by a Department of Housing and Urban Development study as one of the most successfully racially integrated neighborhoods in America. But it will take a lot more hard work to grapple with the still-unresolved, intertwined issues of race and class. Whether that will happen remains to be seen, particularly given the disinterest of the nation's white majority and elected officials in questions of racial justice, especially for African Americans.

THE OBSTACLES TO achieving racial equality over the twentieth century were high—and many were never fully surmounted. The desegregation of northern public accommodations was undermined by massive disinvestment in black communities. The successful battle for civil rights in the workplace was complicated by the restructuring of the post–World War II American economy. Just as blacks got a foot in the door in many industries, jobs and capital fled northern cities for mostly white suburbs and small towns, and, increasingly, to the Sunbelt and abroad. The movement to eradicate discrimination in the housing market was confounded by the mass movement of whites to suburbia. The call for equal education was compromised by the persistence of locally funded, politically balkanized schools. The movement for community control of politics and economics had unintended consequences: Those with the fewest resources gained control of places that were hemorrhaging capital, population, and tax revenue. Civil rights activists often struggled against the odds to forge lasting coalitions. Interracial efforts met with indifference and hostility; intraracial efforts were often hobbled by political infighting. And public officials proved to be fickle: sometimes allying themselves with the goal of racial equality, at other times throwing up hurdles to its success. The activists who fought for racial justice over the long twentieth century differed in strategies and goals. But they knew that just because battles are uphill does not mean they are worth conceding. The struggle for racial equality in the North continues.

ACKNOWLEDGMENTS

Sweet Land of Liberty stands on the shoulders of long-forgotten journalists, most of them black, who covered the northern freedom struggle and draws from the surviving records of civil rights groups on the local, regional, and national levels. It builds on the creative work of scholars who have recently begun the painstaking reconstruction of the history of northern racial inequality, local civil rights activism, and grassroots politics. To those who wrote history's first draft and to those who are writing its second and third drafts, I am greatly indebted. And to those librarians and archivists who preserve the past's many fragments and keep them accessible, often against the odds, I am thankful.

Scholarship is ultimately a collective endeavor. Several colleagues and friends read my drafts. Thanks especially to Sarah Flynn, Risa Goluboff, Steven Hahn, Thomas F. Jackson, Will Murphy, Daryl Scott, Bryant Simon, and John Skrentny for their detailed comments. Tom Pitoniak deserves special credit for his incisive copyediting. Brian Balogh, Lea Beresford, Lizabeth Cohen, Sally Gordon, Jacqueline Jones, Michael B. Katz, and Ira Katznelson offered invaluable support along the way. Geri Thoma has been an extraordinary agent, reader, and advocate. I have also benefited greatly from comments, criticism, and suggestions from activists and academics and students who have heard me present parts of this book in seminars, conference papers, and lectures over the last several years. My analysis of social movements, inequality, and politics is richer for all of my conversations with a remarkable group of grassroots activists and tireless policy advocates I have encountered, especially in Detroit, Philadelphia, and Washington.

Most of the research here is my own, though I have had some help. Thanks to Tina Collins, Kim Gallon, Erik Gellman, Clemmie Harris, Andrew Goodman, Leah Gordon, Chin Jou, Elizabeth Moselle, Julia Rabig, Peter Siskind, and Karen Tani for sharing their research with me and helping me track down sources, and Rachel Guberman for her help with images.

For financial support, I thank the Alphonse Fletcher, Sr., Foundation, the John Simon Guggenheim Foundation, the American Philosophical Society, the American Council of Learned Societies, and the University of Pennsylvania. I wrote much of this book at the Institute for Advanced Study in Princeton, a year for which I am especially grateful.

Dana, Anna, and Jack are always here for me. I shout for joy in thanks for the three most remarkable people I know.

Mount Airy, Philadelphia
December 2007

NOTES

ABBREVIATIONS USED IN NOTES

AD	Gunnar Myrdal, *An American Dilemma: The Negro Problem and Modern Democracy* (New York, 1944)
AESL	Arthur and Elizabeth Schlesinger Library, Radcliffe Institute for Advanced Study, Cambridge, Massachusetts
AFSC-AD-CR	American Friends Service Committee, American Division, Community Relations Section, AFSC Archives, Philadelphia, Pennsylvania
AHR	*American Historical Review*
ALUA	Archives of Labor and Urban Affairs, Walter P. Reuther Library, Wayne State University, Detroit, Michigan
AMP	August Meier Papers, SCRBC
AQ	*American Quarterly*
BA	*Black America*
BAA	Baltimore *Afro-American*
BCCT	*Bucks County Courier-Times*
BJP	Black Journalists Oral History Project, CUOHP
BP	*Black Panther*
BPPH	Black Panther Party of Harlem Papers, SCRBC
BSB	*Bay State Banner* (Boston)
BW	*Business Week*
BWOHP	*The Black Women Oral History Project from the Arthur and Elizabeth Schlesinger Library on the History of Women in America, Radcliffe College*, ed. Ruth Edmonds Hill, 10 vols. (Westport, Conn., 1991)
CCP	*Cleveland Call and Post*
CD	*Chicago Defender*
C-L	*CORE-Lator* (Congress of Racial Equality)
CORE	Congress of Racial Equality Papers, microform
CRC	Civil Rights Congress of Michigan Collection, ALUA
CRWH	*Civil Rights, the White House, and the Justice Department, 1945–1968*, ed. Michael Belknap, 20 vols. (New York, 1991)
CT	*Chicago Tribune*

CUOHP Columbia University Oral History Project, New York, New York
DFP *Detroit Free Press*
DN *Detroit News*
DNAACP Detroit Branch NAACP Papers, ALUA
DUL Detroit Urban League Papers, MHC
DW *Daily Worker*
FCP Fellowship Commission Papers, TUUA
GBP Gloria L. Brown Papers, MHC
GPM *Greater Philadelphia Magazine*
HEQ *History of Education Quarterly*
HFM Henry Ford Museum, Dearborn, Michigan
HLMP Henry Lee Moon Papers, Western Reserve Historical Society, Cleveland, Ohio
HPN *Harrisburg Patriot-News*
IN *Illustrated News*
INS Interracial News Service, National Council of Churches
JAEH *Journal of American Ethnic History*
JAH *Journal of American History*
JCPL Jimmy Carter Presidential Library, Atlanta, Georgia
JES *Journal of Educational Sociology*
JFKL John F. Kennedy Presidential Library, Boston, Massachusetts
JFK-POF John F. Kennedy, President's Office File, JFKL
JNE *Journal of Negro Education*
JNH *Journal of Negro History*
JPH *Journal of Policy History*
JTK John T. Kelsey Papers, MHC
JUH *Journal of Urban History*
JWPP Justine Wise Polier Papers, AESL
LAT *Los Angeles Times*
LBJ-CR *Civil Rights During the Johnson Administration: A Collection from the Holdings of the Lyndon Baines Johnson Library, Austin, Texas,* microfilm, ed. Steven Lawson (University Publications of America, 1984–1987)
LBJL Lyndon Baines Johnson Library, Austin, Texas
LC Library of Congress, Washington, D.C.
LDP Leon DeMeunier Papers, MHC
LH *Labor History*
MC *Michigan Chronicle*
MCVA Miller Center for Public Affairs, University of Virginia, Charlottesville, Virginia
MHC Michigan Historical Collections, Bentley Library, University of Michigan, Ann Arbor
MSRC Moorland-Spingarn Research Center, Howard University, Washington, D.C.

NA *New America*

NAACP National Association for the Advancement of Colored People Papers, LC

NAACP-M *National Association for the Advancement of Colored People Papers,* microfilm, ed. August Meier, John H. Bracey, et al. (Frederick, Md., 1987–)

NACCD *Report of the National Advisory Commission on Civil Disorders* (New York, 1968)

NC *New City*

ND *Negro Digest*

NJH *New Jersey History*

NNC National Negro Congress

NRSS *New Rochelle Standard-Star*

NS *Nation's Schools*

NUL National Urban League

NY *The New Yorker*

NYAN New York *Amsterdam News*

NYHT *New York Herald Tribune*

NYP *New York Post*

NYT *The New York Times*

OH Oral history

OP *Oakland Post*

PB Philadelphia *Bulletin*

PC *Pittsburgh Courier*

PCN *Plainfield Courier-News*

PDN *Philadelphia Daily News*

PG *Pennsylvania Guardian*

PH *Pennsylvania History*

PHC Plainfield History Collection, Plainfield Public Library, Plainfield, New Jersey

PI *The Philadelphia Inquirer*

PMLK *Papers of Martin Luther King, Jr.,* ed. Clayborne Carson et al., 5 vols. (Berkeley and Los Angeles, 1992–)

PMP Pauli Murray Papers, AESL

PNAACP Philadelphia Branch NAACP Papers, TUUA

PSA Pennsylvania State Archives, Harrisburg, Pennsylvania

PT *The Philadelphia Tribune*

PUL Philadelphia Urban League Papers, TUUA

RA *Radical America*

RAM *Black Power Movement Microfilm Collection: Part 3: Papers of the Revolutionary Action Movement, 1962–1996,* ed. Muhammad Ahmad, Ernie Allen, and John H. Bracey (Bethesda, Md., 2003)

RCR *Reporting Civil Rights,* ed. Library of America, 2 vols. (New York, 2003)

RFW   *Black Power Movement Microfilm Collection: Part 2: Papers of Robert Franklin Williams*, ed. Timothy Tyson (Bethesda, Md., 2002)

RHR   *Radical History Review*

RJB   Ralph J. Bunche Collection, MSRC

RRP   Ralph Rosenfeld Papers, MHC

RSB   Robert S. Browne Papers, SCRBC

SA   *Social Action*

SCCF   Schomburg Center Clippings Files, microform

SCRBC   Schomburg Center for Research in Black Culture, New York Public Library, New York

SE   Stuart Eizenstat Papers, JCPL

SEP   *The Saturday Evening Post*

SFSR   *San Francisco Sun-Reporter*

SG   *Survey Graphic*

SP   *Social Problems*

SR   *Saturday Review*

TIH   *Trends in Housing*

TNR   *The New Republic*

TSD   *Tri-State Defender*

TSTR   *To Secure These Rights: The Report of President Harry S Truman's Committee on Civil Rights*, ed. Steven Lawson (Boston, 2004)

TUUA   Temple University Urban Archives, Philadelphia

UAQ   *Urban Affairs Quarterly*

USCB   United States Census Bureau

USCCR   United States Commission on Civil Rights

USDL   United States Department of Labor

USNWR   *U.S. News & World Report*

WDL   Workers' Defense League Papers, ALUA

WP   *The Washington Post*

WSJ   *The Wall Street Journal*

YLJ   *The Yale Law Journal*

INTRODUCTION

xiii   **"The racial issue we confront":** Martin Luther King, Jr., "The Rising Tide of Racial Consciousness," address at the Golden Anniversary Conference of the National Urban League, Sept. 6, 1960, *PMLK*, vol. 5, 503–4. For overviews, see Jacquelyn Dowd Hall, "The Long Civil Rights Movement and the Political Uses of the Past," *JAH* 91 (2005), 1233–63; Steven F. Lawson, "Freedom Then, Freedom Now: The Historiography of the Civil Rights Movement," *AHR* 96 (April 1991), 456–71; Adam Fairclough, "Historians and the Civil Rights Movement,"

Journal of American Studies 24 (1990), 387–98; Charles M. Payne, *I've Got the Light of Freedom: The Organizing Tradition and the Mississippi Freedom Struggle* (Berkeley, Calif., 1995), 413–41; Kevin Gaines, "The Historiography of the Struggle for Black Equality since 1945," in Jean-Christophe Agnew and Roy Rosenzweig, eds., *A Companion to Post-1945 America* (Malden, Mass., 2002), 211–34. Some of the best new scholarship is anthologized in Jeanne F. Theoharis and Komozi Woodard, eds., *Freedom North: Black Freedom Struggles Outside the South, 1940–1980* (New York, 2003).

xiv **The Great Migration of blacks:** On the demographics of black migration, see James N. Gregory, *The Southern Diaspora: How the Great Migrations of Black and White Southerners Transformed America* (Chapel Hill, N.C., 2006), 12–19.

xiv **"It is convenient":** *AD*, 600, 1010.

xv **northern whites fiercely proclaimed:** Pete Hamill, "The Revolt of the White Lower-Middle Class," in Louise Kapp Howe, ed., *The White Majority: Between Poverty and Affluence* (New York, 1970), 13–14; Michael Novak, *The Rise of the Unmeltable Ethnics* (New York, 1972), 71–72.

xv **But in both regions:** For recent southern histories that emphasize regional commonalities, see Kevin Kruse, *White Flight: Atlanta and the Making of Modern Conservatism* (Princeton, N.J., 2005); Matthew Lassiter, *The Silent Majority: Suburban Politics in the Sunbelt South* (Princeton, N.J., 2006); James N. Gregory, "Southernizing the American Working Class: Post-War Episodes of Regional and Class Transformation," *LH* 39 (May 1998), with comments by Thomas Sugrue, Grace Elizabeth Hale, and Alex Lichtenstein and response by Gregory.

xv **Impoverishment and exclusion:** Because of the enormous geographic and chronological scope of this book and the lack of a synthetic treatment of the black civil rights struggle in the North, I have chosen to focus on whites and African Americans. This is not to downplay the importance of the history of other groups or their interaction with whites, African Americans, or one another. They are worthy of full histories in their own right. Some of the best recent scholarship on Texas and California, in particular, considers the intersections and tensions among black, Asian, and Latino civil rights struggles. See, for example, Scott Kurashige, "The Many Facets of *Brown:* Integration in a Multicultural Society," *JAH* 91 (2004), 56–68; Thomas A. Guglielmo, "Fighting for Caucasian Rights: Mexicans, Mexican Americans, and the Transnational Struggle for Civil Rights in World War II Texas," *JAH* 92 (2006), 1212–37.

xvi **The very notion of rights:** Rogers M. Smith, "Rights," in Richard Wightman Fox and James Kloppenberg, eds., *A Companion to American Thought* (Oxford, U.K., 1995); Smith, *Civic Ideals* (New Haven, Conn., 1997); Eric Foner, *The Story of American Freedom* (New York, 1998).

xvi **"Second Bill of Rights":** Franklin Delano Roosevelt, "Message to Congress on the State of the Union," Jan. 11, 1944, in *The Public Papers and Addresses of*

Franklin D. Roosevelt, vol. 13 (New York, 1950), 41; Cass Sunstein, *The Second Bill of Rights: FDR's Unfinished Revolution and Why We Need It More Than Ever* (New York, 2004); Elizabeth Borgwardt, *A New Deal for the World: America's Vision for Human Rights* (Cambridge, Mass., 2005).

xviii **Northern activists shared:** Three recent biographies explore the links between North and South: Barbara Ransby, *Ella Baker and the Black Freedom Movement: A Radical Democratic Vision* (Chapel Hill, N.C., 2003); John D'Emilio, *Lost Prophet: The Life and Times of Bayard Rustin* (New York, 2003); Thomas F. Jackson, *From Civil Rights to Human Rights: Martin Luther King, Jr., and the Struggle for Economic Justice* (Philadelphia, 2006).

xix **the fifteen most segregated:** Lewis Mumford Center for Comparative Urban and Regional Research, University at Albany, "Metropolitan Area Rankings: Population for All Ages: Sortable List of Dissimilarity Scores," mumford1 .dyndns.org/cen2000/WholePop/WPsort/sort_d1.html; Gary Orfield and Chung-mei Lee, *Racial Transformation and the Changing Nature of Segregation* (Cambridge, Mass., 2006), Table 11.

xix **"long civil rights movement":** Hall, "Long Civil Rights Movement," 1235.

xx **"in the North the white":** Alexis de Tocqueville, *Democracy in America*, vol. 1 [1835], trans. Arthur Goldhammer, ed. Olivier Zunz (New York, 2004), 396; Ira Berlin and Leslie Harris, eds., *Slavery in New York* (New York, 2005); Leon F. Litwack, *North of Slavery: The Negro in the Free States, 1790–1860* (New York, 1965).

xx **In the wake of the influx:** Eric Arnesen, *Black Protest and the Great Migration* (Boston, 2002); Gregory, *Southern Diaspora*; James R. Grossman, *Land of Hope: Chicago, Black Southerners, and the Great Migration* (Chicago, 1989); Nicholas Lemann, *The Promised Land: The Great Black Migration and How It Changed America* (New York, 1991); Joe W. Trotter, Jr., ed., *The Great Migration in Historical Perspective* (Bloomington, Ind., 1991); Kimberley L. Phillips, *AlabamaNorth: African-American Migrants, Community, and Working-Class Activism in Cleveland, 1915–45* (Urbana, Ill., 1999); Thomas J. Sugrue, *The Origins of the Urban Crisis: Race and Inequality in Postwar Detroit* (Princeton, N.J., 2005); Matthew Countryman, *Up South: Civil Rights and Black Power in Philadelphia* (Philadelphia, 2005); quote from L. D. Reddick, "What the Northern Negro Thinks About Democracy," *JES* 17 (1944), 296.

xxii **Contrary to the conventional story:** Shelby Steele, *White Guilt: How Blacks and Whites Together Destroyed the Promise of the Civil Rights Era* (New York, 2006); Stephan Thernstrom and Abigail Thernstrom, *America in Black and White: One Nation, Indivisible* (New York, 1997); Fred Siegel, *The Future Once Happened Here: New York, D.C., L.A., and the Future of America's Big Cities* (New York, 2000); Thomas and Mary Edsall, *Chain Reaction: The Impact of Race, Rights, and Taxes on American Politics* (New York, 1991); Tamar Jacoby, *Someone Else's House: America's Unfinished Struggle for Integration* (New York, 2000); for alternatives, see Philip A. Klinkner with Rogers M. Smith, *The Unsteady March: The Rise and Decline of Racial Equality in America* (Chicago,

1999); and Michael K. Brown et al., *Whitewashing Race: The Myth of a Color-Blind Society* (Berkeley, Calif., 2003).

xxiii **"Color is not a human":** James Baldwin, *The Fire Next Time* (New York, 1963), 102.

xxiv **"white noose":** "Philadelphia's New Problem," *Time*, Feb. 2, 1958.

xxiv **Several currents:** On this point, see especially Michael C. Dawson, *Black Visions: The Roots of Contemporary African-American Political Ideologies* (Chicago, 2001).

xxvii **collective efforts to accomplish change:** Charles Payne, *I've Got the Light of Freedom* (Berkeley, Calif., 1995).

CHAPTER 1 | "SWEET LAND OF LIBERTY"

3 **"And this will be the day":** Martin Luther King, Jr., "We Shall Overcome," Speech to the March on Washington, Aug. 24, 1963.

3 **Anna Arnold Hedgeman:** Anna Arnold Hedgeman, *The Trumpet Sounds: A Memoir of Negro Leadership* (New York, 1964), 172–73, 176–80; Dorothy Height, "'We Wanted the Voice of a Woman to Be Heard': Black Women and the 1963 March on Washington," in Bettye Collier-Thomas and V. P. Franklin, eds., *Sisters in the Struggle: African American Women in the Civil Rights–Black Power Movement* (New York, 2001), 83–91; James F. Findlay, Jr., *Church People in the Struggle: The National Council of Churches and the Black Freedom Movement, 1950–1970* (New York, 1993), 50; John D'Emilio, *Lost Prophet: The Life and Times of Bayard Rustin* (New York, 2003), 351–52.

5 **raised in Anoka, Minnesota:** Hedgeman, *The Trumpet Sounds*, 7–9; USCB, *Thirteenth Census of the United States: Population*, vol. 2 (Washington, D.C., 1910), 996; USCB, *Fourteenth Census of the United States: Population*, vol. 3 (Washington, D.C., 1920), 519; Jennifer Delton, *Making Minnesota Liberal: Civil Rights and the Transformation of the Democratic Party* (Minneapolis, 2002), 62.

6 **"The most regrettable and almost tragic feature":** Roy Wilkins, "Minnesota: Seat of Satisfaction," *Messenger* (May 1924), reprinted in Tom Lutz and Susanna Ashton, eds., *These "Colored" United States: African American Essays from the 1920s* (New Brunswick, N.J., 1996), 169–73; Hedgeman, *The Trumpet Sounds*, 12; David Vassar Taylor, *African Americans in Minnesota* (St. Paul, 2002), 28–39.

6 **In the 1920s, blacks faced:** Robert M. Fogelson, *Bourgeois Nightmares: Suburbia, 1870–1930* (New Haven, Conn., 2005), 95–103, 125–28; Kenneth T. Jackson, *The Ku Klux Klan in the City* (New York, 1968); Leonard J. Moore, *Citizen Klansmen: The Ku Klux Klan in Indiana, 1921–1928* (Chapel Hill, N.C., 1991).

6 **she took a teaching job:** Hedgeman, *The Trumpet Sounds*, 23, 27; generally see David Tyack, *The One Best System: A History of American Urban Education* (Cambridge, Mass., 1974), 225–28; *NYT*, Jan. 26, 1990; on Rust College, see

James Farmer, *Lay Bare the Heart: An Autobiography of the Civil Rights Movement* (New York, 1985), 34, 37–40, quote 37. James Farmer was a toddler when Hedgeman was at Rust: he was born in 1920.

7 **the YWCA movement:** Janine Marie Denomme, " 'To End This Day of Strife': Churchwomen and the Campaign for Integration, 1920–1970" (Ph.D. diss., University of Pennsylvania, 2001); Nancy Marie Robertson, *Christian Sisterhood, Race Relations, and the YWCA, 1906–46* (Urbana, Ill., 2007); Judith Weisenfeld, *African American Women and Christian Activism: New York's Black YWCA, 1905–1945* (Cambridge, Mass., 1997).

7 **a still-tentative religious interracialist movement:** Roger Axford to Pauli Murray, Aug. 17, 1943, in PMP, Box 102, Folder 1840; Findlay, *Church People in the Struggle*, 18–19; Ronald C. White, Jr., *Liberty and Justice for All: Racial Reform and the Social Gospel (1877–1925)* (Philadelphia, 2002), 257–60; "Upon this Rock: Race Relations Sunday—A Quarter of a Century," *INS* (Sept.–Oct. 1946), 4.

8 **Haltingly, they began to demand:** Denomme, " 'To End This Day of Strife' "; see also White, *Liberty and Justice for All.*

8 **a politics of respectability and race uplift:** Evelyn Brooks Higginbotham, *Righteous Discontent: The Women's Movement in the Black Baptist Church, 1880–1920* (Cambridge, Mass., 1993); Kevin K. Gaines, *Uplifting the Race: Black Leadership, Politics, and Culture in the Twentieth Century* (Chapel Hill, N.C., 1996); Robert S. Gregg, *Sparks from the Anvil of Oppression: Philadelphia's African Methodists and Southern Migrants, 1890–1940* (Philadelphia, 1993); Joe William Trotter, *Black Milwaukee: The Making of an Industrial Proletariat, 1915–1945* (Urbana, Ill., 1985), 123–24, 127–29; Nina Mjagkij, *Light in the Darkness: African Americans and the YMCA, 1852–1946* (Lexington, Ky., 2003).

9 **Black women such as Arnold:** Higginbotham, *Righteous Discontent*; Darlene Clark Hine, "Black Migration to the Urban Midwest: The Gender Dimension, 1915–1945," in Joe William Trotter, Jr., ed., *The Great Migration in Historical Perspective* (Bloomington, Ind., 1991), 127–46; and Hine, " 'We Specialize in the Wholly Impossible': The Philanthropic Work of Black Women," in Kathleen D. McCarthy, ed., *Lady Bountiful Revisited: Women, Philanthropy, and Power* (New Brunswick, N.J., 1990), 70–93.

9 **One of the most established women's groups:** There is an extensive literature on black women's clubs. See especially Beverly Jones, *Quest for Equality* (New York, 1990); Elsa Barkley Brown, "Womanist Consciousness," *Signs* 14 (1989), 610–33; Dorothy Salem, *To Better Our World* (New York, 1990); Deborah Gray White, *Too Heavy a Load: Black Women in Defense of Themselves, 1894–1994* (New York, 1999); V. P. Franklin and Bettye Collier-Thomas, "For the Race in General and Black Women in Particular: The Civil Rights Activities of African American Women's Organizations, 1915–1950," in Collier-Thomas and Franklin, eds., *Sisters in the Struggle*, 21–41; Salem, "NCNW," in Darlene Clark Hine et al., eds., *Black Women in America* (Bloomington, Ind., 1993).

10 **The Great Migration gave a real sense:** Victoria Wolcott, *Remaking Respectability: African American Women in Interwar Detroit* (Chapel Hill, N.C., 2001), 68–72; Elizabeth Lasch-Quinn, *Black Neighbors: Race and the Limits of Reform in the American Settlement House Movement, 1890–1945* (Chapel Hill, N.C., 1993), 131–50.

11 **The Springfield school controversy:** Jackson, *The Ku Klux Klan in the City*, 239; August Meier and Elliott Rudwick, "Early Boycotts of Segregated Schools: The Case of Springfield, Ohio, 1922–23," *AQ* 20 (1968), 744–58; William Wayne Griffin, *African Americans and the Color Line in Ohio, 1915–1930* (Columbus, Ohio, 2005), 44, 117–18, 179–80; Davison M. Douglas, *Jim Crow Moves North: The Battle over Northern School Segregation, 1865–1954* (New York, 2005), 214–16; Wendell P. Dabney, "Ohio—Past and Present," *Messenger* (April 1925), in Lutz and Ashton, *These "Colored" United States*, 222–24.

12 **"There were no signs":** Hedgeman, *The Trumpet Sounds*, 30–34.

12 **"The North and the South":** Hedgeman, *The Trumpet Sounds*, 31, 36, 37, 39; on laundry work, see Herbert R. Northrup, *Organized Labor and the Negro* (New York, 1944), 132; Ethel L. Best and Ethel Erickson, "A Survey of Laundries and Their Women Workers in Twenty-Three Cities," USDL Women's Bureau, *Bulletin* 78 (1930); Arwen Mohun, *Steam Laundries: Gender, Technology, and Work in the United States and Great Britain, 1880–1940* (Baltimore, 1999), esp. ch. 7; *NYT*, Feb. 12, 1949.

12 **No place was more exciting:** Gilbert Osofsky, *Harlem: The Making of a Ghetto: Negro New York, 1890–1930* (New York, 1971); David Levering Lewis, *When Harlem Was in Vogue* (New York, 1982); Nathan Irvin Huggins, *Harlem Renaissance* (New York, 1971); George Hutchinson, *The Harlem Renaissance in Black and White* (Cambridge, Mass., 1995).

13 **The Harlem YWCA:** Hedgeman, *The Trumpet Sounds*, 47–52; White, *Too Heavy a Load*, 129–30; Weisenfeld, *African American Women and Christian Activism*, 163–65, 169; *CD*, Aug. 6, 1932.

13 **Arnold also reveled:** Hedgeman, *The Trumpet Sounds*, 46–47, 66; Sondra Kathryn Wilson, *Meet Me at the Theresa: The Story of Harlem's Most Famous Hotel* (New York, 2004), 115.

13 **in Depression-era Harlem:** Clyde V. Kiser, "Diminishing Family Income: A Possible Cause of the Harlem Riot," *Opportunity*, May 1935, 171–73; Cheryl Greenberg, *"Or Does It Explode?": Black Harlem in the Great Depression* (New York, 1991); Hedgeman, *The Trumpet Sounds*, 55–57.

14 **Many southern migrants:** Steven Hahn, *A Nation Under Our Feet: Black Political Struggles in the Rural South from Slavery to the Great Migration* (Cambridge, Mass., 2003), 468–74.

15 **"No more fear":** Garvey quoted in Lawrence Levine, "Marcus Garvey and the Politics of Revitalization," in John Hope Franklin and August Meier, eds., *Black Leaders of the Twentieth Century* (Urbana, Ill., 1982), 117–18.

15 **Garvey offered a powerful:** Robert A. Hill, ed., *The Marcus Garvey and Uni-*

versal Negro Improvement Association Papers, vol. 1 (Berkeley, Calif., 1983), xxxv–cxvii; E. David Cronon, *Black Moses: The Story of Marcus Garvey and the Universal Negro Improvement Association* (Madison, Wis., 1955); Tony Martin, *Race First: The Ideological and Organizational Struggles of Marcus Garvey and the Universal Negro Improvement Association* (Westport, Conn., 1976); Judith Stein, *The World of Marcus Garvey: Race and Class in Modern Society* (Baton Rouge, La., 1986).

16 **Many former Garvey supporters:** Audley Moore, OH, by Cheryl Townsend Gilkes, June 6, 8, 1978, *BWOHP;* vol. 8, 123. Mark Naison, *Communists in Harlem During the Depression* (Urbana, Ill., 1983), 50, 100–1. The role of the UNIA in the North remains understudied. See, for example, Trotter, *Black Milwaukee,* 125, 134.

16 **Separatist politics:** Michael A. Gomez, *Black Crescent: The Experience and Legacy of African Muslims in the Americas* (New York, 2005), 203–75.

17 **In rapidly growing urban black neighborhoods:** Kenneth T. Kusmer, "The Black Urban Experience in American History," in Darlene Clark Hine, ed., *The State of Afro-American History* (Baton Rouge, La., 1986); Johnson quoted in *AD,* 808.

17 **Even Hedgeman found herself:** *NYT,* July 31, 1966; Anna Arnold Hedgeman, OH, by Katherine Shannon, Aug. 27, 1968, tape 2 transcript, 32, RJB.

17 **"It actually suggests":** Hedgeman, *The Trumpet Sounds,* 51–53.

18 **Founded in 1909:** Most useful are Charles F. Kellogg, *NAACP: A History of the National Association for the Advancement of Colored People* (Baltimore, 1967); Gilbert Jonas, *Freedom's Sword: The NAACP and the Struggle Against Racism in America, 1909–1969* (New York, 2004); Manfred Berg, *"The Ticket to Freedom": The NAACP and the Struggle for Black Political Integration* (Gainesville, Fla., 2005); Kenneth Janken, *White: The Biography of Walter White, Mr. NAACP* (New York, 2003).

18 **The "Young Turks":** See esp. Beth Tompkins Bates, "A New Crowd Challenges the Agenda of the Old Guard in the NAACP, 1933–1941," *AHR* 102 (1997), 340–77.

19 **In August 1933, she joined:** *CD,* Sept. 9, 1933; W.E.B. Du Bois, "Youth and Age at Amenia," *Crisis,* Oct. 1933, 226–27; generally, see Jonathan Scott Holloway, *Confronting the Veil: Abram Harris, Jr., E. Franklin Frazier, and Ralph Bunche, 1919–1941* (Chapel Hill, N.C., 2002), 4–16; David Levering Lewis, *W.E.B. Du Bois: The Fight for Equality and the American Century, 1919–1963* (New York, 2000), 317–24; Raymond Wolters, *Negroes and the Great Depression: The Problem of Economic Recovery* (Westport, Conn., 1970), 219–29.

19 **"I found myself making decisions":** Hedgeman, *The Trumpet Sounds,* 57; Greenberg, *"Or Does It Explode?,"* 65–92.

19 **Fired up by a desire:** Hedgeman, *The Trumpet Sounds,* 56–57; Hedgeman worked briefly in 1933 and 1934 at a YWCA in Philadelphia; Weisenfeld, *African American Women and Christian Activism,* 178–79.

20 **Blacks were disproportionately represented:** Richard Sterner, *The Negro's*

Share: A Study of Income, Consumption, Housing, and Public Assistance (New York, 1943), 220, 222, 412.

20 **jumping from the GOP onto the Roosevelt bandwagon:** There is a large literature on blacks and the New Deal. Indispensable are Harvard Sitkoff, *A New Deal for Blacks* (New York, 1978); Wolters, *Negroes and the Great Depression;* Nancy M. Weiss, *Farewell to the Party of Lincoln: Black Politics in the Age of FDR* (Princeton, N.J., 1983); John B. Kirby, *Black Americans in the Roosevelt Era* (Knoxville, Tenn., 1980); Patricia Sullivan, *Days of Hope: Race and Democracy in the New Deal Era* (Chapel Hill, N.C., 1996); Robert C. Lieberman, *Shifting the Color Line: Race and the American Welfare State* (Cambridge, Mass., 1999); and Mary Poole, *The Segregated Origins of Social Security* (Chapel Hill, N.C., 2006).

21 **maternalist belief in the power of uplift:** *NYT,* March 29, 1954; Linda Gordon, "Black and White Visions of Welfare: Women's Welfare Activism, 1890–1945," *JAH* 78 (1991), 559–90. Hedgeman was one of sixty-nine black women studied by Gordon.

21 **"protesting the lack of jobs":** Hedgeman, *The Trumpet Sounds,* 67; Dorothy I. Height, OH, by Polly Cowan, various dates, 1974–76, *BWOHP,* vol. 5, 57.

22 **The secular left in the United States:** Doug Rossinow, *The Left Liberal Tradition in America* (Philadelphia, 2007); Michael Denning, *The Cultural Front: The Laboring of American Culture in the Twentieth Century* (London, 1997), 4–21; Mark Naison, "Remaking America: Communists and Liberals in the Popular Front," in Michael E. Brown et al., eds. *New Studies in the Politics and Culture of U.S. Communism* (New York, 1993), 45–73.

23 **"The Party":** Adam Clayton Powell, Jr., *Marching Blacks* (New York, 1945), 68–69; "Negro Editors on Communism: A Symposium of the American Negro Press," *Crisis,* April 1932, 117–19, 154–56. Naison, *Communists in Harlem;* Mark Solomon, *The Cry Was Unity: Communists and African Americans, 1917–1936* (Jackson, Miss., 1998); Robin D. G. Kelley, *Freedom Dreams: The Black Radical Imagination* (Boston, 2002), 44–51.

23 **the CP directed its energies toward the South:** Glenda Elizabeth Gilmore, *Defying Dixie: The Radical Roots of Civil Rights, 1919–1950* (New York, 2008); Robin D. G. Kelley, *Hammer and Hoe: Alabama Communists During the Great Depression* (Chapel Hill, N.C., 1990); Dan T. Carter, *Scottsboro: A Tragedy of the American South* (Baton Rouge, La., 1969); James Goodman, *Stories of Scottsboro* (New York, 1995).

24 **Unemployed Councils:** Daniel Leab, "'United We Eat': The Creation and Organization of the Unemployed Councils in 1930," *LH* 8 (1967); Roy Rosenzweig, "Organizing the Unemployed: The Early Years of the Great Depression," *RA* 10 (1976), 37–60.

24 **Key to the strategy was coalition building:** Naison, *Communists in Harlem,* 169–72; Ford, quoted in Wilson Record, *The Negro and the Communist Party* (Chapel Hill, N.C., 1951), 135; Audley Moore, OH, by Cheryl Townsend Gilkes, June 6, 8, 1978, in *BWOHP,* vol. 8; *CD,* Aug. 9, 1941, Jan. 1, 1944.

25 **Party members were tireless:** Naison, *Communists in Harlem;* Sitkoff, *A New Deal for Blacks,* 139–68; Martha Biondi, *To Stand and Fight: The Struggle for Civil Rights in Postwar New York City* (Cambridge, Mass., 2003); and for a rich debate about the Communist Party and race, see Eric Arnesen, "No 'Graver Danger': Black Anticommunism, the Communist Party, and the Race Question," *Labor* 3 (2006), 13–52, with responses by John Earl Haynes, Kenneth Janken, Martha Biondi, Carol Anderson, Arnesen, ibid., 53–79.

25 **debated the relationship of racial and class solidarity:** Max Schactman, *Race and Revolution* (1933), ed. Christopher Phelps (New York, 2003); George Breitman, ed., *Leon Trotsky on Black Nationalism and Self-Determination* (New York, 1967); Scott McLemee, ed., *C.L.R. James on the Negro Question* (Jackson, Miss., 1996).

26 **shared a broad, international perspective:** Penny von Eschen, *Race Against Empire* (Ithaca, N.Y., 1997); William R. Scott, *The Sons of Sheba's Race: African-Americans and the Italo-Ethiopian War, 1935–41* (Bloomington, Ind., 1993); Naison, *Communists in Harlem,* 173–77; Michael Thurston, " 'Bombed in Spain': Langston Hughes, the Black Press, and the Spanish Civil War," in Todd Vogel, ed., *The Black Press: New Literary and Historical Essays* (New Brunswick, N.J., 2001), 140–58; Roi Ottley, *New World A-Coming: Inside Black America* (Boston, 1942), 285; David Anthony, *Max Yergan: Race Man, Internationalist, Cold Warrior* (New York, 2006).

27 **"The majority of the miserably poor":** Hedgeman, *The Trumpet Sounds,* 67, 88–89; Mark Stern, "Poverty and Family Composition," in Michael B. Katz, ed., *The "Underclass" Debate: Views from History* (Princeton, N.J., 1993), 234. Figure from 1940 census, USDL, Women's Bureau, *Negro Women War Workers,* Bulletin 205 (Washington, D.C., 1946), 18; Evelyn Macon, OH, by Vivian Morris (1939), in Ann Banks, ed., *First-Person America* (New York, 1980), 126; Mohun, *Steam Laundries,* 175–77; Jacqueline Jones, *Labor of Love, Labor of Sorrow: Black Women, Work, and the Family from the Civil War to the Present* (New York, 1985), 217–20.

27 **In 1935, Baker paired up:** Ella Baker and Marvel Cooke, "The Bronx Slave Market," *Crisis,* Nov. 1935, 330; Barbara Ransby, *Ella Baker and the Black Freedom Movement: A Radical Democratic Vision* (Chapel Hill, N.C., 2003), 70–78.

28 **Hedgeman joined in the challenge:** Hedgeman, *The Trumpet Sounds,* 68–69; Weisenfeld, *African American Women and Christian Activism,* 180–81; generally, Phyllis Palmer, *Domesticity and Dirt: Housewives and Domestic Servants in the United States, 1920–45* (Philadelphia, 1989), esp. ch. 4; and Elizabeth Clark-Lewis, *Living In, Living Out* (Washington, D.C., 1994).

28 **executive director of the Brooklyn Y:** *NYAN,* March 5, 1938, May 13, 1939, May 3, 1941; Hedgeman, *The Trumpet Sounds,* 74–79; Erik Gellman, "Death Blow to Jim Crow: The National Negro Congress, 1936–1947" (Ph.D. diss., Northwestern University, 2006), 199–200. Hedgeman appeared on the Brooklyn NNC letterhead as late as 1940. Communication with Erik Gellman, Oct. 13, 2006.

28 **militant protests:** *NYAN*, April 16, 1938, April 27, Nov. 23, 1940; August Meier and Elliott Rudwick, *Along the Color Line: Explorations in the Black Experience* (Urbana, Ill., 1976), 314–32; Trotter, *Black Milwaukee*, 125–27, 134–35; Richard W. Thomas, *Life for Us Is What We Make It: Building Black Community in Detroit, 1915–1945* (Bloomington, Ind., 1992), 194–201; Andor Skotnes, "'Buy Where You Can Work': Boycotting for Jobs in African-American Baltimore, 1933–34," *Journal of Social History* 27 (1994), 735–62.

29 **"symbol of revolt":** Hedgeman, *The Trumpet Sounds*, 74, 75, 79.

29 **"Although all women":** *CD*, May 17, 1941; *NYAN*, Aug. 9, 1941.

30 **During the war:** *NYT*, Jan. 22, March 22, Aug. 4, 1942, Sept. 26, 1943, Feb. 12, 1949, Jan. 26, 1990.

30 **"Negroes may differ":** Roi Ottley, "Negro Morale," *TNR*, Nov. 10, 1941, 614.

CHAPTER 2 | "PRESSURE, MORE PRESSURE AND STILL MORE PRESSURE"

32 **"Dear Fellow Negro Americans":** Randolph, quoted in Philip A. Klinkner with Rogers M. Smith, *The Unsteady March: The Rise and Decline of Racial Equality in America* (Chicago, 1999), 156.

32 **To propose a mass march of blacks:** Lucy Barber, *Marching on Washington: The Forging of an American Political Tradition* (Berkeley, Calif., 2002), 108–40.

33 **"enlisted great sections":** Wilkins quoted in Raymond Wolters, *Negroes and the Great Depression: The Problem of Economic Recovery* (Westport, Conn., 1970), 59; Lester Granger, "The National Negro Congress—An Interpretation," *Opportunity*, May 1936, 151–53; Wilson Record, *The Negro and the Communist Party* (Chapel Hill, N.C., 1951), 153–62.

33 **In its first three years:** Patricia Sullivan, *Days of Hope: Race and Democracy in the New Deal Era* (Chapel Hill, N.C., 1996); Mark Solomon, *The Cry Was Unity: Communists and African Americans, 1917–1936* (Oxford, Miss., 1998), 234–37, 301–4.

34 **"No black workers can be free":** *Resolutions of the National Negro Congress Held in Chicago, Ill., Feb. 14, 15, 16, 1936* (Washington, D.C., 1936), 7–12. Randolph missed the first NNC meeting because of illness; his speech was read to the delegates; *CD*, Feb. 22, 1936.

34 **made unionization a hard sell:** Horace S. Cayton and George S. Mitchell, *Black Workers and the New Unions* (Chapel Hill, N.C., 1939); Bruce Nelson, *Divided We Stand: American Workers and the Struggle for Black Equality* (Princeton, N.J., 2001), 174; August Meier and Elliott Rudwick, *Black Detroit and the Rise of the UAW* (New York, 1979); Thomas J. Sugrue, *The Origins of the Urban Crisis: Race and Inequality in Postwar Detroit* (Princeton, N.J., 1996), 25–26.

35 **the fledgling Congress of Industrial Organizations:** The literature on blacks and the CIO is extensive. Indispensable overviews are Herbert Northrup, *Organized Labor and the Negro* (New York, 1944), esp. 172–231; Robert C. Weaver, *Negro Labor a National Problem* (New York, 1946); Robert H. Zieger, *The CIO,*

1935–55 (Chapel Hill, N.C., 1995), 79–80, 83–85. Invaluable specialized studies include Meier and Rudwick, *Black Detroit;* Eric Arnesen, *Brotherhoods of Color: Black Railroad Workers and the Struggle for Equality* (Cambridge, Mass., 2001); Nelson, *Divided We Stand;* Ruth Needleman, *Black Freedom Fighters in Steel: The Struggle for Democratic Unionism* (Ithaca, N.Y., 2003); Rick Halpern, *Down on the Killing Floor: Black and White Workers in Chicago's Packinghouses, 1904–54* (Urbana, Ill., 1997), esp. 96–129; Roger Horowitz, *"Negro and White, Unite and Fight!" A Social History of Industrial Unionism in Meatpacking, 1930–90* (Urbana, Ill., 1997).

35   **A bellwether of change:** *AD,* 840–41, 1408; Arvarh E. Strickland, *History of the Chicago Urban League* (Urbana, Ill., 1966), 59–60; on the Young Turks, see Jonathan Scott Holloway, *Confronting the Veil: Abram Harris, Jr., E. Franklin Frazier, and Ralph Bunche, 1919–1941* (Chapel Hill, N.C., 2002).

36   **"preach an economic and social gospel":** *CD,* Feb. 28, 1936. A few religious leaders expressed concerns about the leftist taint of the NNC, but they were, for a time, a minority.

36   **"Let us build":** A. Philip Randolph, "The Crisis of the Negro and the Constitution," *Official Proceedings, Second Negro Congress,* 1937, reprinted in Francis Broderick and August Meier, eds., *Negro Protest Thought in the Twentieth Century* (Indianapolis, 1965), 183, 187; Kenneth Robert Janken, *White: The Biography of Walter White, Mr. NAACP* (New York, 2003), 228–31; *NYT,* Feb. 11, 1938.

37   **"slaves of many kinds":** *CD,* Feb. 19, 1938.

37   **the NNC had robust chapters:** Halpern, *Down on the Killing Floor,* 160; Meier and Rudwick, *Black Detroit,* 29, 55–56; Nelson, *Divided We Stand,* 190–192, 202; Beth T. Bates, *Pullman Porters and the Rise of Black Protest Politics in America, 1920–1945* (Chapel Hill, N.C., 2001), 138–42; Lawrence Wittner, "The National Negro Congress: A Reassessment," *AQ* 22 (1970), 883–901; Mark Naison, *Communists in Harlem During the Depression* (Urbana, Ill., 1983), 169–92; Wolters, *Negroes and the Great Depression,* 361; James Wolfinger, *Philadelphia Divided: Race and Politics in the City of Brotherly Love* (Chapel Hill, N.C., 2007), 70–77; Erik Gellman, "'Death Blow to Jim Crow': The National Negro Congress, 1936–1947" (Ph.D. diss., Northwestern University, 2006).

38   **its staunch antifascism:** William R. Scott, *The Sons of Sheba's Race: African-Americans and the Italo-Ethiopian War, 1935–41* (Bloomington, Ind., 1993); Naison, *Communists in Harlem,* 173–77; Michael Thurston, "'Bombed in Spain': Langston Hughes, the Black Press, and the Spanish Civil War," in Todd Vogel, ed., *The Black Press: New Literary and Historical Essays* (New Brunswick, N.J., 2001), 140–58; Roi Ottley, *New World A-Coming: Inside Black America* (Boston, 1942), 285–87.

39   **Torn asunder by its rigid adherence:** *AD,* 817–19, 1401; Record, *The Negro and the Communist Party,* 153–62, 191–99, 248–49; Erik S. Gellman, "'Carthage Must Be Destroyed': Race, City Politics, and the Campaign to Inte-

grate Chicago Transportation Work, 1929–1943," *Labor* 2 (2005), 100–2, argues that the Chicago NNC remained vital after 1940. For a revision of the NNC-Randolph split and a discussion of the NNC's wartime efforts, see Gellman, "'Death Blow to Jim Crow,'" 175–86.

39 **"The organization, led":** St. Clair Drake and Horace R. Cayton, *Black Metropolis: A Study of Negro Life in a Northern City* (New York, 1945), 737–39; Strickland, *History of the Chicago Urban League*, 132–33; Gellman, "'Carthage Must Be Destroyed,'" 92–93.

39 **"the NAACP does not have a mass basis":** Bunche, quoted in Wolters, *Negroes and the Great Depression*, 357; Holloway, *Confronting the Veil*, 94–100; Beth Tompkins Bates, "A New Crowd Challenges the Agenda of the Old Guard in the NAACP, 1933–1941," *AHR* 102 (1997), 340–77.

40 **In Detroit, for example:** Meier and Rudwick, *Black Detroit*, 80–82, 91–92; for another example of prounion activism, see James Wolfinger, "'We Are in the Front Lines of the Battle for Democracy': Carolyn Moore and Black Activism in World War II Philadelphia," *PH* 72 (2005), 1–23.

40 **The NAACP's grassroots insurgency paid off:** E. Franklin Frazier, *The Negro in the United States* (New York, 1949), 507; Manfred Berg, *"The Ticket to Freedom": The NAACP and the Struggle for Black Political Integration* (Gainesville, Fla., 2005), 109–10.

41 **No one had played a more important role:** The scholarship on Randolph is too extensive for full citation here. For useful overviews, see Jervis Anderson, *A. Philip Randolph* (New York, 1972); Paula E. Pfeffer, *A. Philip Randolph: Pioneer of the Civil Rights Movement* (Baton Rouge, La., 1990); Benjamin Quarles, "A. Philip Randolph: Labor Leader at Large," in August Meier and Elliott Rudwick, eds., *Black Leaders of the Twentieth Century* (Urbana, Ill., 1982), 139–66; Eric Arnesen, "A. Philip Randolph: Labor and the New Black Politics," in Arnesen, ed., *The Human Tradition in American Labor History* (Wilmington, Del., 2004), 173–91; Bates, *Pullman Porters*.

41 **"what the Negro worker wants and needs":** Norman Thomas and Oscar DePriest, "The Future of the Black Vote," *Crisis*, Feb. 1931, 45; *NYT*, Oct. 10, 1937; Harvard Sitkoff, *A New Deal for Blacks* (New York, 1978), 161–66.

42 **In 1936, the Socialist Party:** Harry Fleischman, "Workers Defense League," in Mari Jo Buhle et al., eds., *Encyclopedia of the American Left*, 2nd ed. (New York, 1998), 897–98; Aron S. Gilmartin, "Workers Defense League, 1936–1946," in James Peck, ed., *Workers Defense League, Tenth Anniversary Journal* (1946), in SCCF, 005-869. See also chapter 7 below.

42 **advocates of the "Social Gospel":** Ralph E. Luker, *The Social Gospel in Black and White, 1885–1912* (Chapel Hill, N.C., 1998); Ronald C. White, Jr., *Liberty and Justice for All: Racial Reform and the Social Gospel (1877–1925)* (Philadelphia, 2002); Paul A. Carter, *The Decline and Revival of the Social Gospel: Social and Political Liberalism in American Protestant Churches, 1920–40* (Ithaca, N.Y., 1954).

42 **religious and secular leftists found:** James Tracy, *Direct Action: Radical Paci-*

fism from the Union Seven to the Chicago Eight (Chicago, 1996), 14–15; John D'Emilio, *Lost Prophet: The Life and Times of Bayard Rustin* (New York, 2003), 39–71.

43 **Haltingly, they found themselves:** Robert T. Handy, "The American Religious Depression, 1925–1935," *Church History* (March 1960), 3–16; David W. Wills, "An Enduring Distance: Black Americans and the Establishment," in William Hutchinson, ed., *Between the Times: The Travails of the Protestant Establishment in America, 1900–1960* (New York, 1989), 168–92; James F. Findlay, Jr., *Church People in the Struggle: The National Council of Churches and the Black Freedom Movement, 1950–1970* (New York, 1993), 5–6.

43 **a shared "here and now" commitment:** White, *Liberty and Justice for All;* Thomas F. Jackson, *From Civil Rights to Human Rights: Martin Luther King, Jr., and the Struggle for Economic Justice* (Philadelphia, 2006), 25–50.

44 **Randolph's alliance:** Clarence Taylor, *Black Religious Intellectuals: The Fight for Equality from Jim Crow to the 21st Century* (New York, 2002), 11–36; Cynthia Taylor, *A. Philip Randolph: The Religious Journey of an African American Labor Leader* (New York, 2006).

44 **But for blacks:** Richard Sterner, *The Negro's Share: A Study of Income, Consumption, Housing, and Public Assistance* (New York, 1943), 363.

45 **"Well-nigh 99 and 9⁄10 percent":** A. Philip Randolph, "March on Washington Movement Presents Program for Negro," in Rayford Logan, ed., *What the Negro Wants* (Chapel Hill, N.C., 1944), 140.

45 **"To have a 'sense of belonging'":** Ida Coker Clark, "Negro Woman Worker: What Now?," *Opportunity*, Spring 1944; Megan Taylor Shockley, *"We, Too, Are Americans": African American Women in Detroit and Richmond, 1940–54* (Urbana, Ill., 2004), 130.

46 **The NNC belatedly joined:** "The National Negro Congress Supports 'March on Washington' July 1st, 1941," in SCCF, 002-968-1.

46 **"There was every temptation":** Lester B. Granger, "The President, the Negro, and Defense," *Opportunity*, July 1941, 204–7; *BAA*, May 25, 1940; Herbert Garfinkel, *When Negroes March* (Glencoe, Ill., 1959), 33; Daniel Kryder, *Divided Arsenal: Race and the American State During World War II* (New York, 2000), 42–44, 46–47.

47 **"not to intermingle colored and white":** *CD*, Oct. 5, 19, 1940; Anderson, *A. Philip Randolph*, 244, 247–49; Garfinkel, *When Negroes March*, 34.

47 **"National Defense Day":** *NAACP 32nd Annual Report, 1941* (New York, 1942), 38. (The day was Jan. 26, 1941.) Lester B. Granger, "The President, the Negro, and Defense," *Opportunity*, July 1941, 204–7; "The Unprivileged One-Tenth," *TNR*, May 19, 1941, 681; Beulah Amidon, "Negroes and Defense," *SG* (June 1941), 321–26, 359; Walter White, "It's Our Country Too," *SEP*, Dec. 14, 1940, 27ff.

47 **the black press:** E. Franklin Frazier, *The Negro in the United States* (New York, 1949), 512–16, quote 515; Kevin Mumford, "Double V in New Jersey: African-American Civic Culture and Rising Consciousness Against Jim Crow, 1938–

1966," *NJH* 119 (2001), 26; Thomas Sancton, "The Negro Press," *TNR*, April 26, 1943, 558.

48 **the politics of black editors and columnists:** Doxey A. Wilkerson, "The Negro Press," *JNE* 16 (1947), 511–31; *AD*, 47–48, 933; Lewis H. Fenderson, "The Negro Press as a Social Instrument," *JNE* 20 (1951), 181–88; interviews with John H. Murphy III, June 26, 1971, Cecil B. Newman, Aug. 26, 1971, Al Sweeney, June 22, 1972, in BJP; Pegler quoted in Ottley, *New World A-Coming*, 269; the best account of the white press and civil rights is Gene Roberts and Hank Klibanoff, *The Race Beat: The Press, the Civil Rights Struggle, and the Awakening of a Nation* (New York, 2006).

48 **The Sleeping Car Porters:** Bates, *Pullman Porters*; Arnesen, *Brotherhoods of Color*, 84–115; Melinda Chateauvert, *Marching Together: Women of the Brotherhood of Sleeping Car Porters* (Urbana, Ill., 1998); and Deborah Gray White, *Too Heavy a Load: Black Women in Defense of Themselves* (New York, 1999), 160–75.

49 **Randolph made no idle threat:** Anderson, *A. Philip Randolph*, 250–51; Pauli Murray, "Answers to Questionnaire on March on Washington Movement," n.d. [ca. 1955], in PMP, Box 73, Folder 1269.

49 **defection of blacks from the Republicans:** *NYT*, Oct. 26, 1936; Drake and Cayton, *Black Metropolis*, 355; Nancy M. Weiss, *Farewell to the Party of Lincoln: Black Politics in the Age of FDR* (Princeton, N.J., 1983), 272.

50 **The fate of the New Deal:** Ira Katznelson, *When Affirmative Action Was White* (New York, 2005); Robert Zangrando, *The NAACP Crusade Against Lynching* (Philadelphia, 1980).

50 **"Let Jesus lead you and Roosevelt feed you!":** Chicago minister, quoted in Drake and Cayton, *Black Metropolis*, 354; on shifting support for the GOP, see Weiss, *Farewell to the Party of Lincoln*, 29–33, 288.

50 **"For the first time in their lives":** "The Roosevelt Record," *Crisis*, Nov. 1940, 343; Sitkoff, *A New Deal for Blacks*, 66–70, 76–77; Allida M. Black, "Championing a Champion: Eleanor Roosevelt and the Marian Anderson 'Freedom Concert,'" *Presidential Studies Quarterly* 20 (1990), 719–36; Scott A. Sandage, "A Marble House Divided: The Lincoln Memorial, Civil Rights, and the Politics of Memory, 1939–63," in Charles M. Payne and Adam Green, eds., *Time Longer than Rope: A Century of African American Activism, 1850–1950* (New York, 2003), 499–506.

51 **Northern blacks had a mixed experience:** Charles S. Johnson, *Patterns of Negro Segregation* (New York, 1943), 36; Margaret Weir, *Politics and Jobs: The Boundaries of Employment Policy in the United States* (Princeton, N.J., 1992); Jill Quadagno, *The Transformation of Old Age Security: Class and Politics in the American Welfare State* (Chicago, 1988); Mary Poole, *The Segregated Origins of Social Security* (Chapel Hill, N.C., 2006).

52 **And their fate was left to local:** Ira Katznelson, Kim Geiger, and Daniel Kryder, "Limiting Liberalism: The Southern Veto in Congress, 1933–1950," *Political Science Quarterly* 108 (Sept. 1993), 283–306; Jill Quadagno, "From Old Age Assis-

tance to Supplemental Security Income: The Political Economy of Relief in the South, 1935–1972," in Margaret Weir, Ann Orloff, and Theda Skocpol, eds., *The Politics of Social Policy in the United States* (Princeton, N.J., 1988), 235–63; Bruce Schulman, *From Cotton Belt to Sunbelt: Federal Policy and the Economic Development of the South, 1938–1980* (New York, 1991); Alan Brinkley, "The New Deal and Southern Politics," in James C. Cobb and Michael Namorato, eds., *The New Deal and the South* (Jackson, Miss., 1984), 97–117; Robert C. Lieberman, *Shifting the Color Line: Race and the American Welfare State* (Cambridge, Mass., 1998), 7. On race and welfare, see also Jill Quadagno, *The Color of Welfare: How Racism Undermined the War on Poverty* (New York, 1994); Michael K. Brown, *Race, Money, and the Welfare State* (Ithaca, N.Y., 1999); for a skeptical analysis, see Gareth Davies and Martha Derthick, "Race and Social Welfare Policy: The Social Security Act of 1935," *Political Science Quarterly* 112 (1997), 217–35.

52 **Job relief programs:** Sterner, *The Negro's Share*, 222, 273, 276, 280, 283, 412.

52 **housing policies discriminated most overtly:** Gail Radford, *Modern Housing for America: Policy Struggles in the New Deal Era* (Chicago, 1996); Sitkoff, *A New Deal for Blacks*, 67–68; Kenneth T. Jackson, *Crabgrass Frontier: The Suburbanization of the United States* (New York, 1985); Arnold Hirsch, *Making the Second Ghetto: Race and Housing in Chicago, 1940–60* (New York, 1983); Sugrue, *The Origins of the Urban Crisis*, 56–88.

53 **the newly created Civil Liberties Unit:** Brian Balogh, Joanna Grisinger, and Philip Zelikow, "Making Democracy Work: A Brief History of Twentieth-Century Federal Executive Reorganization," Miller Center Working Paper in American Political Development, University of Virginia, July 22, 2002, chart 2; Risa Goluboff, *The Lost Promise of Civil Rights* (Cambridge, Mass., 2007).

53 **New Deal labor legislation:** Arnesen, *Brotherhoods of Color*, 86–87; Weiss, *Farewell to the Party of Lincoln*, 163–66; Dona Cooper Hamilton and Charles V. Hamilton, *The Dual Agenda: Race and Social Welfare Policies of Civil Rights Organizations* (New York, 1997), 33–34; Paul Moreno, *Black Americans and Organized Labor: A New History* (Baton Rouge, La., 2006), 171–73.

54 **"four freedoms":** *CD*, March 22, 1941; Franklin Delano Roosevelt, "Message to Congress on the State of the Union," Jan. 11, 1944, in *The Public Papers and Addresses of Franklin D. Roosevelt*, vol. 13 (New York, 1950), 41. On the centrality of notions of security to the New Deal, see Lizabeth Cohen, *Making a New Deal: Industrial Workers in Chicago, 1919–1939* (New York, 1990); generally see Elizabeth Borgwardt, *A New Deal for the World: America's Vision for Human Rights* (Cambridge, Mass., 2005).

55 **"We have had none":** *CD*, July 19, 1941.

55 **Above all, wartime sacrifice:** On the impact of war on rights, see especially Klinkner and Smith, *The Unsteady March*; Gary Gerstle, *American Crucible: Race and Nation in the Twentieth Century* (Princeton, N.J., 2001), 187–237.

55 **built momentum for the March:** Bates, *Pullman Porters*, 154–58.

55 **Randolph insisted:** "Negroes Committee to March on Washington for Equal Participation in National Defense," *Black Worker*, May 1941, reprinted in *RCR*,

vol. 1, 4; A. Philip Randolph, "March on Washington Movement Presents Program for the Negro," in Logan, ed., *What the Negro Wants*, 154–55.

56 **The movement ended up:** For a critical view of Randolph's decision to keep the March on Washington Movement all black, see Murray, "Answers to Questionnaire"; see also Bates, *Pullman Porters*, 167–71.

56 **Fearful of the specter:** Barber, *Marching on Washington*, 75–107, 115.

57 **On June 25:** Franklin D. Roosevelt, "Executive Order No. 8802," June 25, 1941, in *The Public Papers and Addresses of Franklin D. Roosevelt*, vol. 10 (New York, 1950), 233–37; Anderson, *A. Philip Randolph*, 252–59; *Militant*, July 5, 12, 1941, reprinted in C. L. R. James et al., *Fighting Racism in World War II* (New York, 1980), 147, 149; *NYAN*, July 5, 1941; *CD*, July 12, 1941.

57 **"Throughout the urban areas":** Roi Ottley, "Negro Morale," *TNR*, Nov. 10, 1941, reprinted in *RCR*, vol. 1, 5; Kryder, *Divided Arsenal*, 67.

CHAPTER 3 | "1776 FOR THE NEGRO"

59 **Gunnar Myrdal's *An American Dilemma*:** *CD*, Jan. 29, 1944; David Southern, *Gunnar Myrdal and Black-White Relations: The Use and Abuse of "An American Dilemma," 1944–1969* (Baton Rouge, La., 1987); Walter Jackson, *Gunnar Myrdal and America's Conscience: Social Engineering and Racial Liberalism, 1938–1987* (Chapel Hill, N.C., 1990).

59 **For those unwilling:** *ND*, Dec. 1943; *CD*, Sept. 2, 1944; Maxwell S. Stewart, *The Negro in America* (New York, 1944).

60 **"*The Negro problem*":** *AD*, xlii, xliii. I have removed the italics with the exception of the first line.

60 **Myrdal had relatively little:** Jackson, *Gunnar Myrdal and America's Conscience*, 127–30.

61 **"have not acquired":** *AD*, 601.

61 **"White Northerners":** *AD*, 600.

61 **"fought with education":** *AD*, 1010.

61 **"We foresee that the trend":** *AD*, 1011. I borrow the metaphor of "South Africa" and "Sweden" from an unpublished talk by Ira Katznelson. Generally, see Ira Katznelson, *When Affirmative Action Was White* (New York, 2005).

62 **"Social engineering":** *AD*, 1023, 1024.

63 **"Negroes," reported:** *Chicago Sun*, Jan. 1, 1943, quoted in Eric Arnesen, *Brotherhoods of Color: Black Railroad Workers and the Struggle for Equality* (Cambridge, Mass., 2001), 193.

63 **Randolph and a diverse group:** A. Philip Randolph, Frank Crosswaith, Anna Arnold Hedgeman, Layle Lane, William Lloyd Ives, Leon Ransom, Pauli Murray, and Albert Hamilton to Franklin Delano Roosevelt, July 17, 1942, in PMP, Box 72, Folder 1251.

64 **"I became a highly trained":** Charles H. King, Jr., *Fire in My Bones*, rev. ed. (Grand Rapids, Mich., 1986), 16–18, 182; Lucille B. Milner, "Jim Crow in the

Army," *TNR*, March 13, 1944, 341. The best overview is Bernard C. Nalty, *Strength for the Fight: A History of Black Americans in the Military* (New York, 1986), 125–217.

64 **"I will give no blood":** Anna Arnold Hedgeman, *The Trumpet Sounds: A Memoir of Negro Leadership* (New York, 1964), 81–83.

64 **Jim Crow extended:** *NYT*, Aug. 19, 1941, April 3, 4, 1942; Michael C. C. Adams, *The Best War Ever: America in World War II* (Baltimore, 1994), 83.

65 **"almost guerilla-like warfare":** Pauli Murray, "Negroes Are Fed Up," *Common Sense* (Aug. 1943), 274–76.

65 **black and white youths clashed:** George Lipsitz, *Rainbow at Midnight: Labor and Culture in the 1940s* (Urbana, Ill., 1994), 69–98; Mauricio Mazon, *The Zoot Suit Riots* (Austin, Texas, 1984); Robin D. G. Kelley, *Race Rebels: Culture, Politics, and the Black Working Class* (New York, 1996), 161–82.

66 **The black rebellion even made:** Alan Clive, *State of War: Michigan in World War II* (Ann Arbor, Mich., 1979), 156; Thomas J. Sugrue, *The Origins of the Urban Crisis: Race and Inequality in Postwar Detroit* (Princeton, N.J., 1996), 28–29; Bryant Simon, "Fearing Eleanor: Racial Anxieties and Wartime Rumors in the American South, 1940–1945," in Glenn T. Eskew, *Labor in the Modern South* (Athens, Ga., 2001), 83–101; Gretchen Lemke-Santangelo, *Abiding Courage: African American Migrant Women and the East Bay Community* (Chapel Hill, N.C., 1996), 107–9.

66 **the new Sojourner Truth Homes:** Louis E. Martin, "The Truth About Sojourner Truth," *Crisis*, April 1942, 112–13; "Sojourner Truth Housing," ibid., 137–38; Dominic J. Capeci, Jr., *Race Relations in Wartime Detroit: The Sojourner Truth Housing Controversy of 1942* (Philadelphia, 1984), 80, 88; Sugrue, *The Origins of the Urban Crisis*, 73–75; Seven Mile-Fenelon Improvement Association, poster, "WE DEMAND OUR RIGHTS," CRC, Box 66; Charles Abrams, *Forbidden Neighbors: A Study of Prejudice in Housing* (New York, 1955), 95; Clive, *State of War*, 145–50.

67 **"Detroit is dynamite":** "Detroit Is Dynamite," *Life*, Aug. 17, 1942, 15; Harvard Sitkoff, "The Detroit Race Riot of 1943," *Michigan History* 53 (Fall 1969), 183–206; Dominic J. Capeci, Jr., and Martha Wilkerson, *Layered Violence: The Detroit Rioters of 1943* (Jackson, Miss., 1991); Surveys Division, Office of Special Services, Office of War Information, "Opinions in Detroit Thirty-six Hours after the Race Riots," Special Memorandum No. 64, June 30, 1943, in LBJ-CR, Part 5: Reel 19, frame 588.

68 **Detroit's "Gestapo":** Thurgood Marshall, "The Gestapo in Detroit," *Crisis*, Oct. 1943, 232ff.

68 **Just a month later:** Dominic J. Capeci, Jr., *The Harlem Riot of 1943* (Philadelphia, 1977); Marilynn S. Johnson, *Street Justice: A History of Police Violence in New York City* (Boston, 2003), 191–203, offers an excellent discussion of the context of the riot.

69 **"The angry mob":** Ralph Ellison, "Eyewitness Story of Riot: False Rumors Spurred Mob," *NYP*, Aug. 2, 1943, reprinted in *RCR*, vol. 1, 50.

69 **"We know you live":** Langston Hughes, "Letter to White Shopkeepers," *CD*, Aug. 14, 1943; see also Hughes, "Suggestions to White Shopkeepers," *CD*, Aug. 21, 1943, both reprinted in Christopher De Santis, ed., *Langston Hughes and the Chicago Defender* (Urbana, Ill., 1995), 99–103; "Harlem Riot," *Crisis*, Sept. 1943, 181; *Militant*, Aug. 7, 1943, reprinted in C. L. R. James et al., *Fighting Racism in World War II* (New York, 1980), 347–55.

69 **"people who participated":** Pauli Murray to Lina [Caroline Ware], n.d. [1943], PMP, Box 102, Folder 840. See also Murray, "And the Riots Came," *The Call*, and "Negroes are Fed Up," *Common Sense* (Aug. 1943).

70 **"Why, in these months":** Thomas Sancton, "The Race Riots," *TNR*, July 5, 1943, 12.

70 **"The recent outbreaks":** *NYT*, July 21, 1943.

70 **"What'd you get, black boy":** Pauli Murray, "Mr. Roosevelt Regrets," *Crisis*, Aug. 1943, 252.

70 **"discrimination in employment":** L. D. Reddick, "What the Northern Negro Thinks About Democracy," *JES* 17 (1944), 301.

71 **The order itself:** John Brecher, "8802 Blues," *TNR*, Feb. 22, 1943, 249.

71 **a galvanic effect:** Andrew E. Kersten, *Race, Jobs, and the War: The FEPC in the Midwest, 1941–46* (Urbana, Ill., 2000).

72 **Some of the most vocal advocates:** Mindy Thompson, "The National Negro Labor Council: A History," American Institute for Marxist Studies, Occasional Paper Series No. 27 (1978), 4–5; Martha Biondi, *To Stand and Fight: The Struggle for Civil Rights in Postwar New York City* (Cambridge, Mass., 2003), 8–10.

72 **the Forest-Johnson tendency:** Grace Lee Boggs, *Living for Change: An Autobiography* (Minneapolis, 1998); Charles Denby, *Indignant Heart: A Black Worker's Journal* (1952, rept. Detroit, 1989); Martin Glaberman, *Wartime Strikes* (Detroit, 1980), 62–81.

73 **At the center was C. L. R. James:** James et al., *Fighting Racism in World War II*; Paul Buhle, *Marxism in the United States*, rev. ed. (New York, 1991), 201–5; Scott McLemee, ed., *C. L. R. James on the Negro Question* (Jackson, Miss., 1996). McLemee's excellent introduction is the best overview of James's thinking on race.

73 **The most visible:** Pauli Murray to A. Philip Randolph, July 24, 1942, in PMP, Box 72, Folder 265; A. Philip Randolph, "Why Should We March?" *SG* (Nov. 1942), 488–89; "Blackout Harlem: June 16th!," *Black Worker*, June 1942; "25,000 Jam Madison Square Garden," *Militant*, June 20, 1942; and "Report from Saint Louis," *Militant*, July 4, 1942, both in James et al., *Fighting Racism in World War II*, 213–17; Report on March on Washington Policy Conference, Sept. 25–27, 1942, in PMP, Box 72, Folder 266; Murray, "Answers to Questionnaire on March on Washington Movement," n.d. [circa 1955], in PMP 73:1269.

74 **MOWM activists gathered in Detroit:** "8 Point Program of the March on Washington Movement," n.d., PMP, Box 72, Folder 264; on rights language generally see Elizabeth Borgwardt, *A New Deal for the World: America's Vision for Human Rights* (Cambridge, Mass., 2005).

75 **In Detroit, on April 11, 1943:** "20,000 Members in 1943," *Crisis*, May 1943, 140, 143, 154; Beth T. Bates, "'Double V for Victory' Mobilizes Black Detroit, 1941—1946," in Jeanne F. Theoharis and Komozi Woodard, eds., *Freedom North: Black Freedom Struggles Outside the South, 1940–1980* (New York, 2003), 21–22, 26–27.

76 **the FEPC won a new lease on life:** There is much debate over the impact of the FEPC on wartime hiring. See Kersten, *Race, Jobs, and the War*, 143–44; Merl Reed, *Seedtime for the Modern Civil Rights Movement: The President's Committee on Fair Employment Practice, 1941–46* (Baton Rouge, La., 1991), 347–57.

76 **the second great migration:** Robert C. Weaver, *Negro Labor: A National Problem* (New York, 1946), 78–93; James Gregory, *Southern Diaspora: How the Great Migrations of Black and White Southerners Transformed America* (Chapel Hill, N.C., 2005), 13–16, 32.

77 **"these changes":** Robert C. Weaver, *The Negro Ghetto* (New York, 1948), 79–81; Weaver, *Negro Labor*, 48.

77 **"It may seem odd to hear":** Horace R. Cayton, "Fighting for White Folks," *Nation*, Sept. 26, 1942, 267; Reddick, "What the Northern Negro Thinks About Democracy," 304–6; on black internationalist intellectuals, see Penny von Eschen, *Race Against Empire: Black Americans and Anticolonialism, 1923–1957* (Ithaca, N.Y., 1997). On the importance of wars in shaping racial politics, see Philip A. Klinkner with Rogers M. Smith, *The Unsteady March: The Rise and Decline of Racial Equality in America* (Chicago, 1999).

79 **"truly a war of universal liberation":** Louis E. Martin, "To Be or Not to Be a Liberal," *Crisis*, Sept. 1942, 286.

79 **"it is 1776 for the Negro":** Thomas Sancton, "Something's Happened to the Negro," *TNR*, Feb. 8, 1943, 176.

79 **what the war meant:** Robert Westbrook, "'I Want a Girl, Just Like the Girl That Married Harry James': American Women and the Problem of Political Obligation in World War II," *AQ* 42 (1990), 587–614; Adam Clayton Powell, Jr., *Marching Blacks* (New York, 1945), 121.

79 **"There are thirteen million":** "Huge Rally, Harlem Blackout," *Call*, June 19, 1942, SCCF, 002-968-1.

79 **"History and tradition combine":** Gloster Current, "Let's Get Ten Thousand," *Crisis*, Sept. 1942, 293; *DW*, March 7, 1941; Marshall, "The Gestapo in Detroit," 233; "Jim Crow Uber Alles," *Crisis*, Oct. 1943, 309; "Michigan Sudetenland," *Crisis*, Dec. 1943, 372.

80 **"We brown women of America":** Hortense Johnson and Leotha Hackshaw, "What My Job Means to Me," *Opportunity*, April 1943.

81 *I believe in democracy*: Rhoza Walker, "I Believe in Democracy So Much," *Crisis*, Sept. 1942, 280.

81 **"resentment and despair":** Martin, "To Be or Not to Be a Liberal," 285–86; Albert Parker, "Negroes in the Postwar World" (Pioneer Publishers Pamphlet, 1942), in James et al., *Fighting Racism in World War II*, 300; *PC*, Dec. 19, 1942;

Alfred McClung Lee and Norman D. Humphrey, *Race Riot* (New York, 1943), 7–8.

82 **Until the 1960s:** Jackson, *Gunnar Myrdal and America's Conscience*, 257–61; Oliver C. Cox, "An American Dilemma: A Mystical Approach to the Study of Race Relations," *JNE* 14 (1945), 132–48, quote 132.

83 **"Most of them":** H. H. Giles, "The Present Status and Programs of Private Intergroup Relations Agencies," *JNE* 20 (1951), 413–14, 418.

CHAPTER 4 | "BALANCE OF POWER"

87 **Henry Lee Moon:** *CCP*, Sept. 16, 1950; HLMP, Box 1, Folder 1; on Moon family activity, see especially HLMP, Box 2. Kimberley L. Phillips, *AlabamaNorth: African-American Migrants, Community, and Working-Class Activism in Cleveland, 1915–45* (Urbana, Ill., 1999), 3, 188, 218–19.

87 **Moon's career mirrored:** *NYAN*, March 3, June 15, Oct. 5, 1932; *CCP*, March 8, 1944, in HLMP, Box 1, Folder 2; Henry Lee Moon, "Women Under the Soviets," *Crisis*, April 1934, in HLMP, Box 1, Folder 3; Mark Naison, *Communists in Harlem During the Depression* (Urbana, Ill., 1983), 68, 73–74; *NYAN*, Dec. 28, 1935, Aug. 22, 1936.

88 **"claims of the Negro":** Henry Lee Moon, "Racial Aspects of Federal Public Relations Programs," *Phylon* 4 (1943), 68, 69.

88 **"remains silent":** *NYT*, June 14, Oct. 5, 1932, Oct. 18, 1936.

88 **The alliance of civil rights groups and industrial unions:** Weaver, *Negro Labor*, 294–95; Roger Horowitz, *"Negro and White, Unite and Fight!" A Social History of Industrial Unionism in Meatpacking, 1930–90* (Urbana, Ill., 1997); Rick Halpern, *Down on the Killing Floor: Black and White Workers in Chicago's Packinghouses, 1904–54* (Urbana, Ill., 1998); Steve Rosswurm, ed., *The CIO's Left-Led Unions* (New Brunswick, N.J., 1992); Nelson Lichtenstein, "Life at the Rouge: A Cycle of Workers' Control," in Charles Stephenson and Robert Asher, eds., *Life and Labor: Dimensions of American Working-Class History* (Albany, N.Y., 1986), 251–53; Maurice Zeitlin and Judith Stepan-Norris, *Left Out: Reds and America's Industrial Unions* (Cambridge, U.K., 2002).

89 **Committed to the left-liberal side:** *PC*, Sept. 23, 1944; Patricia Sullivan, *Days of Hope: Race and Democracy in the New Deal Era* (Chapel Hill, N.C., 1996), 169–91; Robert H. Zieger, *The CIO, 1935–55* (Chapel Hill, N.C., 1995), 181–88; Henry Lee Moon, *Balance of Power: The Negro Vote* (Garden City, N.Y., 1948), 140–45.

89 **Moon penned:** Henry Lee Moon, "How the Negroes Voted," *Nation*, Nov. 25, 1944, 640, offers an early version of his book's argument; Moon, *Balance of Power*, 12, 213.

90 **The power of Moon's book:** Roy Wilkins with Tom Matthews, *Standing Fast: The Autobiography of Roy Wilkins* (New York, 1982), 200; *NYT*, July 4, 16,

1948; Kenneth O'Reilly, *Nixon's Piano: Presidents and Racial Politics from Washington to Clinton* (New York, 1995), 156. Versions of Moon's argument had circulated in black and liberal circles for years, giving them even more credibility. See, for example, Roi Ottley, *New World A-Coming: Inside Black America* (New York, 1943), 203–4; Edward A. Harris, "The Negro Faces November," *TNR*, Aug. 28, 1944, 241–43; *CD*, Dec. 2, 1944, in HLMP, Box 1, Folder 2.

91 **As the war drew to a close:** On seniority, see Weaver, *Negro Labor*, 281–305.

91 **Leading the call:** *DW*, Oct. 7, 8, 1944; NNC, Proceedings of the Conference on Postwar Employment, Jan. 13, 1945, NNC, Vertical File, Tamiment Library, New York University, cited in Martha Biondi, *To Stand and Fight: The Struggle for Civil Rights in Postwar New York City* (Cambridge, Mass., 2003), 22; for further discussion, see ibid., 22–26.

91 **By contrast, most unionists:** *MC*, Nov. 18, 1944; Fair Practices Seniority Statement, July 14, 1947, and correction, July 30, 1947, UAW Fair Practices Department Papers, Box 3, Folder 3-3, ALUA; Weaver, *Negro Labor*, 302–4. See also Marshall Stevenson, "Points of Departure, Acts of Resolve: Black-Jewish Relations in Detroit, 1937–1962" (Ph.D. diss., University of Michigan, 1988), 287–88; Leslie S. Perry to Roy Wilkins, Dec. 27, 1944, in NAACP Group II-A, Box 257; "Super-Seniority Exposed," *Workers' Defense League Bulletin*, Fall 1945, in MSRC, Vertical File: Organization: Workers' Defense League; "Left of Center," *TNR*, July 11, 1949; *Ford Facts*, Dec. 22, 1951, ALUA; Nancy MacLean, *Freedom Is Not Enough: The Opening of the American Workplace* (Cambridge, Mass., 2006), 29.

92 **However, African American women:** Ruth Milkman, *Gender at Work* (Urbana, Ill., 1987), 104–12, 130–44; Jacqueline Jones, *Labor of Love, Labor of Sorrow: Black Women, Work, and the Family from Slavery to the Present* (New York, 1985), 256–63.

93 **many CIO unions created:** August Meier and Elliott Rudwick, *Black Detroit and the Rise of the UAW* (New York, 1979), 208–21; Kevin Boyle, "'There Are No Sorrows the Union Cannot Heal': The Struggle for Racial Equality in the UAW, 1940–60," *LH* 36 (1995), 5–23; Richard L. Rowan, *The Negro in the Steel Industry* (Philadelphia, 1968), 54–73.

93 **Hedgeman directed the National Council:** Anna Arnold Hedgeman, *The Trumpet Sounds: A Memoir of Negro Leadership* (New York, 1964), 87–95; Herbert Garfinkel, *When Negroes March* (Glencoe, Ill., 1959), 141, 145–46, 150–55; Cheryl Lynn Greenberg, *Troubling the Waters: Black-Jewish Relations in the American Century* (Princeton, N.J., 2006), 125; *NYT*, Jan. 5, 1947.

93 **a "damnable" law:** *CD*, Jan. 5, 1946; Garfinkel, *When Negroes March*, 158–60.

94 **more militant pro-FEPC activists:** *CD*, Feb. 16, 1946; "Sham Battle," *Crisis*, March 1946, 72; J. W. Ivy, "FEPC: Its Feckless Friends," *Crisis*, March 1946, 73–74; "Along the NAACP Battlefront: Politics," *Crisis*, March 1946, 86; Garfinkel, *When Negroes March*, 158–60; Paula E. Pfeffer, *A. Philip Randolph: Pioneer of the Civil Rights Movement* (Baton Rouge, La., 1990), 108–18.

94 **"FEPC was a frail war-baby":** Winifred Rauschenbusch, "Jobs Without Creed

or Color," WDL, June 1, 1945, 19, 20, in MSRC, Vertical File: Organization: Workers' Defense League; *CD*, Feb. 9, 1946; Anthony S. Chen, "From Fair Employment to Equal Opportunity Employment and Beyond: Affirmative Action and Civil Rights Politics in the New Deal Order, 1941–1972" (Ph.D. diss., University of California, Berkeley, 2002), 49, 113; Will Maslow, "FEPC—A Case History in Parliamentary Maneuver," *University of Chicago Law Review* 13 (1946), 418–22.

95 **By the 1940s, the Republican Party:** Nancy M. Weiss, *Farewell to the Party of Lincoln: Black Politics in the Age of FDR* (Princeton, N.J., 1983), 271–72; Wendell Willkie, *One World* (New York, 1943), 148; St. Clair Drake and Horace Cayton, in *Black Metropolis: A Study of Negro Life in a Northern City* (New York, 1945), 355, praised Willkie as a "champion" of civil rights.

96 **At best, Republicans argued:** Duane Lockard, *Toward Equal Opportunity: A Study of State and Local Antidiscrimination Laws* (London, 1968), 46–57; *PC*, Dec. 22, 1945; *CD*, Dec. 17, 1949.

96 **"The large Negro vote":** *CD*, March 9, 1946; "How Your Congressman Stood on FEPC," *Crisis*, Oct. 1946, 308.

96 **the biggest political target of all:** On Truman's travails (but little mention of black voters), see Alonzo M. Hamby, *Man of the People: A Life of Harry S. Truman* (New York, 1995), 361–86, 418–38; for a more critical view, see Michael Goldfield, *The Color of Politics: Race and the Mainsprings of American Politics* (New York, 1997), 249–56; Wilkins, *Standing Fast*, 200.

97 **"You will enjoy and profit from it":** Wilkins, *Standing Fast*, 200; Hamby, *Man of the People*, 214–15; Burton J. Bernstein, "Ambiguous Legacy: The Truman Administration and Civil Rights," in Bernstein, ed., *Politics and Policies of the Truman Administration* (New York, 1970), 288.

98 **"untested haberdasher":** Wilkins, *Standing Fast*, 192. The literature on Truman's civil rights policies is extensive. For a useful overview, see Philip A. Klinkner with Rogers M. Smith, *The Unsteady March: The Rise and Decline of Racial Equality in America* (Chicago, 1999), 204–26; William C. Berman, *The Politics of Civil Rights in the Truman Administration* (Columbus, Ohio, 1970); Donald R. McCoy and Richard T. Ruetten, *Quest and Response: Minority Rights and the Truman Administration* (Lawrence, Kans., 1973).

98 **Truman faced a wave:** Steven Lawson, "Introduction," *TSTR*, 9.

99 **In December 1946:** Steven Lawson, "Introduction," *TSTR*, 20.

99 **"The central theme":** *TSTR*, 50, 54, 93, 101, 119, 141, 158, 159, 160.

100 **Compounding Truman's concerns:** Cecelia Van Auken, "The Negro Press in the 1948 Presidential Election," *Journalism Quarterly* 36 (Dec. 1949), 431–35.

100 **Adding to the pressure:** James Q. Wilson, *Negro Politics: The Search for Leadership* (Glencoe, Ill., 1960), 78–80; Hedgeman, *The Trumpet Sounds*, 95–96; *CD*, July 24, Sept. 18, Oct. 16, 1948.

101 **"general without an army":** *CD*, Nov. 13, 1948; Henry Lee Moon, "What Chance for Civil Rights?" *Crisis*, Feb. 1949, 42–45. Quote from Clark Clifford campaign memorandum, Aug. 17, 1948, in Zachary Karabell, *The Last Cam-*

paign: How Harry Truman Won the 1948 Election (New York, 2001), 192; Van Auken, "The Negro Press," 434; "The Negro Prefers Truman," *TNR*, Nov. 22, 1948, 8.

102 **In January 1950, four thousand:** "The Civil Rights Mobilization," *Crisis*, Feb. 1950, 100–11; "Comments on the Civil Rights Mobilization," *Crisis*, March 1950, 167–68.

102 **Pundits offered variations:** For examples, see *NYT*, Aug. 10, 1952; Henry Lee Moon, "The Negro Break-Away from the Democrats," *TNR*, Dec. 3, 1956, 17; Moon quote in *CCP*, March 22, 1958.

103 **"It is a matter of record":** Moon, *Balance of Power*, 127, 128.

103 **To be sure, Communists were inconsistent:** Wallace Lee, "Have Communists Quit Fighting for Negro Rights?" *ND*, Dec. 1944, 66, with replies by William L. Patterson, George Schuyler, Benjamin A. Davis, Horace Cayton, and James W. Ford, ibid., 60–70. On wartime issues, see Maurice Isserman, *Which Side Were You On? The American Communist Party During the Second World War* (Middletown, Conn., 1982), 141–43; Biondi, *To Stand and Fight*, makes an argument for the centrality of Communists in postwar New York's civil rights movement. For a more critical assessment, see Eric Arnesen, "No 'Graver Danger': Black Anticommunism, the Communist Party, and the Race Question," *Labor* 3 (2006), 13–52.

103 **Communists and various Socialists:** Robert Korstad and Nelson Lichtenstein, "Opportunities Found and Lost: Labor, Radicals, and the Early Civil Rights Movement," *JAH* 75 (1988), 786–811.

103 **NAACP branches:** Matthew Countryman, *Up South: Civil Rights and Black Power in Philadelphia* (Philadelphia, 2005), 35–44; Randal Maurice Jelks, *African Americans in the Furniture City: The Struggle for Civil Rights in Grand Rapids* (Urbana, Ill., 2006), 132–38.

104 **leftists of all varieties came under siege:** Steve Rosswurm, "An Overview and Assessment of the CIO's Expelled Unions," in Rosswurm, ed., *The CIO's Left-Led Unions* (New Brunswick, N.J., 1992), 1–17; Ellen Schrecker, *Many Are the Crimes: McCarthyism in America* (New York, 1998); Biondi, *To Stand and Fight*, 147–53; Joshua Freeman, *Working-Class New York: Life and Labor Since World War II* (New York, 2000), 72–95.

104 **In many NAACP branches:** Countryman, *Up South*, 35–44; Jelks, *African Americans in the Furniture City*, 132–38; Thomas J. Sugrue, *The Origins of the Urban Crisis: Race and Inequality in Postwar Detroit*, Princeton Classics edition (Princeton, N.J., 2005), 80, 82; NAACP-M, Part 1, Reel 2, frame 246. On NAACP fears about the leftist taint, see Manfred Berg, *"The Ticket to Freedom": The NAACP and the Struggle for Black Political Integration* (Gainesville, Fla., 2005), 131–32.

105 **The Cold War rationale:** There is an extensive body of scholarship on the Cold War and civil rights. The most important books are Brenda Gayle Plummer, *Rising Wind: Black Americans and U.S. Foreign Affairs, 1935–1960* (Chapel Hill, N.C., 1996); Mary L. Dudziak, *Cold War Civil Rights: Race and the*

Image of American Democracy (Princeton, N.J., 2000); Thomas Borstelmann, *The Cold War and the Color Line: American Race Relations in the Global Arena* (Cambridge, Mass., 2001); Brenda Gayle Plummer, ed., *Window on Freedom: Race, Civil Rights, and Foreign Affairs, 1945–1988* (Chapel Hill, N.C., 2003), 93–113; Azza Salama Layton, *International Politics and Civil Rights Policies in the United States, 1941–1960* (New York, 2000).

105 **"the attempts of various groups":** Gilbert Jonas, *Freedom's Sword: The NAACP and the Struggle Against Racism in America, 1909–1969* (New York, 2005), 143–44, 148; David Levering Lewis, *W. E. B. Du Bois: The Fight for Equality and the American Century, 1919–1963* (New York, 2000), 496–553; Martin Duberman, *Paul Robeson: A Biography* (New York, 1988); NAACP-M, Part 1, Reel 2, frames 248–51; Berg, *"The Ticket to Freedom,"* 132–33; Biondi, *To Stand and Fight,* 155–61.

106 **Bruising factional disputes:** Korstad and Lichtenstein, "Opportunities Found and Lost"; Beth T. Bates, "'Double V for Victory' Mobilizes Black Detroit, 1941–1946," in Jeanne F. Theoharis and Komozi Woodard, eds., *Freedom North: Black Freedom Struggles Outside the South, 1940–1980* (New York, 2003), 21, 25, 28; Angela D. Dillard, "Religion and Radicalism: The Reverend Albert B. Cleage, Jr., and the Rise of Black Christian Nationalism in Detroit," ibid., 160; generally, Stevenson, "Points of Departure, Acts of Resolve," 246–327; for other cities, see Countryman, *Up South,* 35–44; Biondi, *To Stand and Fight,* 165–71.

106 **had lost much of its activist edge:** Paul Jacobs, "The NAACP's New Direction," *TNR,* July 16, 1956, 9–11; Wilson, *Negro Politics,* 281–84; *PC,* July 19, 1958.

107 **The Urban League:** *CD,* Sept. 17, 1949; Lester Granger (1956), cited in Greenberg, *Troubling the Waters,* 189.

107 **One was the Civil Rights Congress:** For a comprehensive overview of the CRC's activities, see Gerald Horne, *Communist Front? The Civil Rights Congress, 1946–1956* (Rutherford, N.J., 1988); for local examples, see Robert O. Self, *American Babylon: Race and the Struggle for Postwar Oakland* (Princeton, N.J., 2003), 77–78; Biondi, *To Stand and Fight,* 72–73; Sugrue, *The Origins of the Urban Crisis,* 170–73; Josh Sides, "'You Understand My Condition': The Civil Rights Congress in the Los Angeles African American Community, 1946–1952," *Pacific Historical Review* 67 (1998), 233–57.

108 **In 1951, the CRC presented:** Civil Rights Congress, "We Charge Genocide" (New York, 1951); *CD,* Sept. 21, 1946, Aug. 16, Oct. 25, 1947; Carol Anderson, "Bleached Souls and Red Negroes: The NAACP and Black Communists in the Early Cold War, 1948–1952," in Plummer, ed., *Window on Freedom,* 93–113, offers a critical account of the CRC petition.

108 **"Out of the inhuman black ghettos":** "We Charge Genocide," xiv, 8, 138, 140, 142.

109 **"advocate, abet, advise":** Alien Registration Act, 18 U.S.C. 2385 (1940).

109 **"leftist labor movement":** Coleman A. Young with Lonnie Wheeler, *Hard*

Stuff: The Autobiography of Coleman Young (New York, 1994), 113; "News Release National Negro Labor Council," 1953, "Give Us This Day Our Daily Bread," both in NAACP, Group II-A, Box 336; Mindy Thompson, "The National Negro Labor Council: A History," American Institute for Marxist Studies, Occasional Paper Series No. 27 (1978); Philip S. Foner, *Organized Labor and the Black Worker, 1619–1981*, 2nd ed. (New York, 1982), 301–2; Biondi, *To Stand and Fight*, 263–68.

110 **Tainted red:** "Rough Draft for Article on NNLC," NAACP, Group II-A, Box 336; Stevenson, "Points of Departure, Acts of Resolve," 272; Young interview in Studs Terkel, ed., *American Dreams Lost and Found* (New York, 1980), 363; Martin Halpern, " 'I'm Fighting for Freedom': Coleman Young, HUAC, and the Detroit African American Community," *JAEH* 17 (1997), 19–38.

110 **"a few years before":** Dorothy Height, OH, CUOHP, 133, 138, 139, 141, 142.

111 **"Important national policies":** Moon, *Balance of Power*, 146; *PC*, Dec. 8 and 22, 1945; Rauschenbush, "Jobs Without Creed or Color," made a forceful argument for local and state activism; generally, see Thomas J. Sugrue, " 'All Politics Is Local': The Persistence of Localism in Twentieth Century America," in Meg Jacobs, William Novak, and Julian Zelizer, eds., *The Democratic Experiment: New Directions in American Political History* (Princeton, N.J., 2003), 301–26; Chen, "From Fair Employment," 118.

112 **As their black constituencies grew:** Ralph Bunche, "The Negro in the Political Life of the United States," *JNE* 10 (1941), 567–84; On Kelly, see Drake and Cayton, *Black Metropolis*, 353–59; Arnold R. Hirsch, "The Cook County Democratic Machine and the Dilemma of Race, 1931–1987," in Richard M. Bernard, ed., *Snowbelt Cities: Metropolitan Politics in the Northeast and Midwest Since World War II* (Bloomington, Ind., 1987), 63–90; *PC*, Nov. 3, 10, 1945. Dominic J. Capeci, Jr., *Race Relations in Wartime Detroit* (Philadelphia, 1984), 16–20, 22, 29; Sugrue, *The Origins of the Urban Crisis*, 110–12.

113 **kept blacks on city payrolls:** Sugrue, *The Origins of the Urban Crisis*, 80–81; Moon, *Balance of Power*, 149–56. This followed well-laid channels of urban machine politics, where jobs were allocated on the basis of loyalty rather than some abstract classical liberal conception of "merit."

113 **"were looking to score":** Wilkins, *Standing Fast*, 201; Bernstein, "Ambiguous Legacy," 288–89; Moon, *Balance of Power*, 197–99.

113 **The model law was New York's:** Paul Moreno, *From Direct Action to Affirmative Action: Fair Employment Law and Policy in America, 1933–1972* (Baton Rouge, La., 1997), 107–11; Lockard, *Toward Equal Opportunity*, 41–42; Anthony S. Chen, " 'The Hitlerian Rule of Quotas': Racial Conservatism and the Politics of Fair Employment Legislation in New York State, 1941–1945," *JAH* 92 (2006), 1238–64.

114 **During the war, Jewish groups:** Greenberg, *Troubling the Waters*, 90–100, 136–39; Joshua M. Zeitz, *White Ethnic New York: Jews, Catholics, and the Shaping of Postwar Politics* (Chapel Hill, N.C., 2007), 14; Biondi, *To Stand and Fight*, 18–21.

114 **Antifascism united:** Sugrue, *The Origins of the Urban Crisis*, 171–73; Sidney Fine, *"Expanding the Frontiers of Civil Rights": Michigan, 1948–1968* (Detroit, 2000), 17, 19; Eric Ledell Smith and Kenneth C. Wolensky, "A Novel Public Policy: Pennsylvania's Fair Employment Practices Act of 1955," *PH* 69 (Fall 2002), 504–5.

115 **their denunciation of "quotas":** Chen, "The Hitlerian Rule of Quotas," 1256–57.

115 **The politics of New Jersey's 1947:** *NYT,* Jan. 21, 1947, July 9, 1947; Moon, *Balance of Power*, 10, 36, 198; see also Davison M. Douglas, *Jim Crow Moves North: The Battle over Northern School Segregation, 1865–1954* (New York, 2005), 241.

116 **When the NAACP demanded:** *NYT,* July 2, 9, 20, Aug. 6, 14, 21, Nov. 5, 1947; "New Jersey Among Torchbearers for Justice," *INS* (Fall 1947), 1.

116 **In Philadelphia, rapid growth:** B. R. Brazeal, "The Present Status and Programs of Fair Employment Practices Commissions—Federal, State, and Municipal," *JNE* 20:3 (1951), 394; Vincent P. Franklin, *The Education of Black Philadelphia* (Philadelphia, 1979), 161–62; James Wolfinger, "'An Equal Opportunity to Make a Living—and a Life': The FEPC and Postwar Black Politics," *Labor* 4 (2007), 65–94; City of Philadelphia, Fair Employment Practice Ordinance, in PNAACP, Box 8, Folder 6-157; "Provisions of the Commission on Human Relations," *Philadelphia Home Rule Charter* (Philadelphia, 1959), Sections 4-700 and 4-701; Commission on Human Relations, Staff Responsibilities and Procedure, n.d., PNAACP, Box 4, Folder 6/I/95.

117 **"the Commissar or the Gestapo":** Smith and Wolensky, "A Novel Public Policy," 510.

117 **Free enterprise, in their view:** Elizabeth A. Fones-Wolf, *Selling Free Enterprise: The Business Assault on Labor and Liberalism, 1945–60* (Urbana, Ill., 1994); MacLean, *Freedom Is Not Enough*, 30–31, 50.

118 **"If I apply for a job":** George Fulton to Albert Cobo, Oct. 27, 1951, Detroit Mayor's Papers (1951), Box 4, Folder: FEPC, Detroit Public Library; Smith and Wolensky, "A Novel Public Policy"; Louis Kesselman, *The Social Politics of FEPC: A Study in Reform Pressure Movements* (Chapel Hill, N.C., 1948), 170–73; Fine, *"Expanding the Frontiers of Civil Rights,"* 47, 55.

118 **"conceived in the halls":** Fine, *"Expanding the Frontiers of Civil Rights,"* 55.

118 **"Force is always":** "Brotherhood by Statute is Short of Perfection," *SEP,* Feb. 18, 1950, 10; Fine, *"Expanding the Frontiers of Civil Rights,"* 47; Benson Ford to Walter P. Reuther, in *United Automobile Worker*, May 1953; *UAW-CIO Fair Practices Fact Sheet* 6(7) (March–April 1953), 2, and 8:2 (March–April 1954), ALUA, 1, 5. On Eisenhower, see Robert F. Burk, *The Eisenhower Administration and Black Civil Rights* (Knoxville, Tenn., 1984), 171; Russell L. Riley, *The Presidency and the Politics of Racial Equality* (New York, 1999), 175–200.

119 **"intransigent stand":** Herbert R. Northrup, "Progress Without Federal Compulsion: Arguing the Case for Compromise Methods," *Commentary*, Sept. 1952, 206–11.

119 **FEP bills ground their way:** Lockard, *Toward Equal Opportunity*, 16–72; Anthony S. Chen, "The Passage of State Fair Employment Legislation: An Event-History Analysis with Time-Constant and Time-Varying Covariates," Institute for Industrial Relations Working Paper Series, University of California, Berkeley, 2001; William Collins, "The Labor Market Impact of State-Level Anti-Discrimination Laws, 1940–60," *Industrial and Labor Relations Review* 56 (2003), 244–72.

119 **State FEP laws had:** Chen, "The Passage of State Fair Employment Legislation," 7; Bureau of National Affairs, *State Fair Employment Laws and their Administration* (Washington, D.C., 1964).

120 **A typical state FEP law was Pennsylvania's:** "Death of FEPC—A Drama in 3 Acts," *PB*, June 19, 1955; "A Brief Record of the 1955 Legislative Effort," PSA, MG-207, Subject File: Carton 13, File: FEP—Reports, Pamphlets; "Legislature Passes FEP Bill," *Legal Intelligencer*, Oct. 26, 1955; Lockard, *Toward Equal Opportunity*, 76–97.

120 **Underfunded and understaffed:** City of Philadelphia Commission on Human Relations, *Annual Report*, 1953, in PNAACP, Box 4: Folder 6/I/98; Pennsylvania Human Relations Commission, *Seventh Annual Report, 1962* (Harrisburg, 1963), 25–26; George Schermer, "Effectiveness of Equal Opportunity Legislation," in Herbert R. Northrup and Richard L. Rowan, eds., *The Negro and Employment Opportunity: Problems and Practices* (Ann Arbor, Mich., 1965), 74–75, 79–81; Herbert Hill, "Twenty Years of State Fair Employment Practice Commissions: A Critical Analysis with Recommendations," *Buffalo Law Review* 14 (1964), 22–69; cf. Collins, "The Labor Market Impact."

121 **In 1947, when the Brooklyn Dodgers:** Jackie Robinson's story has been told countless times. The best accounts are Jules Tygiel, *Baseball's Great Experiment: Jackie Robinson and His Legacy* (New York, 1983), and Arnold Rampersad, *Jackie Robinson: A Biography* (New York, 1997). On players' support for integration, see Paul D. Moreno, *Black Americans and Organized Labor: A New History* (Baton Rouge, La., 2006), 224.

121 **"We no longer think":** Lester Granger, "A New Problem for Negroes—Integration," in Arnold M. Rose, ed., *Race Prejudice and Discrimination: Readings in Intergroup Relations in the United States* (New York, 1951), 586. The standard histories of the Urban League are Guichard Parris and Lester Brooks, *Blacks in the City: A History of the National Urban League* (Boston, 1971), and Nancy J. Weiss, *The National Urban League, 1910–1940* (New York, 1974); for local case studies, see Sugrue, *The Origins of the Urban Crisis*, 165–70; Nina Mjagkij, "Behind the Scenes: The Cincinnati Urban League, 1948–63," in Henry Louis Taylor, ed., *Race in the City: Work, Community, and Protest in Cincinnati, 1820–1970* (Urbana, Ill., 1993), 280–94; Arvarh E. Strickland, *History of the Chicago Urban League* (Urbana, Ill., 1966).

122 **a "merit employment" program:** M. T. Puryear, "Merit Employment: Unfinished Business," *SA* (Dec. 1962), 4–13. The program's origins and history are documented extensively in AFSC-AD-CR, various years.

122 **Philadelphia's grassroots campaign:** "A Comprehensive Report of Administrative and Program Improvements of the Armstrong Association," Feb. 1, 1955, PUL, Box 2, Folder 30; Memorandum, To: DeHaven Hinkson from Wayne L. Hopkins, Subject: A Partial List of Philadelphia . . . Concerns with Whom Negro Workers Were Placed, ibid., Box 11, Folder 196. For detailed lists, see Reports of the Employment Department for the Months of May 1954, June 1954, Dec. 1955, Jan. 1956, Feb. 1957, May 1957, in ibid., Box 11, Folder 197.

123 **an "educational program":** "Activities of CEJO, 1949–50," news release, May 16, 1949, in FCP, Box 34, Folder 5; CEJO, Memorandum: Job Opportunities in the Banking Industry for Minority Groups, Aug. 16, 1950, PNAACP, Box 6, Folder I/27A; Memorandum to Executive Committee Members of CEJO, Subject: Report #2—Bank Project, in PNAACP, Box 5, Folder 6/II/117; *CEJO News Letter* [Jan. 1955], ibid.; CEJO Program for 1952–53, ibid.; Burton I. Gordin to Charles Shorter, Aug. 4, 1955, with attached press release, PNAACP, Box 4, Folder 6/I/95; Germantown Committee on Merit Employment letter, Oct. 29, 1959, PUL, Box 2, Folder I/39.

123 **Philadelphia's six major department stores:** Patricia A. Cooper, "The Limits of Persuasion: Race Reformers and the Department Store Campaign in Philadelphia, 1945–1948," *Pennsylvania Magazine of History and Biography* 126 (2002), 97–126; "What the Branches Are Doing," *Crisis*, Dec. 1946, 375–76; News Release—Fair Employment Practices in Department Stores Committee, FCP, Box 34, Folder 5; Wayne Hopkins et al. to Thomas Wriggins, Jr., Oct. 20, 1953, PNAACP, Box 5, Folder 6/I/117; draft letter, Charles Shorter to Lewis C. Davis et al., n.d., ibid.; Walter C. Wynn to Mal James, Oct. 18, 1954, ibid.; Charles A. Shorter to Lewis C. Davis, Oct. 29, 1954, ibid.

124 **Black unemployment in Philadelphia:** City of Philadelphia, Commission on Human Relations, *Philadelphia's Non-White Population 1960, Report No. 3: Socioeconomic Data* (Philadelphia, 1962); Zachary Yale Dyckman, "An Analysis of Negro Employment in the Building Trades" (Ph.D. diss., University of Pennsylvania, 1971), 202.

124 **"a shift of power":** Warner Bloomberg, Jr., "Negroes in the North," *TNR*, June 18, 1956, 13–15.

125 **"an upsurge among Negroes":** *PC*, May 28, 1960.

125 **"Negro trade unionists":** *PC*, May 28, 1960.

125 **In 1959, Randolph founded:** *PC*, April 20, 1960, Nov. 18, Dec. 2, 1961.

125 **Trade Union Leadership Council:** *PC*, May 21, June 11, Sept. 24, 1960.

125 **In 1960, the TULC endorsed:** *PC*, Sept. 10, 1960.

126 **"the solemn campaign pledges":** *PC*, Jan. 18, 1961.

126 **"The old clichés":** TULC Open Letter to George Meany, *Vanguard* (1962), cited in Steve Babson, *Working Detroit: The Making of a Union Town* (Detroit, 1986), 166; Open Letter to Meany, Reuther, and [August] Scholle: "All Unemployed Need Action for Jobs Now," *NA*, Aug. 10, 1963.

126 **the Reverend Leon H. Sullivan:** Leon H. Sullivan, *Build, Brother, Build* (Philadelphia, 1969), 44–52; Countryman, *Up South*, 83–86; August Meier and

Elliott Rudwick, "Early Boycotts of Segregated Schools: The East Orange, New Jersey, Experience, 1899–1906," *HEQ* 4 (1967), 22–35; and Meier and Rudwick, *Along the Color Line: Explorations in the Black Experience* (Urbana, Ill., 1976), 291, 303, 310, 313. On the persistence of uplift ideas, see Clarence Taylor, *Black Religious Intellectuals: The Fight for Equality from Jim Crow to the 21st Century* (New York, 2002), 40–41.

127 **insurgents throughout the North:** William E. Nelson, Jr., and Philip J. Meranto, *Electing Black Mayors: Political Action in the Black Community* (Columbus, Ohio, 1977), 188–90; Report on the Boycott of the Tropical Hut Restaurant, Nov. 21–22, 1958, in NAACP-M, Part 20, Reel 11, frames 279–81; NAACP Bronx Branch, Press Release, Dec. 27, 1958, in NAACP-M, Part 20, Reel 10, Frame 295.

127 **"Selective Patronage" campaign:** Sullivan, *Build, Brother, Build,* 45–51; Countryman, *Up South,* 83–86.

128 **The 400 Ministers:** Judge F. Allen to Mr. [Lewis] Carter, June 23, 1960, PUL, Box 2, Folder 22; Lewis J. Carter, Jr., to Robert L. Taylor, Aug. 10, 1960, ibid.; *PT,* June 6, 1960, Aug. 7, 1960; Sullivan, *Build, Brother, Build,* 83–84; "Nationally Known Breyer's Ice Cream Company Capitulates," n.d. [ca. March 1962], Folder: Philadelphia: Jan.–June 1962, NAACP, Group III, Box C137; "Spreading Negro Boycott," *GPM,* May 1962, 53–58; *PG,* Feb. 8, 1963.

128 **Selective patronage advocates:** Hannah Lees, "The Not-Buying Power of Philadelphia Negroes," *Reporter,* May 11, 1961, 33–35; Sullivan, *Build, Brother, Build,* 65–84, esp. 74, 79; Matthew J. Countryman, "Civil Rights and Black Power in Philadelphia, 1940–1971" (Ph.D. diss., Duke University, 1998), 168–91.

128 **Word of the Philadelphia protests:** Chester Branch, NAACP, "A Statement of Policy," NAACP, Group III, Box C136, Folder: Philadelphia, April–Aug. 1961; Sullivan, *Build, Brother, Build,* 74, 76–77; *PC,* Jan. 5, 19, 1963; J. Archie Hargraves, "The Bedford Stuyvesant Ministers' Movement," *SA* (Dec. 1962), 23–29; August Meier and Elliott Rudwick, *CORE: A Study in the Civil Rights Movement, 1942–1968* (Urbana, Ill., 1975), 121, 187–88, 199; on Sullivan and King, see Thomas F. Jackson, *From Civil Rights to Human Rights: Martin Luther King, Jr., and the Struggle for Economic Justice* (Philadelphia, 2006), 138; Countryman, *Up South,* 112; Stacy Kinlock Sewell, "The 'Not-Buying Power' of the Black Community: Urban Boycotts and Equal Employment Opportunity, 1960–1964," *Journal of African American History* 89 (2004), 135–51; *PC,* Aug. 10, 1963.

CHAPTER 5 | "NO PLACE FOR COLORED"

130 **In June 1950, Martin Luther King, Jr.:** *PMLK,* vol. 1, 327–29; Stephen B. Oates, *Let the Trumpet Sound: A Life of Martin Luther King, Jr.* (New York, 1982), 29; Marion Thompson Wright, "New Jersey Laws and the Negro," *JNH*

28 (April 1943), 192–94; Marion Thompson Wright, "Extending Civil Rights in New Jersey Through the Division Against Segregation," *JNH* 38 (Jan. 1953), 91–107.

130 **"We can go anywhere":** *PMLK*, vol. 1, 112.

131 **"very complexity and uncertainty":** Charles S. Johnson, *Patterns of Negro Segregation* (New York, 1943), 6; "50 Loop Restaurants," CORE, Series 3, Reel 8, frames 905–6; St. Clair Drake and Horace Cayton, *Black Metropolis: A Study of Negro Life in a Northern City* (New York, 1945), 103.

131 **a chatty article:** Horace Cayton, "America's 10 Best Cities for Negroes," *ND*, Oct. 1947, 8–10; see also Ruth Danenhower Wilson, "Negroes in Greater New York," *TNR*, July 16, 1945, 74.

131 **"As for sleeping":** Langston Hughes, "The Snake in the House," *CD*, Oct. 16, 1943, reprinted in Christopher De Santis, ed., *Langston Hughes and the Chicago Defender* (Urbana, Ill., 1995), 104.

131 **"with racism twenty-four hours a day":** Interview with Kermit Bailer, in Elaine Latzman Moon, ed., *Untold Tales, Unsung Heroes: An Oral History of Detroit's African American Community, 1918–1967* (Detroit, 1993), 180–81.

132 **"They said: 'I'm tired' ":** Ashby, quoted in Lizabeth Cohen, *A Consumers' Republic: The Politics of Mass Consumption in Postwar America* (New York, 2003), 180.

132 **Travelers faced particular risks:** Cayton, "America's 10 Best Cities for Negroes," 4–5; *The Negro Motorist Green-Book* (New York, 1949), 1, HFM; Patricia L. Pilling, "Segregation: Cottage Rental in Michigan," *Phylon* 25 (1964), 191–201; Mark S. Foster, "In the Face of 'Jim Crow': Prosperous Blacks and Vacations, Travel, and Outdoor Leisure, 1890–1945," *JNH* 84:2 (Spring 1999), 142; Horace Sutton, "Negro Vacations: A Billion Dollar Business," *ND*, July 1950, 25; Drake and Cayton, *Black Metropolis*, 106.

133 **Even celebrities:** *CD*, Jan. 25, 1936; Johnson, *Patterns of Negro Segregation*, 6, 58, 200–1; Nancy J. Weiss, *Whitney M. Young, Jr., and the Struggle for Civil Rights* (Princeton, N.J., 1989), 41; Mary Dudziak, "Josephine Baker, Racial Protest, and the Cold War," *JAH* 81 (1994), 548; L. D. Reddick, "What the Northern Negro Thinks About Democracy," *JES* 17 (1944), 301; George Schuyler, "Jim Crow in the North," *American Mercury* 68 (June 1949), 66–70, reprinted in Jeffrey B. Leak, ed., *Rac(e)ing to the Right: Selected Essays of George S. Schuyler* (Knoxville, Tenn., 2001), 53–59; Sutton, "Negro Vacations," 26; Langston Hughes, "Fooling Our White Folks," *ND*, April 1950, 38–41; Pilling, "Segregation," 191–201; *CD*, Nov. 20, 1940, Dec. 27, 1941, Sept. 24, 1949.

133 **By World War II, eighteen northern states:** Those states were California, Colorado, Connecticut, Illinois, Indiana, Iowa, Kansas, Massachusetts, Michigan, Minnesota, Nebraska, New Jersey, New York, Ohio, Pennsylvania, Rhode Island, Washington, and Wisconsin. See *AD*, 630, 1366–67; Milton R. Konvitz and Theodore Leskes, *A Century of Civil Rights* (New York, 1962), 155–59. By 1959, six more states, all in the West, had passed laws forbidding discrimination in restaurants. See *NYAN*, Aug. 22, 1959.

134 **"despite the absence of Jim Crow laws":** Reddick, "What the Northern
Negro Thinks About Democracy," 296, 301; *Norfolk Journal and Guide*, May
21, 1960 (thanks to Chin Jou for this citation); Sidney Fine, *"Expanding the
Frontiers of Civil Rights": Michigan, 1948–1968* (Detroit, 2000), 11–12, 29,
105–8, 221–22.

134 **"The law is on the Negro's side":** Reddick, "What the Northern Negro
Thinks," 301.

135 **consumerist rights consciousness:** For a discussion of these issues, see
Cohen, *A Consumers' Republic*, 166–91, though Cohen overstates the centrality
of consumerism to postwar black protest, and Cotten Seiler, " 'So That We as a
Race Might Have Something Authentic to Travel By': African American Auto-
mobility and Cold-War Liberalism," *AQ* 58 (2006), 1091–1117.

135 **"all you had to do":** Juanita Nelson interview, Aug. 1967, AMP, Box 56, Folder
12; see also Wanda Penny interview, Oct. 1965, AMP, Box 57, Folder 1.

135 **Protestors found their staunchest allies:** Doxey A. Wilkerson, "The Negro
Press," *JNE* 16 (1947), 511–31; *AD*, 933; Lewis H. Fenderson, "The Negro Press
as a Social Instrument," *JNE* 20 (1951), 181–88; John H. Murphy III, OH, June
26, 1971, Cecil B. Newman, OH, Aug. 26, 1971, Al Sweeney, OH, June 22, 1972,
BJP; "Jo Baker Snubbed at Stork Club," *Jet*, Nov. 1, 1951, 4; on *Ebony* and *Jet*,
see Adam Green, *Selling the Race: Culture, Community, and Black Chicago,
1940–1955* (Chicago, 2007), esp. ch. 5. On the indifference of the white press,
see Gene Roberts and Hank Klibanoff, *The Race Beat: The Press, the Civil
Rights Struggle, and the Awakening of a Nation* (New York, 2006), 5–6, 12–23.

136 **programming on "Negro issues":** Saul Carson, "On the Air: Conscience as a
Guide," *TNR*, Feb. 14, 1949, 26; Barbara Dianne Savage, *Broadcasting Freedom: Radio, War, and the Politics of Race, 1938–1948* (Chapel Hill, N.C., 1999);
Elizabeth Fones-Wolf, *Waves of Opposition: Labor and the Struggle for Democratic Radio* (Urbana, Ill., 2006), 104, 178–79, 233.

136 **radio began to complement the press:** Kathy M. Newman, "The Forgotten
Fifteen Million: Black Radio, the 'Negro Market,' and the Civil Rights Move-
ment," *RHR* 76 (2000), 115–36; Robert E. Weems, Jr., *Desegregating the Dollar:
African American Consumer Activism in the Twentieth Century* (New York,
1998), 41–49. Black radio in the North is understudied. For a model, see Brian
Ward, *Radio and the Struggle for Civil Rights in the South* (Gainesville, Fla.,
2004); Fones-Wolf, *Waves of Opposition*, 189–91; Nick Salvatore, *Singing in a
Strange Land: C. L. Franklin, the Black Church, and the Transformation of
America* (New York, 2005), 152–55; James Spady, *Georgie Woods: I'm Only a
Man: The Life Story of a Mass Communicator, Promoter, Civil Rights Activist*
(Philadelphia, 1992).

138 **Movie theaters were among:** Richard Butsch, "American Movie Audiences in
the 1930s," *International Labor and Working-Class History* 59 (Spring 2001),
107; David Nasaw, *Going Out: The Rise and Fall of Public Amusements* (New
York, 1993), 221–50.

139 **Civil rights activists did not merely:** Thomas Cripps, *"Amos 'n' Andy* and the

Debate over American Racial Integration," in John E. O'Connor, ed., *American History/American Television* (New York, 1983), 33–54; Melvin Ely, *The Adventures of Amos 'n' Andy* (New York, 1991), 228–36; Nasaw, *Going Out*, 225.

139 **"Many theaters in the North"**: *AD*, 613; Joe William Trotter, *Black Milwaukee: The Making of an Industrial Proletariat, 1915–1945* (Urbana, Ill., 1985), 116–17; Johnson, *Patterns of Negro Segregation*, 75; George M. Houser, *Erasing the Color Line* (New York, 1951), 42–43, in CORE, Series 6, Reel 49, frames 286–318; Marjorie House to All Students, Feb. 24, 1961, NAACP-M, Part 20, Reel 11, frame 305, and related clippings and letters, frames 297–313; Bryant Simon, "Segregated Fantasies: Race, Public Space, and the Life and Death of the Movie Business in Atlantic City, New Jersey, 1945–2000," in Jefferson Cowie and Joseph Heathcott, eds., *Beyond the Ruins: The Meanings of Deindustrialization* (Ithaca, N.Y., 2003), 66–70, 78–79.

139 **In cinema, as with so many other**: Lizabeth Cohen, *Making a New Deal: Industrial Workers in Chicago, 1919–1939* (New York, 1990), 123, 125; Drake and Cayton, *Black Metropolis*, 100, 106.

140 **Philadelphia's battle**: Kenneth W. Mack, "Rethinking Civil Rights Lawyering and Politics in the Era Before Brown," *YLJ* 115 (2005), 294–95.

141 **RKO opened its doors**: William A. McClain, "Cincinnati's Theater Doors Are Opened," *Crisis*, Dec. 1941, 382–83, 389.

142 **"For many years"**: Langston Hughes, "Encounter at the Counter," *CD*, March 30, 1946, reprinted in De Santis, *Langston Hughes*, 57–58.

142 **But local customs, even in chain stores**: Johnson, *Patterns of Negro Segregation*, 59–63; Drake and Cayton, *Black Metropolis*, 102, 106–7; George Schuyler, "Jim Crow in the North," *American Mercury* (1949), reprinted in Leak, ed., *Rac(e)ing to the Right*.

143 **bars and restaurants around large factories**: *PC*, Dec. 15, 1945; Madelon Powers, *Faces Along the Bar: Lore and Order in the Workingman's Saloon, 1870–1920* (Chicago, 1999).

144 **"the emphasis was on public accommodations"**: Wanda Penny interview, Oct. 1965, AMP, Box 57, Folder 1.

144 **suburbs such as Plainfield, New Jersey**: *Northtown Survey on Human Relations* (1947), 72–74, PHC. See also Thomas J. Sugrue and Andrew Goodman, "Plainfield Burning: Black Rebellion in the Suburban North," *JUH* 33 (2007), 571.

144 **James Farmer, Bayard Rustin, and George Houser**: James Farmer, *Lay Bare the Heart: An Autobiography of the Civil Rights Movement* (New York, 1985), 83–116; James Tracy, *Direct Action: Radical Pacifism from the Union Eight to the Chicago Seven* (Chicago, 1996); John D'Emilio, *Lost Prophet: The Life and Times of Bayard Rustin* (New York, 2003).

145 **a common benefactor**: August Meier and Elliott Rudwick, *CORE: A Study in the Civil Rights Movement, 1942–1968* (Urbana, Ill., 1975), 4–7; Tracy, *Direct Action*, 4–6; Farmer, *Lay Bare the Heart*, 88; Nat Hentoff, *Peace Agitator: The Story of A. J. Muste* (New York, 1963); Jo Ann Ooiman Robinson, *Abraham*

Went Out: A Biography of A. J. Muste (Philadelphia, 1981); Meier and Rudwick, *CORE;* 4–7; Maurice Isserman, *If I Had a Hammer* (New York, 1987), 127–37; Tracy, *Direct Action,* 18–20.

146 **CORE activists:** Meier and Rudwick, *CORE,* 7–21; Kenneth Ives, ed., *Black Quakers: Brief Biographies* (Chicago, 1995), 93–95.

146 **In late 1942, they chose two targets:** "History of the Stoners Case," CORE, Series 3, Reel 8, frames 704–5; James Robinson, interview by Elliott Rudwick, Aug. 1967, AMP, Box 57, Folder 4; Meier and Rudwick, *CORE,* 13–14; *CD,* June 19, 1943.

146 **"the [Jack Spratt] case":** James Russell Robinson to Night Manager of Jack Spratt Coffee House, May 14, 1942, CORE, Series 3, Reel 8, frame 697.

147 **"trained and disciplined groups":** "Report on March on Washington Policy Conference, Detroit, Sept. 25–27, 1942," 13, PMP, Box 72, Folder 1266; A. Philip Randolph, "Is Civil Disobedience Practical?" *ND,* March 1943, 27–29; A. Philip Randolph, "March on Washington Movement Presents Program for the Negro," in Rayford W. Logan, ed., *What the Negro Wants* (Chapel Hill, N.C., 1944), 149–50; *CD,* June 26, 1943.

147 **"investigation, negotiation":** Catherine Raymond and George M. Houser, "CORE Techniques and Restaurant Discrimination," n.d. [circa 1948], CORE, Series 6, Reel 49, frames 377–86.

147 **But other left-wing activists:** August Meier and Elliott Rudwick, *Along the Color Line: Explorations in the Black Experience* (Urbana, Ill., 1976), 339–41, 351, 354–55; Renee Romano, *Race Mixing: Black-White Marriage in Postwar America* (Cambridge, Mass., 2003), 117–19; Gerald Zahavi, "Passionate Commitments: Race, Sex, and Communism at Schenectady General Electric, 1932–1954," *JAH* 83 (1996), 514–48; Harvard Sitkoff, *A New Deal for Blacks* (New York, 1978), 157–58; Workers' Defense League News Service, Dec. 13, 1945, and *Workers Defense Bulletin,* Summer 1946, in MSRC, Vertical File: Organization: Workers' Defense League.

148 **In Detroit, the battle:** Charles Denby, *Indignant Heart: A Black Worker's Journal* (1952, rept. Detroit, 1989), 95; Nelson Lichtenstein, *The Most Dangerous Man in Detroit: Walter P. Reuther and the Fate of American Labor* (New York, 1995), 206–11. The taboo against male-female interracial socialization was a major one, even ten years later. See Kevin Boyle, "The Kiss: Racial and Gender Conflict in a 1950s Automobile Factory," *JAH* 84 (1997), 496–523.

148 **drive "to break down the restaurants":** *MC,* Aug. 18, 1944; Denby, *Indignant Heart,* 99–100; Domenic J. Capeci, Jr., *Race Relations in Wartime Detroit: The Sojourner Truth Housing Controversy of 1942* (Philadelphia, 1984), 65–66; interview with James Boggs in Moon, ed., *Untold Tales, Unsung Heroes,* 154.

149 **Throughout the North, ordinary blacks:** "Along the NAACP Battlefront," *Crisis,* Oct. 1946, 313; "What the Branches Are Doing," *Crisis,* Aug. 1947, 251; "Along the NAACP Battlefront," *Crisis,* Sept. 1947, 278–79.

149 **One customer denied service:** "What the Branches Are Doing," *Crisis,* April 1946, 120–21. On the Ferguson case, see *CD,* May 18, 1946; Martha Biondi, *To*

Stand and Fight: The Struggle for Civil Rights in Postwar New York City (Cambridge, Mass., 2003), 62–63; *CD*, Aug. 24, 1946.

149 **a "how to" manual:** "Along the NAACP Battlefront," *Crisis*, Oct. 1946, 313.

150 **"persons usually regarded":** Sol Rabkin, "Racial Desegregation in Places of Public Accommodation," *JNE* 23 (1954), 251.

150 **In places as diverse:** For some examples, see *CD*, Jan. 12, March 19, 23, May 18, July 13, 1935, Jan. 22, Sept. 3, 1938, May 9, 1942, Feb. 6, 1943, Dec. 9, 1944, March 11, 1950; Meier and Rudwick, *Along the Color Line*, 339–41, 351, 354–55; *PC*, Dec. 15, 1945; *AD*, 528, 662; interview with Ernest C. Dillard, Sr. in Moon, ed., *Untold Tales, Unsung Heroes*, 158–59; Davison M. Douglas, *Jim Crow Moves North: The Battle over Northern School Segregation, 1865–1954* (New York, 2005), 135; "Report of the Connecticut Interracial Commission, 1947–48," *JNE* 18:2 (Spring 1949), 195.

151 **One of the most important was "testing":** "What the Branches Are Doing," *Crisis*, Jan. 1947, 23; Robert A. Burnham, "The Mayor's Friendly Relations Committee: Cultural Pluralism and the Struggle for Black Advancement," in Henry Louis Taylor, ed., *Race and the City: Work, Community, and Protest in Cincinnati, 1820–1970* (Urbana, Ill., 1993), 267–69; Meier and Rudwick, *CORE*, 44, 58.

151 **After a spate of discrimination complaints:** *NYT*, March 19, 23, 1951, June 16, 1952, June 9, 1960; *CD*, June 28, 1952; see also Cheryl Lynn Greenberg, *Troubling the Waters: Black-Jewish Relations in the American Century* (Princeton, N.J., 2006), 155–56; Chin Jou, "Daring to Dine in the Jim Crow North: The Problem of Eating and Restaurant Discrimination in Postwar New York City," unpublished paper, Princeton University, Feb. 2, 2004, in author's possession; *Norfolk Journal and Guide*, May 21, 1960 (thanks to Chin Jou for this citation).

152 **it took sustained pressure:** *CD*, March 7, July 25, 1953, June 11, 1955, May 18, 1957; *PC*, May 30, June 6, Oct. 10, 1953.

152 **a group of students in Wichita:** *CD*, Aug. 30, 1958; Ronald Walters, "Standing Up in America's Heartland: 1950s Civil Rights Movement History in Wichita, Kansas," *American Visions* (Feb.–March, 1993), 20–23; Gretchen Cassel Eick, *Dissent in Wichita: The Civil Rights Movement in the Midwest, 1954–1972* (Urbana, Ill., 2001), 1–11.

153 **Finally, in 1960, Kansas City activists:** Edgar Chasteen, "Public Accommodations: Social Movements in Conflict," *Phylon* 30 (1969), 234–50.

153 **"To a great extent":** *CD*, May 19, 1956; *Moms Mabley Breaks It Up*, Chess LP 1472, quoted in Lawrence W. Levine, *Black Culture and Black Consciousness: Afro-American Folk Thought from Slavery to Freedom* (New York, 1977), 365.

154 **Beaches—places of seminudity:** Rose Zeligs, "Growth in Intergroup Attitudes During Brotherhood Week," *JNE* 19:1 (Winter 1950), 94–102; Kevin Mumford, "Double V in New Jersey: African American Civic Culture and Rising Consciousness Against Jim Crow, 1938–1966," *NJH* 119 (2001), 38–41; Victoria W. Wolcott, "Recreation and Race in the Postwar City: Buffalo's 1956 Crystal Beach Riot," *JAH* 93 (2006), 63–90; Bryant Simon, *Boardwalk of*

Dreams: Atlantic City and the Fate of Urban America (New York, 2004), 40–41; *CD*, June 18, 25, 1966.

154 **sparked by incidents at beaches:** William Tuttle, *Race Riot: Chicago in the Red Summer of 1919* (New York, 1970); Alfred McClung Lee and Norman D. Humphrey, *Race Riot* (New York, 1943), esp. 20–71; Marilynn Johnson, "Gender, Race, and Rumours: Re-examining the 1943 Race Riots," *Gender and History* 10 (1998), 252–77; Wolcott, "Recreation and Race in the Postwar City," *NYT*, July 9, 1961; "Transcript of Interviews," LBJ-CR, Part 5, Reel 26, frame 0027; *NACCD*, 76.

155 **Jim Crow parks, pools, and beaches:** Drake and Cayton, *Black Metropolis*, 103–6; Houser, *Erasing the Color Line*, 32–34.

156 **At Palisades Park:** *CD*, Sept. 15, 1945, Aug. 24, Sept. 7, 1946, Aug. 2, 1947, Aug. 20, 1949; Biondi, *To Stand and Fight*, 82–84; Workers' Defense League News Service, Nov. 10, 1948, and Dec. 22, 1948, in MSRC, Vertical File: Organization: Workers' Defense League.

156 **Bimini Baths:** Houser, *Erasing the Color Line*, 34–35; Mario T. Garcia, ed., *Memories of Chicano History: The Life and Narrative of Bert Corona* (Berkeley, 1994), 86; *LAT*, July 3, 1952.

157 **to desegregate Pittsburgh's pools:** *PC*, Jan. 28, 1950, June 6, 13, 20, 1953, July 18, 1953, Feb. 5, 2000; Laurence Glasco, "Double Burden: The Black Experience in Pittsburgh," in Samuel P. Hays, ed., *City at the Point: Essays on the Social History of Pittsburgh* (Pittsburgh, 1989), 93.

157 **Chicago's Tuley Park:** *Chi-CORE News*, Oct. 18, 1947, in CORE, Series 3, Reel 8, frame 755.

157 **Chicago's Calumet Park:** *CD*, July 31, 1957; generally, see Andrew J. Diamond, "Hoodlums, Rebels, and Vice Lords: Street Gangs, Youth Subcultures, and Race in Chicago, 1919–1968" (Ph.D. diss., University of Michigan, 2004), 369–72.

158 **In the aftermath:** *CD*, July 29, Aug. 24, Sept. 4, 1957; Meeting at AFSC Office, Aug. 1, 1957, to Discuss Race Disorders in Chicago AFSC-AD-CR, 1957, Box: Community Relations Projects Section, Folder: Housing Chicago: USCCR, *1961 Report, Book 5: Justice* (Washington, D.C., 1961), 40.

158 **Bob-Lo Island:** "Along the NAACP Battlefront," *Crisis*, Sept. 1946, 280; Megan Taylor Shockley, *"We, Too, Are Americans": African American Women in Detroit and Richmond, 1940–54* (Urbana, Ill., 2004), 176; *Bob-Lo Excursion Co. v. People of State of Michigan*, 333 U.S. 28 (1948).

159 **Coney Island amusement park:** *CD*, March 10, 1951, April 19, July 26, 1952, May 31, June 3, 1961; "Amusement Park Completes Integration After 9 Years," *C-L* 90 (June 1963); Michael Washington, "The Stirrings of the Modern Civil Rights Movement in Cincinnati, Ohio, 1943–1953," in Jeanne F. Theoharis and Komozi Woodard, eds., *Groundwork: Local Black Freedom Movements in America* (New York, 2005), 224–29.

159 **would influence activists in the South:** John M. Glen, *Highlander: No Ordinary School, 1932–1962* (Lexington, Ky., 1988); *PMLK*, vol. 5, 466; Barbara

Ransby, *Ella Baker and the Black Freedom Movement: A Radical Democratic Vision* (Chapel Hill, N.C., 2003); *King Encyclopedia*, s.v. "Vivian, Cordy Tindell," www.stanford.edu/group/King/about_king/encyclopedia/vivian_ct.htm.

160 **south of the Mason-Dixon Line:** "Stand Ins at Movies," *C-L* (Mar. 1961); Jim Peck, "Cracking the Color Line: Nonviolent Direct Action Methods of Eliminating Racial Discrimination," n.d. [ca. early 1960s], in CORE, Series 6, Reel 49, frames 344–57; Kevin M. Kruse, *White Flight: Atlanta and the Making of Modern Conservatism* (Princeton, N.J., 2005); Glenn Eskew, *But for Birmingham: The Local and National Movements in the Civil Rights Struggle* (Chapel Hill, N.C., 1997); Rabkin, "Racial Desegregation in Places of Public Accommodation," 249–61.

160 **a beginning, not an end:** Seiler, "So That We as a Race," 1109; Irving Babow, "Restrictive Practices in Public Accommodations in a Northern Community," *Phylon* 24 (1963), 5–12; "Confidential Report of Dearborn (Michigan) 'Freedom Ride Project,'" July 14, 1961, in CORE, Series 5, Reel 41, frames 120–22.

161 **The battle to open up:** *CD*, Aug. 2, 1947; *C-L 91* (Aug. 1961); Simon, *Boardwalk of Dreams*, 116–31.

161 **parks closed by the dozens:** *CD*, July 28, 1966, March 25, 1968; Nasaw, *Going Out*, 248–50, 253–55.

161 **Left behind:** Alison Isenberg, *Downtown America: A History of the Place and the People Who Made It* (Chicago, 2004), 203–54.

CHAPTER 6 | "GOD HAVE PITY ON SUCH A CITY"

163 **The Brook School, a ramshackle:** *CD*, Sept. 18, 1943; *NYT*, Sept. 10, 24, 30, 1943, Oct. 1, 4, 12, 19, 1943; *CD*, Oct. 30, 1943.

163 **Thurgood Marshall escorted:** *Ramapo Independent*, Sept. 9, 1943; *CD*, Sept. 18, 1943; *NYT*, Sept. 10, 1943; "Jim Crow Enrolls for New Term in Hillburn Schools," n.d., NAACP, Group II-B, Box 144.

164 **Like many older towns:** Report on Hillburn School, Oct. 22, 1943, in NAACP, Group II-B, Box 144.

164 **Hillburn represented racially divided:** William T. Andrews, Report on Visit to Hillburn, Feb. 2, 1931, NAACP, Group II-L, Box 36; *Ramapo Independent*, Sept. 9, 1943; *NYHT*, Sept. 30, 1943.

165 **In 1930, T. N. Alexander:** Memorandum to Mr. [Walter] White from Mr. Andrews, Aug. 4, 1930; Mr. Pickens to Mr. White, July 14, 1931; *Evening News*, Feb. 20, 27, 1932, all in NAACP, Group II-L, Box 36.

165 **When parents struck:** "Segregation Charge Made at Hillburn," n.d., NAACP, Group II-B, Box 144.

166 **many initiated by local NAACP branches:** On the NAACP role in northern school cases generally, see Davison M. Douglas, *Jim Crow Moves North: The Battle over Northern School Segregation, 1865–1954* (New York, 2005), 188–95, 238.

166   **The two-pronged attack:** "Segregation of Pupils Story Stirs Residents of Hill-burn," NAACP, Group II-B, Box 144; *NYHT,* Sept. 30, 1943; *New York World Telegram,* Oct. 1, 1943; NAACP Press Release, Oct. 1, 1943, in NAACP, Group II-B, Box 144; "Hillburn Negroes Firm: Set Up School in Church," in ibid.; *Journal-News* (Westchester County, N.Y.), May 12, 2002; "Stand Firm in Fight on Brook School," [*CCP?*] clipping, Oct. 9, 1943, in AMP, Box 92, Folder 10.

166   **Hillburn's black uprising:** "Town's Negroes Strike Against Jim Crow School," *PM,* Sept. 9, 1943; "Upstate Town Hit by Racial Row," *New York Daily News,* Sept. 13, 1943; "Showdown Is Due of Jim Crow School," *PM,* n.d., in NAACP, Group II-B, Box 144.

167   **The boycott was covered extensively:** In addition to articles above, see *PT,* Oct. 9, 1943; *CD,* Sept. 18, 25, Oct. 2, 16, 30, 1943; *NAACP Annual Report, 1943* (New York, 1944), 9–10.

167   **"astonishingly 'southern' viewpoint":** NAACP Press Release, Sept. 10, 1943, in NAACP, Group II-B, Box 144.

167   **"Mississippi Jim Crowism":** *PM,* Sept. 17, 1943; *CD,* Sept. 25, 1943.

167   **"God have pity":** "Hillburn—The Fair," poetry by Countee Cullen, music by Waldemar Hille, Highlander Folk School. Copy in NAACP, Group II-B, Box 144.

168   **more than twenty thousand posters:** "HILLBURN AND HATTIESBURG," and "JIM CROW BLOCKS SCHOOL HOUSE DOOR," NAACP Press Release, Sept. 25, 1943; Memorandum for the Files, Re: Mass Meeting Held at Golden Gate Ballroom, all in NAACP, Group II-A, Box 227; *People's Voice,* Oct. 9, 1943; *NYAN,* Oct. 9, 1943; *CD,* Oct. 16, 1943.

168   **By mid-October:** *PM,* Oct. 19, 1943; *NYT,* Oct. 19, 1943; "Possible Program at Hillburn," NAACP, Group II-B, Box 144; "Confidential Report on Hillburn School," ibid.; "Hillburn's Attack on Jim Crow," *Crisis,* Oct. 1943, 308–9.

169   **statewide and national implications:** "Schools and Democracy," *INS,* Nov. 1943, 3; *CD,* Oct. 30, 1943, Feb. 12, 1944, March 18, 1944.

169   **flooded into the national NAACP:** See letters and telegrams re Hillburn in NAACP, Group II-B, Box 144; for an alternative view on black protest as wholly local and uncoordinated, see August Meier and Elliott Rudwick, *Along the Color Line: Explorations in the Black Experience* (Urbana, Ill., 1976), 378–82.

169   **largely forgotten:** The lack of scholarly attention to school boycotts in the North is quite astounding. An essential starting point is Douglas, *Jim Crow Moves North,* which focuses primarily on the nineteenth and first half of the twentieth centuries. See also August Meier and Elliott Rudwick, "Early Boycotts of Segregated Schools: The Alton, Illinois, Case, 1897–1908," *JNE* 36 (1967), 394–402, "Early Boycotts of Segregated Schools: The East Orange, New Jersey, Experience, 1899–1906," *HEQ* 4 (1967), 22–35, and "Early Boycotts of Segregated Schools: The Case of Springfield, Ohio, 1922–23," *AQ* 20 (1968), 744–58. They list, but do not examine in any detail, more recent boycotts in "The Origins of Nonviolent Direct Action in Afro-American Protest: A Note on

Historical Discontinuities," in Meier and Rudwick, eds., *Along the Color Line*, 312–14, 359–62, 376–77.

170 **the dramatic expansion of American public education:** USCB, *Historical Statistics of the United States: Colonial Times to 1970, Part I* (Washington, D.C., 1976), 379.

170 **educational boom from the outside:** Michael W. Homel, *Down from Equality: Black Chicagoans and the Public Schools, 1920–41* (Urbana, Ill., 1984); Michael B. Katz and Mark J. Stern, *One Nation Divisible: What America Was and What It Is Becoming* (New York, 2005), 60.

171 **"tendencies toward structural separateness":** Doxey Wilkerson, "The Status of Negro Education" (1940), cited in David Tyack, *The One Best System: A History of American Urban Education* (Cambridge, Mass., 1974), 229; Charles S. Johnson, *Patterns of Negro Segregation* (New York, 1943), 12–22; Noma Jensen, "Are Negroes Integrated into our Northern School Systems?," June 20, 1946, in NAACP, Group II-A, Box 244.

171 **Black students found themselves:** Tyack, *The One Best System*, 217–29, quote 217; James R. Grossman, *Land of Hope: Chicago, Black Southerners, and the Great Migration* (Chicago, 1989), 251–52. On Chicago generally, see Homel, *Down from Equality;* Jeffrey Mirel, *The Rise and Fall of an Urban School System: Detroit, 1907–81* (Ann Arbor, Mich., 1993), 191, 255–56, 400; Gladys Tignor Peterson, "The Present Status of the Negro Separate School as Defined by Court Decisions," *JNE* 4 (1935), 351–74; Joint Committee of the National Education Association and the American Teachers Association, *Legal Status of Segregated Schools* (Washington, D.C., and Montgomery, Ala., 1954), 9–13.

172 **Northern school districts:** Max Wolff, "Segregation in the Schools of Gary, Indiana," *JES* 36 (1963), 251–61; Neil Betten and Raymond Mohl, "The Evolution of Racism in an Industrial City, 1906–1940: A Case Study of Gary, Indiana," *JNH* 59 (1974), 51–64; Richard B. Pierce, *Polite Protest: The Political Economy of Race in Indianapolis* (Bloomington, Ind., 2005), 26–55; *Cleveland Plain Dealer*, Sept. 18, 1954; *Cleveland Press*, March 20–24, 1956, in AMP, Box 92, Folder 12; Memo from Arnold de Mille, Sept. 28, 1954, in NAACP, Group II-A, Box 227; "Hillsboro, Ohio," *C-L* 67 (Feb. 1956), in NAACP, Group III-A, Box 201; *Clemons v. Board of Education of Hillsboro, Ohio*, 228 F.2d. 853 (1956).

172 **"theoretically, the Negro":** W.E.B. Du Bois, "Does the Negro Need Separate Schools?", *JNE* 4:3 (July 1935), 328–29, 335; *CD*, Oct. 6, 13, 1945; Du Bois to Marian S. Williams, Aug. 31, 1945, in Herbert Aptheker, ed., *The Correspondence of W. E. B. Du Bois*, vol. 3 (Amherst, Mass., 1978), 49–50; Douglas, *Jim Crow Moves North*, 195–205.

173 **Joining Du Bois in his skepticism:** Douglas, *Jim Crow Moves North*, 109–11, 172–86.

174 **"relatively small number":** Robin M. Williams, Jr., and Margaret W. Ryan, eds., *Schools in Transition: Community Experiences in Desegregation* (Chapel Hill, N.C., 1954), 240.

175 **black enclaves:** Leonard Blumberg and Michael Lalli, "Little Ghettoes: A
Study of Negroes in the Suburbs," *Phylon* 27:2 (1966), 117–31; Andrew Weise,
"The Other Suburbanites: African American Suburbanization Before 1950,"
JAH (1999), 1495–1524; *Encarta Africana*, 2nd ed., CD-ROM, "Suburbaniza-
tion and African Americans" (by Thomas J. Sugrue); Rosalyn Baxandall and
Elizabeth Ewen, *Picture Windows: How the Suburbs Happened* (New York,
2000), 172–90.

176 **the state was a microcosm:** Wendel A. White et al., *Small Towns, Black Lives:
African American Communities in Southern New Jersey* (Oceanville, N.J.,
2003); Clement Alexander Price, *Freedom Not Far Distant: A Documentary History of Afro-Americans in New Jersey* (Newark, N.J., 1980).

176 **New Jersey had been a hotbed of protests:** Meier and Rudwick, *Along the
Color Line*, 310, 312–14.

176 **In the case of one New Jersey town:** Horace Mann Bond, "The Extent and
Character of Separate Schools in the United States," *JNE* 4:3 (July 1935),
326–27.

176 **New Jersey's battle:** *CD*, June 17, 1939; Marion Thompson Wright, "New Jersey Leads in the Struggle for Educational Integration," *JES* 26 (1953), 401–17.

177 **When the Trenton activists:** Press Release from Milton Konvitz, Re: Briefs
Filed in Trenton Case, Jan. 26, 1944, in NAACP, Group II-B, Folder 143; *Ex Rel
Hedgepeth v. Board of Education of the City of Trenton*; *NYT*, Feb. 1, 1944;
"New Jersey School Admits Bias," Dec. 7, 1945, in MSRC, Vertical File: Educa-
tion, New Jersey; *CD*, Oct. 9, 1943, Oct. 12, 1946; generally, see Kevin Mum-
ford, "Double V in New Jersey: African American Civic Culture and Rising
Consciousness Against Jim Crow, 1938–1966," *NJH* 119 (2001), 22–56.

177 **In 1947, it released a grim survey:** "Survey—Public School Systems in New
Jersey, 1947," "Indications of Discrimination in the Public Schools of New Jer-
sey, 1947," and "Segregation Fought in Jersey Schools," April 11, 1947, all in
NAACP, Group II-B, Folder 143.

178 **The complete overhaul of New Jersey's laws:** For a detailed discussion of
New Jersey's constitution, see ch. 4; see also Douglas, *Jim Crow Moves North*,
241–42.

178 **In 1947, black parents in Long Branch:** John K. Weiss, "All the Town's Children," *TNR*, Nov. 17, 1947, 14.

178 **Facing pressure to desegregate:** *CD*, June 12, July 24, 1948, April 16, 1949;
NYT, Sept. 8, 1949; *PT*, Sept. 10, 1949; *BAA*, Sept. 17, 1949; Williams and Ryan,
eds., *Schools in Transition*, 169–72; "New Jersey Schools," *Crisis*, Dec. 1954,
607; Jack Washington, *The Long Journey Home: A Bicentennial History of the
Black Community of Princeton, New Jersey* (Trenton, N.J., 2005), 193–200.

179 **metropolitan New York:** Martha Biondi, *To Stand and Fight: The Struggle for
Civil Rights in Postwar New York City* (Cambridge, Mass., 2003), 15, 272, 279;
Joshua B. Freeman, *Working-Class New York: Life and Labor Since World
War II* (New York, 2000), 57–58; Paul Milkman, *PM: A New Deal in Journal-
ism, 1940–48* (New Brunswick, N.J., 1997).

180 **NAACP attorney Constance Baker Motley:** Constance Baker Motley, *Equal Justice Under Law: An Autobiography* (New York, 1998), 71.

180 **Born in 1921, Motley:** Motley, *Equal Justice Under Law,* 9–70.

180 **At the beginning of the 1949 school year:** *NYT,* Sept. 15, 17, 24, Nov. 28, 1949; *PT,* Sept. 27, 1949; *BAA,* Sept. 24, 1949; *NYAN,* Sept. 24, 1949, in AMP, Box 92, Folder 10; *CD,* Oct. 1, 1949.

181 **"school boards are not under compulsion":** *NYAN,* Sept. 3, 1949.

181 **Parents of white children:** *PT,* June 6, 1950; *Savannah Tribune,* Jan. 26, Aug. 23, 1951, copies in AMP, Box 92, Folder 11.

181 **By 1962, two of Hempstead's:** *NYT,* Feb. 16, 1962; *Branche v. Board of Education of Town of Hempstead,* 204 F. Supp. 150 (1962).

181 **In May 1954, the U.S. Supreme Court:** *Brown v. Board of Education of Topeka,* 347 U.S. 483 (1954); for reactions, see, for example, *CD,* Oct. 29, 1956. The North is virtually absent from otherwise excellent accounts of the case and its reception. See, for example, Michael J. Klarman, *From Jim Crow to Civil Rights: The Supreme Court and the Struggle for Racial Equality* (New York, 2004), and James T. Patterson, *Brown v. Board of Education: A Civil Rights Milestone and Its Troubled Legacy* (New York, 2001).

182 **"Separate educational facilities":** *Brown v. Board,* at 495.

182 **"generates a feeling of inferiority":** *Brown v. Board,* at 494; National Association of Intergroup Relations Officials (NAIRO), Commission on School Integration, *Public School Segregation and Integration in the North: Analysis and Proposals* (Washington, D.C., 1963), 35; see generally Daryl M. Scott, "Postwar Pluralism, *Brown v. Board of Education,* and the Origins of Multicultural Education," *JAH* 91 (2004), 69–82; Ellen Herman, *The Romance of American Psychology: Political Culture in the Age of Experts* (Berkeley, 1995), esp. 174–207.

183 **No sooner had *Brown* been decided:** June Shagaloff to Henry L. Moon, Jan. 27, 1955, and "Pennsylvania Town Integrates Schools," NAACP Press Release, Feb. 3, 1955; *Harrisburg Evening News,* Aug. 4, 1954; *York Gazette and Daily,* June 29, July 1, 2, 6, 7, 1954; Elwood Chisom to Robert Carter, Aug. 10, 1954, all in NAACP, Group II-A, Box 228.

183 **Even in the absence:** *NYT,* Feb. 10, 1957; "The Facts of de Facto," *Time,* Aug. 2, 1963; G. W. Foster, Jr., "The North and West Have Problems, Too," *SR,* April 20, 1963; Alfred McClung Lee, "The Impact of Segregated Housing on Public Schools," in William W. Brickman and Stanley Lehrer, eds., *The Countdown on Segregated Education* (New York, 1960), 78.

184 **"the problem [of unequal education]":** *CD,* Sept. 19, 1956.

185 **"has become as deeply embedded":** Will Maslow and Richard Cohen, "School Segregation Northern Style," Public Affairs Pamphlet No. 316, Aug. 1961, 10, in SCCF, 004-102; "Should All Northern Schools Be Integrated?" *Time,* Sept. 7, 1962.

185 **"the nearer Negroes get":** NAIRO, *Public School Segregation and Integration in the North,* 23; see also generally Meyer Weinberg, *Race and Place: A Legal History of the Neighborhood School* (Washington, D.C., 1967).

185 **what constituted a neighborhood:** Gerald Gamm, *Urban Exodus: Why the Jews Left Boston and the Catholics Stayed* (Cambridge, Mass., 1999); John McGreevy, *Parish Boundaries: The Catholic Encounter with Race in the Twentieth-Century Urban North* (Chicago, 1996).

186 **The boundaries that mattered:** On boundaries in Chicago, see Homel, *Down from Equality*, 35–40; on the Emlen School case, see USCCR, *Civil Rights USA: Public Schools, Cities in the North and West* (Washington, D.C., 1962), 131ff.

186 **There was nothing fixed:** Mirel, *The Rise and Fall of an Urban School System*, 258–62; Michael Clapper, "School Design, Site Selection, and the Political Geography of Race in Postwar Philadelphia," *Journal of Planning History* 5 (2006), 241–63; Homel, *Down from Equality*, 35–40; *AD*, 630.

187 **Not all school districts gerrymandered:** Johnson, *Patterns of Segregation*, 24–25, 193; USCCR, *Civil Rights USA*, 12–13, 17, 142–53, 171; for examples of transfers in Chicago, see Homel, *Down from Equality*, 40–41.

187 **Preserving racial boundaries:** St. Clair Drake and Horace Cayton, *Black Metropolis: A Study of Negro Life in a Northern City* (New York, 1945), 202; USCCR, *Civil Rights USA*, 223–24; St. Clair Drake, "The Social and Economic Status of the Negro in the United States," *Daedalus* 94 (Fall 1965), 783.

188 **By the late 1950s and early 1960s:** Foster, "The North and West Have Problems, Too."

188 **Harlem seemed a natural place:** Gerald Markowitz and David Rosner, *Children, Race, and Power: Kenneth and Mamie Clark's Northside Center* (Charlottesville, Va., 1996), 90–110; Barbara Ransby, *Ella Baker and the Black Freedom Movement: A Radical Democratic Vision* (Chapel Hill, N.C., 2003), 151–56; Biondi, *To Stand and Fight*, 241–49.

189 **Bernice Skipwith and Shirley Rector:** Sylvan G. Feldstein and Bernard Mackler, "De Facto School Segregation in the North: The Case of *In re Skipwith*," *Howard Law Journal* 35 (Spring 1969), 384–86, 395; Timothy B. Tyson, *Radio Free Dixie: Robert F. Williams and the Roots of Black Power* (Chapel Hill, N.C., 1999), 189–90; and esp. Adina Back, "Exposing the 'Whole Segregation Myth': The Harlem Nine and New York City's School Desegregation Battles," in Jeanne F. Theoharis and Komozi Woodard, eds., *Freedom North: Black Freedom Struggles Outside the South, 1940–1980* (New York, 2003), 65–91.

190 **The case of Skipwith and Rector ended up:** *In the Matter of Charlene Skipwith, Sheldon Rector*, Domestic Relations Court, City of New York, Justine Wise Polier, Dec. 15, 1958, in JWPP, Box 21, Folder 248; for coverage, see *NYT*, Dec. 16, 1958; *USNWR*, Jan. 9, 1959; Naomi Levine, "Attacking Segregation in the North," *Congress Bi-Weekly*, Jan. 10, 1959, 10–12; letters to Polier, esp. JWPP, Box 21, Folder 249; Feldstein and Mackler, "De Facto School Segregation in the North," 416–19; Cheryl Lynn Greenberg, *Troubling the Waters: Black-Jewish Relations in the American Century* (Princeton, N.J., 2006), 123.

190 **nearby New Rochelle:** USCCR, *Civil Rights USA*, 52–55; John Kaplan, "Segregation Litigation and the Schools—Part I: The New Rochelle Experience," *Northwestern Law Review* 58:1 (March–April 1964), 5–7.

191 **In 1930, NAACP officials had opposed:** Leon Scott et al. to Board of Education, Jan. 9, 1930, NAACP, Group II-B, Box 144; USCCR, *Education: 1961: Report 2* (Washington, D.C., 1962), 102.

191 **In the late 1940s, New Rochelle activists:** Resolution Adopted by the Board of Directors of the Council for Unity, Dec. 16, 1948; Citizen's Committee for Lincoln School, "A Report of the Findings Relative to Lincoln School," Jan. 11, 1949; Statement of the Council of Unity to the Board of Education, Jan. 11, 1949; *NRSS*, Feb. 26, 1949; all in NAACP, Group II-B, Box 144; Memorandum to Miss Black from Marian Wynn Perry, Apr. 29, 1949, RE: New Rochelle School and New Rochelle Housing Situations, NAACP, Group II-A, Box 518.

191 **At a lengthy, contentious school board meeting:** *NRSS*, Jan. 12, 1949; Resolution of Board of Education, Jan. 12, 1949, in NAACP, Group II-B, Box 144.

192 **In late 1949, they filed a lawsuit:** Memorandum from Mrs. Motley, RE: New Rochelle School Case, Nov. 7, 1949, ibid.; Hearing Scheduled in NAACP New Rochelle School Fight, Jan. 12, 1950, ibid.

192 **When the New Rochelle school district:** *NYT*, Dec. 20, 1956, March 23, May 12, 1957; Kaplan, "Segregation Litigation," 9; *NYT*, Oct. 6, 8, 1959; *NYT*, Dec. 2, 3, 1959, Jan. 9, May 21, 25, 1960.

192 **Paul Zuber:** Marya Mannes, "School Trouble in Harlem," *Reporter*, Feb. 5, 1959; *CD*, Aug. 23, 1962.

193 **"I feel that at Lincoln School":** Kaplan, "Segregation Litigation," 16.

193 **A group of parents would attempt:** *CD*, Sept. 24, 1960.

193 **Herbert Clish, the superintendent:** *NYT*, Sept. 15, 16, 20, 1960.

194 **The New Rochelle protests accelerated:** *NRSS*, Sept. 26, 1960; *BAA*, Oct. 8, 1960: Memorandum from Gloster Current to Roy Wilkins et al., Oct. 13, 1960, NAACP-M, Part 3-D, Reel 6, frames 798–99 (hereafter Current-Wilkins memo).

194 **played the international card:** *NYT*, Sept. 26, 1960; *NRSS*, Sept. 26, 1960; *NYT*, Sept. 29, Oct. 6, 10, 18, 1960; Current-Wilkins memo, 799–801.

195 **"The schools," argued Clish:** *NYT*, Oct. 2, 1960.

196 **"Nothing makes my blood boil more":** *CD*, Aug. 7, 1961; "The Facts of de Facto," *Time*, Aug. 2, 1963.

196 **The core of Zuber's complaint:** USCCR, *Civil Rights USA*, 39–40, 45.

196 **At trial, however:** Kaplan, "Segregation Litigation," 34; Henry E. Garrett, "The Equalitarian Dogma," *Mankind Quarterly* 1 (1961), 253–57; Garrett, "Racial Differences and Witchhunting," *Science*, March 16, 1962, 984.

197 **Federal judge Irving Kaufman . . . heard the case:** *Taylor v. Board of Education of City School District of City of New Rochelle*, 195 F. Supp. 231 (1961); *NYT*, Jan. 25, 1961; Kaufman later argued that he did "not strike down the neighborhood school policy . . . as an abstract proposition." See *NYT*, March 8, 1961.

198 **The New Rochelle boycotters were jubilant:** *NYT*, Jan. 26, 1961; New York CORE to Dear Friend, April 4, 1961, NAACP, Group III-A, Box 201; *CD*, Aug. 7, 1961.

198 **School district officials:** Memorandum: to Messrs. Wilkins and Current, from Herbert L. Wright, May 3, 1961, NAACP, Group III-A, Box 201; Northern Committee for School Integration to Dear Friend, April 13, 1961, *CD*, Aug. 7, 1961; Kaplan, "Segregation Litigation," 63, 65; *Taylor v. Board of Education*, 294 F.2d 36 (2d Cir. 1961); 368 U.S. 940 (1961); NAIRO, *Public School Segregation and Integration*, 5; USCCR, *Public Education: 1963 Staff Report* (Dec. 1963), 102–4; *NYT*, June 1, 1986.

198 **The New Rochelle victory rippled:** *NYT*, March 19, 1962; Paul Dannis and Leona Farrington to Roy Wilkins, Nov. 30, 1962, NAACP-M, Part 3-D, Reel 6, frame 872; Paul Dannis to Roy Wilkins, March 9, 1963, NAACP-M, Part 3-D, Reel 6, frame 874.

199 ***Taylor v. Board of Education* also launched:** *CD*, Aug. 7, 23, 1961, Sept. 2, 6, 25, 1961, Oct. 16, 1961; Robert L. Carter, *A Matter of Law: A Memoir of Struggle in the Cause of Equal Rights* (New York, 2005), 165, 169–77.

199 **The results of challenges:** Robert Dentler, "Barriers to Northern School Desegregation," *Daedalus* 95 (Winter 1966), 45–63.

CHAPTER 7 | "NO RIGHT MORE ELEMENTAL"

200 **massive suburban developments:** On Levittown, see Herbert Gans, *The Levittowners: Ways of Life and Politics in a New Suburban Community* (New York, 1969); Kenneth T. Jackson, *Crabgrass Frontier: The Suburbanization of the United States* (New York, 1985), 234–38; Barbara Kelly, *Expanding the Dream: Building and Rebuilding Levittown* (Albany, N.Y., 1993).

201 **"land of rats and roaches":** Hughes, quoted in Charles Payne, "'You Duh Man': African Americans in the Twentieth Century," in Harvard Sitkoff, ed., *Perspectives on Modern America: Making Sense of the Twentieth Century* (New York, 2001), 183.

201 **"We can solve a housing problem":** "'Perfect Planning' at Levittown, Pa.," NAACP, Group II-A, Box 161.

201 **"among the basic consumer goods":** Robert C. Weaver, "Chicago: A City of Covenants," *Crisis*, July 1946, 76.

201 **Many smaller towns and suburbs:** Andrew Wiese, *Places of Their Own: African American Suburbanization in the Twentieth Century* (Chicago, 2004).

202 **"sundown towns":** James W. Loewen, *Sundown Towns: A Hidden Dimension of American Racism* (New York, 2005); *Buchanan v. Warley*, 245 U.S. 60 (1917).

202 **restrictive covenants controlled:** Robert M. Fogelson, *Bourgeois Nightmares: Suburbia, 1870–1930* (New Haven, Conn., 2005); Thomas J. Sugrue, "The Geography of Fear," *Nation*, Feb. 27, 2006, 32; "Iron Ring in Housing," *Crisis*, July 1940, 205; Robert C. Weaver, "Chicago: A City of Covenants," *Crisis*, March 1946, 75–78, 93; Patricia Burgess Stach, "Deed Restrictions and Subdivision Development in Columbus, Ohio, 1900–70," *JUH* 15 (1988), 42–68; Wendy

Plotkin, "Racial and Religious Covenants in the U.S. and Canada," www
.public.asu.edu/~wplotkin/DeedsWeb/.

203 **"should never be instrumental":** Charles Abrams, *Forbidden Neighbors: A
Study of Prejudice in Housing* (New York, 1955), 156.

203 **Federal housing programs:** David Freund, "Marketing the Free Market: State
Intervention and the Politics of Prosperity in Metropolitan America," in
Kevin M. Kruse and Thomas J. Sugrue, eds., *The New Suburban History*
(Chicago, 2006), 11–32; Jackson, *Crabgrass Frontier*, 190–218.

204 **"neighborhood security maps":** Kenneth T. Jackson, "Race, Ethnicity, and
Real Estate Appraisal: The Home Owners Loan Corporation and the Federal
Housing Administration," *JUH* 6 (1980), 419–52, offers the most detailed his-
tory of FHA policies. For a recent study, see Colin Gordon, *Mapping Decline: St.
Louis and the Fate of the American City* (Philadelphia, 2008).

204 **bloody battlegrounds:** Thomas J. Sugrue, *The Origins of the Urban Crisis:
Race and Inequality in Postwar Detroit* (Princeton, N.J., 1996), chs. 3, 8, 9;
Arnold R. Hirsch, *Making the Second Ghetto: Race and Housing in Chicago,
1940–1960* (New York, 1983); James Wolfinger, *Philadelphia Divided: Race
and Politics in the City of Brotherly Love* (Chapel Hill, N.C., 2007), 179–202;
Stephen Grant Meyer, *As Long As They Don't Move Next Door: Segregation and
Racial Conflict in American Neighborhoods* (Lanham, Md., 2000), offers the
most comprehensive account.

205 **The mass migration of whites:** John F. Kain, "The Big Cities' Big Problem,"
in Louis A. Ferman, Joyce L. Kornbluh, and J. A. Miller, eds., *Negroes and Jobs*
(Ann Arbor, Mich., 1968), 242.

205 **massive suburban growth:** The scholarship on suburbanization is too extensive to cite here. The most comprehensive account remains Jackson, *Crabgrass
Frontier*. For recent revisions, see Lizabeth Cohen, *A Consumers' Republic: The
Politics of Mass Consumption in Postwar America* (New York, 2003), 193–290,
and Kruse and Sugrue, *The New Suburban History*.

206 **political scientist Robert Wood found:** Robert Wood, *1400 Governments: The
Political Economy of the New York Metropolitan Region* (Cambridge, Mass.,
1961).

206 **In modern America, still an intensely localistic:** Jon C. Teaford, *City and
Suburb: The Political Fragmentation of Metropolitan America* (Baltimore,
1979); Thomas J. Sugrue, "All Politics Is Local: The Persistence of Localism in
Twentieth-Century America," in Meg Jacobs, William J. Novak, and Julian
Zelizer, eds., *The Democratic Experiment: New Directions in American Political
History* (Princeton, N.J., 2003), 301–26; Phil Ethington, "Mapping the Local
State," *JUH* 27 (2001), 686–702; Nancy Burns, *The Formation of American
Local Governments: Private Values in Public Institutions* (New York, 1994);
Gerald E. Frug, *City Making: Building Communities Without Building Walls*
(Princeton, N.J., 1999); and Richard Thompson Ford, "The Boundaries of
Race: Political Geography in Legal Analysis," in Kimberle Crenshaw et al., eds.,

Critical Race Theory: The Key Writings That Formed the Movement (New York, 1995), 449–64.

207 **"In the North":** *AD*, 600, 602.

207 **the NAACP defended Ossian Sweet:** The definitive account is Kevin Boyle, *Arc of Justice: A Saga of Race, Civil Rights, and Murder in the Jazz Age* (New York, 2004).

207 **"There is no right more elemental":** "Iron Ring in Housing," *Crisis*, July 1940, 205.

207 **challenge to restrictive covenants:** "Conference Resolutions," *Crisis*, Sept. 1941, 296; *Hansberry v. Lee*, 311 U.S. 32 (1940); Lorraine Hansberry, *A Raisin in the Sun* (1959; rept. New York, 2004); "What the Branches Are Doing," *Crisis*, Dec. 1946, 375; *Sipes v. McGhee*, 316 Mich. 614. See case-related materials in NAACP, Group II-B, Boxes 135–37. Generally, see Clement E. Vose, *Caucasians Only: The Supreme Court, the NAACP, and the Restrictive Covenant Cases* (Berkeley, Calif., 1959).

208 **NAACP lawyers developed:** Mark V. Tushnet, *Making Civil Rights Law: Thurgood Marshall and the Supreme Court, 1936–1961* (New York, 1994), 88–89.

208 **the 1948 *Shelley v. Kraemer* case:** *Shelley v. Kraemer*, 334 U.S. 1 (1948); *PC*, May 8, 1948, *MC*, May 8, 1948, *CD*, May 8, 1948; "Answer to the Gentlemen," *TNR*, May 17, 1948, 5; "The Houses We Live In," *INS* (Early Summer 1948), 3; Tushnet, *Making Civil Rights Law*, 81–98.

208 **"aided upper-middle-class blacks":** Constance Baker Motley, *Equal Justice Under Law: An Autobiography* (New York, 1998), 67; "Equality in Housing," *TNR*, Dec. 19, 1949, 7–8; Arnold R. Hirsch, "Choosing Segregation: Federal Housing Policy Between *Shelley* and *Brown*," in John Bauman et al., eds., *From Tenements to the Taylor Homes: In Search of an Urban Housing Policy in Twentieth-Century America* (University Park, Pa., 2000).

209 **the fingerprints of public policy:** David M. P. Freund, *Colored Property: State Policy and White Racial Politics in Suburban America* (Chicago, 2007).

210 **New York's Stuyvesant Town:** "'Eminent' Domain: A 'Walled City,'" *INS* (July 1943), 3–4; *PC*, May 19, 1943; *Dorsey v. Stuyvesant Town*, 87 N.E.2d 541 (N.Y. 1949); cert. denied, 339 U.S. 981 (1950); A. Scott Henderson, *Housing and the Democratic Ideal: The Life and Thought of Charles Abrams* (New York, 2000), 136–45; Martha Biondi, *To Stand and Fight: The Struggle for Civil Rights in Postwar New York City* (Cambridge, Mass., 2003), 121–36; Joel Schwartz, *The New York Approach: Robert Moses and the Redevelopment of the Inner City* (Columbus, Ohio, 1993), 84–107.

210 **activists turned their attention to William Levitt:** *NYT*, March 18, 19, 1949; *C.E.D. Newsletter*, Jan. 1954, in NAACP, Group II-A, Box 314; Biondi, *To Stand and Fight*, 230.

211 **Unchecked by the FHA:** "Left of Center," *TNR*, July, 11, 1949, 11; *Ross v. Levitt and Sons*, NAACP-M, Part 1, Supplement 1, Reel 2, frames 146, 153, 172–73, 188; Memorandum from Constance Baker Motley to Messrs. Wilkins et al., Feb. 1, 1952, Re: Committee to End Discrimination in Levittown Campaign

and *Mid-Island Properties v. Harold Johnson and Dulcie M. Johnson and William Cotter*, NAACP, Group II-A, Box 314.

211 **"Mr. Levitt," the NAACP attorney reported:** Memorandum to Mrs. Motley from Roy Wilkins, Aug. 22, 1951; Constance Baker Motley, Memorandum to Mr. Wilkins, Re: Conference on Levittown, Pennsylvania, Nov. 9, 1951; Motley to Vashti Norwood, Nov. 5, 1951, in NAACP, Group II-A, Box 161.

212 **Fine summarized the official position:** Report of the Secretary, NAACP-M, Part 1, Supplement 1, Reel 2, frames 80, 97, 111, 209.

212 **their efforts were fruitless:** Constance Baker Motley to Joseph Bolden, Feb. 26, 1952; Arthur Johnson to To Whom it May Concern, Aug. 27, 1952; NAACP, Group II-A, Box 161; correspondence between C. F. Hood (U.S. Steel president) and Walter White and E. M. Moore (U.S. Steel vice president) and Walter White; Walter White to Dwight D. Eisenhower, Jan. 12, 1954, all in NAACP, Group II-A, Box 161.

212 **filed a federal lawsuit:** NAACP-M, Part I, Supplement 1, Reel 2, frames 840, 849, 860, 872; "Discrimination in Housing," *Crisis*, Feb. 1954, 96–97; "Levitt Hauled into Federal Court," *Crisis*, March 1955, 158–59, 190; *DW*, Jan. 23, 1955; *Arthur L. Johnson et al. v. Levitt & Sons, Inc. et al.*, 131 F. Supp. 114 (E.D. Pa. 1955), 116. See, generally, Arnold R. Hirsch, "Less than Plessy: The Inner City, Suburbs, and State-Sanctioned Residential Segregation in the Age of Brown," in Kruse and Sugrue, eds., *The New Suburban History*, 33–56.

213 **"The right to equality":** Charles Abrams, "The Limits of Law," *Commentary*, Oct. 1952, 402, cited in Henderson, *Housing and the Democratic Ideal*, 144; see also Charles Abrams, OH, interview by B. Swerdloff, esp. 22, 25, 31–32, CUOHP.

213 **"vicious circle":** *AD*, 1023, 1024.

214 **A burgeoning subdiscipline in postwar psychology:** Robin M. Williams, Jr., *The Reduction of Intergroup Tension: A Survey of Research on the Problems of Ethnic, Racial, and Religious Group Relations* (New York, 1947); Robert M. McIver, *The More Perfect Union: A Program for the Control of Inter-group Discrimination in the United States* (New York, 1948); Bruno Bettelheim and Morris Janowitz, "Ethnic Tolerance: A Function of Social and Personal Control," *American Journal of Sociology* 55 (1949), 137–46; Theodore Adorno et al., *The Authoritarian Personality* (New York, 1950); Arnold M. Rose, "Intergroup Relations vs. Prejudice: Theory for the Study of Social Change," *SP* 4 (1957), 174. On Myrdal and psychology, see Daryl Michael Scott, "Postwar Pluralism, *Brown v. Board of Education*, and the Origins of Multicultural Education," *JAH* 91 (2004); 77–78; Ruth Feldstein, *Motherhood in Black and White: Race and Sex in American Liberalism, 1930–1965* (Ithaca, N.Y., 2000), 44–49.

214 **Dr. Frederic Wertham:** Robert Bendiner, "Psychiatry Comes to Harlem," *ND*, Sept. 1948, 77–85; Ausubel, quoted in Daryl Michael Scott, *Contempt and Pity: Social Policy and the Image of the Damaged Black Psyche, 1880–1996* (Chapel Hill, N.C., 1997), 81; Abram Kardiner and Lionel Ovesey, *The Mark of Oppression* (New York, 1951).

214 **Sociologists and psychologists viewed:** Thomas F. Pettigrew, ed., *A Profile of the Negro American* (Princeton, N.J., 1964), 15–25, 146–47, quotes 16, 146; Guy B. Johnson, "The Negro and Crime," in Arnold M. Rose, ed., *Race Prejudice and Discrimination: Readings in Intergroup Relations in the United States* (New York, 1951), 413, 420. See also Feldstein, *Motherhood in Black and White*, 53–60.

215 **"segregation creates slum behavior":** Mozell Hill, "The Metropolis and Juvenile Delinquency," *JNE* 28 (1959), 283, 284; *IN*, Dec. 11, 1961.

215 **Social psychologists provided:** See Gerald Markowitz and David Rosner, *Children, Race, and Power: Kenneth and Mamie Clark's Northside Center* (Charlottesville, Va., 1996); Gerald N. Grob, "Psychiatry and Social Activism: The Politics of a Specialty in Postwar America," *Bulletin of the History of Medicine* 60 (1986), 477–501; August Meier and Elliott Rudwick, *CORE: A Study in the Civil Rights Movement, 1942–1968* (Urbana, 1975); Herbert Kelman, interview, June 1972, AMP, Box 56, Folder 9; Scott, *Contempt and Pity*, 107–8.

216 **social science made its way:** Alice O'Connor, *Social Science for What? Philanthropy and the Social Question in a World Turned Rightside Up* (New York, 2007), 79–89; Thomas C. Reeves, *Freedom and the Foundation: The Fund for the Republic in the Era of McCarthyism* (New York, 1969).

216 **NCDH quickly became:** Juliet Z. Saltman, *Open Housing as a Social Movement: Challenge, Conflict, and Change* (Lexington, Mass., 1971), 29–31, 33–39, 41–53; *Fair Housing Handbook* (New York, 1963); I have read the entire run of *Trends in Housing (TIH)*.

217 **"Prejudice," argued one article:** Mary Jane Ward, "Does Prejudice Cause Mental Illness?," *ND*, April 1949, 6; Betsy Emmons, "The Psychiatrists Look at Race Hate," *ND*, July 1948, 32; Jerome Himelhoch, "The Study of Man: Is There a Bigot Personality?" *Commentary*, March 1947, 277–84; for examples of the popularization of psychology generally, see Ellen Herman, *The Romance of American Psychology: Political Culture in the Age of Experts* (Berkeley, 1995), esp. 174–207; Eva Moskowitz, *In Therapy We Trust: America's Obsession with Self-Fulfillment* (Baltimore, 2001).

217 **"grow up self-respecting":** *TIH*, March–April 1960.

217 **In a series of articles:** Herman Long, "Facts and Fantasies in Integrated Housing," *SA* (Nov. 1957), 10–13; Galen R. Weaver, "Effects of Open Housing on Marriage," *SA* (Nov. 1957), 15.

217 **Despite their grim vision:** Alice O'Connor, *Poverty Knowledge: Social Science, Social Policy, and the Poor in Twentieth-Century U.S. History* (Princeton, N.J., 2001), 88–89; Morton Deutsch and Mary Evans Collins, "Interracial Housing and Changes in Attitudes," in Rose, ed., *Race Prejudice and Discrimination*, 555–64; Gordon W. Allport, *The Nature of Prejudice* (Cambridge, Mass., 1954).

218 **"The future direction":** *PC*, Sept. 1, 1962.

219 **"segregation subjects sections":** *Syracuse Post-Standard*, Jan. 30, 1954.

219 **A small cadre of liberal Protestants:** "Race Relations Sunday Comes of Age," *INS* (March 1943), 1; "Upon This Rock: Race Relations Sunday—A Quarter of

a Century," *INS* (Sept.–Oct. 1946), 4; Helen Huntington Smith, "Do You Know Your Neighbor?," *ND*, July 1948, 41–49 (originally published in *Women's Home Companion*); Rose Zeligs, "Growth in Intergroup Attitudes During Brotherhood Week," *JNE* 19 (1950), 94–102; Dan W. Dodson, "Public Intergroup Relations Agencies," *JNE* 20 (1951), 403–4.

220 **"If Negroes are integrated":** Charles Abrams, "Race Bias in Housing, Part II: Will Interracial Housing Work?" *Nation*, Aug. 2, 1947, 122.

220 **The Quakers had long been:** Jean Soderlund, *Quakers and Slavery: A Divided Spirit* (Princeton, N.J., 1989); Rachel Davis DuBois, *All This and Something More: Pioneering in Intercultural Education: An Autobiography* (Bryn Mawr, Pa., 1984); *Faith and Practice of the Philadelphia Yearly Meeting of the Religious Society of Friends: A Book of Christian Discipline* (Philadelphia, 1955), 37; *Race and Conscience in America: A Review Prepared for the American Friends Service Committee* (Norman, Okla., 1959), iii; Martha L. Deed, "Steps Toward a Quaker Testimony on Racial Equality," *INS* (Sept.–Oct. 1965).

221 **they pushed aggressively for racial equality:** Brian Ward, "Broadcasting Truth to Power: The American Friends Service Committee and the Early Southern Freedom Movement," *Quaker History* 10 (2005), 87–108; William H. Chafe, *Civilities and Civil Rights: Greensboro, North Carolina, and the Black Struggle for Freedom* (New York, 1980); Gerald Jonas, "A Reporter at Large: The American Friends Service Committee: Part I: A Common Concept of Justice," *NY*, March 13, 1971, 94ff., on Chicago; see also "Part II: A Valuable Prototype," *NY*, March 20, 1971, 99ff. Material on Chicago, Milpitas, Columbus, and Syracuse in AFSC-AD-CR, various years.

222 **No sooner did Levittown:** Allen Ward, "Levittown, Pa.: Negroes Not Wanted," *Bucks County Traveler*, June 1954, 12, 27.

222 **In July 1954, Reinheimer met with:** Memorandum from Jane Reinheimer, Subject: Visit with Joseph and Minnie Hitov, July 15, 1954, in AFSC-AD-CR, 1954, Box: Community Relations Housing A–Z, Folder: Visits; Memo from Jane Reinheimer, Sept. 3, 1954; Memo from Jane Reinheimer, April 7, 1955; "Organizations Working for Integrated Housing," *SA* (Nov. 1957), 30–31.

223 **"equal status":** Allport, *The Nature of Prejudice*, ch. 16.

223 **Finding blacks to move into Levittown:** Memos from Jane Reinheimer, May 26, Aug. 9, 16, Sept. 1, 1954; Memo from Jacques Wilmore, Sept. 22, 1954, in AFSC-AD-CR, 1954, Box: Housing A–Z; Memo from Jane Reinheimer, April 11, Aug. 3, Nov. 10, 1955; Kent Larrabee to Dear Friend, Nov. 25, 1955. One activist involved in the effort to integrate Long Island's Levittown noted that CORE looked for a "Paragon of the middle class." See Mrs. Mark Dodson interview, June 1971, AMP, Box 56, Folder 5; Lewis Wechsler, *The First Stone: A Memoir of the Racial Integration of Levittown, Pennsylvania* (Chicago, 2004), 13–16.

224 **Despite the best efforts:** Report of Philadelphia Housing Opportunities Program, Jan. 1953–Apr. 1954, AFSC-AD-CR, 1954, Folder: Housing: General; Memo from Jane Reinheimer, April 11, 1955; "Some What's, Why's, How's, and

Where's About the AFSC Housing Opportunities Program," May 21, 1958, in AFSC-AD-CR, 1958, Folder: Housing Program: General.

224 **Finally, in 1957, William and Daisy Myers:** Job Opportunities Personnel Data Form, AFSC-AD-CR, 1958; *NYT*, Aug. 22, 1957; Wechsler, *The First Stone*, 17–19; Daisy Myers, *Sticks 'n' Stones: The Myers Family in Levittown* (York, Pa., 2005), 23–24, on the interview process, which she remembers entailed some "relevant" and "stupid" questions.

224 **More than two thousand white Levittowners:** Daisy Myers with Linda Shopes, "Breaking Down Barriers," *Pennsylvania Heritage* 28 (Summer 2002), 6–13; *NYP*, Aug. 19, 1957.

224 **Several white Levittowners:** F[lorence] Kite, "Levittown: A Few Notes," Nov. 12, 1957, Barbara Moffett to Lewis Wechsler, Aug. 16, 1957, in AFSC-AD-CR, 1957, Folder: Housing: Lower Bucks County; "Used in P.R.," Aug. 15, 1957, NAACP Press Release, Aug. 22, 1957; Memorandum to Mr. Wilkins et al., from Calvin Banks, Aug. 23, 1957, all in NAACP, Group III-A, Folder 167; Wechsler, *The First Stone.*

225 **A several-week siege followed:** *PT*, Aug. 17, 20, 24, 1957; *NYP*, Aug. 20, 1957; *BCCT*, Aug. 20, 21, 1957; Walter F. Moses to Joseph P. Madden, Sept. 19, 1957; Colgan to Pa. State Department of Insurance, Sept. 16, 1957; Thomas Colgan, OH, Jan. 29, 1991, AFSC; Thomas Colgan to Howard W. McKinney, Sept. 16, 1957; Memo, Barbara Moffatt to Tom Colgan, Sept. 13, 1957, Subject: Where the Levittown Police Protection Matter Stands, all in AFSC-AD-CR, 1957, Folder: Housing: Lower Bucks County; *NYT*, Sept. 25, 26, 27, 1957; NAACP-M, Part 1, Supplement 2, Reel 1, frame 464; Wechsler, *The First Stone*, 65; Myers, *Sticks 'n' Stones*, offers a powerful first-person account.

226 **A wide range of white-dominated:** Kite, "Levittown"; AFSC Role in Levittown, Oct. 11, 1957; Memo to Mike Yarrow from Tom Colgan, Oct. 24, 1957; Lydia Wolcox to Ron Turner, Dec. 16, 1957; Memo to Tom Colgan from Mike Yarrow, Dec. 20, 1957; Thomas Colgan to Robert James, Dec. 11, 1957; Colgan to Joan and Ron Turner, Nov. 7, 1957; Tom Colgan to Daisy and Bill Myers, Feb. 28, 1957; Colgan to Daisy and Bill Myers, June 4, 1958, AFSC-AD-CR, 1958, Folder: Housing: Lower Bucks County; *PT*, Aug. 24, 1957; *DW*, Aug. 25, 1957; *NYHT*, Sept. 21, 1957; Albert Vorspan, "Segregation and Social Justice," *American Judaism* (Jan. 1958), 10–11.

226 **A cadre of white neighbors:** *PT*, Aug. 20, 1957; Kite, "Levittown"; "One Neighbor to Another: A Statement of Principle and Aims," Dogwood Hollow Neighbors, Levittown, Pa., and Memo to Thelma Babbitt from Tom Colgan, Nov. 20, 1957, in AFSC-AD-CR, 1957, Folder: Community Relations Program: General; *DW*, Aug. 20, 22, 25, Sept. 4, 1957; "Experience in Interracial Living," *SA* (Nov. 1957), 21–22.

226 **But even if most Levittowners:** *BCCT*, Aug. 21, 1957; *BCCT*, Aug. 29, 1957; "Integration Troubles Beset Northern Town," *Life*, Sept. 2, 1957; *DW*, Sept. 4, 1957; Memo to Barbara Moffett from Tom Colgan, Oct. 24, 1957; Thomas Col-

gan to Wayne Dockhorn, Nov. 4, 1957; Wechsler, *The First Stone*, 63–65; letters from Mrs. Edward Valent, Art Clay, "A Levittowner" and "Levittown White Democrat," to Governor George Leader, Aug. 1957, in George Leader Papers, Subject File: Levittown State Police Action, Carton 43, PSA (thanks to Peter Siskind for these citations); on Catholic responses, see also Dennis Clark, "A Tale of Two Levittowns," *NC*, May 15, 1963, 4–5.

227 **In addition, several Myers supporters:** Memo to M. Behrman et al. from Lydia Wilcox, Sept. 13, 1957; *PT*, Aug. 24, 1957; Memo to Thelma Babbitt from Tom Colgan, Nov. 20, 1957; Memo to Thelma Babbitt from Tom Colgan, Dec. 19, 1957; Barbara Moffett to Fred Manthey, Nov. 29, 1957; Memo from Tom Colgan, Re: Rev. Mr. Fred Manthey, Nov. 27, 1957; Memo, Thelma Babbitt to CR Staff, Feb. 4, 1958, in AFSC-AD-CR, 1958, Box: Community Relations, Folder: Projects: Housing Program 1958 Reports. Mandel got a police guard at his Philadelphia home because of threats on his life. See *PT*, Aug. 24, 1957.

227 **to find another black family:** *PT*, Aug. 20, 24, Sept. 7, Oct. 26, 1957; Memo to Thelma Babbitt from Tom Colgan, Re: Real Estate Transfers, Nov. 20, 1957; Memo to Thelma Babbitt from Tom Colgan, Dec. 5, 1957; Memo to CR Staff from Thelma Babbitt, April 18, 1958; Report of Events Surrounding the Move of the Second Negro Family to Levittown, Pa., Aug. 6, 1958, in AFSC-AD-CR, Folder: Housing: General.

228 **Now that Levittown had been:** "After the Storm, What Happens to Values," *BW*, Aug. 31, 1957; Memo to Community Relations Staff, from Thelma Babbitt, Nov. 14, 1958, in AFSC-AD-CR, 1958, Folder: Projects: Housing Program 1958 Reports.

228 **In Cicero, Illinois:** Byron S. Miller, "Cicero's Covenants," *TNR*, Aug. 6, 1951, 11–13; Gregory Squires et al., *Chicago: Race, Class, and the Response to Urban Decline* (Philadelphia, 1987), 120.

228 **Mayor Orville Hubbard of Dearborn, Michigan:** *CD*, Dec. 30, 1944; Sugrue, *The Origins of the Urban Crisis*, 76–77; Abrams, *Forbidden Neighbors*, 99–101; David L. Good, *Orvie: The Dictator of Dearborn: The Rise and Reign of Orville L. Hubbard* (Detroit, 1989); quote from Lester Velie, "Housing: Detroit's Time Bomb," *Collier's*, Nov. 23, 1946, 75–76; *PC*, July 6, 1963.

229 **suburbs of Columbus, Ohio:** Memo, AFSC Ohio-Michigan Region, Aug. 31, 1956, Re: Cross-Burning in Columbus, AFSC-AD-CR, 1956, Folder: Housing: Columbus.

229 **the massive Lincoln Village:** Barbee Durham to Murray Lincoln, May 27, 1954; Edward Bennett to Edward Wagner, Feb. 10, 1954; Memo on Lincoln Village, Nov. 12, 1954, in AFSC-AD-CR, 1954, Folder: Housing: Columbus.

229 **In Swarthmore, Pennsylvania:** Allan C. Wood to Members of the Swarthmore Property Owners Association, n.d. [1955]; Allan C. Wood to President and Members of Borough Council, March 14, 1955; Memo to File from Jane Reinheimer, July 28, 1955; AFSC-AD-CR, 1955, Folder: Housing: Swarthmore.

230 **In 1958, when Clarence and Margaret Yarrow:** Norman Jones et al. to

Clarence Yarrow, July 3, 1958, J. Russell Smith to Henry J. Cadbury, July 21, 1958, both in AFSC-AD-CR, 1958, Folder: Projects Housing Program General, 1958.

230 **Concord Park, Pennsylvania:** Brochure: "Concord Park Homes, Inc. Presents the Arizona," in AFSC-AD-CR, 1954, Folder: Morris Milgram.

230 **the vision of Morris Milgram:** Morris Milgram, OH, interviewed by John Britton, March 7, 1968, RJB; *NYT*, Apr. 27, Oct. 11, Nov. 3, 14, 1934; Dec. 21, 1937; June 26, 1938; Feb. 12, June 13, 1939; *Westfield v. Milgram*, 122 N.J.L. (1939) 221. Milgram's conviction for "canvassing" was overturned on appeal. "Weaned on socialist tracts" from Marvin Weisbord, "Homes Without Hate," *Progressive*, Jan. 1961. For a brief overview of the WDL, see Harry Fleischman, "Workers Defense League," in Mari Jo Buhle et al., eds., *Encyclopedia of the American Left*, 2nd ed. (New York, 1998), 897–98; Harvard Sitkoff, *A New Deal for Blacks* (New York, 1978), 165–66; *Last-Minute News*, March 10, 1939, June 24, 1940, and *Workers' Defense Bulletin* (Nov. 1940) in PMP, Box 72, Folder 1248; Richard B. Sherman, *The Case of Odell Waller and Virginia Justice, 1940–42* (Knoxville, Tenn., 1992), 186–87; Morris Milgram comments in "Civil Disobedience: Is It the Answer to Jim Crow: A Symposium," *Non-Violent Action News Bulletin* 2/3, n.d. [ca. 1943], 12–13, PMP, Box 72, Folder 1264; Anna Arnold Hedgeman, *The Trumpet Sounds: A Memoir of Negro Leadership* (New York, 1964), 81; Pauli Murray, *Song in a Weary Throat: An American Pilgrimage* (New York, 1987), 150–76; Herbert Garfinkel, *When Negroes March: The March on Washington Movement in the Organizational Politics for FEPC* (Glencoe, Ill., 1959), 99; Aron S. Gilmartin, "Workers Defense League, 1936–1946," in James Peck, ed., *Workers Defense League, Tenth Anniversary Journal* (1946) in SCCF, 005-869; James Farmer, *Lay Bare the Heart: An Autobiography of the Civil Rights Movement* (New York, 1985), 162.

231 **After the war, Milgram shifted gears:** Paul Buhle, *Marxism in the United States*, rev. ed. (New York, 1991), 199–205; Milgram family holiday letter, 1952, in NAACP, Group II-A, Box 161; "To Build Brotherhood," *Fellowship*, Feb. 1956, reprinted in AFSC-AD-CR, 1956, Folder: Housing: Concord Park. Open housing researchers George and Eunice Grier euphemistically described Milgram as a "professional defender of labor and minority rights" and a " 'crusader' for social justice" but only mentioned his affiliation to the NAACP. See Eunice and George Grier, *Privately Developed Interracial Housing: An Analysis from Experience*, Special Research Report to the Commission on Race and Housing (Berkeley, Calif., 1960), 45. Milgram remained a board member of the WDL. See Workers' Defense League letterhead, Oct. 17, 1962, PMP, Box 72, Folder 1252.

232 **At the WDL, Milgram had grown:** Murray, *Song in a Weary Throat*, 181; Morris Milgram to Pauli Murray, Feb. 27, 1945, PMP, Box 72, Folder 1263; Grier and Grier, *Privately Developed Interracial Housing*, 47–48.

232 **When his father-in-law died:** *NYT*, Nov. 21, 1954, March 10, 1957, June 26,

1997; Morris Milgram, *Good Neighborhood: The Challenge of Open Housing* (New York, 1977), 54–57.

232 **But Milgram was greeted:** Morris Milgram to Pauli Murray, July 15, Aug. 23, 1952, PMP, Box 98, Folder 1741; Milgram to George Houser, April 27, 1953, and attached memo, CORE, Part 3, Reel 12, frames 384–86; Milgram to Houser, Feb. 23, 1954, CORE, Part 3, Reel 12, frames 393–95; Eunice and George Grier, "Interim Summary Report: Concord Park: A Pioneer Attempt at Privately-Built Sales Housing for Interracial Occupancy," Jan. 1955, in AFSC-AD-CR, 1955, Folder: Housing: Concord Park; Albert Vorspan, "A Builder with a Vision," *Congress Weekly*, June 16, 1958, 14; Grier and Grier, *Privately Developed Interracial Housing*, 47–48.

233 **The novelty of Concord Park:** William M. Dwyer, "Experiment in Housing," *Commonweal*, Aug. 12, 1955, 465–66; Milgram, *Good Neighborhood*, 56–57.

234 **a quota of home sales:** Grier and Grier, "Interim Summary Report"; "Private Open-Occupancy Housing: Confidential—Not for Publication," NAACP, Group III-A, Box 167; Morris Milgram, "Where Housing Development Is Open to All: The Story of Two 'Open' Developments," *Hotel and Club Voice*, Nov. 1957, 16–17, in SCCF, 002-334; Grier and Grier, *Privately Developed Interracial Housing*, 68–75, quote 69; Oscar Cohen, "The Case for Benign Quotas in Housing," *Phylon* 21 (1960), 20–29; James Farmer, *Freedom—When?* (New York, 1965), 115–16. For a rich discussion of quotas, see Mark Santow, "Saul Alinsky and the Dilemmas of Race in the Postwar City" (Ph.D. diss., University of Pennsylvania, 2000), ch. 4.

234 **Attracting whites was hard work:** *TIH* (Apr.–May 1957); Marilyn Rosenthal Loeb, "Living in an Inter-Racial Community," *Barnard Alumnae Magazine*, Summer 1960, 6–7; Summary of Remarks by Morris Milgram, National Urban League Conference, Sept. 8, 1955, AFSC-AD-CR, 1955, Folder: Housing: Concord Park; *PT*, Oct. 29, 1957; *USA Today*, Aug. 4, 1997; "New Levittown," *Crisis*, June–July 1958, 345; "MCP Pioneers Integrated Housing," undated article in NAACP, Group III-A, Box 162; *PI*, Oct. 9, 2000.

235 **"Here is proof":** Paul Blanshard, Jr., "County's New Concord Homes Project May Dispel Fancied Fears About Mixed Housing," *Delaware Valley Advance*, March 31, April 7, 1954, in NAACP, Group II-A, Box 315; Concord Park Homes, Inc. Progress Report, Oct. 1956, in NAACP, Group III-A, Box 167; *NYT*, March 10, 1957; *Congress Weekly*, April 1, 1957; *PT*, Oct. 29, 1957.

236 **Most of Milgram's projects:** "Bucks County Gets Its First Interracial Subdivision," *House and Home*, April 1955; Milgram to Amicus Most, May 18, 1956, NAACP, Group III-A, Box 169; *TIH* (March–April 1958).

236 **Over the next decade:** A. Philip Randolph to Roy Wilkins, April 28, 1958 (probably ghostwritten by Milgram), and related letters, in NAACP, Group III-A, Box 161; Memo to Barbara Moffett from Ed Holmgren, Jan. 28, 1957; Memos to Barbara Moffett from Ed Holmgren, Feb. 18, 25, 1957; AFSC, Chicago Regional Office, Minutes of Meeting, March 7, 1957, all in AFSC-AD-

CR, 1957, Folder: Housing: Chicago; *CD*, March 4, 1957; "Putting Principles into Practice: Facts About Modern Community Developers," July 1958, in PMP, Box 98, Folder 1745.

237 **A small village in 1950, Deerfield tripled:** USCB, *1950 Census of Population* (Washington, D.C., 1952); *1960 Census of Population* (Washington, D.C., 1962).

237 **Chicago's North Shore:** Michael Ebner, *Creating Chicago's North Shore* (Chicago, 1988), 234–36, 242; Glencohen in Anthony Lewis, *Portrait of a Decade: The Second American Revolution* (New York, 1964), 249.

237 **In Deerfield, as in so much:** Weisbord, "Homes Without Hate"; generally, see Richard Babcock, *The Zoning Game: Municipal Practices and Policies* (Madison, Wis., 1966).

238 **the community exploded:** *CD*, Nov. 18, 1959; *NYT*, Nov. 28, 1959; Morris Milgram, Memo to MCD Stockholders and Friends, Dec. 23, 1959, in NAACP, Group III-A, Box 158; *TIH* (Nov.–Dec. 1959); Weisbord, "Homes Without Hate"; *PC*, Dec. 26, 1959, Jan. 1, 1960.

238 **At town meetings:** For a description of the "uproar," see *Progress Development Corporation v. James C. Mitchell et al.*, 286 F.2d 222 (1961), at 226, Jan. 4, 1961; see also *PC*, Dec. 5, 1959; on *Ebony* and Trumbull Park, see Adam Green, *Selling the Race: Culture, Community, and Black Chicago, 1940–55* (Chicago, 2007), 183–90.

239 **hatched a scheme to stop Progress:** "Northern Segregationists," *TNR*, Dec. 28, 1959, 5–6; *TIH* (Nov.–Dec. 1959); USCCR, *1961 Report, Book 3: Housing* (Washington, D.C., 1961), 133, 195.

239 **Milgram and Progress sued Deerfield:** Morris Milgram to Pauli Murray, June 19, July 29, 1958; see also legal materials, all in PMP, Box 98, Folder 1745; Meeting of N.Y. Members, Board of Freedom of Residence Fund, Oct. 31, 1961, in NAACP, Group III-A, Box 158.

240 **"the amalgamation":** *Augusta Courier*, Jan. 4, 1960, in NAACP, Group III-A, Box 158. See also Weisbord, "Homes Without Hate."

240 **an uphill legal battle:** *PC*, Jan. 2, 1960; *TIH* (Jan.–Feb. 1960); Confidential Memo to David Scull from Morris Milgram, Aug. 2, 1961, NAACP, Group III-A, Box 162; *Deerfield Park District, Appellee, v. Progress Development Corporation et al., Appellants*, 26 Ill. 2nd 296 (1962).

241 **Milgram also filed a civil rights lawsuit:** *Progress Development Corporation v. James C. Mitchell et al.*, March 4, 1960, 182 F. Supp. 681 (1960), 699.

241 **harsh judgment for Milgram and his project:** *Progress v. Mitchell*, at 700, 707, 709–10; *Chicago Daily News*, March 5, 1960; *CT*, March 5, 1960; Joint Memorandum, American Jewish Committee and Anti-Defamation League, Subject: Progress Development Corporation, March 29, 1960, in NAACP, Group III-A, Box 158; *Jewish Advocate*, Jan. 12, 1961.

241 **Milgram's attorneys appealed:** *CD*, Jan. 5, July 29, 1961; *CT*, Jan. 5, 1961; Deerfield Litigation, Confidential Summary of Litigation to Date, Oct. 19, 1961, and Memo, Re: Deerfield Litigation, Nov. 20, 1961, in NAACP, Group III-A, Box 158.

242 **As the Deerfield cases wended:** Murray, *Song in a Weary Throat*, 379; Thomas F. Jackson, *From Civil Rights to Human Rights: Martin Luther King, Jr., and the Struggle for Economic Justice* (Philadelphia, 2006), 126–27; *NYT*, Jan. 6, 1961, Dec. 1, 1962; Memo from Mildred Bond, April 19, 1963, NAACP, Group III-A, Box 158; Joseph B. Robison to Robert F. Kennedy, April 26, 1963, in NAACP, Group III-A, Box 162; *PC*, May 1, 1963. See also Milgram, *Good Neighborhood*, 60–63, and "Modern Community Developers," Confidential Memo, Feb. 9, 1965, in NAACP, Group III-A, Box 162; Roy Wilkins, "Investment: Direct Action for Housing Integration," *Crisis*, Jan.–Feb 1967.

243 **"open occupancy":** *INS*, Nov.–Dec. 1958 and March–April 1959; "Churches Call for Open Occupancy Housing," *SA* (Nov. 1957), 22–23.

243 **"Christians can make their love real":** "Love in Deed and in Truth," Message for Race Relations Sunday, Feb. 14, 1960, *INS* (Jan.–Feb. 1960), 1–2; "The Neighborhood Stabilization Program," *INS* (July–Aug. 1961); "Resources for Worship," *SA* (Nov. 1957), 25. See also "A Litany for Grace and Race," *SA* (May 1963), 28–30; Buell G. Gallagher, "The Secure Community," *SA* (Oct. 1957), 5–9.

244 **Jewish organizations funded:** H. H. Giles, "The Present Status and Programs of Private Intergroup Relations Agencies," *JNE* 20 (1951), 420, 424; Cheryl Lynn Greenberg, *Troubling the Waters: Black-Jewish Relations in the American Century* (Princeton, 2006), 139–46; Charles Abrams, OH, CUOHP.

245 **"God cares how we think":** "The Christian Faith and Public Opinion," *SA* (Feb. 1952), 1–43, quotes 5, 15, 41; see also Giles, "The Present Status," 415, 417, 419.

245 **When Dr. Arthur Falls:** "Experience in Interracial Living," *SA* (Nov. 1957), 17, 20.

245 **mobilizing the liberal press:** Walter White, "How Detroit Fights Race Hatred," *SEP*, July 18, 1953, 26–27; Ellsworth Rosen, "When a Negro Moves Next Door," *SEP*, April 4, 1959.

246 **film and theatrical productions:** "The Arts," *SA* (Nov. 1957), 24.

246 **commissioned filmmaker Nathan Zucker:** *TIH* (March–April 1958); Meyer, *As Long as They Don't Move Next Door*, 145–48; Giles, "The Present Status," 417; Alfred A. Kraemer and Oscar Lee, "And What About the Fellowship," *INS* (Sept.–Oct. 1963); Greenberg, *Troubling the Waters*, 140–41.

246 **the open housing pledge or covenant campaign:** *TIH* (Aug. 1956); "A Planned Dispersion Pattern—An Answer to the Ghetto," *INS* (Sept.–Oct. 1958), 4; "Advertising Good Will Through Open Occupancy Pledge Covenants," *INS* (May–June 1961); "Confrontation in the Local Church," *INS* (Jan.–Feb. 1962); *NYT*, Feb. 2, 1961; James A. Tillman, Jr., "Quest for Fair Housing and Community-Wide Religious Involvement: A Case History," *SA* (May 1963), 16–28; Henry B. Clark, "Open Housing Covenant Campaigns," *Christianity and Crisis*, Feb. 17, 1964, 13–16; *NYT*, March 12, 1967.

247 **"There have been enough resolutions":** Philip Johnson, *Call Me Neighbor, Call Me Friend* (Garden City, N.Y., 1965), 6.

247 **In 1965, just two years after Milgram exhausted:** *CD*, July 31, 1965.

247 **Survey researcher Paul Sheatsley examined:** Paul B. Sheatsley, "White Attitudes Toward the Negro," *Daedalus* (Winter 1966), 222; see also Thomas Pettigrew, "Complexity and Change in American Racial Patterns: A Social Psychological View," in Talcott Parsons and Kenneth B. Clark, eds., *The Negro American* (Boston, 1966); Charles Abrams, OH, CUOHP.

248 **"the net effect of economic factors":** Karl E. Taeuber and Alma F. Taeuber, *Negroes in Cities* (Chicago, 1965), 94.

249 **The balkanization of postwar metropolitan America:** Sugrue, *The Origins of the Urban Crisis*, Appendix A, for data on sixteen northern cities; Duane Lockard, *Toward Equal Opportunity: A Study of State and Local Antidiscrimination Laws* (London, 1968), 103.

CHAPTER 8 | "NEW FRONTIER"

253 **Whitney M. Young, Jr.:** Dennis C. Dickerson, *Militant Mediator: Whitney M. Young, Jr.* (Lexington, Ky., 1998); Nancy J. Weiss, *Whitney M. Young, Jr., and the Struggle for Civil Rights* (Princeton, N.J., 1989).

254 **"good, educated, church-going":** "I'm Liberal but . . . ," April 8, 1961, quoted in Dickerson, *Militant Mediator*, 133; *PC*, Nov. 4, 1961.

254 **"the masses of Negroes":** *TSD*, Jan. 20, 1960. The standard histories of the Urban League are Guichard Parris and Lester Brooks, *Blacks in the City: A History of the National Urban League* (Boston, 1971), and Nancy J. Weiss, *The National Urban League, 1910–1940* (New York, 1974).

254 **Radical activists denounced:** *TSD*, July 30, 1960; Ossie Sykes, "Urban League: Servant of Two Masters," *Liberator*, Feb. 1964, 17; *PC*, Nov. 5, 1960 (on airline stewardesses); *PC*, March 17, 1962; on Urban League programs, see George B. Nesbitt, "The Negro Race Relations Expert and Negro Community Leadership," *JNE* 21 (1952), 148–60, quote 160; Nina Mjagkij, "Behind the Scenes: The Cincinnati Urban League, 1948–63," in Henry Louis Taylor, ed., *Race and the City: Work, Community and Protest in Cincinnati, 1820–1970* (Urbana, Ill., 1993), 280–94; Thomas J. Sugrue, *The Origins of the Urban Crisis: Race and Inequality in Postwar Detroit* (Princeton, N.J., 1996), 165–70; Arvarh E. Strickland, *History of the Chicago Urban League* (Urbana, Ill., 1966).

255 **"On an economic level":** *NYT*, Oct. 6, 1963; National Urban League, *Economic and Social Status of the Negro in the United States* (New York, 1961).

255 **black America was at a turning point:** USCB, *Statistical Abstract of the United States* (Washington, D.C., 1961), 24, 30; for a useful overview, see Marion Hayes, "A Century of Change: Negroes in the U.S. Economy, 1860–1960," *Monthly Labor Review* (Dec. 1962), reprinted in Louis Ferman et al., eds., *Negroes and Jobs* (Ann Arbor, Mich., 1968), 53–65.

256 **In nearly every other realm:** Allen B. Batchelder, "Decline in the Relative Income of Negro Men," in Ferman et al., eds., *Negroes and Jobs*, 71, 74, 84. Black-

white unemployment ratios were higher for men than women. See Dorothy K. Newman et al., *Protest, Politics, and Prosperity: Black Americans and White Institutions, 1940–75* (New York, 1978), esp. Table 2-6; Sidney M. Peck, "The Economic Situation of Negro Labor," in Julius Jacobson, ed., *The Negro and the American Labor Movement* (New York, 1968), 218.

257 **The industrial cities:** Sugrue, *The Origins of the Urban Crisis*, ch. 4; Roger Horowitz, *"Negro and White, Unite and Fight!" A Social History of Industrial Unionism in Meatpacking, 1930–90* (Urbana, Ill., 1997), 245–58; Joshua Freeman, *Working-Class New York: Life and Labor Since World War II* (New York, 2000), 146–47, 161; *PC*, May 27, 1961; Robert Self, *American Babylon: Race and the Struggle for Postwar Oakland* (Princeton, N.J., 2003).

257 **In one of the greatest ironies:** Eric Arnesen, *Brotherhoods of Color: Black Railroad Workers and the Struggle for Equality* (Cambridge, Mass., 2001), 237; Jefferson Cowie and Joseph Heathcott, eds., *Beyond the Ruins: The Meanings of Deindustrialization* (Ithaca, N.Y., 2003); Jefferson Cowie, *Capital Moves: RCA's Seventy-Year Quest for Cheap Labor* (Ithaca, N.Y., 1999); Bruce Schulman, *From Cotton Belt to Sunbelt: Federal Policy, Economic Development, and the Transformation of the South, 1938–1980* (New York, 1991).

258 **By every economic measure:** Ferman et al., eds., *Negroes and Jobs*, 18–20, 65, 72–76; Arthur M. Ross and Herbert Hill, eds., *Employment, Race, and Poverty* (New York, 1967), 30, 61; George H. Gallup, *The Gallup Poll: Public Opinion, 1935–1971*, vol. 3 (New York, 1972), 1769.

258 **whites had some significant economic advantages:** Ferman et al., eds., *Negroes and Jobs*, 47, 195, 248–51.

258 **Northern metropolitan areas were as segregated:** Sugrue, *The Origins of the Urban Crisis*, Appendix A; Kenneth T. Jackson, *Crabgrass Frontier: The Suburbanization of the United States* (New York, 1985).

259 **urban renewal projects and highways:** Jon Teaford, *Rough Road to Renaissance* (Baltimore, 1990); F. James Davis, "The Effects of Freeway Displacement on a Northern City," *Phylon* 26 (1965), 209–15; Robert Caro, *The Power Broker: Robert Moses and the Fall of New York* (New York, 1974), 839–94; Raymond A. Mohl, "Race and Space in the Modern City: Interstate-95 and the Black Community in Miami," in Arnold R. Hirsch and Raymond A. Mohl, eds., *Urban Policy in Twentieth-Century America* (New Brunswick, N.J., 1993), 134–39, offers a detailed account of urban highway projects, many in the North.

259 **Many of the nation's most vital:** Margaret Pugh O'Mara, *Cities of Knowledge: Cold War Science and the Search for the Next Silicon Valley* (Princeton, N.J., 2005), 142–81; Sugrue, *The Origins of the Urban Crisis*, 47–48; Alison Isenberg, *Downtown America: A History of the Place and the People Who Made It* (Chicago, 2004), 201.

260 **There were some advantages:** Rashi Fein, "An Economic and Social Profile of the Negro American," in Talcott Parsons and Kenneth B. Clark, ed., *The Negro American* (Boston, 1966), 123–26.

260 **public housing projects:** Arnold Hirsch, *Making the Second Ghetto: Race and Housing in Chicago, 1940–1960* (New York, 1983); Thomas O'Connor, *Building a New Boston: Politics and Urban Renewal, 1950 to 1970* (Boston, 1993), 123–24; John Bauman, *Public Housing, Race, and Renewal: Urban Planning in Philadelphia, 1920–1974* (Philadelphia, 1987).

261 **the street corners of inner cities:** Elliot Liebow, *Tally's Corner: A Study of Negro Streetcorner Men* (Boston, 1967); Elijah Anderson, *A Place on the Corner* (Chicago, 1978); Sugrue, *The Origins of the Urban Crisis*, 119–21, 261; Mayor's Committee—Community Action for Youth Reports, Chapter 2: "Target Area Youth: Their Life Style," in DNAACP, Part 1, Box 23.

262 **Dotting black neighborhoods ... were churches:** Black urban religious institutions in the mid–twentieth century are understudied. Two good starting points are Clarence Taylor, *The Black Churches of Brooklyn* (New York, 1994), and Angela D. Dillard, *Faith in the City: Preaching Radical Social Change in Detroit* (Ann Arbor, Mich., 2007).

262 **"bottom of the pile Negroes":** Malcolm X as told to Alex Haley, *The Autobiography of Malcolm X* (1964; rept. New York, 1973), 183, 199; "Militant Stand Marked Leader," *BAA*, March 6, 1965. The best overviews are C. Eric Lincoln, *The Black Muslims in America* (1961), 3rd ed. (Grand Rapids, Mich., and Trenton, N.J., 1994), and Michael A. Gomez, *Black Crescent: The Experience and Legacy of African Muslims in the Americas* (New York, 2005).

263 **"today's world is floating":** *BAA*, Feb. 20, 1960, cited in Lincoln, *Black Muslims*, 84; Karl Evanzz, *The Messenger: The Rise and Fall of Elijah Muhammad* (New York, 1999), 67–69, 72–77, claims that Fard was David Ford, a follower of Noble Drew Ali. See also Claude A. Clegg III, *An Original Man: The Life and Times of Elijah Muhammad* (New York, 1997), 14–40.

264 **The Nation did not rely:** Evanzz, *The Messenger*, 173, in Clegg, *An Original Man*, 98–100.

264 **created a rich cultural infrastructure:** James Gregory, *The Southern Diaspora: How the Great Migrations of Black and White Southerners Transformed America* (Chapel Hill, N.C., 2005), 113–52; Adam Green, *Selling the Race: Culture, Community, and Black Chicago, 1940–55* (Chicago, 2007); Suzanne E. Smith, *Dancing in the Streets: Motown and the Cultural Politics of Black Detroit* (Cambridge, Mass., 1999).

265 **the new political demography:** Campbell Gibson and Kay Jung, "Historical Census Statistics on Population Totals by Race, 1790–1990, for Large Cities," www.census.gov/population/www/documentation/twps0076.pdf.

265 **Other than blanketing:** Theodore H. White, *The Making of the President, 1960,* (New York, 1961), 323. A recent and excellent critical assessment of Kennedy's civil rights politics is Nick Bryant, *The Bystander: John F. Kennedy and the Struggle for Black Equality* (New York, 2006), which highlights Kennedy's indifference to and inconstancy on the matter of civil rights, but downplays black activists' perceptions of the Democratic Party and Kennedy administration as open

to change. A similar argument can be found in Mark Stern, *Calculating Visions: Kennedy, Johnson, and Civil Rights* (New Brunswick, N.J., 1992).

266 **"the strongest pronunciation":** *PC*, July 23, 1960.

266 **a climate of policy experimentation:** Carl Brauer, "Kennedy, Johnson, and the War on Poverty," *JAH* 69 (1982), 98–119; Alice O'Connor, *Poverty Knowledge: Social Science, Social Policy, and the Poor in Twentieth-Century U.S. History* (Princeton, 2001), 139–65; Sar A. Levitan, *Federal Aid to Depressed Areas* (Baltimore, 1964).

267 **Executive Order 10925:** John David Skrentny, *The Minority Rights Revolution* (Cambridge, Mass., 2002), 101–3; Remarks of the President at the Meeting . . . of the President's Committee for Equal Employment Opportunity, April 11, 1961, in *CRWH*, vol. 5, 49; Statement by Vice President Lyndon B. Johnson at the Organizational Meeting, April 11, 1961, ibid., 51.

267 **The federal government alone employed:** *PC*, Feb. 17, 1962.

267 **first task was to gather hard data:** Skrentny, *The Minority Rights Revolution*, 101–2; Robert Troutman to John F. Kennedy, Aug. 22, 1962, *CRWH*, vol. 5, 116; Plans for Progress Report to the President, Aug. 20, 1962, in ibid., 119.

268 **The committee was flooded:** *PC*, April 22, 1961.

268 **"comprehensive investigations":** Memo from John Feild to Arthur Goldberg, June 22, 1962, *CRWH*, vol. 5, 95; *PC*, June 3, 1961.

268 **Using the PCEEO as a weapon:** *PC*, Dec. 9, 1961, April 21, July 14, 1962.

268 **policy innovation:** Hugh Davis Graham, *The Civil Rights Era: Origins and Development of National Policy, 1960–1972* (New York, 1990), 42.

269 **altering the composition of their workforces:** Pattern-Changing Results of Complaint Investigations, Sept. 1962, in *CRWH*, vol. 5., 127, 128; Addendum to Sept. 1962 Report, Nov. 15, 1962, ibid., 152; Report of Labor Liaison Division, Nov. 15, 1962, in ibid., 156; *PC*, April 28, 1962.

269 **In its first year, federal agencies hired:** *PC*, Nov. 24, 1962.

270 **Even less promising:** USCCR, *The Fifty States Report* (Washington, D.C., 1961); *NYT*, Oct. 29, Nov. 21, 1958.

270 **series of visits:** *CD*, Nov. 12, 26, Dec. 12, 1960, July 3, 13, Nov. 29, 1961.

270 **The commission had a master publicist:** *Time*, Feb. 9, 1962; Theodore Martin Hesburgh, *God, Country, Notre Dame: The Autobiography of Theodore M. Hesburgh* (South Bend, Ind., 2000).

270 **Its findings for northern cities:** *NYT*, Feb. 2, 1959, Nov. 17, June 11, 1961, Dec. 2, 1962.

271 **"no single, limited approach":** *NYT*, Nov. 17, 1961.

272 **Leading the efforts:** Weiss, *Whitney M. Young, Jr.*, 143–45; *PC*, Aug. 10, 1963.

272 **"compensatory" programs:** *PC*, Nov. 4, 1961.

272 **Audley "Queen Mother" Moore:** *CD*, April 16, 1938, April 26, 1941, Jan. 1, 1944, Jan. 5, 1946, Jan. 25, 1947.

272 **"Without Reparations":** "Why Reparations?" n.d. [circa 1963]; thanks to Merlin Chowkwanyun for this document. See also Third International Confer-

ence on Black Power, "Reparations: Queen Mother Moore," RAM, Reel 11, frame 867; Stokely Carmichael with Ekwueme Michael Thelwell, *Ready for Revolution: The Life and Struggles of Stokely Carmichael (Kwame Ture)* (New York, 2003), 100; Martha Biondi, "The Rise of the Reparations Movement," *RHR* 87 (Fall 2003), 7; Mary Frances Berry, *My Face Is Black, Is True: Callie House and the Struggle for Ex-Slave Reparations* (New York, 2005).

273 **Young continued to defend:** *PC*, June 15, 1963; *NYT*, May 15, June 10, 16, 1963; *PC*, Aug. 24, 1963; *TSD*, Aug. 24, 1963; Whitney M. Young, Jr., *To Be Equal* (New York, 1964), 21–32.

274 **"We have generously":** "Urban League Plan for Middle Class," *NA*, Feb. 14, 1964; "The Negro Revolt," *American Child*, Nov. 1963; Graham, *The Civil Rights Era*, 111–13. Graham argues that Young gave up the compensatory rhetoric, but he did not. For examples, see *PC*, Sept. 19, 1964; *CD*, Jan. 30, 1965.

274 **Young's shift in emphasis resounded:** *NYT*, Oct. 6, 1963; William Brink and Louis Harris, *The Negro Revolution in America* (New York, 1963), 116–17. By comparison, 93 percent of northern blacks had a positive view of the NAACP. About the same percentage of blacks (65) viewed the SCLC positively; 61 percent viewed CORE favorably. It was noteworthy that the disapproval rating for the Urban League (13 percent) was higher than that of CORE (7 percent), the NAACP (3 percent), and the SCLC (8 percent).

274 **"nonviolent assault":** A. Philip Randolph, "The Cruel Deception," *NA*, Sept. 5, 1960; on the democratic left and civil rights, see especially Thomas F. Jackson, *From Civil Rights to Human Rights: Martin Luther King, Jr., and the Struggle for Economic Justice* (Philadelphia, 2006).

275 **His ideas exploded into the public eye:** Michael Harrington, *The Other America: Poverty in the United States* (New York, 1962); Maurice Isserman, *The Other American: The Life of Michael Harrington* (New York, 2000), 157–61, 182–87, 194–99.

276 **had a galvanic effect:** Dwight Macdonald, "Our Invisible Poor," *NY*, Jan. 19, 1963, 82–132; Isserman, *The Other American*, 208–9.

276 **"The crisis confronting":** A. Philip Randolph, "The Unfinished Revolution," *Progressive*, Dec. 1962, 20–25.

276 **How to balance:** "Urban League Plan for Middle Class," *NA*, Feb. 14, 1964.

276 **"It has become increasingly obvious":** Sam Bottone, "Preferential Treatment Vital: Attack on Immediate Job Bias Problem," *NA*, March 28, 1964.

277 **"slum families":** "The Challenge of Jobless Youth: Report of the President's Committee on Youth Employment," April 1963, SCCF, 005-480; O'Connor, *Poverty Knowledge*, 141–42; Margaret Weir, *Politics and Jobs: The Boundaries of Employment Policy in the United States* (Princeton, N.J., 1992), 54–58, 63–67.

277 **Manpower Development and Training Act:** James Sundquist, *Politics and Policy: The Eisenhower, Kennedy, and Johnson Years* (Washington, D.C., 1968), 85–91; Jill Quadagno, *The Color of Welfare: How Racism Undermined the War on Poverty* (New York, 1994), 70–76.

278 **local civil rights activists took up job training:** Ossie Davis to Friend, June 1963; "Jobs and Hope," June 1963; Dennis A. Derryck, "Minority Youth Can Be Apprentices," in *Occupational Outlook Quarterly* (Dec. 1967), 7–10; all in SCCF, 005-869.

278 **Proponents of job training:** Allen J. Matusow, *The Unraveling of America: A History of Liberalism in the 1960s* (New York, 1984), 104; Sundquist, *Politics and Policy*, 85–91; *PC*, April 7, 1964. Chicago provides many good examples. See *CD*, Jan. 20, Feb. 27, April 10, June 5, 12, July 19, 1965.

279 **most zealous proponent:** Leon H. Sullivan, *Build, Brother, Build* (Philadelphia, 1969); *PC*, Aug. 10, 1963; "Hail Pastor as OIC Founder," *Ebony*, May 1964, 35–36.

279 **"Sullivan has just almost":** The Martin Luther King, Jr., FBI File, Part II: The King-Levison File. Surveillance of Telephones in Stanley Levison's Residence, Sub-file 9, Vol. 6, Reel 6, frames 0001–0006. Thanks to Thomas F. Jackson for this citation. For a positive comparison to Washington, see *PC*, Aug. 15, 1964.

279 **But Sullivan also attracted:** *PC*, Aug. 10, 1963; Matthew J. Countryman, *Up South: Civil Rights and Black Power in Philadelphia* (Philadelphia, 2005), 112–14; Bernard E. Anderson, *The Opportunities Industrialization Centers: A Decade of Community-Based Manpower Services* (Philadelphia, 1976).

280 **But events in the South:** Taylor Branch, *Parting the Waters: America in the King Years* (New York, 1987), offers a powerful overview of the southern freedom struggle up through 1963; on Kennedy's limitations, see Mary Dudziak, *Cold War Civil Rights: Race and the Image of American Democracy* (Princeton, N.J., 2000), ch. 4; Skrentny, *The Minority Rights Revolution*, esp. 33–35; Raymond Arsenault, *Freedom Riders: 1961 and the Struggle for Racial Justice* (New York, 2006); Bryant, *The Bystander*.

281 **Nationwide, it had no more:** August Meier and Elliot Rudwick, *Along the Color Line: Explorations in the Black Experience* (Urbana, Ill., 1976), 249.

281 **"released waves of dammed-up energy":** Lerone Bennett, Jr., "What Sit-Downs Mean to America," *Ebony*, June 1960, 35; *CD*, April 5, 1960.

281 **"With the success of the sit-ins":** James Robinson interview, Dec. 1967, AMP, Box 57, Folder 4; Marvin Rich interview, Dec. 21, 1970, AMP, Box 57, Folder 3.

281 **Inspired by the southern sit-ins:** Anna Holden to Morris Abram, April 3, 1961; *Michigan Daily*, March 25, 1961; "Second Call for Kresge Action," April 26, 1961; "Freedom Sing" press release, June 16, 1961; *Michigan Daily*, July 11, 12, 1961; *Ann Arbor News*, July 10, 1961; *DN*, July 26, 1961; *News and Letters*, Aug. 1961; all in LDP; Message to All AADAC Members and Friends, 1960, in CORE, Series 5, Reel 21, frame 528. For similar protests in Kent, Ohio, led by Kent State University students, see NAACP-M, Part 20, Reel 11, frames 287–89.

282 **an increasingly militant edge:** Ollie Leeds interview, April 28, 1971, AMP, Box 56, Folder 10; "Civil Rights Battle: Northern Style," *Ebony*, March 1963, 96ff; Brian Purnell, "'Drive a While for Freedom': Brooklyn CORE's 1964 Stall-in and Public Discourses on Protest Violence," in Jeanne Theoharis and

Komozi Woodard, ed., *Groundwork: Local Black Freedom Movements in America* (New York, 2005), 45–75.

282 **breathed new life into the open housing movement:** *TIH* (May–June 1960); *TIH* (July–Aug. 1960); *TIH* (Nov.–Dec. 1961); *NYAN*, Jan. 20, 1962; *TIH* (May–June 1962).

283 **an executive order prohibiting:** *TIH* (Sept.–Oct. 1962); *TIH* (March–April 1963); *TIH* (July–Aug. 1963); see also *CD*, May 13, 1963.

283 **Nothing in the order prevented:** *TIH* (Nov.–Dec. 1961); Juliet Z. Saltman, *Open Housing as a Social Movement: Challenge, Conflict, and Change* (Lexington, Mass., 1971), 34; Nicholas deB. Katzenbach, Memorandum for the President, Re: Reorganization of Civil Rights Responsibilities, Sept. 20, 1965, in *CRWH*, vol. 5, 213; Graham, *The Civil Rights Era*, 259; AFSC, *Report to the President: AFSC Experience and Recommendations Re: Executive Order 11063 on Equal Opportunity in Housing* (Philadelphia, 1967).

283 **"Futile would be the traditional":** Robert S. Browne, "Toward Decreasing Racial Strife in the North," RSB, Box 22, Folder 2; Herman H. Long, "Beyond Tokenism," *SA* (Sept. 1963), 11.

284 **"Words and declarations":** Alfred A. Kraemer and Oscar Lee, "And What About the Fellowship?," *INS* (Sept.–Oct. 1963); Dennis Clark, "The Siege of a Social Problem," *INS* (March–April 1963).

284 **took up the call:** *TIH* (July–Aug. 1961); *TIH* (Sept.–Oct. 1961); *TIH* (Jan.–Feb. 1962); *New Haven Core-Lator* (Jan. 1962), in NAACP, Group III, Box A-201; *CD*, Jan. 16, 1965.

284 **The largest-scale CORE efforts:** Meier and Rudwick, *CORE*, 184; "A Tale of Three Cities on Housing," *C-L* 86 (Feb. 1961); Louis Smith interview, June 1971, AMP, Box 57, Folder 6; on Cleveland, see Arthur Evans interview, March 13, 1971, AMP, Box 56, Folder 5; on Windowshop efforts in Los Angeles and Columbus, see William Fischer, "A Housing Program Developed by the 1961 CORE Housing Institute," in LDP, Box 1; also Mildred Pitts Walker, "Nigger Go Home—Where?," *Liberator*, July 1963, 7–18.

CHAPTER 9 | "FIRES OF FRUSTRATION AND DISCORD"

286 **Wilkins and black conservative columnist George Schuyler:** *PC*, Jan. 5, 1963; *CD*, Jan. 2, 1963.

287 **"Let us, for once":** James Baldwin, "Not 100 Years of Freedom," *Liberator*, Jan. 1963, 7.

287 **the growing sense of impatience:** *PC*, Jan. 12, 1963; Lincoln Lynch to Marv [Rich], Jan. 8, 1963, CORE, Series 5, Reel 22, frame 923; "Long Island CORE and the Civil Rights War, 1963," CORE, Series 5, Reel 22, frames 939–40.

287 **"frightening suddenness":** *CD*, June 8, 1963; conversation with Herbert Hill, June 6, 1963, AMP, Box 56, Folder 8; on Gardner Taylor, see Clarence Taylor, *Black Religious Intellectuals: The Fight for Equality from Jim Crow to the 21st*

Century (New York, 2002), 38–42; Norman Hill interview, June 21, 1963, AMP, Box 56, Folder 8; *PC*, June 29, 1963; *CD*, May 2, 1963; *BAA*, June 22, 1963.

288 **"permanently unemployed mass"**: *NYT*, July 3, 1963.

288 **"In this one hundredth year"**: "Outgrowing the Ghetto Mind," *Ebony*, Aug. 1963, 98.

288 **"Suddenly it seems"**: *NYT*, Aug. 12, 1963.

290 **Early spring brought**: *PC*, April 27, May 11, 25, June 8, 1963; *CD*, May 13, 1963; *WSJ*, May 17, 1963.

291 **But many northerners took home**: *CD*, May 15, June 1, 1963; *PC*, May 18, 1963; "Revolution in Harlem Streets," *NA*, Sept. 24, 1963; Nat Hentoff, *The New Equality* (New York, 1964), 49; *IN*, May 27, Sept. 16, 1963.

292 **to battles on their home front**: Bayard Rustin, "Birmingham Leads to New Stage of Struggle," *NA*, June 18, 1963.

292 **wave of protests shook Philadelphia**: Thomas J. Sugrue, "Affirmative Action from Below: The Building Trades, Civil Rights, and the Struggle for Racial Equality in the North, 1945–1969," *JAH* 91 (2004), 145–73.

292 **The most visible leader**: Gaeton Fonzi, "Cecil Storms In," *GPM* (July 1963), 21–23, 45–57; *NYT*, Sept. 2, 1964.

293 **"arrogant foul mouth radical"**: James R. Moses to Roy Wilkins, [received] Sept. 16, 1964, NAACP, Group III, Box C137, Folder: Philadelphia, July–Sept. 1964; for an example of Moore's reputation among the poor, see *NYT Sunday Magazine*, Aug. 2, 1964.

293 **"His method"**: *NYT*, Sept. 2, 1964.

293 **Within months at the helm**: Press Release, n.d. [July 23, 1963], Subject: 30th Street Post Office and Robert C. Nix, NAACP, Group III, Box C137; Press Release, July 30, 1963, Subject: NAACP and Bus Company Reach Agreement, ibid.; Press Release, Sept. 19, 1963, Subject: U.S. Army Electronics Material Agency, ibid.; PNAACP Press Release, n.d. [1964], in NAACP, Group III, Box C137; *NYT*, Aug. 15, 1963, Sept. 2, 1964; "Pennsylvania: 'The Goddam Boss,'" *Time*, Sept. 11, 1964.

293 **he came out fighting**: *PG*, Jan. 25, Feb. 8, June 7, 1963; Fonzi, "Cecil Storms In," 45. See also Matthew Countryman, *Up South: Civil Rights and Black Power in Philadelphia* (Philadelphia, 2005), 120–79.

294 **The Philadelphia protests**: *PT*, June 1, 1963; *PB*, May 27, 30, 1963; *PC*, June 1, 8, 1963.

294 **"They're all getting tough"**: Meeting, May 20, 1963, 11:25 a.m., transcribed in Jonathan Rosenberg and Zachary Karabell, eds., *Kennedy, Johnson, and the Quest for Justice: The Civil Rights Tapes* (New York, 2003), 117.

295 **A week later, concerned**: *NYT*, May 26, 1963; *PC*, June 8, 1963; "Kennedy and Baldwin," *TNR*, June 15, 1963, 3–4; James Baldwin, "Lorraine Hansberry at the Summit," *Freedomways* (1979), reprinted in Esther Cooper Jackson, *Freedomways Reader: Prophets in Their Own Country* (Boulder, Colo., 2000), 77–81.

295 **On June 4, just as the first wave**: Statement by the President on Equal Em-

ployment Opportunity, June 4, 1963, in *Public Papers of the President of the United States: John F. Kennedy, 1963* (Washington, D.C., 1964), 439; *PB*, June 4, 1963; *NYT*, June 5, 1963; Lee C. White, Memorandum for the President, June 4, 1963, Folder: Civil Rights: General, 1/1/63–6/4/63, JFK-POF, Box 97; see also Robert Dallek, *An Unfinished Life: John F. Kennedy, 1917–1963* (Boston, 2003), 601.

295 **"fires of frustration and discord":** Radio and Television Report to the American People on Civil Rights, June 11, 1963, in *Public Papers of the President of the United States: John F. Kennedy, 1963* (Washington, D.C., 1964), 468–71; *NYT*, June 12, 1963.

296 **"large segments of the Negro population":** G. Mennen Williams, Memorandum for the President, June 15, 1963, in *CRWH*, vol. 1, p. 433.

296 **The White House stepped up its efforts:** Thompson Powers, "Memorandum for Lee White," June 7, 1963, Robert F. Kennedy Papers, Box 9, Folder: Civil Rights, 6/1–6/15/63, JFKL. The five "danger spots" were Atlanta, Chicago, Detroit, Los Angeles, and Philadelphia. See also Willard Wirtz, Memorandum to the Attorney General, June 5, 1963, Folder: Civil Rights: Governmental Agencies, Box 11, ibid.; Willard Wirtz to Robert F. Kennedy, June 12, 1963, ibid.; Willard Wirtz, Memorandum for the President, June 13, 1963, JFK-POF, Box 97, Folder: Civil Rights Meeting with Union Leaders; White House Press Release, "Executive Order 11114," June 22, 1963, Tile Layers Union Local 6 Papers, Box 8, Folder 55, TUUA; Hugh Davis Graham, *The Civil Rights Era: Origins and Development of National Policy, 1960–1972* (New York, 1990), 66–67, 85, 279. See, generally, Herbert H. Haines, *Black Radicals and the Civil Rights Mainstream* (Knoxville, Tenn., 1988), 157–65.

297 **"we have a right to expect":** "The Time-Life Broadcast Civil Rights 'Spots' Project," JFK-POF, Box 97, Folder: Civil Rights General, 9/63–10/63.

297 **Between May 19 and July 1:** *CD*, July 27, 1963.

297 **In Englewood, New Jersey:** *PC*, May 11, June 1, 1963; Gerald Walker, "Englewood and the Northern Dilemma," *Nation*, July 8, 1963, 9. See also ch. 13.

297 **In school districts large and small:** Jeanne Theoharis, "'I'd Rather Go to School in the South': How Boston's School Desegregation Complicates the Civil Rights Paradigm," in Jeanne F. Theoharis and Komozi Woodard, eds., *Freedom North: Black Freedom Struggles Outside the South, 1940–1980* (New York, 2003), 131; USCCR, *Public Education: 1963 Staff Report* (Dec. 1963), 91–94; *NYT*, June 21, 1963; *CD*, Nov. 19, 1963.

298 **A growing insurgency in Chicago:** *CD*, June 20, 1963; Hoyt W. Fuller, "Rise of the Negro Militant," *Nation*, Sept. 14, 1963.

298 **"Walk to Freedom March":** *BW*, June 29, 1963, reprinted in *IN*, July 8, 1963; Nelson Lichtenstein, *The Most Dangerous Man in Detroit: Walter Reuther and the Fate of American Labor* (New York, 1995), 381; *PC*, July 13, 1963; *MC*, June 29, July 6, 1963; *DFP*, June 24, 1963; *BW*, July 30, 1963, cited in B. J. Widick, *Detroit: City of Race and Class Violence* (New York, 1972), 157; Martin Luther

King, Jr., speech at the Great March on Detroit, June 23, 1963, available at www.stanford.edu/group/King/publications/speeches.

299 **deep divisions over politics and strategy:** Angela D. Dillard, "Religion and Radicalism: The Reverend Albert B. Cleage, Jr., and the Rise of Black Christian Nationalism in Detroit," in Theoharis and Woodard, eds., *Freedom North*, 166–69; Nick Salvatore, *Singing in a Strange Land: C. L. Franklin, the Black Church, and the Transformation of America* (New York, 2005), 251–54; Suzanne E. Smith, *Dancing in the Streets: Motown and the Cultural Politics of Black Detroit* (Cambridge, Mass., 1999), 21–53.

299 **"I do not identify myself":** *IN*, March 4, 1963.

300 **Cleage was a rising star:** For background on Cleage, see Angela D. Dillard, *Faith in the City: Preaching Radical Social Change in Detroit* (Ann Arbor, Mich., 2007), 237–85, and Hiley Ward, *Prophet of a Black Nation* (New York, 1969).

300 **"spends too much time":** *IN*, May 27, June 10, 1963.

300 **He also challenged:** *PC* (Detroit edition), Feb. 3, 10, 1962; *PC*, Oct. 13, 1962; *IN*, Jan. 14, Feb. 4, 18, April 1, 8, 1963; Jeffrey Mirel, *The Rise and Fall of an Urban School System: Detroit, 1907–81* (Ann Arbor, Mich., 1993), 264–65, 267–69; Grace Lee Boggs, *Living for Change: An Autobiography* (Minneapolis, 1998), 122.

300 **Despite his skepticism:** *IN*, June 10, 1963; *CD*, June 3, 1963; Boggs, *Living for Change*, 124.

301 **Just a few months after:** *Militant*, Oct. 21, 1963; Sterling Gray, "Man of the Year, Albert B. Cleage, Jr.: Architect of a Revolution," *Liberator*, Dec. 1963, 8–9; Albert B. Cleage, Jr., *Black Christian Nationalism: New Directions for the Black Church* (New York, 1972), 105–7; Salvatore, *Singing in a Strange Land*, 216–18, 241–44.

301 **a string of demonstrations throughout the Northeast:** *NYT*, June 9, 1963; *PC*, June 22, 29, July 27, Aug. 10, 1963; John Cumbler, *A Social History of Economic Decline: Business, Politics and Work in Trenton* (New Brunswick, N.J., 1989), 173–74; August Meier and Elliott Rudwick, *CORE: A Study in the Civil Rights Movement, 1942–1968* (Urbana, Ill., 1975), 227–28, 231, 236–37, 371; Graham, *The Civil Rights Era*, 66–67, 85, 279; Clarence Taylor, *Black Churches of Brooklyn* (New York, 1994), 139–63; *NYT*, June 18, July 23, Aug. 1, 1963; *PC*, June 22, Aug. 10, 1963; "Revolution in Harlem Streets," *NA*, Sept. 24, 1963.

302 **a total of 1,412 separate:** William Brink and Louis Harris, *The Negro Revolution in America* (New York, 1963), 46.

302 **On July Fourth, thirty thousand:** *CD*, July 6, 1963; *BAA*, July 8, 1963; "The Demonstrators," *NC*, July 15, 1963, 2–3; "Chicago No 'Wonderful Town' for Negroes," *NA*, Oct. 21, 1963; Maxwell C. Stanford, "Revolutionary Action Movement (RAM): A Case Study of an Urban Revolutionary Movement in Western Capitalist Society" (M.A. thesis, Atlanta University, 1986), 85–86, available at www.ulib

.csuohio.edu/research/portals/blackpower/stanford.pdf; Brink and Harris, *The Negro Revolution in America*, 108–9.

302 **Even the icons:** *CD*, July 6, 1963; "Civil Rights: 'The Awful Roar,'" *Time*, Aug. 30, 1963, 13–14; "1963: Year of Violence," *Liberator*, Jan. 1964, 7; *TSD*, July 20, Aug. 10, 1963; Taylor Branch, *Pillar of Fire: America in the King Years, 1963–65* (New York, 1998), 115; *CD*, Feb. 19, 1963.

303 **antipolice demonstrations:** "Youthful Black Leaders in Phila. Fight Back Against a Frame-up," ca. 1963, RAM, Reel 6, frame 594; "Philadelphia Shamed, Black Militants Framed," *Liberator*, Sept. 1963, 8; Peter Levy, *Civil War on Race Street: The Civil Rights Movement in Cambridge, Maryland* (Gainesville, Fla., 2003); *CD*, July 18, 1963; *NYT*, Aug. 26, 1963; *CD*, Aug. 14, 1963; "The Demonstrators," *NC*, July 15, 1963, 2–3; "Chicago No 'Wonderful Town' for Negroes," *NA*, Oct. 21, 1963.

304 **At Harlem's Speakers' Corner:** "Revolution in Harlem Streets," *NA*, Sept. 24, 1963.

304 **In mid-June, a protest:** *NYT*, June 18, 1963; *PC*, June 22, 1963.

304 **In Detroit, seven hundred protestors:** *IN*, July 22, 1963; *MC*, July 13, 1963; Sidney Fine, *Violence in the Model City: The Cavanagh Administration, Race Relations, and the Detroit Riot of 1967* (Ann Arbor, Mich., 1988), 106.

304 **The situation was even tenser:** *CD*, Oct. 30, 1963; Countryman, *Up South*, 155–56; "Wanted Dead or Alive," RAM, Reel 12, Frame 134.

304 **"Looks as if we have Birmingham":** *PC*, Feb. 23, March 2, Nov. 23, 1963.

305 **police departments began preparing:** *CD*, Aug. 3, 1963; *TSD*, Aug. 10, 1963.

305 **"White folks ain't going to":** *NYT*, Aug. 12, 1963.

305 **"Violence seems to be the only way":** *TSD*, Aug. 10, 1963.

305 **"new people":** James R. Robinson interview, April 28, 1971, AMP, Box 57, Folder 4.

305 **The iconic event:** Brink and Harris, *The Negro Revolution in America*, 26–27, 46–47; Juan Williams, "40th Anniversary of the March on Washington: A Great Day in Washington," *Crisis*, July–Aug. 2003, 24–30.

306 **"symbolic protest":** *IN*, Aug. 19, 1963.

306 **Black militants largely joined:** Malcolm X as told to Alex Haley, *The Autobiography of Malcolm X* (1964; rept. New York, 1973), 278; Michael Thelwell, "The August 28th March on Washington: The Castrated Giant" (1964), reprinted in Thelwell, *Duties, Pleasures, and Conflicts* (Amherst, Mass., 1987), 59; James Forman, *The Making of Black Revolutionaries: A Personal Account* (New York, 1972), 331.

307 **"largest delegation was composed of labor groups":** *PC*, Sept. 7, 1963; "Groundswell for March," *NA*, Aug. 10, 1963.

307 **Many unions whose rank and file marched:** Roger Horowitz; *"Negro and White, Unite and Fight!" A Social History of Industrial Unionism in Meatpacking, 1930–90* (Urbana, Ill., 1997), 254–55; Thomas J. Sugrue, *The Origins of the Urban Crisis: Race and Inequality in Postwar Detroit* (Princeton, N.J., 1996), 144; Minna Ziskind, "Labor Conflict in the Suburbs: Organizing Retail in Metropoli-

tan New York, 1954–1958," *International Labor and Working-Class History* 64 (Oct. 2003), 55–73; *NYT*, Aug. 29, 1963; Reuther quoted in Kevin Boyle, *The UAW and the Heyday of American Liberalism, 1945–1968* (Ithaca, N.Y., 1995), 180; "March's Radical Demands Point Way for Struggle," *NA*, Sept. 24, 1963.

308 **"challenge" the "Uncle Tom leaders":** "Let Us March ON Washington," *Liberator*, Aug. 1963, 2.

308 **New York's Umbra group:** James Edward Smethurst, *The Black Arts Movement: Literary Nationalism in the 1960s and 1970s* (Chapel Hill, N.C., 2005), 149.

308 **a clash aboard a bus:** Hentoff, *The New Equality*, 28.

309 **Lynn used the march to launch:** Freedom Now Party, "The Declaration of Washington," Aug. 28, 1963, in SCCF, 001-848; *NYT*, Aug. 24, 1963; *PC*, Aug. 31, 1963; *IN*, Sept. 2, 30, 1963; *Militant*, Sept. 30, 1963; William Worthy, "An All Black Party," *Liberator*, Oct. 1963, 18–19; on Lynn's background, see *CD*, Dec. 5, 1942, Apr. 26, 1947, June 6, 1959.

309 **"I observed that circus":** *Autobiography of Malcolm X*, 280; Forman, *The Making of Black Revolutionaries*, 333; Branch, *Pillar of Fire*, 130–31; *PC*, Sept. 7, 1963; C. E. Wilson, "The Pilgrimage," *Liberator*, Sept. 1963, 5.

309 **growing in prominence and popularity:** C. Eric Lincoln, *The Black Muslims in America* (1961), 3rd ed. (Grand Rapids, Mich., and Trenton, N.J., 1994), 2. The *Newsweek* survey was conducted door-to-door and on the streets in sixty predominantly black neighborhoods throughout the country, and all but six of the 158 interviewers were black. It is possible that the class composition of the survey team (mostly professionals without "personal attitudes" that might "distort the results") might have led to a selection bias in the survey, lowering the approval rates for the Nation somewhat. It was also striking, however, that a sizeable minority of northern blacks surveyed "were not sure" about either the "Black Muslims" (35 percent) or Elijah Muhammad (50 percent). See Brink and Harris, *The Negro Revolution in America*, 118–22, and, on the survey's method, 11–17. Charlie L. Russell, "Black Muslims in Crisis," *Liberator*, Nov. 1963, 12.

310 **"House Negroes" and "Uncle Toms":** "Message to the Grassroots," in George Breitman, ed., *Malcolm X Speaks: Selected Speeches and Statements* (New York, 1965); Albert Cleage, "Myths About Malcolm X," speech delivered in Detroit, Feb. 24, 1967, reprinted in John Henrik Clarke, ed., *Malcolm X: The Man and His Times* (New York, 1969), 13–26.

310 **"There's no such thing as a nonviolent":** "Message to the Grassroots," 9; *CD*, Nov. 21, 1963; for a scathing discussion of the speech, see Salvatore, *Singing in a Strange Land*, 263–64; by contrast, see Smith, *Dancing in the Streets*, 54–59, 85–88.

310 **"80 percent Muslims":** James Boggs and Grace Lee Boggs, "Detroit: Birth of a Nation," *National Guardian*, Oct. 7, 1967; Marvin Rich, interview, June 1963, AMP, Box 57, Folder 3, italics in original; on the nonreligious appeal of the Nation of Islam after Malcolm X's death, see Ula Taylor, "Elijah Muhammad's Nation of Islam: Separatism, Regendering, and a Secular Approach to Black

Power after Malcolm X (1965–75)," in Theoharis and Woodard, eds., *Freedom North*, 178.

311 **"much publicized 'Black Revolt'"**: *IN*, Nov. 25, Dec. 9, 1963.

CHAPTER 10 | "LONG HOT SUMMERS"

313 **"one of those mild-mannered, slow-burning"**: *NYT*, June 22, 1967.

313 **odyssey of protest**: *PC*, Aug. 3, 1963; *NYAN*, July 27, Aug. 3, 10; Sept. 7, 14, 28, Oct. 5, 1963; "Rochdale Village Demonstration," *Crisis*, Nov. 1963, 547; *PC*, Oct. 5, 1963; August Meier and Elliott Rudwick, *CORE: A Study in the Civil Rights Movement, 1942–1968* (Urbana, Ill., 1975), 237; *NYT*, July 29, Sept. 6, Nov. 15, 1963, June 22, 1967.

313 **The Rochdale Movement**: *PC*, Sept. 14, Oct. 26, Nov. 9, Dec. 7, 1963; *NYAN*, Nov. 16, 1963.

314 **Rochdale Movement activists repudiated the liberalism**: *PC*, Jan. 11, 1964; *NYAN*, Dec. 7, 1963; *NYT*, June 22, 1967.

315 **Cleveland had long been a bastion**: Kimberley L. Phillips, *AlabamaNorth: African-American Migrants, Community, and Working-Class Activism in Cleveland, 1915–45* (Urbana, Ill., 1999); Don Freeman, "The Cleveland Story," *Liberator*, June 1963, 11, 18; "Report from Cleveland," *Liberator*, Nov. 1963, 5; James Smethurst, *The Black Arts Movement: Literary Nationalism in the 1960s and 1970s* (Chapel Hill, N.C., 2005), 215–21.

316 **the young RAM activists**: On the origins of RAM, see Maxwell C. Stanford, "Revolutionary Action Movement (RAM): A Case Study of an Urban Revolutionary Movement in Western Capitalist Society" (M.A. thesis, Atlanta University, 1986), available at www.ulib.csuohio.edu/research/portals/blackpower/stanford.pdf.

316 **key figures in black power**: *TSD*, June 27, July 25, 1959; Timothy B. Tyson, *Radio Free Dixie: Robert F. Williams and the Roots of Black Power* (Chapel Hill, N.C., 1999), 149–65, 215–16; Thomas F. Jackson, *From Civil Rights to Human Rights: Martin Luther King, Jr., and the Struggle for Economic Justice* (Philadelphia, 2007), 106–7; Robert F. Williams, *Negroes with Guns* (New York, 1962), 5.

317 **brought a discussion of black self-defense**: *PC*, July 2, 1960, Aug. 5, Sept. 9, 1961 (quote), Sept. 16, 1961; Raymond Arsenault, *Freedom Riders: 1961 and the Struggle for Racial Justice* (New York, 2006), 404–18; Tyson, *Radio Free Dixie*, 220–86. Williams was less well known to the general public because of the thin national news media coverage of him. See Jenny Walker, "A Media Made Movement? Black Violence and Nonviolence in the Historiography of the Civil Rights Movement," in Brian Ward, ed., *Media, Culture, and the Modern African American Freedom Struggle* (Gainesville, Fla., 2001), 50–52.

318 **in the heart of a freedom struggle**: *PC*, Sept. 22, 1962, June 8, 1963; Williams, *Negroes with Guns*; Penny M. von Eschen, *Race Against Empire: Black Ameri-*

cans and Anticolonialism, 1937–1957 (Ithaca, N.Y., 1997); Robin D. G. Kelley, *Freedom Dreams: The Black Radical Imagination* (Boston, 2002), esp. 36–109.

318 **Williams corresponded with Stanford:** For an early example of connections between Stanford and Williams, see Robert F. Williams to Max Stanford, Dec. 17, 1963, RFW, Reel 1, frames 790–91; Kelley, *Freedom Dreams*, 72.

318 **a natural networker:** On Cleveland, see David Cohen phone conversation, July 25, 1971, AMP, Box 56, Folder 3; Arthur Evans interview, March 13, 1971, AMP, Box 56, Folder 5, mentions the Monroe Defense Committee in Cleveland's CORE chapter but does not bring up Stanford; Grace Lee Boggs, *Living for Change* (Minneapolis, 1998), 125, 135; Max Stanford, "As Others See It," *Muhammad Speaks*, Aug. 16, 1963; William W. Sales, Jr., *From Civil Rights to Black Liberation: Malcolm X and the Organization of Afro-American Unity* (Boston, 1994), 99–100, 105–6; Matthew Countryman, *Up South: Civil Rights and Black Power in Philadelphia* (Philadelphia, 2005), 110.

319 **In 1963, RAM emerged into the public eye:** "Youthful Black Leaders in Phila. Fight Back Against a Frame-Up," ca. 1963, RAM, Reel 6, frame 594; "Philadelphia Shamed, Black Militants Framed," *Liberator*, Sept. 1963, 8; Max Stanford, FBI File, Memo, Sept. 25, 1964, RAM, Reel 4; Max Stanford, M.A. thesis draft, sent to John Bracey and Ernie Allen for comment (May 1979), RAM, Reel 3, frames 106–10; cartoon, *BA* (Nov.–Dec. 1963), 3.

319 **"The Negro cannot integrate":** Charles W. Johnson, Jr., "The White Man's Heaven Is the Black Man's Hell," *BA* (Fall 1964), 20, RAM, Reel 12, frame 694.

319 **RAM's rhetoric:** Johnson, "The White Man's Heaven"; Max Stanford, "Revolutionary Nationalism and the Afro-American Liberation Movement," *BA* (Nov.–Dec. 1963), in RAM, Reel 12, frame 658; Wanda Marshall, "Integration, Separation, or What?," *BA* (Nov.–Dec. 1963), 11–18, in RAM, Reel 12, frames 664, 672; for a discussion of Stanford's relationship to Maoism, see Kelley, *Freedom Dreams*, 77–83.

320 **"prerequisite to a *genuine* Black Revolution":** Don Freeman, "Black Youth and Afro-American Liberation," *BA* (Fall 1964), RAM, Reel 12, frames 674–99.

320 **the Black Arts movement:** Smethurst, *The Black Arts Movement*.

321 **"We are afraid to walk the streets":** William Woodley, "The Latest Victim," *BA* (Nov.–Dec. 1963), RAM, Reel 12, frame 656.

321 **"get rid of traitors":** "The Black Guard," RAM, Reel 5, frame 596.

321 **"guerilla youth force":** Orientation to a Black Mass Movement, RAM, Reel 1, frame 261; on organization of black ghetto youth, RAM, Reel 5, frame 787; Max Stanford, curriculum vitae, RAM, Reel 1; FBI memo, July 16, 1965, RAM, Reel 4; "Three Black Power Groups Linked to Rioting," RAM, Reel 12, frame 145; *NYT*, July 29, 1966; "Carmichael Supports RAM," *Human Events*, Aug. 6, 1966, RAM, Reel 12, frame 137; Lance Hill, *The Deacons for Defense: Armed Resistance and the Civil Rights Movement* (Chapel Hill, N.C., 2004), 221–24; *BAA*, Nov. 27, 1965; *PC*, April 9, 1966 (on Deacons move north); Robinson, *CD*, July 31, 1965.

321 **Still, RAM kept looking:** "The Twelve Point Program of RAM," 1964, in RAM, Reel 5, frame 730; "Notes on an Afroamerican Student Movement," 1965, RAM, Reel 8, frame 369; Max Stanford, "Revolutionary Nationalism and the Afroamerican Student," *Liberator,* Jan. 1965; RAM, "The Los Angeles War Cry: 'Burn, Baby, Burn,'" n.d., RAM, Reel 6; "The Battle of Watts: An Analysis and Statement by the Revolutionary Action Movement" (1965), RAM, Reel 1, frame 289 ff.; *OP,* Dec. 3, 1972.

322 **Ferguson also took heat:** *NYT,* June 22, 1967; Gladys Harrington, who chained herself to the crane at the Rochdale Village protest, also complained that her fellow CORE members chastised her for the tactic. See James R. Robinson interview, April 28, 1971, AMP, Box 57, Folder 4. Ferguson led another wave of protests against Billy Banjo in 1965. See RAM, Reel 6, frames 738ff.

322 **drawn powerfully to Malcolm X:** "First Person: The Price of Freedom: Herman Ferguson," *Souls* 7:1 (Winter 2005), 84–106; *PC,* Dec. 7, 1963.

322 **Malcolm X grew disaffected:** Malcolm X as told to Alex Haley, *The Autobiography of Malcolm X* (1964; rept. New York, 1973); William W. Sales, *From Civil Rights to Black Liberation: Malcolm X and the Organization of Afro-America Unity* (Boston, 1994), esp. ch. 5.

323 **Ferguson was never:** *NYT,* Sept. 22, 1996; "First Person," 98–99; Sales, *From Civil Rights to Black Liberation,* 109, 114, 121.

324 **most notably the Socialist Workers' Party:** Strikingly, the Socialist Workers' Party edition of Malcolm's speeches included just one delivered before his break with Elijah Muhammad—his 1963 "Message to the Grassroots," in Detroit in November 1963. The rest of the collection includes speeches from 1964 and 1965. George Breitman, ed., *Malcolm X Speaks* (New York, 1965). The party's various publishing arms continued to publish editions of Malcolm's speeches and books about Malcolm well into the 1970s; they were a major moneymaker for the small Socialist sect. See also Smethurst, *The Black Arts Movement,* 145–47.

324 **To a great extent, Malcolm was:** Carlos E. Russell, "Exclusive Interview with Brother Malcolm X," *Liberator,* May 1964, 13; on Malcolm X and memory, see Len Holt, "Malcolm X the Mirror," *Liberator,* Feb. 1965; Ossie Davis, "Our Shining Black Prince: Eulogy Delivered at the Funeral of Malcolm X, Faith Temple Church of God," Feb. 27, 1965, in John Henrik Clarke, ed., *Malcolm X* (New York, 1969), xi–xii. The essays in Clarke, *Malcolm X,* and in Joe Wood, ed., *Malcolm: In Our Own Image* (New York, 1993), convey the heterogeneity of interpretations of his life and its meaning; see also William L. Van Deburg, *Black Camelot: African-American Culture Heroes in Their Times, 1960–1980* (Chicago, 1997), 76–78.

325 **In the summer of 1964, black residents:** *NYT,* July 17, 18, 19, 20, 22, 23, 1964; Carvin Eison, *July '64,* Image/Word/Sound Films, 2004; on postriot Rochester, see R.D.G. Wadhwani, "Kodak, FIGHT, and the Definition of Civil Rights in Rochester, New York," *Historian* 60 (1997), 59–75.

326 **Of the 163 uprisings in the summer of 1967:** For a list of places of riot outbreaks in 1967, see *NACCD*, 323–24; population figures from 1970 USCB, *1970
Census of Population*, vol. 1, parts 1–50, *Characteristics of the Population* (Washington, D.C., 1973).

326 **The form, scale, and duration:** Material in this and the following paragraph
summarizes the findings of the Kerner Commission. See *NACCD*.

327 **By the early 1960s, complaints:** USCCR, *1961 Report, Book 5: Justice* (Washington, D.C., 1961), 5–28; Marilynn S. Johnson, *Street Justice: A History of Police Violence in New York City* (Boston, 2003), 229–34; Robert Fogelson,
Violence as Protest: A Study of Riots and Ghettos (Garden City, N.Y., 1971),
57–58; James Baldwin, *Nobody Knows My Name* (New York, 1962), 67; *NACCD*,
206.

328 **"Without such cases to report":** Louis E. Lomax, *The Negro Revolt* (New
York, 1962), 59.

328 **When police arrested and beat:** *PC*, Sept. 9, 1961; *NYAN*, Dec. 6, 1962.

328 **routinely strip-searched all women:** *CD*, June 5, 1965.

329 **"The Negro mass in the North":** Meeting, May 20, 1963, 11:25 a.m., transcribed in Jonathan Rosenberg and Zachary Karabell, eds., *Kennedy, Johnson,
and the Quest for Justice: The Civil Rights Tapes* (New York, 2003), 120.

329 **collisions between young black men and the police:** *AD*, 527, 542, 1342.
Myrdal, admitting that he had no quantitative data to back up his point, as-
serted that police brutality was less common in the North than in the South.
See also Elliott M. Rudwick, "Police Work and the Negro," *Journal of Criminal
Law, Criminology, and Police Science* 50 (1960), 596–99, and Robert M. Fogel-
son, "From Resentment to Confrontation: The Police, the Negroes, and the
Outbreak of the Nineteen-Sixties Riots," *Political Science Quarterly* 83 (1968),
217–47.

329 **The scarcity of black police officers:** Robert M. Fogelson, *Big City Police*
(Cambridge, Mass., 1977), 247–53, 256–60.

330 **Police departments remained:** *NACCD*, 322; *CD*, Aug. 21, 1965; Johnson,
Street Justice, 202–3, 236–37; Sidney Fine, *Violence in the Model City: The Ca-
vanagh Administration, Race Relations, and the Detroit Riot of 1967* (Ann
Arbor, Mich., 1988), 108–9.

330 **"Colored citizens cannot":** *BAA*, Sept. 10, 1966.

330 **overt expression of racist sentiments:** Thomas J. Sugrue and Andrew M.
Goodman, "Plainfield Burning: Black Rebellion in the Suburban North," *JUH*
33 (2007), 574–75; Fine, *Violence in the Model City*, 95–96.

331 **Only a minority of blacks:** *Supplemental Studies for the National Advisory
Committee on Civil Disorders* (Washington, D.C., 1968), 42–44, 217–43; Larry
Dillard, interview (1968) in Bob Blauner, *Black Lives, White Lives: Three
Decades of Race Relations in America* (Berkeley, Calif., 1989), 113; Lomax, *The
Negro Revolt*, 59–60; generally, see Harlan Hahn and Joe R. Feagin, "Riot-
Precipitating Police Practices: Attitudes in Urban Ghettos," *Phylon* 31 (1970),
183–93.

332 **Blacks regularly complained:** Fine, *Violence in the Model City*, 99.

332 **"Right now":** Harold Sampson interview (1968), in Blauner, *Black Lives, White Lives*, 118.

332 **Rumors played a crucial role:** On the power of rumors, see *NACCD*, 69; generally, Patricia A. Turner, *I Heard It Through the Grapevine: Rumor in African-American Culture* (Berkeley, Calif., 1993), 45–53.

333 **"Listen, man":** *BAA*, Aug. 28, 1965.

333 **"I don't understand all this talk":** Lawrence Stewart, "Eyewitness Newark," *Militant*, July 24, 1967.

333 **"That set had a tag on it":** *PCN*, July 14, 1967.

333 **"just a group of kids":** Commission interview of Plainfield youths, conducted by Steve Kurzman and Steve Weiner, LBJ-CR, Part 5, Reel 26, frame 00112.

333 **Rioters targeted nearly every type:** Mutual Loan Research Bureau, "The Detroit Report," Sept. 13, 1967, in LBJ-CR, Part 5, Reel 9, frames 885–86.

333 **were not unscathed:** On the looting of black-owned stores, see *PT*, July 25, 29, Aug. 8, 1967, and Stewart, "Eyewitness Newark." See also Alison Isenberg, *Downtown America: A History of the Place and the People Who Made It* (Chicago, 2004), 235–36.

335 **As Watts burned:** RAM, "The Los Angeles War Cry: 'Burn, Baby, Burn,' " n.d., RAM, Reel 5; "The Battle of Watts: An Analysis and Statement by the Revolutionary Action Movement" (1965), RAM, Reel 1, frame 289ff.; Richard Price and Rob Stewart, "Watts, LA: A First Hand Report: Rebellion Without Ideology," *Liberator*, Sept. 1965, 6; H. Rap Brown, "The Black Revolution Will Not Be Stopped," *Liberator*, Sept. 1967, 3; Derrick Morrison, "Eyewitness Detroit," *Militant*, Aug. 7, 1967; George Novak, "The Black Uprisings—1967," *Militant*, Sept. 4, 1967.

335 **honing their skills for the impending:** Frank Donner, *Protectors of Privilege: Red Squads and Police Repression in Urban America* (Berkeley, Calif., 1990), 176. On rifle clubs, see point three of "The 12 Point Program of RAM" (1964), in RAM, Reel 5, frame 730; *NYT*, March 15, 1964; "Malcolm X: Self-Defense vs. Submission," *Liberator*, April 1964, 3; Malcolm X, "The Ballot or the Bullet," in Breitman, *Malcolm Speaks*, 23–24; Hill, *Deacons for Defense*, 223; Fine, *Violence in the Model City*, 26. Ferguson's involvement with the Jamaica Rifle Club was closely monitored by the FBI. See Confidential Investigation of Jamaica Rifle and Pistol Club, RAM, Reel 6, frames 856–61.

335 **"We have to learn to fight":** Diane C. Fujino, *Heartbeat of Struggle: The Revolutionary Life of Yuri Kochiyama* (Minneapolis, 2005), 200; Interoffice Memorandum, to Mr. Nelson from Mr. Wilson, Subject: Report on Attendance of City-Wide Citizens Action Committee, Oct. 12, 1967, in LBJ-CR, Part 5, Reel 24, frame 38.

335 **attracted the attention of the FBI:** See Stanford's FBI files in RAM, Reel 4, frames 2–736; quotes from FBI memo, March 9, 1965, and appendix; FBI memo, July 16, 1965. Herman Ferguson's FBI files, released for his trial, are almost useless. Vast sections are redacted. See RAM, Reel 7, frames 1–363.

336 **"created a climate of unrest":** FBI press release, in LBJ-CR, Part 5, Reel 9, frame 540.

336 **"overthrow the Government":** *NYT*, Nov. 5, 1967.

337 **grew increasingly disaffected:** Tyson, *Radio Free Dixie*, 297; James Forman, *The Making of Black Revolutionaries: A Personal Account* (New York, 1972), 440; Sales, *From Civil Rights to Black Liberation*, 130; Peniel E. Joseph, *Waiting 'til the Midnight Hour: A Narrative History of Black Power in America* (New York, 2006), 108, 124.

337 **By 1966, some SNCC activists:** Joseph, *Waiting 'til the Midnight Hour*, 132–73; Stokely Carmichael with Ekwueme Michael Thelwell, *Ready for Revolution: The Life and Struggles of Stokely Carmichael (Kwame Ture)* (New York, 2003), 524.

338 **"scare the daylights":** *BAA*, July 23, 1966; Gilbert Jonas, *Freedom's Sword: The NAACP and the Struggle Against Racism in America, 1909–1969* (New York, 2005), 383.

339 **Was black power a movement?:** On the breadth of black power, see Dean E. Robinson, *Black Nationalism in American Politics and Thought* (Cambridge, U.K., 2001), 73; and generally, Jeffrey O. G. Ogbar, *Black Power: Radical Politics and African American Identity* (Baltimore, 2004), and Joseph, *Waiting 'til the Midnight Hour*.

339 **"SNCC has formally chosen":** *BAA*, June 11, 1966.

339 **"the other side of the old coin":** *BAA*, Sept. 17, 1966.

339 **In a "manifesto":** *NYT*, Oct. 14, 1966; *BAA*, Oct. 22, 1966; *CD*, Oct. 29, 1966; see also "Crisis and Commitment," *Crisis*, Oct. 1966, 474.

340 **"force the nation to see":** *BAA*, July 16, 1966.

340 **"Other ethnic groups":** *BAA*, July 23, 1966.

340 **a black power summit:** *NYT*, Sept. 4, 8, 1966; *CD*, Sept. 6, Oct. 10, 1966.

340 **"The cup is running over":** *BAA*, July 9, 1966.

340 **"turning away from a slavish":** *BAA*, July 16, 1966.

340 **"no clear, solid center":** Carmichael with Thelwell, *Ready for Revolution*, 549.

341 **An instant celebrity, Carmichael spent:** *NYAN*, Sept. 3, 1966; *Paterson Morning Call*, Aug. 11, 1966, copy in RAM, Reel 4, frame 162; "Carmichael Supports RAM," in ibid., Reel 12, frame 137; *BAA*, Sept. 24, 1966. On the complex relationship of RAM, Carmichael, and the Panthers, see Stanford, "Revolutionary Action Movement," 119–22.

341 **formed their own Black Panther organizations:** The Black Panthers have generated more scholarship than any other black radical organization. The best recent work includes Judson L. Jeffries, "An Unexamined Chapter of Black Panther History," in Jeffries, ed., *Black Power: In the Belly of the Beast* (Urbana, Ill., 2005), 185–224; Jon Rice, "The World of the Illinois Panthers," in Jeanne F. Theoharis and Komozi Woodard, eds., *Freedom North: Black Freedom Struggles Outside the South, 1940–1980* (New York, 2003); and Jama Lazerow and Yohuru Williams, eds., *In Search of the Black Panther Party: New Perspectives on a Revolutionary Movement* (Durham, N.C., 2006).

342 **Seale had been affiliated:** Stanford claimed that Seale was "purged" from RAM for "drunkenness and irresponsibility"; Stanford, "Revolutionary Action Movement," 122. The Black Panther Party Platform has been widely reprinted. Here I quote from Black Panther Party 10-Point Program (handwritten), BPPH, Box 1, Folder 3.

343 **their singular focus on the criminal justice system:** The topic of blacks' historical relationship to the police and the criminal justice system, particularly in the twentieth century, has been woefully understudied. For two important contributions, see Martha Biondi, *To Stand and Fight: The Struggle for Civil Rights in Postwar New York City* (Cambridge, Mass., 2003), 60–78, 197–202; Johnson, *Street Justice*, esp. 181–276.

343 **"What is a pig?":** *BP*, Oct. 19, 1968; my thinking about pigs has been influenced by Peter Stallybrass and Allon White, *The Politics and Poetics of Transgression* (Ithaca, N.Y., 1986), esp. 44–59.

343 **children's coloring book:** Reginald Major, *A Panther Is a Black Cat* (New York, 1971), 87.

343 **the category of pig was capacious:** For a broad sample, see *BP*, Sept. 7, Oct. 19, 26, Nov. 16, 1968, Jan. 25, Mar. 31, 1969; Douglas quote from *BP*, May 18, 1968; on Douglas, see Major, *A Panther Is a Black Cat*, 139–43, and Sam Durant, ed., *Black Panther: The Revolutionary Art of Emory Douglas* (New York, 2007); also Brian Ward, "Jazz and Soul, Race and Class, Cultural Nationalists and Black Panthers: A Black Power Debate Revisited," in Ward, ed., *Media, Culture, and the Modern African American Freedom Struggle*, 180–82.

344 **Eugene McCarthy removed a mask:** *BP*, Nov. 2, 1968; the use of *pig* to refer to police officers may or may not have been the distinct contribution of the Black Panthers, but whether or not it was, the Panthers certainly popularized the term through repetition. See JoNina M. Abron, "Raising the Consciousness of the People: The Black Panther Intercommunal News Service, 1967–1980," in Ken Wachsberger, ed., *Voices from the Underground: Insider Histories of the Vietnam Era Underground Press* (Tempe, Ariz., 1993), 351; Rodger Streitmatter, "*Black Panther* Newspaper: A Militant Voice, a Salient Vision," in Todd Vogel, ed., *The Black Press: New Literary and Historical Essays* (New Brunswick, N.J., 2001), 232–33, 235, 239. For other cartoons discussed, see *BP*, Nov. 16, Dec. 21, 1968, March 3, 16, 1969.

344 **In a dramatic act of protest:** Simon Wendt, "The Roots of Black Power? Armed Resistance and the Radicalization of the Civil Rights Movement," in Peniel Joseph, ed., *The Black Power Movement: Rethinking the Civil Rights—Black Power Era* (New York, 2006), 160–63. Cf Bridgette Baldwin, "In the Shadow of the Gun: The Black Panther, the Ninth Amendment, and the Discourses of Violence," in Lazerow and Williams, ed., *In Search of the Black Panther Party*, 67–96.

344 **"Wherever they went":** Jean Genet, *Prisoner of Love* (Middletown, Conn., 1992), 85, quoted in Nikhil Pal Singh, "The Black Panthers and the 'Undeveloped Country' of the Left," in Charles E. Jones, ed., *The Black Panther Party*

Reconsidered (Baltimore, 1998), 82, and 82–87 more generally on the performative nature of Panther politics.

345 **"is a dramatization":** *BAA*, April 4, 1970; for an assessment of Stewart's career, see *NYT*, April 10, 2002; see also G. Louis Heath, ed., *Off the Pigs: The History and Literature of the Black Panther Party* (Metuchen, N.J., 1976), 66.

345 **Black Panther politics:** Nikhil Pal Singh, *Black Is a Country: Race and the Unfinished Struggle for Democracy* (Cambridge, Mass., 2004), 202–6.

346 **"I was feeling proud, man":** *NACCD*, 133; Interoffice Memorandum to Mr. Wilson from Tom Popp, Re: interviews 10/12, in LBJ-CR, Part 5, Reel 24, frame 195.

346 **Many black residents in Plainfield:** Office of the Assistant Deputy Director for Research, LBJ-CR, Part 5, Reel 7, frame 253.

347 **"the black community has generally interpreted":** David O. Sears, "Black Attitudes Toward the Political System in the Aftermath of the Watts Riots," *Midwest Journal of Political Science* 13 (1969), 515–44, quote 517. See also David O. Sears and T. M. Tomlinson, "Riot Ideology in Los Angeles: A Study in Negro Attitudes," *Social Science Quarterly* 49 (1968), 485–503; Joe R. Feagin and Paul B. Sheatsley, "Ghetto Resident Appraisals of a Riot," *Public Opinion Quarterly* 32 (1968), 352–62.

347 **"A significant consequence":** *NACCD*, 130; *Supplemental Studies*, 217–43.

347 **Survey researchers made:** *NACCD*, 121–35; T. M. Tomlinson, "The Development of a Riot Ideology Among Urban Negroes," in Allen Grimshaw, ed., *Racial Violence in the United States* (Chicago, 1969), 226–31; Nathan Kaplan, "The New Ghetto Man: A Review of Recent Empirical Studies," in David Boesel and Peter Rossi, eds., *Cities Under Siege: An Anatomy of the Ghetto Riots, 1964–1968* (New York, 1971), 353–54.

348 **"two societies, one black, one white":** *NACCD*, 1.

348 **Social scientists offered:** Fogelson, *Violence as Protest*, 86–90; E. L. Quarantelli and Russell R. Dynes, "Property Norms and Looting: Their Patterns in Community Crises," *Phylon* 31 (1970), 138–72; Lizabeth Cohen, *A Consumers' Republic: The Politics of Consumption in Postwar America* (New York, 2003), 373–78.

348 **emphasized "frustrated expectations":** Jack A. Bloom, "Ghetto Revolts, Black Power, and the Limits of the Civil Rights Coalition," in Raymond D'Angelo, ed., *The American Civil Rights Movement: Readings and Interpretations* (New York, 2001), 383–408; James A. Geschwender, "Civil Rights Protest and Riots: A Disappearing Distinction," *Social Science Quarterly* 49 (1968), 474–84, takes the suggestion a step further and argues that the riots were an extension of the civil rights movement.

349 **"outbreaks of animal spirits":** Edward C. Banfield, "Rioting Mainly for Fun and Profit," in James Q. Wilson, ed., *The Metropolitan Enigma* (Cambridge, Mass., 1968), 312–41.

350 **"Those cats":** *BAA*, Sept. 11, 1965.

351 **demands for law and order:** Michael Flamm, *Law and Order: Street Crime, Urban Unrest, and the Crisis of Liberalism in the 1960s* (New York, 2005).

351 **"indiscriminate use of force":** *NACCD*, 335; Albert Bergesen, "Race Riots of 1967: An Analysis of Police Violence in Detroit and Newark," *Journal of Black Studies* 12 (1982), 261–74.

351 **In Detroit, four white police officers:** John Hersey, *The Algiers Motel Incident* (New York, 1968).

351 **"any possibility of neutralizing":** Kenneth T. O'Reilly, *Racial Matters: The FBI's Secret File on Black America* (New York, 1989), 277, 280–81; Ward Churchill and Jim Vander Wall, *Agents of Repression: The FBI's Secret Wars Against the Black Panther Party and the American Indian Movement*, 2nd ed. (Boston, 2002), 45–47. Churchill and Vander Wall inaccurately identify Maxwell Stanford as Maxwell Sanford.

352 **"deliberate frame-up attempt":** Max Stanford to Roy Wilkins, July 5, 1967, NAACP-M, Part 28, Series B, Reel 7, frame 543; Roy Wilkins, *Standing Fast* (New York, 1982), 325; "Wanted: Who? All the Black Youth! Why? To Take Care of Business," flyer, Aug. 27, 1967, in RAM, Reel 6; *Crusader* 9:3 (Dec. 1967), in RFW, Reel 11, frame 194; see also *Crusader* (Summer 1969), in RFW, Reel 11, frame 231; for another defense of Ferguson, see Lawrence P. Neal, "An Open Letter to Roy Wilkins," *Liberator*, Aug. 1967, 4–7; *NYAN*, June 24, July 1, 1967, June 22, 1968; *CD*, June 17, 1968.

352 **While the conspiracy case:** *NYT*, Feb. 25, March 11, 1968; "The White Power Conspiracy," Sept. 1968, RAM, Reel 1, frames 518–23.

352 **Ferguson also joined forces:** *NYT*, June 22, 1967, June 4, Oct. 4, 1968, April 4, 1989.

353 **"to expose, disrupt, misdirect":** Memorandum to Special Agent in Charge, Albany, New York, from J. Edgar Hoover, Aug. 25, 1967, reprinted in William L. Van Deburg, ed., *Modern Black Nationalism: From Marcus Garvey to Louis Farrakhan* (New York, 1997), 134–35. The memo singled out "Stokely Carmichael, H. Rap Brown, Elijah Mohammad [*sic*], and Maxwell Stanford." See also Airtel to SAC Albany, Re: Counterintelligence Program, March 4, 1968, RAM, Reel 7, frames 470–74.

353 **the FBI planted informants:** O'Reilly, *Racial Matters*, 261–324.

353 **sometimes retaliated violently:** *NYT*, Dec. 6, 9, 10, 1969; *CD*, Dec. 10, 13, 15, 1969.

354 **New Haven's Panther chapter:** The New Haven murders are discussed extensively in Paul Bass and Douglas W. Rae, *Murder in the Model City: The Black Panthers, Yale, and the Redemption of a Killer* (New York, 2006), and Yohuru Williams, *Black Politics/White Power: Civil Rights, Black Power, and the Black Panthers in New Haven* (New York, 2000); O'Reilly, *Racial Matters*, 261–324.

354 **"the media will not report":** William Worthy, "The Black Power Establishment," *Esquire*, Dec. 1967.

354 **Above all, black power:** Komozi Woodard, "It's Nation Time in NewArk: Amiri Baraka and the Black Power Experiment in New Jersey," in Theoharis and Woodard, eds., *Freedom North*, 287, perceptively writes, "Because the

Black Power movement was experimental, the critical study of Black Power politics must begin with an inquiry into its most important experiments."

CHAPTER 11 | "UNCONDITIONAL WAR"

356 **"Unfortunately, many Americans":** Lyndon Baines Johnson, State of the Union Address, Jan. 8, 1964, available at millercenter.virginia.edu/scripps/diglibrary/prezspeeches/johnson/lbj_1964_0108.html; Yarmolinsky, quoted in Dona Cooper Hamilton and Charles V. Hamilton, *The Dual Agenda: Race and Social Welfare Policies of Civil Rights Organizations* (New York, 1997), 157; Carl Brauer, "Kennedy, Johnson, and the War on Poverty," *JAH* 69 (1982), 113–19.

357 **When Johnson took office:** Bruce Schulman, *Lyndon B. Johnson and American Liberalism* (Boston, 1995), document 5; Dorothy K. Newman et al., *Protest, Politics, and Prosperity: Black Americans and White Institutions* (New York, 1978), Tables 2.6 and 7.2.

357 **In 1963, a remarkable 83 percent:** William Brink and Louis Harris, *Black and White: A Study of U.S. Racial Attitudes Today* (New York, 1967), appendix D, 240, 242; Peter Goldman, *Report from Black America* (New York, 1969), 147–48, 256.

359 **Housing was, however, too hot an issue:** Ismail Alsheik and Leonard S. Rubinowitz, "A Missing Piece: Fair Housing and the 1964 Civil Rights Act," *Howard Law Journal* 48 (2005), 841–911.

359 **"character or use" of a property:** Duane Lockard, *Toward Equal Opportunity: A Study of State and Local Antidiscrimination Laws* (London, 1968), 111–12.

359 **By the early 1960s, Realtors:** *The 50 States Report Submitted to the U.S. Commission on Civil Rights by the State Advisory Committees* (Washington, D.C., 1961), 71, 143, 263–64; on the use of free enterprise rhetoric, see David Freund, "Marketing the Free Market: State Intervention and the Politics of Prosperity in Metropolitan America," in Kevin M. Kruse and Thomas J. Sugrue, eds., *The New Suburban History* (Chicago, 2006), 11–32.

359 **Opponents of fair-housing laws:** *TIH* (Nov.–Dec. 1963); Thomas J. Sugrue, *The Origins of the Urban Crisis: Race and Inequality in Postwar Detroit* (Princeton, N.J., 1996), 226–28; Bruce A. Miller, "Anti–Open Housing Laws: A Historical Anomaly?," *University of Detroit Law Review* 43 (Dec. 1965), 165–72; Thomas W. Casstevens, "The Defeat of Berkeley's Fair Housing Ordinance," in Lynn W. Eley and Thomas W. Casstevens, eds., *The Politics of Fair Housing Legislation* (San Francisco, 1968), 187–236.

360 **A measure forbidding employment discrimination:** *NYT*, Feb. 1, 2, 1964.

360 **The proposed civil rights bill's Title VII:** Judith Stein, *Running Steel, Running America: Race, Economic Policy, and the Decline of Liberalism* (Chapel Hill, N.C., 1998), 82–87; Hugh Davis Graham, *The Civil Rights Era: Origins*

and Development of National Policy, 1960–1972 (New York, 1990), 95–99, 129–32, 139–41; John David Skrentny, *The Ironies of Affirmative Action: Politics, Justice, and Culture in America* (Chicago, 1996), 120–21.

361 **"Now the responsibility":** *PC*, June 27, 1964; *NYT*, April 13, May 5, 1964; Civil Rights Act of 1964, Pub L. 88-352, 78 Stat. 241; Clifford Alexander, OH, with Joe B. Frantz, June 4, 1973, LBJ-CR, Part 3, Reel 1, frame 100.

361 **Black opinion on the Civil Rights Act:** *CD*, June 22, 1964; *PC*, June 27, Aug. 8, 1964; *NYAN*, July 18, 1964.

362 **Whatever they thought:** *PC*, Aug. 15, 1964; *PT*, July 24, 1965; Nancy MacLean, *Freedom Is Not Enough: The Opening of the American Workplace* (Cambridge, Mass., 2006), 76–113; Thomas J. Sugrue, "Affirmative Action from Below: Civil Rights, the Building Trades, and the Politics of Racial Equality in the North, 1945–1969," *JAH* 91 (2004), 145–73; David Podoff to NAACP, April 2, 1965, in NAACP-M, Part 21, Reel 13, frame 1024.

362 **Throughout the North, activists:** S. Arthur Spiegel, "Affirmative Action in Cincinnati," *Cincinnati Historical Society Bulletin* 37 (1979), 78–88; George Lipsitz, *Life in the Struggle: Ivory Perry and the Culture of Opposition* (Philadelphia, 1988), 85; Herbert Hill, "The Racial Practices of Organized Labor: The Contemporary Record," in Julius Jacobson, ed., *The Negro and the American Labor Movement* (New York, 1968), 303–20; *PB*, Jan. 20, 1964; see also Vertical File: Building Trades Unions NYC, SCCF, 002-761; *NYT*, Feb. 2, June 28, 1967; Memorandum from Edward C. Sylvester, Jr., to David Rose, Oct. 6, 1967, in LBJ-CR, Part 1, Reel 11, frames 159–60; Cecil B. Moore, interview by John Britton, Sept. 26, 1967, 10, RJB.

363 **In 1965, President Johnson issued:** Exec. Order No. 11,246, 30 Fed. Reg. 12319 (Sept. 24, 1965); Memorandum to Philadelphia Federal Executive Board from Warren Phelan, Oct. 27, 1967, Box 34, Folder 1, FCP; James E. Jones, "The Bugaboo of Racial Quotas," *Wisconsin Law Review* 34 (1970), 343–48; Sugrue, "Affirmative Action from Below," 170.

363 **Straddling the fence proved difficult:** Zachary Yale Dykman, "An Analysis of Negro Employment in the Building Trades" (Ph.D. diss., University of Pennsylvania, 1971), 205; Graham, *The Civil Rights Era*, 330, 540, n. 35–36.

364 **But they held out hope that Johnson:** *CD*, Feb. 29, 1964; Dennis C. Dickerson, *Militant Mediator: Whitney M. Young, Jr.* (Lexington, Ky., 1998), 246–61.

365 **"the problems require much more":** On Humphrey, see Stein, *Running Steel*, 76–78, 87, and generally, Timothy N. Thurber, *The Politics of Equality: Hubert H. Humphrey and the African American Freedom Struggle* (New York, 1999).

365 **How much more—and what form:** Mark I. Gelfand, "The War on Poverty," in Robert A. Divine, ed., *The Johnson Years*, vol. 1, *Foreign Policy, the Great Society, and the White House* (Lawrence, Kans., 1987), 128, 147, n. 6. The best brief overview is Nicholas Lemann, *The Promised Land: The Great Black Migration and How It Changed America* (New York, 1991), 109–222.

365 **"young men ... whose background"**: Transcript, Morris Abram, OH, Interview II, May 3, 1984, by Michael Gillette, Internet Copy, LBJL.

366 **"A multi-billion dollar"**: Bayard Rustin, "From Protest to Coalition Politics," *Commentary*, Feb. 1965, 25–31.

366 **hoped to solve poverty on the cheap**: James Sundquist, *Politics and Policy: The Eisenhower, Kennedy, and Johnson Years* (Washington, D.C., 1968), 144–45, 148–49; Michael K. Brown, *Race, Money, and the American Welfare State* (Ithaca, N.Y., 1999), 232–60.

366 **"urban kids and ghetto kids"**: Transcript, Stewart L. Udall, OH, Interview I, April 18, 1969, by Joe B. Frantz, Internet Copy, LBJL.

366 **"These are not simply camps"**: Lyndon B. Johnson, message to Congress, March 16, 1964, www.presidency.ucsb.edu/ws/?pid=26109.

366 **To make sure that everyone got the point**: *PC*, Jan. 9, 30, April 10, 1965; *CD*, Jan. 30, 1965; Alice O'Connor, *Poverty Knowledge: Social Science, Social Policy, and the Poor in Twentieth-Century U.S. History* (Princeton, N.J. 2001), 169, 176–77.

366 **Above all, Job Corps boosters**: *CD*, April 17, Nov. 15, 1965; *BAA*, Nov. 20, 1965; *NYT*, Nov. 18, 1965; Peter Schrag, "Kilmer: Portrait of a Job Corps Center," *SR*, March 16, 1968; *BAA*, April 26, 1969.

367 **Unlike Job Corps, CAP**: James T. Patterson, *America's Struggle Against Poverty in the Twentieth Century* (Cambridge, Mass., 2000), 147; Lemann, *The Promised Land*, 164–70.

367 **CAP started with a simple, radical idea**: For an intelligent discussion of these issues, see Sidney M. Milkis, "Lyndon Johnson, the Great Society, and the 'Twilight' of the Modern Presidency," in Milkis and Jerome Mileur, eds., *The Great Society and the High Tide of Liberalism* (Amherst, Mass., 2005), 1–49.

368 **The War on Poverty opened up**: Alice O'Connor, "Community Action, Urban Reform, and the Fight Against Poverty: The Ford Foundation's Gray Areas Program," *JUH* 22 (1996), 586–625; Allen J. Matusow, *The Unraveling of America: A History of Liberalism in the 1960s* (New York, 1984), 122–26, 243–69; Daniel Patrick Moynihan, *Maximum Feasible Misunderstanding: Community Action in the War on Poverty* (New York, 1969); Michael B. Katz, *The Undeserving Poor: From the War on Poverty to the War on Welfare* (New York, 1989), 95–101.

368 **"block-by-block effort"**: C. E. Wilson, "Towards Black Community Power," *Liberator*, March 1964, 9–11. Material in this and the next paragraph draws from Thomas J. Sugrue, "All Politics Is Local: The Persistence of Localism in Twentieth-Century America," in Meg Jacobs, William Novak, and Julian Zelizer, eds., *The Democratic Experiment: New Directions in American Political History* (Princeton, N.J., 2003), 301–26; see also Thomas F. Jackson, "The State, the Movement, and the Urban Poor: The War on Poverty and Political Mobilization in the 1960s," in Katz, ed., *The "Underclass" Debate*, 403–39; Alan Altshuler, *Community Control: The Black Demand for Participation in Large American Cities* (Indianapolis, 1970); for the emphasis on "community" in a

wide range of social movements during the 1960s, see Howard Brick, *Age of Contradiction: American Thought and Culture in the 1960s* (Ithaca, N.Y., 2000), 98–123.

369 **"The time has come":** *CD*, March 13, 1965.

369 **"Let blacks do it themselves":** W. H. Ferry, "The Case for a New Federalism," *SR*, June 15, 1968, 15.

369 **"BLACK POWER MEANS":** "UNITY—BLACK POWER," pamphlet in BPPH, Folder 1/9.

369 **Countless neighborhood groups:** Clayton Riley, "Cement Roots Action in Harlem," *Liberator*, Aug. 1964, 10–11; "Now in Watts, LA," *Liberator*, Dec. 1965, 11.

370 **CORE led the way in bridging:** Richard Brown interview, May 1970, AMP, Box 56, Folder 12; Frank Merande interview, Dec. 17, 1970, AMP, Box 56, Folder 12; "Detroit CORE's Campaign to End Employment Discrimination and Tokenism at AAA," ca. August 1964, in RRP, Folder 1; Gloria Brown to Floyd, Dec. 3, 1966, GBP, Folder 1; Tommie Moore, "An Editorial," *The Newspaper*, Feb. 21, 1966, in ibid.; Bernard Mandel interview, April 25, 1970, AMP, Box 56, Folder 12.

370 **not limited to radicals:** *PC*, Oct. 31, 1964; John Morsell, interview, May 1969, AMP, Box 56, Folder 12.

371 **In the first year of the War on Poverty:** On CAP, see Alice O'Connor, "Swimming Against the Tide: A Brief History of Federal Policy in Poor Communities," in Ronald F. Ferguson and William T. Dickens, eds., *Urban Problems and Community Development* (Washington, D.C., 1999), 100–4; Altshuler, *Community Control*, 111; Matusow, *The Unraveling of America*, 244–46.

371 **"the pilot program for the entire":** *PC*, Sept. 11, 1965.

371 **"has rejected as policy makers":** *BAA*, Jan. 9, 23, 1965.

371 **In New York City:** *PT*, Feb. 22, 1965.

371 **"a non-white person should have":** *PT*, Jan. 16, 1965.

372 **Conspiracy theories:** Richard A. Keiser, *Subordination or Empowerment? African-American Leadership and the Struggle for Urban Political Power* (New York, 1997), 99–101; Matusow, *The Unraveling of America*, 256–57.

372 **By 1968, Philadelphia's War on Poverty:** *PT*, Jan. 5, 1965; *BAA*, March 20, 1965; *PT*, Feb. 9, 1968; Matthew Countryman, *Up South: Civil Rights and Black Power in Philadelphia* (Philadelphia, 2005), 300.

372 **One of the central questions:** *PB*, May 27, 1965; Arthur Shostak, "Promoting Participation of the Poor: Philadelphia's Antipoverty Program," *Social Work* 11 (1965), 64–72; see also Countryman, *Up South*, 296–300, and Matusow, *The Unraveling of America*, 256–57.

372 **In Boston, thirteen:** *BAA*, May 1, 1965; Stephan Thernstrom, *Poverty, Planning, and Politics in the New Boston: The Origins of ABCD* (New York, 1969), 188–89.

372 **In Cleveland, where only one:** *PT*, Aug. 21, 1965; *BAA*, Aug. 21, 1965.

373 **In Norwalk, Connecticut:** *BAA*, Aug. 7, 1965.

373 **In Chester, Pennsylvania:** *PT*, May 9, 1967.

373 **And in Plainfield, New Jersey:** Interview with Plainfield Councilman Harvey Judkins, conducted by Steve Kurzman and Steve Weiner, LBJ-CR, Part 5, Reel 26, frame 00417; *PT*, May 9, 1967.

373 **Detroit and Chicago served as studies:** Paul E. Peterson and J. David Greenstone, *Race and Authority in Urban Politics: Community Participation and the War on Poverty* (Chicago, 1976), 19–24, 34–39; *NA*, Feb. 20, 1966.

373 **In cities with strong political machines:** Matusow, *The Unraveling of America*, 248–49.

374 **criticism from the right:** *CD*, Dec. 4, 1965; *BAA*, Jan. 8, 1966; *NYT*, Feb. 2, 1969; Moynihan, *Maximum Feasible Misunderstanding*, 182.

374 **As Watts burned:** Lyndon Johnson, phone conversation with John McCone, Aug. 18, 1965, Tape WH6508.05, Citation #8550, Recordings of Telephone Conversations—White House Series, Recordings and Transcripts of Conversations and Meetings, LBJL, Transcript prepared by the Presidential Recordings Program, MCVA; Johnson phone conversation with Martin Luther King, Jr., Aug. 20, 1965, 5:10 p.m., Tape WH6508.07, Citation #8578, Recordings of Telephone Conversations—White House Series, Recordings and Transcripts of Conversations and Meetings, LBJL, Transcript prepared by the Presidential Recordings Program, MCVA.

375 **"we must shed ourselves":** *NYT*, June 29, 1965.

375 **"With its titanic rhetoric":** Penn Kemble, "Report on CCAP Conference: Problems of Anti-Poverty Coalition," *NA*, April 22, 1966, 3.

375 **Black activists also denounced:** *PT*, July 17, 1965; Daniel H. Watts, "War on Poverty: Or How I Stop Eating and Learned to Love Starvation," *Liberator*, May 1966, 3.

375 **In November 1965, more than two hundred:** *PC*, Nov. 20, 1965; *NYT*, Nov. 18, 1965.

376 **"A Freedom Budget for All Americans":** A. Philip Randolph Institute, "A Freedom Budget for All Americans," in Louis A. Ferman, Joyce L. Kornbluh, and J. A. Miller, *Negroes and Jobs* (Ann Arbor, Mich., 1968), 551, 552, 554; *NYT*, Oct. 27, 28, 1966; *CD*, Dec. 3, 1966; John D'Emilio, *Lost Prophet: The Life and Times of Bayard Rustin* (New York, 2003), 430–38.

377 **the Freedom Budget provided common ground:** *CD*, Nov. 30, 1965, Oct. 27, Nov. 26, 1966, Feb. 7, 1967; *BSB*, Nov. 23, 1967.

377 **not a propitious moment:** *NYT*, Nov. 10, 1966; Matusow, *The Unraveling of America*, 214–15.

378 **Community Action struggled:** *WSJ*, Dec. 19, 1974; *NYT*, April 10, 1975.

378 **"Has the program become":** "Scandal in the Job Corps," *Reader's Digest*, Feb. 1967, 119; "Job Corps Comes Up to a Test," *BW*, Oct. 14, 1967; *CD*, Oct. 13, 1966; "First Year of Job Corps," brochure and undated article [ca. 1969], SCCF, 005-453; *BAA*, April 19, 1969; *CD*, Jan. 30, 1973.

378 **"training in family life":** *PC*, Jan. 30, 1965.

378 **a controversial report:** Lee Rainwater and William L. Yancey, eds., *The*

Moynihan Report and the Politics of Controversy (Cambridge, Mass., 1967), includes the full report and many responses to it; Ruth Feldstein, *Motherhood in Black and White: Race and Sex in American Liberalism, 1930–1965* (Ithaca, N.Y., 2000), 139–52; Steve Estes, *I Am a Man! Race, Manhood, and the Civil Rights Movement* (Chapel Hill, N.C., 2005), 110–13, 125–27.

379 **Black opinion on the Moynihan report was mixed:** *CD*, Oct. 2, Nov. 27, Dec. 6, 10, 1965; see generally, Yancey and Rainwater, *The Moynihan Report*.

379 **"from Rosa Parks to Harriet Tubman":** Alvin Brooks, interview, n.d., AMP, Box 56, Folder 2. There is an ellipsis in front of "Bates" in the interview transcript, which I filled with "Daisy," who headed the Arkansas NAACP and moved to national prominence as a key figure in the Little Rock desegregation battle in 1957.

380 **a new masculine leadership:** Walter Brooks, interview, Aug. 1971, AMP, Box 56, Folder 2; Roy Innis, interview, Oct. 4, 1971, AMP, Box 56, Folder 9; Doris Innis, interview, Oct. 12, 1971, AMP, Box 56, Folder 9; Gloria Brown, interview, July 10, 1971, AMP, Box 56, Folder 2.

380 **advocated a politics of "protection":** Farah Jasmine Griffin, "'Ironies of the Saint': Malcolm X, Black Women, and the Price of Protection," in Bettye Collier-Thomas and V. P. Franklin, eds., *Sisters in the Struggle: African American Women in the Civil Rights–Black Power Movement* (New York, 2001), 214–29; Malcolm X as told to Alex Haley, *The Autobiography of Malcolm X* (1964; rept. New York, 1973), 93: Estes, *I Am A Man!*, 88–106; see also C. Eric Lincoln, *The Black Muslims in America* (1961), 3rd ed. (Grand Rapids, Mich., and Trenton, N.J., 1994), 30; Daniel Matlin, "'Lift Up Yr Self!': Reinterpreting Amiri Baraka (LeRoi Jones), Black Power, and the Uplift Tradition," *JAH* 93 (2006), 91–116.

380 **"Where are the warriors":** Ronald Snellings, "All My Yesterdays," *BA*, vol. 1, no. 3, RAM, Reel 2.

381 **"What makes a woman appealing":** Clyde Halisi, ed., *The Quotable Karenga* (Los Angeles, 1967), 27–28; for discussions of Karenga's gender theory, see Tracye Matthews, "'No One Ever Asks, What a Man's Place in the Revolution Is': Gender and the Politics of the Black Panther Party 1966–1971," in Charles E. Jones, ed., *The Black Panther Party Reconsidered* (Baltimore, 1998), 271–73; Scot Brown, "The Politics of Culture: The US Organization and the Quest for Black 'Unity,'" in Jeanne F. Theoharis and Komozi Woodard, eds., *Freedom North: Black Freedom Struggles Outside the South, 1940–1980* (New York, 2003), 223–53.

381 **"It was but a short step":** Paula Giddings, *When and Where I Enter: The Impact of Black Women on Race and Sex in America* (New York, 1984), 314–24, quote 318; Dorothy Burnham, "Biology and Gender: False Theories About Women and Blacks," *Freedomways* (1978), in Esther Cooper Jackson, ed., *Freedomways Reader: Prophets in Their Own Country* (Boulder, Colo., 2000), 248–52; Sara Evans, *Personal Politics: The Roots of Women's Liberation in the Civil Rights Movement* (New York, 1979); Ruth Rosen, *The World Split Open:*

How the Modern Women's Movement Changed America (New York, 2000), 115–21, 145–48, 276–85.

381 **The gender essentialism . . . came under siege:** Betty Frank Lomax, "Afro-American Woman: Growth Deferred," *Liberator*, May 1966, 18; Louise Moore, "Black Women vs. Black Men," *Liberator*, Aug. 1966, 16–17; Jean Carey Bond and Pat Peery, "Has the Black Man Been Castrated?" *Liberator*, May 1969, 5.

382 **Evelyn Rodgers accused:** Evelyn Rodgers, "Sisters—Stop Castrating the Black Man," *Liberator*, May 1966, 21.

382 **America's two-tiered welfare state:** Linda Gordon, *Pitied but Not Entitled: Single Mothers and the History of Welfare* (Cambridge, Mass., 1994); Alice Kessler-Harris, *In Pursuit of Equity: Men, Women, and the Quest for Economic Citizenship in Twentieth-Century America* (New York, 2001); Katz, *The Undeserving Poor*; Theda Skocpol, "The Limits of the New Deal System and the Roots of Contemporary Welfare Dilemmas," in Margaret Weir, Ann Orloff, and Theda Skocpol, eds., *The Politics of Social Policy in the United States* (Princeton, N.J., 1988), 295–98.

383 **To supplement meager welfare checks:** Carol Stack, *All Our Kin: Strategies for Survival in a Black Community* (New York, 1974); Kathryn Edin and Laura Lein, *Making Ends Meet: How Single Mothers Survive Welfare and Low-Wage Work* (New York, 1997).

383 **In 1961, in the six northern states:** State welfare data by race for 1948, 1953, 1961, and 1967 from Frances Fox Piven and Richard A. Cloward, *Regulating the Poor: The Functions of Public Welfare* (New York, 1971), Statistical Source Table 4.

383 **growing unpopularity of the program:** *NYT*, Feb. 14, 1952; more generally, see Michael B. Katz and Lorrin R. Thomas, "The Invention of Welfare in America," *JPH* 10 (1998), 399–418.

384 **the national stage in Newburgh:** Lisa Levenstein, "From Innocent Children to Unwanted Migrants and Unwed Moms: Two Chapters in the Public Discourse on Welfare in the United States, 1960–1961," *Journal of Women's History* 11 (2000), 10–33.

384 **In Illinois, the state halted:** "Chaos in Chicago: Democracy Northern Style," *Liberator*, May 1963, 10–11; *CD*, Feb. 27, March 6, April 29, 1963; *NYT*, May 1, 1963.

384 **Similar arguments over welfare:** *NYT*, April 7, 1963, Jan. 1, July 12, 1964; *WSJ*, Oct. 6, 1964.

385 **Welfare authorities policed:** Winifred Bell, *Aid to Dependent Children* (New York, 1965), is an essential guide to state welfare practices.

385 **"Just because they suspect":** *CD*, Jan. 1, Feb. 26, 1966.

386 **By the early 1960s, welfare mothers joined:** *WSJ*, Oct. 6, 1964, March 18, 1966; *LAT*, July 24, Sept. 6, 1966; *NYT*, Aug. 4, 1966; Belinda Robnett, *How Long? How Long?: African-American Women in the Struggle for Civil Rights* (New York, 1997), 19–23.

386 **Boston's MAW:** The material in this and the following paragraph draws from *BSB*, Oct. 9, 1965, July 9, 16, Aug. 20, 1966, June 10, Oct. 5, Nov. 2, 1967; *BAA*, Sept. 24, 1966.

387 **A cadre of social workers:** "A Manifesto for a More Humane Welfare System," *SA* (Nov. 1966), 28–29; Felicia Kornbluh, *The Battle for Welfare Rights: Politics and Poverty in Modern America* (Philadelphia, 2007), 44–45; Daniel Walkowitz, *Working with Class: Social Workers and the Politics of Middle-Class Identity* (Chapel Hill, N.C., 1999), 263–64.

388 **organizing efforts of George Wiley:** Nick Kotz and Mary Lynn Kotz, *A Passion for Equality: George Wiley and the Movement* (New York, 1977), 25–85; Kornbluh, *The Battle for Welfare Rights*, 28–29.

388 **Wiley rose in prominence in CORE:** George Wiley, interview, Feb. 29, 1964, AMP, Box 57, Folder 7; Kotz and Kotz, *A Passion for Equality*, 165–77; August Meier and Elliott Rudwick, *CORE: A Study in the Civil Rights Movement, 1942–1968* (Urbana, Ill., 1975), 406–8.

389 **Johnnie Tillmon:** Deborah Gray White, *Too Heavy a Load: Black Women in Defense of Themselves* (New York, 1999), 223–27; Annelise Orleck, *Storming Caesars Palace: How Black Mothers Fought Their Own War on Poverty* (Boston, 2005), 109–10; Kotz and Kotz, *A Passion for Equality*, 219–21.

389 **eyes on both the local and the national:** Kotz and Kotz, *Passion for Equality*, 181–220.

390 **"This is part of a national":** *BAA*, July 9, Sept. 3, Sept. 24, 1966; *NYT*, July 1, Aug. 31, Sept. 16, 1966.

390 **mobilizing the poor:** Richard Cloward and Frances Fox Piven, "A Strategy to End Poverty," *Nation*, May 2, 1966, 510; see generally, Frances F. Piven and Richard Cloward, *Poor People's Movements: Why They Succeed, How They Fail* (New York, 1977); Kotz and Kotz, *Passion for Equality*, 181–88.

391 **experimenting with legal programs:** Karen Tani, "*Fleming v. Nestor:* Anticommunism, the Welfare State, and the Making of 'New Property,'" unpublished research paper, University of Pennsylvania; Edgar S. Cahn and Jean Cahn, "The War on Poverty: A Civilian Perspective," *YLJ* 73 (1964); Earl Johnson, Jr., *Justice and Reform: The Formative Years of the American Legal Services Program* (New Brunswick, N.J., 1978), 21–23; Peter Marris and Martin Rein, *The Dilemmas of Social Reform: Poverty and Community Action in the United States*, 2nd ed. (Chicago, 1973), 14–32, 171–77; Scott Stossel, *Sarge: The Life and Times of Sargent Shriver* (Washington, D.C., 2004).

391 **"provide the means":** Johnson, *Justice and Reform*, 75, citing a speech by Bamberger to the annual meeting of the National Legal Aid and Defender Association.

391 **"further the cause of justice":** "Neighborhood Law Offices: The New Wave in Legal Services for the Poor," *Harvard Law Review* 80 (1967), 806; Pub. Law. No. 90-122, 81 Stat. 672, 698 (1967).

392 **By 1971, the Legal Services program:** *BAA*, Oct. 9, 1971; for examples of legal services efforts, see *CD*, Nov. 27, 1965, Dec. 10, 1966, March 29, 1967.

392 **viewed themselves as the legal arm of grassroots:** Matusow, *The Unraveling of America*, 266–67; Richard M. Pious, "Policy and Public Administration: The Legal Services Programs in the War on Poverty," *Politics and Society* 2 (1971), 365–91; *BAA*, April 15, Oct. 9, 1971.

392 **But few welfare rights organizers drew:** Martha F. Davis, *Brutal Need: Lawyers and the Welfare Rights Movement, 1960–1973* (New Haven, Conn., 1993); Kornbluh, *The Battle for Welfare Rights*, 68–77, 172–76.

393 **The most important welfare rights cases:** *King v. Smith*, 392 U.S. 309 (1968), *Lewis v. Martin*, 397 U.S. 552 (1970); *Shapiro v. Thompson*, 394 U.S. 618 (1968); *Goldberg v. Kelly*, 397 U.S. 254 (1970); *Dandridge v. Williams*, 397 U.S. 471 (1970); Premilla Nadasen, *Welfare Warriors: The Welfare Rights Movement in the United States* (New York, 2005), 59–63; Kornbluh, *The Battle for Welfare Rights*, 176.

394 **"mingling with the crowd":** *LAT*, May 13, 1968.

394 **They were frustrated at the indignities:** Kotz and Kotz, *A Passion for Equality*, 235–36; John Bauman, *Public Housing, Race, and Renewal in Philadelphia, 1920–1974* (Philadelphia, 1987); Lisa Levenstein, "The Gendered Roots of Modern Urban Poverty: Poor Women and Public Institutions in Post–World War II Philadelphia" (Ph.D. diss., University of Wisconsin, Madison, 2002). For a bleaker picture of life in the projects, see John Bauman, Norman P. Hummon, and Edward K. Muller, "Public Housing, Isolation and the Underclass: Philadelphia's Richard Allen Homes, 1942–1965," *JUH* 17 (1991), 264–92.

394 **Like Doris Bland and Johnnie Tillmon:** Levenstein, "Gendered Roots"; Kotz and Kotz, *A Passion for Equality*, 235; Nadasen, *Welfare Warriors*, 59–63, 132.

395 **an ambitious agenda:** Felicia Kornbluh, "'To Fulfill Their Rightly Needs': Consumerism and the National Welfare Rights Movement," *RHR* 69 (1997), 76–113; Nadasen, *Welfare Warriors*, 67, 109–11; Countryman, *Up South*, 278–82.

395 **Under Jones, the PWRO fused:** *PT*, June 23, July 18, Aug. 25, 1970; *PI*, Nov. 22, 1981.

396 **The welfare rights movement played:** Patterson, *America's Struggle Against Poverty*, 171, 178–83; Michael B. Katz, *In the Shadow of the Poorhouse: A Social History of Welfare in America*, Tenth Anniversary Edition (New York, 1996), 275, 276, 278; Frances Fox Piven and Richard Cloward, *Regulating the Poor: The Functions of Public Welfare*, 2nd ed. (New York, 1993), 330–37; Mark Stern, "Poverty and Family Composition Since 1940," in Michael B. Katz, ed., *The "Underclass" Debate: Views from History* (Princeton, N.J., 1993), 238–40; John E. Schwarz, *America's Hidden Success: A Reassessment of Public Policy from Kennedy to Reagan*, rev. ed. (New York, 1988), 24–36.

397 **"Nixon couldn't live like this":** *PT*, April 18, June 2, 1970.

397 **Nixon's FAP:** *PT*, April 18, 1970. On FAP, see Daniel Patrick Moynihan, *The Politics of a Guaranteed Income* (New York, 1973), 230–31, and Gareth Davies, *From Opportunity to Entitlement: The Transformation and Decline of Great Society Liberalism* (Lawrence, Kans., 1996), 211–43.

398 **significant increase of women:** Rhonda Y. Williams, *The Politics of Public Housing: Black Women's Struggles Against Urban Inequality* (New York, 2004), 162–64; Countryman, *Up South*, 298.

398 **In addition, the War on Poverty solidified:** Paul E. Peterson and J. David Greenstone, "Citizen Participation and Racial Change: The Mobilization of Low-Income Communities Through Community Action," in Robert Haveman, ed., *A Decade of Federal Anti-Poverty Programs* (New York, 1977), 241–78; Michael B. Katz and Mark J. Stern, *One Nation Divisible: What America Was and What It Is Becoming* (New York, 2005), 91–93; Frances Fox Piven and Richard Cloward, "The Politics of the Great Society," in Milkis and Mileur, eds., *The Great Society and the High Tide of Liberalism*, 263–64; Gloster Current, interview, ca. Feb 1, 1966, in AMP, Box 56, Folder 4.

399 **"very localized neighborhood uplift":** "Freedom Budget," *NA*, Oct. 31, 1966.

CHAPTER 12 | "THE BLACK MAN'S LAND"

400 **"Melting pot Harlem":** Langston Hughes, "My Early Days in Harlem," *Freedomways* (1963), reprinted in Esther Cooper Jackson, *Freedomways Reader: Prophets in Their Own Country* (Boulder, Colo., 2000), 319–20; *NYT*, July 26, 1964; *CD*, May 28, 1963; *TIH* (Feb. 1967); *WSJ*, July 20, 1964. Allon Schoener, ed., *Harlem on My Mind* (New York, 1968) offers an evocative portrayal.

401 **"the Black Man's Land":** Grace Boggs and James Boggs, "The City Is the Black Man's Land," *Monthly Review* 17 (April 1966), 35–46.

401 **"wellsprings of future progress":** *NYT*, April 19, 1966.

402 **Jesse Gray was a tough survivor:** Mark Naison, "The Rent Strikes in New York," *RA* 1(3) (Nov.–Dec. 1967), 18–21, quote 19; Gerald Horne, *Red Seas: Ferdinand Smith and Radical Black Sailors in the United States and Jamaica* (New York, 2005), 188; Horne, *Black Liberation/Red Scare: Ben Davis and the Communist Party* (Newark, Del., 1994), 259–60; J. H. O'Dell, "Looking Back on Operation Dixie," *Labor Notes* (April 2005), 5; Michael Lipsky, *Protest in City Politics: Rent Strikes, Housing, and the Power of the Poor* (Chicago, 1970), 55–56; *NYAN*, Feb. 6, 1954, Feb 19, 1955; *NYT*, Oct. 25, 1954; "Mayoral Circus," *Libertarian Forum: A Monthly Newsletter* 5(3) (March 1973), 1.

403 **Tenants' movements and housing organizations:** Lisa Levenstein, "The Gendered Roots of Modern Urban Poverty: Poor Women and Public Institutions in Post–World War II Philadelphia" (Ph.D. diss., University of Wisconsin, Madison, 2002); Rhonda Y. Williams, *The Politics of Public Housing: Black Women's Struggles Against Urban Inequality* (New York, 2004); Roberta Feldman, Susan Stall, and Patricia A. Wright, " 'The Community Needs to Be Built by Us': Women Organizing in Chicago Public Housing," in Nancy Naples, ed., *Community Activism and Feminist Politics* (New York, 1998), 257–74.

404 **one of the grimmest sections of Harlem:** Ronald Lawson and Stephen E. Barton, "Sex Roles in Social Movements: A Case Study of the Tenant Movement

in New York City," *Signs* 6 (1980), 230–47; quotes about Harlem from *CD*, Feb. 6, 1965; Lipsky, *Protest in City Politics*, 78–80.

404 **little army of tenants:** *NYAN*, July 4, 8, Aug. 8, Dec. 15, 1959; *NYT*, July 2, 27, 1959, Dec. 29, 1960.

404 **"No Heat, No Rent!":** *PC*, July 27, 1963.

405 **New York's tenant protests peaked:** *NYT*, Aug. 4, Oct. 29, Nov. 5, Dec. 1, 2, 30, 31, 1963, Jan. 1, Feb. 1, 1964; *NYAN*, Oct. 25, 1963; *CD*, Dec. 31, 1963, Feb. 17, 1964; *PC*, Oct. 12, Dec. 14, 1963, Jan. 4 (on media strategy), Feb. 29, May 2, 1964; "Rent Strike: Concerning the Community Council on Harlem," *NY*, Jan. 25, 1964, 19–20; generally, see Joel Schwartz, "The New York City Rent Strikes of 1963–1964," *Social Service Review* 57 (Dec. 1983), and "Tenant Power in the Liberal City, 1943–1971," in Ronald Lawson, ed., *The Tenant Movement in New York City, 1904–1984* (New Brunswick, N.J., 1986), ch. 4.

405 **Gray's media strategy paid off:** *IN*, Dec. 23, 1963; *PC*, Nov. 30, Dec. 7, 1963; "Rent Strike," *Ebony*, April 1964, 112–20; *PC*, May 16, 1964; "Rent Strikes Hit Cleveland Ghetto," *NA*, Jan. 31, 1964; "Chicago Boycott," *NA*, Feb. 28, 1964.

405 **"People unite in struggle":** *Newsweek*, Dec. 30, 1963, 17–18; *NYT*, Dec. 23, 1963.

406 **"People ask me why I spend":** Quoted in Lipsky, *Protest in City Politics*, 57.

406 **"racial basis":** *PC*, Feb. 23, March 9, 1963.

406 **into the circle of Malcolm X:** *PC*, March 28, 1964; *CD*, March 30, 1964.

406 **protests against police brutality:** *PC*, May 16, 1964.

406 **"There's only one thing":** *NYT*, July 20, 1964.

406 **A late July court order:** *NYT*, July 28, 30, Aug. 8, 11, Sept. 18, 1964.

406 **"It's always very easy":** Gray, Nov. 29, 1964, speech at OAAU, quoted in George Breitman, ed., *Malcolm X Speaks: Selected Speeches and Statements* (New York, 1965), 89; on Gray and RAM, see *NYT*, July 24, 1966 (the *NYT* incorrectly identified Maxwell Stanford as Robert Stanford).

407 **And the burgeoning student left joined:** Jennifer Frost, *An Interracial Movement of the Poor: Community Organizing and the New Left* (New York, 2001); "Rent Revolt," *NA*, Jan. 10, 1964.

407 **"picketing all day":** Doris Innis, interview, Oct. 12, 1971, AMP, Box 56, Folder 9. On Gray's influence on CORE, see Norman Hill, interview, Dec. 15, 1970, AMP, Box 56, Folder 8; Donald Roberts, interview, July 9, 1971, AMP, Box 57, Folder 4; see also Schwartz, "The New York City Rent Strikes of 1963–64," 174–79, 181–82, 185. CORE joined tenants' organizing efforts in Harlem in the summer of 1963; see *PC*, July 20, 27, 1963; August Meier and Elliott Rudwick, *CORE: A Study in the Civil Rights Movement, 1942–1968* (Urbana, Ill., 1975), 244–46; Naison, "The Rent Strikes in New York," 27–28, 42–50.

407 **"what was really needed":** Frank Merande, interview, Dec. 17, 1970, AMP, Box 56, Folder 12.

407 **tenant organizing as a vehicle:** For an early example, see *New York CORE Action* (Jan. 1963), in CORE, Series 5, Reel 23, frame 225; *CD*, Dec. 3, 1963; Nor-

man Hill, interview, Dec. 15, 1970, AMP, Box 56, Folder 8; Donald Roberts, interview, July 9, 1971, AMP, Box 57, Folder 4; Ralph and Janice Rosenfeld, interviews, July 9–10, 1971, AMP, Box 57, Folder 4; Press Release, Oct. 28, 1966, and *CORE News*, Jan. 1967, GBP; Bernard Mandel, interview, April 25, 1970, AMP, Box 56, Folder 12.

408 **In the mid-1960s:** *TIH* (Feb. 1967).

408 **Even when they were organized:** Donald Roberts, interview, July 9, 1971, in AMP, Box 57, Folder 4; Rosenfeld interviews; Phyllis Ryan, interview, n.d., AMP, Box 57, Folder 4; *Tenant Council News*, June 4, 1965, in RRP, Folder 1.

408 **"small numbers and the doubt":** *NYT*, May 17, 1967.

408 **One activist, Carolyn Foster:** "Power to the People, Joan," March 15, 1970, and undated entry in "FREE HUEY BLACK PANTHER PARTY, HOUSING COORDINATOR" notebook, BPPH, Folder 1/12; flyer, "These two avaricious, racist slumlords . . ." in BPPH, Folder 1/19.

409 **To be sure, the Panthers did some:** "Students Research Lead Poisoning," *People's Community News*, May 24, 1970, in BPPH, Folder 1/19; "Free Health Center," ibid.; *BP*, Feb. 21, 1970; *PT*, March 24, May 9, 1970; "Free Breakfast for School Children," "Free Breakfast Program—Tool of Liberation," and "Community Medical Clinic," BPPH, Folder 1/20; JoNina M. Abron, "'Serving the People': The Survival Programs of the Black Panther Party," in Charles E. Jones, ed., *The Black Panther Party Reconsidered* (Baltimore, 1998), 177–92; Reginald Major, *A Panther Is a Black Cat* (New York, 1971), 85–88; Steve Estes, *I Am a Man!*, 171–73. For a useful overview of diverse community-based programs over the twentieth century, see Robert Halpern, *Rebuilding the Inner City: A History of Neighborhood Initiatives to Address Poverty in the United States* (New York, 1995), 149–94.

409 **professionalization of protest:** *NYT*, Aug. 21, 1967. For an example of ongoing efforts, see Andrew Feffer, "The Land Belongs to the People: Reframing Urban Protest in Post-Sixties Philadelphia," in Van Gosse and Richard Moser, eds., *The World the Sixties Made: Politics and Culture in Recent America* (Philadelphia, 2003), 67–99.

410 **"I do not have a flag":** *NYT*, Aug. 20, 1958.

411 **"freedom fighters":** *CD*, June 17, 1963; *NYAN*, June 22, 1963.

411 **New York's newly revitalized CORE chapter:** Meier and Rudwick, *CORE*, 125.

411 **In 1961, Funnyé led:** *CD*, July 19, 1961; *PC*, Aug. 5, 1961; "Rental Office Sit In," *C-L* 93 (Dec. 1961).

411 **the New York CORE chapter grew increasingly militant:** Meier and Rudwick, *CORE*, 228, 235, 236–37.

411 **Funnyé had a knack:** *CD*, March 12, 1962; *PC*, Sept. 14, 1963; Feb. 8, 1964; *NYAN*, Aug. 31, Sept. 28, 1963, April 4, 1964; "Action Backed Drive Gets Negroes on TV," *C-L* (Feb. 1964); Meier and Rudwick, *CORE*, 239; Clarence Funnyé to Roy Wilkins, Nov. 6, 1964, in NAACP-M, Part 21, Reel 13, frame 959.

412 **GM executives met:** *PC*, April 4, 1964.

412 **demonstrations in Albany:** *NYT*, March 10, 1964.

412 **Funnyé's militant integrationism put him:** "Action Now for Jobs and Free-dom—A Program for New York CORE," CORE, Series 5, Reel 41, frames 1055–56; untitled memo, CORE, Series 5, Reel 41, frames 948–50.

412 **"away from the 'sit in' approach":** *NYAN*, Nov. 21, 1964; *PC*, Dec. 5, 1964.

413 **At CORE's 1965 national convention:** New York CORE Report to the 1965 Convention, cited in Meier and Rudwick, *CORE*, 379–80; see also Leilah Danielson, "The 'Two-Ness' of the Movement: James Farmer, Nonviolence, and Black Nationalism," *Peace and Change* 29 (2004), 431–52, esp. 444–45.

413 **"Black Power," stated CORE:** Quoted in Robert L. Allen, *Black Awakening in Capitalist America: An Analytic History* (New York, 1969), 65; *NYAN*, Jan. 14, 1967; Clarence Funnyé, "Deghettoization," *Architectural Forum*, April 1969, 74–77.

413 **"back streets and alleys":** *NYT*, July 5, 1966; *CD*, July 5, 1966.

413 **He joined forces with the open housing movement:** *TIH* (Sept.–Oct. 1965); *NYT*, Nov. 17, 1964; *NYAN*, Jan. 14, 1967; *TIH* (May–July 1968); *CD*, Sept. 21, 1968; *TIH* (March–April 1969).

414 **"massive nationwide effort":** *PC*, Oct. 17, 1964.

414 **NCDH's efforts were more ambitious:** *TIH* (May–June 1965); *TIH* (Sept.–Oct. 1965); *TIH* (Feb. 1968).

414 **"Do the planners believe":** *NYT*, Feb. 13, 1965, Sept. 19, 1971.

415 **"unled Negro communities":** *PC*, Aug. 21, 1965.

415 **King was not always greeted warmly:** Taylor Branch, *Pillar of Fire: America in the King Years, 1963–1965* (New York, 1998), 423, 447; James F. Findlay, Jr., *Church People in the Struggle: The National Council of Churches and the Black Freedom Movement, 1950–1970* (New York, 1993), 170–71; *PC*, Aug. 21, 1965.

415 **King began testing the waters:** *BAA*, July 17, 24, 31, 1965; Matthew Country-man, *Up South: Civil Rights and Black Power in Philadelphia* (Philadelphia, 2005), 174–77; Cecil B. Moore, interview by John Britton, Sept. 26, 1967, quote 29, also 36–37, RJB.

415 **That led King to turn to Chicago:** Thomas F. Jackson, *From Civil Rights to Human Rights: Martin Luther King, Jr., and the Struggle for Economic Justice* (Philadelphia, 2007), 276–307; James R. Ralph, Jr., *Northern Protest: Martin Luther King, Jr., Chicago, and the Civil Rights Movement* (Cambridge, Mass., 1993); Mark Santow, "Saul Alinsky and the Dilemmas of Race in the Post-war City" (Ph.D. diss., University of Pennsylvania, 2000).

416 **civil rights community impressed King:** *CD*, June 19, July 24, 31, Sept. 4, 1965; Santow, "Saul Alinsky and the Dilemmas of Race." On moderation of black leadership in Chicago, see esp. James Q. Wilson, *Negro Politics: The Search for Leadership* (Glencoe, Ill., 1960), 230–50.

416 **Chicago was also one of the most racially:** William Peters, "Race War in Chicago," *TNR*, Jan. 9, 1950, 10–12. Arnold R. Hirsch, *Making the Second Ghetto: Race and Housing in Chicago, 1940–1960* (New York, 1983), is the de-

finitive history. See also Arnold R. Hirsch, "Massive Resistance in the Urban North: Trumbull Park, Chicago, 1953–1966," *JAH* 82 (1995), 522–50; Amanda Seligman, *Block by Block: Neighborhoods and Public Policy on Chicago's West Side* (Chicago, 2005); "Mayor Daley Meets the Movement," *Nation,* Aug. 30, 1965, 92–95; more generally on Chicago, see the excellent accounts by Ralph, *Northern Protest;* Adam Cohen and Elizabeth Taylor, *American Pharaoh: Mayor Richard J. Daley: His Battle for Chicago and the Nation* (Boston, 2000); and Alan B. Anderson and George W. Pickering, *Confronting the Color Line: The Broken Promise of the Civil Rights Movement in Chicago* (Athens, Ga., 1986).

417 **King and local activists prepared the Chicago campaign:** *CD,* Sept. 4, Oct. 9, 1965; Jan. 8, 1966; *BAA,* Jan. 15, 1966.

417 **"the only dignified, sincere":** *BAA,* March 12, 1966.

417 **It was impossible for a celebrity:** *CD,* Jan. 29, 1966; Cohen and Taylor, *American Pharaoh,* 362; Jon Rice, "The World of the Illinois Panthers," in Jeanne F. Theoharis and Komozi Woodard, *Freedom North: Black Freedom Struggles Outside the South, 1940–1980* (New York, 2003), 42.

418 **"All clear-thinking Negroes":** *CD,* May 1, 1965.

418 **King could not dampen the anger and violence:** *CT,* July 11, 1966; Rice, "The World of the Illinois Panthers," 45; *CD,* July 9, 16, 23, 1966; *NACCD,* 38–39.

419 **obstacles from Chicago's political leadership:** *CD,* July 31, 1965, July 18, 1966; *BAA,* March 5, 19, 1966.

419 **that King faced among Chicago's whites:** *NYT,* Aug. 24, 1966.

419 **"I wish I were an Alabama trooper":** David L. Lewis, *King: A Critical Biography* (New York, 1970), 339.

420 **But Chicago's grassroots activists:** Ralph, *Northern Protest,* 220–35.

420 **not atypical of the urban North:** Stephen Grant Meyer, *As Long as They Don't Move Next Door: Segregation and Racial Conflict in American Neighborhoods* (Lanham, Md., 2000), offers a comprehensive overview; *BAA,* Dec. 18, 1965; Raymond Berens, "Welcome to Folcroft," *GPM* (Oct. 1963), 77–85; James Hecht, *Because It Is Right: Integration in Housing* (Boston, 1970), 154; "HUD's Failure in Warren, Michigan," in Louis H. Masotti and Jeffrey K. Hadden, eds., *Suburbia in Transition* (New York, 1974), 154–57; Richard David Riddle, "The Rise of the 'Reagan Democrats' in Warren, Michigan, 1964–1984." (Ph.D. diss., Wayne State University, 1998).

420 **"White inaction has turned":** *BSB,* Oct. 1, 1966.

420 **"if reformers can be persuaded":** Frances Fox Piven and Richard A. Cloward, "Desegregated Housing: Who Pays for the Reformer's Ideal?" *TNR,* Dec. 17, 1966, 17–22, quote 22.

421 **Whites in many wealthy, segregated:** Hecht, *Because It Is Right,* 138–42.

421 **Birmingham, Michigan:** *NYT,* April 2, 1968.

421 **"The guy who said":** *NYT,* May 20, 1970.

421 **A small number of countercultural whites:** "A Planned Dispersion Pattern—An Answer to the Ghetto," *INS* (Sept.–Oct. 1958), 4; *TIH* (May–June

1960); Suleiman Osman, "The Birth of Postmodern New York: Gentrification, Postindustrialization, and Race in South Brooklyn, 1950–1980" (Ph.D. diss., Harvard University, 2006); Juliet Z. Saltman, *Open Housing as a Social Movement: Challenge, Conflict, and Change* (Lexington, Mass., 1971).

421 **an unacknowledged class politics:** Gordon Allport, *The Nature of Prejudice* (Cambridge, Mass., 1954), ch. 16; Eleanor Paperno Wolf and Charles N. Lebeaux, *Change and Renewal in an Urban Community: Five Case Studies of Detroit* (New York, 1969).

422 **"limiting the amount":** George Grier and Eunice Grier, *Equality and Beyond: Housing Segregation and the Goals of the Great Society* (Chicago, 1966), 72–75.

422 **"The Great Society":** *PC*, June 5, 1965; *CD*, Sept. 28, 1965.

422 **Methodically, NCDH supporters:** On NCDH lobbying efforts, see various issues of *TIH*, 1965–68.

423 **the Fair Housing Act:** *WSJ*, Feb. 8, 1968; Douglas S. Massey and Nancy A. Denton, *American Apartheid: Segregation and the Making of the Underclass* (Cambridge, Mass., 1993), 192–200; Hugh Davis Graham, "The Surprising Career of Federal Fair Housing Law," *JPH* 12 (2000), 217–19.

423 **"The practice of closed housing":** *BAA*, Dec. 18, 1965; *WSJ*, June 21, 1967.

423 **Title VIII faced similar problems:** *PC*, Jan. 19, 1963; *CD*, Jan. 16, 1965; *BSB*, June 29, 1967; Duane Lockard, *Toward Equal Opportunity: A Study of State and Local Antidiscrimination Laws* (London, 1968), 117–33; Massey and Denton, *American Apartheid*, 195–200; Robert G. Schwemm, "Private Enforcement of the Fair Housing Act," *Yale Law and Policy Review* 6 (1988), 375–92.

423 **"Fair Housing Flop":** *WSJ*, Feb. 2, 1965.

424 **"Negroes don't come out":** *BSB*, Feb. 25, 1967.

424 **In Chicago, HOME:** *TSD*, April 21, 1961; Carol Kleiman, "Breaking the Housing Barrier," *Renewal* (April–May 1964), 14–17; "Mission in Suburbia," *Renewal* (April 1965), 14–16.

424 **"both the advantages of living":** *CD*, Dec. 4, 1965.

424 **"there is no political force":** *NYT*, June 1, 1971.

425 **"sterile, futile struggle":** *IN*, Dec. 4, 1961, Dec. 9, 1963.

425 **"Integration up to this point":** Quoted in Peter Goldman, *Report from Black America* (New York, 1969), 186.

425 **"I'm for the black communities":** Quoted in Goldman, *Report from Black America*, 189.

426 **"brothers who, faced":** *CD*, Nov. 19, 1968.

426 **"A soldier afraid to confront":** *NYT*, Aug. 7, 1966.

426 **"less like a colony":** Funnyé, quoted in Jackie Robinson with Alfred Duckett, *I Never Had It Made: An Autobiography of Jackie Robinson* (1972; rept. New York, 2003), 189.

426 **"only reinforce the ghetto":** *OP*, May 8, 1969; *NYAN*, May 24, 1969.

426 **"a new form of militancy":** *SFSR*, May 3, 1969.

427 **"the ultimate logic":** Casey Mann et al., "The Separatists' Fantasy: A Reply," *Liberator*, April 1969, 9.

427 **Funnyé was heartened by a robust debate:** *TIH* (May 1969).

427 **"conservative, reformist, integrationist":** Roy Innis, interview, Oct. 4, 1971, AMP, Box 56, Folder 9.

427 **"community nationalism":** Michael C. Dawson, *Black Visions: The Roots of Contemporary African-American Political Ideologies* (Chicago, 2001), 100–2.

428 **buying black:** C. Eric Lincoln, *The Black Muslims in America*, 3rd ed. (Grand Rapids, Mich., and Trenton, N.J., 1994), 88–89; *BAA*, Aug. 1, 1970. A concise overview of the history of black capitalism is Manning Marable, *How Capitalism Underdeveloped Black America* (Boston, 1983), 133–67.

428 **"Why should white people":** Malcolm X, cited in William L. Van Deburg, *New Day in Babylon: The Black Power Movement and American Culture, 1965–1975* (Chicago, 1992), 113.

428 **"Black Economic Front":** Third International Conference on Black Power: Economics, Robert (Sonny) Carson Chairman, Aug. 31, 1968, RAM, Reel 11, frames 856, 864, 865; Hiley H. Ward, *Prophet of the Black Nation* (Philadelphia, 1969), 204–5; U.S. Small Business Administration, *Annual Report 1969* (Washington, D.C., 1970), in Mansel G. Blackford, *A History of Small Business in America*, 2nd ed. (Chapel Hill, N.C., 2003), 150. On Vaughn's bookstore, see Sidney Fine, *Violence in the Model City: The Cavanagh Administration, Race Relations, and the Detroit Riot of 1967* (Ann Arbor, Mich., 1988), 29, 244. For other cooperative efforts, see Theora Makeda, "A Challenge for Black Leadership," *Liberator*, June 1967, 8–11.

429 **One of the most celebrated:** Peter Bailey, "N.E.G.R.O. Charts New Path to Freedom," *Ebony*, April 1968, 49, 53.

429 **CORE founder James Farmer:** from a speech at Cornell quoted in Tamar Jacoby, *Someone Else's House: America's Unfinished Struggle for Integration* (New York, 1999), 55.

430 **community development corporations:** For an excellent discussion of CDCs written at the time, see Geoffrey Faux, *CDCs: New Hope for the Inner City* (New York, 1971). A recent, favorable appraisal is Alexander von Hoffman, *House by House, Block by Block: The Rebirth of America's Urban Neighborhoods* (New York, 2002).

431 **"strongly based":** Robert S. Browne, "Economics Within a Nationalist Context," Oct. 5, 1971, RSB, Box 22, Folder 21.

431 **CDCs would allow:** See Frances Fox Piven and Richard M. Cloward, eds., *The Politics of Turmoil: Essays on Poverty, Race, and the Urban Crisis* (New York, 1972), 177ff., which includes a debate between Funnyé and Piven and Cloward on community control and deghettoization.

431 **"There has been a gradual":** *The Negro Handbook* (Chicago, 1966), 215; Allen, *Black Awakening in Capitalist America*, 154.

431 **"Black dollars buy less":** Alex Poinsett, "The Economics of Liberation," *Ebony*, Aug. 1969, 150–54.

432 **To woo black shoppers:** Even the number of traditional "race" businesses, in-

cluding funeral homes, barbershops, and restaurants, steadily declined. See Allen, *Black Awakening in Capitalist America*, 154. On the difficulties facing small black-owned businesses in Harlem, see Carlos E. Russell, "Problems of Selling Black," *Liberator*, Oct. 1964, 14–15; more generally, see Alison Isenberg, *Downtown America: A History of the Place and the People Who Made It* (Chicago, 2004), 224–54.

432 **"Blacks, entering as novices":** Robert S. Browne, "Although there has been no shortage . . . ," untitled manuscript, ca. 1973, RSB, Box 24, Folder 12.

432 **"Owning and operating":** Makeda, "A Challenge for Black Leadership," 10; for a larger discussion of this process, see Isenberg, *Downtown America*.

433 **"compensatory capitalism":** *CD*, Oct. 8, 1968.

433 **"white strings":** W. H. Ferry, "The Case for a New Federalism," *SR;* June 15, 1968, 17.

433 **While some black power groups:** Tom Wolfe, *Radical Chic and Mau-Mauing the Flak Catchers* (New York, 1971).

434 **Ford was bankrolling:** *BAA*, March 29, 1969; Karen Ferguson, "Organizing the Ghetto: The Ford Foundation, CORE, and White Power in the Black Power Era, 1967–1969," *JUH* 34 (2007), 67–100.

434 **Calls for reparations:** *CD*, Sept. 2, 1967; Mary Frances Berry, *My Face Is Black Is True;* Robin D. G. Kelley, *Freedom Dreams: The Black Radical Imagination* (Boston, 2002), 110–34.

434 **"what the white man owes us":** Third International Conference on Black Power, "Reparations: Queen Mother Moore," RAM, Reel 11, frame 867; Stokely Carmichael with Ekwueme Michael Thelwell, *Ready for Revolution: The Life and Struggles of Stokely Carmichael (Kwame Ture)* (New York, 2003), 100; Audley Moore, OH, by Cheryl Townsend Gilkes, June 6, 8, 1978, BWOHP, vol. 8, 153, 171, 176; Martha Biondi, "The Rise of the Reparations Movement," *RHR* 87 (Fall 2003), 7.

435 **Joining Moore in the demand:** Robert Sherrill, "We Also Want Four Hundred Billion Dollars Back Pay," *Esquire*, Jan. 1969, 72, 75; *BAA*, Feb. 8, 1969, Jan. 17, 1970; Kelley, *Freedom Dreams*, 124–28; see also Van Deburg, *New Day in Babylon*, 145–49; Ollie Leeds, "The Separatists' Fantasy," *Liberator*, Feb. 1969, 4–8.

435 **"That's a cheap price":** *CD*, June 14, 1969.

435 **The Manifesto did not call:** For a transcript of the Black Manifesto, see Robert S. Lecky and H. Elliott Wright, *Black Manifesto: Religion, Racism, and Reparations* (New York, 1969), 114–26; *CD*, May 5, 1969; *NYT*, May 9, 1969.

436 **On May 4, he interrupted services:** Donald H. Elliott, "Inclusiveness in Riverside Church," *SA* (Sept. 1963), 36–39; *CD*, May 10, 12, 1969; Albert B. Cleage, Jr., *Black Christian Nationalism: New Directions for the Black Church* (New York, 1972), 145.

436 **but showed up at Riverside Church again:** James Forman, *The Making of Black Revolutionaries: A Personal Account* (New York, 1972), 546–50; *NYT*, May 10, 12, 1969.

436 **Riverside's pastor:** Dr. Ernest Campbell, WRVR-FM, New York, broadcast, May 10, 1969, reprinted in Lecky and Wright, *Black Manifesto*, 127–32.

436 **"Judgment day was at hand":** *NYT*, May 3, 1969.

437 **they took to the road:** See, for example, *CD*, May 12, 1969; *BAA*, July 12, 26, Aug. 2, 1969.

437 **By July, the Manifesto:** *BAA*, July 19, 1969.

437 **A Gallup poll:** George Gallup, *The Gallup Poll: Public Opinion, 1935–1971*, vol. 3 (New York, 1972), 2200.

437 **More conservative church leaders:** *NYT*, May 3, 5, 7, 16, 1969; *BAA*, July 5, 12, 1969; Countryman, *Up South*, 268–71.

437 **"should be taken literally":** Ronald Goetz, "The Black Manifesto: The Great White Hope," *Christian Century*, June 18, 1969, 832–33.

438 **"existence of the Black Manifesto:** "Response of the Archdiocese, May 21, 1969," in Lecky and Wright, *Black Manifesto*, 145–47; *NYT*, May 22, 1969; *BAA*, July 5, Aug. 16, 1969. More generally, see Findlay, *Church People in the Struggle*, 199–236.

438 **generated intense debate among blacks:** *NYT*, May 7, 1969; *BAA*, May 31, 1969; Cleage, *Black Christian Nationalism*, 146.

438 **"Religion and so-called Christianity":** Forman, *The Making of Black Revolutionaries*, 546.

438 **Conservative black churchmen:** *CD*, May 24, 29, 1969; *BAA*, July 26, Aug. 23, 30, Sept. 20, 27, 1969; Lecky and Wright, *Black Manifesto*, 11–14; Gallup, *The Gallup Poll*, 2200.

438 **Forman also took a hit from the left:** *BAA*, July 19, 1969; Audley Moore, OH, 153.

438 **Other black leaders:** *NYT*, May 9, 1969; *BAA*, May 31, June 14, July 5, 12, 19, 26, 1969.

439 **nearly 21 percent in a 1969 survey:** Gallup, *The Gallup Poll*, 2200.

439 **In Philadelphia, the Episcopal Church:** Richard G. Schneider, "The Black Manifesto and the Episcopal Church in Philadelphia: A Skirmish in the Struggle for Justice" (University of Pennsylvania, College of General Studies, Capstone Project, July 16, 2001); *PB*, May 18, 1970; Robert L. DeWitt, "1964–74: Decade of Crisis in a Stormy See," *Witness* (July 1984), 7, quoted in Schneider, "The Black Manifesto," 70, n. 28; "Advocate of Social Justice Bishop DeWitt Dies," Episcopal News Service, Nov. 26, 2003.

439 **"by whatever name":** *CD*, Sept. 8, 1969.

439 **The United Methodists allocated:** *BAA*, July 5, 1969, June 20, 1970; Forman, *The Making of Black Revolutionaries*, 548, 549.

440 **Progress Plaza:** Leon H. Sullivan, *Build, Brother, Build* (Philadelphia, 1969), 162–66; Stephanie Dyer, "Progress Plaza: Black Power in a Shopping Mall," unpublished paper, 2005, in author's possession.

440 **When business writer:** Jules Cohn, "Is Business Meeting the Challenge of Urban Affairs?" *Harvard Business Review* 48:2 (1970), 68–82; see more gener-

ally, Herbert H. Haines, *Black Radicals and the Civil Rights Mainstream* (Knoxville, Tenn., 1988), 106–13.

441 **"Never before in our nation's past":** "The Urban Coalition," *Ebony*, Nov. 1967, 131ff. On Newark efforts, see Julia Rabig, "Broken Deal: Devolution, Development, and Civil Society in Newark, New Jersey, 1960–1990" (Ph.D. diss., University of Pennsylvania, 2007), ch. 3.

441 **National Alliance of Businessmen:** *BAA*, Jan. 18, 1969.

441 **Life Insurance Committee:** *NYT*, Sept. 14, 1967; March 24, Sept. 16, Dec. 11, 1968; Jan. 2, Oct. 12, 1969; *BAA*, Oct. 11, 1969.

441 **Local business leaders also launched:** Heather Thompson, *Whose Detroit: Politics, Labor, and Race in a Modern American City* (Ithaca, N.Y., 2001), 73–75; *BAA*, March 9, 1969; George W. Corner, "The Black Coalition: An Experiment in Racial Cooperation, Philadelphia, 1968," *Proceedings of the American Philosophical Society* 120:3 (1976), 178–86.

441 **"I for one am not knocking":** Leeds, "The Separatists' Fantasy," 5.

442 **"much of the black militant talk":** Richard M. Nixon, "Bridges to Human Dignity," April 25, 1968, quoted in Dean J. Kotlowski, *Nixon's Civil Rights: Politics, Principle, and Policy* (Cambridge, Mass., 2001), 129.

442 **"get skinned for this":** John McClaughry, "Black Ownership and National Politics," in American Assembly, Columbia University, *Black Economic Development* (Englewood Cliffs, N.J., 1969), 39; "Roy Innis: From Left-Wing Radical to Right-Wing Extremist," *Journal of Blacks in Higher Education*, 39 (April 30, 2003), 69.

442 **"Black Americans":** Nixon, "Bridges to Human Dignity," CBS television address, April 25, 1968, cited in Faux, *CDCs*, 42; Richard M. Nixon, Presidential Nomination Acceptance Speech, Aug. 8, 1968, Miami Beach, Florida, available at www.presidency.ucsb.edu/ws/index.php?pid=25968.

442 **"put the administration":** Kotlowski, *Nixon's Civil Rights*, 135; *BAA*, March 15, 1969.

443 **a careful political calculus:** John David Skrentny, *The Ironies of Affirmative Action: Politics, Justice, and Culture in America* (Chicago, 1996), 143–50; Paul Frymer, *Uneasy Alliances: Race and Party Competition in America* (Princeton, N.J., 1999), 100–4; Lewis A. Randolph and Robert E. Weems, Jr., "The Ideological Origins of Richard M. Nixon's 'Black Capitalism' Initiative," *Review of Black Political Economy* 29 (1) (Summer 2001), 49–61; *WSJ*, Dec. 5, 1968.

443 **prominent black allies:** Bruce Kesler, "Nixon and Black Power," *Liberator*, Sept. 1968, 14; Daniel H. Watts, "The Vote," *Liberator*, Oct. 1968, 3; Daniel Watts, "Richard Nixon," *Liberator*, Dec. 1968, 3. For rejoinders see letters from Wm. Pierson, *Liberator*, Oct. 1968, 22; Benjamin Dupuy, *Liberator*, Nov. 1968, 22; J. Jasper Caldwell, Jr., with reply by Daniel Watts, *Liberator*, Jan. 1969, 22; on Jackson, *CD*, Nov. 2, 1970; in 1971, Jackson endorsed Daley's Republican opponent for mayor; see *CD*, April 6, 8, 10, 1971; *NYT*, Dec. 1, 1968; WSJ, Oct. 13, 1969, Oct. 27, 1972.

444 **To be sure, African American public opinion:** *PT,* March 10, 18, June 30, 1970; *BAA,* March 8, May 3, 1969.

444 **"sees nothing dangerous":** *BP,* June 7, 1969.

444 **Eldridge Cleaver denounced:** *BP,* May 19, 1970, Nov. 22, 1969.

444 **Not surprisingly, Nixon:** Kotlowski, *Nixon's Civil Rights,* 179; on Nixon and the Panthers, see also Huey P. Newton, "The Black Panthers," in *The Black Revolution: An Ebony Special Issue* (Chicago, 1970), 130–31.

444 **Of all Nixon's critics, Clarence Funnyé:** *BAA,* May 3, 1969; *NYAN,* May 24, July 5, 1969; *NYT,* Feb. 18, 1971.

445 **"The harsh facts of housing economics":** *NYT,* May 16, 1971.

445 **Around the North:** Peter Siskind, "Suburban Growth and Its Discontents: The Logic and Limits of Reform on the Postwar Northeast Corridor," in Kevin M. Kruse and Thomas J. Sugrue, eds., *The New Suburban History* (Chicago, 2006), 161–82; Charles M. Haar and Demetrius S. Iatridis, *Housing the Poor in Suburbia: Public Policy at the Grass Roots* (Cambridge, Mass., 1974); *Southern Burlington County NAACP v. Mount Laurel Township,* 336 A.2d. (N.J., 1975); David Kirp et al., *Our Town: Race, Housing, and the Soul of Suburbia* (New Brunswick, N.J., 1995); Charles M. Haar, *Suburbs Under Siege: Race, Space, and Audacious Judges* (Princeton, N.J., 1996); Howard Gillette, *Camden After the Fall: Decline and Renewal in a Post-Industrial City* (Philadelphia, 2005), 95–119, 160–87.

445 **There were some glimmers of hope:** Carole Goodwin, *The Oak Park Strategy: Community Control of Racial Change* (Chicago, 1979); W. Dennis Keating, *The Suburban Racial Dilemma: Housing and Neighborhoods* (Philadelphia, 1994), 96–113.

445 **Chicago housing discrimination lawsuit:** *Hills v. Gautreaux,* 425 U.S. 284 (1976); Leonard S. Rubinowitz and James E. Rosenbaum, *Crossing the Class and Color Lines: From Public Housing to White Suburbia* (Chicago, 2000); Alexander Polikoff, *Waiting for Gautreaux: A Story of Segregation, Housing, and the Black Ghetto* (Evanston, Ill., 2006); *Encarta Africana,* 2nd ed., CD-ROM s.v. "Suburbanization and African Americans" (by Thomas J. Sugrue); Annemette Sorensen, Karl E. Taeuber, and Leslie J. Hollingsworth, Jr., "Indices of Residential Racial Segregation for American Cities, 1940–1970," *Sociological Focus* 8 (1975), 128–30; Massey and Denton, *American Apartheid,* 222.

447 **Clarence Funnyé died:** *NYT,* Sept. 13, 22, 1970; *BSB,* Sept. 24, 1970; *TIH,* Year End Report, 1970.

447 **Jesse Gray, on the other hand:** *CD,* Aug. 30, Sept. 4, 1973; *BSB,* March 15, 1973; *NYT,* June 16, 1970, April 4, Nov. 9, 1972, March 1, 1973, Feb. 22, Sept. 19, 1974, March 6, June 6, 1976, Sept. 30, 1977.

CHAPTER 13 | "IT'S NOT THE BUS, IT'S US"

449 **Verda Bradley:** *DN,* May 16, 2004 (she is called Virda in the *News* article but appears as Verda in court records).

449 **when employers used educational:** Patricia Cayo Sexton, *Education and Income: Inequalities of Opportunity in Our Public Schools* (New York, 1961), 11–18.

449 **Detroit's public schools were in crisis:** *Findings and Recommendations of the Citizens Advisory Committee on Equal Educational Opportunities,* abridged ed. (Detroit, 1962), 100; Denton Watson, "The Detroit School Challenge," *Crisis,* June–July 1974, 188–93; Sidney Fine, *Violence in the Model City: The Cavanagh Administration, Race Relations, and the Detroit Riot of 1967* (Ann Arbor, Mich., 1988), 42–43; Eleanor Paperno Wolf, *Trial and Error: The Detroit School Segregation Case* (Detroit, 1981), 165; Ed Simkins, interview, by John J. Ursu, n.d. [Fall 1967], LBJ-CR, Part 5, Reel 24, frame 215.

450 **"We were upset":** Quotes from *DN,* May 16, 2004, and Tamar Jacoby, *Someone Else's House: America's Unfinished Struggle for Integration* (New York, 2000), 271.

451 **Federal school desegregation litigation:** Michael W. Combs, "The Federal Judiciary and Northern School Segregation: Judicial Management in Perspective," *Journal of Law and Education* 12 (1984), 345–46. For a useful discussion of the fluidity of activists' stands toward education, see Jack Dougherty, *More Than One Struggle: The Evolution of Black School Reform in Milwaukee* (Chapel Hill, N.C., 2004).

451 **two cases loomed:** See chapter 6, above. "School Desegregation, A Northern Problem," *INS* (Sept.–Oct. 1961); Will Maslow, "De Facto Public School Segregation," *Villanova Law Review* 6 (Spring 1961), 353–76.

451 **"Parents with a segregation grouse":** *PC,* March 17, 1962.

451 **"The truth is that":** Paul Zuber, "The 'de Facto Segregation' Hoax," *Liberator,* Aug. 1963, 8.

452 **In the aftermath:** *BAA,* May 25, 1963; *CD,* Dec. 15, 1956, Sept. 21, 1957, Sept. 27, 1958; "De Facto Segregation in Chicago Public Schools," NAACP-M, Part 3D, Reel 5, frames 036ff.; Theodore Barry to Roy Wilkins, July 29, 1958, NAACP-M, Part 3D, Reel 5, frame 082.

452 **The push for school desegregation:** Michael W. Homel, *Down from Equality: Black Chicagoans and the Public Schools, 1920–41* (Urbana, Ill., 1984), 134–85; Anne Meis Knupfer, *The Chicago Black Renaissance and Women's Activism* (Urbana, Ill., 2006), 74–92; *CD,* Aug. 23, Sept. 2, 18, Oct. 2, 1961; June Shagaloff to Roy Wilkins et al., Nov. 10, 1961, NAACP-M, Part 3, Reel 5, frame 098; Gloster Current to S. S. Morris, Oct. 16, 1961, NAACP-M, Part 3D, Reel 4, frames 401–2.

453 **When seventeen protestors:** "Chicago Parents Arrested in School Demonstrations," NAACP-M, Part 3D, Reel 5, frame 110; *CD,* Jan. 8, 17, 27, 1962.

453 **protests took on a life of their own:** *CD,* Nov. 27, 1962, Jan. 30, July 20, Aug. 17, 24, 31, 1963; "Should All Northern Schools Be Integrated?" *Time,* Sept. 7, 1962; "Chicago No 'Wonderful Town' for Negroes," *NA,* Oct. 21, 1963; generally, see August Meier and Elliott Rudwick, *CORE: A Study in the Civil Rights Movement, 1942–1968* (Urbana, Ill., 1975), 247–48.

453 **Zuber's lawsuit skidded:** *Webb v. Board of Ed. of City of Chicago*, 223 F. Supp. 466 (N.D. Ill. 1963); Naomi Brodkey, "Public Schools Crisis: Chicago Style," *NC*, Dec. 15, 1963, 4–8.

454 **Englewood, New Jersey, activists:** *NYT*, Sept. 4, 1954; Bergen County Branch NAACP to Dr. Stearns et al., June 12, 1961, in NAACP-M, Part 3D, Reel 6, frames 009–12.

454 **outraged national NAACP officials:** Calvin D. Banks to Gloster Current, Oct. 4, 1961, NAACP-M, Part 3D, Reel 6, frame 26; June Shagaloff, memo to Mr. Wilkins, Oct. 18, 1961, NAACP-M, Part 3D, Reel 6, frame 30; Gloster Current to Roy Wilkins, Jan. 19, 1962, NAACP-M, Part 3D, Reel 6, frame 42.

455 **the "Englewood Movement":** June Shagaloff, Memorandum: Background Information on School Desegregation in New Jersey, n.d., NAACP-M, Part 3D, Reel 6, frame 142; Press Release, Feb. 2, 1962 and flyers, CORE, Series 5, Reel 41, frames 353, 356, 368; *PC*, Feb. 10, 17, Aug. 18, 1962; *CD*, Aug. 4, 8, 9, Sept. 5, 13, 1962; *NYAN*, Feb. 24, March 3, May 26, 1962; *Newark Evening News*, May 18, 1962; *NYT*, Feb. 2, 3, May 23, Aug. 7, 1962; *DW*, Feb. 13, 1962; Meier and Rudwick, *CORE*, 193.

455 **"Residents of expensive homes":** Paul Zuber, "The Problem of Segregation in Northern Public Schools," *Liberator*, Oct. 1962, 10; *NYHT*, Aug. 19, 1962.

455 **"the only difference":** Zuber, "The Problem of Segregation"; *CD*, Aug. 23, 27, 1962.

456 **Englewood Movement's increasing militancy:** *CD*, Aug. 4, 8, 9, 11, 27, 1962; Suzanne Platof to Patricia Hainey, Feb. 13, 1962, CORE, Series 5, Reel 22, frames 629–30.

456 **Although Malcolm decided:** Milton Galamison, "Some Lessons from the Struggle on the Englewood Plantation," *Liberator*, March 1962, 2; *CD*, Aug. 9, 20, 1962; *NYHT*, July 28, 1962, in NAACP-M, Part 3D, Reel 6, frame 081; *NYT*, Aug. 8, 27, 1962, *New York Herald-American*, May 20, 1963, in SCCF, 001–638; USCCR, *Public Education: 1963 Staff Report* (Washington, D.C., 1963), 92; *NYT*, July 3, 1963.

456 **"This is a new Negro":** *CD*, Sept. 13, 1962.

457 **The NAACP legal team worried:** *PC*, Feb. 24, March 3, 17, 1962; *NYAN*, April 21, Dec. 1, 1962.

457 **"there is one lesson to be learned":** Current to Wilkins, NAACP-M, Part 3D, Reel 6, frame 045.

457 **By pushing at the boundaries:** Constance Baker Motley, *Equal Justice Under the Law: An Autobiography* (New York, 1998), 127.

457 **Carter turned northward:** Robert L. Carter, *A Matter of Law: A Memoir of Struggle in the Cause of Equal Rights* (New York, 2005); Jack Greenberg, *Crusaders in the Courts: How a Dedicated Band of Lawyers Fought for the Civil Rights Revolution* (New York, 1994), 293–98.

458 **The "Land of Lincoln":** August Meier and Elliott Rudwick, "Early Boycotts of Segregated Schools: The Alton, Illinois, Case, 1897–1908," *JNE* 36 (1967), 394–402; Elliott Rudwick, *Race Riot at East Saint Louis, July 2, 1917* (Urbana,

Ill., 1982); James W. Loewen, *Sundown Towns: A Hidden Dimension of American Racism* (New York, 2005), 60–65; Davison M. Douglas, *Jim Crow Moves North: The Battle over Northern School Segregation, 1865–1954* (New York, 2005), 245.

458 **Shagaloff's first stop:** *CD*, Feb. 16, Sept. 13, 27, Oct. 18, 1952; June Shagaloff, OH, interviewed by Robert E. Martin, Sept. 5, 1968, RJB; Len Schroeter, "Force and Violence in Illinois," *Nation*, Feb. 9, 1952, 124–26; "Explosive School Situation," *Crisis*, March 1952, 143–44; "Southern Exposure," *Crisis*, April 1952, 208–13; June Shagaloff, "A Study of Community Acceptance of Desegregation in Two Areas," *JNE* 23 (1954), 330–38; Douglas, *Jim Crow Moves North*, 245–55; John P. Jackson, Jr., "Creating a Consensus: Psychologists, the Supreme Court, and School Desegregation, 1952–55," *Journal of Social Issues* 54 (1998), 143–77.

459 **Carter and Shagaloff shared:** John Morsell, interview, Jan. 31, 1964, AMP, Box 56, Folder 2. Morsell described them as "most extreme" on the matter of northern school desegregation.

459 **"Segregation in education":** Resolutions on Northern Public Schools Adopted by the 52nd Annual Convention of the NAACP, July 15, 1961, NAACP-M, Part 3D, Reel 4, frame 393.

459 **activists responded to Shagaloff:** Shagaloff, OH, 32, 41; Dougherty, *More than One Struggle*, 76, 92–93.

459 **"It is our intention":** *CD*, Aug. 28, 1962.

460 **Shagaloff advised many:** June Shagaloff, NAACP Memorandum: Public School Desegregation in the North and West, Jan. 1963, SCCF, 004-102.

460 **While civil rights groups protested:** The NAACP litigation campaign in the North in the early 1960s is scarcely mentioned in Jack Greenberg's memoirs, in large part because he and the LDF focused primarily on southern cases. Greenberg mentions his involvement in New Rochelle's case in one sentence and an endnote, and discusses the Denver school desegregation case and, briefly, the litigation that led to *Milliken v. Bradley*. See Greenberg, *Crusaders in the Courts*, 291, 392–94, 565; Zuber, "The 'de Facto Segregation' Hoax," 8; Shagaloff, OH, 39; see also Maslow, "De Facto Public School Segregation"; Robert L. Carter, "De Facto School Segregation: An Examination of the Legal and Constitutional Questions Presented," *Western Reserve Law Review* 16 (1965), 502–25.

461 **When the Gary, Indiana, school district:** "Abandon School Site After NAACP Protest," NAACP-M, Part 3D, Reel D, frame 16; *CD*, May 2, 3, 1962.

461 **Gary's NAACP:** *CD*, May 12, June 6, 1962; "NAACP Files School Suit in Gary, Ind.," June 15, 1962, in NAACP-M, Part 3D, Reel 5, frame 118; William E. Nelson, Jr., and Philip J. Meranto, *Electing Black Mayors: Political Action in the Black Community* (Columbus, Ohio, 1977), 176; *CD*, Feb. 13, 1963.

461 **Gary was a natural site:** Robin M. Williams and Margaret W. Ryan, eds., *Schools in Transition: Community Experiences in Desegregation* (Chapel Hill, N.C., 1954), 50, 112–16; James H. Tipton, *Community in Crisis: The Elimination*

of Segregation from a Public School System (New York, 1953); June Shagaloff, memorandum to Charles Ross et al., July 1962, NAACP-M, Part 3D, Reel 5, frame 120; see, generally, Raymond A. Mohl and Neil Betten, *Steel City: Urban and Ethnic Patterns in Gary, Indiana, 1906–1950* (New York, 1986).

462 **Judge F. Ryan Duffy ruled:** *Bell v. School City of Gary, Indiana,* 324 F.2d 209; *CD,* Nov. 5, 26, 1963; "Court Excuses Accidental Segregation," *NS* (May 1963), 88.

462 **"The NAACP":** *PC,* Aug. 17, 1963.

463 **At the same time, however:** Max Wolff, *A Study of Racial Imbalance in the Plainfield Public Schools: The Facts, Effects, and Remedies,* Prepared for the Lay Advisory Committee to the Plainfield, N.J., Board of Education, June 15, 1962, and Decision of the New Jersey Board of Education in *Booker v. Plainfield Board of Education,* Feb. 5, 1964, both in PHC; *Booker v. Board of Education of Plainfield,* 212 A.2d, 45 N.J. 161 (1965); *Vetere v. Allen,* 15 N.Y.2d. 259 (1965); see also Robert L. Herbst, "The Legal Struggle to Integrate Schools in the North," *Annals of the American Academy of Political and Social Science* 407 (May 1973), 47–48.

463 **stepped up their protests:** Jeanne Theoharis, " 'I'd Rather Go to School in the South': How Boston's School Desegregation Complicates the Civil Rights Paradigm," in Jeanne F. Theoharis and Komozi Woodard, eds., *Freedom North: Black Freedom Struggles Outside the South, 1940–1980* (New York, 2003), 132; *NYT,* Feb. 4, 1964; "NYC School Boycott Huge Success," *NA,* Feb. 14, 1964.

463 **"the tokenism of transfers":** "Boycott Against Tokenism," *NA,* Jan. 31, 1964.

464 **Later that year, black students:** "Death in Cleveland, but No Equality," *NA,* April 14, 1964.

464 **Growing pressure to desegregate:** *NYT,* Jan. 12, 1966; American Association of School Administrators, *School Racial Policy* (Washington, D.C., 1966), 21–28; "Schools Face New Desegregation Phase," *NS* (March 1966), 80–82; "Princeton Plan: New Jersey's Hope," *NS* (Nov. 1966), 65.

464 **"Increasing numbers of young Negroes":** *NYT,* Feb. 23, 1969.

465 **A typical one was Plainfield:** Decision of the New Jersey Board of Education in *Booker v. Plainfield Board of Education,* Feb. 5, 1964, PHC; Commission interview with Dr. Noble Hiebert, superintendent, Plainfield Schools, conducted by Steve Kurzman and Steve Weiner, LBJ-CR, Part 5, Reel 26, Frame 00172; Commission interview with Alfred Schmidt, Director, Plainfield Building Commission, conducted by Steve Kurzman and Steve Weiner, LBJ-CR, Part 5, Reel 26, frame 00110; transcript of interviews, LBJ-CR, Part 5, Reel 26, frames 00264, 00272; John R. Logan, "The State of Public School Integration," available at www.s4.brown.edu/schoolsegregation/index.htm.

465 **On one hand, white attitudes:** Herbert Hyman and Paul B. Sheatsley, "Attitudes Toward Segregation," *Scientific American* (Dec. 1956), 35–39; "Mixed Schools: How Northern Parents Feel," *USNWR,* March 23, 1959; Stewart Alsop and Oliver Quayle, "What Northerners Really Think About Negroes," *SEP,* Sept. 7, 1963, 17–21; NAIRO, Commission on School Integration, *Public School*

Segregation and Integration in the North: Analysis and Proposals (Washington, D.C., 1963), 29–30.

466　**thousands of white parents:** "Racial Crisis Ahead for Neighborhood Schools," *USNWR*, July 8, 1963, 48; Jerald E. Podair, *The Strike That Changed New York: Blacks, Whites, and the Ocean Hill–Brownsville Crisis* (New Haven, Conn., 2002), 26–30.

466　**"discrimination against the majority":** "The Facts of de Facto," *Time*, Aug. 2, 1963.

467　**"When 10,000 Queens white mothers":** Doris Innis, interview, Oct. 12, 1971, AMP, Box 56, Folder 9.

467　**"high impact, low probability":** C. E. Wilson, "Why Don't Public Schools Teach Our Children, Part 1," *Liberator*, March 1965, 4; C. E. Wilson, "Why Don't Public Schools Teach Our Children, Part 2," *Liberator*, April 1965, 12.

468　**The localistic nature of public education:** Thomas J. Sugrue, "All Politics Is Local: The Persistence of Localism in Twentieth-Century America," in Meg Jacobs et al., eds., *The Democratic Experiment: New Directions in American Political History* (Princeton, N.J., 2003), 301–26; Lizabeth Cohen, *A Consumers' Republic: The Politics of Mass Consumption in Postwar America* (New York, 2003), 231–35, 240–51.

468　**"culturally deprived" students:** USCCR, *Public Education: 1963 Staff Report*, 124–25, 127–29; *IRCD Bulletin*, Sept. 1965, in NAACP-M, Part 3, Reel D4, frame 658; Doxey A. Wilkerson, "School Integration, Compensatory Education, and the Civil Rights Movement in the North," *JNE* 34 (1965), 300–9.

469　**none held out more promise:** Elementary and Secondary Education Act of 1965, Pub. L. 89-10, 79 Stat. 27.

470　**"This is the precise moment":** *Congressional Record* 111 (March 24, 1965), 5735, cited in James Sundquist, *Politics and Policy: The Eisenhower, Kennedy, and Johnson Years* (Washington, D.C., 1968), 215; Patrick McGuinn and Frederick Hess, "Freedom from Ignorance?: The Great Society and the Evolution of the Elementary and Secondary Education Act of 1965," in Sidney Milkis and Jerome Mileur, eds., *The Great Society and the High Tide of Liberalism* (Amherst, Mass., 2005), 295.

470　**"educational parks":** *PC*, Feb. 15, June 27, 1964, Oct. 30, 1965; *CD*, Jan. 15, 1966, April 17, Dec. 14, 1967; LeRoy B. Allen, "Replications of the Educational Park Concept for the Disadvantaged," *JNE* 40 (1971), 225–32; "Pittsburgh's Goal: Educational Parks," *NS* (Nov. 1966).

471　**"Now, about this school integration":** S.A.L., "Through Women's Eyes: What I Want for Junnie," *Liberator*, Oct. 1964, 20–21; Wilson, "Why Don't Public Schools Teach, Part 2," 15; "New Jersey Feels Black Power Push," *NS*, Nov. 1966, 65.

472　**"Only by strong assertive action":** Alvin F. Poussaint, "Education and Black Self-Image," *Freedomways* (1968), in Esther Cooper Jackson, ed., *Freedomways Reader: Prophets in Their Own Country* (Boulder, Colo., 2000), 224–25; *CD*, Feb. 27, Sept. 28, 1963.

472 **Civil rights activists had long campaigned:** *CD*, Feb. 17, March 31, 1923, Jan. 24, 1931.

473 **The intercultural education movement:** David Tyack, *Seeking Common Ground: Public Schools in a Diverse Society* (Cambridge, Mass., 2003), 81; Nicholas V. Montalto, *A History of the Intercultural Education Movement, 1924–1941* (New York, 1982); *CD*, Dec. 4, 8, 1962; phone interview with Richard Tyler, Oct. 19, 2005.

473 **"Survival Curriculum":** *NYT*, March 17, 1968. A year and a half earlier, Maxwell Stanford had argued for the creation of "liberation schools" as an alternative to white-dominated education. See *BAA*, Sept. 24, 1966.

473 **African-focused curriculum:** *CD*, March 9, 1968; Jonathan Zimmerman, "*Brown*-ing the American Textbook: History, Psychology, and the Origins of Modern Multiculturalism," *HEQ* 44 (2004), 46–69; see also Daryl M. Scott, "Postwar Pluralism, *Brown v. Board of Education*, and the Origins of Multicultural Education," *JAH* 91 (2004), 80–82, though Scott draws too sharp a distinction between pluralists and black power and calls for "racially separate" education.

474 **"You cannot give pride":** Kenneth Clark, "Ghetto Education," *Center Magazine*, Nov. 1968, 1, cited in Zimmerman, "*Brown*-ing the American Textbook," 69.

475 **overcome by administrative reorganization:** Heather Lewis, "More than Half a Loaf: Everyday Governance and Democratic Action in the 1960s," paper presented to MCVA, May 5, 2006.

475 **The Harlem school became the proving ground:** *CD*, Sept. 22, 27, 1966.

475 **New York's Ocean Hill–Brownsville:** The Ocean Hill–Brownsville controversy generated a huge literature. The most important studies are Martin Mayer, *The Teachers Strike, New York, 1968* (New York, 1969); Marilyn Gittell and Maurice Berube, eds., *Confrontation at Ocean Hill–Brownsville* (New York, 1969); Podair, *The Strike That Changed New York*; Daniel H. Perlstein, *Justice, Justice: School Politics and the Eclipse of Liberalism* (New York, 2004). For background, see Wendell Pritchett, *Brownsville, Brooklyn: Blacks, Jews, and the Changing Face of the Ghetto* (Chicago, 2002).

476 **a version of community control remained in place:** Heather A. Lewis, "Protest, Place and Pedagogy: New York City's Community Control Movement and Its Aftermath, 1966–1996" (Ph.D. diss., New York University, 2006).

477 **But for all the attention:** Peter Goldman, *Report from Black America* (New York, 1970), 267–68, 270; NAACP quote from Alan A. Altshuler, *Community Control: The Black Demand for Participation in Large American Cities* (Indianapolis, 1970), 60–61.

478 **"it is freedom of choice":** *Deal v. Cincinnati Board of Education*, 369 F.2d. 55 (1966).

478 **"equal educational opportunity":** *Hobson v. Hansen*, 269 F. Supp. 40 (1967); Beatrice A. Moulton, "*Hobson v. Hansen:* The de Facto Limits on Judicial Power," *Stanford Law Review* 20 (1967–68), 1249–68.

478 **In 1958, a federal judge dismissed:** *Henry v. Godsell,* 165 F. Supp. 87 (1958); see also USCCR, *Five Communities: Their Search for Equal Education,* Clearinghouse Publication 37 (Dec. 1972), 16–19.

479 **"intentionally utilized the power":** *Davis v. School District of the City of Pontiac,* 309 F. Supp. 734 (1970).

479 **White Pontiac exploded:** USCCR, *Five Communities,* 19–23; USCCR, *School Desegregation in Ten Communities,* Clearinghouse Publication 43 (June 1973), 15–18, 21. A sympathetic account of NAG is Jacoby, *Someone Else's House,* 259–61, 265–69.

480 **Supreme Court decision involving the Denver:** *Keyes v. Denver School District #1,* 413 U.S. 931 (1973). For accounts of *Keyes,* see Herbst, "The Legal Struggle to Integrate Schools," 44, 59–60; James T. Patterson, *Brown v. Board of Education: A Civil Rights Milestone and Its Troubled Legacy* (New York, 2001), 160–62.

480 *Keyes* **had potentially:** *Keyes* also had far-reaching implications beyond the scope of this study by considering black and Hispanic plaintiffs together when considering patterns of segregation.

481 *Keyes* **was overshadowed:** *BAA,* June 8, 1963; Jeffrey Mirel, *The Rise and Fall of an Urban School System: Detroit, 1907–81* (Ann Arbor, Mich., 1993), 188–89, 192–93, 258–59, 261; Paul R. Dimond, *Beyond Busing: Inside the Challenge to Urban Segregation* (Ann Arbor, Mich., 1985), 61–63; Fine, *Violence in the Model City,* 7–9, 43–50; Will Maslow, "De Facto Public School Segregation," in Hubert H. Humphrey, ed., *School Desegregation: Documents and Commentaries* (New York, 1964), 164.

481 **Detroit activists, both black and white:** William R. Grant, "Community Control Versus Integration—The Case of Detroit," *Public Interest* (Summer 1971); Dimond, *Beyond Busing,* 26–27; Fine, *Violence in the Model City,* 437; Wolf, *Trial and Error,* 147–57.

481 **While the decentralization:** Mirel, *The Rise and Fall of an Urban School System,* 338–45; Joe T. Darden et al., *Detroit: Race and Uneven Development* (Philadelphia, 1987), 221–28.

482 **"Governmental actions and inaction":** *Bradley v. Milliken,* 338 F. Supp. 582 (1971), at 587. The best discussion of the case remains Dimond, *Beyond Busing,* esp. 26–118.

482 **Roth found evidence:** *Bradley v. Milliken,* 345 F. Supp. 914 (1972); *Milliken v. Bradley,* 418 U.S. 717 (1974), 733.

483 **Of all the education rulings:** John Kelsey to constituents, June 1972, JTK, Box 1; "I Am Opposed to Bussing. What Can I Do?" in Shirley Wohlfield Papers, Box 1, Folder: *Bradley v. Milliken,* MHC; USCCR, *Your Child and Busing,* Clearinghouse Publication 36 (May 1972), 7; Jennifer Hochschild, *The New American Dilemma: Liberal Democracy and School Desegregation* (New Haven, Conn., 1984), 216, n. 67; Bond, quoted in Theoharis, "'I'd Rather Go to School in the South,'" 142.

483 **"We believe 'forced busing'":** *"Hi" Neighbor,* newsletter of the Outer–Van

Dyke Home Owners Association (Aug. 1975), copy in Carmen Roberts Papers, MHC; Maryann Shankin to John Kelsey, April 14, 1976, in JTK, Box 1, Folder: Busing Correspondence, 1976; Rickie Solinger, "Poisonous Choice," in Molly Ladd-Taylor and Lauri Umansky, eds., *"Bad" Mothers: The Politics of Blame in Twentieth-Century America* (New York, 1998), 381–402.

484 **"It will be interesting":** John Bennett to John Kelsey, June 29, 1972, JTK, Box 1, Folder: Busing Correspondence, 1972; *DN*, May 10, 16, 17, 1972; Statement of Election Returns, Presidential Primary Election, May 16, 1972, microfilm, Office of the Wayne County Clerk, City County Building, Detroit; Dan T. Carter, *The Politics of Rage: George Wallace, the Origins of the New American Conservatism, and the Transformation of American Politics* (New York, 1995), 434, 445.

484 **Those who continued to support:** *WSJ*, Nov. 24, 1971; R. Bruce Dodd, "Dissenting Opinion: A Profile of Abner Mikva," *University of Chicago Alumni Magazine*, Aug. 1996, available at http://magazine.uchicago.edu/9608/9608Mikva.html; Michael O'Brien, *Philip Hart: The Conscience of the Senate* (East Lansing, Mich., 1995), 184–88.

485 **"indoctrinated with lies":** *BP*, April 25, 1970; Steering Committee, National Black Political Convention, Press Release, March 28, 1972 in RJB, Box 19, Folder 1; *NYT*, March 14, 1972; *WP*, March 21, 1972; Earl Ofari, "Problems for Black Politicians," *Guardian*, June 21, 1972.

485 **Black Detroiters:** *DFP*, Oct. 21, 22, 1974; see also *WP*, Sept. 2, 1975.

486 **The state and forty-four suburban school districts:** Dimond, *Beyond Busing*, 99–110.

486 **In its controversial 5–4 decision:** *Milliken v. Bradley*, 418 U.S. 717 (1974), at 741–42, 815; *DFP*, July 26, 1974.

487 **Through the 1960s, Boston's whites:** "Police Idle as NAACP Is Stoned in Boston Parade," NAACP Press Release, March 20, 1964, in NAACP, Part 20, Reel 11, frame 281; Gerald Gamm, *Urban Exodus: Why the Jews Left Boston and the Catholics Stayed* (Cambridge, Mass., 1999); Katherine L. Bradbury et al., *Urban Decline and the Future of American Cities* (Washington, D.C., 1982), 50–51.

488 **When Judge Arthur Garrity:** J. Anthony Lukas, *Common Ground: A Turbulent Decade in the Lives of Three American Families* (New York, 1986); Ronald Formisano, *Boston Against Busing: Race, Class, and Ethnicity in the 1960s and 1970s* (Chapel Hill, N.C., 1991); and, more critically, James Green, "In Search of Common Ground," *RA* 20:5 (1987), 40–60; Jeanne Theoharis, " 'We Saved the City': Black Struggles Against Educational Inequality in Boston, 1960–76," *RHR* 81 (2001), 61–93.

489 **"Substantial desegregation":** Jennifer L. Hochschild and Nathan Scovronick, *The American Dream and the Public Schools* (New York, 2003), 35.

489 **"The insistence on integrating":** Derrick A. Bell, "Serving Two Masters: Integration Ideals and Client Interests in School Desegregation Litigation," *YLJ* 85 (1976), 470–516; Bell, "School Desegregation: Seeking Victory Among the

Ashes," *Freedomways* (1977), in Jackson, ed., *Freedomways Reader*, 229–32; Elizabeth Higginbotham, *Too Much to Ask: Black Women in the Era of Integration* (Chapel Hill, N.C., 2001), 48–54.

490 **What remained deeply entrenched:** For a useful summary, see Harvey Kantor and Barbara Brenzel, "Urban Education and the Truly Disadvantaged: The Historical Roots of the Contemporary Crisis," in Katz, ed., *The "Underclass" Debate*, 366–402.

491 **In its 1973 decision:** *San Antonio Independent School District v. Rodriguez*, 411 U.S. 1 (1973); James T. Patterson, *Brown v. Board of Education: A Civil Rights Milestone and Its Troubled Legacy* (New York, 2001), 177–78; Cohen, *A Consumers' Republic*, 240–50; Hochschild and Scovronick, *The American Dream and the Public Schools*, 26.

491 **No place better demonstrated:** Thomas J. Sugrue, "Expert Report of Thomas J. Sugrue," *University of Michigan Journal of Race and the Law* 5 (Fall 1999), 289; Gary Orfield, Susan Eaton, and the Harvard Project on School Desegregation, *Dismantling Desegregation: The Quiet Reversal of Brown v. Board of Education* (New York, 1996).

491 **these basic measures were abysmal:** *DN*, Oct. 24, 2004; Detroit City School District MEAP Scores, Class of 2004, available at http://mdoe.state.mi.us/oeaa.

491 **Verda Bradley's son Ronald:** *DFP*, Sept. 29, 1992; *DN*, May 16, 2004.

CHAPTER 14 | "FIGHTING FOR OUR LIVES"

493 **funeral of state senator Roxanne Jones:** *PDN*, May 20, 31, 1996; *PI*, May 21, 1996; *PT*, May 21, 31, 1996.

494 **In 1967, when Roxanne Jones:** See chapter 11 above.

494 **"The marching has stopped":** Donald H. McGannon and Vernon E. Jordan, Jr., "Introduction," in *When the Marching Stopped: An Analysis of Black Issues in the '70s* (New York, 1973), iii, iv.

495 **Other longtime activists:** Zuber joined the faculty of Rensselaer Polytechnic Institute; Brown founded the Black Economic Research Center; Maxwell Stanford converted to Islam in 1970, changed his name to Muhammad Ahmad, and studied at Atlanta University and the University of Massachusetts, Amherst.

496 **waning influence of the black press:** Circulation had steadily declined since the 1950s. See Ronald N. Jacobs, *Race, Media and the Decline of Civil Society: From Watts to Rodney King* (New York, 2000), esp. 48–53.

496 **offered lengthy interviews:** Selected episodes of *American Black Journal* are online at http://matrix.msu.edu/~abj/.

496 **Media images of blacks and poverty:** Martin Gilens, *Why Americans Hate Welfare: Race, Media, and the Politics of Antipoverty Policy* (Chicago, 1999).

496 **In the celebrity-obsessed:** Norman Kelley, *The Head Negro in Charge Syndrome: The Dead End of Black Politics* (New York, 2004); Adolph L. Reed, Jr., *The Jesse Jackson Phenomenon: The Crisis of Purpose in Afro-American Politics*

(New Haven, Conn., 1986); Dean E. Robinson, *Black Nationalism in American Politics and Thought* (Cambridge, U.K., 2001), 122–25.

498 **A deep strain of antistatism:** *BSB*, Feb. 17, 1972; *OP*, Jan. 13, Feb. 17, 1972.

498 **"black imitators who deal":** *TSD*, Mar. 11, 1972.

498 **National Black Political Convention:** National Black Political Convention State Convenors, and National Support Committee, in RSB, Box 19, Folder 1; *CD*, March 9, 18, 1972; *TSD*, April 8, 1972; James B. Lane, "Black Political Power and Its Limits: Gary Mayor Richard G. Hatcher's Administration, 1968–87," in David R. Colburn and Jeffrey S. Adler, eds., *African-American Mayors: Race, Politics, and the American City* (Urbana, Ill., 2001), 57–79; William Strickland, "The Gary Convention and the Crisis of American Politics," *Black Worker*, Oct. 1972, 22 (that issue also includes articles on the convention by Ronald Walters, William Clay, Amiri Baraka, and Charles Hamilton). The best overview of the convention in its context is Komozi Woodard, *A Nation Within a Nation: Amiri Baraka (LeRoi Jones) and Black Power* (Chapel Hill, N.C., 1999), 159–218.

498 **The proceedings in Gary:** *NYT*, March 10, 14, 1972; *WSJ*, March 14, 1972; *WP*, March 16, 1972; *SFSR*, March 18, 1972.

499 **a lengthy and controversial blueprint:** "The National Black Political Agenda," in Komozi Woodard, Randolph Boehm, and Daniel Lewis, eds., *The Black Power Movement, Part 1: Amiri Baraka from Black Arts to Black Radicalism* (Bethesda, Md., 2000), reel 3; *Eyes on the Prize II: America at the Racial Crossroads*, Episode 11: "Ain't Gonna Shuffle No More" (PBS/Blackside, 1990).

499 **Of major civil rights groups:** *NYT*, March 10, May 17, 1972; *SFSR*, March 18, 1972; *CD*, May 22, 1972; *BSB*, May 25, 1972.

500 **"elitism and conservatism":** Earl Ofari, "Problems for Black Politicians," *Guardian*, June 21, 1972.

500 **"Political action is an essential":** Richard Hatcher, Keynote Address, March 11, 1972, in RSB, Box 19, Folder 3; *LAT*, March 12, 15, 1972; *NYT*, March 12, 1972; *CD*, March 13, 1972.

501 **But efforts to create race-conscious:** Robert Self, *American Babylon: Race and the Struggle for Postwar Oakland* (Princeton, N.J., 2003), 298–309; Heather Thompson, *Whose Detroit?: Politics, Race, and Labor in a Modern American City* (Ithaca, N.Y., 2001), 193–94, 211; National Research Council, *A Common Destiny: Blacks and American Society* (Washington, D.C., 1989), 219, 234–37.

501 **The 1970s witnessed a stunning increase:** Calculated from National Research Council, *A Common Destiny*, Table 5-10, 238. For a longer view, see USCB, *Statistical Abstract of the United States* (Washington, D.C., 2006), Table 403.

502 **But the Republicans:** *BSB*, June 16, 1970; *WSJ*, Oct. 27, 1972; Paul Frymer, *Uneasy Alliances: Race and Party Competition in America* (Princeton, 1999), 100–4; National Research Council, *A Common Destiny*, 235–37.

503 **"a Negro first and a Democrat second":** Heather A. Thompson, "Rethinking the Collapse of Postwar Liberalism: The Rise of Mayor Coleman Young and the

Politics of Race in Detroit," in Colburn and Adler, eds., *African-American Mayors*, 234.

503 **Black mayoral candidates:** John F. Bauman. "W. Wilson Goode: The Black Mayor as Urban Entrepreneur," *JNH* 77 (1992), 141–58; Colburn and Adler, eds., *African-American Mayors;* Raphael J. Sonenshein, *Politics in Black and White: Race and Power in Los Angeles* (Princeton, N.J., 1993); Mary Summers and Philip A. Klinkner, "The Daniels Election in New Haven and the Failure of the Deracialization Hypothesis," *UAQ* 27 (1991), 202–15.

503 **With few exceptions, black mayors:** John H. Mollenkopf, *The Contested City* (Princeton, N.J., 1983); Adolph Reed, Jr., *Stirrings in the Jug: Black Politics in the Post-Segregation Era* (Minneapolis, 1999), 79–115.

504 **he had no problem accommodating:** Thompson, "Rethinking the Collapse," 223–48; David Fasenfest, "Community Politics and Urban Redevelopment: Poletown, Detroit, and General Motors," *UAQ* 22 (1986), 101–23; June Manning Thomas, "Detroit: The Centrifugal City," in Gregory D. Squires, ed., *Unequal Partnerships: The Political Economy of Urban Redevelopment in Postwar America* (New Brunswick, N.J., 1989), 149–53; Bill McGraw et al., eds., *The Quotations of Mayor Coleman A. Young* (Detroit, 1991), 72.

504 **As mayor, however, Goode:** Bauman, "W. Wilson Goode," 141–58. For Goode's version of the story, see W. Wilson Goode, *In Goode Faith* (Philadelphia, 1992).

505 **black political power still had:** Peter J. Eisinger, "Affirmative Action in Municipal Employment: The Impact of Black Political Power," *American Political Science Review* 76 (1982), 380–92; Eisinger, "The Economic Conditions of Black Employment in Municipal Bureaucracies," *American Journal of Political Science* 26 (1982), 754–71; Dennis Deslippe, "'Do Whites Have Rights?' White Detroit Policemen and 'Reverse Discrimination' Protests in the 1970s," *JAH* 93 (2004), 932–60; Stephan Thernstrom and Abigail Thernstrom, *America in Black and White: One Nation Indivisible* (New York, 1997), 188–89; National Research Council, *A Common Destiny*, 244; Michael B. Katz and Mark J. Stern, *One Nation Divisible: What America Was and What It Is Becoming* (New York, 2005), 91–93.

505 **To a great extent, black economic:** John David Skrentny, *The Ironies of Affirmative Action: Politics, Justice, and Culture in America* (Chicago, 1996), and *The Minority Rights Revolution* (Cambridge, Mass., 2002); Judith Stein, *Running Steel, Running America: Race, Economic Policy, and the Decline of Liberalism* (Chapel Hill, N.C., 1998), 148–52; William Safire, *Before the Fall: An Inside View of the Pre-Watergate White House* (Garden City, N.Y., 1975); Dean Kotlowski, *Nixon's Civil Rights: Politics, Principle, and Policy* (Cambridge, Mass., 2001), 97–124; Joan Hoff, *Nixon Reconsidered* (New York, 1994), 90–92; *Contractors Assn. of Eastern Pennsylvania v. Schultz*, 311 F. Supp. 1002 (1970); 442 F.2d 159 (1971); cert. denied, 404 U.S. 854 (1971); William B. Gould, *Black Workers in White Unions: Job Discrimination in the United States* (Ithaca, N.Y., 1977), 297–362; Steven M. Gillon, *"That's Not What We Meant to Do": Reform*

and Its Unintended Consequences in Twentieth-Century America (New York, 2000), 147.

506 **the extent to which affirmative action opened:** Terry H. Anderson, *In Pursuit of Fairness: A History of Affirmative Action* (New York, 2004), offers a balanced discussion of the intense, voluminous debate; Nancy MacLean, *Freedom Is Not Enough: The Opening of the American Workplace* (Cambridge, Mass., 2006), 333–47; Erin Kelly and Frank Dobbin, "How Affirmative Action Became Diversity Management: Employer Response to Antidiscrimination Law, 1961–1996," in John David Skrentny, ed., *Color Lines: Affirmative Action, Immigration, and Civil Rights Options for America* (Chicago, 2001), 87–117.

506 **divergent black and white opinions:** Lee Sigelman and Susan Welch, *Black Americans' Views of Racial Inequality: The Dream Deferred* (New York, 1991); James R. Kluegel, "Trends in Whites' Explanations of the Gap in Black-White Socioeconomic Status, 1977–1989," *American Sociological Review* 55 (1990), 512–25; Jennifer Hochschild, *Facing Up to the American Dream: Race, Class, and the Soul of the Nation* (Princeton, N.J., 1995), 61, 63, 68.

507 **In 1978, the Supreme Court split badly:** *Regents of the University of California v. Bakke*, 438 U.S. 265 (1978); on "societal discrimination," see Powell's opinion in *Wygant v. Jackson Board of Education*, 476 U.S. 267 (1986), 276; Skrentny, *Color Lines*, 11. For a succinct overview, see Howard Ball, *The Bakke Case: Race, Education, and Affirmative Action* (Lawrence, Kans., 2000).

508 **In his stand-alone opinion:** *Regents v. Bakke*, esp. 311–19.

508 **diversity became a goal in its own right:** Erin Kelly and Frank Dobbin, "How Affirmative Action Became Diversity Management," *American Behavioral Scientist* 41 (1998), 960–83, Elizabeth Lasch-Quinn, *Race Experts: How Racial Etiquette, Sensitivity Training, and New Age Therapy Hijacked the Civil Rights Revolution* (New York, 2001), is rather polemical and overlooks continuities with postwar psychological and moral understandings of prejudice and reform but is nonetheless useful.

509 **no correlations between self-esteem and educational success:** Tom Loveless, *The 2006 Brown Center Report on American Education* (Washington, D.C., 2006).

510 **The Court set the bar of proof so high:** *Fullilove v. Klutznick*, 481 U.S. 472 (1980); *Richmond v. J. A. Croson Co.*, 488 U.S. 469 (1989); *Adarand v. Pena*, 515 U.S. 200 (1995).

510 **Rather than engaging in a head-on:** John David Skrentny, "Walking a Fine Line: Republican Efforts to End Affirmative Action," in Mark Landy et al., eds., *Seeking the Center* (Washington, D.C., 2001), 132–71; Hanes Walton, Jr., *When the Marching Stopped: The Politics of Civil Rights Regulatory Agencies* (Albany, N.Y., 1988).

511 **the rise in black suburbanization:** *NYT*, June 14, 1992, Aug. 15, 1994, July 27, 1996; Joshua B. Freeman, *Working-Class New York: Life and Labor Since World War II* (New York, 2000), 295; Andrew Wiese, " 'The House I Live In': Race, Class, and African American Suburban Dreams in the Postwar United States,"

in Kevin M. Kruse and Thomas J. Sugrue, eds., *The New Suburban History* (Chicago, 2005), 99–119; Sheryll Cashin, *The Failure of Integration: How Race and Class Are Undermining the American Dream* (New York, 2004), esp. 128–66.

511 **Southfield, Michigan, is a case in point:** Joe T. Darden et al., *Detroit: Race and Uneven Development* (Philadelphia, 1987), 147–49; National Center for Educational Statistics, *Michigan School District Data Book* (1989–90); *K–12 Public Education in Michigan: Selected Characteristics and Services by County and School District* (Lansing, Mich., 1997); *DN*, Jan. 21, 1997.

511 **Segregated suburbs were:** Douglas S. Massey and Nancy A. Denton, *American Apartheid: Segregation and the Making of the Underclass* (Cambridge, Mass., 1993), 84–87; Reynolds Farley, Elaine L. Fielding, and Maria Krysan, "The Residential Preferences of Blacks and Whites: A Four-Metropolis Analysis," *Housing Policy Debate* 8 (1997), 763–800; Reynolds Farley et al., "Continued Racial Residential Segregation in Detroit: 'Chocolate City, Vanilla Suburbs' Revisited," *Journal of Housing Research* 4 (1993), 1–38; Reynolds Farley et al., "Stereotypes and Segregation: Neighborhoods in the Detroit Area," *American Journal of Sociology* 100 (1994), 751–52.

512 **In most metropolitan areas:** William Julius Wilson, *The Declining Significance of Race* (Chicago, 1978), made the most forceful argument about the growing separation of working- and middle-class blacks. For an alternative, see Thomas J. Sugrue, *The Origins of the Urban Crisis* (Princeton, N.J., 1996), ch. 6. More generally, see Reynolds Farley, "Residential Segregation of Social and Economic Groups Among Blacks, 1970–1980," in Christopher Jencks and Paul Peterson, eds., *The Urban Underclass* (Washington, D.C., 1991), 274–98; Mary Pattillo, "Sweet Mothers and Gangbangers: Managing Crime in a Black Middle-Class Neighborhood," *Social Forces* 76 (1998), 751; Bart Landry, *The New Black Middle Class* (Berkeley, Calif., 1987), 181–86; Richard D. Alba, John R. Logan, and Paul E. Bellair, "Living with Crime: The Implications of Racial/Ethnic Differences in Suburban Location," *Social Forces* 73 (1994), 427. Wilson now acknowledges the precariousness of middle-class life in the inner city. See William Julius Wilson and Richard Taub, *There Goes the Neighborhood: Racial, Ethnic, and Class Tensions in Four Chicago Neighborhoods and Their Meaning for America* (New York, 2006).

512 **In the last three decades of:** *Encarta Africana*, 2nd ed., CD-ROM, s.v. "Suburbanization and African Americans" (by Thomas J. Sugrue); on Roosevelt, *NYT*, Dec. 28, 1969, and Jonathan Kozol, *The Shame of the Nation: The Restoration of Apartheid Schooling in America* (New York, 2005), 150–60; on Hempstead, see *NYT*, June 5, 16, 2002. See also Myron Orfield, *American Metropolitics: The New Suburban Reality* (Washington, D.C., 2002).

513 **studies of housing discrimination:** Diana Pearce, "Gatekeepers and Homeseekers: Institutionalized Patterns in Racial Steering," *SP* 26 (1979), 325–42; Michael Fix and Raymond J. Struyk, eds., *Clear and Convincing Evidence: Measurement of Discrimination in America* (Washington, D.C., 1993).

513 **the problems facing urban blacks:** "Cities in Peril," *USNWR*, April 7, 1975, 29; William Baer, "On the Death of Cities," *Public Interest* 45 (Fall 1976); on the sense of crisis in the 1970s, see Robert A. Beauregard, *Voices of Decline: The Postwar Fate of U.S. Cities* (Oxford, U.K., 1993), 219–45; Jon Teaford, *The Rough Road to Renaissance: Urban Revitalization in America, 1940–1985* (Baltimore, 1990), 200–31; this paragraph draws from Thomas J. Sugrue, "Carter's Urban Policy Crisis," in Gary M. Fink and Hugh Davis Graham, eds., *The Carter Presidency: Policy Choices in the Post–New Deal Era* (Lawrence, Kans., 1998), 137.

514 **stark decline in labor force participation:** Richard B. Freeman and Harry J. Holzer, eds., *The Black Youth Employment Crisis* (Chicago, 1986); Troy Duster, "Postindustrialism and Youth Employment: African Americans as Harbingers," in Katherine McFate, Roger Lawson, and William Julius Wilson, eds., *Poverty, Inequality, and the Future of Social Policy: Western States in the New World Order* (New York, 1995), 466–73; Richard Freeman, "Crime and the Employment of Disadvantaged Youth," in George Peterson and Wayne Vroman, eds., *Urban Labor Markets and Job Opportunities* (Washington, D.C., 1992); Marie Gottschalk, *The Prison and the Gallows: The Politics of Mass Incarceration in America* (New York, 2006), 2.

514 **persistent workplace discrimination:** Joleen Kirschenman and Kathryn M. Neckerman, " 'We'd Love to Hire Them, But . . .': The Meaning of Race for Employers," in Jencks and Peterson, eds., *The Urban Underclass;* Joleen Kirschenman, Philip Moss, and Chris Tilly, "Space as a Signal, Space as a Barrier: How Employers Map and Use Space in Four Metropolitan Labor Markets," Russell Sage Foundation Working Paper 89; Philip Moss and Chris Tilly, "Raised Hurdles for Black Men: Evidence from Interviews with Employers," Russell Sage Foundation Working Paper 81; Harry Holzer, *What Employers Want: Job Prospects for the Less Educated* (New York, 1996).

515 **perverse incentives of welfare:** Charles Murray, *Losing Ground: American Social Policy, 1950–1980* (New York, 1984); the most nuanced discussion of the public policy worries about unwed teens is Maris Vinovskis, *An "Epidemic" of Adolescent Pregnancy: Some Historical and Policy Considerations* (New York, 1988), 23–37.

515 **Arguments about the underclass:** Ken Auletta, *The Underclass* (New York, 1982); Adolph Reed, "The Underclass as Myth and Symbol," *RA* 24 (1992), 21–40; Michael B. Katz, "The 'Underclass' as a Metaphor of Social Transformation," in Katz, ed., *The "Underclass" Debate: Views from History* (Princeton, 1993), 3–23; Herbert Gans, *The War Against the Poor* (New York, 1995).

516 **expanded the mandate of the welfare rights:** On welfare rights after the early 1970s, see Todd Shaw, " 'We Refused to Lay Down Our Spears': The Persistence of Welfare Rights Activism, 1966–1996," in Ollie A. Johnson III and Karin L. Stanford, eds., *Black Political Organizations in the Post–Civil Rights Era* (New Brunswick, N.J., 2002), 170–92; Annelise Orleck, *Storming Caesars Palace: How Black Mothers Fought Their Own War on Poverty* (Boston, 2005).

516 **Despite those grim statistics:** Philadelphia City Planning Commission, *North Philadelphia Databook* (Philadelphia, 1986), 13, 19, 31, 33, 80.

516 **the neighborhood's many churches:** *PT,* May 9, July 18, 1970; Philadelphia City Planning Commission, "North Philadelphia Plan Draft," Sept. 1986, in author's possession, 13; Paul M. Washington, *"Other Sheep I Have": The Autobiography of Father Paul M. Washington* (Philadelphia, 1994); generally, Camilo Jose Vergara, *How the Other Half Worships* (New Brunswick, N.J., 2005); Clifford J. Green, *Churches, Cities, and Human Community* (Grand Rapids, Mich., 1994).

518 **Every major northeastern:** John D. Kasarda, "Urban Change and Minority Opportunities," in Paul E. Peterson., ed., *The New Urban Reality* (Washington, D.C., 1985), Table 1; "Delaware Valley Data: Employment, 1970–1993," Delaware Valley Regional Planning Commission, *Data Bulletin* 50 (Sept. 1995), 21; Carolyn Adams et al., *Philadelphia: Neighborhoods, Division, and Conflict in a Postindustrial City* (Philadelphia, 1991), 107–10.

518 **As jobs disappeared:** Sudhir Alladi Venkatesh, *Off the Books: The Underground Economy of the Urban Poor* (Cambridge, Mass., 2006).

518 **image of "welfare queens":** *NYT,* Feb. 15, 29, 1976, Dec. 27, 1983; *CD,* Nov. 14, 30, 1974, Feb. 17, 19, 1975.

519 **were far less likely to own cars:** *North Philadelphia Databook,* 42–43. See, generally, Thomas J. Sugrue, "Driving While Black: The Car and Race Relations in Modern America," *Automobile in American Life and Society,* University of Michigan–Dearborn/Henry Ford Museum, 2005, www.autolife.umd.umich.edu/Race/R_Casestudy/R_Casestudy1.htm.

519 **"spatial mismatch":** John F. Kain, "Housing Segregation, Negro Employment, and Metropolitan Decentralization," *Quarterly Journal of Economics* 82 (May 1968), 175–97; Yale Rabin, "Highways as a Barrier to Equal Access," *Annals* 407 (1973), 69; Keith R. Ihlanfeldt and David L. Sjoquist, "Job Accessibility and Racial Differences in Youth Employment Rates," *American Economic Review* 80 (1990), 267–76, documents mismatch in Philadelphia; see also Margaret Pugh, "Barriers to Work: The Spatial Divide Between Jobs and Welfare Recipients in Metropolitan Areas," Brookings Institution, Center for Metropolitan and Urban Policy Working Paper, Sept. 1998; John Pucher and John L. Renne, "Socioeconomics of Urban Travel: Evidence from the 2001 NHTS," *Transportation Quarterly* 57:3 (Summer 2003), 49–77.

520 **The most rapid job growth:** Adams et al., *Philadelphia,* 165–69; Thomas J. Sugrue, "The Structures of Urban Poverty: The Reorganization of Space and Work in Three Periods of American History," in Katz, ed., *The "Underclass" Debate,* 85–117.

520 **poor people found themselves:** Paul A. Jargowsky, *Poverty and Place: Ghettos, Barrios, and the American City* (New York, 1997), 44–49, 223; Paul A. Jargowsky and Mary Jo Bane, "Ghetto Poverty in the United States, 1970–1980," in Jencks and Peterson, eds., *The Urban Underclass,* Table 3, 248.

521 **By contrast, outlying parts:** William Schneider, "The Suburban Century Be-

gins," *Atlantic* 270 (July 1992), 33–44; Margaret Weir, "Urban Poverty and Defensive Localism," *Dissent* (Summer 1994), 337–42; generally, Kevin M. Kruse and Thomas J. Sugrue eds., *The New Suburban History* (Chicago, 2006).

521 **Surrounding Philadelphia:** Council of the Great City Schools, *Adequate Funding of Urban Schools:* Part I: *An Analysis of Funding to the Philadelphia Public Schools* (Washington, D.C., 1998).

522 **The Nixon administration took:** A. James Reichley, *Conservatives in an Age of Change: The Nixon and Ford Administrations* (Washington, D.C., 1981), 154–73, quote 166.

522 **"urban Marshall Plan":** *NYT,* June 14, July 27, 1977; Marcy Kaptur, exit interview, tape recording, JCPL, memorandum for Stuart Eizenstat and Bert Carp from Marcy Kaptur, Sept. 29, 1977, in SE, Box 307, Folder: Urban Policy (1) 9/77; see also materials in ibid., Box 311, Folder: Urban and Regional Policy Group; JC [Jimmy Carter] to Pat Harris and Stuart Eizenstat, Feb. 16, 1978, in ibid., Box 310, Folder: Urban Policy (Most Active); see generally, Sugrue, "Carter's Urban Policy Crisis," 137–57.

523 **When he visited New York's:** *NYT,* Oct. 6, 13, 1977; Memorandum for the President, Nov. 20, 1977, from Jack Watson and Bruce Kirschenbaum, Subject: Status Report on the South Bronx, SE, Box 308, Folder: Urban Policy (Most Active); Jill Jonnes, *We're Still Here: The Rise, Fall, and Resurrection of the South Bronx* (Boston, 1986), 311–23.

523 **When Carter finally announced:** Memorandum from Ralph Schlosstein to Stu Eizenstat, May 3, 1978, in SE, Box 310, Folder: Urban Policy (Most Active); handwritten note from B [Bert Carp] to Stu [Eizenstat], May 26, 1978; attached to Memorandum for Hamilton Jordan et al. from Jack Watson and Bruce Kirschenbaum, Subject: Presdiential Urban Trip. SE, Box 309, Folder: Urban Policy (Most Active); *NYAN,* April 1, 1978; *NYT,* April 2, 16, Dec. 5, 1978, Jan 11, 21, 27, 1979; Alice O'Connor, "Swimming Against the Tide: A Brief History of Federal Policy in Poor Communities," in Ronald F. Ferguson and William T. Dickens, eds., *Urban Problems and Community Development* (Washington, D.C., 1999), 108–13.

523 **continued in the Reagan administration:** John Mollenkopf, "Urban Policy at the Crossroads," in Margaret Weir, ed., *The Social Divide: Political Parties and the Future of Activist Government* (Washington, D.C., 1998), 469–70; Abbott, quoted in Jeffrey S. Adler, "Introduction," in Colburn and Adler, eds., *African-American Mayors,* 8.

524 **domestic agenda was cutting welfare:** Michael K. Brown, "Gutting the Great Society: Black Economic Progress and the Budget Cuts," *Urban League Review* 7 (1982), 11–24; Henry Aaron, "Non-Defense Programs," in Joseph A. Pechman, ed., *Setting National Priorities: The 1983 Budget* (Washington, D.C., 1982), 101–50; Carl Abbott, *Urban America in the Modern Age* (Arlington Heights, Ill., 1992), 131; Kathryn J. Edin and Laura Lein, *Making Ends Meet* (New York, 1998). Michael B. Katz, *Improving Poor People: The Welfare State,*

the "Underclass," and Urban Schools as History (Princeton, N.J., 1995), 144–72.

524 **Roxanne Jones's home state:** Michael B. Katz, *In the Shadow of the Poorhouse: A Social History of Welfare in America* (New York, 1996), 293–94.

525 **"Oh my God!":** *PI*, Feb. 7, 1982.

525 **In 1983, Jones's organization:** *PI*, July 10, 1983, Jan. 27, 1984; *NYT*, June 6, 1983.

525 **Still, indefatigable:** *PI*, June 19, July 10, Sept. 16, Oct. 3, 1983.

525 **quixotic campaign for the state senate:** *PI*, April 11, Nov. 7, 1984, Jan. 2, 1985; *Washington Informer*, May 22, 1985; *NYT*, Jan. 1, 1980; Andrew Feffer, "The Land Belongs to the People: Reframing Urban Protest in Post–Civil Rights Philadelphia," in Van Gosse and Richard Moser, eds., *The World the 60s Made: Politics and Culture in Recent America* (Philadelphia, 2003), 80–81, 83–86; Matthew Countryman, *Up South: Civil Rights and Black Power in Philadelphia* (Philadelphia, 2005), 320–22.

526 **Over the next eleven years:** *PI*, Feb. 5, 1985, March 15, June 22, 1988, April 18, 1992; *HPN*, Dec. 27, 1989, June 3, 1996.

527 **high-profile cases:** George Jackson, *Soledad Brother* (New York, 1970); Assata Shakur, *Assata: An Autobiography* (London, 1987); Mumia Abu-Jamal, *Live from Death Row* (New York, 1996).

528 **Nationwide, the proportion:** Figures from Jencks, *Rethinking Social Policy* 77. See also Rebecca M. Blank, "The Employment Strategy: Public Policies to Increase Work and Earnings," in Sheldon H. Danziger et al., eds., *Confronting Poverty: Prescriptions for Change* (New York, 1994), 179–180.

528 **"The special status of blacks":** Greenberg quoted in Thomas Edsall and Mary Edsall, *Chain Reaction: The Impact of Race, Rights, and Taxes on American Politics* (New York, 1992), 182.

529 **So long as the Democrats were perceived:** Peter Brown, *Minority Party: Why the Democrats Face Defeat in 1992 and Beyond* (Washington, D.C., 1991); Edsall and Edsall, *Chain Reaction*; Jim Sleeper, *The Closest of Strangers: Liberalism and the Politics of Race in New York* (New York, 1990); Stanley Greenberg, *Middle-Class Dreams: The Politics and Power of the New American Majority* (New York, 1995); Michael Tomasky, *Left for Dead: The Life, Death, and Possible Resurrection of Progressive Politics in America* (New York, 1996); Kenneth S. Baer, *Reinventing Democrats: The Politics of Liberalism from Reagan to Clinton* (Lawrence, Kans., 2000); for critical analyses, see Philip A. Klinkner with Rogers M. Smith, *The Unsteady March: The Rise and Decline of Racial Equality in America* (Chicago, 1999), 303–5, 308–16; Adolph Reed, "Race and the Disruption of the New Deal Coalition," *UAQ* 27 (1991), 326–33; Felicia A. Kornbluh, "Why Gingrich? Welfare Rights and Racial Politics, 1965–1995," in Judith Jackson Fossett and Jeffrey A. Tucker, eds., *Race Consciousness: African-American Studies for the New Century* (New York, 1997), 193–207.

529 **The Democrats were outflanked:** "Personal Responsibility Act," in Ed Gilles-

pie and Bob Schellhas, eds., *Contract with America* (New York, 1994), 65–77; R. Kent Weaver, "Ending Welfare As We Know It," in Weir, ed., *The Social Divide*, 361–416.

529 **empowered by a provision:** Mollenkopf, "Urban Policy at the Crossroads," 464–505.

530 **they made local experiments the basis:** Michael B. Katz, *The Price of Citizenship: Redefining the American Welfare State* (New York, 2001), 77–136.

530 **"There is a need":** *NYT,* April 16, 1995; "A Long Line for Fast Food Jobs," *BW,* July 31, 1995, 30; Katherine Newman, *No Shame in My Game: The Working Poor in the Inner City* (New York, 1999).

530 **In her last weeks:** *HPN,* June 3, 1996; Daniel Gitterman, Joanne Spetz, and Matt Fellowes, "The Other Side of the Ledger: Federal Health Spending in Metropolitan Economies," Discussion Paper, Brookings Institution Metropolitan Policy Program, Sept. 2004, www.brook.edu/metro/pubs/20040917_gitterman.htm.

531 **"Nine dollars":** *PT,* May 21, 1996.

531 **President Bill Clinton signed:** Public Law 104-193, August 22, 1996, 110 Stat. 2105.

531 **In its first ten years:** *PT,* June 23, 1995, *PDN,* May 20, 1996; Carmen deNavas Walt, Bernadette D. Proctor, and Jessica Smith, USCB, Current Population Reports P60-233, *Income, Poverty, and Health Insurance Coverage in the United States: 2006* (Washington, D.C., 2007), Figure 3; Sharon Hays, *Flat Broke with Children: Women in the Age of Welfare Reform* (New York, 2002); Jason DeParle, *American Dream: Three Women, Ten Kids, and a Nation's Drive to End Welfare* (New York, 2004); Ellen Reese, *Backlash Against Welfare Mothers: Past and Present* (Berkeley, Calif., 2005).

EPILOGUE

533 **Even though West Mount Airy:** *PI,* March 25, 1999; *PDN,* March 25, 1999.

533 **West Mount Airy remains:** For an overview of the extensive body of work on West Mount Airy (and adjacent East Mount Airy), see Mt. Airy Historical Awareness Committee, Mount Airy Biblography, www.wman.net/mtairybiblio.pdf. The best overview is Barbara Ferman et al., "West Mount Airy, Philadelphia," *Cityscape* 4:2 (1998), 29–59.

534 **"blacks believe it works only":** Jennifer Hochschild, *Facing Up to the American Dream: Race, Class, and the Soul of the Nation* (Princeton, 1995), 68.

535 **Whites and blacks alike value:** Pew Research Center, *Optimism About Black Progress Declines: A Social and Demographic Trends Report* (Washington, D.C., 2007), 54, available at http://pewsocialtrends.org/assets/pdf/Race.pdf, hereafter referred to as Pew Report. See "The Compelling Need for Diversity in Higher Education," available at www.vpcomm.umich.edu/admissions and *Gratz v. Bollinger,* 539 U.S. 244 (2003).

535 **By contrast, blacks:** Lee Sigelman and Susan Welch, *Black Americans' Views of Racial Inequality: The Dream Deferred* (New York, 1991); Hochschild, *Facing Up to the American Dream*, 61; Pew Report, 16–18.

535 **By sizeable numbers, blacks report:** Pew Report, 30.

535 **matters of law and order:** Susan Welch et al., "Justice for All: Still an American Dilemma," in Obie Clayton, Jr., ed., *An American Dilemma Revisited: Race Relations in a Changing World* (New York, 1996), 216–22; *WP*, Oct. 8, 1995; Pew Report, 9.

536 **disagree over remedies:** Donald R. Kinder and Lynn M. Sanders, *Divided by Color: Racial Politics and Democratic Ideals* (Chicago, 1996), 27–31; Pew Report, 10.

536 **Multi-City Study of Urban Inequality:** Alice O'Connor, Chris Tilly, and Lawrence Bobo, eds., *Urban Inequality: Evidence from Four Cities* (New York, 2001).

537 **In 1963:** Thomas J. Sugrue, *The Origins of the Urban Crisis: Race and Inequality in Postwar Detroit* (Princeton, N.J., 1996), 105.

537 **A glance at black professions:** USCB, *1960 Census of Population: Michigan*, vol. 1, part 24 (Washington, D.C., 1963), Table 122; *1970 Census of Population: Michigan*, vol. 1, part 24 (Washington, D.C., 1973), Table 171; *1980 Census of Population: Michigan*, vol. 1, part 24 (Washington, D.C., 1983), Table 219; *1990 Census of Population and Housing: Equal Employment Opportunity File*, CD-ROM (Washington, D.C., 1992). Data from 1990 includes the entire Experienced Civilian Labor Force.

537 **more diverse workforces:** Genevieve Capowski, "Managing Diversity," *Management Review* 85:6 (1996), 13–20; Joel Makower, "Managing Diversity in the Workplace," *Business and Society Review* (Winter 1995), 48–54; David A. Thomas and Robin J. Ely, "Making Differences Matter: A New Paradigm for Managing Diversity," *Harvard Business Review* 74(9) (Sept.–Oct. 1996), 79–80.

538 **economically insecure:** USCB, *Income, Earnings, and Poverty from the 2006 American Community Survey* (Washington, D.C., 2007).

538 **The most persistent feature:** Diana Pearce, "Gatekeepers and Homeseekers: Institutionalized Patterns in Racial Steering," *SP* 26 (1979), 325–42; Douglas J. Massey and Nancy A. Denton, *American Apartheid: Segregation and the Making of the Underclass* (Cambridge, Mass., 1993), 98–104; John Yinger, *Housing Discrimination Study: Incidence of Discrimination and Variation in Discriminatory Behavior* (Washington, D.C., 1991); Michael Fix and Raymond J. Struyk, eds., *Clear and Convincing Evidence: Measurement of Discrimination in America* (Washington, D.C., 1993).

539 **"Even if black incomes":** Massey and Denton, *American Apartheid*, 84–87, Table 4.1.

539 **The starkest racial disparities:** USCB, "Net Worth and Asset Ownership of Households: 1998 and 2000," *Current Population Reports*, Household Studies (May 2003), 12. On the black-white gap, see Thomas M. Shapiro, *The Hidden Cost of Being African-American: How Wealth Perpetuates Inequality* (New

York, 2004); Dalton Conley, *Being Black, Living in the Red: Race, Wealth, and Social Policy in America* (Berkeley, Calif., 1999); and Melvin L. Oliver and Thomas M. Shapiro, *Black Wealth, White Wealth: A New Perspective on Racial Inequality* (New York, 1997).

539 **gaps in health and life expectancy:** National Center for Health Statistics, *Health, United States 2006*, Table 27, www.cdc.gov/nchs/data/hus/hus06.pdf.

539 **The gap in homicide rates:** *Healthy United States 2006*, Table 45; William J. Bennett et al., *Body Count: Moral Poverty and How to Win America's War Against Crime and Drugs* (New York, 1996), 66.

541 **"the white race in America":** Reinhold Niebuhr, *Moral Man and Immoral Society* (New York, 1936), 253.

542 **microcosm in West Mount Airy:** USCB, Census 2000 Summary File 1, for Philadelphia tracts 232–37, available at www.factfinder.census.gov; Ferman, "West Mount Airy"; *PT*, Feb. 4, 2007.

INDEX

ABOUT THE AUTHOR

THOMAS J. SUGRUE is a historian at the University of Pennsylvania, where he is currently Edmund J. and Louise W. Kahn Professor of History and Sociology. Sugrue's first book, *The Origins of the Urban Crisis*, won the prestigious Bancroft Prize in American History, the President's Book Award of the Social Science History Association, the Philip Taft Prize in Labor History, and the Urban History Association Prize for Best Book in North American Urban History. He has also published essays and reviews in *The Washington Post, The Nation, London Review of Books, Chicago Tribune, The Philadelphia Inquirer,* and *Detroit Free Press*.

ABOUT THE TYPE

This book was set in Bodoni, a typeface designed by Giambattista Bodoni (1740–1813), the renowned Italian printer and type designer. Bodoni originally based his letter forms on those of the Frenchman Fournier, and created his type to have beautiful contrasts between light and dark.